Middle School 3-2
학교시험 완벽대비

KB087308

2학기 전과정

# 적중 100 plus

영어 기출문제집

## 중3
미래 │ 최연희

*Best Collection*

# 구성과 특징

교과서의 주요 학습 내용을 중심으로 학습 영역별 특성에 맞춰 단계별로 다양한 학습 기회를 제공하여
단원별 학습능력 평가는 물론 중간 및 기말고사 시험 등에 완벽하게 대비할 수 있도록 내용을 구성

## Words & Expressions

Step1    Key Words 단원별 핵심 단어 설명 및 풀이
        Key Expression 단원별 핵심 숙어 및 관용어 설명
        Word Power 반대 또는 비슷한 뜻 단어 배우기
        English Dictionary 영어로 배우는 영어 단어

Step2    실력평가 단원별 수시평가 대비 주관식, 객관식 문제풀이

Step3    서술형 대비 학업성취도 및 수행능력평가 대비 서술형 문제풀이

## Conversation

Step1    핵심 의사소통 소통에 필요한 주요 표현 방법 요약
        핵심 Check 기본적인 표현 방법 및 활용능력 확인

Step2    대화문 익히기 교과서 대화문 심층 분석 및 확인

Step3    교과서 확인학습 빈칸 채우기를 통한 문장 완성 능력 확인

Step4    기본평가 시험대비 기초 학습 능력 평가

Step5    실력평가 단원별 수시평가 대비 주관식, 객관식 문제풀이

Step6    서술형 대비 학업성취도 및 수행능력평가 대비 서술형 문제풀이

## Grammar

Step1    주요 문법 단원별 주요 문법 사항과 예문을 알기 쉽게 설명
        핵심 Check 기본 문법사항에 대한 이해 여부 확인

Step2    기본평가 시험대비 기초 학습 능력 평가

Step3    실력평가 단원별 수시평가 대비 주관식, 객관식 문제풀이

Step4    서술형 대비 학업성취도 및 수행능력평가 대비 서술형 문제풀이

## Reading

Step1    구문 분석 단원별로 제시된 문장에 대한 구문별 분석과 내용 설명
        확인문제 문장에 대한 기본적인 이해와 인지능력 확인

Step2    확인학습A 빈칸 채우기를 통한 문장 완성 능력 확인

Step3    확인학습B 제시된 우리말을 영어로 완성하여 작문 능력 키우기

Step4    실력평가 단원별 수시평가 대비 주관식, 객관식 문제풀이

Step5    서술형 대비 학업성취도 및 수행능력평가 대비 서술형 문제풀이
        교과서 구석구석 교과서에 나오는 기타 문장까지 완벽 학습

# Composition

## |영역별 핵심문제|

단어 및 어휘, 대화문, 문법, 독해 등 각 영역별 기출문제의 출제 유형을 분석하여 실전에 대비하고 연습할 수 있도록 문제를 배열

## |단원별 예상문제|

기출문제를 분석한 후 새로운 시험 출제 경향을 더하여 새롭게 출제될 수 있는 문제를 포함하여 시험에 완벽하게 대비할 수 있도록 준비

## |서술형 실전 및 창의사고력 문제|

학교 시험에서 점차 늘어나는 서술형 시험에 집중 대비하고 고득점을 취득하는데 만전을 기하기 위한 학습 코너

## |단원별 모의고사|

영역별, 단계별 학습을 모두 마친 후 실전 연습을 위한 모의고사

INSIGHT
on the textbook

교과서 파헤치기

- **단어Test1~3** 영어 단어 우리말 쓰기, 우리말을 영어 단어로 쓰기, 영영풀이에 해당하는 단어와 우리말 쓰기
- **대화문Test1~2** 대화문 빈칸 완성 및 전체 대화문 쓰기
- **본문Test1~5** 빈칸 완성, 우리말 쓰기, 문장 배열연습, 영어 작문하기 복습 등 단계별 반복 학습을 통해 교과서 지문에 대한 완벽한 습득
- **구석구석지문Test1~2** 지문 빈칸 완성 및 전문 영어로 쓰기

# Lesson 4

# This Is Korea

 **의사소통 기능**

- 궁금한 것 묻고 답하기
  A: I wonder why he is running.
  B: I think he is late for school.

- 설명 요청하기
  A: Could you explain what this is?
  B: It's a traditional Korean hat. It's called a gat.

**언어 형식**

- '과거완료' had + 과거분사
  She kept laughing even after she **had been** in the water for over five hours.

- 간접의문문
  They didn't understand **why I wanted to take their pictures**.

# Words & Expressions

## Key Words

- **ad** [æd] 명 광고 (= advertisement)
- **attend** [əténd] 동 참석하다
- **audience** [ɔ́:diəns] 명 청중
- **audio guide** 음성 안내기
- **bakery** [béikəri] 명 빵집
- **beat** [bi:t] 명 (북 등을 치는) 소리, (심장의) 고동
- **black-and-white** 형 (사진, TV 등) 흑백의
- **bookstore** [búkstər] 명 서점
- **breadwinner** [brédwinər] 명 생계를 책임지는 사람, 가장
- **breathe** [bri:ð] 동 호흡하다
- **bridge** [bridʒ] 명 교량, 다리
- **community** [kəmjú:nəti] 명 지역 공동체
- **complete** [kəmplí:t] 동 완성[완료]하다
- **continue** [kəntínju:] 동 계속하다
- **copy machine** 복사기
- **destroy** [distrɔ́i] 동 파괴하다
- **device** [diváis] 명 기구
- **diver** [dáivər] 명 잠수부
- **environment** [inváiərənmənt] 명 환경
- **exhibition** [èksəbíʃən] 명 전시회, 박람회
- **female** [fí:meil] 형 여성의
- **good harvest** 풍년
- **greenhouse** [grí:nhàus] 명 온실
- **harvest** [há:rvist] 동 수확하다
- **heritage** [héritidʒ] 명 유산
- **intangible** [inténdʒəbl] 형 무형의, 만질 수 없는

- **jellyfish** [dʒélifiʃ] 명 해파리
- **marine** [mərí:n] 형 해양의, 바다의
- **moved** [mu:vd] 형 감동받은
- **nationwide** [néiʃənwàid] 형 전국적인
- **overseas** [óuvərsiz] 부 해외로, 해외에
- **overwork** [óuvərwərk] 동 과로하다
- **past** [pæst] 형 지나간 명 과거
- **path** [pæθ] 명 경로, 길
- **photographer** [fətágrəfər] 명 사진작가
- **press** [pres] 동 누르다 명 언론, 기자
- **promote** [prəmóut] 동 홍보하다, 촉진하다
- **realize** [rí:làiz] 동 깨닫다, 인식하다
- **seafood** [sí:fud] 명 해산물
- **several** [sévərəl] 형 몇몇의
- **suitable** [sú:təbl] 형 적합한, 적절한
- **sunshine** [sánʃain] 명 햇빛
- **tightly** [táitli] 부 단단히, 꽉
- **traditional** [trədíʃənl] 형 전통적인
- **trail** [treil] 명 좁은 길
- **underground** [ándərgráund] 형 지하의
- **underwater** [ándərwɔ́tər] 형 수중의, 물속에서
- **volcanic** [vɑlkǽnik] 형 화산의, 화산 작용에 의한
- **waterfall** [wɔ́tərfɔl] 명 폭포
- **wetsuit** [wétsu:t] 명 잠수용 고무옷, 잠수복
- **worldwide** [wɔ́rldwaid] 부 세계적으로

## Key Expressions

- **a couple of** 두 서너 개의
- **a little bit** 조금, 약간
- **an intangible cultural treasure** 무형문화재
- **be good for** ~에 유익하다
- **be suitable for** ~에 적절하다
- **check ~ out** ~을 확인하다, ~을 조사하다
- **cheer up** 힘을 북돋아 주다, 격려하다
- **get into** ~에 들어가다
- **give (someone) a call** 전화를 걸다
- **give (someone) a hand** 거들어 주다, 돕다
- **give a presentation** 발표하다

- **give a talk** 강의하다, 연설하다
- **go on vacation** 휴가 가다
- **happen to** 우연히 ~하다
- **keep -ing** 계속해서 ~하다
- **make double-sided copies** 양면 복사를 하다
- **take a photo** 사진을 찍다
- **walk along** ~을 따라 걷다
- **Why don't we ~?** ~하는 것이 어때?
- **Why not?** 왜 안 되겠어?, 좋고말고.
- **wish for** ~을 기원하다
- **would like to** ~하고 싶다

## Word Power

※ 서로 비슷한 뜻을 가진 어휘

- □ **ad** 광고(**advertisement**) : **commercial** 광고
- □ **device** 기구 : **tool** 도구
- □ **moved** 감동받은 : **touched** 감동받은
- □ **several** 몇몇의 : **a few** 몇몇의

- □ **borrow** 빌리다 : **rent** 임대하다
- □ **environment** 환경 : **surroundings** 환경
- □ **path** 경로, 길 : **trail** 좁은 길
- □ **suitable** 적합한, 적절한 : **proper** 적절한

※ 서로 반대되는 뜻을 가진 어휘

- □ **borrow** 빌리다 ↔ **lend** 빌려주다
- □ **nationwide** 전국적인 ↔ **local** 지역적인

- □ **female** 여성의 ↔ **male** 남성의
- □ **suitable** 적합한 ↔ **unsuitable** 부적절한

※ 동사 – 명사

- □ **attend** 참석하다 – **attendance** 참석
- □ **continue** 계속하다 – **continuity** 연속
- □ **explain** 설명하다 – **explanation** 설명
- □ **realize** 깨닫다 – **realization** 깨달음

- □ **breathe** 호흡하다 – **breath** 호흡
- □ **destroy** 파괴하다 – **destruction** 파괴
- □ **promote** 홍보하다 – **promotion** 홍보

※ 형용사 – 명사

- □ **good** 좋은 – **goodness** 선량함
- □ **aware** 알고 있는 – **awareness** 인식
- □ **weak** 약한 – **weakness** 약함
- □ **polite** 예의 바른 – **politeness** 예의 바름
- □ **sad** 슬픈 – **sadness** 슬픔

- □ **ill** 아픔 – **illness** 질병
- □ **fair** 공정한 – **fairness** 공정함
- □ **kind** 친절한 – **kindness** 친절
- □ **happy** 행복한 – **happiness** 행복
- □ **dark** 어두운 – **darkness** 어둠

## English Dictionary

- □ **ad** 광고 (= **advertisement**)
  → a picture, set of words, or a short film, intended to persuade people to buy
  사람들이 사도록 설득하려고 의도된 사진, 어구, 또는 짧은 영상

- □ **beat** (북 등을 치는) 소리
  → one of a series of regular movements or hitting actions 일련의 규칙적인 움직임 또는 치는 동작 중의 하나

- □ **breadwinner** 생계를 책임지는 사람, 가장
  → the member of a family who earns the money to support the others 가족을 부양하려고 돈을 버는 가족 구성원

- □ **breathe** 호흡하다
  → to take air into your lungs and send it out again
  폐로 공기를 들여보내고 그것을 다시 내보내다

- □ **community** 지역 공동체
  → the people who live in the same area, town, etc.
  같은 지역이나 마을 등에 사는 사람들

- □ **heritage** 유산
  → the traditional beliefs, values, customs of a family, country, or society
  한 가족, 국가, 사회의 전통적인 믿음, 가치관, 관습

- □ **intangible** 무형의, 만질 수 없는
  → having value but not existing physically
  가치가 있지만 물리적으로 존재하지는 않는

- □ **overseas** 해외의
  → to or in a foreign country that is across the sea
  바다 건너 있는 외국으로 가거나 외국에 있는

**01** 다음 짝지어진 단어의 관계가 같도록 빈칸에 알맞은 말을 쓰시오.

> female : male = _____ : borrow

**02** 다음 영영풀이가 가리키는 것을 고르시오.

> having value but not existing physically

① underground    ② traditional
③ volcanic    ④ marine
⑤ intangible

**03** 다음 중 밑줄 친 부분의 뜻풀이가 바르지 않은 것은?

① All the audience stood up and gave the performer a big hand. (청중)
② We can't breathe in outer space. (호흡하다)
③ It is an important part of community life. (공동체)
④ She invited me to her photo exhibition. (전시회)
⑤ The trip was a great experience. (실험)

**04** 다음 우리말에 맞게 빈칸에 알맞은 말을 쓰시오. (철자가 주어진 경우, 그 철자로 시작하여 쓸 것.)

(1) 심해 잠수를 위해 잠수복을 가져와라.
➡ Bring a w_____ for deep sea diving.
(2) 그 영화는 전세계적으로 유명해졌다.
➡ The movie has become famous w_____.

(3) 그들은 지역 신문에 광고를 실었다.
➡ They put an _____ in the local paper.
(4) 우리는 강 위에 놓인 다리를 건넜다.
➡ We crossed the _____ over the river.

**서답형**
**05** 다음 문장의 빈칸에 들어갈 말을 〈보기〉에서 골라 알맞은 형태로 쓰시오.

> ┤ 보기 ├
> cheer up / wish for / get into / be good for / walk along

(1) Walking _____ your health.
(2) I _____ lots of interests for our new products.
(3) _____! You can do better next time.
(4) If you _____ the street, you can find the post office.
(5) It is hard to _____ the medical school.

**06** 다음 주어진 문장의 밑줄 친 press와 같은 의미로 쓰인 것은?

> Please press the start button.

① Jack blamed the press photographers for violating his privacy.
② Which switch should I press to turn it off?
③ Some people don't believe the press reports.
④ They are fighting for the freedom of the press.
⑤ The car accident in my town was reported in the press.

**01** 다음 짝지어진 단어의 관계가 같도록 빈칸에 알맞은 말을 쓰시오.

> thin : thick = future : _____

**02** 다음 우리말에 맞게 빈칸에 알맞은 말을 쓰시오. (철자가 주어진 경우, 그 철자로 시작하여 쓸 것.)

(1) 길은 단풍잎으로 덮여 있었다.
➡ The p_____ was covered with colorful leaves.

(2) 전 지역 공동체가 바이러스에 대해 걱정했다.
➡ The whole _____ was concerned about the virus.

(3) 그 밴드는 그들의 새로운 앨범을 홍보할 필요가 있다.
➡ The band needs to p_____ their new album.

(4) 해파리를 본 적이 있나요?
➡ Have you ever seen the _____?

**03** 다음 우리말과 일치하도록 주어진 단어를 모두 배열하여 완성하시오.

(1) 우리는 작년에 풍년이 들었다.
(last / harvest / had / we / a / good / year)
➡ _____

(2) 돈이 항상 행복을 가져다주지는 않는다.
(does / happiness / money / not / bring / always)
➡ _____

(3) 우리의 국가적 유산이 화재에 의해 파괴되었다.
(was / by / the / our / heritage / destroyed / fire / national)
➡ _____

**04** 다음 우리말을 주어진 단어를 이용하여 영작하시오.

(1) 우리는 한 시간 동안 길을 따라 걸었다. (along, for, street)
➡ _____
_____

(2) 이 책은 초등학생들에게 적합하다. (suitable, elementary)
➡ _____
_____

(3) 종이를 절약하기 위해 양면 복사를 하자. (let's, save)
➡ _____
_____

**05** 다음 문장의 빈칸에 들어갈 말을 〈보기〉에서 골라 쓰시오.

> ┤ 보기 ├
> realize / promote / underwater / volcanic / several

(1) This campaign will _____ the education for all ages.

(2) He didn't _____ that he was acting differently.

(3) I go hiking _____ times a month.

(4) The _____ photographer is diving into the sea.

(5) Dokdo was created from _____ activity.

# Conversation

**①** 궁금한 것 묻고 답하기

> **A** I wonder why he is running. 왜 그가 달리고 있는지 궁금해.
> **B** I think he is late for school. 내 생각엔 그가 학교에 늦은 것 같아.

■ 궁금증을 표현할 때 wonder(궁금하다), curious(궁금한, 호기심이 많은), want to know(알고 싶다) 등의 표현을 이용하여 'I wonder ~.'라고 말한다. 이때 어순은 'I wonder+의문사+주어+동사 ~.', 'I wonder+if/whether+주어+동사 ~.'이다. 또한 궁금한 내용을 'I want to know ~.', 'I don't know why ~.'로 표현할 수 있다.

■ 'Can I ~?', 'Can/Could you ~?' 등과 같이 요구/요청을 나타내는 조동사 표현을 사용하여 'Can I ask you ~?' 또는 'Can you tell me ~?'와 같이 궁금한 점에 대하여 물어볼 수 있다. 그 외에 궁금증을 나타낼 때는 'Do you know ~?' 등을 사용할 수도 있다.

■ 궁금함을 나타낼 때 'I wonder ~.' 대신에 쓸 수 있는 표현으로 'I'm curious ~.' 또는 'I want to know ~.' 등이 있다. 'I'm curious'와 명사구를 같이 쓸 때는 'I'm curious about+명사구'이고, 명사절과 함께 쓸 때는 'I'm curious if/whether ~.' 또는 'I'm curious 의문사+주어+동사'이다.

### 궁금한 것 묻고 답하기

- I'm wondering + if/whether 주어+동사/의문사절. ~인지 궁금하다.
- Can you tell me ~? ~에 대해 말해 줄 수 있니?
- Can I ask you + 의문사절? ~에 대하여 물어봐도 되니?
- I'm curious if/whether 주어+동사. ~가 궁금하다.
- I want to know 명사구/명사절. ~을 알고 싶다.
- I'd be very interested to ~. 나는 ~에 매우 관심이 많다.

### 핵심 Check

**1.** 밑줄 친 우리말을 괄호 안에 주어진 어휘를 이용하여 영작하시오.

G: Wow, look at the bridge in this ad.
<u>어디에서 찍은 사진인지 궁금하네.</u> (the photo, taken)

B: That's Gwangandaegyo in Busan.

G: How do you know that?

B: I went there with my family last summer.

➡ _____

## ② 설명 요청하기

> **A** Could you explain what this is? 이게 무엇인지 설명해 줄 수 있니?
>
> **B** It's a traditional Korean hat. It's called a gat. 그것은 한국의 전통적인 모자야. 갓이라고 불러.

■ 상대방에게 궁금한 내용에 대한 설명을 요청할 때는 '설명하다, 말하다'의 의미를 가지는 동사 'explain', 'tell' 또는 'give information' 등의 표현을 사용하여 'Could/Can you explain 의문사절?', 'Could/Can you tell me more about ~?'라고 표현한다. Could 대신 Would, Can, Will 등을 사용할 수 있고, 'Do you mind if I ask you to explain ~?'이라고 말할 수도 있다.

■ 상대방의 말을 듣고 추가로 더 많이 설명해 달라고 할 때는 'Could/Can you tell me more about it?' 이라고 한다. 좀 더 공손하게 표현하여 Can 대신에 Could나 Would를 사용할 수도 있다. tell 대신에 explain을 써서 'Could/Can you explain that more, please?'라고 할 수 있다.

■ 상대방이 말하는 의도를 모르거나 사용하는 단어의 뜻을 몰라서 설명을 요청할 때 쓰는 표현은 'What does that mean?(그것이 무슨 뜻입니까?)', 'What do you mean by that?(그것이 무슨 뜻이니?)' 등이다. 상대방의 말을 알아듣지 못했을 때는 'I'm not following you.(잘 알아듣지 못하겠습니다.)', 'I don't get it.(제대로 이해를 못하겠어요.)' 등의 표현을 사용하여 상대방이 다시 설명을 하도록 요청할 수도 있다.

### 설명 요청하기

- Could/Can you explain what this is? 이게 무엇인지 설명해 줄 수 있니?
- Could/Can you tell me more about it? 그것에 대해 좀 더 말해 줄 수 있니?
- I think I need some more information about it. 그것에 대해 정보가 더 필요한 것 같아.
- Could you give me more information? 좀 더 정보를 주시겠습니까?
- Could you be more specific? 좀 더 구체적으로 말해 주시겠습니까?
- What is the meaning of that exactly? 그게 정확하게 무슨 뜻입니까?

### 핵심 Check

**2.** 다음 대화를 자연스러운 순서로 배열하시오.

B: Excuse me, I'd like to use a copy machine.

(A) Sure. Press the button for double-sided copies, and then press the start button.

(B) Could you explain how to make double-sided copies?

(C) O.K. You can use this machine.

B: Thank you.

➡ _____

**Listen & Speak 1 A-2**

B: Look over there. ❶I wonder why there are so many people waiting in line.

G: They're waiting to ❷get into the new bakery there.

B: Why? Is ❸it famous?

G: Yes. ❸It was on a TV program.

B: Really? We should try their bread then.

G: Sure.

B: 저기 좀 봐. 왜 저렇게 많은 사람들이 줄을 서서 기다리고 있는지 궁금하네.

G: 새로 생긴 제과점에 들어가려고 기다리고 있는 거야.

B: 왜? 유명한 곳이야?

G: 맞아. TV 프로그램에 나왔어.

B: 정말? 그럼 우리 저곳의 빵을 먹어 봐야겠다.

G: 그래.

❶ 궁금한 것을 묻는 표현으로 'I want to know why there are so many people waiting in line.' 등으로 바꾸어 쓸 수 있다.

❷ get into: ~에 들어가다

❸ It은 The new bakery를 가리킨다.

**Check(√) True or False**

(1) The boy wants to know why there are lots of people waiting in line.　　T ☐　F ☐

(2) The new bakery became famous after it was on a TV program.　　T ☐　F ☐

**Communicate A**

Jaden: Do you hear that? I wonder where that music is coming from.

Yuri: I think it's coming from over there. Do you want to go and ❶check it out?

Jaden: Yes, I love that strong beat. Is it ❷traditional Korean music?

Yuri: Yes, it's called nongak. It's a kind of ❸community band music.

Jaden: Nongak? ❹Could you explain a little bit more about it?

Yuri: It's traditionally used to ❺cheer up farmers and ❻wish for a good harvest.

Jaden: I see. Look! Some people are dancing to the rhythm.

Yuri: Yes, that's a big part of nongak. Dancing together completes the music.

Jaden: Let's join them.

Yuri: Sure. Why not?

Jaden: 저거 들리니? 저 음악이 어디서 오는 것인지 궁금하네.

유리: 저기서 나오는 것 같은데. 가서 확인해 볼래?

Jaden: 그래. 저 강한 비트가 마음에 들어. 이게 한국의 전통 음악이니?

유리: 맞아. 농악이라고 해. 공동체 악단 음악의 한 종류야.

Jaden: 농악? 그것에 대해 좀 더 설명해 줄래?

유리: 그건 전통적으로 농부들의 힘을 북돋아 주고 풍년을 기원하기 위해 사용되었어.

Jaden: 그렇구나. 봐! 몇몇 사람들이 리듬에 맞춰 춤추고 있어.

유리: 그래. 그게 농악의 큰 부분이야. 함께 춤추는 것이 음악을 완성하지.

Jaden: 저들과 함께 하자.

유리: 물론이야. 왜 안 되겠어?

❶ check (something) out: ~을 확인하다, 조사하다　　❷ traditional: 전통적인　　❸ community: 지역 공동체

❹ 상대방에게 궁금한 내용에 대한 설명을 요청할 때 쓰는 표현으로 'Could you tell me a little bit more about it?' 등으로 바꾸어 쓸 수 있다.

❺ cheer up: 격려하다　　❻ wish for: ~을 기원하다

**Check(√) True or False**

(3) Jaden and Yuri are listening to nongak.　　T ☐　F ☐

(4) The strong beat is a big part of nongak.　　T ☐　F ☐

### Listen & Speak 1 A-1

**G:** Wow, look at the ❶bridge in this ❷ad. I wonder where the photo was taken.

**B:** That's Gwangandaegyo in Busan.

**G:** How do you know that?

**B:** I went ❸there with my family last summer.

❶ bridge: 다리
❷ ad(= advertisement): 광고
❸ there는 Gwangandaegyo in Busan을 가리킨다.

### Listen & Speak 2 A-1

**W:** Excuse me, ❶I'd like to ❷borrow ❸an audio guide.

**M:** Here you are.

**W:** ❹Could you explain how to use ❺it?

**M:** Sure. Press this button, and it'll tell you what to do.

❶ would like to ~: ~하고 싶다
❷ borrow: 빌리다
❸ audio guide: 음성 안내기
❹ 'Could you tell me how to use it?' 등으로 바꾸어 표현할 수 있다.
❺ it은 the audio guide를 가리킨다.

### Listen & Speak 2 A-2

**B:** Are you going somewhere this summer?

**G:** I'm going to Jejudo to ❶walk along the Jeju Olle Trail.

**B:** The Jeju Olle Trail? Could you explain what ❷that is?

**G:** It's a long hiking ❸path around Jejudo.

**B:** Oh, I see. I hope you enjoy your trip!

❶ walk along: ~을 따라 걷다
❷ that은 the Jeju Olle Trail을 가리킨다.
❸ path: 길

### Progress Check 1

**W:** Look over there. ❶I wonder why there are so many cars on the road.

**M:** Lots of people are ❷going on vacation this weekend.

**W:** Really? Then, ❸why don't we go somewhere, too?

**M:** O.K.

❶ 궁금한 것을 묻는 표현으로 'Could you tell me why there are so many cars on the road?'로 바꾸어 표현할 수 있다.
❷ go on vacation: 휴가를 가다
❸ why don't we ~? = how about ~? = what about ~? = ~하는 게 어때?

### Progress Check 2

**B:** Excuse me, I'd like to use a ❶copy machine.

**W:** O.K. You can use ❷this machine.

**B:** Could you explain how to ❸make double-sided copies?

**W:** Sure. ❹Press the button for double-sided copies, and then press the start button.

**B:** Thank you.

❶ copy machine: 복사기
❷ this machine은 복사기를 가리킨다.
❸ make double-sided copies: 양면 복사를 하다
❹ press: 누르다

● 다음 우리말과 일치하도록 빈칸에 알맞은 말을 쓰시오.

### Listen & Speak 1 A-1

G: Wow, look at the _____ in this _____. I wonder _____ _____ _____ _____ _____.

B: That's Gwangandaegyo in Busan.

G: _____ do you know that?

B: I went there _____ my family _____ _____.

해석

G: 와, 이 광고에 나오는 다리 좀 봐. 어디에서 찍은 사진인지 궁금하네.
B: 부산의 광안대교야.
G: 그걸 어떻게 아니?
B: 작년 여름에 우리 가족들과 그곳에 갔었거든.

### Listen & Speak 1 A-2

B: Look over there. _____ _____ _____ there are so many people _____ _____ _____.

G: They're waiting to _____ _____ the new bakery there.

B: Why? Is it _____?

G: Yes. It was _____ a TV program.

B: Really? We should _____ their bread then.

G: Sure.

B: 저기 좀 봐. 왜 저렇게 많은 사람들이 줄을 서서 기다리고 있는지 궁금하네.
G: 새로 생긴 제과점에 들어가려고 기다리고 있는 거야.
B: 왜? 유명한 곳이야?
G: 맞아. TV 프로그램에 나왔어.
B: 정말? 그럼 우리 저곳의 빵을 먹어 봐야겠다.
G: 그래.

### Listen & Speak 2 A-1

W: Excuse me, _____ _____ _____ _____ an audio guide.

M: Here you are.

W: Could you _____ _____ _____ _____ _____?

M: Sure. _____ this button, and it'll tell you _____ _____ _____.

W: 실례합니다, 음성 가이드를 대여하고 싶은데요.
M: 여기 있습니다.
W: 어떻게 사용하는지 설명해 주실 수 있나요?
M: 물론이죠. 이 버튼을 누르면, 무엇을 해야 할지 말해 줄 겁니다.

### Listen & Speak 2 A-2

B: Are you going _____ this summer?

G: I'm going to Jejudo to _____ _____ the Jeju Olle Trail.

B: The Jeju Olle Trail? _____ _____ _____ what that is?

G: It's a _____ _____ _____ around Jejudo.

B: Oh, I see. I hope you _____ _____ _____ !

B: 이번 여름에 어디 갈 거야?
G: 제주 올레길을 따라 걸으러 제주도에 갈 거야.
B: 제주 올레길? 그게 무엇인지 설명해 줄래?
G: 제주도 둘레에 있는 긴 하이킹 코스야.
B: 오, 그렇구나. 즐거운 여행이 되길 바랄게!

해석

## Communicate A

**Jaden:** Do you hear that? _____ _____ _____ that music is coming from.

**Yuri:** I think it's coming from over there. Do you want to go and _____ _____ _____ ?

**Jaden:** Yes, I love that _____ _____ . Is it _____ Korean music?

**Yuri:** Yes, it's called nongak. It's a kind of _____ band music.

**Jaden:** Nongak? _____ _____ _____ a little bit more about it?

**Yuri:** It's _____ used to _____ _____ farmers and wish for a _____ _____ .

**Jaden:** I see. Look! Some people are dancing to the _____ .

**Yuri:** Yes, that's a big part of nongak. Dancing together _____ the music.

**Jaden:** Let's join them.

**Yuri:** Sure. _____ _____ ?

Jaden: 저거 들리니? 저 음악이 어디서 오는 것인지 궁금하네.

유리: 저기서 나오는 것 같은데. 가서 확인해 볼래?

Jaden: 그래, 저 강한 비트가 마음에 들어. 그게 한국의 전통 음악이니?

유리: 맞아, 농악이라고 해. 공동체 악단 음악의 한 종류야.

Jaden: 농악? 그것에 대해 좀 더 설명해 줄래?

유리: 그건 전통적으로 농부들의 힘을 북돋아 주고 풍년을 기원하기 위해 사용되었어.

Jaden: 그렇구나. 봐! 몇몇 사람들이 리듬에 맞춰 춤추고 있어.

유리: 그래, 그게 농악의 큰 부분이야. 함께 춤추는 것이 음악을 완성하지.

Jaden: 저들과 함께 하자.

유리: 물론이야. 왜 안 되겠어?

## Progress Check 1

**W:** Look over there. _____ _____ _____ _____ _____ _____ _____ _____ on the road.

**M:** Lots of people are _____ _____ _____ this weekend.

**W:** Really? Then, _____ _____ _____ go somewhere, too?

**M:** O.K.

W: 저기 좀 봐요. 도로에 왜 저렇게 차가 많은지 궁금하네요.

M: 많은 사람들이 이번 주말에 휴가를 가거든요.

W: 정말요? 그럼, 우리도 어디 가는 게 어떤가요?

M: 좋아요.

## Progress Check 2

**B:** Excuse me, I'd like to use a _____ _____ .

**W:** O.K. You can use this machine.

**B:** Could you explain _____ _____ _____ _____ _____ _____ ?

**W:** Sure. _____ the button for double-sided copies, and then _____ the start button.

**B:** Thank you.

B: 실례합니다, 복사기를 좀 쓰고 싶은데요.

W: 알겠어요. 이 기계를 써도 돼요.

B: 어떻게 양면 복사를 하는지 설명해 주실 수 있나요?

W: 물론이죠. 양면 복사 버튼을 누르고, 시작 버튼을 누르세요.

B: 감사합니다.

[01~02] 다음 대화를 읽고 물음에 답하시오.

G: Wow, look at the bridge in this ad. (A)<u>I wonder where was the photo taken.</u>
B: That's Gwangandaegyo in Busan.
G: (B)<u>그걸 어떻게 아니?</u>
B: I went there with my family last summer.

**01** 위 대화의 밑줄 친 (A)를 어법상 바르게 고치시오.

➡ _____

**02** 위 대화의 밑줄 친 우리말 (B)를 5 단어로 영작하시오.

➡ _____

[03~04] 다음 대화를 읽고 물음에 답하시오.

Tom: Are you going somewhere this summer?
Jane: I'm going to Jejudo to walk along the Jeju Olle Trail.
Tom: The Jeju Olle Trail? (A)<u>Could you explain what that is?</u> (tell)
Jane: It's a long hiking path around Jejudo.
Tom: Oh, I see. I hope you enjoy your trip!

**03** 위 대화의 밑줄 친 (A)와 의미가 같도록 주어진 단어를 사용하여 바꿔 쓰시오.

➡ _____

**04** 위 대화의 내용과 일치하지 <u>않는</u> 것은?

① Jane은 이번 여름에 제주도에 갈 예정이다.
② Jane은 제주도에서 올레길을 걸을 것이다.
③ 올레길은 제주도 둘레에 있는 긴 하이킹 코스이다.
④ Tom은 Jane이 즐거운 여행을 하길 바란다.
⑤ Tom은 이미 올레길에 대해 잘 알고 있다.

**01** 다음 대화가 자연스럽게 이어지도록 순서대로 배열하시오.

> Look over there. I wonder why there are so many people waiting in line.

> (A) Sure.
> (B) Yes. It was on a TV program.
> (C) Why? Is it famous?
> (D) Really? We should try their bread then.
> (E) They're waiting to get into the new bakery there.

➡ _____

다음 대화의 빈칸 (A)에 들어갈 말로 적절하지 <u>않은</u> 것은?

> W: Excuse me, I'd like to borrow an audio guide.
> M: Here you are.
> W: _____(A)_____
> M: Sure. Press this button, and it'll tell you what to do.

① Could you explain how to use it?
② Can you tell me how to use it?
③ Could you give me more information about how to use it?
④ Could you be more specific about how to use it?
⑤ What do you mean by that?

[03~04] 다음 대화를 읽고 물음에 답하시오.

> G: Wow, ⓐ<u>look</u> at the bridge in this ad. I wonder where the photo ⓑ<u>took</u>.
> B: That's Gwangandaegyo ⓒ<u>in</u> Busan.
> G: How do you know ⓓ<u>that</u>?
> B: I went ⓔ<u>there</u> with my family last summer.

**03** 위 대화의 밑줄 친 ⓐ~ⓔ 중 어법상 <u>틀린</u> 것을 찾아 바르게 고치시오.

➡ _____

**04** 위 대화의 내용과 일치하지 <u>않는</u> 것은?

① The girl and the boy are watching the ad.
② There is a bridge in the ad.
③ The girl wants to know where the photo of the bridge was taken.
④ The boy visited Busan with his family last summer.
⑤ The girl wants to take a photo of the bridge.

[05~06] 다음 대화를 읽고 물음에 답하시오.

> Brian: Look over there. I wonder why there are so many people (A)[waited / waiting] in line.
> Sujin: They're waiting to (B)[get into / get out] the new bakery there.
> Brian: Why? Is it famous?
> Sujin: Yes. It was (C)[on / off] a TV program.
> Brian: Really? We should try their bread then.
> Sujin: Sure.

**05** 위 대화의 (A)~(C)에 들어갈 말로 바르게 짝지어진 것은?

|  | (A) | (B) | (C) |
|---|---|---|---|
| ① | waited | get into | on |
| ② | waited | get out | off |
| ③ | waiting | get out | on |
| ④ | waiting | get out | off |
| ⑤ | waiting | get into | on |

**06** 위 대화의 내용과 일치하지 <u>않는</u> 것은?

① Brian은 왜 많은 사람들이 줄을 서서 기다리고 있는지 궁금하다.

② 새로 생긴 제과점에 들어가려고 많은 사람들이 줄을 서 있다.

③ 새로 생긴 제과점이 TV 프로그램에 나왔다.

④ Brian은 새로 생긴 제과점의 빵을 먹어 보고 싶다.

⑤ Brian과 수진은 함께 제과점 앞에서 줄을 서서 기다리고 있었다.

서답형

**07** 다음 대화가 자연스럽게 이어지도록 순서대로 배열하시오.

(A) Thank you.

(B) O.K. You can use this machine.

(C) Excuse me, I'd like to use a copy machine.

(D) Could you explain how to make double-sided copies?

(E) Sure. Press the button for double-sided copies, and then press the start button.

➡ _____

[08~09] 다음 대화를 읽고 물음에 답하시오.

Jaden: Do you hear that? (a)<u>I wonder where that music is coming from.</u>

Yuri: I think it's coming from over there. Do you want to go and check it out?

Jaden: Yes, I love that strong beat. Is it traditional Korean music?

Yuri: Yes, it's called nongak. It's a kind of community band music.

Jaden: Nongak? Could you explain a little bit more about it?

Yuri: It's traditionally used to cheer up farmers and wish for a good harvest.

Jaden: I see. Look! Some people are dancing to the rhythm.

Yuri: Yes, that's a big part of nongak. (b)<u>함께 춤추는 것이 음악을 완성하지.</u> (together)

Jaden: Let's join them.

Yuri: Sure. Why not?

**08** 위 대화의 밑줄 친 (a)와 바꾸어 쓸 수 있는 것을 고르시오.

① I don't know where that music is coming from.

② I'm sure where that music is coming from.

③ It's not certain where that music is coming from.

④ I want to know where that music is coming from.

⑤ I've been told where that music is coming from.

**09** 위 대화의 밑줄 친 (b)를 주어진 단어를 사용하여 5 단어로 영작하시오.

➡ _____

**10** 다음 짝지어진 대화가 <u>어색한</u> 것은?

① A: Look at the boy. I wonder why he is running.

B: I think he is late for school.

② A: Look at her. I wonder why she looks surprised.

B: I think she saw a celebrity.

③ A: Could you explain what this is?

B: It's a traditional Korean hairpin. It's called a binyeo.

④ A: Can you tell me how to use this machine?

B: Sure. Press this button first.

⑤ A: I want to know where the photo was taken.

B: Thank you for your great efforts.

**[01~02]** 다음 대화를 읽고 물음에 답하시오.

W: Excuse me, I'd like to borrow an audio guide.
M: Here you are.
W: _____
M: Sure. Press this button, and it'll tell you what to do.

**01** 위 대화의 빈칸에 들어갈 말을 주어진 단어를 배열하여 영작하시오.

you / how / it / could / to / explain / use

➡ _____

**02** What does the woman get to know after pressing the button?

➡ _____

**03** 다음 대화의 내용과 일치하도록 빈칸을 완성하시오.

Brian: Look over there. I wonder why there are so many people waiting in line.
Sujin: They're waiting to get into the new bakery there.
Brian: Why? Is it famous?
Sujin: Yes. It was on a TV program.
Brian: Really? We should try their bread then.
Sujin: Sure.

Brian and Sujin saw many people ( A ) _____ in front of ( B ) _____. People wanted to ( C ) _____ there. The new bakery was so popular because (D) _____. Brian and Sujin wanted to try its bread together.

**[04~05]** 다음 대화를 읽고 물음에 답하시오.

Jaden: Do you hear that? I wonder where that music is coming from.
Yuri: I think it's coming from over there. Do you want to go and check it out?
Jaden: Yes, I love that strong beat. Is it traditional Korean music?
Yuri: Yes, it's called nongak. It's a kind of community band music.
Jaden: Nongak? Could you explain a little bit more about it?
Yuri: It's traditionally used to cheer up farmers and wish for a good harvest.
Jaden: I see. Look! Some people are dancing to the rhythm.
Yuri: Yes, that's a big part of nongak. Dancing together completes the music.
Jaden: Let's join them.
Yuri: Sure. Why not?

**04** 위 대화를 읽고 빈칸에 알맞은 말을 써 넣으시오.

VISIT Korea

About Korea | **Culture** | Food | Travel | More

Nongak …
• is a community __(1)__ music
• has __(2)__ beats
• cheers up __(3)__
• wishes for a good __(4)__

➡ (1) _____ (2) _____ (3) _____
(4) _____

**05** What are Jaden and Yuri going to do after the conversation?

➡ _____
_____

# Grammar

### ① '과거완료' had + 과거분사

- Until then, I **had** only **seen** black-and-white photos of haenyeo.
  그때까지, 나는 흑백 사진 속의 해녀만 보았었다.　　　그녀는 다섯 시간이 넘도록 물속에 있은 후에도 계속 웃었다.

- She kept laughing even after she **had been** in the water for over five hours.

■ 과거완료시제는 'had+과거분사' 형태로 표현하며, 과거의 어느 시점을 기준으로 그 이전에 일어난 동작이나 상태를 나타낸다.

- Somi went shopping at the local market after she **had gone** swimming at Hyeopjae Beach.
  소미는 협재 해변으로 수영하러 간 후, 지역 시장으로 쇼핑하러 갔다.

■ 과거의 특정 시점을 기준으로 그 이전에 일어난 동작의 완료, 경험, 계속, 결과를 나타낸다.

(1) 완료: '막 ~했었다'는 의미로 과거 이전에 시작된 동작이 과거의 어느 시점에 완료된 일을 나타낸다. 보통 already, yet 등의 부사와 함께 쓰인다.

- When I arrived, the class **had** already **begun**. 내가 도착했을 때, 수업이 벌써 시작됐다.

(2) 경험: '~한 적이 있었다'는 의미로 과거 이전부터 과거의 어느 시점까지의 경험을 나타낸다. 보통 never, ever, once, twice, before 등의 부사(구)와 함께 쓰인다.

- Barbara recognized the suspect immediately, for she **had met** him online before.
  Barbara는 그 용의자를 즉시 알아봤는데, 전에 온라인상에서 그를 만난 적이 있었기 때문이었다.

(3) 결과: '(과거 이전에) ~해서, 그 결과 …했다'는 의미로 과거 이전의 동작이 과거의 어느 시점의 결과에 영향을 미치는 것을 나타낸다.

- He **had gone** to work when I called. 내가 전화했을 때, 그는 (이미) 출근했다.

(4) 계속: '계속 ~하고 있었다'는 의미로 과거 이전부터 과거의 어느 시점까지 계속되는 동작이나 상태를 나타낸다. 보통 since, for 등과 함께 쓰인다.

- Tiffany **had waited** for her brother for 2 years when he returned.
  그녀의 오빠가 돌아왔을 때, Tiffany는 오빠를 2년 동안이나 기다렸었다.

■ 부정문은 'had+not[never]+과거분사', 의문문은 'Had+주어+과거분사 ~?', 과거 어느 시점을 기준으로 전부터 진행 중인 동작을 강조할 때는 과거완료진행형 'had+been+V-ing'을 쓴다.

- She **had never won** an Academy Award by then. 그녀는 그 때까지 아카데미상을 탄 적이 없었다.

- **Had they met** the director before? 그들이 전에 감독을 만난 적이 있었나요?

- I **had been watching** a movie until you came to see me. 당신이 나를 보러올 때까지 나는 영화를 보고 있었다.

### 핵심 Check

1. 괄호 안에서 알맞은 말을 고르시오.

(1) My family (has / had) lived in Seoul before we moved to Busan.

(2) Suji had never seen wild animals until she (visits / visited) the zoo.

## ② 간접의문문

> - They didn't understand **why I wanted to take their pictures.**
> 그들은 내가 왜 그들의 사진을 찍으려고 하는지 이해하지 못했다.
>
> - Please tell us **what you're planning to do in the future.**
> 앞으로 계획하고 있는 것에 대해 말씀해 주세요.

■ 간접의문문은 의문문이 다른 문장의 일부가 된 형태로 '의문사+주어+동사' 형태로 쓰며, 이때 의문사가 접속사 역할을 한다.

- I want to know. + Where is he from?
  → I want to know **where he is from**. 나는 그가 어디에서 왔는지 알고 싶다.
- I wonder. + Why did she leave so early?
  → I wonder **why she left so early**. 나는 그녀가 왜 그렇게 빨리 떠났는지 궁금하다.

■ 의문문의 '동사+주어'의 어순이, 간접의문문에서 '주어+동사'의 어순이 되지만, 의문사가 주어인 의문문은 어순의 변화가 생길 수 없다.

- My teacher will tell us. + Who called the police?
  → My teacher will tell us **who called the police**.
  나의 선생님은 누가 경찰에게 전화를 했는지 우리에게 말해 줄 것이다.

■ 의문사가 없는 경우, **if** 또는 **whether**가 '~인지 (아닌지)'라는 의미의 명사절을 이끈다.

- I don't know. + Does she like me?
  → I don't know **if[whether] she likes me**. 나는 그녀가 나를 좋아하는지 알지 못한다.
- Tell us. + Is the lady married or not?
  → Tell us **if[whether] the lady is married or not**. 그 숙녀분이 결혼했는지 안 했는지를 우리에게 말해 주시오.

■ 생각이나 추측, 상상, 믿음 등을 나타내는 동사들(think, believe, guess, suppose, imagine)이 쓰인 문장에서 의문사가 이끄는 간접의문문이 목적어가 될 때, 간접의문문의 의문사를 문장 맨 앞으로 보낸다. 이 경우, 의문사가 문두로 가도, 어순은 '주어+동사'이다.

- Do you believe? + What does he have in his bag?
  → **What** do you believe **he has in his bag**? 당신은 그의 가방 속에 그가 무엇을 가지고 있다고 생각합니까?
- Do you think? + Who is going to marry you?
  → **Who** do you think **is going to marry you**? 당신은 누가 당신과 결혼할 것이라고 생각합니까?

## 핵심 Check

**2.** 다음 문장에서 어법상 <u>틀린</u> 부분을 찾아 바르게 고쳐 쓰시오.

(1) I wonder when will she make us the cookie. ➡ _____

(2) Nobody knows why was Sarah so upset. ➡ _____

**01** 다음 빈칸에 들어갈 말로 알맞은 것은?

Parker was sure he _____ his laptop on the table last night, but he couldn't find it.

① put          ② puts          ③ has put

④ to put          ⑤ had put

**02** 다음 두 문장을 한 문장으로 바꿔 쓸 때, 빈칸에 들어갈 말로 가장 적절한 것은?

• Does Andy know?

• Is that bus going to the airport?

→ Does Andy know _____ that bus is going to the airport?

① where          ② but          ③ if          ④ how          ⑤ so

**03** 다음 밑줄 친 부분 중 어법상 옳은 것을 고르시오.

① The old man had lived in the town for 40 years until now.

② The plane has already taken off when I reached the airport.

③ The police had found his wallet that was left under the desk.

④ She opened the box that Miles had sent a week before.

⑤ Nora has gone to London before her husband came back.

**04** 다음 두 문장을 간접의문문을 이용하여 한 문장으로 만들 때, 빈칸에 알맞은 말을 써 넣으시오.

(1) The reporter asked.

   How did she become interested in taking photos?

   ➡ The reporter _____ _____ _____ _____ _____ in taking photos.

(2) Could you tell us?

   What is so special about haenyeo?

   ➡ Could you _____ _____ _____ _____ _____ _____ about haenyeo?

**01** 밑줄 친 부분이 어법상 어색한 것은?

① After all the animals <u>had left</u> the burning woods, she felt relieved.

② The violinist <u>played</u> such a beautiful song that the audience gave her an endless applause that night.

③ Lucy asked the man how to fix the phone that <u>has broken</u> down.

④ The professor <u>had</u> just <u>left</u> the hall when the politician appeared.

⑤ Caroline ate the cookies that her grandma <u>had made</u> for her.

[02~03] 다음 우리말을 어법상 알맞게 영작한 것을 고르시오.

**02**

| 그게 무엇인지 설명해 주시겠어요? |

① Could you explain that what it is?

② Could you explain that what that is?

③ Could you explain what is that?

④ Could you explain that what is that?

⑤ Could you explain what that is?

**03**

| 왜 저렇게 많은 사람들이 줄을 서서 기다리고 있는지 궁금하다. |

① I wonder why so many people there waiting in line.

② I wonder why are there so many people waiting in line.

③ I wonder why do so many people are waiting in line.

④ I wonder why there are so many people waiting in line.

⑤ I wonder why there are so many people are waiting in line.

[04~05] 다음 중 어법상 옳은 것을 고르시오.

**04** ① Jinsu had read the article about the history of Jeju for the last 3 years.

② William lived in New York before he had moved to San Francisco.

③ Kevin required that Minsu had completed the report.

④ He lost the watch which he had bought the day before.

⑤ I am hungry since I had not eaten anything so far.

**05** ① Could you tell us more about what so special is about haenyeo?

② Does Julie know which subject do I like?

③ Do you imagine how old she is?

④ Tell me what is your favorite food.

⑤ Do you want to ask your English teacher what the sentence means?

서답형

**06** 다음 문장에서 어법상 어색한 단어 한 개를 찾아서 고치시오.

| It had been raining since Miranda went to Spain to learn tango. |

_____ ➡ _____

**07** 다음 두 문장을 의미가 같도록 한 문장으로 바꿔 쓸 때 적절하지 않은 것은?

① I'd like to know. + When did Louise apply for the scholarship?
→ I'd like to know when Louise applied for the scholarship.

② May I ask you? + How much are the souvenir photos?
→ May I ask you how much the souvenir photos are?

③ David asked Emma. + Why was she angry with him?
→ David asked Emma why she was angry with him.

④ Could you tell us? + What did Frank buy at the mall?
→ Could you tell us what Frank bought at the mall?

⑤ Susan is wondering. + Who took away her kids' toys?
→ Susan is wondering who her kids' toys took away.

**08** 다음 중 밑줄 친 과거완료의 용법이 〈보기〉와 같은 것은?

┌─ 보기 ─┐
He <u>had</u> already <u>found</u> out the secret of the mystery cube when I asked him.
└─────┘

① Tiffany <u>had lived</u> in Busan for 7 months before she moved to Daegu.

② Anna <u>had</u> never <u>been</u> fat by the time she started learning swimming.

③ My cousin <u>had been</u> sick in bed for a week when I visited him.

④ I didn't know how long he <u>had waited</u> for me at the gate the other day.

⑤ Jordan <u>had</u> not <u>finished</u> the work when everyone was about to go out.

**09** 다음 중 밑줄 친 부분의 쓰임이 〈보기〉와 같은 것은?

┌─ 보기 ─┐
Chanho should not miss such a good opportunity <u>if</u> he wants to win the game.
└─────┘

① Does anybody know <u>if</u> the handsome guy over there has a girlfriend?

② I'm sure the company will succeed <u>if</u> it expands their market in Asia.

③ All of us were not sure <u>if</u> Peter's answer was right or wrong.

④ Taste the food to determine <u>if</u> more salt is required.

⑤ Sarah wondered <u>if</u> Ted would come to the party without the invitation.

**10** 다음 두 문장을 한 문장으로 만들 때 가장 적절한 것은?

• Do you think?
• Why did the haenyeo look happy?

① Do you think why did the haenyeo look happy?

② Do you think why the haenyeo looked happy?

③ Why do you think did the haenyeo look happy?

④ Why do you think the haenyeo looked happy?

⑤ Why do you think the haenyeo did looked happy?

**[11~12]** 다음 중 어법상 옳은 문장은?

**11**
① Cecilia had lost the necklace which I bought for her.
② You can't see the snowman anymore as it had melted this morning.
③ When we were about to leave home, my uncle had already arrived.
④ The passengers have been seated before the plane took off.
⑤ William has never seen the wallaby until he visited Australia.

**12** 중요
① Do you think where Clara first met her husband?
② Could you please tell us what did your action mean?
③ I wonder whether did anyone see the boy walking along the beach.
④ Do you know how the writer of these books old is?
⑤ Let me know what they are drinking.

서답형
**[13~14]** 우리말과 일치하도록 괄호 안에 주어진 어구를 바르게 배열하시오.

**13**
기자는 많은 고객들이 돈가스를 먹으려고 줄을 서서 상당한 시간을 보냈다고 말했다. (돈가스: pork cutlet)
→ The reporter said that (lining up, time, had spent, in order to, quite a long, many, eat, customers, pork cutlet).

➡ The reporter said that _____

_____.

**14**
당신은 그 절들이 왜 유명하다고 생각합니까?
(the temples, you, famous, why, are, do, think)?

➡ _____

서답형
**15** 다음 그림을 보고 자연스러운 문장이 되도록 괄호 안에 주어진 어구를 바르게 배열하여 빈칸을 완성하시오.

(1)

➡ Jiho _____

_____. (fly, could, asked, people, in the sky, his sister, why, not)

(2)

➡ Pooh _____

_____. (a hive, told, touched, he, that morning, his friend, had, that)

**01** 다음 우리말과 일치하도록 괄호 안에 주어진 어구를 바르게 배열하여 문장을 완성하시오.

(1) 그 기업은 몇몇 프랑스인들이 전에 훔쳐갔었던 한국의 많은 보물들을 수집했다.

➡ The company _____

_____.

(before, French, stolen, collected, many, that, had, Korean treasures, some)

(2) 수민이는 어떻게 자신이 해녀를 전 세계적으로 홍보할 수 있을지 궁금하다.

➡ Sumin _____

_____. (the haenyeo, wonders, can, worldwide, promote, how, she)

(3) Jim이 출장에서 돌아왔을 때, 그는 누군가가 자신의 집에 침입했었던 것을 발견했다.

➡ When Jim came back from a business trip, _____

_____. (his house, found, broken, he, someone, into, had)

(4) 그 사진 작가가 어디에서 이 사진들을 찍었는지 추측할 수 있습니까?

➡ _____

these pictures? (guess, took, can, the photographer, where, you)

**02** 다음 〈보기〉와 같이 간접의문문을 활용하여 빈칸을 채우시오.

┌─ 보기 ─┐

When does the post office close?

→ Do you know when the post office closes?

(1) How could they get to the meeting on time?

➡ Do you know _____

_____?

(2) Which boy did the girl next to Jane choose at the blind date?

➡ Can you tell me _____

_____?

(3) Hasn't Shrek learned German yet?

➡ Do you know _____

_____?

(4) Where did Alex find the baby tiger?

➡ Let her figure out _____

_____.

(5) How old does the new employee look?

➡ How old do you think _____

_____?

**03** 다음 사진을 참고하여 우리말에 맞게, 괄호 안에 주어진 어구를 활용하되, 과거완료시제를 써서 빈칸을 채우시오.

그 날까지 나는 흑백 사진들 속의 아주 지친 모습의 해녀만 봤었다. (who, haenyeo, photos, only see, black-and-white photos)

➡ Until the day, I _____

_____

looked very tired.

**04** 다음 문장에서 어법상 어색한 것을 바르게 고쳐 다시 쓰시오.

(1) Can you tell me where was the magician when he disappeared?

➡ _____

(2) Does the young student know how the hotel is far?

➡ _____

(3) Do you know could I take pictures of haenyeo?

➡ _____

(4) They didn't understand why did the girl want to take their pictures.

➡ _____

(5) Tell me what did Zin Kim promise the haenyeo.

➡ _____

(6) I wonder why is Jejudo not suitable for farming.

➡ _____

**05** 주어진 우리말을 〈조건〉에 맞게 영작하시오.

┌ 조건 ┐
1. 부정 의미의 과거완료시제를 쓸 것.
2. The haenyeo를 포함, 총 18 단어로 쓸 것.
3. 숫자도 영어로 쓸 것.
4. the photographer, think, her picture, pretty, until, that, she, take 등을 활용할 것.
5. ago를 가장 마지막 단어로 할 것.

그 사진작가가 12년 전에 그녀의 사진을 찍을 때까지, 그 해녀는 자신이 예쁘다고 생각하지 않았었다.

➡ _____

**06** 괄호 안에 주어진 어휘를 활용하여 글자 수대로 다음 우리말을 영작하시오.

(1) Tom은 해녀들이 어떤 호흡장치도 없이 어떻게 물속에 그렇게나 오래 머무를 수 있는지 궁금했다. (how, stay, wonder, so long, without, breathing devices, haenyeo, for, any, could, 16 단어)

➡ _____

(2) 그들은 너무 많은 해양 생물을 채취하는 것이 바다를 어떻게 파괴할 수 있는지 연구하고 있다. (how, can, are, study, marine life, destroy, catching, too much, the ocean, 13 단어)

➡ _____

(3) 마녀는 거울에게 세상에서 가장 아름다운 여자가 누구인지 물었다. (who, woman, the witch, in the world, beautiful, was, ask, the mirror, 14 단어)

➡ _____

(4) 엄마 염소는 아기들이 늑대에게 언제 문을 열어 준 것인지 몰랐다. (when, to, the door, the mother goat, open, not know, the wolf, the babies, 15 단어)

➡ _____

## Haenyeo, Female Divers of Korea

For the past several years, the underwater photographer Zin Kim has promoted the culture of Jeju haenyeo worldwide. Haenyeo are Korean female divers who harvest seafood without any breathing devices. Their culture made UNESCO's Intangible Cultural Heritage list in 2016. At her studio last week, Zin Kim was interviewed about her experience of taking pictures of haenyeo.

**Q. How did you become interested in taking photos of haenyeo?**

One day, I happened to take pictures of a haenyeo. I was surprised to find that she was enjoying her job. Until then, I had only seen black-and-white photos of haenyeo who looked very tired. However, she kept laughing even after she had been in the water for over five hours. I realized then that I should take pictures of haenyeo.

**Q. You take beautiful pictures of them, but isn't it difficult to take pictures of haenyeo?**

At first, they didn't understand why I wanted to take their pictures. They didn't think they looked pretty in their wetsuits. So, I said to them, "You're very special. I want to show your culture to the world." They opened up to me then. Of course, I also promised them that I would make them look beautiful in my pictures.

---

female 여성의, 암컷의

past 지나간

several 몇몇의

underwater 수중의, 물속에서

photographer 사진작가

promote 홍보하다, 촉진하다

worldwide 세계적으로

breathe 호흡하다

intangible 무형의, 만질 수 없는

heritage 유산

experience 경험

happen to 우연히 ~하다

black-and-white (사진, TV 등) 흑백의

realize 깨닫다, 인식하다

wetsuit 잠수용 고무 옷

---

### 확인문제

● 다음 문장이 본문의 내용과 일치하면 T, 일치하지 <u>않으면</u> F를 쓰시오.

1 Zin Kim is the underwater photographer. ☐

2 Haenyeo are Korean female divers who harvest seafood with breathing devices. ☐

3 At first, haenyeo understood why Zin Kim wanted to take their pictures. ☐

4 Haenyeo didn't think they looked pretty in their wetsuits. ☐

5 Zin Kim wants to show the culture of Korea to the world. ☐

**Q. Could you tell us more about haenyeo? What's so special about them?**

I can tell you three things. First, haenyeo are a symbol of strong women. Jejudo, which is a volcanic island, is not suitable for farming, 계속적 용법의 관계대명사. which가 Jejudo를 받아서 그에 대한 추가 설명을 덧붙이고 있다. so many haenyeo have become the breadwinners for their families. Second, haenyeo form their own communities and help each other. For example, more-experienced haenyeo train less-experienced haenyeo. more(부사)+experienced(형용사)가 haenyeo를 꾸며 주고 있음. less(부사)+experienced(형용사)가 haenyeo를 꾸며 주고 있음. Third, because they stay in the water without any breathing devices, haenyeo can't catch a lot of seafood. This is good for the underwater be good for: ~에 좋다 environment. Catching too much marine life at one time in one place 동명사 주어   = It can destroy the ocean to catch too much marine life at one time can destroy the ocean.   in one place.

**Q. Lastly, please tell us what you're planning to do in the future.**
'What are you planning to do ~?'라는 의문문이 tell의 직접목적어로 쓰여 간접의문문이 된 형태
I once attended an overseas exhibition with a couple of haenyeo
   attended at(×)                          2~3명[개]
to give a talk about their lives. When I finished my talk, one of the
to부정사의 부사적 용법(목적)
haenyeo held my hand tightly. She said to me, "Thank you so much.
        = me by the
I've never known in my whole life that I was such a special person."
경험 용법                          such+a+형용사+명사
She was crying with happiness. Everyone in the audience was deeply
moved. I can never forget that moment, so I'll continue to take pictures
= touched                                      = taking
of haenyeo. I want to tell more beautiful stories about them to many
                            tell은 to를 사용하여 3형식으로 바꿀 수 있다.
more people in the world.

volcanic 화산의, 화산 작용에 의한
suitable 적합한, 적절한
breadwinner 생계를 책임지는 사람, 가장
experienced 경험이 있는
marine 해양의, 바다의
once 한 번, 한때, 옛날
attend 참석하다
overseas 해외의
exhibition 전시회, 박람회
give a talk 강의하다, 연설하다
tightly 단단히, 꽉
audience 청중

**확인문제**

● 다음 문장이 본문의 내용과 일치하면 T, 일치하지 않으면 F를 쓰시오.

1 Many haenyeo have become the breadwinners for their families. ☐

2 Haenyeo can catch a lot of seafood at one time. ☐

3 Catching too much marine life at one time in one place can destroy the ocean. ☐

4 A couple of haenyeo attendeded an overseas exhibition and gave a talk about their lives. ☐

5 One of the haenyeo said that she had never known in her whole life that she was such a special person. ☐

● 우리말을 참고하여 빈칸에 알맞은 말을 쓰시오.

**1** Haenyeo, _____ _____ of Korea

**2** For the past several years, the _____ _____ Zin Kim _____ _____ the culture of Jeju haenyeo worldwide.

**3** Haenyeo are Korean female divers who harvest seafood _____ _____ _____ _____.

**4** Their culture _____ _____ _____ _____ _____ in 2016.

**5** At her studio last week, Zin Kim _____ _____ about her experience of taking pictures of haenyeo.

**6** Q. How did you _____ _____ _____ taking photos of haenyeo?

**7** One day, I _____ _____ take pictures of a haenyeo.

**8** I _____ _____ _____ _____ _____ that she was enjoying her job.

**9** Until then, I had only seen black-and-white photos of haenyeo who _____ _____ _____.

**10** However, she _____ _____ even after she had been in the water for over five hours.

**11** I realized then that I _____ _____ pictures of haenyeo.

**12** Q. You take beautiful pictures of them, but _____ _____ _____ to take pictures of haenyeo?

**13** At first, they didn't understand _____ _____ _____ to take their pictures.

**14** They didn't think they looked pretty _____ _____ _____.

**15** So, I said to them, "You're _____ _____.

**16** I want to _____ your culture _____ the world."

**17** They _____ _____ to me then.

**18** Of course, I also promised them that I would _____ _____ look _____ in my pictures.

| | |
|---|---|
| 1 | 해녀, 한국의 여성 잠수부 |
| 2 | 지난 몇 년 동안, 수중 사진작가 Zin Kim은 제주 해녀 문화를 전 세계에 홍보해 왔다. |
| 3 | 해녀는 어떤 호흡 장치도 사용하지 않고 해산물을 채취하는 한국의 여성 잠수부들이다. |
| 4 | 그들의 문화는 2016년에 유네스코 무형문화유산에 등재되었다. |
| 5 | 지난주 그녀의 작업실에서, Zin Kim과 해녀의 사진을 찍는 그녀의 경험에 대해 인터뷰를 했다. |
| 6 | Q. 어떻게 해녀의 사진을 찍는 것에 관심을 가지게 되었나요? |
| 7 | 어느 날, 저는 우연히 한 해녀의 사진을 찍게 되었어요. |
| 8 | 저는 그녀가 자신의 일을 즐겁게 하는 것을 보고 놀랐습니다. |
| 9 | 그때까지, 저는 흑백 사진 속의 아주 지친 모습의 해녀만 봐 왔죠. |
| 10 | 하지만, 그녀는 다섯 시간이 넘도록 물속에 있은 후에도 계속 웃었어요. |
| 11 | 저는 그때 해녀의 사진을 찍어야겠다고 깨달았어요. |
| 12 | Q. 작가님은 아름다운 해녀 사진들을 찍으시는데, 그들의 사진을 찍는 것이 어렵진 않으신가요? |
| 13 | 처음에, 그들은 제가 왜 자신들의 사진을 찍으려고 하는지 이해하지 못했어요. |
| 14 | 그들은 잠수복을 입은 자신들의 모습이 예뻐 보인다고 생각하지 않았으니까요. |
| 15 | 그래서, 제가 그들에게 말했죠. "여러분들은 아주 특별해요. |
| 16 | 저는 여러분의 문화를 세계에 알리고 싶어요." |
| 17 | 그들은 그때 제게 마음을 열었어요. |
| 18 | 물론, 저 또한 그들에게 제 사진 속에서 그들을 아름답게 보이도록 하겠다고 약속했지요. |

**19** Q. Could you tell us _____ _____ haenyeo?

**20** What's _____ _____ about them?

**21** I _____ _____ _____ three things.

**22** First, haenyeo are a symbol of _____ _____.

**23** Jejudo, which is a volcanic island, _____ _____ _____ _____ farming, so many haenyeo have become _____ _____ _____ their families.

**24** Second, haenyeo _____ their own communities and help _____ _____.

**25** For example, _____ haenyeo train _____ haenyeo.

**26** Third, because they stay in the water _____ any breathing devices, haenyeo _____ _____ a lot of seafood.

**27** This _____ _____ _____ the underwater environment.

**28** Catching too much marine life _____ _____ _____ _____ _____ _____ can destroy the ocean.

**29** Q. Lastly, please tell us what you're _____ _____ _____ in the future.

**30** I once _____ an overseas exhibition with a couple of haenyeo to _____ _____ _____ about their lives.

**31** When I finished my talk, one of the haenyeo _____ _____ _____ tightly.

**32** She said to me, "Thank you _____ _____.

**33** I've never known in my whole life that I was _____ _____ _____ _____."

**34** She was crying _____ _____.

**35** Everyone in the audience _____ _____ _____.

**36** I _____ _____ _____ that moment, so I'll continue to take pictures of haenyeo.

**37** I want to tell _____ _____ _____ _____ to many more people in the world.

**19** Q. 해녀에 대해서 더 말씀해 주시겠어요?

**20** 그들은 무엇이 그렇게 특별한가요?

**21** 세 가지를 말씀 드릴게요.

**22** 첫 번째로, 해녀들은 강인한 여성의 상징이에요.

**23** 제주도는 화산섬이고, 이는 농사에 적합하지 않아서 많은 해녀들이 가족들의 생계비를 버는 가장이 되어 왔어요.

**24** 둘째로, 해녀들은 그들 자신의 공동체를 조직하고 서로 도와요.

**25** 예를 들어, 경험이 더 많은 해녀들이 경험이 적은 해녀들을 훈련시키지요.

**26** 세 번째로, 어떤 호흡 장치도 사용하지 않고 물속에 머물기 때문에, 해녀는 많은 해산물을 채취할 수가 없어요.

**27** 이것은 수중 환경에 좋은 것이지요.

**28** 한 번에 한 장소에서 너무 많은 해양생물을 채취하는 것은 바다를 파괴할 수 있으니까요.

**29** Q. 마지막으로, 앞으로 계획하고 있는 것에 대해 말씀해 주세요.

**30** 예전에 두 명의 해녀들과 함께 그들의 삶에 대해 이야기하기 위해 해외에서 열리는 박람회에 참가한 적이 있어요.

**31** 제가 연설을 마쳤을 때, 해녀 중 한 분이 제 손을 꼭 잡았어요.

**32** 그분이 말했죠, "너무 고마워.

**33** 내 평생 내가 이렇게 특별한 사람이라는 걸 미처 알지 못했어."

**34** 그녀는 행복해서 울고 있었어요.

**35** 청중들 모두가 깊은 감동을 받았어요.

**36** 전 그 순간을 절대 잊을 수가 없기 때문에 해녀의 사진을 계속해서 찍을 거예요.

**37** 저는 그들에 대한 더 많은 아름다운 이야기들을 세계의 더 많은 사람들에게 알려 주고 싶어요.

● 우리말을 참고하여 본문을 영작하시오.

**1** 해녀, 한국의 여성 잠수부
➡ _____

**2** 지난 몇 년 동안, 수중 사진작가 Zin Kim은 제주 해녀 문화를 전 세계에 홍보해 왔다.
➡ _____
_____

**3** 해녀는 어떤 호흡 장치도 사용하지 않고 해산물을 채취하는 한국의 여성 잠수부들이다.
➡ _____

**4** 그들의 문화는 2016년에 유네스코 무형문화유산에 등재되었다.
➡ _____

**5** 지난주 그녀의 작업실에서, Zin Kim과 해녀의 사진을 찍는 그녀의 경험에 대해 인터뷰를 했다.
➡ _____

**6** Q. 어떻게 해녀의 사진을 찍는 것에 관심을 가지게 되었나요?
➡ _____

**7** 어느 날, 저는 우연히 한 해녀의 사진을 찍게 되었어요.
➡ _____

**8** 저는 그녀가 자신의 일을 즐겁게 하는 것을 보고 놀랐습니다.
➡ _____

**9** 그때까지, 저는 흑백 사진 속의 아주 지친 모습의 해녀만 봐 왔죠.
➡ _____

**10** 하지만, 그녀는 다섯 시간이 넘도록 물속에 있은 후에도 계속 웃었어요.
➡ _____

**11** 저는 그때 해녀의 사진을 찍어야겠다고 깨달았어요.
➡ _____

**12** Q. 작가님은 아름다운 해녀 사진들을 찍으시는데, 그들의 사진을 찍는 것이 어렵진 않으신가요?
➡ _____

**13** 처음에, 그들은 제가 왜 자신들의 사진을 찍으려고 하는지 이해하지 못했어요.
➡ _____

**14** 그들은 잠수복을 입은 자신들의 모습이 예뻐 보인다고 생각하지 않았으니까요.
➡ _____

**15** 그래서, 제가 그들에게 말했죠, "여러분들은 아주 특별해요.
➡ _____

**16** 저는 여러분의 문화를 세계에 알리고 싶어요."
➡ _____

**17** 그들은 그때 제게 마음을 열었어요.
➡ _____

**18** 물론, 저 또한 그들에게 제 사진 속에서 그들을 아름답게 보이도록 하겠다고 약속했지요.
➡ _____

**19** Q. 해녀에 대해서 더 말씀해 주시겠어요?
➡ _____

**20** 그들은 무엇이 그렇게 특별한가요?

➡ _____

**21** 세 가지를 말씀 드릴게요.

➡ _____

**22** 첫 번째로, 해녀들은 강인한 여성의 상징이에요.

➡ _____

**23** 제주도는 화산섬이고, 이는 농사에 적합하지 않아서 많은 해녀들이 가족들의 생계비를 버는
가장이 되어 왔어요.

➡ _____

_____

**24** 둘째로, 해녀들은 그들 자신의 공동체를 조직하고 서로 도와요.

➡ _____

**25** 예를 들어, 경험이 더 많은 해녀들이 경험이 적은 해녀들을 훈련시키지요.

➡ _____

**26** 세 번째로, 어떤 호흡 장치도 사용하지 않고 물속에 머물기 때문에, 해녀는 많은 해산물을 채취할
수가 없어요.

➡ _____

_____

**27** 이것은 수중 환경에 좋은 것이지요.

➡ _____

**28** 한 번에 한 장소에서 너무 많은 해양생물을 채취하는 것은 바다를 파괴할 수 있으니까요.

➡ _____

**29** Q. 마지막으로, 앞으로 계획하고 있는 것에 대해 말씀해 주세요.

➡ _____

**30** 예전에 두 명의 해녀들과 함께 그들의 삶에 대해 이야기하기 위해 해외에서 열리는 박람회에
참가한 적이 있어요.

➡ _____

**31** 제가 연설을 마쳤을 때, 해녀 중 한 분이 제 손을 꼭 잡았어요.

➡ _____

**32** 그분이 말했죠, "너무 고마워.

➡ _____

**33** 내 평생 내가 이렇게 특별한 사람이라는 걸 미처 알지 못했어."

➡ _____

**34** 그녀는 행복해서 울고 있었어요.

➡ _____

**35** 청중들 모두가 깊은 감동을 받았어요.

➡ _____

**36** 전 그 순간을 절대 잊을 수가 없기 때문에 해녀의 사진을 계속해서 찍을 거예요.

➡ _____

**37** 저는 그들에 대한 더 많은 아름다운 이야기들을 세계의 더 많은 사람들에게 알려 주고 싶어요.

➡ _____

**[01~03] 다음 글을 읽고 물음에 답하시오.**

For the past several years, the underwater photographer Zin Kim has promoted the culture of Jeju haenyeo worldwide. Haenyeo are Korean female divers ⓐ_____ harvest seafood without any breathing devices. Their culture ⓑ<u>made</u> UNESCO's Intangible Cultural Heritage list in 2016. At her studio last week, Zin Kim was interviewed about her experience of taking pictures of haenyeo.

**01** 위 글의 빈칸 ⓐ에 들어갈 알맞은 말을 <u>모두</u> 고르시오.

① which　　② who　　③ what
④ that　　⑤ whom

**02** 위 글의 밑줄 친 ⓑmade와 같은 의미로 쓰인 것을 고르시오.

① She <u>made</u> her own clothes.
② He always <u>made</u> me laugh.
③ She <u>made</u> him her assistant.
④ They <u>made</u> me repeat the whole story.
⑤ Jones <u>made</u> a professor in five years.

**03** 중요 According to the passage, which is NOT true?

① Zin Kim is an underwater photographer.
② Zin Kim has promoted the culture of Jeju haenyeo worldwide for the past several years.
③ Haenyeo are Korean female divers.
④ Haenyeo harvest seafood with the help of breathing devices.
⑤ Haenyeo's culture has been UNESCO's Intangible Cultural Heritage since 2016.

**[04~06] 다음 글을 읽고 물음에 답하시오.**

Q. _____ ⓐ _____

One day, I happened to take pictures of a haenyeo. I was surprised to find that she was enjoying her job. Until then, I had only seen black-and-white photos of haenyeo who looked very tired. However, she kept _____ ⓑ _____ even after she ⓒ<u>had been</u> in the water for over five hours. I realized then that I should take pictures of haenyeo.

**04** 중요 위 글의 빈칸 ⓐ에 들어갈 알맞은 질문을 고르시오.

① Could you tell us more about haenyeo?
② What's so special about haenyeo?
③ How did you become interested in taking photos of haenyeo?
④ What do you want to do in the future?
⑤ Is it difficult to take pictures of haenyeo?

**서답형**
**05** 위 글의 빈칸 ⓑ에 laugh를 알맞은 형태로 쓰시오.

➡ _____

**06** 아래 〈보기〉에서 위 글의 밑줄 친 ⓒhad been과 과거완료의 용법이 <u>다른</u> 것의 개수를 고르시오.

─ 보기 ─
① I <u>had</u> just <u>finished</u> my homework when she came.
② He <u>had lived</u> there for ten years when his father died.
③ I found that I <u>had lost</u> my wallet on the subway.
④ The train <u>had</u> already <u>left</u> when he got to the station.
⑤ They <u>had</u> never <u>met</u> a student like him before.

① 1개　② 2개　③ 3개　④ 4개　⑤ 5개

[07~09] 다음 글을 읽고 물음에 답하시오.

**Q. You take beautiful pictures of them, but isn't it difficult to take pictures of haenyeo?**

(①) At first, ⓐ그들은 제가 왜 자신들의 사진을 찍으려고 하는지 이해하지 못했어요. (②) They didn't think they looked pretty in their wetsuits. (③) So, I said to them, "You're very special. (④) I want to show your culture to the world." (⑤) Of course, I also promised them that I would make them look beautiful in my pictures.

**07** 위 글의 흐름으로 보아, 주어진 문장이 들어가기에 가장 적절한 곳은?

> They opened up to me then.

①        ②        ③        ④        ⑤

**08** 위 글의 제목으로 알맞은 것을 고르시오.

① Why Do You Want to Take Pictures of Haenyeo?

② Wow! Haenyeo Let Me Show Their Culture through Pictures!

③ Why Is It Important to Show Haenyeo's Culture?

④ Are You Interested in Taking Pictures of Haenyeo?

⑤ How Can You Make Haenyeo Look Beautiful in Your Pictures?

**09** 위 글의 밑줄 친 ⓐ의 우리말에 맞게 주어진 어휘를 이용하여 10 단어로 영작하시오.

> why, their pictures

➡ _____

_____

[10~13] 다음 글을 읽고 물음에 답하시오.

**Q. Lastly, please tell us what you're planning to do in the future.**

I once (A)[attended / attended to] an overseas exhibition with a couple of haenyeo to give a talk about their lives. When I finished my talk, one of the haenyeo held my hand tightly. She said to me, "Thank you so much. ⓐI've never known in my whole life that I was (B)[so / such] a special person." She was crying with happiness. Everyone in the audience was deeply moved. I can never forget that moment, (C)[as / so] I'll continue to take pictures of haenyeo. I want to tell more beautiful stories about them to many more people in the world.      <I: Zin Kim>

서답형
**10** 위 글의 괄호 (A)~(C)에서 문맥이나 어법상 알맞은 낱말을 골라 쓰시오.

➡ (A) _____ (B) _____ (C) _____

**11** 위 글의 분위기로 가장 알맞은 것을 고르시오.

① confusing        ② interesting

③ depressing       ④ boring

⑤ touching

**12** Which question CANNOT be answered after reading the passage?

① With whom did Zin Kim attend an overseas exhibition?

② Why did Zin Kim attend an overseas exhibition?

③ When Zin Kim finished her talk, what did one of the haenyeo tell her?

④ How long has Zin Kim taken pictures of haenyeo?

⑤ What does Zin Kim want to tell to many more people in the world?

**13** 위 글의 밑줄 친 ⓐ의 현재완료와 용법이 같은 것을 모두 고르시오.

① I have just bought my watch.

② I have been to England twice.

③ Have you ever seen a panda?

④ Have you finished it yet?

⑤ Alice has lived in New York since January.

[14~17] 다음 글을 읽고 물음에 답하시오.

> **Q. Could you tell us more about haenyeo? What's so special about them?**
>
> I can tell you three things. First, haenyeo are a symbol of strong women. (A)Jejudo, that is a volcanic island, is not suitable for farming, so many haenyeo have become the ⓐ for their families. Second, haenyeo form their own communities and help each other. For example, more-experienced haenyeo train less-experienced haenyeo. Third, because they stay in the water without any breathing devices, haenyeo can't catch a lot of seafood. (B)This is good for the underwater environment. Catching too much marine life at one time in one place can destroy the ocean.

**14** 주어진 영영풀이를 참고하여 빈칸 ⓐ에 철자 b로 시작하는 단어를 쓰시오.

> the people who earn the money that the family need for essential things

➡ _____

**15** 위 글의 밑줄 친 (A)에서 어법상 틀린 부분을 찾아 고치시오.

_____ ➡ _____

**16** 위 글의 밑줄 친 (B)This가 가리키는 것을 본문에서 찾아 쓰시오.

➡ _____

**17** 위 글의 주제로 알맞은 것을 고르시오.

① haenyeo as the subject of pictures

② what is special about haenyeo

③ haenyeo as a symbol of strong women

④ the hard lives of the breadwinners

⑤ the way haenyeo form their own communities

[18~21] 다음 글을 읽고 물음에 답하시오.

> **Q. ①You take beautiful pictures of them, but isn't it difficult to take pictures of haenyeo?**
>
> At first, ②they didn't understand why I wanted to take ③their pictures. They didn't think they looked pretty ⓐ their wetsuits. So, I said to ④them, "⑤You're very special. I want to show your culture ⓑ the world." They opened up to me then. Of course, ⓒI also promised them that I would make them looking beautiful in my pictures.
>
> <I: Zin Kim>

**18** 위 글의 빈칸 ⓐ와 ⓑ에 들어갈 전치사가 바르게 짝지어진 것은?

|  | ⓐ | ⓑ |  | ⓐ | ⓑ |
|---|---|---|---|---|---|
| ① | for | – from | ② | in | – by |
| ③ | in | – to | ④ | on | – to |
| ⑤ | for | – by |  |  |  |

**19** 밑줄 친 ①~⑤ 중에서 가리키는 대상이 나머지 넷과 <u>다른</u> 것은?

①      ②      ③      ④      ⑤

서답형

**20** 위 글의 밑줄 친 ⓒ에서 어법상 <u>틀린</u> 부분을 찾아 고치시오.

➡ _____ _____

**21** 자신들의 사진을 찍는 것에 대한 해녀들의 심경 변화로 가장 알맞은 것을 고르시오.

① hopeful → nervous
② delighted → upset
③ bored → agreeing
④ puzzled → consenting
⑤ confused → disappointed

[22~25] 다음 글을 읽고 물음에 답하시오.

**Q. Could you tell us more about haenyeo? What's so special about them?**

I can tell you three things. First, haenyeo are a symbol of strong women. (A)Jejudo, which is a volcanic island, is suitable for farming, so many haenyeo have become the breadwinners for their families. Second, haenyeo form their own communities and help each other.   ⓐ  , more-experienced haenyeo train less-experienced haenyeo. Third, because they stay in the water without any (B)breathing devices, haenyeo can't catch a lot of seafood. This is good for the underwater environment. (C)Catching too much marine life at one time in one place can destroy the ocean.

**22** 위 글의 빈칸 ⓐ에 들어갈 알맞은 말을 고르시오.

① Therefore      ② However
③ For example      ④ Moreover
⑤ As a result

서답형

**23** 위 글의 밑줄 친 (A)에서 흐름상 어색한 부분을 찾아 고치시오.

➡ _____ _____

**24** 위 글의 밑줄 친 (B)breathing과 문법적 쓰임이 <u>다른</u> 것을 <u>모두</u> 고르시오.

① He is a <u>walking</u> dictionary.
② Where is my <u>sleeping</u> bag?
③ She is in the <u>waiting</u> room.
④ If you want to smoke, you need to go to a <u>smoking</u> room in the lobby.
⑤ Look at the <u>dancing</u> girl over there.

서답형

**25** 위 글의 밑줄 친 (C)를 다음과 같이 바꿔 쓸 때 빈칸에 들어갈 알맞은 말을 두 단어로 쓰시오.

➡ It can destroy the ocean _____ too much marine life at one time in one place.

[01~03] 다음 글을 읽고 물음에 답하시오.

> **Q. How did you become interested in taking photos of haenyeo?**
>
> ⓐOne day, I happened to take pictures of a haenyeo. I was surprised to find that she was enjoying her job. ⓑUntil then, I have only seen black-and-white photos of haenyeo who looked very tired. However, she kept laughing even after she had been in the water for over five hours. I realized then that I should take pictures of haenyeo. <I: Zin Kim>

**01** 위 글의 밑줄 친 ⓐ를 다음과 같이 바꿔 쓸 때 빈칸에 들어갈 알맞은 말을 두 단어로 쓰시오.

➡ One day, I took pictures of a haenyeo _____ (또는 _____).

**02** 위 글의 밑줄 친 ⓑ에서 어법상 틀린 부분을 찾아 고치시오.

_____ ➡ _____

**03** 다음 빈칸 (A)와 (B)에 알맞은 단어를 넣어 Zin Kim이 해녀의 사진을 찍는 것에 관심을 가지게 된 계기를 완성하시오.

> When Zin Kim happened to take pictures of a haenyeo, she was (A)_____ her job and kept (B)_____ even after she had been in the water for over five hours. Zin Kim was surprised at that and decided to take pictures of haenyeo.

[04~06] 다음 글을 읽고 물음에 답하시오.

> (A)[During / For] the past several years, the underwater photographer Zin Kim has promoted the culture of Jeju haenyeo worldwide. Haenyeo are Korean female divers who harvest seafood without (B)[any / no] breathing devices. ⓐTheir culture made UNESCO's (C)[Tangible / Intangible] Cultural Heritage list in ⓑ2016. At her studio last week, Zin Kim was interviewed about her experience of taking pictures of haenyeo.

**04** 위 글의 괄호 (A)~(C)에서 문맥이나 어법상 알맞은 낱말을 골라 쓰시오.

➡ (A) _____ (B) _____ (C) _____

**05** 위 글의 밑줄 친 ⓐTheir가 가리키는 것을 본문에서 찾아 쓰시오.

➡ _____

**06** 위 글의 밑줄 친 ⓑ2016을 영어로 읽는 법을 쓰시오.

➡ _____

[07~09] 다음 글을 읽고 물음에 답하시오.

> **Q. Could you tell us more about haenyeo? What's so special about them?**
>
> I can tell you three things. First, haenyeo are a symbol of strong women. Jejudo, which is a volcanic island, is not suitable for farming, so many haenyeo have become the breadwinners for their families. Second, haenyeo form their own communities and

help each other. For example, more-experienced haenyeo train less-experienced haenyeo. Third, because they stay in the water without any breathing devices, haenyeo can't catch a lot of seafood. This is good for the underwater environment. Catching too much ____ⓐ____ life at one time in one place can destroy the ocean.

**07** 주어진 영영풀이를 참고하여 빈칸 ⓐ에 철자 m으로 시작하는 단어를 쓰시오.

> relating to the sea or to the animals and plants that live in the sea

➡ _____

**08** Why is the way haenyeo catch seafood good for the underwater environment? Fill in the blanks (A) and (B) with suitable words.

> Because they stay in the water without any (A)_____ _____, haenyeo (B)_____ _____ a lot of seafood.

**09** 해녀에 대한 특별한 점 3가지를 우리말로 쓰시오.

➡ (1) _____
   (2) _____
   (3) _____
       _____

[10~13] 다음 글을 읽고 물음에 답하시오.

**Q. Lastly, please tell us ____ⓐ____.**
I once attended an overseas exhibition with a couple of haenyeo to give a talk about their lives. When I finished my talk, ⓑone of the haenyeo held my hand tightly. She

said to me, "Thank you so much. I've never known in my whole life that I was such a special person." She was crying with happiness. Everyone in the audience was deeply ⓒmoved. I can never forget that moment, so I'll continue to take pictures of haenyeo. I want to tell more beautiful stories about them to many more people in the world.                    <I: Zin Kim>

**10** 다음 주어진 의문문을 위 글의 빈칸 ⓐ에 알맞은 순서로 배열하여 쓰시오.

> What are you planning to do in the future?

➡ _____

**11** 위 글의 밑줄 친 ⓑ를 다음과 같이 바꿔 쓸 때 빈칸에 들어갈 알맞은 단어를 쓰시오.

➡ one of the haenyeo held _____ by the hand tightly

**12** 위 글의 밑줄 친 ⓒmoved와 바꿔 쓸 수 있는 말을 쓰시오.

➡ _____

**13** 위 글의 내용과 일치하도록 다음 빈칸 (A)와 (B)에 알맞은 단어를 쓰시오.

> Zin Kim will continue to (A)_____ _____ of haenyeo as she can never forget the moment when one of the haenyeo thanked her. She wants to tell (B)_____ _____ _____ about haenyeo to many more people in the world.

**Communicate – B Talk and Play**

**A:** I wonder what these are.

<u>간접의문문 어순으로 '의문사+주어+동사'의 순서로 이어진다.</u>

**B:** They're called songpyeon.

**A:** Could you explain more about <u>them</u>?

= songpyeon

**B:** They're traditional Korean rice cakes.

구문해설 • traditional: 전통적인

해석

A: 나는 이것들이 무엇인지 궁금해.

B: 그것들은 송편이라고 불려.

A: 이것에 대해 좀 더 설명해 줄래?

B: 그것들은 전통적인 한국 떡이야.

**After You Read A**

**A Photographer Who Loves Haenyeo**

Zin Kim, an underwater photographer, <u>has promoted</u> the culture of Jeju

현재완료(계속적 용법)

haenyeo worldwide. She decided to <u>take pictures of them</u> when she met a

= take their pictures

haenyeo <u>who</u> was enjoying her job. <u>It</u> was not easy <u>taking</u> their pictures at

관계대명사(주격)   가주어   진주어(동명사)

first. However, when she told them <u>that</u> she wanted to show their culture to the

접속사(명사절)

world, the haenyeo <u>finally</u> opened their minds. At an overseas exhibition, she

부사(동사 수식)   → its(×) 주의 haenyeo는 복수(a haenyeo는 단수)

gave a talk about the lives of haenyeo. After her speech, <u>one of the haenyeo</u>

one of the 복수명사+단수동사

<u>was</u> crying with happiness. Zin Kim said that she <u>would</u> continue to take

시제 일치(will과거)

pictures of haenyeo.

구문해설 • underwater: 수중의, 물속의   • promote: 홍보하다, 촉진하다   • overseas: 해외의
• exhibition: 전시회

**해녀를 사랑하는 사진작가**

수중 사진작가 김진은 전 세계에 제주의 해녀 문화를 홍보해 왔다. 그녀는 자신의 일을 즐기고 있었던 한 해녀를 만났을 때, 그들의 사진을 찍기로 결심했다. 처음에는 그들의 사진을 찍는 것이 쉽지 않았다. 그러나, 그녀가 세상 사람들에게 그들의 문화를 보여주고 싶다고 그들에게 말했을 때, 마침내 해녀들은 마음을 열었다. 한 해외 전시회에서 그녀는 해녀들의 삶에 대해 강연했다. 그녀의 연설이 끝나자 해녀들 중 한 사람은 기쁨의 눈물을 흘렸다. 김진은 앞으로도 해녀들의 사진 찍는 일을 계속할 것이라고 말했다.

**Write**

Kim Minho is a barista. He makes coffee drinks <u>for a living</u>. He became a

for a living: 밥벌이로, 생계 수단으로

barista after he <u>had found</u> out about his passion for coffee. His favorite part of

바리스타가 되기 전에 발견한 것이므로, 과거완료시제를 사용

his job is <u>decorating</u> coffee with hot milk and <u>watching</u> his customers <u>enjoying</u>

동명사 보어   동명사 보어   지각동사 whatching의 목적격보어로 쓰인 현재분사

it. He is planning <u>to open</u> his own coffee shop.

opening(×)

구문해설 • barista: 바리스타, 커피 내리는 사람   • find out: 발견하다, 찾다   • passion: 열정, 흥미
• decorate: 장식하다, 꾸미다   • customer: 손님

김민호는 바리스타이다. 그의 직업은 커피 음료를 만드는 것이다. 그는 커피에 대한 그의 열정을 발견한 후에 바리스타가 되었다. 그의 직업에서 그가 가장 좋아하는 부분은 뜨거운 우유로 커피를 장식하고 그의 손님들이 그것을 즐기는 것을 보는 것이다. 그는 자신의 커피점을 열 계획이다.

**01** 다음 짝지어진 단어의 관계가 같도록 빈칸에 알맞은 말을 쓰시오.

> dark : darkness = happy : _____

**02** 다음 영영풀이가 가리키는 것을 고르시오.

> the member of a family who earns the money to support the others

① baker      ② breadwinner
③ diver      ④ audience
⑤ presenter

**03** 다음 중 밑줄 친 부분의 뜻풀이가 바르지 <u>않은</u> 것은?

① Could you <u>explain</u> more about it? (설명하다)
② There are a lot of <u>female</u> teachers in Korea. (여성의)
③ I'm planning an <u>overseas</u> trip. (해외의)
④ I have been on a trip for the <u>past</u> few days. (지나간)
⑤ She is walking along the <u>path</u>. (신뢰)

**04** 다음 우리말에 맞게 빈칸에 알맞은 말을 쓰시오.

(1) 너는 어디로 휴가를 가고 싶니?
➡ Where do you want to _____?
(2) 제가 두 서너 개의 질문을 하겠습니다.
➡ I'm going to ask _____ questions.
(3) 이 음악은 군인들을 격려하기 위해 만들어졌다.
➡ This music was made to _____ soldiers.

(4) 질문이 있다면 제게 전화주세요.
➡ _____ me _____ if you have any questions.

**05** 다음 문장의 빈칸에 들어갈 말을 <보기>에서 골라 쓰시오.

> ┤ 보기 ├
> heritage / greenhouse / device / breathe / overwork

(1) Her _____ and stress caused her to be ill.
(2) In winter, farmers grow vegetables in their _____.
(3) Cotton clothing allows your skin to _____.
(4) They tried to invent a _____ to measure brain activity during sleep.
(5) We should protect our national _____.

**[06~07]** 다음 대화를 읽고 물음에 답하시오.

Jack: Excuse me, I'd like to use a copy machine.
Sue: O.K. You can use this machine.
Jack: Could you explain how to make double-sided copies?
Sue: Sure. Press the button for double-sided copies, and then press the start button.
Jack: Thank you.

**06** What does Jack want to make?

➡ _____

**07** What will Jack do before pressing the start button?

➡ _____

[08~09] 다음 대화를 읽고 물음에 답하시오.

> Tom: Are you going somewhere this summer? (A)
>
> Jane: I'm going to Jejudo to walk along the Jeju Olle Trail. (B)
>
> Tom: The Jeju Olle Trail? (C)
>
> Jane: It's a long hiking path around Jejudo. (D)
>
> Tom: Oh, I see. I hope you enjoy your trip! (E)

**08** 위 대화의 (A)~(E) 중 주어진 문장이 들어가기에 가장 적절한 곳은?

> Could you explain what that is?

① (A)  ② (B)  ③ (C)  ④ (D)  ⑤ (E)

**09** 위 대화를 읽고 대답할 수 없는 것은?

① Where is Jane going to visit this summer?

② What is the Jeju Olle Trail?

③ Why does Jane want to visit Jejudo?

④ What does Tom hope for Jane?

⑤ What does Tom want to do in Jejudo?

[10~12] 다음 대화를 읽고 물음에 답하시오.

> Jaden: Do you hear that? I wonder where that music is coming from.
>
> Yuri: I think it's coming from over there. Do you want to go and ⓐcheck out it?
>
> Jaden: Yes, I love ⓑthat strong beat. Is it traditional Korean music?
>
> Yuri: Yes, it's ⓒcalled nongak. It's a kind of community band music.
>
> Jaden: Nongak? Could you explain a little bit more about it?
>
> Yuri: It's traditionally used to cheer up farmers and ⓓwish for a good harvest.

> Jaden: I see. Look! Some people are dancing to the rhythm.
>
> Yuri: Yes, that's a big part of nongak. Dancing together ⓔcompletes the music.
>
> Jaden: Let's join them.
>
> Yuri: Sure. Why not?

**10** 위 대화의 밑줄 친 ⓐ~ⓔ 중 어법상 어색한 것을 찾아 바르게 고치시오.

➡ _____

**11** 위 대화에서 다음 주어진 영영풀이가 가리키는 말을 찾아 쓰시오.

> one of a series of regular movements or hitting actions

➡ _____

**12** 위 대화의 내용과 일치하지 않는 것은?

① Jaden은 들려오는 음악의 강한 비트가 마음에 든다.

② Jaden과 유리는 농악을 듣고 있다.

③ 농악은 공동체 악단 음악의 한 종류이다.

④ 농악은 전통적으로 농부들의 힘을 북돋아 주고 풍년을 기원하기 위해 사용되었다.

⑤ 리듬은 농악의 큰 부분으로서 음악을 완성한다.

**13** 다음 대화를 참고하여 주어진 빈칸에 적절한 단어를 쓰시오.

> Philip: Sam, have you ever eaten cheese fondue made with Swiss style?
>
> Sam: Yes, two times.
>
> Philip: When did you first eat it?
>
> Sam: Before I graduated from the college.

➡ Sam _____ _____ cheese fondue before he graduated from the college.

**[14~15]** 다음 중 어법상 어색한 문장을 모두 고르시오.

**14**
① The people can't even guess where are the monsters from.
② The participants don't understand why the speaker is interested in.
③ Mom doesn't know whether Jamie and Esther are coming.
④ When do you think the researcher will complete the project?
⑤ There's no one knowing when the car accident happened.

**15**
① I wonder why she didn't choose me as her colleague.
② Do you know who made these yummy cookies and drinks?
③ Would you tell me when did he leave the office?
④ Do you think when Tracy will come back for her original position?
⑤ Do you have any idea how long it will take to get to the wedding?

**16** 다음 그림을 보고 괄호 안의 단어를 배열하여 빈칸을 알맞게 채우시오.

(1)

➡ Junho is _____
_____. (which, go, thinking, should, he, to, about, university)

(2)

➡ Ye-eun is _____
_____. (when, stop, will, the, wondering, rain)

**17** 다음 괄호 안에서 어법상 알맞은 것을 고르시오.

(1) Sven dropped the carrot that Olaf (had pulled / has pulled) out of the field in the snow.

(2) Last week, we learned that Kennedy (had been killed / was killed) by gunshot in 1963.

(3) The rock band (has already gone / had already gone) to New York before their fans got informed of the news.

(4) Some film lovers around the world said that they (have been / had been) learning Korean to watch *Parasite* without subtitles.

(5) An invitation was sent to the girl after the prince (had seen / has seen) her dancing on the street.

(6) I wonder when the angels (had appeared / appeared / has appeared) to the nuns.

**18** 다음 쇼핑몰의 안내 페이지와 〈보기〉의 질문을 참고하여 알맞은 내용을 골라 빈칸에 간접의문문을 써 넣으시오.

---

Fresh Daddy Grocery

• Open Hours: 10a.m. ~ 8p.m.
• Address: 123 Ilsan, Goyang
• Nearby Station: Daewha (line 3)
• Contact: mngr@freshdaddy.co.kr

---

┤ 보기 ├

• Is there any subway station near the store?
• What time does the store open?
• How can we contact the store manager?
• Where is the store located?

---

(1) Do you know _____?
   → The store opens at 10 a.m.
(2) Can you tell me _____
   _____?
   → By e-mail. mngr@freshdaddy.co.kr.
(3) Tell me _____.
   → Fresh Daddy Grocery is at 123 Ilsan, Goyang.
(4) Do you know _____
   _____?
   → Yes, the nearest subway station from the store is Daewha on line 3.

**19** 다음 각 문장의 밑줄 친 부분이 과거완료시제의 용법 중 어떤 것에 해당하는지 〈보기〉에서 찾아 기호를 쓰시오.

┤ 보기 ├

ⓐ 완료    ⓑ 경험    ⓒ 결과    ⓓ 계속

(1) I had never seen the desert until I went to Sahara last year. ( _____ )
(2) As soon as she came back to her desk, she felt something had gone from her drawer. ( _____ )

(3) Before the boss came up, Jessica had finished her report. ( _____ )
(4) The lady couldn't notice the old man since she had lost her sight. ( _____ )
(5) By the time the teacher found something strange, Michael had already completed his reading. ( _____ )
(6) Jacob had lived in Daejeon for 4 years by last year. ( _____ )
(7) Bong had won several awards before winning the Academy Award. ( _____ )
(8) The girl had stayed in the dormitory until her parents came to visit her. ( _____ )

**20** 다음 그림과 스케줄 표를 보고 과거완료시제를 활용하여, 빈칸에 알맞은 말을 써 넣으시오.

---

Today's Schedule

• Vanessa – clean the windows and wash the dishes
• Sally – give the dog some food and water the plant

---

(1) When Mom came home, she found _____
   _____.
(2) When Mom came home, she found _____
   _____.

**21** 다음 우리말에 맞도록 괄호 안에 주어진 어휘를 알맞게 배열하시오.

(1) 수진이는 왜 자신이 다른 나라에 가서 요리법을 배워야 하는지 이해할 수 없었다. (had to, in, how, why, to cook, she, learn, another country)

➡ Sujin couldn't understand _____

_____.

(2) 비행기에 남은 좌석이 있는지 확인해 주시겠어요? (seats, there, the plane, left, any, on, are, if)

➡ Could you check _____

_____?

**Reading**

**[22~24] 다음 글을 읽고 물음에 답하시오.**

**Q. Could you tell us more about haenyeo? What's so special about them?**

I can tell you three things. First, haenyeo are a symbol of strong women. Jejudo, which is a volcanic island, is not suitable ⓐ farming, so many haenyeo have become the breadwinners ⓑ their families. Second, haenyeo form their own communities and help each other. For example, more-experienced haenyeo train less-experienced haenyeo. Third, because they stay in the water without any breathing devices, haenyeo can't catch a lot of seafood. This is good for the underwater environment. ⓒCatching too much marine life at one time in one place can destroy the ocean.

**22** 위 글의 빈칸 ⓐ와 ⓑ에 공통으로 들어갈 알맞은 전치사를 고르시오.

① to      ② on      ③ for

④ in      ⑤ at

**23** 위 글의 밑줄 친 ⓒCatching과 문법적 쓰임이 같은 것을 모두 고르시오.

① Our cat is good at catching mice.

② Do you know the man catching fish?

③ I think I'm catching a cold.

④ My hobby is catching the fish.

⑤ I saw a woman catching a butterfly.

**24** According to the passage, which is NOT true?

① Haenyeo are a symbol of strong women.

② Jejudo is a volcanic island.

③ Haenyeo form their own communities.

④ Haenyeo stay in the water with no breathing devices.

⑤ Haenyeo can catch a lot of seafood at one time.

**[25~26] 다음 글을 읽고 물음에 답하시오.**

**Q. Lastly, please tell us what you're planning to do in the future.**

I once attended an overseas exhibition with a couple of haenyeo to give a talk about their lives. When I finished my talk, one of the haenyeo held my hand tightly. She said to me, "Thank you so much. I've never known in my whole life that I was such a special person." She was crying with happiness. Everyone in the audience was deeply ⓐmoved. I can never forget that moment, so I'll continue to take pictures of haenyeo. I want to tell more beautiful stories about them to many more people in the world.        <I: Zin Kim>.

**25** 위 글의 밑줄 친 ⓐmoved와 같은 의미로 쓰인 것을 고르시오.

① He moved towards the window.
② The sight moved me to tears.
③ We moved to the country last week.
④ The ship moved before the wind.
⑤ I moved that a vote should be taken on this.

**26** 위 글의 주제로 알맞은 것을 고르시오.

① an overseas exhibition Zin Kim attended
② giving a talk about haenyeo's lives
③ Zin Kim's plan in the future
④ the happiness of one of the haenyeo
⑤ beautiful stories about haenyeo

**27** 위 글의 빈칸 ⓐ에 들어갈 알맞은 말을 고르시오.

① That is
② Moreover
③ Thus
④ For example
⑤ However

**28** 위 글의 종류로 알맞은 것을 고르시오.

① review
② book report
③ diary
④ article
⑤ autobiography

**29** Which question CANNOT be answered after reading the passage?

① What does Zin Kim do?
② How did Zin Kim take pictures of haenyeo?
③ When did Zin Kim decide to take pictures of haenyeo?
④ Was it easy to take pictures of haenyeo at first?
⑤ What did Zin Kim want to show to the world?

**[27~29]** 다음 글을 읽고 물음에 답하시오.

### A Photographer Who Loves Haenyeo

Zin Kim, an underwater photographer, has promoted the culture of Jeju haenyeo worldwide. She decided to take pictures of them when she met a haenyeo who was enjoying her job.

It was not easy taking their pictures at first. ____ⓐ____, when she told them that she wanted to show their culture to the world, the haenyeo finally opened their minds.

At an overseas exhibition, she gave a talk about the lives of haenyeo. After her speech, one of the haenyeo was crying with happiness. Zin Kim said that she would continue to take pictures of haenyeo.

출제율 95%

**01** 다음 문장의 빈칸에 공통으로 들어갈 말을 고르시오.

> • The manager will _____ a presentation on the new items.
> • Can you _____ me your hand?
> • I usually _____ a call to my grandmother every week.

① give ② take ③ keep
④ like ⑤ check

출제율 90%

**02** 다음 대화가 자연스럽게 이어지도록 순서대로 배열하시오.

> (A) Really? Then, why don't we go somewhere, too?
> (B) O.K.
> (C) Lots of people are going on vacation this weekend.
> (D) Look over there. I wonder why there are so many cars on the road.

➡ _____

**[03~04]** 다음 대화를 읽고 물음에 답하시오.

Jaden: Do you hear that? I wonder where that music is coming from.
Yuri: (A) I think it's coming from over there. Do you want to go and check it out?
Jaden: Yes, I love that strong beat. Is it traditional Korean music?
Yuri: (B) It's a kind of community band music.
Jaden: Nongak? Could you explain a little bit more about it?
Yuri: (C) It's traditionally used to cheer up farmers and wish for a good harvest.
Jaden: (D) I see. Look! Some people are dancing to the rhythm.

Yuri: Yes, that's a big part of nongak. Dancing together completes the music.
Jaden: (E) Let's join them.
Yuri: Sure. Why not?

출제율 95%

**03** 위 대화의 (A)~(E) 중 주어진 문장이 들어가기에 적절한 곳은?

> Yes, it's called nongak.

① (A) ② (B) ③ (C) ④ (D) ⑤ (E)

출제율 100%

**04** 위 대화를 읽고 대답할 수 <u>없는</u> 것은?

① Where is the strong beat coming from?
② What is nongak?
③ What are some people doing to the rhythm?
④ What is a big part of nongak?
⑤ What kind of dancing can complete the music?

**[05~06]** 다음 대화를 읽고 물음에 답하시오.

W: Excuse me, I'd like to borrow an audio guide.
M: Here you are.
W: Could you explain how to use it?
M: Sure. Press this button, and it'll tell you what to do.

출제율 90%

**05** What does the woman want to do?

➡ _____

출제율 90%

**06** What should the woman do to use the audio guide?

➡ _____

**[07~08]** 다음 대화를 읽고 물음에 답하시오.

> Emma: Look over there. (A)도로에 왜 저렇게 차가 많은지 궁금하네요.
>
> Mike: Lots of people are going on vacation this weekend.
>
> Emma: Really? Then, (B)why don't we go somewhere, too? (how)
>
> Mike: O.K.

**07** 위 대화의 밑줄 친 (A)의 우리말을 〈보기〉에 주어진 단어들을 <u>모두</u> 배열하여 영작하시오.

> ┤ 보기 ├
>
> there / wonder / on / I / the / cars / so / are / road / why /many

➡ _____

**08** 위 대화의 밑줄 친 (B)와 의도가 같도록 주어진 단어를 사용하여 다시 쓰시오.

➡ _____

**09** 다음 대화가 자연스럽게 이어지도록 순서대로 배열하시오.

> (A) How do you know that?
> (B) That's Gwangandaegyo in Busan.
> (C) I went there with my family last summer.
> (D) Wow, look at the bridge in this ad. I wonder where the photo was taken.

➡ _____

**[10~11]** 다음 대화를 읽고 물음에 답하시오.

> Jack: Excuse me, I'd like to use a copy machine.
>
> Sue: O.K. You can use this machine.
>
> Jack: 어떻게 양면 복사를 하는지 설명해 주실 수 있나요?
>
> Sue: Sure. Press the button for double-sided copies, and then press the start button.
>
> Jack: Thank you.

**10** 위 대화의 밑줄 친 우리말을 〈보기〉에 주어진 단어를 알맞게 배열하여 영작하시오.

> ┤ 보기 ├
>
> how / you / copies / explain / could / make / double-sided / to

➡ _____
_____

**11** 위 대화의 내용과 일치하지 <u>않는</u> 것은?

① Jack wants to use a copy machine.
② Jack wants to make double-sided copies.
③ Sue knows how to make double-sided copies.
④ Jack should press the two buttons to make double-sided copies.
⑤ Jack should press the start button at first.

**12** 다음 우리말을 바르게 영작한 것은?

> 당신은 Paul이 무슨 음악을 듣고 있다고 생각합니까?

① What music do you suppose Paul is listening to?
② What do you suppose music is Paul listening to?
③ Do you suppose what music is Paul listening to?
④ Is what music you suppose Paul listening to?
⑤ What music do you suppose is Paul listening to?

**13** 〈보기〉와 같이 과거완료시제를 이용하여, 두 문장을 괄호 안에 주어진 접속사로 시작하는 한 문장으로 만드시오.

> ┤ 보기 ├
>
> All the Korean film fans shouted for joy. Bong won the Academy Awards. (because)
> → Because Bong had won the Academy Awards, all the Korean film fans shouted for joy.

(1) Susan promised her teacher not to throw away used batteries. She learned the importance of recycling. (after)

➡ _____

_____

_____

(2) Sunwoo lay in his room all day long. He sprained his ankle during the basketball game. (before)

➡ _____

_____

_____

**14** 다음 빈칸에 들어가기에 어색한 문장을 모두 골라 번호를 쓰고 알맞게 고쳐 다시 쓰시오.

> Do you know _____ ?

ⓐ when does the shopping mall close
ⓑ where the nearest subway station is
ⓒ what kind of movie was she watching
ⓓ what does she usually do on Sundays
ⓔ how many toys there are in the room
ⓕ what time does the show begin

➡ _____

_____

_____

**15** 다음 중 어법상 올바른 문장을 모두 고르면? (정답 2개)

① His family happened to know that Brian has worked hard only to be taken to hospital the day before.
② The first half of the match already started when we had arrived at the stadium.
③ Most Asians felt proud that Director Bong has won the grand prize at the Cannes Film Festival for the film.
④ Marty returned the umbrella which she had borrowed from the restaurant.
⑤ The flower looked much fresher than before because it had rained the day before.

**16** 다음 그림을 보고, 내용에 맞게 〈보기〉에서 알맞은 단어를 각각 선택하여 어법에 맞게 빈칸에 채워 넣으시오.

> ┤ 보기 ├
>
> • already / much / often / how → 1회씩 사용
> • gain / eat / weigh → 1회씩 사용, 어형변화 가능
> • had / he → 2회씩 사용

> The bulldog wanted to know _____ _____ _____ _____. He was surprised to find that _____ _____ _____ _____ weight before he stood on the scale. He regretted that he _____ _____ _____ some snacks before going to bed.

**17** 출제율90%

다음 우리말과 그 영작이 바르게 짝지어지지 <u>않은</u> 것은?

① 네가 몇 시에 올 것인지 궁금하다.

→ I wonder what time you will come.

② 누가 그 강아지를 내게 줬는지 말해줘.

→ Tell me who gave me the puppy.

③ 그녀가 무슨 드레스를 입었는지 기억이 안 난다.

→ I can't remember what dress she put on.

④ 그녀가 몇 살이라고 짐작하니?

→ Do you guess how old she is?

⑤ 수민이가 왜 날 싫어하는지 몰라.

→ I don't know why Sumin hates me.

**[18~20]** 다음 글을 읽고 물음에 답하시오.

> **Q. How did you become interested in taking photos of haenyeo?**
>
> One day, I happened to take pictures of a haenyeo. I was surprised to find that she was enjoying her job. Until then, I had only seen black-and-white photos of haenyeo who looked very tired. ___ⓐ___, she kept laughing even after she had been in the water for over five hours. I realized then that I should take pictures of haenyeo. <I: Zin Kim>

**18** 출제율95%

위 글의 빈칸 ⓐ에 들어갈 알맞은 말을 고르시오.

① In addition   ② For example

③ That is   ④ However

⑤ Therefore

**19** 출제율100%

위 글의 주제로 알맞은 것을 고르시오.

① how to take pictures of haenyeo

② the hard lives of haenyeo

③ the reason Zin Kim became interested in taking photos of haenyeo

④ the difficulty of taking pictures of haenyeo

⑤ the most beautiful picture that has ever been taken

**20** 출제율90%

Until she happened to take pictures of a haenyeo, what kind of photos of haenyeo had Zin Kim only seen? Answer in English in a full sentence.

➡ _____

_____

**[21~22]** 다음 글을 읽고 물음에 답하시오.

> **Q. You take beautiful pictures of them, but isn't ⓐit difficult to take pictures of haenyeo?**
>
> At first, they didn't understand why I wanted to take their pictures. They didn't think they looked pretty in their wetsuits. So, I said to them, "You're very special. I want to show your culture to the world." They opened up to me then. Of course, I also promised them that I would make them look beautiful in my pictures. <I: Zin Kim>

**21** 출제율95%

위 글의 밑줄 친 ⓐit과 문법적 쓰임이 같은 것을 고르시오.

① I make it a rule to eat breakfast.

② It is 2 miles from here to the airport.

③ It is I that am to blame.

④ Did you see it?

⑤ It is important for you to have a dream.

**22** According to the passage, which is NOT true?

① Zin Kim takes beautiful pictures of haenyeo.

② From the beginning, Zin Kim had no difficulty in taking pictures of haenyeo.

③ Haenyeo didn't think they looked pretty in their wetsuits.

④ Zin Kim wanted to show haenyeo's culture to the world.

⑤ Zin Kim promised haenyeo that she would make them look beautiful in her pictures.

[23~25] 다음 글을 읽고 물음에 답하시오.

**Q. ⓐLastly, please tell us what you're planning to do in the future.**

I once attended an overseas exhibition with a couple of haenyeo ⓑto give a talk about their lives. (①) She said to me, "Thank you so much. (②) I've never known in my whole life that I was such a special person." (③) She was crying with happiness. (④) Everyone in the audience was deeply moved. (⑤) I can never forget that moment, so I'll continue to take pictures of haenyeo. I want to tell more beautiful stories about them to many more people in the world.

**23** 위 글의 흐름으로 보아, 주어진 문장이 들어가기에 가장 적절한 곳은?

> When I finished my talk, one of the haenyeo held my hand tightly.

①    ②    ③    ④    ⑤

**24** 위 글의 밑줄 친 ⓐLastly와 바꿔 쓸 수 있는 말을 고르시오.

① Eventually    ② Immediately

③ Extremely    ④ Finally

⑤ At last

**25** 위 글의 밑줄 친 ⓑto give와 to부정사의 용법이 다른 것의 개수를 고르시오.

┌─ 보기 ─┐
① She went there to give a talk about it.
② It's your turn to give a talk about it.
③ He is wise enough to give a talk about it.
④ I felt proud to give a talk about it.
⑤ It was exciting to give a talk about it.
└────────┘

① 1개   ② 2개   ③ 3개   ④ 4개   ⑤ 5개

[26~28] 다음 글을 읽고 물음에 답하시오.

Kim Minho is a barista. He makes coffee drinks ____ⓐ____ a living. He became a barista after he had found out about his passion ____ⓑ____ coffee. His favorite part of his job is decorating coffee with hot milk and watching his customers enjoying it. He is planning to open his own coffee shop.

**26** 위 글의 빈칸 ⓐ와 ⓑ에 공통으로 들어갈 알맞은 전치사를 쓰시오.

➡ _____

**27** 주어진 영영풀이에 해당하는 단어를 본문에서 찾아 쓰시오.

> a person who makes and serves coffee in a coffee bar

➡ _____

**28** What's Kim Minho's favorite part of his job? Answer in English beginning with "It's".

➡ _____
_____

[01~03] 다음 대화를 읽고 물음에 답하시오.

Brian: Look over there. I wonder why there are so many people waiting in line.

Sujin: They're waiting to get into the new bakery there.

Brian: Why? Is it famous?

Sujin: Yes. It was on a TV program.

Brian: Really? We should try their bread then.

Sujin: Sure.

**01** Why are so many people waiting in line?

➡ _____

**02** Why is the new bakery famous? (7 words)

➡ _____

**03** What does Brian want to try?

➡ _____

[04~05] 다음 중에서 틀린 문장을 찾아 번호를 쓰고, 바르게 고쳐 문장을 다시 쓰시오.

**04** ① The film director had been tired because he spoke in front of so many people.
② The mechanic told her that someone had touched the tires of her car.
③ Emilia found out that she had lost her smartphone.
④ Julie decided to marry Jake as she had liked him for a long time.
⑤ The accounting manager said he had already completed his financial report.

➡ _____
_____

**05** ① The president wants to know what his secretary bought a week ago.
② I have no idea why the super hero is blamed for the accident.
③ Could you tell us if the injured soldier will come tomorrow morning?
④ Do you think where the police officer caught the thief?
⑤ Does Michael know how you could escape from the prison?

➡ _____
_____

**06** 〈보기〉처럼 괄호 안에 주어진 접속사와 과거완료시제를 이용하여 두 문장을 한 문장으로 쓰시오.

┤ 보기 ├

James was too full to eat more. He ate all three meals by himself. (Because로 시작)

→ Because James had eaten all three meals by himself, he was too full to eat more.

(1) Mary fought off a strange man's attack. She learned taekwondo before. (Because로 시작)

➡ _____
_____
_____

(2) Kevin never thought of quitting drinking. He saw a video of himself being a heavy drinker. (Until로 시작)

➡ _____
_____
_____

[07~09] 다음 글을 읽고 물음에 답하시오.

**Q. You take beautiful pictures of them, but isn't it difficult to take pictures of haenyeo?**

At first, they didn't understand why I wanted to take their pictures. ⓐThey didn't think they looked prettily in their wetsuits. So, I said to them, "You're very special. I want to show your culture to the world." They opened up to me then. Of course, I also promised them that ⓑ내 사진 속에서 그들을 아름답게 보이도록 하겠다.                 <I: Zin Kim>

**07** 위 글의 밑줄 친 ⓐ에서 어법상 틀린 부분을 찾아 고치시오.

_____ ➡ _____

**08** 위 글의 밑줄 친 ⓑ의 우리말에 맞게 주어진 어휘를 알맞게 배열하시오.

> them / pictures / beautiful / make / I / in / would / my / look

➡ _____

**09** Why did Zin Kim want to take pictures of haenyeo? Fill in the blanks (A) and (B) with suitable words.

> Because haenyeo are (A)_____
> _____ and she wanted to (B)_____
> _____ to the world.

[10~12] 다음 글을 읽고 물음에 답하시오.

**Q. Could you tell us more about haenyeo? What's so special about them?**

I can tell you three things. First, haenyeo are a symbol of strong women. Jejudo, which is a volcanic island, is not suitable for farming, so many haenyeo have become the breadwinners for their families. Second, haenyeo form their own communities and help each other. For example, more-experienced haenyeo train less-experienced haenyeo. Third, because they stay in the water (A)[with / without] any breathing devices, haenyeo can't catch a lot of seafood. This is good (B)[at / for] the underwater environment. Catching too much marine life at one time in one place can (C)[destroy / protect] the ocean.

**10** 위 글의 괄호 (A)~(C)에서 문맥상 알맞은 낱말을 골라 쓰시오.

➡ (A) _____ (B) _____ (C) _____

**11** 다음 빈칸 (A)와 (B)에 알맞은 단어를 넣어 해녀들이 그들 자신의 공동체를 조직하고 서로 돕는 한 예를 완성하시오.

> (A)_____ haenyeo are trained
> by (B)_____ haenyeo.

**12** Why is it impossible for haenyeo to catch a lot of seafood at one time? Answer in English beginning with "Because".

➡ _____
_____

**01** 다음 대화를 읽고 대화의 내용과 일치하도록 Jaden의 일기를 완성하시오.

Jaden: Do you hear that? I wonder where that music is coming from.

Yuri: I think it's coming from over there. Do you want to go and check it out?

Jaden: Yes, I love that strong beat. Is it traditional Korean music?

Yuri: Yes, it's called nongak. It's a kind of community band music.

Jaden: Nongak? Could you explain a little bit more about it?

Yuri: It's traditionally used to cheer up farmers and wish for a good harvest.

Jaden: I see. Look! Some people are dancing to the rhythm.

Yuri: Yes, that's a big part of nongak. Dancing together completes the music.

Jaden: Let's join them.

Yuri: Sure. Why not?

---

Walking down the street, I heard music with a (A)_____. I wanted to know (B)_____. Yuri and I found that it was traditional Korean music, called (C)_____. Yuri explained that it's a kind of (D)_____ and traditionally used to (E)_____. It was impressive for me that some people were dancing to the rhythm because dancing was a big part of nongak. Yuri and I joined them and completed the music together.

**02** 다음 그림을 보고, 그림의 상황에 맞게 〈보기〉와 같이 간접의문문을 사용하여 어법에 맞게 자유롭게 영작하시오.

보기

Do you know when you should feed the puppy?
Tell me if you checked our mailbox.

(1) _____

(2) _____

(3) _____

# 단원별 모의고사

**01** 다음 영영풀이가 가리키는 것을 고르시오.

> a picture, set of words, or a short film, intended to persuade people to buy

① advertisement   ② audio guide
③ jellyfish   ④ beat
⑤ sunshine

**02** 다음 주어진 문장의 밑줄 친 beat와 같은 의미로 쓰인 것은?

> This type of music has a strong beat.

① I like the steady beat of the drums.
② He beat me at chess.
③ Hailstones beat against the window.
④ My mother beat dust out of the carpet.
⑤ I heard the sound of beating the door.

**03** 다음 우리말에 맞게 주어진 단어를 활용하여 영작하시오.

(1) 나는 사진작가가 되고 싶다. (photo)
➡ _____

(2) 그녀는 가장 적절한 후보였다. (suit)
➡ _____

(3) 그는 내 손을 꽉 잡았다. (hold, tight)
➡ _____

(4) 나는 소설을 빌리고 싶습니다. (like)
➡ _____

**[04~05]** 다음 대화를 읽고 물음에 답하시오.

> G: Wow, look at the bridge in this ad.
> _____
> B: That's Gwangandaegyo in Busan.
> G: How do you know that?
> B: I went there with my family last summer.

**04** 위 대화의 빈칸에 들어갈 말로 적절하지 <u>않은</u> 것은?

① I wonder where the photo was taken.
② Can you tell me where the photo was taken?
③ Can I ask you where the photo was taken?
④ I want to know where the photo was taken.
⑤ I'm sure where the photo was taken.

**05** Where did the boy visit last summer?

➡ _____
_____

**[06~07]** 다음 대화를 읽고 물음에 답하시오.

> Brian: Look over there. _____
> Sujin: They're waiting to get into the new bakery there.
> Brian: Why? Is it famous?
> Sujin: Yes. It was on a TV program.
> Brian: Really? We should try their bread then.
> Sujin: Sure.

**06** 위 대화의 빈칸에 들어갈 말을 〈보기〉에 주어진 단어들을 배열하여 완성하시오.

> ┤ 보기 ├
> many / in / why / are / wonder / so / I / people / waiting / line / there

➡ _____
_____

**07** 위 대화를 읽고 대답할 수 <u>없는</u> 것은?

① What is Brian wondering?
② Why are many people waiting in line?
③ Why is the new bakery famous?
④ What does Brian want to try?
⑤ When was the new bakery on the TV program?

**08** 다음 대화가 자연스럽게 이어지도록 순서대로 배열하시오.

> (A) It's a long hiking path around Jejudo.
>
> (B) Oh, I see. I hope you enjoy your trip!
>
> (C) Are you going somewhere this summer?
>
> (D) I'm going to Jejudo to walk along the Jeju Olle Trail.
>
> (E) The Jeju Olle Trail? Could you explain what that is?

➡ _____

**[09~10]** 다음 대화를 읽고 물음에 답하시오.

> Emma: Look over there. I wonder why there are so many cars on the road.
>
> Mike: Lots of people are going on vacation this weekend.
>
> Emma: Really? Then, why don't we go somewhere, too?
>
> Mike: O.K.

**09** Why are so many cars on the road?

➡ _____

_____

**10** What did Emma suggest to Mike?

➡ _____

**11** 다음 짝지어진 대화가 <u>어색한</u> 것은?

① A: I'm wondering why he got upset.
　B: I think he had a fight with his brother.

② A: Can you tell me what they are?
　B: They're called songpyeon.

③ A: Could you tell me about them?
　B: They're traditional Korea rice cakes.

④ A: Would you give me more information?
　B: Sure. Let's take a look at this book together.

⑤ A: I'm curious why she looks so sad.
　B: I'm not following you.

**12** 다음 주어진 우리말을 영작한 것으로 옳은 것은?

> 이것이 무엇인지 설명해 주시겠어요?

① Can you explain what is this?

② Could you explain what this is?

③ Could you explain that what this?

④ What could you explain this is?

⑤ What could you explain is this?

**13** 다음 두 문장을 한 문장으로 만들 때 빈칸에 들어갈 말로 가장 알맞은 것은?

> • He was infected by the virus.
>
> • He stayed at the center of the disease for 3 months.
>
> → He was infected by the virus because _____

① he might stay at the center of the disease for 3 months.

② had he stayed at the center of the disease for 3 months.

③ he has stayed at the center of the disease for 3 months.

④ he had stayed at the center of the disease for 3 months.

⑤ he could have stayed at the center of the disease for 3 months.

**14** 다음 중 밑줄 친 부분의 쓰임이 나머지 넷과 <u>다른</u> 것은?

① Mr. Baker doesn't know <u>where the post office is located</u>.

② Mina asked me <u>what time the bank would close</u>.

③ I wonder <u>when my girlfriend will come to France</u>.

④ The executives of the company don't understand <u>why the facility is required</u>.

⑤ Let everybody know about the man <u>who won the Oscars</u> yesterday.

**15** 다음 그림을 보고, 주어진 단어들을 알맞게 배열하여 영작하되, 과거완료시제를 반드시 포함하시오. (동사를 변형)

(the woman, put, the fish, really, if)

➡ James wondered _____

_____ in the fish-shaped bun.

**16** 다음에 등장하는 사람과 직업에 대한 안내문을 읽고 괄호 안에 주어진 어휘를 알맞게 배열하여 빈칸 (A)와 (B)를 채우시오.

Yori became a content creator (A)_____

_____(gotten, she, after, views, had, 20,000) on her first video clip on WeTube. Her favorite part of her job is (B)_____

_____(about, what, sharing, special, Korean food, is) with many people around the world.

**[17~18]** 다음 글을 읽고 물음에 답하시오.

**Q. How did you become interested in taking photos of haenyeo?**

One day, I happened to take pictures of a haenyeo. I was surprised ⓐ<u>to find</u> that she was enjoying her job. Until then, I had only seen black-and-white photos of haenyeo who looked very tired. However, she kept laughing even after she had been in the water for over five hours. I realized then that I should take pictures of haenyeo.   <I: Zin Kim>

**17** 위 글의 밑줄 친 ⓐ<u>to find</u>와 to부정사의 용법이 같은 것을 <u>모두</u> 고르시오.

① She was too tired <u>to find</u> it.

② Do you know how <u>to find</u> it?

③ I was eager <u>to find</u> it.

④ Tell me the way <u>to find</u> it.

⑤ Is it difficult <u>to find</u> it?

**18** According to the passage, which is NOT true?

① Zin Kim happened to take pictures of a haenyeo.

② The haenyeo was enjoying her job.

③ Before Zin Kim took pictures of a haenyeo, she had seen many colorful photos of haenyeo.

④ The haenyeo Zin Kim took pictures of kept laughing even after she had been in the water for over five hours.

⑤ At that time, Zin Kim realized that she should take pictures of haenyeo.

**[19~21]** 다음 글을 읽고 물음에 답하시오.

**Q. Could you tell us more about haenyeo?**

_____ ⓐ _____

I can tell you three things. First, haenyeo are a symbol of strong women. Jejudo, which is a volcanic island, is not suitable for farming, so ⓑ많은 해녀들이 가족들의 생계비를 버는 가장이 되어 왔어요. (①) Second, haenyeo form their own communities and help each other. (②) For example, more-experienced haenyeo train less-experienced haenyeo. (③) Third, because they stay in the water without any breathing devices, haenyeo can't catch a lot of seafood. (④) Catching too much marine life at one time in one place can destroy the ocean. (⑤)

**19** 위 글의 빈칸 ⓐ에 들어갈 알맞은 질문을 고르시오.

① What's so special about them?
② How did you become interested in taking photos of them?
③ Isn't it difficult to take their pictures?
④ What's the secret of holding their breath?
⑤ What are you planning to do in the future?

**20** 위 글의 흐름으로 보아, 주어진 문장이 들어가기에 가장 적절한 곳은?

> This is good for the underwater environment.

①        ②        ③        ④        ⑤

**21** 위 글의 밑줄 친 ⓑ의 우리말에 맞게 9 단어로 영작하시오.

➡ _____

_____

**[22~24]** 다음 글을 읽고 물음에 답하시오.

Yori is a content creator about traditional Korean food. She posts her video clips about making and eating Korean food. She became a content creator after she had gotten ⓐ20,000 views on her first video clip on WeTube. Her favorite part of her job is sharing ⓑwhat is special about Korean food with many people around the world. She is planning to write a cookbook on Korean food.

**22** 위 글의 밑줄 친 ⓐ를 영어로 읽는 법을 쓰시오.

➡ _____

**23** 위 글의 밑줄 친 ⓑwhat과 바꿔 쓸 수 있는 말을 세 단어로 쓰시오.

➡ _____

**24** 위 글을 읽고 답할 수 <u>없는</u> 질문을 고르시오.

① What does Yori do?
② How did Yori become a content creator?
③ When did Yori get 20,000 views on her first video clip on WeTube?
④ What is Yori's favorite part of her job?
⑤ What is Yori planning to do in the future?

# A Journey into Your Mind

 **의사소통 기능**

- 걱정하기
  I'm worried about Sports Day.
- 의무 부인하기
  You don't have to clean the classroom.

 **언어 형식**

- 분사구문
  **Feeling** nervous, Jisu was carefully studying her notes in her chair.
- not only ~ but also ...
  His rival became **not only** a political supporter **but also** a good friend.

# Words & Expressions

## Key Words

- **actually** [ǽktʃuəli] 부 실제로
- **anxious** [ǽŋkʃəs] 형 불안해하는
- **apart** [əpáːrt] 부 (거리 · 공간 · 시간상으로) 떨어져
- **behavior** [bihéivjər] 명 행동
- **bored** [bɔːrd] 형 지루해하는
- **carefully** [kɛ́ərfəli] 부 조심스럽게
- **chew** [tʃuː] 동 (음식을) 씹다
- **competition** [kàmpətíʃən] 명 경쟁, 대회
- **confident** [kánfədənt] 형 자신감 있는
- **convenient** [kənvíːnjənt] 형 편리한
- **decide** [disáid] 동 결심하다
- **enemy** [énəmi] 명 적
- **famously** [féiməsli] 부 유명하게
- **graduate** [grǽdʒuət] 동 졸업하다
- **guess** [ges] 동 추측하다
- **helpless** [hélplis] 형 무력한
- **hip** [hip] 명 엉덩이, 허리께
- **instead** [instéd] 부 대신에
- **judge** [dʒʌdʒ] 동 판단하다
- **lend** [lend] 동 빌려주다
- **lucky** [lʌ́ki] 형 행운인, 운이 좋은
- **Mexican** [méksikən] 형 멕시코 출신의, 멕시코의
- **mind** [maind] 명 마음, 정신

- **nervous** [nə́ːrvəs] 형 불안해하는
- **place** [pleis] 동 놓다, 두다
- **political** [pəlítikəl] 형 정치적인
- **practice** [prǽktis] 동 연습하다
- **prepare** [pripɛ́ər] 동 준비하다
- **presentation** [prèzəntéiʃən] 명 발표
- **professional** [prəféʃənl] 형 전문적인
- **psychologist** [saikálədʒist] 명 심리학자
- **psychology** [saikálədʒi] 명 심리학
- **rare** [rɛər] 형 드문, 희귀한
- **relax** [rilǽks] 동 휴식을 취하다
- **relay** [ríːlei] 명 이어달리기
- **relieved** [rilíːvd] 형 안도하는
- **rival** [ráivəl] 명 경쟁자
- **seafood** [síːfud] 명 해산물, 해물
- **solution** [səlúːʃən] 명 해결책
- **Sports Day** 운동회
- **stranger** [stréindʒər] 명 낯선 사람
- **stressful** [strésfəl] 형 스트레스가 많은
- **study** [stʌ́di] 명 과목, 연구
- **supporter** [səpɔ́ːrtər] 명 지원자
- **unique** [juːníːk] 형 독특한

## Key Expressions

- **according to** ~에 따르면
- **be good at** ~을 잘하다
- **be worried about** ~을 걱정하다
- **by oneself** 혼자서
- **chances are that** 아마 ~일 것이다
- **clear one's mind** 마음을 가다듬다, 마음을 맑게 하다
- **come over** (장소에) 들르다
- **come up with** (해답 등을) 찾아내다, 내놓다
- **do ~ a favor** ~에게 호의를 베풀다
- **get off** 내리다
- **get up** 일어나다
- **have no idea** 알지 못하다
- **I can't wait!** 너무 기다려져!
- **in front of** ~의 앞에
- **make a presentation** 발표하다

- **make a reservation** 예약하다
- **not ~ anymore** 더 이상 ~가 아닌
- **not ~ at all** 결코 ~가 아닌
- **not only A but also B** A뿐만 아니라 B도 또한
- **put too much pressure on** ~에게 너무 많은 부담을 주다
- **Shall we ~?** ~할까요?
- **stand tall** 당당해 보이다, 우뚝 서다
- **with one's feet apart** 양발을 벌린 채로
- **stop by** ~에 들르다
- **strangely enough** 매우 이상하게도
- **turn A into B** A를 B로 바꾸다
- **What if ~?** ~하면 어쩌지?
- **Why don't you ~?** ~하지 않겠니?
- **Why not?** 좋죠!

## Word Power

### ※ 서로 비슷한 뜻을 가진 어휘

- [ ] **actually** 실제로 : **really** 실제로
- [ ] **carefully** 조심스럽게 : **attentively** 주의 깊게
- [ ] **guess** 추측하다 : **suppose** 추측하다
- [ ] **lucky** 운이 좋은 : **fortunate** 운 좋은

- [ ] **anxious** 불안해하는 : **nervous** 불안해하는
- [ ] **confident** 자신감 있는 : **convinced** 확신하는
- [ ] **helpless** 무력한 : **powerless** 힘없는
- [ ] **place** 놓다, 두다 : **put** 두다

### ※ 서로 반대되는 뜻을 가진 어휘

- [ ] **carefully** 조심스럽게 ↔ **carelessly** 부주의하게
- [ ] **convenient** 편리한 ↔ **inconvenient** 불편한
- [ ] **lend** 빌려주다 ↔ **borrow** 빌리다
- [ ] **rare** 드문, 희귀한 ↔ **common** 흔한

- [ ] **certain** 확실한 ↔ **uncertain** 불확실한
- [ ] **enemy** 적 ↔ **friend** 친구
- [ ] **lucky** 운이 좋은 ↔ **unlucky** 운이 나쁜

### ※ 명사 − 형용사

- [ ] **beauty** 아름다움 − **beautiful** 아름다운
- [ ] **care** 보살핌, 조심 − **careful** 조심스러운
- [ ] **thought** 생각 − **thoughtful** 신중한
- [ ] **hope** 희망 − **hopeful** 희망찬
- [ ] **person** 사람 − **personal** 개인적인
- [ ] **nation** 국가 − **national** 국가적인

- [ ] **color** 색 − **colorful** 다채로운
- [ ] **success** 성공 − **successful** 성공적인
- [ ] **power** 힘 − **powerful** 힘 있는
- [ ] **stress** 스트레스 − **stressful** 스트레스가 많은
- [ ] **option** 선택 − **optional** 선택적인
- [ ] **tradition** 전통 − **traditional** 전통적인

### ※ Word Partner (collocations)

- [ ] **come back** 돌아오다
- [ ] **come over** (장소에) 들르다
- [ ] **come to a decision** 결정을 내리다
- [ ] **come to an end** 끝내다

- [ ] **come first** 최우선이다
- [ ] **come prepared** 준비해 오다
- [ ] **come to an agreement** 합의에 이르다
- [ ] **come up with** 생각해 내다

## English Dictionary

- [ ] **bake** 굽다
  → to cook something using dry heat, in an oven
  오븐에서 열을 이용해서 어떤 것을 요리하다
- [ ] **chew** (음식을) 씹다
  → to bite food several times before swallowing it
  삼키기 전에 음식을 몇 번 물다
- [ ] **convenient** 편리한
  → useful to you because it saves you time
  시간을 덜어주기 때문에 쓸모가 있는
- [ ] **enemy** 적
  → someone who hates you and wants to harm you
  당신을 싫어하며 당신에게 해를 끼치고 싶어 하는 사람
- [ ] **graduate** 졸업하다
  → to complete your education at a college, school, etc.
  대학이나 학교 등에서 교육을 끝내다
- [ ] **presentation** 발표
  → an event at which you describe or explain a new product or idea
  새로운 상품이나 생각을 묘사하거나 설명하는 행사
- [ ] **psychology** 심리학
  → the study of the mind and how it influences people's behavior
  사람의 마음과 그것이 행동에 영향을 미치는 방식을 연구하는 학문

**01** 다음 짝지어진 단어의 관계가 같도록 빈칸에 알맞은 말을 주어진 철자로 시작하여 쓰시오.

carefully : carelessly = common : r_____

**02** 다음 영영풀이가 가리키는 것을 고르시오.

the study of the mind and how it influences people's behavior

① politics
② psychology
③ psychologist
④ presentation
⑤ solution

**03** 다음 중 밑줄 친 부분의 뜻풀이가 바르지 않은 것은?

① He decided to retire because of the political scandals. (정치적인)
② Wild flowers are becoming rare. (드문, 귀한)
③ You should not judge a man by his appearance. (판단하다)
④ She was in a relaxed and confident mood. (편안한)
⑤ The man is responsible for a very professional job. (전문적인)

**04** 다음 주어진 문장의 밑줄 친 judge와 같은 의미로 쓰인 것은?

Don't judge a book by its cover.

① Chris was asked to judge the singing competition.
② He was brought before the judge.

③ It's difficult to judge how long the journey will take.
④ Mr. White will judge this case.
⑤ We can't judge whether what you're doing well or not.

**05** 다음 문장에 공통으로 들어갈 말을 고르시오.

• When will you _____ back?
• My twin sister tried to _____ up with a unique idea.
• We would love to have you _____ over and celebrate with us.

① go
② get
③ lend
④ decide
⑤ come

서답형

**06** 다음 우리말에 맞게 빈칸에 알맞은 말을 쓰시오.

(1) 당신은 그것들을 적어도 1미터는 떨어뜨려 놓아야 합니다.
➡ You should place them at least one meter _____.

(2) 아이들은 그들의 잘한 행동에 대해 사탕을 받았다.
➡ Children were given sweets for their good _____.

(3) Jack은 양 허리께에 손을 대고 서 있다.
➡ Jack is standing with his hands on his _____.

(4) 대부분의 별들은 사람의 시야에 보이지 않는다.
➡ Most stars are _____ to human sight.

**01** 다음 짝지어진 단어의 관계가 같도록 빈칸에 알맞은 말을 쓰시오.

> person : personal = care : _____

**02** 다음 우리말에 맞게 빈칸에 알맞은 말을 쓰시오.

(1) 아마 그는 회의에 늦을 것이다.

➡ _____ _____ _____ he will be late for the meeting.

(2) 매우 이상하게도, 나는 전혀 불안하지 않다.

➡ _____ _____, I don't feel nervous at all.

(3) 항상 당당해 보이고 리더가 되어라.

➡ Always _____ _____ and be a leader.

(4) 나는 혼자서 이 모든 것을 할 수 없다.

➡ I can't do it all _____ _____.

**03** 다음 우리말을 주어진 단어를 이용하여 영작하시오.

(1) 나는 전문적인 심리학자가 되고 싶다. (become)

➡ _____

(2) 아이들은 쉽게 지루해한다. (get, bored)

➡ _____

(3) 내 개는 종종 내 신발을 씹는다. (shoes)

➡ _____

(4) 네 자신을 믿어라, 그리고 자신감을 가져라. (be, in)

➡ _____

**04** 다음 문장의 빈칸에 들어갈 말을 〈보기〉에서 골라 쓰시오.

> ┌─── 보기 ───┐
> rivals / seat / judge / loudly / law

(1) Do not _____ a book by its cover.

(2) People say it is Murphy's _____ when something goes wrong.

(3) When I am happy, I sing _____.

(4) The two teams have been _____ since the first match.

(5) You don't have to sit in your _____.

**05** 우리말과 일치하도록 주어진 단어를 모두 배열하여 영작하시오.

(1) 그의 그림 실력은 거의 전문가적이다. (skills / professional / are / his / almost / drawing)

➡ _____

_____

(2) 그녀가 예약하는 걸 잊어버리면 어떡하죠? (she / make / a / if / what / reservation / to / forgets)

➡ _____

(3) 나는 마음을 가다듬기 위해 산책하기로 결심했다. (to / a / to / my / I / take / mind / decided / walk / clear)

➡ _____

(4) 두 발을 벌리고 서서 손바닥은 위로 향하게 하라. (upwards / stand / feet / your / your / facing / apart / hands / with / and)

➡ _____

_____

# Conversation

## ① 걱정하기

> • I'm worried about Sports Day. 난 운동회가 걱정돼.

■ 걱정이 된다는 것을 나타내는 표현은 'I'm worried ~(나는 ~가 걱정돼.)' 또는 'I'm concerned ~(나는 ~가 걱정돼.)'라고 한다. 걱정을 나타내는 nervous 또는 문제를 나타내는 trouble을 써서 'I'm nervous about ~', 'I'm in trouble ~'이라고 할 수도 있다.

■ 걱정이 되는 것이 두려움이나 무서움을 포함하고 있을 때는 scared, frightened, terrified 등을 써서 'I'm scared ~', 'I'm frightened ~', 'I'm terrified ~' 등으로 나타내기도 한다. 이 말에 공감할 때는 'Me, too.(나도 그래.)'라고 한다.

■ 걱정이 되는 내용을 덧붙일 때는 전치사 about나 접속사 that을 써서 'I'm worried about ~' 또는 'I'm worried that ~'이라고 한다. about 뒤에는 명사나 동명사를 쓰고 that 뒤에는 주어, 동사가 있는 절을 쓴다.

### 걱정하기

| | |
|---|---|
| • I'm worried about 명사 / that 주어+동사 ~. | 나는 ~가 걱정돼. |
| • I'm concerned about ~. | 나는 ~가 걱정이야. |
| • I'm afraid that ~ . | 나는 ~가 걱정돼. |
| • I'm nervous about ~. | 나는 ~가 불안해. |
| • I'm anxious about ~. | 나는 ~가 걱정이야. |

### 핵심 Check

**1.** 다음 밑줄 친 (A)의 우리말과 일치하도록 주어진 어휘를 포함하여 영어로 쓰시오.

**G:** What happened to your shoes? Aren't they new?

**B:** Yes, but my dog chewed them. He does it all the time. (A)<u>난 그가 걱정돼</u>. (worried, him)

**G:** He was probably bored. Why don't you play with him more often?

**B:** O.K, I will. I hope he will stop chewing my shoes.

➡ _____

## ② 의무 부인하기

> • **You don't have to clean the classroom.** 너는 교실을 청소할 필요가 없어.

■ '~해야 한다'는 뜻의 의무를 나타내는 표현은 'You have to+동사원형(~해야 한다)', 'You must+동사원형(~해야 한다)', 'You should/ought to+동사원형(~해야 한다)', 'You need to+동사원형(~할 필요가 있다)' 등이다.

■ 의무를 나타내는 'have to'를 부정하여 'don't/doesn't have to+동사원형'이 되면 의무를 부인하여 '~할 필요가 없다'는 뜻으로 'don't need to+동사원형'과 비슷한 의미가 된다. 'There is no need to+동사원형'도 '~할 필요가 없다.'는 의미로 의무를 부인하는 표현이다. must, should는 긍정 표현일 때는 의무를 나타내지만, 'must not', 'should not'처럼 부정이 되면 '~해서는 안 된다'는 의미의 금지를 나타내는 표현이 된다.

■ 그 외에 의무를 나타내는 표현으로 'be supposed to+동사원형(~해야 한다, ~하기로 되어 있다)'가 있고, 'have to'를 강조하여 'have got to+동사원형(~해야 한다)'이 있다. 'be not supposed to'는 '~해서는 안 된다'는 의미의 금지 표현이다.

### 의무 부인하기

• You don't have to ~.  ~할 필요가 없다.
• You don't need to ~.  ~할 필요가 없다.
• There's no need to ~.  ~할 필요가 없다.

### 핵심 Check

2. 다음 대화의 밑줄 친 (A)의 우리말에 해당하는 적절한 표현을 쓰시오.

A: I'm going to the school library. Do I have to bring my student ID?

B: (A)아니, 그럴 필요 없어.

➡ _____ / _____

3. 다음 대화를 자연스러운 순서로 배열하시오.

M: Shall we have seafood spaghetti for dinner?

(A) You don't have to do that. We already have what we need.

(B) Oh, I see. Then, I'll be back home by 6 to help you cook.

(C) Sure. I'll stop by the store on the way home.

➡ _____

**Listen and Speak 1 A-1**

G: What happened to your shoes? Aren't ❶they new?

B: Yes, but my dog chewed them. ❷He does it all the time. ❸I'm worried about ❷him.

G: He was probably ❹bored. ❺Why don't you play with him more often?

B: O.K., I will. I hope he will ❻stop chewing my shoes.

G: 신발이 왜 그래? 새것 아니었어?

B: 맞는데, 내 개가 씹어 버렸어. 항상 그렇게 해. 그 개가 걱정돼.

G: 아마 심심했을 거야. 개와 더 자주 놀아 주는 게 어때?

B: 알겠어, 그럴게. 그 개가 내 신발 씹는 걸 그만두면 좋겠네.

❶ they는 your shoes를 가리킨다.　　❷ He와 him은 my dog을 가리킨다.

❸ 걱정이 된다는 것을 나타내는 표현으로 'I'm concerned about him.' 또는 'I'm anxious about him.'으로 바꾸어 표현할 수 있다.

❹ bored: 지루해하는

❺ 'Why don't you ~?'는 무언가를 제안하는 표현으로 'How about ~?' 또는 'What about ~?' 등으로 바꾸어 표현할 수 있다.

❻ stop+ing: ~하던 것을 멈추다, stop+to부정사: ~하기 위해 멈추다

**Check(√) True or False**

(1) The boy's dog chewed his new shoes.　　T ☐ F ☐

(2) The boy is going to play with his dog if his dog stops chewing his shoes.　　T ☐ F ☐

**Communicate A**

Yuri: Hi, Jaden. Sports Day is next Friday. ❶I can't wait!

Jaden: Really? I'm actually worried about ❷it.

Yuri: Why? ❸Aren't you good at sports?

Jaden: Yes, I am, but I'm worried about the 800-meter relay.

Yuri: What do you mean?

Jaden: I'm the last runner. ❹What if our team loses because of me?

Yuri: I think you're ❺putting too much pressure on yourself.

Jaden: Really? Don't you think I should practice every day?

Yuri: No, you don't have to do that. It's just a school race. It's not about winning or losing.

Jaden: I guess you're right, Yuri. I'm lucky to have a friend like you.

유리: 안녕, Jaden. 운동회가 다음 주 금요일이야. 너무 기다려져!

Jaden: 정말? 난 사실 걱정돼.

유리: 왜? 너 운동 잘하지 않아?

Jaden: 응, 그렇긴 하지만, 800미터 릴레이가 걱정돼.

유리: 무슨 뜻이니?

Jaden: 내가 마지막 주자거든. 나 때문에 우리 팀이 지면 어쩌지?

유리: 넌 네 스스로에게 너무 많은 압박을 주고 있는 것 같아.

Jaden: 그래? 내가 매일 연습해야 한다고 생각하지 않니?

유리: 아니, 그럴 필요 없어. 그냥 학교 경기일 뿐인걸. 이기고 지고에 관한 게 아냐.

Jaden: 네 말이 맞는 것 같다. 유리야. 너 같은 친구를 둬서 다행이야.

❶ 'I can't wait!'은 '너무 기다려져!'라고 기대감을 나타내는 표현으로 'I'm looking forward to it.' 등으로 바꾸어 표현할 수 있다.

❷ it은 'Sports Day'를 가리킨다.　　❸ be good at ~: ~을 잘하다

❹ What if ~?: '~하면 어쩌지?'라는 의미를 나타낸다.　　❺ put too much pressure on: ~에게 너무 많은 부담을 주다

**Check(√) True or False**

(3) Jaden is going to take part in the 800-meter relay as the last runner.　　T ☐ F ☐

(4) Yuri focuses on the importance of winning at the race.　　T ☐ F ☐

### Listen and Speak 1 A-2

**B:** You look a bit ❶nervous.

**G:** I'm worried about my swimming ❷ competition this Saturday.

**B:** Don't worry. You're ❸such a good swimmer. Just relax and enjoy yourself!

**G:** Thanks. I feel much better now.

❶ nervous: 긴장된
❷ competition: 대회
❸ such a(n)+형용사+명사

### Listen and Speak 2 A-1

**B:** Mom, what time are we going to ❶Grandma's place tomorrow morning?

**W:** About 8 a.m. I'm going to ❷bake cookies for ❸her before we go.

**B:** Then, should I ❹get up early to help you?

**W:** ❺You don't have to. Your dad will help me.

**B:** O.K, then. Good night, Mom!

❶ place: 주택, 집
❷ bake: 굽다
❸ her는 Grandma를 가리킨다.
❹ get up: 일어나다
❺ 의무를 부인하는 표현으로 'You don't need to.'로 바꾸어 표현할 수 있다.

### Listen and Speak 2 A-2

**W:** Shall we try that new Mexican restaurant tomorrow?

**M:** ❶Why not? I'll call the restaurant to ❷make a reservation for us.

**W:** You don't have to call them. You can ❸do it online.

**M:** Oh, I see. How ❹convenient!

❶ 'Why not?'은 '좋죠!'라는 동의의 표현이다.
❷ make a reservation: 예약하다
❸ do it = make a reservation
❹ convenient: 편리한

### Progress Check 1

**B:** You look ❶a bit nervous.

**G:** Well, I'm worried about my ❷presentation in history class.

**B:** Don't worry. ❸You've prepared ❹a lot. You'll ❺do a great job.

**G:** Thanks. I feel much better now.

❶ a bit: 조금
❷ presentation: 발표
❸ have p.p. 형태로 현재완료 시제를 나타낸다. prepare: 준비하다
❹ a lot: 많이
❺ do a great job: 잘하다

### Progress Check 2

**M:** ❶Shall we have ❷seafood spaghetti for dinner?

**W:** Sure. I'll ❸stop by the store ❹on the way home.

**M:** You don't have to ❺do that. We already have what we need.

**W:** Oh, I see. Then, I'll ❻be back home by 6 to help you cook.

❶ Shall we ~?: 우리 ~할까요?
❷ seafood: 해산물
❸ stop by: ~에 들르다 (= drop by)
❹ on the way home: 집에 가는 길에
❺ do that = stop by the store
❻ be back home: 집에 돌아오다

● 다음 우리말과 일치하도록 빈칸에 알맞은 말을 쓰시오.

### Listen & Speak 1 A-1

G: What _____ _____ your shoes? Aren't they new?

B: Yes, but my dog _____ them. He does it _____ _____ _____. I'm _____ _____ him.

G: He was probably _____. _____ _____ _____ play with him more often?

B: O.K., I will. I _____ he will stop _____ my shoes.

해석

G: 신발이 왜 그래? 새것 아니었어?

B: 맞는데, 내 개가 씹어 버렸어. 항상 그렇게 해. 그 개가 걱정돼.

G: 아마 심심했었을 거야. 개와 더 자주 놀아 주는 게 어때?

B: 알겠어, 그럴게. 그 개가 내 신발 씹는 걸 그만두면 좋겠네.

### Listen & Speak 1 A-2

B: You look a bit _____.

G: I'm worried about my _____ _____ this Saturday.

B: Don't _____. You're such a good swimmer. Just _____ and _____ yourself!

G: Thanks. I feel much _____ now.

B: 너 좀 긴장한 것 같아 보이는데.

G: 이번 토요일에 있는 수영 대회가 걱정돼.

B: 걱정 마. 너는 수영을 아주 잘 하잖아. 그냥 긴장을 풀고 즐겨!

G: 고마워. 기분이 훨씬 괜찮아졌어.

### Listen & Speak 2 A-1

B: Mom, _____ _____ are we going to Grandma's place tomorrow morning?

W: About 8 a.m. I'm going to _____ _____ for her before we go.

B: Then, should I _____ _____ early to help you?

W: You _____ _____ _____. Your dad will help me.

B: O.K, then. Good night, Mom!

B: 엄마, 우리 내일 아침 몇 시에 할머니 댁에 가나요?

W: 8시쯤에. 가기 전에 할머니를 위해 쿠키를 구울 거란다.

B: 그럼, 제가 일찍 일어나서 도와드릴까요?

W: 그럴 필요 없단다. 아빠가 도와주실 거야.

B: 알겠어요, 그럼. 안녕히 주무세요, 엄마!

### Listen & Speak 2 A-2

W: _____ _____ _____ that new Mexican restaurant tomorrow?

M: _____ not? I'll call the restaurant to _____ _____ _____ for us.

W: You _____ _____ call them. You can do it _____.

M: Oh, I see. How _____!

W: 우리 내일 새로 생긴 멕시코 레스토랑에 가 볼까요?

M: 좋죠! 레스토랑에 전화해서 예약해 둘게요.

W: 전화할 필요 없어요. 온라인으로 할 수 있거든요.

M: 오, 그렇군요. 정말 편리하네요!

## Communicate A

**Yuri:** Hi, Jaden. Sports Day is next Friday. I can't _____!

**Jaden:** Really? I'm actually _____ about it.

**Yuri:** Why? Aren't you _____ _____ sports?

**Jaden:** Yes, I am, but I'm worried about the 800-meter _____.

**Yuri:** _____ do you _____?

**Jaden:** I'm the _____ _____. _____ _____ our team loses because of me?

**Yuri:** I think you're _____ _____ _____ _____ _____ yourself.

**Jaden:** Really? Don't you think I should _____ every day?

**Yuri:** No, you _____ _____ _____ _____ that. It's just a school race. It's not about _____ or _____.

**Jaden:** I guess you're _____, Yuri. I'm _____ to have a friend like you.

## Progress Check 1

**B:** You look a bit _____.

**G:** Well, I'm worried about my _____ in _____ class.

**B:** Don't worry. You've _____ a lot. You'll _____ a great _____.

**G:** Thanks. I _____ _____ _____ now.

## Progress Check 2

**M:** Shall we have _____ _____ for dinner?

**W:** Sure. I'll _____ _____ the store _____ _____ _____ home.

**M:** _____ _____ _____ _____ do that. We already have _____ we need.

**W:** Oh, I see. Then, I'll be _____ home by 6 to _____ you _____.

해석

유리: 안녕, Jaden. 운동회가 다음 주 금요일이야. 너무 기다려져!
Jaden: 정말? 난 사실 걱정돼.
유리: 왜? 너 운동 잘하지 않아?
Jaden: 응, 그렇긴 하지만, 800미터 릴레이가 걱정돼.
유리: 무슨 뜻이니?
Jaden: 내가 마지막 주자거든. 나 때문에 우리 팀이 지면 어쩌지?
유리: 넌 네 스스로에게 너무 많은 압박을 주고 있는 것 같아.
Jaden: 그래? 내가 매일 연습해야 한다고 생각하지 않니?
유리: 아니, 그럴 필요 없어. 그냥 학교 경기일 뿐인걸. 이기고 지고에 관한 게 아냐.
Jaden: 네 말이 맞는 것 같아, 유리야. 너 같은 친구를 둬서 다행이야.

B: 너 좀 긴장한 것 같다.
G: 그게, 역사 수업 시간에 내가 할 발표가 걱정돼.
B: 걱정 마. 많이 준비했잖아. 잘할 거야.
G: 고마워. 기분이 훨씬 나아졌어.

M: 우리 저녁으로 해물 스파게티를 먹을까요?
W: 좋아요. 집에 오는 길에 가게에 들를게요.
M: 그럴 필요 없어요. 필요한 건 이미 가지고 있거든요.
W: 오, 그렇군요. 그럼, 6시까지 돌아와서 요리하는 걸 도울게요.

[01~02] 다음 대화를 읽고 물음에 답하시오.

Jane: What ⓐhappened to your shoes? Aren't they new?

Brian: Yes, but my dog ⓑchewed them. He does it all the time. I'm ⓒworried about him.

Jane: He was probably ⓓbored. Why don't you play with him more often?

Brian: O.K., I will. I hope he will stop ⓔto chew my shoes

**01** 위 대화의 ⓐ~ⓔ중 어색한 것을 찾아 바르게 고치시오.

➡ _____

**02** 위 대화의 내용과 일치하지 않는 것은?

① Brian의 새 신발이 망가졌다.

② Brian의 개가 Brian의 신발을 처음으로 씹었다.

③ Brian은 그의 개가 걱정이 된다.

④ Jane은 Brian에게 개와 더 자주 놀아줄 것을 제안했다.

⑤ Brian은 그의 개가 신발을 씹는 걸 그만 두길 바란다.

[03~04] 다음 대화를 읽고 물음에 답하시오.

B: You look a bit nervous.

G: I'm worried about my swimming competition this Saturday.

B: Don't worry. You're such a good swimmer. Just relax and enjoy yourself!

G: Thanks. I feel much better now.

**03** What's the matter with the girl?

➡ _____

**04** What does the boy advise the girl to do?

➡ _____

[01~03] 다음 대화를 읽고 물음에 답하시오.

Jane: What happened to your shoes? Aren't they new?

Brian: Yes, but my dog chewed them. He does it all the time. (A)I'm worried about him.

Jane: He was probably bored. (B)Why don't you play with him more often? (about, how)

Brian: O.K., I will. I hope he will stop chewing my shoes.

**01** 위 대화의 밑줄 친 (A)와 바꾸어 쓸 수 있는 것을 <u>모두</u> 고르시오.

① I'm anxious about him.

② I'm fond of him.

③ I'm concerned about him.

④ I'm tired of him.

⑤ I'm glad to see him.

**02** 위 대화의 밑줄 친 (B)와 의미가 같도록 주어진 단어를 사용하여 다시 쓰시오.

➡ _____

**03** 위 대화를 읽고 대답할 수 <u>없는</u> 것은?

① What's the problem with Brian's shoes?

② Who chewed Brian's shoes?

③ What is Brian worried about?

④ What does Jane suggest to Brian?

⑤ When did Brian buy his shoes?

[04~05] 다음 대화를 읽고 물음에 답하시오.

B: You look a bit ___(A)___.

G: I'm worried about my swimming competition this Saturday.

B: Don't worry. You're such a good swimmer. Just relax and enjoy yourself!

G: Thanks. I feel much better now.

**04** 위 대화의 빈칸 (A)에 들어갈 말로 적절한 것은?

① satisfied　　　② excited

③ happy　　　　④ pleased

⑤ nervous

**05** 위 대화에 나타난 여자의 심경 변화로 적절한 것은?

① worried → relieved

② nervous → disappointed

③ worried → lonely

④ nervous → lonely

⑤ disappointed → worried

**06** 다음 대화가 자연스럽게 이어지도록 순서대로 배열하시오.

(A) O.K, then. Good night, Mom!

(B) Then, should I get up early to help you?

(C) About 8 a.m. I'm going to bake cookies for her before we go.

(D) You don't have to. Your dad will help me.

(E) Mom, what time are we going to Grandma's place tomorrow morning?

➡ _____

**[07~08]** 다음 대화를 읽고 물음에 답하시오.

Emily: Shall we try that new Mexican restaurant tomorrow?

Tom: Why not? I'll call the restaurant to make a reservation for us.

Emily: You don't have to call them. You can do it online.

Tom: Oh, I see. How convenient!

서답형

**07** What does Emily suggest doing?

➡ _____

서답형

**08** Why doesn't Tom need to call the restaurant to make a reservation? (6 words)

➡ _____

**[09~10]** 다음 대화를 읽고 물음에 답하시오.

Yuri: Hi, Jaden. Sports Day is next Friday. I can't wait!

Jaden: Really? I'm actually worried about it.

Yuri: Why? Aren't you good at sports?

Jaden: Yes, I am, but I'm (A)[concerned / concerning] about the 800-meter relay.

Yuri: What do you mean?

Jaden: I'm the last runner. What if our team loses (B)[because / because of] me?

Yuri: I think you're putting too much pressure on (C)[you / yourself].

Jaden: Really? Don't you think I should practice every day?

Yuri: No, you don't have to do that. It's just a school race. It's not about winning or losing.

Jaden: I guess you're right, Yuri. I'm lucky to have a friend like you.

**09** 위 대화의 (A)~(C)에 들어갈 말이 바르게 짝지어진 것은?

|     | (A) | (B) | (C) |
|-----|-----|-----|-----|
| ① | concerned | because | you |
| ② | concerned | because of | yourself |
| ③ | concerned | because of | you |
| ④ | concerning | because of | yourself |
| ⑤ | concerning | because | you |

중요

**10** 위 대화를 읽고 대답할 수 <u>없는</u> 것은?

① When is Sports Day?

② What is Jaden worried about?

③ How has Jaden's feeling changed?

④ Should Jaden practice for the 800-meter relay every day?

⑤ Who is the first runner of the 800-meter relay?

**11** 다음 짝지어진 대화가 <u>어색한</u> 것은?

① A: I'm worried about Sports Day. I'm not good at sports.

B: I know how you feel, but try to enjoy it.

② A: I'm concerned about my brother. He gets angry so often these days.

B: How about trying to calm him down?

③ A: I'm worried about my English speaking test.

B: Don't worry. You've prepared a lot. You can make it.

④ A: I'm anxious about my future.

B: You're such a good student! Everything will be fine.

⑤ A: I'm nervous about my presentation in English class.

B: I feel much better now. Thanks a lot.

**01** 다음 대화가 자연스럽게 이어지도록 순서대로 배열하시오.

> (A) Thanks. I feel much better now.
> (B) You look a bit nervous.
> (C) Don't worry. You've prepared a lot. You'll do a great job.
> (D) Well, I'm worried about my presentation in history class.

➡ _____

[02~04] 다음 대화를 읽고 물음에 답하시오.

> Jack: Mom, what time are we going to Grandma's place tomorrow morning?
> Mom: About 8 a.m. I'm going to bake cookies for her before we go.
> Jack: Then, should I get up early to help you?
> Mom: You don't have to. Your dad will help me.
> Jack: O.K, then. Good night, Mom!

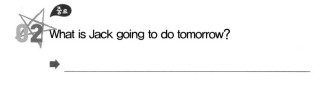 What is Jack going to do tomorrow?

➡ _____

**03** What is Jack's mom going to do before she visits Jack's grandma's place?

➡ _____

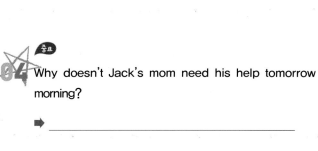 Why doesn't Jack's mom need his help tomorrow morning?

➡ _____
_____

**05**  다음 대화의 내용과 일치하도록 Jaden의 일기를 완성하시오.

> Yuri: Hi, Jaden. Sports Day is next Friday. I can't wait!
> Jaden: Really? I'm actually worried about it.
> Yuri: Why? Aren't you good at sports?
> Jaden: Yes, I am, but I'm worried about the 800-meter relay.
> Yuri: What do you mean?
> Jaden: I'm the last runner. What if our team loses because of me?
> Yuri: I think you're putting too much pressure on yourself.
> Jaden: Really? Don't you think I should practice every day?
> Yuri: No, you don't have to do that. It's just a school race. It's not about winning or losing.
> Jaden: I guess you're right, Yuri. I'm lucky to have a friend like you.

> Mon, June 15th, 2020
> Today, I was so concerned about Sports Day. I was chosen as the (A)_____ of the 800-meter relay. All my classmates believed that I can do it very well. But I felt so burdened. I was worried that (B)_____ . I talked about it to Yuri and she said that I was putting too (C)_____ on myself. Actually, I was thinking whether (D)_____ every day or not. Yuri advised me not to do so, because it's just a school race, not about (E)_____ . I was encouraged by her a lot. I really appreciated her today.

# Grammar
교과서

## ❶ 분사구문

> • **Feeling** nervous, Jisu was carefully studying her notes in her chair.
> 지수는 긴장이 되어, 의자에 앉아 자신의 필기를 열심히 들여다보고 있었다.

- 종속접속사가 이끄는 부사절을 분사를 이용하여 간략한 부사구로 바꾼 것이다.
  - **While I was walking** on the street, I saw my teacher.
  - = **Walking** on the street, I saw my teacher. 거리를 걷고 있었을 때, 나는 선생님을 봤다.

- 부사구와 주절의 관계에 따라 양보, 동시동작, 이유, 시간, 조건 등의 의미로 쓰인다.
  - (1) 양보: **Although he is** over 90, the businessman runs faster than the young.
    - = **Being** over 90, the businessman runs faster than the young.
      비록 그 사업가는 90세가 넘었지만, 젊은 사람들보다 빨리 뛴다.
  - (2) 동시동작(부대상황): **While she sat** on the bed, she watched TV.
    - = **Sitting** on the bed, she watched TV. 침대에 앉아서 그녀는 TV를 시청했다.
  - (3) 이유: **As he was** tired, Harry went to bed early.
    - = **Being tired**, Harry went to bed early. 피곤했기 때문에, Harry는 일찍 잠자리에 들었다.
  - (4) 시간: **When she doesn't work**, she enjoys the board games.
    - = **Not working**, she enjoys the board games. 일하지 않을 때, 그녀는 보드게임을 즐긴다.
  - (5) 조건: **If you take** a taxi, you'll get to the party on time.
    - = **Taking** a taxi, you'll get to the party on time. 택시를 타면, 파티에 제 시간에 도착할 거야.

- 종속절의 시제가 주절보다 앞선 경우, 완료분사구문을 사용한다.
  - **As she had done** it before, Susan knew how to fix the copy machine.
    - = **Having done** it before, Susan knew how to fix the copy machine.

- 주절과 종속절의 주어가 다를 경우, 분사구문의 주어를 남겨 두는 것을 독립분사구문이라고 하며, 일반인이 주어일 경우에는 생략 가능하다. (비인칭 독립분사구문)
  - (1) 독립분사구문: **As it was** cloudy, we couldn't go on a field trip.
    - = **It being** cloudy, we couldn't go on a field trip. 날이 흐려서, 소풍을 갈 수 없었다.
  - (2) 비인칭 독립분사구문: **generally speaking**(일반적으로 말해), **considering**(~를 고려하면)
  - (3) with+목적어+분사: Mom fell asleep **with the TV turned on**. (TV를 켠 채로)

### 핵심 Check

1. 다음 괄호 안에서 알맞은 말을 고르시오.

   (1) (Feeling / Felt) worried, Jake drove to the subway station to pick her up.

   (2) With night (come / coming) on, it got colder and colder.

## ② 상관접속사 not only ~ but also ...

> • His rival became **not only** a political supporter **but also** a good friend.
> 그의 경쟁자는 정치적 지원자 뿐만 아니라 좋은 친구가 되었다.

■ 상관접속사 'not only A but also B'는 'A뿐만 아니라 B도 또한'이라는 뜻이며, 'B as well as A'로 바꿀 수 있다. 접속사이므로 A와 B 자리에 명사뿐만 아니라 동사, 형용사, 준동사 등 어떤 것이든 올 수 있으며, A에 동사가 오면 B에도 동사가 와야 한다.

　• My mom is **not only** a good cook **but also** a great painter.
　　= My mom is a great painter as well as a good cook. 우리 어머니는 훌륭한 요리사일 뿐만 아니라 대단한 화가이기도 하다.

■ 상관접속사의 종류와 주어로 쓰일 때의 수 일치

　(1) Not only A but also B(= B as well as A): A뿐만 아니라 B도 또한 (B에 일치)
　　• **Not only** they **but also** she wants the job. 그들뿐만 아니라 그녀도 그 일을 원한다.
　　　= She **as well as** they **wants** the job.

　(2) Not A but B: A가 아니라 B (B에 일치)
　　• **Not** they **but** she **wants** the job. 그들이 아니라 그녀가 그 일을 원한다.

　(3) Both A and B: A와 B 둘 다 (복수 주어)
　　• **Both** they **and** she **want** the job. 그들과 그녀 모두 다 그 일을 원한다.

　(4) Either A or B: A 또는 B 둘 중 하나 (동사와 가까운 주어에 일치)
　　• **Either** they **or** she **wants** the job. 그들 또는 그녀 둘 중 하나는 그 일을 원한다.

　(5) Neither A nor B: A도 B도 아닌 (동사와 가까운 주어에 일치)
　　• **Neither** they **nor** she **wants** the job. 그들도 그녀도 그 일을 원하지 않는다.

■ Not only가 주어가 아닌 동사를 받을 경우 문두에 오면 도치가 일어난다.
　• **Not only** is he wise, **but also** he is kind. 그는 현명할 뿐만 아니라 친절하다.
　• **Not only** could she read the book, **but also** she could memorize it.
　　그녀는 그 책을 읽을 수 있었을 뿐만 아니라 그 책을 외울 수도 있었다.

■ not only ~ but also에서 only 대신 just, simply 등을 쓸 수 있고, also는 생략해서 쓰기도 한다.
　• The fairy was **not just** wise **but** beautiful. 그 요정은 지혜로울 뿐만 아니라 아름다웠다.

### 핵심 Check

**2.** 다음 문장에서 어법상 **틀린** 부분을 찾아 바르게 고쳐 쓰시오.

　(1) Andy not only plays but also teach the guitar. ➡ _____

　(2) Not only you but also he are responsible for the problem. ➡ _____

**01** 다음 빈칸에 들어갈 말로 알맞은 것은?

> Mina is not only a good listener but also _____.

① sings well　　　② beautiful　　　③ has a sense of humor
④ poor at hearing　　⑤ a great leader

**02** 다음 부사절을 분사구문으로 바꿔 쓸 때, 빈칸에 들어갈 말로 가장 적절한 것은?

> As he wanted to make his dad feel better, Harry smiled brightly at him.
> → _____ to make his dad feel better, Harry smiled brightly at him.

① He wanting　　　② As he wanting　　　③ Wanting
④ Having wanted　　⑤ Being wanting

**03** 다음 중 어법상 옳지 <u>않은</u> 것을 고르시오.

① She is both generous and intelligent.
② Frank's friends not only sing well but also paint well.
③ He is interested either in soccer or in hockey.
④ Kevin not only writes well but also dancing well.
⑤ Nora has not only the dolls but also their house.

**04** 다음 분사구문을 접속사가 이끄는 부사절로 만들 때, 빈칸에 알맞은 말을 써 넣으시오.

(1) Listening to music, John cleaned his room.
　➡ While _____ _____ _____ _____, John cleaned his room.

(2) Feeling lonely, she called her mother in New York.
　➡ As _____ _____ _____, she called her mother in New York.

(3) Being small and weak, Ron has enough courage to complete the difficult mission before him.
　➡ _____ _____ _____ _____ _____ _____, Ron has enough courage to complete the difficult mission before him.

**01** 다음 중 어법상 <u>어색한</u> 것은?

① Not only your friends but also my uncle have those problems.
② The violinist not only played a beautiful song but also gave a great influence on young kids.
③ Lucy has lived not only in France but also in Egypt.
④ Not only the professor but also the student is working on the project.
⑤ Caroline ate not only the cookies but also the jams that her mother made.

[02~03] 다음 우리말을 알맞게 영작한 것을 고르시오.

**02**

> 그는 눈을 감은 채로 걷고 있었다.

① He was walking his eyes closing.
② He was closing his eyes and walking.
③ He walked and closed his eyes.
④ He was walking closed his eyes with.
⑤ He was walking with his eyes closed.

**03**

> 많은 사람들을 괴롭혔는데도 불구하고, Tom은 부자로 잘 살았다.

① Even though he having bullied many people, Tom lived well off.
② Although he bullying many people, Tom lived well off.
③ Having bullied many people, Tom living well off.
④ Though having bullied many people, Tom lived well off.
⑤ He had bullied many people, though Tom lived well off.

[04~05] 다음 중 어법상 옳은 것을 고르시오.

**04** ① Both Jinsu and his sister is reading the article about the history of Jeju.
② Not only William but also Bentley have lived in New York since last year.
③ Kevin bought Minsu not only the laptop but also a bag.
④ I don't have neither a pen nor a pencil.
⑤ Not only I am hungry but also can't move a little.

**05** ① Not only Mary but also Chris speak Spanish well.
② Not only the students but also the teacher know who the girl is.
③ Not only he but also you is wrong.
④ Tell me not only what you like but also she likes to go.
⑤ Elizabeth not only teaches swimming but also sells a lot of swim suits.

서답형
**06** 다음 문장에서 어법상 <u>어색한</u> 단어 한 개를 찾아서 고치시오.

> Exhausting after the hard work, Paula laid herself down on the bed on coming home.

_____ ➡ _____

**07** 다음 두 문장을 의미가 같도록 한 문장으로 바꿔 쓸 때 적절하지 <u>않은</u> 것은?

① Tom likes the book. + Jimmy likes the book, too.
→ Not only Tom but also Jimmy likes the book.

② Cory listens to the radio program. + Sean listens to the radio program, too.
→ Both Cory and Sean listens to the radio program.

③ One of the two students, Martha or Sue, may have the answer sheet.
→ Either Martha or Sue may have the answer sheet.

④ Kim doesn't know the way home. Her cousins don't know the way home, either.
→ Neither Kim nor her cousins know the way home.

⑤ Sharon could solve the quiz. + Sharon could pass the exam as well.
→ Sharon could not only solve the quiz but also pass the exam.

**08** 다음 중 밑줄 친 분사구문의 용법이 〈보기〉와 같은 것은?

┌─ 보기 ─┐
<u>Born</u> in America, Sam isn't good at speaking English.
└────────┘

① <u>Living</u> in Busan for over 10 years, Rena can't understand the conversation between Busan citizens.

② <u>Finishing</u> her homework, Anna went outside to meet her boyfriend.

③ <u>Having</u> nothing special to do, I just called Robert.

④ <u>Not knowing</u> how long she waited for me, I was surprised at her cold hands.

⑤ <u>Turning</u> left at first corner, you can find the post office.

**09** 다음 〈보기〉의 문장과 가장 가까운 뜻을 가진 문장을 고르시오.

┌─ 보기 ─┐
Not only Josh but also Mina doesn't like smoking as well as drinking.
└────────┘

① Both Josh and Mina don't like smoking but drinking.

② Neither Josh nor Mina likes both smoking and drinking.

③ Either Josh or Mina doesn't like smoking nor drinking.

④ Neither Josh nor Mina doesn't like smoking but also drinking.

⑤ Both Josh and Mina hate not smoking but drinking.

**10** 다음 주어진 분사구문을 접속사를 이용한 부사절로 만들 때 가장 적절한 것은?

The disease having come from China, Chinese government blames Korea.

① Since the disease comes from China, Chinese government blames Korea.

② Although the disease comes from China, Chinese government blames Korea.

③ If the disease came from China, Chinese government blames Korea.

④ Though the disease came from China, Chinese government blames Korea.

⑤ While the disease comes from China, Chinese government blames Korea.

[11~12] 다음 중 어법상 옳은 문장은?

**11**
① Cecilia had lost not only the necklace and also the rings.
② You can not only see the snowman but also likes the colder weather in winter.
③ My uncle not only arrived earlier but also prepared our dinner.
④ Not only the passengers were surprised but also irritated.
⑤ William likes only the pen but also the notebooks.

**12**
① Both Clara or her husband watched the movie *Parasite*.
② Can either you nor the doctor please explain us what worsens the situation?
③ Not only I but also David wonder whether the speaker is telling the truth.
④ I think either you or your mom know how the problem was solved.
⑤ Eliza loves not only Raynold but also me.

서답형
[13~14] 우리말과 일치하도록 괄호 안에 주어진 단어들을 바르게 배열하시오.

**13**
아주 오래 전에 나무와 마른 풀로 지어졌기 때문에, 그 집은 항상 화재의 위험에 노출되어 있다.
→ (wood, grass, having, and, built, of, been, dry) so long ago, the house is always exposed to the danger of fire.

➡ _____

**14**
또 다시 회의에 늦고 싶지 않았기 때문에, 그녀는 지하철역으로 최대한 빨리 뛰었다.
(be, for, not, the meeting, to, wanting, late) again, she ran to the subway station as fast as she could.

➡ _____

서답형
**15** 다음 그림을 보고 자연스러운 문장이 되도록 괄호 안에 주어진 단어를 바르게 배열하여 빈칸을 완성하시오.

(1)

➡ After _____
_____, (tall, Wonder Woman, for, a few, standing, minutes, like), Jisu didn't feel nervous anymore.

(2)

➡ Jenny was _____
_____ a splash on the street. (for, by, school, only, not, but, late, hit, also)

**01** 다음 우리말과 일치하도록 괄호 안에 주어진 단어들을 바르게 배열하여 문장을 완성하시오.

(1) 마음을 정리하고 싶기 때문에, Kobe는 혼자 하루 여행을 떠나기로 결정했다. (his, to, wanting, mind, clear)

➡ _____, Kobe decided to take a day trip by himself.

(2) 당신은 자신에 대한 확신이 생길 뿐만 아니라, 다른 사람이 보기에도 자신감에 차 보일 것이다. (look, feel, only, about, confident, sure, not, also, yourself, but)

➡ You will _____

_____ to other people.

(3) 경쟁자를 친구로 만들고 싶다면, 경쟁자에게 부탁을 하라. (into, a rival, turn, wanting, a friend, to)

➡ _____,

ask your rival to do you a favor.

**02** 다음 〈보기〉에 있는 접속사를 한 번씩만 사용하여, 각 밑줄 친 분사구문을 부사절로 바꾸시오. (단, 진행형 표현은 쓸 수 없다.)

┌─────── 보기 ───────┐
while   because   when   if   though
└─────────────────────┘

(1) Graduating from high school next year, Tammy wants to become a professional farmer.

➡ _____

_____

(2) Being sick all day long, I could complete the difficult project.

➡ _____

_____

(3) Having a problem that you cannot share with your family or friends, try talking to a stranger.

➡ _____

_____

(4) Listening to the radio, Henry cleaned his guitars.

➡ _____

_____

(5) Not having to worry about being judged, we often tell strangers about our problems.

➡ _____

_____

**03** 다음 글을 읽고, 질문에 답하시오.

┌─────────────────────────────────────┐
The hardest time in my life was my first grade in middle school. When my family moved to another city, I had to go to a new school. (A)As I didn't have any friends at school, I felt sad and lonely. One day, I asked one of my classmates to show me her notes. (B)(she, help, become, good friend) From this experience, I have learned that asking for help is a good way to make friends.
└─────────────────────────────────────┘

(1) 밑줄 친 (A)를 접속사가 없는 분사구문으로 바꾸되 'no'를 사용하시오.

➡ _____

(2) (B)의 괄호 속에 밑줄 친 단어들과 not only ~ but also를 활용해, 문맥에 맞게 영작하시오. (시제에 주의할 것)

➡ _____

_____

(3) 위에 나온 단어들을 활용하여, 다음 우리말을 7 단어의 분사구문으로 영작하시오.
'도움을 청하면, 당신은 친구를 사귈 수 있다.'

➡ _____

**04** 주어진 어구를 이용하여 〈조건〉에 맞게 영작하시오.

┌─ 조건 ─
1. 'not only A but also B'를 사용할 것.
2. 주어진 단어를 활용하되, 괄호 안의 글자 수 조건에 맞출 것.
└

(1) Minju's mom, good doctor, great cook (13 단어)

➡ _____

_____

(2) Harry, speak Spanish, dance well (9 단어)

➡ _____

_____

(3) Seohyun, beautiful, very kind (9 단어)

➡ _____

_____

(4) Frank, his parents, nice (9 단어)

➡ _____

_____

**05** 다음 문장에서 어법상 <u>어색한</u> 단어를 하나씩만 찾아 바르게 고치시오.

(1) Not only does she believe that she has to get a perfect score on every test but also she study without sleeping.

➡ _____ ➡ _____

(2) Both my cat and your puppy is sick now.

_____ ➡ _____

(3) Either Ms. Brown or her sons is responsible for the problem.

_____ ➡ _____

(4) The new job she got lately was not only difficult but also too stress.

_____ ➡ _____

(5) I wonder why not only Jejudo but also the islands in the south coast is crowded with visitors these days.

_____ ➡ _____

**06** 다음 그림을 보고 괄호 안의 단어를 배열하여 빈칸을 알맞게 채우시오.

(1)

➡ The reason I recommend this restaurant is

_____. (food, only, healthy, its, not, that, also, is, but, delicious)

(2)

➡ _____

to the local governor. (the farmer, donated, picked, huge, carrot, having, it, a)

## Psychology Answers Your Questions

Do you think you have a unique problem? Chances are that many other people have the same problem. Psychology is the study of the human mind and behavior, so it can help you find a solution to your problem.

### How do I become less nervous?

It was five minutes before Jisu's big presentation in front of the whole class. Feeling nervous, Jisu was carefully studying her notes in her chair. Then, her teacher came over and told her to stand tall like Wonder Woman. After standing tall for a few minutes, Jisu did not feel nervous anymore. In fact, she was confident that she would make a great presentation. According to Amy Cuddy, a famous psychologist, we can become more confident just by standing tall for two minutes before stressful events. Our bodies change our minds, and our minds can change our behavior. Do you want to feel confident? Stand with your feet apart, and place your hands on your hips. You will not only feel sure about yourself but also look confident to other people.

psychology 심리학
unique 유일무이한, 독특한
chances are that 아마 ~일 것이다
mind 마음, 정신
behavior 행동
solution 해법, 해결책
stand tall 당당해 보이다, 우뚝 서다
confident 자신감 있는
apart (거리·공간·시간상으로) 떨어져
hip 엉덩이, 허리께

📎 확인문제

● 다음 문장이 본문의 내용과 일치하면 T, 일치하지 않으면 F를 쓰시오.

1 Only you have a unique problem. ☐

2 Psychology is the study of the human mind and behavior. ☐

3 After standing tall like Wonder Woman, Jisu felt confident. ☐

4 Our minds can't change our behavior. ☐

## Who can help me feel better?

When he graduates from high school next year, Taeho wants to become a professional farmer. However, he has never told anyone about it. He is worried that his parents or his friends will not understand. Wanting to clear his mind, Taeho decided to take a day trip on a train by himself. On the train, he told a complete stranger sitting beside him about his problem. He had no idea why he did it. However, he felt much better when he got off the train. Strangely enough, we often tell strangers about our problems just like Taeho. That is because we do not have to worry about being judged or seeing them again. If you have a problem that you cannot share with your family or friends, try talking to a stranger. You will feel much better.

## How do I turn a rival into a friend?

Benjamin Franklin once had a political rival who did not like him at all. Franklin wanted to become friends with him, so he came up with a plan. His rival had a rare book. Franklin asked his rival to lend him the book for a few days. When Franklin returned the book, he thanked him deeply. Since that day, his rival became not only a political supporter but also a good friend. Franklin famously said, "Enemies who do you one favor will want to do more." If you want to turn a rival into a friend, don't do your rival a favor. Instead, ask your rival to do you a favor.

graduate 졸업하다
professional 전문적인, 직업의
clear one's mind 마음을 가다듬다, 마음을 맑게 하다
by oneself 혼자
judge 판단하다
political 정치와 관련된, 정치적인
rival 경쟁자, 경쟁 상대
come up with (해답 등을) 찾아내다, 내놓다
rare 드문, 희귀한, 살짝 익힌
do ~ a favor ~에게 호의를 베풀다

### 확인문제

● 다음 문장이 본문의 내용과 일치하면 T, 일치하지 않으면 F를 쓰시오.

1  Taeho has never told anyone about what he wants to be. ☐

2  Taeho told his friends about his future hope. ☐

3  Franklin borrowed a rare book from his rival. ☐

4  Franklin's rival remained his political rival. ☐

• 우리말을 참고하여 빈칸에 알맞은 말을 쓰시오.

**1** _____ Answers Your Questions

**2** Do you think you have a _____ problem?

**3** _____ _____ that many other people have the same problem.

**4** Psychology is the study of the _____ _____ and _____, _____ it can help you _____ a solution _____ your problem.

**5** How do I _____ _____ nervous?

**6** It was five minutes before Jisu's _____ _____ in front of the _____ _____.

**7** _____ nervous, Jisu was _____ _____ her notes in her chair.

**8** Then, her teacher _____ _____ and told her _____ _____ _____ like Wonder Woman.

**9** After _____ _____ for a few minutes, Jisu did _____ feel nervous _____.

**10** _____ _____, she was _____ _____ she would _____ a great presentation.

**11** According to Amy Cuddy, a famous psychologist, we can _____ more confident just _____ _____ _____ for two minutes before _____ _____.

**12** Our _____ change our _____, and our _____ can change our _____.

**13** Do you want to _____ _____?

**14** Stand with your feet _____, and _____ your hands _____ your hips.

**15** You will _____ _____ _____ _____ about yourself _____ _____ _____ _____ to other people.

**16** Who can help me _____ better?

**17** When he _____ _____ high school next year, Taeho wants to become a _____ farmer.

**18** _____, he _____ _____ anyone about it.

**1** 심리학이 당신의 물음에 답하다

**2** 여러분은 당신만의 유일무이한 고민을 가지고 있다고 생각하는가?

**3** 아마 많은 다른 사람들이 여러분과 똑같은 고민을 가지고 있을 것이다.

**4** 심리학은 인간의 마음과 행동에 관한 연구이며, 따라서 여러분이 문제에 대한 해결책을 찾는 데 도움을 줄 수 있다.

**5** 어떻게 하면 긴장을 덜 할 수 있나요?

**6** 지수가 반 전체 앞에서 발표를 하기 5분 전이었다.

**7** 지수는 긴장이 되어, 의자에 앉아 자신의 필기를 열심히 들여다보고 있었다.

**8** 그때 선생님이 다가와서는 원더우먼처럼 꼿꼿이 서 있어 보라고 말했다.

**9** 그렇게 몇 분을 우뚝 선 후에, 지수는 더 이상 긴장되지 않았다.

**10** 사실, 그녀는 발표를 멋있게 할 수 있을 것이라는 자신감이 생겼다.

**11** 유명한 심리학자인 Amy Cuddy에 의하면, 우리는 스트레스를 받는 상황 이전에 2분 정도 꼿꼿이 서 있는 것만으로도 자신감이 더 생길 수 있다고 한다.

**12** 우리의 몸은 마음을 바꾸고, 마음은 우리의 행동을 바꿀 수 있다.

**13** 자신감이 생기기를 원하는가?

**14** 양발을 벌리고, 허리께에 손을 올려 보아라.

**15** 자신에 대한 확신이 생길 뿐만 아니라 다른 사람이 보기에도 자신감에 차 보인다.

**16** 누가 내 기분을 낫게 해 줄 수 있나요?

**17** 내년에 고등학교를 졸업한 이후에 태호는 전문적인 농부가 되고 싶어 한다.

**18** 하지만, 누구에게도 그것에 대해 한 번도 말하지 않았다.

**19** He is _____ _____ his parents or his friends _____ _____ _____ .

**20** _____ to _____ _____ _____ , Taeho decided _____ _____ a day trip on a train _____ _____ .

**21** On the train, he told a _____ stranger _____ beside him about his problem.

**22** He had no idea _____ _____ _____ _____ _____ .

**23** _____ , he _____ _____ _____ when he got off the train.

**24** _____ _____ , we often tell strangers about our problems just like Taeho.

**25** That is _____ we do not have to worry about _____ _____ or _____ them again.

**26** If you have a problem _____ you cannot _____ _____ your family or friends, try _____ to a stranger.

**27** You will _____ _____ better.

**28** How do I _____ a _____ _____ a friend?

**29** Benjamin Franklin once had a political rival _____ did _____ like him _____ _____ .

**30** Franklin wanted to _____ _____ _____ him, so he _____ _____ _____ a plan.

**31** His rival had a _____ book.

**32** Franklin asked his rival _____ _____ him the book for _____ _____ _____ .

**33** When Franklin returned the book, he thanked him _____ .

**34** _____ that day, his rival became _____ _____ a political supporter _____ _____ a good friend.

**35** Franklin famously said, "Enemies _____ _____ _____ _____ will want to do more."

**36** If you want to _____ a rival _____ a friend, don't _____ _____ _____ .

**37** _____ , ask your rival _____ _____ you a favor.

**19** 그는 부모님이나 친구들이 이해하지 못할까 걱정이 된다.

**20** 마음을 정리하기 위해서, 태호는 혼자 하루 기차 여행을 떠나기로 결심했다.

**21** 기차에서, 그는 옆에 앉은 전혀 모르는 사람에게 자신의 고민에 대해서 말했다.

**22** 그는 자신이 왜 그랬는지 알 수 없었다.

**23** 그러나, 기차에서 내릴 때 기분이 훨씬 좋아졌다.

**24** 정말 이상하게도, 우리는 태호처럼 우리의 문제에 대해 낯선 사람에게 말할 때가 있다.

**25** 그것은 우리가 평가받거나 그 사람을 다시 볼 것이라는 걱정을 할 필요가 없기 때문이다.

**26** 만약 가족이나 친구들과도 나눌 수 없는 고민이 있다면, 낯선 이에게 말해 보아라.

**27** 기분이 훨씬 나아질 것이다.

**28** 라이벌을 어떻게 친구로 만들 수 있을까요?

**29** Benjamin Franklin에게는 한때 그를 전혀 좋아하지 않는 정치적 경쟁자가 있었다.

**30** Franklin은 그와 친구가 되고 싶어서, 계획을 세웠다.

**31** 그의 경쟁자는 희귀한 책을 가지고 있었다.

**32** Franklin은 그의 정적에게 그 책을 며칠 동안 빌려달라고 부탁했다.

**33** Franklin이 그 책을 돌려줄 때, 그는 그에게 진심으로 감사를 표했다.

**34** 그날 이후로, 그의 경쟁자는 정치적인 후원자뿐만 아니라 좋은 친구가 되었다.

**35** Franklin은 "당신을 한 번 도운 적은 더 돕고 싶어 하게 된다."라는 유명한 말을 했다.

**36** 여러분이 경쟁자를 친구로 만들고 싶다면, 경쟁자의 부탁을 들어주지 마라.

**37** 대신, 경쟁자에게 부탁을 해 보아라.

● 우리말을 참고하여 본문을 영작하시오.

**1** 심리학이 당신의 물음에 답하다

➡ _____

**2** 여러분은 당신만의 유일무이한 고민을 가지고 있다고 생각하는가?

➡ _____

**3** 아마 많은 다른 사람들이 여러분과 똑같은 고민을 가지고 있을 것이다.

➡ _____

**4** 심리학은 인간의 마음과 행동에 관한 연구이며, 따라서 여러분이 문제에 대한 해결책을 찾는 데 도움을 줄 수 있다.

➡ _____

_____

**5** 어떻게 하면 긴장을 덜 할 수 있나요?

➡ _____

**6** 지수가 반 전체 앞에서 발표를 하기 5분 전이었다.

➡ _____

**7** 지수는 긴장이 되어, 의자에 앉아 자신의 필기를 열심히 들여다보고 있었다.

➡ _____

**8** 그때 선생님이 다가와서는 원더우먼처럼 꼿꼿이 서 있어 보라고 말했다.

➡ _____

**9** 그렇게 몇 분을 우뚝 선 후에, 지수는 더 이상 긴장되지 않았다.

➡ _____

**10** 사실, 그녀는 발표를 멋있게 할 수 있을 것이라는 자신감이 생겼다.

➡ _____

**11** 유명한 심리학자인 Amy Cuddy에 의하면, 우리는 스트레스를 받는 상황 이전에 2분 정도 꼿꼿이 서 있는 것만으로도 자신감이 더 생길 수 있다고 한다.

➡ _____

_____

**12** 우리의 몸은 마음을 바꾸고, 마음은 우리의 행동을 바꿀 수 있다.

➡ _____

**13** 자신감이 생기기를 원하는가?

➡ _____

**14** 양발을 벌리고, 허리께에 손을 올려 보아라.

➡ _____

**15** 자신에 대한 확신이 생길 뿐만 아니라 다른 사람이 보기에도 자신감에 차 보인다.

➡ _____

**16** 누가 내 기분을 낮게 해 줄 수 있나요?

➡ _____

**17** 내년에 고등학교를 졸업한 이후에 태호는 전문적인 농부가 되고 싶어 한다.

➡ _____

**18** 하지만, 누구에게도 그것에 대해 한 번도 말하지 않았다.
➡ _____

**19** 그는 부모님이나 친구들이 이해하지 못할까 걱정이 된다.
➡ _____

**20** 마음을 정리하기 위해서, 태호는 혼자 하루 기차 여행을 떠나기로 결심했다.
➡ _____

**21** 기차에서, 그는 옆에 앉은 전혀 모르는 사람에게 자신의 고민에 대해서 말했다.
➡ _____

**22** 그는 자신이 왜 그랬는지 알 수 없었다.
➡ _____

**23** 그러나, 기차에서 내릴 때 기분이 훨씬 좋아졌다.
➡ _____

**24** 정말 이상하게도, 우리는 태호처럼 우리의 문제에 대해 낯선 사람에게 말할 때가 있다.
➡ _____

**25** 그것은 우리가 평가받거나 그 사람을 다시 볼 것이라는 걱정을 할 필요가 없기 때문이다.
➡ _____

**26** 만약 가족이나 친구들과도 나눌 수 없는 고민이 있다면, 낯선 이에게 말해 보아라.
➡ _____

**27** 기분이 훨씬 나아질 것이다.
➡ _____

**28** 라이벌을 어떻게 친구로 만들 수 있을까요?
➡ _____

**29** Benjamin Franklin에게는 한때 그를 전혀 좋아하지 않는 정치적 경쟁자가 있었다.
➡ _____

**30** Franklin은 그와 친구가 되고 싶어서, 계획을 세웠다.
➡ _____

**31** 그의 경쟁자는 희귀한 책을 가지고 있었다.
➡ _____

**32** Franklin은 그의 정적에게 그 책을 며칠 동안 빌려달라고 부탁했다.
➡ _____

**33** Franklin이 그 책을 돌려줄 때, 그는 그에게 진심으로 감사를 표했다.
➡ _____

**34** 그날 이후로, 그의 경쟁자는 정치적인 후원자뿐만 아니라 좋은 친구가 되었다.
➡ _____

**35** Franklin은 "당신을 한 번 도운 적은 더 돕고 싶어 하게 된다."라는 유명한 말을 했다.
➡ _____

**36** 여러분이 경쟁자를 친구로 만들고 싶다면, 경쟁자의 부탁을 들어주지 마라.
➡ _____

**37** 대신, 경쟁자에게 부탁을 해 보아라.
➡ _____

[01~03] 다음 글을 읽고 물음에 답하시오.

Do you think you have a ⓐunique problem? Chances are that many other people have the same problem. Psychology is the study of the human mind and behavior, so it can help you find a solution to your problem.

_____(A)_____

It was five minutes before Jisu's big presentation in front of the whole class. Feeling ⓑnervous, Jisu was carefully studying her notes in her chair. Then, her teacher came over and told her to stand tall like Wonder Woman. After standing tall for a few minutes, Jisu did not feel nervous anymore. In fact, she was confident that she would make a great presentation. According to Amy Cuddy, a famous ⓒpsychology, we can become more confident just by standing tall for two minutes before stressful events. Our bodies change our minds, and our minds can change our behavior. Do you want to feel confident? Stand with your feet ⓓapart, and place your hands on your hips. You will not only feel sure about yourself but also look ⓔconfident to other people.

**01** 위 글의 빈칸 (A)에 들어갈 알맞은 말을 고르시오.

① Why do we become nervous?
② How do I become less nervous?
③ How do I turn a rival into a friend?
④ How do we feel better?
⑤ Who can help me feel better?

**02** 위 글의 밑줄 친 ⓐ~ⓔ 중 잘못 쓰인 것을 고르시오.

① ⓐ  ② ⓑ  ③ ⓒ  ④ ⓓ  ⑤ ⓔ

**03** According to the passage, which is NOT true?

① Many people probably have the same problem as we do.
② Psychology can help us find a solution to our problem.
③ Jisu was going to make a big presentation in front of the whole class.
④ Jisu's teacher asked her to stand still for a few minutes.
⑤ Our bodies change our minds, and our minds can change our behavior.

[04~06] 다음 글을 읽고 물음에 답하시오.

How do I turn a rival into a friend?

Benjamin Franklin once had a political rival who did not like ①him at all. Franklin wanted to become friends with ②him, so ③he came up with a plan. His rival had a rare book. Franklin asked his rival to lend ④him the book for a few days. When Franklin returned the book, he thanked him deeply. Since that day, ⑤his rival became not only a political supporter but also a good friend. Franklin famously said, "Enemies ___ⓐ___ do you one favor will want to do more." If you want to turn a rival into a friend, don't do your rival a favor. Instead, ask your rival ___ⓑ___ you a favor.

**04** 위 글의 빈칸 ⓐ에 들어갈 알맞은 말을 모두 고르시오.

① that  ② what  ③ which
④ whose  ⑤ who

서답형

**05** 빈칸 ⓑ에 do를 알맞은 형태로 쓰시오.

➡ _____

**06** 위 글의 밑줄 친 ①~⑤ 중에서 가리키는 대상이 다른 것을 고르시오.

①      ②      ③      ④      ⑤

[07~09] 다음 글을 읽고 물음에 답하시오.

Who can help me feel better?

When he graduates from high school next year, Taeho wants to become a professional farmer. (①) He is worried that his parents or his friends will not understand. (②) Wanting to clear his mind, Taeho decided to take a day trip on a train ____ⓐ____. (③) On the train, he told a complete stranger sitting beside him about his problem. (④) He had no idea why he did it. (⑤) However, he felt much better when he got off the train. Strangely enough, we often tell strangers about our problems just like Taeho. ⓑThat is why we do not have to worry about being judged or seeing them again. If you have a problem that you cannot share with your family or friends, try talking to a stranger. You will feel much better.

**07** 위 글의 흐름으로 보아, 주어진 문장이 들어가기에 가장 적절한 곳은?

> However, he has never told anyone about it.

①      ②      ③      ④      ⑤

서답형

**08** 위 글의 빈칸 ⓐ에 'alone'과 같은 뜻의 말을 두 단어로 어법에 맞게 쓰시오.

➡ _____

서답형

**09** 위 글의 밑줄 친 ⓑ에서 어색한 것을 찾아 바르게 고쳐 쓰시오.

_____ ➡ _____

[10~13] 다음 글을 읽고 물음에 답하시오.

Do you think you have a unique problem? ____ⓐ____ are that many other people have the same problem. Psychology is the study of the human mind and behavior, so it can help you find a solution to your problem.

How do I become (A)[less / more] nervous?

It was five minutes before Jisu's big presentation in front of the whole class. ⓑFeeling nervous, Jisu was carefully studying her notes in her chair. Then, her teacher came over and told her to stand tall like Wonder Woman. After standing tall for a few minutes, Jisu did not feel nervous anymore. In fact, she was confident that she would make a great presentation. According to Amy Cuddy, a famous psychologist, we can become more (B)[nervous / confident] just by standing tall for two minutes before stressful events. Our bodies change our minds, and our minds can change our behavior. Do you want to feel confident? Stand with your feet (C)[apart / together], and place your hands on your hips. You will not only feel sure about yourself but also look confident to other people.

**10** 위 글의 괄호 (A)~(C)에서 문맥이나 어법상 알맞은 낱말을 골라 쓰시오.

➡ (A) _____ (B) _____ (C) _____

**11** 위 글의 빈칸 ⓐ에 알맞은 말을 쓰시오.

➡ _____

## 12 위 글의 밑줄 친 ⓑFeeling과 쓰임이 같은 것을 고르시오.

① I watched Kate underline{singing} on the stage.

② He was underline{enjoying} himself at the camp.

③ When young, Lindsey was good at underline{playing} the piano.

④ underline{Drinking} water is good for your health.

⑤ underline{Returning} the book, Franklin thanked him deeply.

## 13 Which question CANNOT be answered after reading the passage?

① What is Amy Cuddy?

② How can we become less nervous?

③ What is the advice of Jisu's teacher?

④ Why do our bodies change our minds?

⑤ How long did Jisu stand tall?

**[14~16]** 다음 글을 읽고 물음에 답하시오.

---
(A)
_____

Benjamin Franklin once had a political rival who did not like him at all. Franklin wanted to become friends with him, so he came up with a plan. His rival had a rare book. Franklin asked his rival to lend him the book for _____ⓐ_____ days. When Franklin returned the book, he thanked him deeply. Since that day, ⓑunderline{his rival became not only a political supporter but also a good friend.} Franklin famously said, "Enemies who do you one favor will want to do more." If you want to turn a rival into a friend, don't do your rival a favor. Instead, ask your rival to do you a favor.

## 14 위 글의 빈칸 (A)에 들어갈 말로 적절한 것은?

① How did Benjamin approach his political rival?

② How do I turn a rival into a friend?

③ Why do we need to turn a rival into a friend?

④ Don't ask your rival to do you a favor.

⑤ Why did Benjamin need to borrow the book?

## 15 위 글의 빈칸 ⓐ에 들어갈 말로 알맞은 것은?

① little          ② a little          ③ a lot

④ few          ⑤ a few

서답형

## 16 위 글의 밑줄 친 ⓑ를 'as well as'를 이용하여 바꿔 쓰시오.

➡ _____

_____

**[17~20]** 다음 글을 읽고 물음에 답하시오.

---
Who can help me feel better?

When he graduates from high school next year, Taeho wants to become a _____ⓐ_____ farmer. However, he has never told anyone about it. He is worried that his parents or his friends will not understand. Wanting to clear his mind, Taeho decided to take a day trip on a train by himself. On the train, he told a complete stranger sitting beside him about his problem. He had no idea why he did it. _____ⓑ_____, he felt much better when he got off the train. Strangely enough, we often tell strangers about our problems just like Taeho. That is because we do not have to worry about being judged or seeing them again. If you have a problem that you cannot share with your family or friends, try talking to a stranger. You will feel (A)underline{much} better.

**서답형**

**17** 주어진 영영풀이의 빈칸에 해당하는 말을 빈칸 ⓐ에 철자 p 로 시작하여 쓰시오.

> _____ people have jobs that require advanced education or training

➡ _____

**18** 빈칸 ⓑ에 들어갈 알맞은 말을 고르시오.

① Moreover　　② For example

③ Therefore　　④ However

⑤ In addition

**19** 위 글의 밑줄 친 (A)much와 바꿔 쓸 수 없는 말을 고르시오.

① very　　② a lot

③ even　　④ still

⑤ far

**중요**

**20** Which question CANNOT be answered after reading the passage?

① What does Taeho want to become when he graduates from high school next year?

② To whom has Taeho told about his wish?

③ Why did Taeho tell a complete stranger sitting beside him about his problem?

④ Why did Taeho decide to take a day trip on a train by himself?

⑤ How can we feel better when we have a problem?

[21~23] 다음 글을 읽고 물음에 답하시오.

How do I become ___ⓐ___ nervous?

It was five minutes before Jisu's big presentation in front of the whole class. Feeling nervous, Jisu was carefully studying her notes in her chair. Then, her teacher came over and told her to stand tall like Wonder Woman. (A)After standing tall for a few minutes, Jisu did not feel nervous no more. In fact, she was confident that she would make a great presentation. According to Amy Cuddy, a famous psychologist, we can become more confident just by (B)standing tall for two minutes before stressful events. Our bodies change our minds, and our minds can change our behavior. Do you want to feel confident? Stand with your feet apart, and place your hands on your hips. You will not only feel sure about yourself but also look confident to other people.

**21** 위 글의 빈칸 ⓐ에 들어갈 알맞은 말을 고르시오.

① few　　② little　　③ less

④ more　　⑤ very

**서답형**

**22** 위 글의 밑줄 친 (A)에서 흐름상 어색한 부분을 찾아 고치시오.

_____ ➡ _____

**23** 위 글의 밑줄 친 (B)standing과 문법적 쓰임이 다른 것을 모두 고르시오.

① He was standing by the gate.

② Standing on my hands was difficult.

③ Her punishment was standing silently.

④ She looked so miserable, standing there in the rain.

⑤ Standing under the sun was terrible.

[01~03] 다음 글을 읽고 물음에 답하시오.

(A)Who can help me feel better?

When he graduates from high school next year, Taeho wants to become a professional farmer. However, he has never told anyone about it. He is worried that his parents or his friends will not understand. Wanting to clear his mind, Taeho decided to take a day trip on a train by himself. On the train, he told a complete stranger sitting beside him about his problem. He had no idea why he did it. However, he felt much better when he got off the train. ⓐ정말 이상하게도, we often tell strangers about our problems just like Taeho. (B)That is because we do not have to worry about being judged or seeing them again. If you have a problem that you cannot share with your family or friends, try talking to a stranger. You will feel much better.

**01** 위 글의 밑줄 친 (A)의 답이 될 수 있는 것을 본문에서 찾아 세 단어를 쓰시오.

➡ _____

**02** 밑줄 친 ⓐ의 우리말에 맞게 enough를 이용하여 두 단어를 쓰시오.

➡ _____

**03** 위 글의 밑줄 친 (B)That이 가리키는 것을 본문에서 찾아 쓰시오.

➡ _____

[04~06] 다음 글을 읽고 물음에 답하시오.

Do you think you have a unique problem? Chances are that many other people have the same problem. Psychology is the study of the human mind and behavior, so it can help you find a solution to your problem.

How do I become less nervous?

It was five minutes before Jisu's big presentation in front of the whole class. ⓐ Feeling nervous, Jisu was carefully studying her notes in her chair. Then, her teacher came over and told her to stand tall like Wonder Woman. After standing tall for a few minutes, Jisu did not feel nervous anymore. In fact, she was confident that she would make a great presentation. According to Amy Cuddy, a famous psychologist, we can become more confident just by standing tall for two minutes before stressful events. Our bodies change our minds, and our minds can change our behavior. Do you want to feel confident? Stand with your feet apart, and place your hands on your hips. You will not only feel sure about yourself but also look confident to other people.

**04** Why can psychology help us find a solution to our problem?

➡ _____
_____

**05** How can we get to be more confident?

➡ _____
_____

**06** 위 글의 밑줄 친 ⓐFeeling을 부사절로 고쳐 쓰시오.

➡ _____

[07~09] 다음 글을 읽고 물음에 답하시오.

How do I turn a rival into a friend?

Benjamin Franklin once had a political rival who did not like him at all. Franklin wanted to become friends ___ⓐ___ him, so he came up ___ⓐ___ a plan. His rival had a rare book. Franklin asked his rival to lend him the book for a few days. ⓑWhen Franklin returned the book, he thanked him deep. Since that day, ⓒhis rival became not only a political supporter but also a good friend. Franklin famously said, "Enemies who do you one favor will want to do more." If you want to turn a rival into a friend, don't do your rival a favor. Instead, ask your rival to do you a favor.

**07** 위 글의 빈칸 ⓐ에 공통으로 들어갈 전치사를 쓰시오.

➡ _____

**08** 위 글의 밑줄 친 ⓑ에서 어색한 부분을 찾아 고치시오.

_____ ➡ _____

**09** 위 글의 밑줄 친 ⓒ를 'as well as'를 이용하여 바꿔 쓰시오.

➡ _____

_____

[10~13] 다음 글을 읽고 물음에 답하시오.

Who can help me feel better?

When he graduates from high school next year, Taeho wants to become a professional farmer. However, he has never told anyone about ⓐit. He is worried that his parents or his friends will not understand. (A)[Wanting / Wanted] to clear his mind, Taeho decided to take a day trip on a train by himself. On the train, he told a complete stranger (B)[sat / sitting] beside him about his problem. ⓑ그는 자신이 왜 그랬는지 알 수 없었다. However, he felt much better when he got off the train. Strangely enough, we often tell strangers about our problems just like Taeho. That is because we do not have to worry about (C) [being judged / judging] or seeing them again. If you have a problem that you cannot share with your family or friends, try talking to a stranger. You will feel much better.

**10** 위 글의 괄호 (A)~(C)에서 문맥이나 어법상 알맞은 낱말을 고르시오.

➡ (A) _____ (B) _____ (C) _____

**11** 위 글의 밑줄 친 ⓐit이 가리키는 것을 본문에서 찾아 쓰시오.

➡ _____

**12** 위 글의 밑줄 친 ⓑ의 우리말을 주어진 어휘를 이용하여 영작하시오. (no, idea, it)

➡ _____

**13** 위 글의 내용과 일치하도록 다음 빈칸 (A)와 (B)에 알맞은 단어를 쓰시오.

Taeho wants to become a professional farmer, but he is worried that his parents or his friends will not understand. While taking a day trip on a train by himself, he told (A)_____ _____ _____ about his problem. He didn't know why he did it. But he felt (B)_____ _____ when he got off the train.

### Listen & Speak 2 – B Think and Talk

A: What don't I have to do on Stress-Free Day?

B: You don't have to clean the classroom.
<u>= You don't need to</u>

C: You don't have to come to school by 8:30.

구문해설 • stress-free: 스트레스가 없는

해석

A: 스트레스가 없는 날에 무엇을 할 필요가 없을까?

B: 너는 교실 청소를 할 필요가 없어.

C: 너는 8:30분까지 학교에 올 필요가 없어.

### Link

How confident do you feel about yourself? <u>Wanting to find the answer</u>
분사구문(= As[Because] we wanted)
to this question, we created a test <u>about</u> confidence. Thirty students <u>took the</u>
[행위 · 동작 · 작용의 대상] ~에 대하여                                                      시험[검사]을 치르다
<u>test</u>. The average score was nine. Eighteen students scored <u>above</u> the average
[초과] ~ 이상인[으로]
score. <u>Thus</u>, sixty percent of the students felt quite confident about <u>themselves</u>.
결과를 이끄는 연결어                                                                              them(×)

구문해설 • confident: 자신감이 있는  • confidence: 자신감  • average: 평균; 평균의

당신은 스스로에 대해 얼마나 확신이 있나요? 질문에 대한 답을 찾고 싶어, 우리는 자신감에 대한 검사지를 만들었습니다. 30명의 학생들이 검사를 했습니다. 평균적인 점수는 9점이었습니다. 18명의 학생들이 평균 점수를 넘었습니다. 따라서, 학생들의 60%가 그들 스스로에 대해 꽤 자신감을 갖고 있습니다.

### Write

**The hardest time in my life**

The <u>hardest</u> time in my life was <u>when</u> my grandmother passed away five years
최상급                                                  the time when: ~할 때
ago. When I was <u>younger</u>, she took care of me most of the time. <u>Not having</u>
비교 대상 없는 비교급(자기 자신)                                    = As[Because] I didn't have her around의 분사구문
<u>her around</u>, I <u>felt sad and lonely</u>. One day, I found my grandmother's diary.
                                            지각동사+형용사
<u>She not only wrote</u> a lot about her memories but also <u>wished</u> that I <u>would lead</u>
(= Not only did she write ~, but also <u>she</u> wished)                        병렬 구조            will의 과거형(시제 일치)
a happy life. From this experience, I <u>have learned</u> that I should try to <u>be happy</u>
                    부사구                      현재완료
<u>just as she wished</u>.
be 형용사 just as(접속사) S+wished: S가 원했던 것처럼 ~하다

구문해설 • pass away: 죽다  • have ~ around: ~가 곁에 있다  • just as: ~가 …한 것과 같이

**내 삶에서 가장 힘들었던 순간**

내 삶에서 가장 힘들었던 순간은 5년 전 할머니께서 돌아가셨을 때였다. 내가 더 어렸을 때, 그녀는 대부분의 시간 동안 나를 돌봐주셨다. 그녀가 곁에 없어서, 나는 슬프고 외로웠다. 어느 날, 나는 할머니의 일기장을 발견했다. 그녀는 그녀의 기억에 대해 많이 적었을 뿐만 아니라, 내가 행복한 삶을 살기를 바랐다. 이 경험을 통해, 나는 그녀가 원했던 것처럼 행복해지려고 노력해야 한다는 것을 배웠다.

## 영역별 핵심문제

**01** 다음 짝지어진 단어의 관계가 같도록 빈칸에 알맞은 말을 쓰시오.

> tradition : traditional = success : _____

**02** 다음 영영풀이가 가리키는 것을 고르시오.

> to complete your education at a college, school, etc.

① graduate      ② judge
③ guess      ④ decide
⑤ prepare

**03** 다음 중 밑줄 친 부분의 뜻풀이가 바르지 <u>않은</u> 것은?

① I want to be a specialist in child <u>psychology</u>. (심리학)
② We blamed his bad <u>behavior</u>. (행동)
③ Do you have a better <u>solution</u>? (해결책)
④ He drew a <u>unique</u> picture on the wall. (독특한)
⑤ The two houses stand 500 meters <u>apart</u>. (가까이)

**04** 다음 우리말에 맞게 빈칸에 알맞은 말을 쓰시오. (철자가 주어진 것은 그 철자로 시작할 것.)

(1) 그녀는 아마 며칠 후에 떠날 것이다.
➡ She will p_____ leave in a few days.

(2) 너는 그 문제에 대해 좀 전문적인 조언을 얻을 필요가 있다.
➡ You need to get some _____ advice about that problem.

(3) 나는 사람의 마음에 관심이 있어서, 대학에서 심리학을 공부할 것이다.
➡ I am interested in the human mind, so I will study _____ in college.

(4) 그녀는 희귀한 병을 가졌다.
➡ She has a r_____ disease.

**05** 다음 문장의 빈칸에 들어갈 말을 〈보기〉에서 골라 쓰시오.

> ┤ 보기 ├
> chances are that / get off / stop by / stand tall / make a presentation

(1) Are you going to _____ at the meeting?
(2) Could you _____ the store for some bread on the way home?
(3) Go out into the real world and _____, my students!
(4) _____ our team will win the championship.
(5) We need to _____ at the next station.

**06** 다음 문장에 공통으로 들어갈 말을 고르시오.

> • I can't handle this project _____ myself.
> • Would you stop _____ my office and do me a favor?
> • I'll be back home _____ 6 to help you.

① by      ② with
③ from      ④ to
⑤ of

**Conversation**

**[07~09] 다음 대화를 읽고 물음에 답하시오.**

Minsu: Shall we have seafood spaghetti ⓐfor dinner?

Emma: Sure. I'll (A)stop by the store ⓑon the way home.

Minsu: You don't have ⓒto do that. We already have ⓓwhat we need.

Emma: Oh, I see. Then, I'll be back home by 6 to ⓔhelp you cooking.

**07** 위 대화의 밑줄 친 ⓐ~ⓔ 중 어법상 틀린 것을 찾아 바르게 고치시오.

_____ ➡ _____

**08** 위 대화의 밑줄 친 (A)와 바꾸어 쓸 수 있는 것은?

① drop
② chew
③ get
④ decide
⑤ judge

**09** 위 대화의 내용과 일치하지 않는 것은?

① 민수는 Emma에게 저녁에 해산물 스파게티 먹을 것을 제안했다.
② Emma는 집에 오는 길에 가게에 들를 것이다.
③ 민수는 이미 스파게티에 필요한 것을 갖고 있다.
④ Emma는 6시까지 집에 돌아올 것이다.
⑤ Emma는 민수가 요리하는 것을 도울 것이다.

**[10~11] 다음 대화를 읽고 물음에 답하시오.**

B: You look a bit nervous.

G: Well, _____ (A)

B: Don't worry. You've prepared a lot. You'll do a great job.

G: Thanks. I feel much better now.

**10** 위 대화의 빈칸 (A)에 들어갈 말을 주어진 단어를 모두 배열하여 영작하시오.

┌─ 보기 ─┐
history class / about / in / presentation / worried / I'm / my
└────────┘

➡ _____

**11** 위 대화의 내용과 일치하지 않는 것은?

① 소녀는 약간 긴장되어 보인다.
② 소녀는 역사 시간에 할 발표를 걱정한다.
③ 소녀는 발표 준비를 많이 했다.
④ 소녀는 소년 덕분에 기분이 훨씬 나아졌다.
⑤ 소년은 소녀의 발표를 칭찬하였다.

**12** 다음 대화가 자연스럽게 이어지도록 순서대로 배열하시오.

(A) Oh, I see. How convenient!
(B) You don't have to call them. You can do it online.
(C) Shall we try that new Mexican restaurant tomorrow?
(D) Why not? I'll call the restaurant to make a reservation for us.

➡ _____

**[13~14] 다음 대화를 읽고 물음에 답하시오.**

Jane: What happened to your shoes? Aren't they new?

Brian: Yes, but my dog chewed them. He does it all the time. I'm worried about him.

Jane: He was probably bored. Why don't you play with him more often?

Brian: O.K., I will. I hope he will stop chewing my shoes.

**13** What happened to Brian's shoes?

➡ _____

**14** What does Jane advise Brian to do?

➡ _____

(2)

➡ Jiho has decided _____

_____. (to go, nor, to get,

college, neither, to, a job)

**Grammar**

**15** 다음 문장의 밑줄 친 분사구문을 부사절로 바르게 바꾼 것은?

> Living alone in this big apartment, I rarely feel lonely.

① Because I live in this big apartment,
② While I'm living in this big apartment,
③ If I live in this big apartment,
④ Though I live in this big apartment,
⑤ Unless I live in this big apartment,

**16** 다음 그림을 보고 괄호 안의 단어를 배열하여 빈칸을 알맞게 채우시오. (단, 단어 배열은 그림의 왼쪽에서 오른쪽임.)

(1)

➡ _____

on the spider web. (in, the honeybee, are, the ladybug, both, and, trouble)

**17** 다음 중 어법상 어색한 문장을 모두 고르시오.

① Not only can people guess the story but they also know the ending.
② Both the participants or the researchers were satisfied with the result.
③ Either Jamie and Esther is coming today.
④ I can't even imagine not only when but also where the event will happen.
⑤ Neither Thomas nor his team members were present at the meeting.

**18** 다음 괄호 안에서 어법상 알맞은 것을 고르시오.

(1) Not only Sammy but also Olga (like / likes) the soup so much.
(2) Maria required that the dance teams should practice not only singing but also (to dance / dancing).
(3) Either Kennedy (or / nor) Jason should complete the assignment by tomorrow.
(4) Either the recording engineers or the music director (is / are) going to direct the song production.
(5) Not the angels but the devil (appear / appears) before the sad soul.

**19** 다음 문장의 밑줄 친 부사절을 분사구문으로 알맞게 바꾼 것을 고르시오.

> <u>As she doesn't have anyone around to encourage her,</u> Joanne felt even more lonely.

① As she having not anyone around to encourage her,

② There being someone around to encourage her,

③ Having not anyone around to encourage her,

④ As having not anyone around to encourage her,

⑤ Not having anyone around to encourage her,

**20** 다음 밑줄 친 부분 중 어법상 어색한 것을 고르시오.

① <u>Not having money</u>, Robert couldn't buy the birthday present for his wife.

② <u>Raining all day</u>, the club members stayed at home and watched their video clips.

③ <u>Being tired</u>, Sonya went to bed early.

④ <u>Finding the book he had lost</u>, I called him to come over to my place.

⑤ <u>Frankly speaking</u>, the prime minster of Japan seemed like an idiot.

**Reading**

[21~22] 다음 글을 읽고 물음에 답하시오.

Do you think you have a unique problem? Chances are that many other people have the same problem. Psychology is the study of the human mind and behavior, so it can help you find a solution ___ⓐ___ your problem.

How do I become less nervous?

It was five minutes before Jisu's big presentation in front of the whole class. Feeling nervous, Jisu was carefully studying her notes in her chair. Then, her teacher came over and told her ___ⓑ___ stand tall like Wonder Woman. After standing tall for a few minutes, Jisu did not feel nervous anymore. ___ⓒ___, she was confident that she would make a great presentation.

**21** 위 글의 빈칸 ⓐ와 ⓑ에 공통으로 들어갈 알맞은 전치사를 고르시오.

① to        ② on        ③ for

④ in        ⑤ at

**22** 위 글의 빈칸 ⓒ에 알맞은 것을 고르시오.

① For example      ② However

③ In addition      ④ In fact

⑤ Thus

[23~25] 다음 글을 읽고 물음에 답하시오.

Who can help me feel better?

When he graduates from high school next year, Taeho wants to become a professional farmer. However, he has never told anyone about it. He is worried that his parents or his friends will not understand. ⓐWanting to clear his mind, Taeho decided to take a day trip on a train by himself. On the train, he told a complete stranger sitting beside him about his problem. He had no idea why he did it. However, he felt much better when he got off the train. Strangely enough, we often tell strangers about our problems just like Taeho. That is because we do not have to worry about being judged or seeing them again. If you have a problem that you cannot share with your family or friends, try talking to a stranger. You will feel much better.

**23** 위 글의 주제로 알맞은 것을 고르시오.

① how to meet a complete stranger
② how to feel better when we have a problem
③ how to clear our mind
④ why Taeho wants to be a professional farmer
⑤ why we tell a teacher about our problem

**24** 밑줄 친 ⓐ를 부사절로 알맞게 고친 것을 고르시오.

① As he wants to clear his mind
② Because he wanted to clear his mind
③ Though he wanted to clear his mind
④ If he wanted to clear his mind
⑤ After he wanted to clear his mind

**25** According to the passage, which is NOT true?

① Taeho wants to become a professional farmer after graduation from high school.
② Taeho has never told anyone about becoming a professional farmer.
③ When we have a problem that we cannot share with our family or friends, we will feel much better by trying talking to a stranger.
④ Taeho took a day trip on a train by himself as he wanted to clear his mind.
⑤ Taeho knew why he told a complete stranger about his problem.

[26~29] 다음 글을 읽고 물음에 답하시오.

How do I turn a rival into a friend?

Benjamin Franklin once had a political rival who did not like him at all. (①) Franklin wanted to become friends with him, so he came up with a plan. (②) His rival had a rare book. (③) When Franklin returned the book, he thanked him deeply. (④) Since that day, his rival became not only a political supporter but also a good friend. (⑤) Franklin famously said, "Enemies who do you one favor will want to do more." If you want to turn a rival into a friend, don't do your rival a favor. _____ⓐ_____, ask your rival to do you a favor.

**26** 위 글의 빈칸 ⓐ에 들어갈 말로 알맞은 것을 고르시오.

① However        ② For instance
③ Nonetheless     ④ In fact
⑤ Instead

**27** 위 글의 흐름으로 보아, 주어진 문장이 들어가기에 가장 적절한 곳은?

Franklin asked his rival to lend him the book for a few days.

①        ②        ③        ④        ⑤

**28** 위 글에 나타난 Franklin에 대한 설명으로 가장 적절한 것을 고르시오.

① wicked        ② honest        ③ wise
④ timid         ⑤ evil

**29** What did Franklin's political rival do for Franklin? Answer in English with 7 words.

➡ _____

**01** 출제율 90%

다음 영영풀이가 가리키는 것을 고르시오.

> someone who hates you and wants to harm you

① stranger
② supporter
③ psychologist
④ rival
⑤ enemy

**02** 출제율 95%

다음 우리말을 주어진 단어를 이용하여 영작하시오.

(1) 네 자신에게 너무 많은 부담을 주지 마라. (pressure, too, on)

　➡ _____

(2) 두 발을 벌리고 서라. (with, feet)

　➡ _____

(3) 내가 식당에 전화해서 예약할게요. (make, restaurant)

　➡ _____

**[03~05]** 다음 대화를 읽고 물음에 답하시오.

Minsu: Shall we have seafood spaghetti for dinner?

Emma: Sure. I'll stop by the store on the way home.

Minsu: You don't have to do that. We already have what we need.

Emma: Oh, I see. Then, I'll be back home by 6 to help you cook.

**03** 출제율 90%

What is Minsu going to cook for dinner?

　➡ _____

**04** 출제율 95%

Why doesn't Emma have to stop by the store?

　➡ _____
　_____

**05** 출제율 90%

By when will Emma be back home to help Minsu?

　➡ _____

**06** 출제율 95%

다음 대화가 자연스럽게 이어지도록 순서대로 배열하시오.

> (A) He was probably bored. Why don't you play with him more often?
> (B) O.K., I will. I hope he will stop chewing my shoes.
> (C) What happened to your shoes? Aren't they new?
> (D) Yes, but my dog chewed them. He does it all the time. I'm worried about him.

　➡ _____

**[07~08]** 다음 대화를 읽고 물음에 답하시오.

Jack: Mom, what time are we going to Grandma's place tomorrow morning?

Mom: About 8 a.m. I'm going to bake cookies for her before we go.

Jack: Then, should I get up early to help you?

Mom: (A)그럴 필요 없단다. (have) Your dad will help me.

Jack: O.K, then. Good night, Mom!

**07** 출제율 90%

위 대화의 밑줄 친 (A)의 우리말을 주어진 단어를 사용하여 영작하시오. (4 words)

　➡ _____

## 08 위 대화의 내용과 일치하지 <u>않는</u> 것은?

① Jack is supposed to visit his grandma with her mother.

② Jack is going to his grandma's place about 8 a.m. tomorrow morning.

③ Jack doesn't need to help his mom tomorrow morning.

④ Jack's mom is planning to bake cookies for Jack's grandma at night.

⑤ Jack's father is going to help Jack's mom to bake cookies.

[09~10] 다음 대화를 읽고 물음에 답하시오.

Yuri: Hi, Jaden. Sports Day is next Friday. I can't wait!

Jaden: Really? I'm actually worried about it.

Yuri: Why? Aren't you good at sports?

Jaden: (A) Yes, I am, but I'm worried about the 800-meter relay.

Yuri: What do you mean?

Jaden: (B) I'm the last runner. What if our team loses because of me?

Yuri: (C) I think you're putting too much pressure on yourself.

Jaden: (D) Really? Don't you think I should practice every day?

Yuri: (E) It's just a school race. It's not about winning or losing.

Jaden: I guess you're right, Yuri. I'm lucky to have a friend like you.

## 09 위 대화의 (A)~(E) 중 주어진 문장이 들어가기에 적절한 곳은?

No, you don't have to do that.

① (A)　② (B)　③ (C)　④ (D)　⑤ (E)

## 10 위 대화의 내용과 일치하지 <u>않는</u> 것은?

① 운동회가 다음 주 금요일이다.

② Jaden은 운동을 잘하지만 800미터 릴레이가 걱정된다.

③ Jaden은 자신 때문에 팀이 질까봐 걱정한다.

④ 유리는 Jaden이 스스로에게 너무 많은 압박을 주고 있는 것 같다고 생각한다.

⑤ 유리는 이기거나 지는 것이 중요한 경기는 아니지만, Jaden이 매일 연습해야 한다고 생각한다.

## 11 다음 대화의 내용과 일치하지 <u>않는</u> 것은?

B: You look a bit nervous.

G: I'm worried about my swimming competition this Saturday.

B: Don't worry. You're such a good swimmer. Just relax and enjoy yourself!

G: Thanks. I feel much better now.

① 소녀는 긴장한 것 같아 보인다.

② 소녀는 다음 주 토요일에 있는 수영대회를 걱정하고 있다.

③ 소녀는 수영을 아주 잘한다.

④ 소년은 소녀에게 긴장을 풀고 즐기라고 하였다.

⑤ 소녀는 소년의 격려 덕분에 기분이 훨씬 괜찮아졌다.

## 12 다음 중 어법상 올바른 문장을 <u>모두</u> 고르면?

① Opened the drawer, he took out a letter.

② There being no bus service, we had to walk all the way home.

③ Worked hard to finish the project in time, Chris was taken to hospital.

④ Knowing not what to do, she asked him for help.

⑤ Director Bong winning the great awards, the fans in Korea felt proud of his films.

**[13~14]** 다음 중 빈칸에 들어갈 수 <u>없는</u> 말을 고르시오.

출제율 100%

## 13

> The princess Elsa in the castle was not only _____ but also generous.

① beautiful    ② friendly    ③ lovely
④ truly       ⑤ wise

출제율 95%

## 14

> My grandmother not only wrote a lot about her memories on her family and friends but also _____.

① wished that I would lead a happy life
② was sure that her children would be happy
③ was satisfied with a quiet life
④ proud of her family members
⑤ wanted to be remembered by us

출제율 95%

## 15 다음 각 문장의 부사절을 알맞은 분사구문으로 전환하시오.

(1) When we use green energy vehicles, we can reduce a good amount of $CO_2$ in the air.

➡ _____, we can reduce a good amount of $CO_2$ in the air.

(2) Because Anne didn't come back, her husband waited for three hours.

➡ _____, her husband waited for three hours.

(3) As Shane had not been invited to the final match, he stayed at home all day long.

➡ _____, Shane stayed at home all day long.

출제율 95%

## 16 다음 중 우리말과 그 영작이 바르게 짝지어지지 <u>않은</u> 것은?

① Ben은 영어뿐만 아니라 중국어도 말할 수 있다.
→ Ben can speak not only English but also Chinese.

② 그 배우는 드라마뿐만 아니라 영화도 찍고 있다.
→ The actor is filming not only a drama but also a movie.

③ 아이들뿐만 아니라 그들의 엄마도 펭수를 좋아한다.
→ Not only the kids but also their mom like Pengsu.

④ BTS는 한국에서뿐만 아니라 일본에서도 콘서트를 열 것이다.
→ BTS will hold a concert not only in Korea but also in Japan.

⑤ 불고기는 맛있을 뿐만 아니라 영양가도 있다.
→ Bulgogi is not only delicious but also nutritious.

**[17~18]** 다음 글을 읽고 물음에 답하시오.

> How confident do you feel about yourself? (A)Wanting to find the answer to this question, we created a test about confidence. Thirty students took the test. The average score was nine. Eighteen students scored above the average score. Thus, ⓐ percent of the students felt quite confident about themselves.

출제율 90%

## 17 위 글의 빈칸 ⓐ에 들어갈 알맞은 말을 영어로 쓰시오.

➡ _____

**18** 위 글의 밑줄 친 (A)를 부사절로 고쳐 쓰시오.

➡ _____

_____

**[19~20]** 다음 글을 읽고 물음에 답하시오.

Do you think you have a ___ⓐ___ problem? (A)아마 많은 다른 사람들이 여러분과 똑같은 고민을 가지고 있을 것이다. Psychology is the study of the human mind and behavior, so it can help you find a solution to your problem.

**19** 주어진 영영풀이에 해당하는 단어를 빈칸 ⓐ에 써 넣으시오.

being the only one of its kind

➡ _____

**20** 위 글의 밑줄 친 (A)의 우리말에 맞게 chances를 이용하여 10 단어로 영작하시오.

➡ _____

_____

**[21~23]** 다음 글을 읽고 물음에 답하시오.

How do I become less nervous?

It was five minutes before Jisu's big presentation in front of the whole class. (①) Feeling nervous, Jisu was carefully studying her notes in her chair. (②) Then, her teacher came over and told her to stand tall like Wonder Woman. (③) In fact, she was confident that she would make a great presentation. (④) According to Amy Cuddy,

a famous psychologist, we can become more confident just by standing tall for two minutes before stressful events. (⑤) Our bodies change our minds, and our minds can change our behavior. Do you want to feel confident? Stand with your feet apart, and place your hands on your hips. ⓐYou will not only feel sure about yourself but also look confident to other people.

**21** 위 글의 흐름으로 보아, 주어진 문장이 들어가기에 가장 적절한 곳은?

After standing tall for a few minutes, Jisu did not feel nervous anymore.

① ② ③ ④ ⑤

**22** What did Jisu's teacher advise Jisu to do?

➡ _____

_____

**23** 위 글의 밑줄 친 ⓐ와 그 뜻이 다른 것을 고르시오.

① You will not only feel sure about yourself but look confident to other people.
② You will not simply feel sure about yourself but look confident to other people.
③ You will not just feel sure about yourself but also look confident to other people.
④ You will not merely feel sure about yourself but also look confident to other people.
⑤ You will not feel sure about yourself but look confident to other people.

**[01~03]** 다음 대화를 읽고 물음에 답하시오.

> **Yuri:** Hi, Jaden. Sports Day is next Friday. I can't wait!
>
> **Jaden:** Really? I'm actually worried about it.
>
> **Yuri:** Why? Aren't you good at sports?
>
> **Jaden:** Yes, I am, but I'm worried about the 800-meter relay.
>
> **Yuri:** What do you mean?
>
> **Jaden:** I'm the last runner. What if our team loses because of me?
>
> **Yuri:** I think you're putting too much pressure on yourself.
>
> **Jaden:** Really? Don't you think I should practice every day?
>
> **Yuri:** No, you don't have to do that. It's just a school race. It's not about winning or losing.
>
> **Jaden:** I guess you're right, Yuri. I'm lucky to have a friend like you.

**01** What is Yuri looking forward to?

➡ _____

**02** As the last runner of the 800-meter relay, what is Jaden worried about?

➡ _____
_____

**03** Why does Yuri think Jaden doesn't have to practice every day?

➡ _____
_____

**04** 다음 우리말에 맞도록 괄호 안에 주어진 어휘를 알맞게 배열하시오.

(1) Bob과 Tom이 길을 걷고 있었을 때, 그들은 Julie가 노래 부르는 것을 봤다. (down, street, walking, the)

➡ _____, Bob and Tom saw Julie singing.

(2) 비록 Jane은 아버지의 뜻을 알지 못했지만, 그가 말한 대로 하기로 결심했다. (what, not, meant, knowing, her father)

➡ _____, Jane decided to do as he told.

(3) 그 비행기에 남은 좌석이 있다면, 나는 오늘 저녁에 LA로 갈 것이다. (seats, there, the plane, left, any, on, being)

➡ _____, I will go to L.A. this evening.

(4) 마음을 정리하고 싶었기 때문에, Karen은 회사를 그만두겠다고 사장에게 말했다. (clear, wanting, mind, to, her)

➡ _____, Karen told the boss that she'd quit the company.

**05** 다음 그림을 보고, 내용에 맞게 〈보기〉에서 알맞은 단어를 각각 선택하여, 어법에 맞게 대화의 빈칸에 채워 넣으시오.

┤ 보기 ├
- not / but / both / only / either / neither / also / nor / and
- 반드시 한 번씩만 사용할 것.
- 빈칸의 위치에 따라 대·소문자 구분할 것.

Jina: You know when Mom's birthday is?

Jihun: Sure. It's in November, isn't it?

Jina: Yeah, on which day?

Jihun: It probably falls on before or after the cookie stick *Pepero* day. So, it's _____ 10th, or 12th?

Jina: _____ 10th _____ 12th is right. It's 18th, just a week after *Pepero* day. _____ _____ Dad _____ _____ you don't care about Mom.

Jihun: Sorry for that. Instead, what should _____ Dad _____ I do?

[06~08] 다음 글을 읽고 물음에 답하시오.

**The hardest time in my life**

The hardest time in my life was when my grandmother passed away five years ago. When I was younger, she took care of me most of the time. ⓐNot having her around, I felt sad and lonely. One day, I found my grandmother's diary. ⓑShe not only wrote a lot about her memories but also wished that I would lead a happy life. From this experience, I have learned that I should try to be happy just as she wished.

**06** 위 글의 밑줄 친 ⓐ를 부사절로 고쳐 쓰시오.

➡ _____

**07** 위 글의 밑줄 친 ⓑ를 not only로 시작하여 바꿔 쓰시오.

➡ _____

**08** 위 글의 필자가 할머니의 일기장을 통해 얻은 교훈을 우리말에 쓰시오.

➡ _____
_____

[09~11] 다음 대화를 읽고 물음에 답하시오.

A: Who ate the cookies?

B: (*Touching his* _____ⓐ_____) I don't know. Maybe the dog ate them.

A: I can tell that you're (A)[lying / laying] because you're touching your _____ⓐ_____ .

C: This is an example of the Pinocchio Effect. People experience the Pinocchio Effect when they tell a lie. (B)[Not only they / Not only do they] feel (C)[even if / as if] their nose is getting hotter, but also the temperature around their eyes (D)[raises / rises].

**09** 위 글의 빈칸 ⓐ에 공통으로 들어갈 알맞은 말을 쓰시오.

➡ _____

**10** Why do people touch their nose when they tell a lie? Fill in the blanks (A) and (B) with suitable words.

Because they feel as if not only their nose is (A)_____ _____, but also the temperature around their eyes (B)_____.

**11** 위 글의 괄호 (A)~(D)에서 문맥상 알맞은 낱말을 골라 쓰시오.

➡ (A) _____ (B) _____
   (C) _____ (D) _____

**01** 다음 대화를 읽고 대화의 내용과 일치하도록 빈칸을 완성하시오.

> Jack: Mom, what time are we going to Grandma's place tomorrow morning?
>
> Mom: About 8 a.m. I'm going to bake cookies for her before we go.
>
> Jack: Then, should I get up early to help you?
>
> Mom: You don't have to. Your dad will help me.
>
> Jack: O.K, then. Good night, Mom!

> I'm looking forward to visiting (A)_____ tomorrow. We're going to leave about 8 a.m tomorrow. My mom is planning to (B)_____ for my grandma. (C)_____ is going to help her early in the morning. I can't wait to see my grandma!

**02** 다음 내용을 바탕으로 다른 사람에게 공감과 조언을 하는 편지의 빈칸을 알맞게 채우시오.

| Situation | Feelings |
|---|---|
| • have just moved to a new school<br>• have nobody to talk to<br>• ask one of my classmates to show me her notes<br>• Asking for help | • lonely<br>• feel like crying<br>• showed me her notes, started to talk about herself<br>• help you make new friends |

> To someone who (A)_____,
> I understand how (B)_____ you might be feeling now. I had to go to a new school like you because my whole family moved to Gunsan, a small city in Korea. (C)_____, I felt like crying on the first day at my new school. However, a small thing made the situation better. I asked one of my classmates to show me her notes. Then, she not only (D)_____. That was how she became my new friend. Asking for help sometimes (E)_____. I wish you all the best.

## 단원별 모의고사

**01** 다음 우리말에 맞게 빈칸을 완성하시오. (철자가 주어진 것은 그 철자로 시작할 것.)

(1) 그녀는 판매를 올리기 위한 새로운 아이디어를 떠올렸다.

➡ She _____ _____ _____ a new idea for increasing sales.

(2) 그는 저녁을 먹으러 우리집에 들렀다.

➡ He c_____ _____ to my house for dinner.

(3) 내가 돌아왔을 때, 이미 모두가 가버렸다.

➡ When I _____ _____, everybody was already gone.

**02** 다음 문장의 빈칸에 들어갈 말을 〈보기〉에서 골라 쓰시오.

┌─ 보기 ─┐

competition / text message / prepare / mind / anxious / unique

(1) He sent a _____ to his dad.

(2) You don't have to be _____ about the exam.

(3) Everyone's fingerprint is _____.

(4) While I cook the pasta, would you _____ the sauce?

(5) I went for a walk to clear my _____.

(6) I'm worried about my swimming _____.

**03** 우리말과 일치하도록 주어진 단어를 배열하여 영작하시오.

(1) 당신은 정치적인 사안에 관심이 있나요?

(the / in / you / are / issue / interested / political)

➡ _____

_____

(2) 당신은 매일 연설 준비를 할 필요가 없어요.

(every day / prepare / you / your / don't / to / speech / have)

➡ _____

_____

(3) 나는 우리의 발표가 전혀 걱정되지 않아.

(worried / about / at / our / all / I'm / presentation / not)

➡ _____

_____

**04** 다음 짝지어진 대화가 <u>어색한</u> 것은?

① A: What don't I have to do on Stress-Free Day?

B: You don't have to clean the classroom.

② A: I'm worried about my grade on the science test.

B: You don't have to be good at every subject.

③ A: I'm concerned about my weight. I think I'm too fat.

B: You don't need to worry about your weight. You look great.

④ A: I'm afraid that I'll make a mistake on my math test.

B: You don't have to worry too much.

⑤ A: I'm worried about my family. We don't talk to each other much these days.

B: You look a bit nervous. You don't need to talk to each other.

**[05~06]** 다음 대화를 읽고 물음에 답하시오.

> B: You look a bit nervous.
>
> G: Well, I'm worried about my presentation in history class.
>
> B: Don't worry. You've prepared a lot. You'll do a great job.
>
> G: Thanks. I feel much better now.

**05** What is the girl concerned about?

➡ _____

_____

**06** Why does the boy think the girl will do a great job?

➡ _____

**07** 다음 대화를 읽고 대답할 수 없는 것은?

> Jack: Mom, what time are we going to Grandma's place tomorrow morning?
>
> Mom: About 8 a.m. I'm going to bake cookies for her before we go.
>
> Jack: Then, should I get up early to help you?
>
> Mom: You don't have to. Your dad will help me.
>
> Jack: O.K, then. Good night, Mom!

① What is Jack going to do with his mom?

② What is Jack's mom going to do for his grandma?

③ Who will help Jack's mom in the morning?

④ When are Jack and his mom going to his grandma's place tomorrow?

⑤ What time is Jack's mom going to get up to bake cookies?

**[08~09]** 다음 대화를 읽고 물음에 답하시오.

> Emily: Shall we try that new Mexican restaurant tomorrow?
>
> Tom: Why not? I'll call the restaurant to _____(A)_____ for us.
>
> Emily: You don't have to call them. You can do it online.
>
> Tom: Oh, I see. How convenient!

**08** 위 대화의 빈칸 (A)에 '예약하다'를 3 단어로 쓰시오.

➡ _____

**09** 위 대화의 내용과 일치하지 않는 것은?

① Emily는 Tom에게 내일 새로 생긴 멕시코 레스토랑에 가자고 제안한다.

② Tom은 멕시코 레스토랑에 가는 것이 별로 마음에 들지 않는다.

③ Tom은 레스토랑에 전화로 예약할 필요가 없다.

④ 레스토랑 예약은 온라인으로 할 수 있다.

⑤ Tom은 온라인 예약이 편리하다고 생각한다.

**10** 다음 대화가 자연스럽게 이어지도록 순서대로 배열하시오.

> (A) Thanks. I feel much better now.
>
> (B) You look a bit nervous.
>
> (C) I'm worried about my swimming competition this Saturday.
>
> (D) Don't worry. You're such a good swimmer. Just relax and enjoy yourself!

➡ _____

**11** 다음 대화의 (A)~(C)에 들어갈 말이 바르게 짝지어진 것은?

> Jane: What happened to your shoes? Aren't they new?
>
> Brian: Yes, but my dog chewed them. He does it all the time. I'm (A)[worrying / worried] about him.
>
> Jane: He was probably (B)[boring / bored]. Why don't you play with him more often?
>
> Brian: O.K., I will. I hope he will stop (C) [to chew / chewing] my shoes.

|   | (A) | (B) | (C) |
|---|-----|-----|-----|
| ① | worrying | boring | to chew |
| ② | worrying | bored | chewing |
| ③ | worried | bored | to chew |
| ④ | worried | bored | chewing |
| ⑤ | worried | boring | to chew |

**12** 다음 대화와 일치하도록 빈칸을 완성하시오.

> B: You look a bit nervous.
>
> G: I'm worried about my swimming competition this Saturday.
>
> B: Don't worry. You're such a good swimmer. Just relax and enjoy yourself!
>
> G: Thanks. I feel much better now.

> The girl looked (A)_____. She was so worried because of (B)_____. It'll be held on (C)_____. The boy already knew she is a good swimmer, so he encouraged her, by saying (D)"_____". Thanks to the boy, the girl felt relieved.

**[13~14]** 다음 주어진 우리말을 영작한 것으로 옳은 것은?

**13**
> 지수는 자신에 대한 확신을 느꼈을 뿐만 아니라, 타인들에게도 자신감에 차 보였다.

① Jisu felt not only sure about herself but looked also confident to other people.

② Not only Jisu felt sure about herself but also other people looked confident.

③ Jisu not only felt sure about herself but looked confident to other people.

④ Not only did feel Jisu sure about herself but she also looked confident to other people.

⑤ Jisu not only felt sure about herself but also looked confidently to other people.

**14**
> Franklin은 기타를 연주할 수 있을 뿐만 아니라, 피아노 조율도 할 수 있다.

① Franklin can play not only the guitar, but also tune the piano.

② Franklin not only can play the guitar, but also can he tune the piano.

③ Not only can Franklin play the guitar, does he also tune the piano.

④ Not only can Franklin play the guitar, but he can tune the piano.

⑤ Not Franklin only can play the guitar, but can he also tune the piano.

**15** 다음 각 문장의 밑줄 친 분사구문을 부사절로 바꿀 때 어법 상 <u>어색한</u> 것은?

① <u>Visiting Vladivostok</u>, she could learn the Russian dance.

→ When she visited Vladivostok,

② <u>Seen from the high sky</u>, the city seems to be made of the lego bricks.

→ If it is seen from the high sky,

③ <u>There being nothing to eat</u>, the mice moved to another city.

→ Since there was nothing to eat,

④ <u>It being cold but fine</u>, we went on a picnic.

→ Though it was cold but fine,

⑤ <u>Completing the final review</u>, Roberto went out for a walk with his pets.

→ After he completed the final review,

**16** 다음 그림을 보고, 주어진 단어들을 알맞게 배열하여 빈칸을 채우시오.

(Sam, Minju, are, joining, and, in, both, interested, a club)

➡ _____

_____ and doing volunteer work.

**17** 다음 각 문장의 밑줄 친 부사절을 분사구문으로 바꾼 것 중 옳은 것은?

① <u>While Babe was watching TV</u>, his pet puppies fell asleep.

→ Watching TV,

② <u>Because she went to bed earlier last night</u>, Reon woke up at dawn.

→ She going to bed earlier last night,

③ <u>If you cut the wrong wire</u>, the box will explode.

→ Cutting the wrong wire,

④ <u>If it is fine tomorrow</u>, we will go fishing in the sea.

→ Being fine tomorrow,

⑤ <u>When it is seen from a spaceship</u>, the Earth is blue.

→ Seen from a spaceship,

[18~19] 다음 중에서 틀린 문장을 찾아 기호를 쓰고, 바르게 고쳐 문장을 다시 쓰시오.

**18** ① Finding the smartphone she had lost, Emilia cried out with joy.

② Someone having touched the tires of her car, Clara didn't use it that morning.

③ Seeing its master, the dog wagged its tail.

④ Julie having seen him before, she decided to make friends with Charles.

⑤ Speaking in front of many people for a long time, the director felt quite tired.

➡ _____

_____

**19** ① Do both Michael and his employees know how the company survived?

② Can either you or your partner explain to me what's happening in this building?

③ Not only you but also they warned us of the danger of the viruses.

④ Not only can he fly the drones, but he also makes some drones himself.

⑤ Neither the president nor his secretaries wants to know the basic causes of the problem.

➡ _____

_____

**[20~22]** 다음 글을 읽고 물음에 답하시오.

①The hardest time in my life was my first grade in middle school. When my family moved to Gunsan, I had to go to a new school. ②Had no friends at school, I felt sad and lonely. One day, I asked one of my ③classmate to show me her notes. She not only helped me but also ④became a good friend. From this experience, I have learned that _____ⓐ_____ is a good way ⑤to make friends.

**20** 위 글의 밑줄 친 ①~⑤에서 어법상 어색한 것을 두 개 골라 바르게 고치고 그 이유를 밝히시오.

➡ _____

이유: _____

_____

**21** 위 글의 빈칸 ⓐ에 알맞은 것을 고르시오.

① asking for help
② keeping silent
③ inquiring questions
④ moving to a new school
⑤ showing notes

**22** According to the passage, which is NOT true?

① The writer had to go to a new school when her family moved to Gunsan.
② The writer's hardest time in her life was her first grade in middle school.
③ The writer had some friends at the new school.
④ One of the writer's classmates not only helped her but also became a good friend.
⑤ The writer learned a good way to make friends.

**[23~25]** 다음 글을 읽고 물음에 답하시오.

_____ⓐ_____

①When he graduates from high school next year, Taeho wants to become a professional farmer. ②Having no friends, he has never told anyone about it. ③He is worried that his parents or his friends will not understand. ④Wanting to clear his mind, Taeho decided to take a day trip on a train by himself. ⑤On the train, he told a complete stranger sitting beside him about his problem. He had no idea why he did it. However, he felt much better when he got off the train. Strangely enough, we often tell strangers about our problems just like Taeho. That is because we do not have to worry about being judged or seeing them again. If you have a problem that you cannot share with your family or friends, try talking to a stranger. You will feel much better.

**23** 위 글의 빈칸 ⓐ에 알맞은 것을 고르시오.

① How do I become less nervous?
② Who can help me feel better?
③ Why has Taeho never told anyone about his problem?
④ How do I turn a rival into a friend?
⑤ How does psychology answer our questions?

**24** Why did Taeho take a day trip on a train by himself?

➡ _____

_____

**25** 위 글의 ①~⑤ 중에서 흐름상 어색한 것을 고르시오.

①          ②          ③          ④          ⑤

# MEMO

## Lesson

# 6

# Find Your Passion

### 🎤 의사소통 기능

- 불만족 표현하기
  I'm not satisfied with this T-shirt.

- 다짐 말하기
  I promise I won't be late again.

### 🎤 언어 형식

- 관계부사
  He wanted to create a place **where** people
  could try his innovative food.

- 접속부사 however, thus
  Some dishes were even decorated with flowers.
  Customers, **however**, were unhappy.
  He wanted to cook much more quickly and easily.
  **Thus**, he invented new machines for his kitchen.

# Words & Expressions

## Key Words

- **actor** [ǽktər] 명 배우
- **appreciate** [əprí:ʃièit] 동 진가를 알아보다, 고마워하다
- **arts high school** 예술 고등학교
- **blueberry** [blú:bèri] 명 블루베리
- **check** [tʃek] 명 계산서
- **complain** [kəmpléin] 동 불평하다
- **completely** [kəmplí:tli] 부 완전하게
- **creative** [kriéitiv] 형 창의적인, 창조적인
- **crush** [krʌʃ] 동 으깨다
- **customer** [kʌ́stəmər] 명 고객, 소비자
- **decide** [disáid] 동 결정하다
- **decorate** [dékərèit] 동 장식하다, 꾸미다
- **device** [diváis] 명 도구
- **dish** [diʃ] 명 음식, 요리
- **draw** [drɔː] 동 그리다
- **fantastic** [fæntǽstik] 형 환상적인
- **few** [fju:] 형 소수의, 거의 없는
- **finish** [fíniʃ] 동 끝마치다
- **fix** [fiks] 동 수리하다
- **form** [fɔːrm] 명 서류
- **fresh** [freʃ] 형 신선한
- **gladly** [glǽdli] 부 기꺼이
- **grand** [grænd] 형 웅장한, 위대한
- **happen** [hǽpən] 동 일어나다
- **honestly** [ánistli] 부 솔직하게, 솔직히

- **inconvenience** [ìnkənví:njəns] 명 불편, 애로
- **innovative** [ínəvèitiv] 형 획기적인
- **inventor** [invéntər] 명 발명가
- **ma'am** [mæm] 명 (여성을 정중히 부르는 말) 부인
- **meal** [mi:l] 명 식사
- **passion** [pǽʃən] 명 열정, 흥미
- **pay** [pei] 동 지불하다, 지급하다
- **promise** [prámis] 동 약속하다, 다짐하다
- **provide** [prəváid] 동 제공하다
- **pursue** [pərsú:] 동 추구하다, 추진하다
- **rare** [rɛər] 형 덜 익은, 살짝 익힌
- **real** [rí:əl] 형 사실적인
- **reason** [rí:zn] 명 이유
- **role** [roul] 명 역할, 배역
- **satisfied** [sǽtisfàid] 형 만족한
- **sell** [sel] 동 팔다
- **slice** [slais] 명 한 조각, 일부
- **successful** [səksésfəl] 형 성공적인
- **supper** [sʌ́pər] 명 만찬, 저녁 식사
- **surely** [ʃúərli] 부 확실히, 분명히
- **tank** [tæŋk] 명 (물 · 기름 등의) 탱크
- **throughout** [θru:áut] 전 ~ 동안 내내
- **unfortunately** [ənfɔ́:rtʃənətli] 부 불행하게도
- **uniquely** [ju:ní:kli] 부 독특하게
- **yet** [jet] 부 아직

## Key Expressions

- **as a result** 결과적으로
- **be interested in** ~에 관심이 있다
- **be used to** ~에 익숙하다
- **do one's best** 최선을 다하다
- **feel like -ing** ~할 마음이 나다
- **fill out** 작성하다
- **have a bite of** 한 입 베어 물다
- **have a look at** ~을 살펴보다
- **not anymore** 더 이상 아니다
- **now that** ~이기 때문에, ~이므로

- **of all time** 역대, 지금껏
- **put ... in charge of ~** ~에게 …의 책임을 맡기다
- **put up** 내붙이다, 게시하다
- **scare away** 겁주어 쫓아내다
- **take charge of** ~의 책임을 지다, ~을 떠맡다
- **take a class** 수업을 듣다
- **take on** ~을 떠맡다
- **That's the reason why ~.** 그것이 ~하는 이유이다.
- **turn off** ~을 끄다

## Word Power

※ 서로 비슷한 뜻을 가진 어휘

- ☐ **check** 계산서 – **bill** 계산서
- ☐ **complain** 불평하다 – **criticize** 비난하다
- ☐ **completely** 완전히 – **thoroughly** 철저하게
- ☐ **creative** 창의적인 – **original** 독창적인
- ☐ **decide** 결정하다 – **determine** 결정하다
- ☐ **fix** 수리하다 – **repair** 수리하다

- ☐ **happen** 일어나다 – **occur** 일어나다
- ☐ **provide** 제공하다 – **supply** 제공하다
- ☐ **pursue** 추구하다 – **seek** 찾다, 추구하다
- ☐ **reason** 이유 – **cause** 원인
- ☐ **supper** 저녁 식사 – **dinner** 저녁 식사
- ☐ **surely** 확실히 – **certainly** 확실하게

※ 서로 반대되는 뜻을 가진 어휘

- ☐ **completely** 완전하게 ↔ **incompletely** 불완전하게
- ☐ **fantastic** 환상적인 ↔ **realistic** 현실적인, 현실성 있는
- ☐ **convenience** 편리함 ↔ **inconvenience** 불편

- ☐ **rare** 덜 익은 ↔ **well-done** 잘 익은
- ☐ **satisfied** 만족한 ↔ **dissatisfied** 불만족한
- ☐ **sell** 팔다 ↔ **purchase** 구입하다

※ 동사 – 명사

- ☐ **appreciate** 진가를 알아보다 – **appreciation** 진가의 인정
- ☐ **complain** 불평하다 – **complaint** 불평
- ☐ **decide** 결정하다 – **decision** 결정
- ☐ **decorate** 장식하다 – **decoration** 장식

- ☐ **innovate** 혁신하다 – **innovation** 혁신
- ☐ **pay** 지불하다 – **payment** 지불
- ☐ **provide** 제공하다 – **provision** 공급
- ☐ **pursue** 추구하다 – **pursuit** 추구

※ 접두사 un-

- ☐ **clear** 명백한 – **unclear** 불확실한
- ☐ **creative** 창의적인 – **uncreative** 창의적이지 않은
- ☐ **easy** 쉬운 – **uneasy** 불편한
- ☐ **fortunate** 행운의 – **unfortunate** 불행한
- ☐ **happy** 행복한 – **unhappy** 불행한

- ☐ **natural** 자연스러운 – **unnatural** 자연스럽지 않은
- ☐ **real** 사실적인 – **unreal** 사실적이지 않은
- ☐ **successful** 성공적인 – **unsuccessful** 성공적이지 않은
- ☐ **usual** 흔한 – **unusual** 흔치 않은

## English Dictionary

- ☐ **appreciate** 진가를 알아보다
  → to like something because one recognizes its good qualities
  어떤 것의 좋은 점을 인정하여 그것을 좋아하다

- ☐ **complain** 불평하다
  → to say that you are annoyed, not satisfied, or unhappy about something or someone
  어떤 것이나 누군가에 대해 짜증나거나 불만족스럽거나 불쾌하다고 말하다

- ☐ **crush** 으깨다
  → to press something so hard that it breaks or is damaged
  어떤 것을 세게 눌러서 깨지거나 손상되게 하다

- ☐ **customer** 고객, 소비자
  → someone who buys goods or services from a shop, company, etc.
  상점, 회사 등으로부터 상품이나 서비스를 구입하는 사람

- ☐ **decorate** 장식하다, 꾸미다
  → to make something look more nice by putting something pretty on it
  어떤 예쁜 것을 올려놓아 어떤 것을 더 좋아 보이게 만들다

- ☐ **fix** 수리하다
  → to repair something that is broken or not working properly
  망가지거나 제대로 작동하지 않는 것을 수리하다

- ☐ **form** 서류
  → an official document with spaces where you write information
  당신이 정보를 적을 여백을 가진 공식적인 문서

- ☐ **pursue** 추구하다, 추진하다
  → to make efforts to achieve a particular aim or result, often over a long period of time
  종종 오랜 시간에 걸쳐, 어떤 특정 목표나 결과를 달성하기 위해 노력하다

- ☐ **rare** 덜 익은, 살짝 익힌
  → cooked a short time; still red inside
  잠깐 요리된; 속이 아직 붉은

**01** 다음 짝지어진 단어의 관계가 같도록 빈칸에 알맞은 말은?

> check – bill : determine – _____

① complain  ② cause  ③ crush
④ device  ⑤ decide

**서답형**

**02** 주어진 영어 설명에 맞게 문장의 빈칸에 알맞은 말을 쓰시오.

> It is unnecessary to _____ the argument any further.

> <영어 설명> to make efforts to achieve a particular aim or result, often over a long period of time

➡ _____

**03** 다음 주어진 단어를 사용하여 자연스러운 문장을 만들 수 없는 것은?

> provide  slice  promise  fix

① I'll see what I can do but I can't _____ anything.
② They're sending an engineer to _____ the phone.
③ I usually have a _____ of bread every morning.
④ Photographs of actors _____ the walls of the restaurant.
⑤ Teachers _____ a model for children to imitate.

**04** 다음 빈칸에 들어갈 알맞은 말을 고르시오.

> Find your _____ and follow your dreams.

① passion  ② device
③ convenience  ④ expression
⑤ contact

**05** 밑줄 친 부분의 의미로 알맞지 <u>않은</u> 것은?

① They managed to <u>scare</u> the bears <u>away</u>. (겁주어 쫓아내다)
② Could you <u>fill out</u> these forms? (작성하다)
③ I <u>was</u> not <u>used to</u> carrying a tray with one hand. (~에 사용되었다)
④ I don't feel ready to <u>take on</u> new responsibilities. (떠맡다)
⑤ To <u>take the class</u>, you have to be able to use a computer. (수업을 듣다)

**06** 다음 빈칸에 공통으로 들어갈 말로 알맞은 것을 고르시오.

> • You will take charge _____ the company.
> • To my thinking, he's one of the greatest comedians _____ all time.

① in  ② of  ③ with
④ at  ⑤ for

**01** 다음 영영풀이에 알맞은 어휘를 〈보기〉에서 찾아 쓰시오.

┌─ 보기 ├─
form    complain
customer    appreciate

(1) to say that you are annoyed, not satisfied, or unhappy about something or someone

➡ _____

(2) someone who buys goods or services from a shop, company, etc.

➡ _____

(3) to like something because one recognizes its good qualities

➡ _____

(4) an official document with spaces where you write information

➡ _____

**02** 다음 짝지어진 두 단어의 관계가 같도록 빈칸에 알맞은 말을 쓰시오.

(1) decide : decision = complain : _____

(2) completely : incompletely
= natural : _____

**03** 다음 우리말에 맞도록 빈칸에 알맞은 말을 쓰시오.

(1) 그것은 획기적인 디자인 덕분에 곧 인기 있게 되었다.

➡ It soon became popular thanks to its _____ design.

(2) 나는 내 방을 꽃으로 장식하고 싶어.

➡ I want to _____ my room with flowers.

(3) 그는 그의 어린 딸에게 안전장치를 만들어 주었다.

➡ He made a safety _____ for his baby daughter.

(4) 그녀는 이 영화에서 주인공을 연기한다.

➡ She plays the main _____ in this movie.

**04** 우리말에 맞게 한 단어를 추가하여 주어진 어구를 알맞게 배열하시오.

(1) 나는 패션에 대한 열정을 갖고 있다.
(a, I, fashion, have, for)

➡ _____

(2) 그 새 식당은 밝고 다채로운 간판을 세웠다.
(the new restaurant, sign, and, bright, up, a, colorful)

➡ _____
_____

(3) 양해해 주셔서 감사드리며 불편을 끼쳐드린 점 사과드립니다.
(we, you, your, understanding, and, inconvenience, thank, apologize, any, for)

➡ _____
_____

(4) 이제 겨울이니까, 나는 주말마다 스키 타러 갈 거야.
(I'm, weekend, winter, it's, now, go, going, skiing, every, to)

➡ _____
_____

# Conversation

교과서

## ① 불만족 표현하기

> **I'm not satisfied with this T-shirt.** 나는 이 티셔츠가 마음에 들지 않아.

■ 'I'm not satisfied with A.'는 '나는 A가 마음에 들지 않는다.'는 의미로 불만족을 나타내는 표현으로, 'I'm not happy with ~.'라고 표현하기도 한다. 불만족을 나타낼 때는 'not satisfied with ~', 'not happy with ~', 'not pleased with ~'와 함께 'unhappy with ~', 'dissatisfied with ~'를 사용하여 'I'm unhappy with ~', 'I'm dissatisfied with ~' 또는 'I don't like ~'라고 할 수도 있다.

■ 불만족에 대하여 물을 때는 'Are you dissatisfied with ~?' 또는 'Are you unhappy with ~?(~이 마음에 안 드니?)' 등과 같은 표현을 사용한다.

■ 고민이나 불만족의 원인을 물어볼 때는 'Is something worrying you?(무슨 걱정거리가 있나요?)' 또는 'Is there something bothering you?(뭔가 걸리는 일이 있나요?)', 'Is there anything wrong?(뭐 잘못된 일 있니?)', 'What happened?(무슨 일 있니?)'와 같은 표현을 사용하고, 무슨 문제가 있는지 물어볼 때는 'Is something wrong?(뭐가 잘못되었니?)' 또는 'What's wrong (with you)?(뭐가 잘못됐나요?)', 'Why are you disappointed?(왜 실망스러운가요?)'와 같은 표현을 쓸 수도 있다.

### 불만족 표현하기

- I'm not satisfied with ~. 나는 ~가 만족스럽지 않아.
- I don't like ~. 나는 ~가 안 좋아.
- I'm not happy with ~. 나는 ~가 마음에 들지 않아.
- I'm unhappy with ~. 나는 ~가 마음에 들지 않아.
- I'm dissatisfied with ~. 나는 ~가 불만스러워요.

### 핵심 Check

1. 다음 밑줄 친 (A)의 우리말과 일치하도록 주어진 표현을 이용하여 영어로 쓰시오.

   **M:** Hello, ma'am. How can I help you?

   **W:** I bought this phone only a week ago, but it sometimes turns off by itself.

   **M:** Oh, I see. May I have a look at it? (Pause) We're sorry for the inconvenience. It'll take a few hours to fix it.

   **W:** (A)그 휴대전화가 만족스럽지 않아요. (the phone, satisfied) I'd like a new one.

   **M:** Of course. I just need to fill out this form.

   ➡ _____

## ② 다짐 말하기

**I promise I won't be late again.** 다시는 늦지 않겠다고 약속할게요.

- 'I promise to ~.'는 '~하겠다고 약속합니다.'의 뜻으로 확실하게 하겠다는 다짐을 나타내는 말이다. promise를 쓸 때는 to부정사나 'that 주어+동사'의 형태가 따라온다. 상대방에게 확실하게 '~하겠다.'는 의미로 확실성을 나타내는 'make sure(확실하게 하다)'를 사용하여 'I will make sure that 주어+동사 ~' 라고 할 수도 있다.

- 다짐이나 확실한 일을 나타내는 표현에는 sure(확실한), certain(확신하는), positive(긍정적인) 등을 사용하여 'I'm sure (that) ~.'이라고 하거나 'I'm certain (that) ~.' 또는 'I'm positive about ~.(나는 ~에 대해 확신한다.)'라고 할 수 있고, '맹세하다'라는 의미의 'swear'를 사용하여 'I swear I will ~.'이라는 표현을 사용할 수 있다.

- '확실하다'라는 의미로 'I'm 100 percent sure.(나는 100% 장담해.)' 또는 'It is obvious/clear that ~.(~ 가 분명하다.)'를 쓰기도 한다. 'bet'은 '내기를 걸다, 틀림없다'의 뜻으로 'I bet that ~.'이라고 하면 '틀림없이 ~이다.'라는 뜻이 된다. 앞으로 할 일이나 일어날 일에 대하여 상대방에게 확신을 주거나, 원하는 것이나 좋은 일이 일어날 것이 확실함을 나타낼 때는 'I have no doubt that ~.(~할 거라고 믿는다., ~을 믿어 의심치 않는다., ~할 거라고 확신한다.)'이라는 표현을 사용한다.

### 다짐 말하기

- I promise to ~. 나는 ~하겠다고 약속해.
- I promise you that I'll ~. 나는 ~하겠다고 약속드릴게요.
- She will make sure that ~. 그녀는 반드시 ~하도록 할 거다.
- He swears he will ~. 그는 ~하겠다고 약속한다.
- I'm sure that ~. 나는 반드시 ~할 것이다.
- I'm certain that ~. 나는 확실히 ~할 것이다.

### 핵심 Check

**2.** 다음 대화의 밑줄 친 (A)의 우리말에 해당하는 적절한 표현을 쓰시오.

B: Mom, I want to take cooking classes.

W: What? I thought you were interested in sports.

B: I was but not anymore. I want to become a chef.

W: Are you sure? Cooking is hard work.

M: Don't worry. (A)최선을 다하겠다고 약속할게요. (do, promise)

W: O.K., then.

➡ _____

### Listen & Speak 1 A-1

B: Wow! Did you draw this?

G: I did. Do you like it?

B: Yes, the bread and the milk ❶look so real. ❷I feel like having a bite of the bread.

G: Thanks, but ❸I'm not satisfied with it. It's not ❹unique.

B: I don't think ❺so. I think it's a fantastic drawing.

---

B: 우와! 이거 네가 그린 거야?
G: 내가 그렸어. 마음에 들어?
B: 응. 빵이랑 우유가 정말 진짜 같아. 빵을 한 입 먹고 싶어지는데.
G: 고마워. 하지만 이건 만족스럽진 않아. 독창적이지 않아.
B: 난 그렇게 생각 안 해. 정말 멋진 그림인 것 같아.

❶ look+형용사: ~하게 보이다
❷ feel like ~ing: ~하고 싶다
❸ 'be not satisfied with'는 불만족을 표현하는 말이다.
❹ unique: 독창적인
❺ so는 'It's not unique.'를 대신하고 있다.

**Check(√) True or False**

(1) The girl is satisfied with what she drew.  T ☐ F ☐

(2) The boy thinks the bread and the milk look so real.  T ☐ F ☐

### Listen & Speak 1 A-2

M: Hello, ma'am. How can I help you?

W: I bought this phone only a week ago, but it sometimes turns off ❶by itself.

M: Oh, I see. May I ❷have a look at it? (*Pause*) We're sorry for the ❸inconvenience. ❹It'll take a few hours to fix it.

W: ❺I'm not satisfied with the phone. I'd like a new ❻one.

M: Of course. I just need to ❼fill out this form.

---

M: 안녕하세요, 고객님. 무엇을 도와드릴까요?
W: 이 휴대전화를 겨우 일주일 전에 샀는데, 가끔 저절로 꺼져요.
M: 오, 그렇군요. 제가 좀 봐도 될까요? 불편을 드려 죄송합니다. 고치는 데 몇 시간 정도 걸릴 거예요.
W: 이 휴대전화가 만족스럽지 않아요. 새것을 원해요.
M: 물론이죠. 이 서류만 작성하면 됩니다.

❶ by itself: 스스로, 저절로 = naturally, automatically(자동으로)
❷ have a look at: ~을 한 번 보다, it은 this phone을 가리킨다.
❸ inconvenience: 불편
❹ take: (시간이) 걸리다, fix: 고치다, 수리하다
❺ 'be not satisfied with'는 불만족을 표현하는 말이다.
❻ one은 phone을 대신해서 쓰인 부정대명사이다.
❼ fill out a form: 서식을 작성하다

**Check(√) True or False**

(3) The woman bought the phone a few weeks ago.  T ☐ F ☐

(4) The man needs to fill out a form.  T ☐ F ☐

**Listen & Speak 2 A-1**

G: Wow, I like this blueberry jam. Where did you buy it?

B: I made it ❶myself.

G: Really? ❷This is better than any other jam I've ever had. You should sell it.

B: Do you think people would want to buy this?

G: Of course. ❸I promise I'll be your first customer.

❶ 강조 용법으로 쓰인 재귀대명사이다.
❷ '비교급+than any other+단수 명사'로 최상급의 의미이다. jam 뒤에는 관계대명사 that이 생략되어 있는 형태로 관계사절이 선행사인 jam을 수식하고 있다.
❸ 다짐을 말할 때 쓰는 표현이다. promise 뒤에는 구체적인 내용을 명사절로 써서 나타내며, "I promise to be your first customer."로 바꿔 쓸 수 있다.

 **Listen & Speak 2 A-2**

B: Mom, I want to go to an arts high school. I want to become an actor.

W: What? I thought you were interested in science.

B: I was but ❶not anymore. I want to become a movie star.

W: Are you sure you want to be an actor?

B: Yes, I'll learn ❷how to act. ❸I promise I'll do my best.

❶ 'not anymore'는 'I'm not interested in science anymore.'에서 중복되는 것을 생략하고 쓴 표현이다.
❷ 'how to act'는 '의문사+to부정사'로 learn의 목적어 역할을 하고 있다.
❸ 다짐을 말할 때 쓰는 표현으로 'I promise to do my best.'로 바꿔 쓸 수 있다.

 **Communicate A**

Man: Are you enjoying your meal?

Woman: Well, the bread was good, and the salad was fresh.

Man: How about your steak?

Woman: Honestly, ❶I'm not satisfied with the steak. It's too ❷rare for me.

Man: I'm sorry. Would you like me to bring you another one?

Woman: ❸That's O.K. I need to be going. Let me just have the check, please.

Man: I'm really sorry. You won't have to pay for the steak.

Woman: O.K. Thanks.

Man: ❹I promise we'll provide you with a better experience next time you visit.

❶ 'be not satisfied with'는 불만족을 표현하는 말이다.
❷ rare: 설익은, 덜 익은
❸ That은 다른 것으로 가져다 주겠다는 앞 문장의 내용을 받고 있다.
❹ 다짐을 말할 때 쓰는 표현이다.

 **Progress Check 1**

M: Hello, ma'am. How can I help you?

W: I got this hat as a gift yesterday, ❶but I'm not satisfied with the color.

M: Oh, I see. We have this hat in different colors.

W: Do you have ❷one in blue?

M: Yes, we ❸do. I'll get ❷one for you.

W: Thanks.

❶ 'be not satisfied with'는 불만족을 표현하는 말이다.
❷ one은 hat을 대신해서 쓰인 부정대명사이다.
❸ do는 'have the hat in blue'를 대신하는 대동사이다.

 **Progress Check 2**

B: Mom, I want to ❶take cooking classes.

W: What? I thought you were interested in sports.

B: I was but ❷not anymore. I want to become a chef.

W: Are you sure? Cooking is hard work.

B: Don't worry. ❸I promise I'll do my best.

W: O.K., ❹then.

❶ take classes: 수업을 듣다
❷ 'not anymore'는 'I'm not interested in sports anymore.'에서 중복되는 것을 생략하고 쓴 표현이다.
❸ 다짐을 말할 때 쓰는 표현으로 'I promise to do my best.'로 바꿔 쓸 수 있다.
❹ then은 'If you promise you'll do your best'를 대신한다고 볼 수 있다.

 **Progress Check 3**

G: Dad, I want to watch a movie on TV now.

M: ❶Have you finished your homework?

G: No, but ❷I promise I'll finish it after I watch TV.

❶ 현재완료의 완료 용법이다.
❷ 다짐을 말할 때 쓰는 표현으로 'I promise to finish it after I watch TV.'로 바꿔 쓸 수 있다.

● 다음 우리말과 일치하도록 빈칸에 알맞은 말을 쓰시오.

### Listen & Speak 1 A-1

B: Wow! Did you draw this?

G: I _____. Do you like _____?

B: Yes, the bread and the milk _____ _____ _____. I _____ _____ _____ _____ _____ the bread.

G: Thanks, but _____ _____ _____ _____ it. It's not _____.

B: I don't think _____. I think it's a _____ _____.

### Listen & Speak 1 A-2

M: Hello, ma'am. _____ _____ I _____ you?

W: I bought this phone _____ _____ _____ _____, but it _____ _____ _____ _____ _____.

M: Oh, I see. May I _____ _____ _____ _____ it? (*Pause*) We're sorry for the _____. It'll _____ a _____ _____ _____ fix it.

W: _____ _____ _____ _____ the phone. I'd like a new _____.

M: Of course. I just need to _____ _____ this _____.

### Listen & Speak 2 A-1

G: Wow, I like this blueberry jam. Where did you buy it?

B: I made it _____.

G: Really? This is _____ _____ _____ _____ _____ I've ever had. You should sell _____.

B: Do you think people _____ want to buy this?

G: Of course. _____ _____ _____ _____ your first customer.

### Listen & Speak 2 A-2

B: Mom, I want to go to an arts high school. I want to become an actor.

W: What? I thought you _____ _____ _____ science.

B: I was but _____ _____. I _____ become a movie star.

W: _____ you _____ you want to be an actor?

B: Yes, I'll learn _____ _____. _____ _____ my best.

B: 우와! 이거 네가 그린 거야?
G: 내가 그렸어. 마음에 들어?
B: 응, 빵이랑 우유가 정말 진짜 같아. 빵을 한 입 먹고 싶어지는데.
G: 고마워, 하지만 이건 만족스럽진 않아. 독창적이지 않아.
B: 난 그렇게 생각 안 해. 정말 멋진 그림인 것 같아.

M: 안녕하세요, 고객님. 무엇을 도와드릴까요?
W: 이 휴대전화를 겨우 일주일 전에 샀는데, 가끔 저절로 꺼져요.
M: 오, 그렇군요. 제가 좀 봐도 될까요? 불편을 드려 죄송합니다. 고치는 데 몇 시간 정도 걸릴 거예요.
W: 그 휴대전화가 만족스럽지 않아요. 새것을 원해요.
M: 물론이죠. 이 서류만 작성하면 됩니다.

G: 우와, 이 블루베리 잼 마음에 든다. 어디서 샀어?
B: 직접 만든 거야.
G: 정말? 내가 지금껏 먹어본 잼 중에 제일 좋아. 팔아도 되겠어.
B: 사람들이 이걸 사길 원할 거라고 생각해?
G: 물론이지. 내가 너의 첫 손님이 되겠다고 약속할게.

B: 엄마, 저 예술 고등학교에 가고 싶어요. 배우가 되고 싶어요.
W: 뭐라고? 네가 과학에 관심이 있다고 생각했는데.
B: 그랬었는데 더는 아니에요. 저는 영화 배우가 되고 싶어요.
W: 배우가 되고 싶은 게 확실하니?
B: 네, 연기하는 방법을 배울 거예요. 최선을 다하겠다고 약속할게요.

### Communicate A

**Man:** Are you enjoying _____ _____?

**Woman:** Well, the bread was _____, and the salad was _____.

**Man:** How _____ your steak?

**Woman:** Honestly, _____ _____ _____ _____ the steak. It's too _____ for me.

**Man:** I'm sorry. Would you like me _____ _____ you _____ _____?

**Woman:** That's O.K. I need to _____ _____. Let me just _____ the _____, please.

**Man:** I'm really sorry. You _____ _____ _____ pay for the steak.

**Woman:** O.K. Thanks.

**Man:** _____ _____ _____ _____ you _____ a better experience next time you visit.

### Progress Check 1

**M:** Hello, ma'am. _____ _____ _____ help you?

**W:** I _____ this hat _____ a gift yesterday, but _____ _____ _____ _____ the color.

**M:** Oh, I see. We have this hat _____ different colors.

**W:** Do you have _____ _____ _____?

**M:** Yes, we _____. I'll _____ _____ for you.

**W:** Thanks.

### Progress Check 2

**B:** Mom, I want to _____ cooking _____.

**W:** What? I thought you were _____ _____ sports.

**B:** I was but _____ _____. I want to become a chef.

**W:** Are you sure? Cooking is hard work.

**B:** Don't _____. _____ _____ _____ _____ my best.

**W:** O.K., _____.

### Progress Check 3

**G:** Dad, I want to watch a movie _____ TV now.

**M:** _____ you _____ your homework?

**G:** No, but _____ _____ _____ _____ it after I watch TV.

남자: 식사가 마음에 드십니까?
여자: 음, 빵은 괜찮았고, 샐러드도 신선했어요.
남자: 스테이크는 어떠세요?
여자: 솔직히, 스테이크는 만족스럽지 않아요. 제겐 너무 덜 익었어요.
남자: 죄송합니다. 다른 것으로 가져다 드릴까요?
여자: 괜찮아요. 가봐야 해서요. 그냥 계산서 좀 갖다주세요.
남자: 정말 죄송합니다. 스테이크 값은 지불하지 않으셔도 됩니다.
여자: 알겠습니다. 감사해요.
남자: 다음에 방문하실 때는 더 좋은 경험을 드릴 것을 약속드릴게요.

M: 안녕하세요, 고객님. 무엇을 도와드릴까요?
W: 어제 이 모자를 선물 받았는데, 색상이 마음에 들지 않아요.
M: 오, 그렇군요. 이 모자로 다른 색상도 있습니다.
W: 파란 것도 있나요?
M: 네, 있습니다. 하나 가져다 드릴게요.
W: 고맙습니다.

B: 엄마, 저 요리 수업을 듣고 싶어요.
W: 뭐? 네가 스포츠에 관심이 있다고 생각했는데.
B: 그랬는데 더는 아니에요. 저는 요리사가 되고 싶어요.
W: 정말이니? 요리는 힘든 일이란다.
B: 걱정하지 마세요. 최선을 다하겠다고 약속할게요.
W: 그래, 그럼.

G: 아빠, 저 지금 TV에서 영화를 보고 싶어요.
M: 숙제는 끝냈니?
G: 아니요, 하지만 TV를 보고 나서 끝낼 것을 약속드릴게요.

**01** 다음 빈칸 (A)에 알맞은 문장을 고르시오.

> B: Wow! Did you draw this?
>
> G: I did. Do you like it?
>
> B: Yes, the bread and the milk look so real. I feel like having a bite of the bread.
>
> G: Thanks, but _____ (A) _____ . It's not unique.
>
> B: I don't think so. I think it's a fantastic drawing.

① I'm pleased with it

② I'm not satisfied with it

③ I think I can make it more real

④ I think it's rather natural

⑤ I think it looks like real bread and milk

**02** 밑줄 친 우리말을 주어진 어구를 이용해 영작하시오.

> G: Wow, I like this blueberry jam. Where did you buy it?
>
> B: I made it myself.
>
> G: Really? This is better than any other jam I've ever had. You should sell it.
>
> B: Do you think people would want to buy this?
>
> G: Of course. <u>내가 너의 첫 손님이 되겠다고 약속할게.</u> (promise, be first customer, 7 단어)

➡ _____

**03** 다음 대화가 자연스럽게 연결되도록 (A)~(D)를 적절하게 배열하시오.

> M: Hello, ma'am. How can I help you?
>
> (A) I'm not satisfied with the phone. I'd like a new one.
>
> (B) Oh, I see. May I have a look at it? (*Pause*) We're sorry for the inconvenience. It'll take a few hours to fix it.
>
> (C) I bought this phone only a week ago, but it sometimes turns off by itself.
>
> (D) Of course. I just need to fill out this form.

➡ _____

**01** 다음 중 짝지어진 대화가 어색한 것은?

① A: Wow! Did you draw this?
 B: Yes, I did. Do you like it?
② A: I'm not satisfied with the phone. I'd like a new one.
 B: Of course. I just need to fill out this form.
③ A: Are you sure you want to be an actor?
 B: Yes, I'll learn how to act. I promise I'll do my best.
④ A: I was but not anymore. I want to become a chef.
 B: I thought you were interested in sports.
⑤ A: Are you enjoying your meal?
 B: Well, the bread was good, and the salad was fresh.

[02~05] 다음 대화를 읽고 물음에 답하시오.

M: Hello, ma'am. How can I help you?
W: I got this hat as a gift yesterday, but I'm not satisfied with _____(A)_____ .
M: Oh, I see. We have this hat in different colors.
W: (a)파란 것도 있나요? (one, have, in)
M: _____(B)_____ I'll get one for you.
W: Thanks.

**02** 빈칸 (A)에 알맞은 말을 고르시오.

① the color    ② the shape
③ its convenience    ④ its size
⑤ its price

**03** 위 대화의 빈칸 (B)에 들어갈 말로 알맞은 말을 we를 포함한 3 단어로 쓰시오.

➡ _____

서답형

**04** 밑줄 친 (a)의 우리말에 맞게 괄호 안에 주어진 어휘를 이용하여 영작하시오.

➡ _____

**05** 위 대화의 내용과 일치하는 것은?

① The man is a customer.
② The woman bought a hat yesterday.
③ The woman is satisfied with the gift.
④ The woman has a blue hat.
⑤ The man will get a hat for the woman.

[06~07] 다음 대화를 읽고 물음에 답하시오.

B: Mom, I want to go to an arts high school. I want to become an actor.
W: What? I thought you were interested in science.
B: I was but (a)더는 아니에요. I want to become a movie star.
W: Are you sure you want to be an actor?
B: Yes, I'll learn how to act. _____(A)_____

**06** 위 대화의 빈칸 (A)에 들어갈 말로 알맞은 것은?

① Do you want me to do my best?
② I don't want to try my best.
③ Let me wish good luck.
④ I hope I'll do my best.
⑤ I promise I'll do my best.

**07** 밑줄 친 (a)의 우리말에 맞게 두 단어로 영작하시오.

➡ _____

**08** 주어진 글 사이에 대화가 자연스럽게 연결되도록 (A)~(D)를 적절하게 배열하시오.

> M: Hello, ma'am. How can I help you?

> (A) Do you have one in blue?
> (B) Oh, I see. We have this hat in different colors.
> (C) I got this hat as a gift yesterday, but I'm not satisfied with the color.
> (D) Yes, we do. I'll get one for you.

> W: Thanks.

➡ _____

[09~12] 다음 대화를 읽고 물음에 답하시오.

Man: Are you enjoying your meal?
Woman: Well, the bread was good, and the salad was fresh.
Man: How about your steak?
Woman: Honestly, _____(A)_____ . It's too rare for me.
Man: I'm sorry. Would you like me to bring you another ___(B)___ ?
Woman: That's O.K. I need to be going. Let me just have the check, please.
Man: I'm really sorry. You won't have to pay for the steak.
Woman: O.K. Thanks.
Man: I promise we'll provide you with a better experience (a)다음에 방문하실 때는.

**09** 위 대화의 빈칸 (A)에 알맞은 말은?

① I enjoyed a lot
② I think this restaurant is very good
③ I think the service is not so good
④ I'm not satisfied with the steak
⑤ it's very good and delicious

**10** 위 대화의 빈칸 (B)에 알맞은 말을 부정대명사를 이용하여 쓰시오.

➡ _____

**11** 위 대화를 읽고 대답할 수 없는 것은?

① What does the woman think about the salad?
② Does the man always serve the steak rare?
③ Did the woman enjoy the steak?
④ Will the woman pay for the steak?
⑤ Will the man serve the woman better next time she visits?

**12** 위 대화의 밑줄 친 (a)의 우리말을 'time'을 이용하여 영작하시오.

➡ _____

**13** 다음 대화의 밑줄 친 부분의 의도로 알맞은 것은?

> G: Dad, I want to watch a movie on TV now.
> M: Have you finished your homework?
> G: No, but I promise I'll finish it after I watch TV.

① 불만족 표현하기　② 희망 표현하기
③ 설명하기　④ 경험 말하기
⑤ 다짐 말하기

[01~03] 다음 대화를 읽고 물음에 답하시오.

Man: Are you enjoying your meal?

Woman: Well, the bread was good, and the salad was fresh.

(A) That's O.K. I need to be going. Let me just have the check, please.

(B) Honestly, I'm not satisfied with the steak. It's too rare for me.

(C) I'm sorry. Would you like me to bring you another one?

(D) How about your steak?

Man: I'm really sorry. (a)스테이크 값은 지불하지 않으셔도 됩니다. (won't, the steak)

Woman: O.K. Thanks.

Man: I promise we'll provide you with a better experience next time you visit.

**01** 위 대화의 (A)~(D)를 알맞은 순서로 배열하시오.

➡ _____

**02** 괄호 안에 주어진 어휘를 이용하여 밑줄 친 우리말 (a)에 맞게 8 단어로 쓰시오.

➡ _____

**03** Why isn't the woman satisfied with the steak? Use the word 'because'.

➡ _____

_____

_____

[04~05] 다음 대화를 읽고 물음에 답하시오.

M: Hello, ma'am. How can I help you?

W: I bought this phone only a week ago, but it sometimes turns off (a)저절로.

M: Oh, I see. May I have a look at it? (Pause) We're sorry for the inconvenience. It'll take a few hours to fix it.

W: _____ (A) _____ I'd like a new one.

M: Of course. I just need to fill out this form.

**04** 위 대화의 빈칸 (A)에 '전화기가 만족스럽지 않음'을 표현하는 말을 6 단어로 쓰시오.

➡ _____

**05** 밑줄 친 (a)의 우리말을 2 단어로 쓰시오.

➡ _____

**06** 다음 대화에서 어법상 어색한 것을 찾아 바르게 고치시오. (2개)

B: Wow! Did you draw this?

G: I was. Do you like it?

B: Yes, the bread and the milk look so real. I feel like to have a bite of the bread.

G: Thanks, but I'm not satisfied with it. It's not unique.

B: I don't think so. I think it's a fantastic drawing.

(1) _____ ➡ _____

(2) _____ ➡ _____

# Grammar

교과서

**1** 관계부사

> • He wanted to create a place **where** people could try his innovative food.
> 그는 사람들이 그의 획기적인 음식을 먹어볼 수 있는 장소를 만들기를 원했다.
>
> • That's the reason **why** he hasn't finished the painting yet.
> 그것이 그가 아직 그림을 끝내지 못한 이유이다.

■ 관계부사는 접속사와 부사의 역할을 동시에 하는 것으로 선행사를 수식한다.
  • I remember **the day**. We first met **on the day**.
  = I remember the day **when** we first met. 나는 우리가 처음 만난 날을 기억한다.
  • That is **the building**. My uncle works **in the building**.
  = That is the building **where** my uncle works. 저기가 나의 삼촌이 일하는 건물이다.

■ 선행사가 장소, 시간, 이유, 방법 등의 명사일 때 전치사와 관계대명사로 표현 가능하며, 생략 등 각각의 용례도 조금씩 다르다.
  (1) 장소(where): This is **the house**. Da Vinci lived **in the house**.
    → This is the house **which[that]** da Vinci lived **in**.
    → This is the house **in which** da Vinci lived. (in that (×))
    → This is the house **where** da Vinci lived. 이곳이 다빈치가 살았던 집이다.
  (2) 시간(when): This is **the day**. Da Vinci was born **on the day**.
    → This is the day **which[that]** da Vinci was born **on**.
    → This is the day **on which** da Vinci was born. (on that (×))
    → This is the day **when** da Vinci was born. 이 날이 다빈치가 태어난 날이다.
  (3) 이유(why): This is **the reason**. Da Vinci is a genius **for the reason**.
    → This is the reason **which[that]** da Vinci is a genius **for**.
    → This is the reason **for which** da Vinci is a genius. (for that (×))
    → This is the reason **why** da Vinci is a genius. 이것이 다빈치가 천재인 이유이다.
    → This is **why** da Vinci is a genius. (the reason 또는 why 둘 중의 하나 생략 가능)
  (4) 방법(how): This is **the way**. Da Vinci escaped **in the way**.
    → This is the way **which[that]** da Vinci escaped **in**.
    → This is the way **in which** da Vinci escaped. (in that (×))
    → This is **the way how** da Vinci escaped.(×) (the way와 how를 같이 쓸 수 없다.
    → This is **the way** da Vinci escaped. 이것이 다빈치가 탈출한 방법이다.
    → This is **how** da Vinci escaped. (the way 또는 how 둘 중의 하나만 써야 한다.)

## 핵심 Check

**1.** 괄호 안에서 알맞은 말을 고르시오.
  (1) Sumi doesn't tell me the reason (why / which) she cried yesterday.
  (2) This is the year (how / when) the teacher decided to start a business.

## ② 접속부사

> • Some dishes were even decorated with flowers. Customers, **however**, were unhappy. 몇몇 음식들은 심지어 꽃으로 장식되었다. 하지만, 손님들은 불만족스러워했다.
>
> • He wanted to cook much more quickly and easily. **Thus**, he invented new machines for his kitchen. 그는 훨씬 더 빠르고 더 쉽게 요리하고 싶어 했다. 따라서 그는 그의 부엌을 위해 새로운 기계들을 발명하였다.

■ 접속부사는 앞에 제시된 문장의 내용을 부가적으로 연결하는 역할을 하며, 앞 문장과 대조되는 상황일 때는 'however'(그러나)와 같은 역접을, 자연스러운 인과 관계일 때는 'thus'(그러므로)와 같은 순접을 쓴다. 또한, 접속부사는 접속사가 아니라 부사이므로 문장들을 직접 연결할 수는 없다. 문장의 접속사 역할을 하는 세미콜론 뒤 또는 문장 맨 앞이나 뒤에서 쉼표와 함께 쓰이며, 문장 중간에 올 때는 앞뒤에 쉼표가 오게 된다.

• David is active, **however**, his son is quiet and shy. David은 활동적이지만, 그의 아들은 조용하고 부끄럼을 탄다.
• The road was blocked. **Thus**, we had to go back. 길이 막혀서, 우리는 되돌아가야 했다.

■ 같은 의미의 문장을 접속사, 접속부사 등으로 표현할 수 있다.

• **Because** it rained yesterday, the ground is wet. 어제 비가 와서, 땅이 젖었다.
= **Because of** the rain yesterday, the ground is wet. 어제 비 때문에, 땅이 젖었다.
= It rained yesterday. **Thus**, the ground is wet. 어제 비가 왔다. 그래서 땅이 젖었다.
• **Though** he was small, he jumped the hurdle. 비록 그는 작았지만, 장애물을 뛰어넘었다.
= He was small. **However**, he jumped the hurdle. 그는 작았다. 하지만 그는 장애물을 뛰어넘었다.

■ 그 밖의 다양한 접속부사나 연결어들의 종류와 의미

(1) 역접: 대조, 양보 (however, still, on the contrary, nevertheless 등)
(2) 인과, 결과 (thus, therefore, so, hence, consequently, as a result)
(3) 예시 (for example, for instance)
(4) 부가, 추가 (in addition, furthermore, moreover 등)
(5) 유사 (likewise, similarly, in the same way 등)

• She didn't like to eat it. **Nevertheless**, she did it.
그녀는 그것을 먹고 싶지 않았다. 그럼에도 불구하고 결국은 그것을 먹었다.

• **For example**, a virus that causes severe symptoms may be less likely to be transmitted.
예를 들어, 심각한 증상을 초래하는 바이러스는 전염이 덜 될지도 모른다.

### 핵심 Check

2. 다음 빈칸에 however 또는 thus를 사용하여 두 문장을 연결하시오.

(1) Mary wants to buy a new pen. _____, she doesn't have enough money.

(2) The soldiers threatened the citizens. _____, the public was very upset.

**01** 다음 빈칸에 들어갈 말로 알맞은 것은?

> The concert was cancelled due to the virus. _____, the singer and her fans were very disappointed.

① However          ② For example          ③ Thus
④ Similarly          ⑤ Instead

**02** 다음 두 문장을 한 문장으로 연결할 때, 각각의 빈칸에 들어갈 알맞은 말을 써 넣으시오.

(1) Tom bought the house. A famous musician lived in the house.
➡ Tom bought the house _____ _____ a famous musician lived.
➡ Tom bought the house _____ a famous musician lived.

(2) I want to know the reason. Mina was angry for the reason.
➡ I want to know the reason _____ _____ Mina was angry.
➡ I want to know the reason _____ Mina was angry.

**03** 다음 밑줄 친 부분 중 어법상 옳지 않은 것을 고르시오.

① That is the restaurant <u>where</u> I found my credit card.
② Venice is the city <u>where</u> Marco Polo was born in.
③ I'm interested in the house <u>where</u> the singer lived.
④ They don't know the reason <u>why</u> their mother left them.
⑤ Eric developed the way in <u>which</u> he could make much money.

**04** 다음 빈칸에 however 또는 thus 중 알맞은 단어를 써 넣으시오.

(1) Megan wanted to buy me coffee. _____, I don't like caffeine.

(2) It is proved that sleep helps with your memory. _____, it is important to get enough sleep to get good grades.

(3) Fred has been sick since last night. He looks more lively than anybody else, _____.

(4) Sharon is a small and weak child. _____, she has the courage enough to fight against injustice.

(5) The film is based on real events. _____, it gives the audience a more realistic feeling.

**01** 다음 중 어법상 <u>어색한</u> 것은?

① Do you remember the day when we first met?

② This is the library where you can enjoy reading 3D books.

③ Sujin will show Peter the way how she could solve the problem.

④ This is the kindergarten where my mom is working.

⑤ Judy is wondering about the reason why her brother is so happy.

**[02~03]** 다음 중 밑줄 친 부분이 문맥상 <u>어색한</u> 것을 고르시오.

**02** ① Clara bought her son a bag that he wanted. <u>However</u>, he didn't seem to be happy with it.

② Ben learned about the importance of the environment. <u>Thus</u>, he decided to save electricity every day.

③ Watson was very hungry; <u>however</u>, he handed out his food to the poor.

④ William has lived next to the park for 3 years. <u>Thus</u>, he has never been there.

⑤ I have never been to Japan. I know and speak Japanese very well, <u>however</u>.

**03** ① Jane can speak Chinese. <u>In addition</u>, she can speak German.

② The movie was very disappointing. <u>Therefore</u>, the actors' performances were excellent.

③ Monkeys do not plan for the future. <u>On the other hand</u>, we human beings live by planning.

④ Anna often feels tired. <u>So</u>, she's going to take vitamins.

⑤ Liz has been learning to swim for 5 years. <u>Nevertheless</u>, she is really bad at swimming.

**[04~05]** 다음 우리말을 어법상 알맞게 영작한 것을 고르시오.

**04** 그 회의가 끝나게 될 시간을 아십니까?

① Do you know when will the meeting be over?

② When do you know the time the meeting will be over?

③ Do you know the time at when the meeting will be over?

④ Do you know the time which the meeting will be over?

⑤ Do you know the time when the meeting will be over?

**05** 이것이 내가 성공한 이유이다.

① This is why I succeeded.

② This is the reason which I succeeded.

③ This is the reason why I succeeded for.

④ This is which I succeeded for.

⑤ This is the reason on which I succeeded.

**서답형**

**06** 다음 〈보기〉에 주어진 단어들을 한 번씩만 사용해서 글의 흐름에 알맞게 빈칸을 채워 넣으시오.

┌─── 보기 ───┐
Therefore, For example, However,
Moreover, Similarly

① Shakespeare invented many words in his works. _____, he took the noun 'elbow' and turned it into the verb.

(2) It was very cold. _____, the wind blew hard.

(3) A son is likely to follow his father. _____, a daughter tends to go after her mother.

(4) Lily has a passive personality. _____, she actively works and raises her voice for the poor.

(5) The world economy became even worse than before. _____, lots of people lost their jobs.

[07~08] 다음 중 글의 흐름상 However 또는 Thus가 바르게 쓰인 문장은?

**07** ① Judy lost David's phone number. However, she couldn't contact him.

② All the passengers saw the accident. Thus, most of them could stay calm.

③ My boyfriend prepared our dinner. However, my family were happy about it.

④ The sea was stormy. Thus, they set sail.

⑤ The teacher explained the solution of the question. However, Lisa felt that the answer was wrong.

**08** ① Both of us watched the movie. Thus, we couldn't understand the story of it.

② The doctor explained that Sarah would be fine. However, I felt relieved.

③ Jerome studied hard not to lose the opportunity. Thus, he finally got the job.

④ Robert fixed the car himself. However, he knew of the car better than anyone.

⑤ Ann asked him a math problem. Thus, he couldn't solve the hard problem.

[09~10] 다음 중 어법상 옳지 <u>않은</u> 문장은?

**09** ① She told me the reason for which her son became a world famous pianist.

② She told me the reason why her son became a world famous pianist.

③ She told me the reason which her son became a world famous pianist for.

④ She told me why her son became a world famous pianist.

⑤ She told me the reason in which her son became a world famous pianist.

**10** ① Michael showed me the way which he escaped from the prison in.

② Michael showed me the way he escaped from the prison.

③ Michael showed me the way in how he escaped from the prison.

④ Michael showed me how he escaped from the prison.

⑤ Michael showed me the way in which he escaped from the prison.

[11~12] 다음 두 문장을 한 문장으로 표현할 때, 빈칸에 들어갈 알맞은 말을 쓰시오.

**서답형**

**11**

> • Jason often goes to the local market.
> • He can find fresh vegetables there.

➡ Jason often goes to the local market _____ he can find fresh vegetables.

**서답형**

**12**

> • Now is the time.
> • The babies go to sleep at the time.

➡ Now is the time _____ the babies go to sleep.

[13~14] 우리말과 일치하도록 괄호 안에 주어진 어구들을 바르게 배열하시오.

**서답형**

**13**

> 나의 어머니는 2차 세계대전이 발생했던 해에 태어나셨다.
> → My (World War Ⅱ, the year, broke, born, was, when, out, in, mother).

➡ My _____ _____.

**서답형**

**14**

> 많은 사람들이 지하철이 30분이나 도착하지 않은 이유를 알고 싶어 한다.
> Many people want to know (has, for, the subway, why, 30 minutes, arrived, not).

➡ Many people want to know _____ _____.

**15** 다음 〈보기〉의 문장과 가장 가까운 뜻을 가진 문장을 고르시오.

> ┤ 보기 ├
> Dahyun had five pieces of pizza and two burgers. She was still hungry, however.

① Since Dahyun had five pieces of pizza and two burgers, she was still hungry.
② As Dahyun had five pieces of pizza and two burgers, she was still hungry.
③ Though Dahyun had five pieces of pizza and two burgers, she was still hungry.
④ Unless Dahyun had five pieces of pizza and two burgers, she was still hungry.
⑤ Once Dahyun had five pieces of pizza and two burgers, she was still hungry.

**서답형**

**16** 다음 그림을 보고 자연스러운 문장이 되도록 괄호 안에 주어진 어구를 바르게 배열하여 빈칸을 완성하시오.

(1)

➡ Seokbong _____ _____, looking at his poor handwriting. (his mother, couldn't understand, them, about, the way, straight, cut)

(2)

➡ My friends were surprised _____ _____. (rich, how, hear, be, I, could, to)

**01** 다음 괄호 안에서 어법상 알맞은 것을 고르시오.

> Da Vinci believed that people would soon appreciate his creative cooking. (However / Thus), that never happened.

**02** 다음 우리말과 일치하도록 괄호 안에 주어진 단어들을 바르게 배열하여 문장을 완성하되, 빈칸에 해당하는 Thus와 However 중에서 문맥상 알맞은 접속부사를 선택하여 문두에 쓰시오.

(1) 다빈치는 몇몇 음식들을 심지어 꽃으로 장식했다. _____, 손님들은 고기 요리에 익숙했기 때문에 불만족스러워했다. (unhappy, customers, because, used, were, were, to, they)

➡ Da Vinci even decorated some foods with flowers. _____

_____ meat dishes.

(2) 그는 훨씬 더 빠르고 더 쉽게 요리하고 싶어 했다. _____, 그는 그의 부엌을 위해 새로운 기계들을 발명했다. (new machines, kitchen, he, for, his, invented)

➡ He wanted to cook much more quickly and easily. _____

_____.

(3) 당신의 몸이 당신의 마음을 바꿀 수 있다. _____, 당신의 마음도 당신의 행동을 바꿀 수 있다. (can, as, your mind, your behavior, change, well)

➡ Your body can change your mind.

_____.

(4) Mina는 마음을 정리하고 싶었다. _____, 그녀는 혼자 하루 여행을 떠나기로 결심했다. (by herself, to take, she, a day trip, decided)

➡ Mina wanted to clear her mind.

_____.

**03** 다음 (A)와 (B) 두 문장을 한 문장으로 연결할 때, 주어진 〈조건〉에 맞게 영작하시오.

— 조건 —
1. (A)의 위에서부터 순서대로 영작할 것.
2. (A)가 앞에 오는 문장일 것.
3. 가급적 '선행사+관계부사'로 영작할 것.
4. 관계부사는 생략하지 말 것. (that은 사용할 수 없음.)

| (A) | (B) |
|---|---|
| They found a special cave. | She could be world famous in the way. |
| The singer told me the way. | I can see the life coming back in the season. |
| My favorite season is spring. | The Korean national football team beat Brazil at the stadium. |
| Please tell your mom the reason. | My first daughter was born on the day. |
| That is the soccer stadium. | You hid the letter from Grace for the reason. |
| I remember the day. | Their ancestors spent the winter in the cave. |

(1) _____

_____

(2) _____

(3) _____

_____

(4) _____

_____

(5) _____

_____

(6) _____

**04** 다음은 어느 백화점 내부의 모습이다. 그림을 참고하여, 관계부사와 각각의 번호에 주어진 표현들을 모두 사용하여 문장을 완성하시오.

① make a hamburger
② put some money
③ talk over tea and coffee
④ write a marketing report

(1) restaurant, she, make a hamburger
➡ A receipt was handed over to a man at _____ .
(2) charity box, a girl, put some money
➡ There was _____
_____ .
(3) the cafe, we, talk over tea and coffee
➡ This was _____
_____ .
(4) laptop, she, write a marketing report
➡ Brenda brought _____
_____ .

**05** 다음 글의 빈칸 (A)~(D)에 들어갈 알맞은 접속부사를 However 또는 Thus만을 사용하여 써 넣으시오.

Da Vinci believed that people would soon appreciate his creative cooking. (A)_____, that never happened. He created machines that could crush vegetables and pull spaghetti. Surely, they were all very innovative. (B)_____, most of them were too big or too difficult to use. Da Vinci never became a successful cook. (C)_____, he showed great interest in cooking throughout his life. Now you know all about his secret passion for cooking. (D)_____, you will never look at *The Last Supper* the same way.

**06** 다음 밑줄 친 ①~⑥에서 어색한 곳을 모두 찾아 고치시오. (단, 본문에 있는 단어만을 사용하여 수정할 것)

When he graduates from high school next year, Taeho wants to become a professional farmer. ①However, he has never told anyone about it. He is worried that his parents or his friends will not understand. ②As he wanted to clear his mind, Taeho decided to take a day trip on a train by himself. On the train, he told a complete stranger sitting beside him about his problem. He didn't know the reason ③why he did it. ④Thus, he felt much better when he got off the train. Strangely enough, we often tell strangers about our problems just like Taeho. That is ⑤because we do not have to worry about being judged or seeing them again. ⑥However, if you have a problem that you cannot share with your family or friends, try talking to a stranger. You will feel much better.

➡ _____

**07** 다음 그림을 보고 괄호 안의 단어를 배열하여 빈칸을 알맞게 채우시오.

(in, with, she, the pool, when, played, the summer vacation)
➡ Minju could never forget _____
_____ her cousins.

## Da Vinci the Cook

Leonardo da Vinci is <u>known as</u> <u>one of the greatest painters</u> of all
time. He was also a great inventor, scientist, and musician. Very <u>few</u>
people, <u>however</u>, know that da Vinci was also a creative cook.

In 1473, <u>twenty-year-old</u> da Vinci worked <u>as</u> a cook at a restaurant in
Florence, Italy. When he took charge of the kitchen, da Vinci changed
the menu completely. He made simple but artistic dishes <u>like</u> fish with
<u>a few</u> carrot slices. Some dishes were <u>even</u> decorated with flowers.
Customers, however, were unhappy because they <u>were used to</u> dishes
with big servings of meat. <u>As a result</u>, da Vinci lost his job.

A few years <u>later</u>, da Vinci opened a restaurant with his friend
Sandro Botticelli. He wanted to create a place <u>where</u> people could try
his innovative food. They put up a beautifully <u>painted</u> sign and made
a uniquely <u>written</u> menu. Da Vinci believed that people would soon
appreciate his creative cooking. Unfortunately, <u>that</u> <u>never happened</u>.

---

**of all time** 역대, 지금껏

**few** 소수의, 거의 없는

**creative** 창의적인, 창조적인

**take charge of** ~의 책임을 지다, ~을 떠맡다

**dish** 음식, 요리

**slice** 한 조각, 일부

**decorate** 장식하다, 꾸미다

**customer** 손님, 고객

**be used to** ~에 익숙하다

**innovative** 획기적인

**put up** 내붙이다, 게시하다

**uniquely** 독특하게

**appreciate** 진가를 알아보다, 고마워하다

**unfortunately** 불행하게도

---

 확인문제

● 다음 문장이 본문의 내용과 일치하면 T, 일치하지 <u>않으면</u> F를 쓰시오.

1  Leonardo da Vinci is known as one of the greatest painters of all time. ☐

2  Customers liked da Vinci's dishes decorated with flowers. ☐

3  Leonardo da Vinci once ran a restaurant with his friend. ☐

4  People appreciated da Vinci's creative cooking. ☐

In the early 1480s, da Vinci began to work for Ludovico Sforza in Milan. He was given many different roles, such as a musician, a painter, and an engineer. He was also put in charge of the kitchen. He was happy to be given another chance to pursue his passion for cooking. Da Vinci did not stop at cooking creative dishes. He wanted to cook much more quickly and easily. Thus, he invented new machines for his kitchen. He created machines that could crush vegetables and pull spaghetti. He even made a device that could scare frogs away from the water tank. Surely, they were all very innovative, but most of them were too big or too difficult to use.

In 1495, Sforza asked da Vinci to make a grand painting, which was based on the last supper of Jesus, on the wall of a church in Milan. Da Vinci gladly took on the project because he had always been interested in food. He spent a lot of time cooking all kinds of food to decide what to put on the table in his picture. "Da Vinci has wasted his time in the kitchen for over a year. That's the reason why he hasn't finished the painting yet," complained the people from the church to Sforza.

Although da Vinci never became a successful cook, he showed great interest in cooking throughout his life. He was not only a great painter but also a creative cook. Now that you know all about his secret passion for cooking, you will never look at *The Last Supper* the same way.

put ... in charge of
…에게 ~의 책임을 맡기다
pursue 추구하다, 추진하다
passion 열정, 흥미
tank (물·기름 등의) 탱크
surely 확실히, 분명히
grand 웅장한, 위대한
supper 만찬, 저녁 식사
take on 떠맡다
reason 이유
complain 불평하다
throughout ~ 동안 내내
now that ~이기 때문에, ~이므로

---

📎 **확인문제**

● 다음 문장이 본문의 내용과 일치하면 T, 일치하지 <u>않으면</u> F를 쓰시오.

1  Da Vinci was happy to be given another chance to pursue his passion for cooking. ☐

2  Da Vinci stopped at cooking creative dishes. ☐

3  Da Vinci never became a successful cook. ☐

4  Da Vinci was not a great painter but a creative cook. ☐

● 우리말을 참고하여 빈칸에 알맞은 말을 쓰시오.

**1** Da Vinci _____ _____

**2** Leonardo da Vinci _____ _____ _____ one of the greatest _____ _____ _____ _____.

**3** He was _____ a great inventor, scientist, and musician.

**4** Very _____ people, _____, know that da Vinci was also a _____ cook.

**5** In 1473, _____ da Vinci worked _____ a cook at a restaurant in Florence, Italy.

**6** When he _____ _____ _____ the kitchen, da Vinci changed the menu _____.

**7** He made simple _____ artistic dishes _____ fish with _____ _____ carrot slices.

**8** Some dishes _____ _____ _____ _____ flowers.

**9** Customers, _____, were unhappy because they _____ _____ _____ dishes with big _____ of meat.

**10** _____ _____ _____, da Vinci lost his job.

**11** _____ _____ years later, da Vinci opened a restaurant with his friend Sandro Botticelli.

**12** He wanted to create a place _____ people could try his _____ food.

**13** They put up a _____ _____ sign and made a _____ _____ menu.

**14** Da Vinci believed that people _____ soon _____ his _____ cooking.

**15** Unfortunately, that never _____.

**1** 요리사 다빈치

**2** 레오나르도 다빈치는 역대 가장 위대한 화가들 중의 한 명으로 알려져 있다.

**3** 그는 또한 위대한 발명가, 과학자, 그리고 음악가였다.

**4** 하지만, 극히 소수의 사람들만이 또한 그가 창의적인 요리사였다는 것을 안다.

**5** 1473년, 스무 살의 레오나르도 다빈치는 이탈리아 플로렌스에 있는 음식점에서 요리사로 일했다.

**6** 그가 부엌을 책임지게 되었을 때, 다빈치는 메뉴를 완전히 바꿔 버렸다.

**7** 그는 약간의 당근 조각을 곁들인 생선과 같이 간단하지만 예술적인 음식을 만들었다.

**8** 몇몇 음식들은 심지어 꽃으로 장식되었다.

**9** 하지만, 손님들은 많은 양의 고기 요리에 익숙했었기 때문에 불만족스러워했다.

**10** 그 결과, 다빈치는 그의 직업을 잃었다.

**11** 몇 년 후, 다빈치는 그의 친구인 산드로 보티첼리와 함께 음식점을 열었다.

**12** 그는 사람들이 그의 획기적인 음식을 먹어 볼 수 있는 장소로 만들기를 원했다.

**13** 그들은 아름답게 그려진 간판을 내걸었고 독특하게 써진 메뉴를 만들었다.

**14** 다빈치는 사람들이 곧 그의 창의적인 요리의 진가를 알아볼 것이라고 믿었다.

**15** 불행히도, 그런 일은 결코 일어나지 않았다.

**16** In the early 1480s, da Vinci began _____ _____ for Ludovico Sforza in Milan.

**17** He _____ _____ many different roles, _____ _____ a musician, a painter, and an engineer.

**18** He _____ also _____ _____ _____ _____ the kitchen.

**19** He was happy _____ _____ _____ _____ chance _____ _____ his passion for cooking.

**20** Da Vinci did not _____ _____ cooking creative dishes.

**21** He wanted to cook _____ _____ quickly and easily.

**22** _____, he invented new machines for his kitchen.

**23** He created machines _____ could crush vegetables and pull spaghetti.

**24** He even made a device _____ could _____ frogs _____ _____ the water tank.

**25** Surely, they were all very innovative, but most of them _____ _____ big or _____ difficult _____ use.

**26** In 1495, Sforza asked da Vinci _____ _____ a grand painting, _____ _____ _____ _____ the last supper of Jesus, on the wall of a church in Milan.

**27** Da Vinci gladly _____ _____ the project because he _____ always _____ interested in food.

**28** He spent _____ _____ _____ time _____ all kinds of food to decide _____ _____ _____ on the table in his picture.

**29** "Da Vinci has wasted his time in the kitchen _____ _____ a year. That's the reason _____ he hasn't finished the painting yet," complained the people from the church _____ Sforza.

**30** _____ da Vinci never became a successful cook, he showed great interest in cooking _____ his life.

**31** He was _____ _____ a great painter _____ _____ a creative cook.

**32** _____ _____ you know all about his secret passion for cooking, you will never look at *The Last Supper* _____ _____ _____.

16 1480년대 초반에, 다빈치는 밀라노에서 루도비코 스포르차를 위해 일하기 시작했다.

17 그는 음악가, 화가, 그리고 공학자와 같은 많은 역할들을 부여받았다.

18 그는 또한 주방을 책임지게 되었다.

19 그는 요리를 향한 그의 열정을 추구할 또 다른 기회를 얻게 되어 행복했다.

20 다빈치는 창의적인 요리를 만드는 것에 멈추지 않았다.

21 그는 훨씬 더 빠르고 쉽게 요리하고 싶어했다.

22 따라서, 그는 그의 주방에서 사용할 새로운 기계들을 발명하였다.

23 그는 채소를 으깨고 스파게티를 뽑는 기계들을 만들었다.

24 그는 심지어 개구리를 겁주어 물탱크에서 쫓아낼 수 있는 기구도 만들었다.

25 확실히 그것들은 모두 매우 획기적이었지만, 그것들 중 대부분은 사용하기에 너무 크거나 너무 어려웠다.

26 1495년, 스포르차는 다빈치에게 웅장한 그림을 밀라노에 있는 교회의 벽에 그려 달라고 부탁했는데, 그것은 예수의 최후의 만찬을 바탕으로 한 것이었다.

27 다빈치는 기꺼이 그 작업을 맡았는데, 그가 항상 음식에 흥미를 가졌기 때문이었다.

28 그는 그림 속 식탁 위에 어떤 음식을 올릴지 결정하기 위해 모든 종류의 음식을 요리하느라 많은 시간을 썼다.

29 "다빈치는 1년 넘게 부엌에서 시간을 낭비해 오고 있습니다. 그것이 그가 아직도 그림을 끝내지 못한 이유입니다."라고 교회 사람들이 스포르차에게 불평을 했다.

30 다빈치는 결코 성공적인 요리사는 되지 못했지만 그는 그의 생애 내내 요리에 대한 큰 흥미를 보여 주었다.

31 그는 훌륭한 화가일 뿐만 아니라 창의적인 요리사였다.

32 이제 여러분은 요리에 대한 그의 비밀스런 열정을 모두 알게 되었기 때문에 〈최후의 만찬〉을 절대 같은 식으로는 보지 않을 것이다.

● 우리말을 참고하여 본문을 영작하시오.

**1** 요리사 다빈치

➡ _____

**2** 레오나르도 다빈치는 역대 가장 위대한 화가들 중의 한 명으로 알려져 있다.

➡ _____

**3** 그는 또한 위대한 발명가, 과학자, 그리고 음악가였다.

➡ _____

**4** 하지만, 극히 소수의 사람들만이 또한 그가 창의적인 요리사였다는 것을 안다.

➡ _____

**5** 1473년, 스무 살의 레오나르도 다빈치는 이탈리아 플로렌스에 있는 음식점에서 요리사로 일했다.

➡ _____

**6** 그가 부엌을 책임지게 되었을 때, 다빈치는 메뉴를 완전히 바꿔 버렸다.

➡ _____

**7** 그는 약간의 당근 조각을 곁들인 생선과 같이 간단하지만 예술적인 음식을 만들었다.

➡ _____

**8** 몇몇 음식들은 심지어 꽃으로 장식되었다.

➡ _____

**9** 하지만, 손님들은 많은 양의 고기 요리에 익숙했었기 때문에 불만족스러워했다.

➡ _____

**10** 그 결과, 다빈치는 그의 직업을 잃었다.

➡ _____

**11** 몇 년 후, 다빈치는 그의 친구인 산드로 보티첼리와 함께 음식점을 열었다.

➡ _____

**12** 그는 사람들이 그의 획기적인 음식을 먹어 볼 수 있는 장소로 만들기를 원했다.

➡ _____

**13** 그들은 아름답게 그려진 간판을 내걸었고 독특하게 써진 메뉴를 만들었다.

➡ _____

**14** 다빈치는 사람들이 곧 그의 창의적인 요리의 진가를 알아볼 것이라고 믿었다.

➡ _____

**15** 불행히도, 그런 일은 결코 일어나지 않았다.

➡ _____

**16** 1480년대 초반에, 다빈치는 밀라노에서 루도비코 스포르차를 위해 일하기 시작했다.

➡ _____

**17** 그는 음악가, 화가, 그리고 공학자와 같은 많은 역할들을 부여받았다.

➡ _____

**18** 그는 또한 주방을 책임지게 되었다.

➤ _____

**19** 그는 요리를 향한 그의 열정을 추구할 또 다른 기회를 얻게 되어 행복했다.

➤ _____

**20** 다빈치는 창의적인 요리를 만드는 것에 멈추지 않았다.

➤ _____

**21** 그는 훨씬 더 빠르고 쉽게 요리하고 싶어했다.

➤ _____

**22** 따라서, 그는 그의 주방에서 사용할 새로운 기계들을 발명하였다.

➤ _____

**23** 그는 채소를 으깨고 스파게티를 뽑는 기계들을 만들었다.

➤ _____

**24** 그는 심지어 개구리를 겁주어 물탱크에서 쫓아낼 수 있는 기구도 만들었다.

➤ _____

**25** 확실히 그것들은 모두 매우 획기적이었지만, 그것들 중 대부분은 사용하기에 너무 크거나 너무 어려웠다.

➤ _____

**26** 1495년, 스포르차는 다빈치에게 웅장한 그림을 밀라노에 있는 교회의 벽에 그려 달라고 부탁했는데, 그것은 예수의 최후의 만찬을 바탕으로 한 것이었다.

➤ _____

_____

**27** 다빈치는 기꺼이 그 작업을 맡았는데, 그가 항상 음식에 흥미를 가졌기 때문이었다.

➤ _____

**28** 그는 그림 속 식탁 위에 어떤 음식을 올릴지 결정하기 위해 모든 종류의 음식을 요리하느라 많은 시간을 썼다.

➤ _____

**29** "다빈치는 1년 넘게 부엌에서 시간을 낭비해 오고 있습니다. 그것이 그가 아직도 그림을 끝내지 못한 이유입니다."라고 교회 사람들이 스포르차에게 불평을 했다.

➤ _____

**30** 다빈치는 결코 성공적인 요리사는 되지 못했지만 그는 그의 생애 내내 요리에 대한 큰 흥미를 보여 주었다.

➤ _____

**31** 그는 훌륭한 화가일 뿐만 아니라 창의적인 요리사였다.

➤ _____

**32** 이제 여러분은 요리에 대한 그의 비밀스런 열정을 모두 알게 되었기 때문에 〈최후의 만찬〉을 절대 같은 식으로는 보지 않을 것이다.

➤ _____

_____

[01~03] 다음 글을 읽고 물음에 답하시오.

Leonardo da Vinci is known as one of the greatest painters of all time. He was also a great inventor, scientist, and musician. Very few people, however, know that da Vinci was also _____(A)_____.

In 1473, twenty-year-old da Vinci worked as a cook at a restaurant in Florence, Italy. When he took charge of the kitchen, da Vinci changed the menu completely. He made simple but artistic dishes like fish with a few carrot slices. Some dishes were even decorated with flowers. Customers, however, were unhappy because they were used to dishes with big servings of meat. As a result, da Vinci lost his job.

A few years later, da Vinci opened a restaurant with his friend Sandro Botticelli. He wanted to create a place where people could try his innovative food. They put up a beautifully painted sign and made a uniquely written menu. Da Vinci believed that people would soon _____(B)_____ his creative cooking. Unfortunately, that never happened.

**01** 위 글의 빈칸 (A)에 들어갈 알맞은 말을 고르시오.

① a good barista
② a creative cook
③ a great psychologist
④ an innovative physician
⑤ a natural philosopher

서답형
**02** 주어진 영영풀이를 참고하여 빈칸 (B)에 들어갈 단어를 철자 a로 시작하여 쓰시오.

to like something because you recognize its good qualities

➡ _____

**03** According to the passage, which is NOT true?

① Da Vinci is known as one of the greatest painters.
② Da Vinci was also a great inventor and musician.
③ Da Vinci made simple but artistic dishes like fish with a few carrot slices.
④ Da Vinci lost his job because customers liked dishes decorated with flowers.
⑤ Da Vinci opened a restaurant with Sandro Botticelli.

[04~06] 다음 글을 읽고 물음에 답하시오.

In the early 1480s, da Vinci began to work for Ludovico Sforza in Milan. He was given many different roles, such as a musician, a painter, and an engineer. He was also put in charge of the kitchen. He was happy to be given another chance to pursue his passion ___ⓐ___ cooking. Da Vinci did not stop at cooking creative dishes. He wanted to cook much more quickly and easily. ___ⓑ___, he invented new machines for his kitchen. He created machines that could crush vegetables and pull spaghetti. He even made a device that could scare frogs away ___ⓒ___ the water tank. Surely, they were all very innovative, but most of them were too big or too difficult ___ⓓ___.

**04** 위 글의 빈칸 ⓐ와 ⓒ에 들어갈 전치사가 바르게 짝지어진 것은?

① on – for
② on – to
③ for – from
④ for – for
⑤ in – from

**05** 위 글의 빈칸 ⓑ에 들어갈 알맞은 말을 고르시오.

① Thus       ② As a result

③ Surely       ④ However

⑤ Unfortunately

**서답형**

**06** 위 글의 빈칸 ⓓ에 use를 알맞은 형태로 쓰시오.

➡ _____

[07~09] 다음 글을 읽고 물음에 답하시오.

In 1495, Sforza asked da Vinci to make a ① <u>grand</u> painting, which was based on the last supper of Jesus, on the wall of a church in Milan.

(A) "Da Vinci has ②<u>wasted</u> his time in the kitchen for over a year. That's the reason why he hasn't finished the painting yet," ③<u>commended</u> the people from the church to Sforza.

(B) He spent a lot of time cooking all kinds of food to decide what to put on the table in his picture.

(C) Da Vinci ④<u>gladly</u> took on the project because he had always been interested in food.

Although da Vinci never became a ⑤ <u>successful</u> cook, he showed great interest in cooking throughout his life. He was not only a great painter but also a creative cook. ___ⓐ___ you know all about his secret passion for cooking, you will never look at *The Last Supper* the same way.

**07** 위 글의 (A)~(C)의 순서로 가장 적절한 것은?

① (A)-(C)-(B)      ② (B)-(A)-(C)

③ (B)-(C)-(A)      ④ (C)-(A)-(B)

⑤ (C)-(B)-(A)

**서답형**

**08** 위 글의 빈칸 ⓐ에 'As' 대신 쓸 수 있는 말을 두 단어로 쓰시오.

➡ _____

**중요**

**09** 위 글의 밑줄 친 ①~⑤에서 문맥상 어색한 것을 고르시오.

①     ②     ③     ④     ⑤

[10~12] 다음 글을 읽고 물음에 답하시오.

Leonardo da Vinci is known as one of the greatest (A)[painter / painters] of all time. He was also a great inventor, scientist, and musician. Very few people, however, know that da Vinci was also a creative cook.

In 1473, twenty-year-old da Vinci worked as a cook at a restaurant in Florence, Italy. When he took charge of the kitchen, da Vinci changed the menu completely. He made simple but artistic dishes like fish with (B)[a few / a little] carrot slices. Some dishes were even decorated with flowers. Customers, however, were unhappy because they were used to dishes with big servings of meat. As a result, da Vinci (C)[got / lost] his job.

A few years later, da Vinci opened a restaurant with his friend Sandro Botticelli. He wanted to create a place where people could try his innovative food. They put up a beautifully painted ⓐ<u>sign</u> and made a uniquely written menu. Da Vinci believed that people would soon appreciate his creative cooking. Unfortunately, that never happened.

**10** 위 글의 괄호 (A)~(C)에서 문맥이나 어법상 알맞은 낱말을 골라 쓰시오.

➡ (A) _____ (B) _____ (C) _____

**11** Which question CANNOT be answered after reading the passage?

① Do many people know that da Vinci was a creative cook?

② What was da Vinci's job in 1473?

③ What did da Vinci do when he took charge of the kitchen?

④ How long did da Vinci work as a cook?

⑤ Why did da Vinci lose his job?

**12** 위 글의 밑줄 친 ⓐsign과 같은 의미로 쓰인 것을 고르시오.

① Headaches may be a sign of stress.

② Many building signs are written in English.

③ He gave a thumbs-up sign.

④ He signed to me to enter the garden.

⑤ There is no sign of habitation.

[13~15] 다음 글을 읽고 물음에 답하시오.

In the early 1480s, da Vinci began to work for Ludovico Sforza in Milan. He was given many different roles, such as a musician, a painter, and an engineer. He was also put in charge of the kitchen. He was happy to be given another chance to pursue his passion for cooking. ⓐDa Vinci did not stop at cooking creative dishes. ⓑHe wanted to cook much more quickly and easily.(only, also) Thus, he invented new machines for his kitchen. He created machines that could crush vegetables and pull spaghetti. He even made a device ⓒ개구리를 겁주어 물탱크에서 쫓아낼 수 있는.(frogs, that, away, could, the water tank, scare, from) Surely, they were all very ___(A)___, but most of them were too big or too difficult to use.

**13** 위 글의 빈칸 (A)에 들어갈 말로 적절한 것은?

① common      ② routine      ③ plain

④ traditional      ⑤ innovative

**14** 위 글의 밑줄 친 문장 ⓐ와 ⓑ를 괄호 안에 주어진 어휘를 이용하여 한 문장으로 쓰시오.

➡ _____

_____

**15** 위 글의 밑줄 친 ⓒ의 우리말에 맞게 괄호 안에 주어진 어휘를 배열하시오.

➡ _____

[16~19] 다음 글을 읽고 물음에 답하시오.

In 1495, Sforza asked da Vinci to make a grand painting, which was based on the last supper of Jesus, on the wall of a church in Milan. Da Vinci gladly took on the project because he had always been interested in food. ⓐ그는 그림 속 식탁 위에 어떤 음식을 올릴지 결정하기 위해 모든 종류의 음식을 요리하느라 많은 시간을 썼다. "Da Vinci has ___(A)___ his time in the kitchen for over a year. That's the reason why he hasn't finished the painting yet," complained the people from the church to Sforza.

___(B)___ da Vinci never became a successful cook, he showed great interest in cooking throughout his life. He was not only a great painter but also a creative cook. Now that you know all about his secret passion for cooking, you will never look at *The Last Supper* the same way.

**16** 위 글의 빈칸 (A)에 들어갈 말로 알맞은 것은?

① saved    ② wasted    ③ kept
④ prevented    ⑤ recovered

**17** 빈칸 (B)에 들어갈 알맞은 말을 고르시오.

① When    ② Since    ③ If
④ Although    ⑤ Unless

서답형

**18** 위 글의 밑줄 친 ⓐ의 우리말에 맞게 주어진 어휘를 배열하시오.

> he, all kinds, on the table, what, time, spent, in his picture, a lot of, cooking, food, decide, put, of, to, to

➡ _____

_____

**19** Which question CANNOT be answered after reading the passage?

① What did da Vinci ask Sforza to do to make a grand painting?
② What was the grand painting based on?
③ Why did da Vinci gladly take on the project?
④ Why did da Vinci spend a lot of time cooking all kinds of food?
⑤ Why will we never look at *The Last Supper* the same way?

[20~22] 다음 글을 읽고 물음에 답하시오.

In the early 1480s, da Vinci began to work for Ludovico Sforza in Milan. He was given many different roles, such as a musician, a painter, and an engineer.

(A) Surely, they were all very innovative, but most of them were too big or too difficult to use.

(B) He was also put in charge of the kitchen. He was happy to be given another chance to ___ⓐ___ his passion for cooking. Da Vinci did not stop at cooking creative dishes. He wanted to cook much more quickly and easily.

(C) Thus, he invented new machines for his kitchen. He created machines that could crush vegetables and pull spaghetti. He even made a device that could scare frogs away from the water tank.

서답형

**20** 주어진 영영풀이에 해당하는 말을 빈칸 ⓐ에 철자 p로 시작하여 쓰시오.

> to make efforts to achieve a particular aim or result, often over a long period of time

➡ _____

**21** 위 글의 (A)~(C)의 순서로 가장 적절한 것은?

① (A)-(C)-(B)    ② (B)-(A)-(C)
③ (B)-(C)-(A)    ④ (C)-(A)-(B)
⑤ (C)-(B)-(A)

**22** 위 글에서 다빈치가 루도비코 스포르차를 위해 한 일에 해당하지 않는 것을 고르시오.

① 과학자    ② 주방장    ③ 화가
④ 기술자    ⑤ 음악가

[01~03] 다음 글을 읽고 물음에 답하시오.

Leonardo da Vinci is known as one of the greatest painters of all time. He was also a great inventor, scientist, and musician. Very few people, however, know that da Vinci was also a creative cook.

In 1473, twenty-year-old da Vinci worked as a cook at a restaurant in Florence, Italy. When he took charge of the kitchen, da Vinci changed the menu completely. He made simple but artistic dishes like fish with a few carrot slices. Some dishes were even decorated with flowers. Customers, however, were unhappy because they were used to dishes with big servings of meat. As a result, da Vinci lost his job.

A few years later, da Vinci opened a restaurant with his friend Sandro Botticelli. ⓐ그는 사람들이 그의 획기적인 음식을 먹어 볼 수 있는 장소로 만들기를 원했다. They put up a beautifully painted sign and made a uniquely written menu. Da Vinci believed that people would soon appreciate his creative cooking. Unfortunately, ⓑthat never happened.

**01** Why did da Vinci lose his job? Answer in English using the words, 'It's because, creative and satisfied.'

➡ _____

_____

**02** 밑줄 친 ⓐ의 우리말에 맞게 'a place, try, innovative'를 이용하여 13 단어로 영작하시오.

➡ _____

_____

**03** 위 글의 밑줄 친 ⓑthat이 가리키는 것을 본문에서 찾아 쓰시오.

➡ _____

[04~06] 다음 글을 읽고 물음에 답하시오.

In the early 1480s, da Vinci began to work for Ludovico Sforza in Milan. He was given many different roles, such as a musician, a painter, and an engineer. He was also put in charge of the kitchen. ⓐHe was happy to be given the other chance to pursue his passion for cooking. Da Vinci did not stop at cooking creative dishes. He wanted to cook much more quickly and easily. Thus, he invented new machines for his kitchen. He created machines that could crush vegetables and pull spaghetti. He even made a device that could scare frogs away from the water tank. Surely, ⓑthey were all very innovative, but most of them were too big or too difficult to use.

**04** What did da Vinci do to cook much more quickly and easily?

➡ _____

**05** 밑줄 친 ⓐ에서 어색한 것을 찾아 바르게 고치시오.

_____ ➡ _____

**06** 위 글의 밑줄 친 ⓑthey가 가리키는 것을 본문에서 찾아 쓰시오.

➡ _____

[07~09] 다음 글을 읽고 물음에 답하시오.

In 1495, Sforza asked da Vinci to make a grand painting, ⓐwhich was based on the last supper of Jesus, on the wall of a church in Milan. Da Vinci gladly took on the project because he had always been interested in food. He spent a lot of time cooking all kinds of food to decide what to put on the table in his picture. "Da Vinci has wasted his time in the kitchen for over a year. That's the reason why he hasn't finished the painting yet," complained the people from the church to Sforza.

Although da Vinci never became a successful cook, he showed great interest in cooking throughout his life. ⓑHe was not only a great painter but also a creative cook. Now that you know all about his secret passion for cooking, you will never look at *The Last Supper* the same way.

**07** 위 글의 밑줄 친 ⓐ를 접속사를 사용하여 바꿔 쓰시오.

➡ _____

**08** 위 글의 밑줄 친 ⓑ를 'as well as'를 이용하여 바꿔 쓰시오.

➡ _____

**09** Why did da Vinci spend a lot of time cooking all kinds of food? Fill in the blank with suitable words.

➡ It was to _____
_____ .

[10~12] 다음 글을 읽고 물음에 답하시오.

In 1473, twenty-year-old da Vinci worked as a cook at a restaurant in Florence, Italy. When he took charge of the kitchen, da Vinci changed the menu (A)[complete / completely]. He made simple but artistic dishes like fish with a few carrot slices. Some dishes were even decorated with flowers. Customers, ____ⓐ____, were (B)[happy / unhappy] because they were used to dishes with big servings of meat. As a result, da Vinci lost his job.

A few years later, da Vinci opened a restaurant with his friend Sandro Botticelli. He wanted to create a place where people could try his innovative food. ⓑThey put up a beautifully painted sign and made a uniquely written menu. Da Vinci believed that people would soon (C)[appreciate / depreciate] his creative cooking. Unfortunately, that never happened.

**10** 위 글의 빈칸 ⓐ에 알맞은 말을 쓰시오.

➡ _____

**11** 위 글의 괄호 (A)~(C)에서 문맥이나 어법상 알맞은 낱말을 고르시오.

➡ (A) _____ (B) _____ (C) _____

**12** 위 글의 밑줄 친 ⓑThey가 가리키는 것을 본문에서 찾아 쓰시오.

➡ _____

해석

## Write

My name is Kim Jieun. I am an artist who uses technology. There was a
　　　　　　　　　　　　　　주격 관계대명사　　　　　　　　　　　　선행사(시간)
special moment when I decided what I wanted to be. Back in 2030, I made
　　　　　　관계부사　　　　관계대명사
a small statue using technology. It was a great chance to learn about using
　　　　　　분사구문　　　　　　　　　　　　　　　형용사적 용법　전치사+동명사
technology for arts. Thus, I decided to go to a technical high school. After I
graduated from high school, I entered Korea Art College and learned more
자동사+전치사　　　　　　　타동사(전치사 불필요)
about arts and technology. This year, I held my first exhibition. I am very
satisfied with my life.
감정을 나타내는 과거분사

구문해설　• statue: 동상　• hold: 개최하다　• exhibition: 전시회　• satisfied with: ～에 만족하는

내 이름은 김지은이다. 나는 기술을 사용하는 예술가다. 내가 예술가가 되기로 결심했을 때 특별한 순간이 있었다. 2030년에, 나는 기술을 사용해 작은 동상을 만들었다. 그것은 예술을 위한 기술을 배우는 데에 아주 좋은 기회였다. 따라서, 나는 기술 고등학교에 진학하기로 결심했다. 고등학교를 졸업한 뒤, 나는 한국 예술 대학에 입학해서 예술과 기술에 대해 더 배웠다. 올해, 나는 내 첫 전시회를 열었다. 나는 내 인생에 매우 만족한다.

## Link

Some people think creativity is the most important thing to consider when
　　　　　　　　　　　　　　　　最상급　　　　　　　　형용사적 용법
they choose their career. They like to come up with new ideas and design new
　　　　　　　　　　　　　　　　명사적 용법(like의 목적어)　　　　　　　　to come과 병렬 관계
things. Thus, they want to work at a place where they can use their creativity.
　　　　　결과를 이끄는 접속부사　　　　　　　　　　　　관계부사(= in which)

구문해설　• creativity: 창의력　• come up with: ～을 생각해 내다

어떤 사람들은 직업을 선택할 때 고려해야 할 가장 중요한 것은 창의력이라고 생각한다. 그들은 새로운 아이디어를 떠올리고 새로운 것들을 구상하기를 좋아한다. 따라서, 그들은 그들의 창의력을 발휘할 수 있는 곳에서 일하기를 원한다.

## Watch and Think Share

Winston Churchill is known for being the Prime Minister of the United
　　　　　　　　　　～로 알려지다
Kingdom during World War II. Very few people, however, know that he
during: 특정 기간 (for 다음에는 보통 숫자로 나타내는 기간이 나옴)　　　　　　　　역접의 접속부사
was also a historian, a painter, and a writer. He even won the Nobel Prize in
　　　　　　　　　　　　　　　　　　　　　　　　　　심지어
Literature in 1953.

구문해설　• Prime Minister: 수상　• historian: 사학자　• the Nobel Prize in Literature: 노벨 문학상

Winston Churchill은 제2차 세계대전 중 영국의 수상이었던 것으로 알려져 있다. 하지만, 극소수의 사람들은 그가 또한 사학자이며, 화가이자, 작가임을 알고 있다. 심지어 그는 1953년에 노벨 문학상을 수상하기도 했다.

## 영역별 핵심문제

**01** 〈보기〉의 밑줄 친 어휘와 같은 의미로 쓰인 것을 고르시오.

> ┤ 보기 ├
> Let me have the check, please.

① Can I have the check, please?
② They carried out security checks at the airport.
③ Would you please check if I filled out this card right?
④ I need to cash this check.
⑤ Cars are checked as they come off the production line.

**02** 다음 대화의 빈칸에 〈영영풀이〉에 해당하는 어휘를 쓰시오.

> A: What are you going to do tomorrow?
> B: I'm going to _____ the Christmas tree.

> <영영 풀이> to make something look more attractive by putting something pretty on it

➡ _____

**03** 괄호 안에 주어진 어휘를 이용하여 빈칸에 알맞게 쓰시오.

> • It is _____ for a large asteroid to come so close to Earth. (usual)
> • _____, I won't be able to attend the meeting. (fortunate)
>
> *asteroid: 소행성

**04** 다음 영영풀이에 해당하는 단어를 주어진 철자로 시작하여 빈칸에 쓰고, 알맞은 것을 골라 문장을 완성하시오.

> • r_____ : why someone decides to do something, or the cause or explanation for something that happens
> • r_____ : cooked a short time; still red inside

(1) Do you have a _____ for being so late?
(2) My father likes _____ meat that is still a little pink inside.

**05** 다음 짝지어진 단어의 관계가 같도록 빈칸에 알맞은 말을 쓰시오. (철자 p로 시작할 것)

> rare : well-done = sell : _____

**06** 다음 문장의 빈칸에 공통으로 들어갈 알맞은 말을 쓰시오.

> • They _____ him in charge of the park.
> • He _____ up a sign saying, "No pets."
> • Fire engines arrived to _____ out a fire.
> • I have a sweater you can _____ on.

**07** 다음 중 짝지어진 대화가 <u>어색한</u> 것은?

① A: I'm not satisfied with this bag.
   B: Why not?
   A: I don't like the color.
② A: These plants are dying.
   B: I'm sorry. I promise I'll water them more often.
③ A: I want to become a movie star.
   B: I promise I'll do my best.
④ A: Have you finished your homework?
   B: No, but I promise I'll finish it after I watch TV.
⑤ A: Do you have this in a smaller size?
   B: No, I'm sorry, but the smaller ones are all sold out. I promise I'll have one for you by next week.

[08~10] 다음 대화를 읽고 물음에 답하시오.

G: Wow, I like this blueberry jam. Where did you buy it?
(A) Do you think people would want to buy this?
(B) Really? This is better than any other jam I've ever had. You should sell it.
(C) I made it myself.
(D) Of course. _____ (a)

**08** 위 대화의 빈칸 (a)에 첫 손님이 되겠다는 다짐을 말하는 표현을 7 단어로 쓰시오.

➡ _____

**09** 주어진 글 다음의 대화가 자연스럽게 연결되도록 (A)~(D)를 순서대로 가장 적절하게 배열한 것은?

① (B) – (A) – (C) – (D)
② (B) – (C) – (A) – (D)
③ (C) – (B) – (A) – (D)
④ (C) – (B) – (D) – (A)
⑤ (C) – (D) – (B) – (A)

**10** 위 대화의 내용과 일치하지 <u>않는</u> 것은?

① 소녀는 블루베리 잼이 마음에 든다.
② 블루베리 잼은 사 온 것이다.
③ 블루베리 잼은 소녀가 먹어본 잼 중에 제일 좋았다.
④ 소녀는 사람들이 블루베리 잼을 사기를 원할 거라고 생각한다.
⑤ 소녀는 첫 손님이 되겠다고 약속한다.

**11** 다음 주어진 문장을 둘로 나눌 때, 원래 문장과 의미가 가장 가까운 것은?

> Although Tracy lived alone in that big apartment, she rarely felt lonely.
> → Tracy lived alone in that big apartment.
> _____, _____.

① Fortunately, she felt lonely.
② Consequently, she rarely felt lonely.
③ Instead, she felt lonely.
④ Nevertheless, she rarely felt lonely.
⑤ Therefore, she rarely felt lonely.

**[12~13]** 다음 중 어법상 <u>어색한</u> 문장을 고르시오.

**12** ① This is the hotel where the singer stayed last week.

② This is the hotel that the singer stayed in last week.

③ This is the hotel which the singer stayed last week.

④ This is the hotel in which the singer stayed last week.

⑤ This is the hotel which the singer stayed in last week.

**13** ① Would you tell us the reason why Sandra hasn't come yet?

② The house where the photographer lived had a beautiful studio.

③ Timothy can't forget the day when Anne left Paris for New York.

④ An auditorium is a large space or building in which is used for events such as meetings or concerts.

⑤ Now is the time when they should start to produce the cure for the disease.

**14** 다음 괄호 안에서 어법상 알맞은 것을 고르시오.

(1) Da Vinci did not feel well. (However / Thus), he still kept painting.

(2) Dr. Kim required that everyone present at the lecture wear a mask. (However / Thus), most of them didn't take it seriously.

(3) Everything she said turned out to be untrue. (However / Thus), many people were disappointed with her.

(4) My grandmother has rarely brushed her teeth after meals. (However / Thus), despite her age of 90, she has healthy teeth.

(5) James was in deep sleep after working all night. (However / Thus), he didn't answer the phone.

(6) Da Vinci had always been interested in food. (However / Thus), when he was asked to make a painting of the last supper of Jesus, he gladly took on the project.

**15** 다음 그림을 보고 괄호 안의 단어를 배열하여 빈칸을 알맞게 채우시오.

(1)

➡ People were not interested in ＿＿＿＿＿＿

＿＿＿＿＿＿＿＿＿＿＿＿＿＿＿. (da Vinci, his, cooking, made, creative, how)

(2)

➡ At school, I like lunchtime best ＿＿＿＿＿

＿＿＿＿＿＿＿＿＿＿＿＿＿＿＿＿＿.

(have, with, can, when, a, my friends, meal, I, delicious)

**[16~17]** 다음 밑줄 친 부분 중 어법상 어색한 것을 고르시오.

**16** ① Let her know <u>how</u> the machines work in such a hot and humid environment.

② That evening was the moment <u>when</u> I fell in love with the princess.

③ I will show you the way <u>how</u> the magician escaped from the steel box.

④ Tom can't forget the day <u>when</u> he first ate cold bean soup noodles.

⑤ Does Sarah know the reason <u>why</u> her husband came here?

**17** ① Venice is the city <u>where</u> Marco used to live in.

② That is the square <u>where</u> I picked up her credit cards.

③ This is the building <u>in which</u> my parents met for the first time.

④ I remember the shop <u>which</u> I bought some souvenirs at.

⑤ The town <u>where</u> she's going to move is not far from here.

**18** 다음 밑줄 친 부분의 쓰임이 〈보기〉와 같은 것은?

> Friday is the day <u>when</u> my daughter goes to the pool to learn swimming.

① Mina was taking a shower <u>when</u> someone visited her.

② I wonder <u>when</u> you will leave here for Africa to volunteer.

③ No one knows <u>when</u> the virus disease could be treated properly.

④ I like the Christmas season <u>when</u> I can meet all my family.

⑤ <u>When</u> does she think she can call me?

**19** 다음 접속부사가 쓰인 두 문장을 한 문장으로 적절하게 바꾼 것을 고르시오.

> His explanation was unclear. Thus, I didn't understand it.

① Although his explanation was unclear, I didn't understand it.

② Whereas his explanation was unclear, I didn't understand it.

③ As soon as his explanation was unclear, I didn't understand it.

④ Since his explanation was unclear, I didn't understand it.

⑤ Unless his explanation was unclear, I didn't understand it.

Reading

**[20~22]** 다음 글을 읽고 물음에 답하시오.

Leonardo da Vinci is known as one of the greatest painters of all time. He was also a great inventor, scientist, and musician. Very _____ⓐ_____ people, however, know that da Vinci was also a creative cook.

In 1473, twenty-year-old da Vinci worked as a cook at a restaurant in Florence, Italy. When he took charge of the kitchen, da Vinci changed the menu completely. (①) He made simple but artistic dishes like fish with a few carrot slices. (②) Some dishes were even decorated with flowers. (③) As a result, da Vinci lost his job.

A few years later, da Vinci opened a restaurant with his friend Sandro Botticelli. (④) He wanted to create a place where people could try his innovative food. (⑤) They put up a beautifully painted sign and made a uniquely written menu. Da Vinci believed that people would soon appreciate his creative cooking. Unfortunately, that never happened.

**20** 위 글의 빈칸 ⓐ에 들어갈 알맞은 말을 고르시오.

① many　　② few　　③ a few
④ little　　⑤ a little

**21** 위 글의 흐름으로 보아, 주어진 문장이 들어가기에 가장 적절한 곳은?

> Customers, however, were unhappy because they were used to dishes with big servings of meat.

①　　②　　③　　④　　⑤

**22** What did da Vinci do when he took charge of the kitchen?

➡ _____

[23~25] 다음 글을 읽고 물음에 답하시오.

In the early 1480s, da Vinci began to work for Ludovico Sforza in Milan. He was given many different roles, ___ⓐ___ a musician, a painter, and an engineer. He was also put in charge of the kitchen. He was happy to be given another chance to pursue his passion for cooking. Da Vinci did not stop at cooking creative dishes. He wanted to cook much more quickly and easily. Thus, he invented new machines for his kitchen. He created machines ___ⓑ___ could crush vegetables and pull spaghetti. He even made a device ___ⓑ___ could scare frogs away from the water tank. Surely, they were all very innovative, but ⓒ그것들 중 대부분은 사용하기에 너무 크거나 너무 어려웠다.

**23** 위 글의 빈칸 ⓐ에 들어갈 말로 like 대신 쓸 수 있는 말을 쓰시오. (two words)

➡ _____

**24** 위 글의 빈칸 ⓑ에 공통으로 들어갈 알맞은 말을 쓰시오.

➡ _____

**25** 위 글의 밑줄 친 ⓒ의 우리말에 맞게 주어진 어휘를 이용하여 11 단어로 영작하시오.

> them, too, most, difficult, use, or

➡ _____

**[26~28]** 다음 글을 읽고 물음에 답하시오.

In 1495, Sforza asked da Vinci to make a grand painting, which was based on the last supper of Jesus, on the wall of a church in Milan. (①) He spent a lot of time cooking all kinds of food to decide what to put on the table in his picture. (②) "Da Vinci has wasted his time in the kitchen for over a year. That's the reason ⓐ he hasn't finished the painting yet," complained the people from the church to Sforza.

(③) Although da Vinci never became a successful cook, he showed great interest in cooking throughout his life. (④) He was not only a great painter but also a creative cook. Now that you know all about his secret passion for cooking, you will never look at *The Last Supper* the same way. (⑤)

**26** 위 글의 빈칸 ⓐ에 들어갈 말로 알맞은 것을 고르시오.

① when     ② where     ③ how
④ why     ⑤ what

**27** 위 글의 흐름으로 보아, 주어진 문장이 들어가기에 가장 적절한 곳은?

> Da Vinci gladly took on the project because he had always been interested in food.

①     ②     ③     ④     ⑤

**28** What was the grand painting based on? Answer in English with 9 words.

➡ _____

**[29~30]** 다음 글을 읽고 물음에 답하시오.

Some people think creativity is the most important thing ⓐto consider when they choose their career. They like to come up with new ideas and design new things. Thus, they want to work at a place ⓑ그들의 창의력을 발휘할 수 있는 곳에서(use, creativity).

**29** 위 글의 밑줄 친 ⓐ와 문법적 쓰임이 같은 것을 고르시오.

① I need some time to consider.
② They sat down to consider the problem.
③ It is important to consider the cost of repairs.
④ I decided to consider the money he borrowed lost.
⑤ Everyone in the office is meeting to consider forming a union.

**30** 위 글의 밑줄 친 ⓑ의 우리말에 맞게 주어진 어휘를 이용하여 6 단어로 영작하시오.

➡ _____

**01** 출제율 90%

다음 중 짝지어진 단어의 관계가 나머지와 다른 것은?

① inconvenience – convenience
② sell – purchase
③ check – bill
④ satisfied – dissatisfied
⑤ creative – uncreative

**02** 출제율 100%

다음 밑줄 친 부분의 의미로 알맞지 않은 것은?

① We would appreciate you letting us know of any problems. (고마워하다)
② I really don't feel like working anymore. (~할 마음이 나다)
③ It's not a quiet island anymore. (더 이상 ~ 아니다)
④ Don't you want to have a bite of this burger? (~을 한 입 베어 물다)
⑤ Now that I finally know I'll take care of you. (이제)

**03** 출제율 95%

다음 빈칸에 공통으로 들어갈 알맞은 말을 쓰시오.

> • I was put in _____ of the office.
> • He took _____ of the farm after his father's death.

**04** 출제율 95%

다음 주어진 우리말에 맞게 빈칸을 채우시오. (철자가 주어진 경우 주어진 철자로 시작할 것)

(1) 그는 역대 최고의 선수라고 불려요.
➡ He is called the greatest player _____ _____ t_____.

(2) Frank는 거리에서 사람들이 자기를 알아보는 것에 익숙해 있다.
➡ Frank is u_____ _____ being recognized in the street.

(3) 코알라는 호주 고유의 동물이다.
➡ The koala is u_____ to Australia.

**[05~07]** 다음 대화를 읽고 물음에 답하시오.

> B: Wow! Did you draw this?
> G: I ⓐdid. Do you like it?
> B: Yes, the bread and the milk look so ⓑreally. (A)빵을 한 입 먹고 싶어지는데.
> G: Thanks, but I'm not satisfied ⓒwith it. It's not ⓓunique.
> B: I don't think ⓔso. I think it's a fantastic drawing.

**05** 출제율 90%

위 대화의 밑줄 친 ⓐ~ⓔ 중 어법상 어색한 것을 고르시오.

① ⓐ  ② ⓑ  ③ ⓒ  ④ ⓓ  ⑤ ⓔ

✏️ 출제율 100%

**06** 위 대화를 읽고 대답할 수 <u>없는</u> 질문을 고르시오.

① Who drew the drawing?

② Does the girl like the drawing?

③ Does the boy think the bread and the milk look so real?

④ Does the boy think the drawing is fantastic?

⑤ What is unique in the drawing?

✏️ 출제율 90%

**07** 위 대화의 밑줄 친 (A)의 우리말에 맞게 영작하시오. (9 단어)

➡ _____

**[08~10]** 다음 대화를 읽고 물음에 답하시오.

> Man: Are you enjoying your meal?
>
> Woman: Well, the bread was good, and the salad was fresh.
>
> Man: How about your steak?
>
> Woman: Honestly, _____ (A) _____.
> It's too rare for me.
>
> Man: I'm sorry. Would you like me to bring you another one?
>
> Woman: That's O.K. I need to be going. Let me just have the check, please.
>
> Man: I'm really sorry. You won't have to pay for the steak.
>
> Woman: O.K. Thanks.
>
> Man: I promise we'll provide you with a better experience next time you visit.

✏️ 출제율 95%

**08** 위 대화의 빈칸 (A)에 들어갈 말로 어울리지 <u>않는</u> 것을 고르시오.

① I'm not pitiful with the steak

② I'm not satisfied with the steak

③ I'm dissatisfied with the steak

④ I'm not happy with the steak

⑤ I don't like the steak

✏️ 출제율 90%

**09** What does the woman ask the man to do?

➡ _____

✏️ 출제율 100%

**10** 위 대화의 내용과 일치하지 <u>않는</u> 것은?

① 여자는 빵에는 만족했고, 샐러드에는 실망했다.

② 여자는 스테이크에 만족하지 않았다.

③ 남자는 다른 스테이크로 가져다 주겠다고 제안한다.

④ 여자는 스테이크 값을 지불하지 않아도 된다.

⑤ 남자는 다음 방문 때는 더 좋은 경험을 드리겠다고 약속한다.

✏️ 출제율 100%

**11** 다음 빈칸에 접속부사 however 또는 thus 중에서 알맞은 것을 선택하여 써 넣으시오.

(1) Leonardo da Vinci is known as one of the greatest painters and also a great inventor, scientist, and musician. Very few people, _____, know that da Vinci was a creative cook.

(2) Customers who saw da Vinci's creative food were unhappy because they were used to dishes with big servings of meat. _____, da Vinci lost his job.

(3) Da Vinci wanted to make creative food much more quickly and easily. _____, he invented new machines that could crush vegetables and pull spaghetti.

(4) Da Vinci never became a successful cook when he lived. _____, he showed great interest in cooking throughout his life.

(5) I have learned all about the secret passion for cooking of da Vinci. _____, I think I will never look at *The Last Supper* the same way as before.

**12** 다음 글의 빈칸 ①~⑤에 들어갈 단어가 <u>잘못된</u> 것은?

In 1495, Sforza asked da Vinci to make a grand painting, ①_____ was based on the last supper of Jesus, on the wall of a church in Milan. Da Vinci gladly took on the project ②_____ he had always been interested in food. He spent a lot of time cooking all kinds of food to decide ③_____ to put on the table in his picture. "Da Vinci has wasted his time in the kitchen for over a year. That's the ④_____ why he hasn't finished the painting ⑤_____," complained the people from the church to Sforza.

① which  ② because  ③ that
④ reason  ⑤ yet

**13** 다음 그림을 보고 괄호 안의 단어를 배열하여 빈칸을 알맞게 채우시오.

People complained that da Vinci wasted too much time on food and that was _____.

(the painting, why, finished, he, earlier, the reason, hadn't)

**14** 다음 두 문장을 가능하다면 선행사와 관계부사를 모두 써서 한 문장으로 쓰시오. (단, 관계부사는 반드시 사용해야 함)

(1) • Jamaica is the country.
 • International reggae festivals take place every summer in Jamaica.
 ➡ _____
 _____

(2) • Show your brother the way.
 • You solved the puzzle in such a short time in that way.
 ➡ _____
 _____

(3) • Everyone but me knows the day.
 • I will be transferred to Jeju island on the day.
 ➡ _____
 _____

(4) • Katherine won't tell her teacher the reason.
 • She ran out of the classroom for that reason.
 ➡ _____
 _____

**15** 다음 그림을 보고 괄호 안의 단어를 배열하여 빈칸을 알맞게 채우시오.

(pizza, people, line up, to eat, have to, all night, where)

➡ That is the famous restaurant _____

_____.

[16~18] 다음 글을 읽고 물음에 답하시오.

Leonardo da Vinci is known as one of the greatest painters of all time. He was also a great inventor, scientist, and musician. Very few people, however, know that da Vinci was also a creative cook.

In 1473, twenty-year-old da Vinci worked as a cook at a restaurant in Florence, Italy. When he took charge of the kitchen, da Vinci changed the menu completely. He made simple but artistic dishes like fish with a few carrot slices. Some dishes were even decorated with flowers. Customers, however, were unhappy because they were ⓐused to dishes with big servings of meat. As a result, da Vinci lost his job.

A few years later, da Vinci opened a restaurant with his friend Sandro Botticelli. _____(A)_____. They put up a beautifully painted sign and made a uniquely written menu. Da Vinci believed that people would soon appreciate his creative cooking. Unfortunately, that never happened.

**16** 위 글의 빈칸 (A)에 주어진 두 문장을 한 문장으로 바꾸어 쓰시오.

- He wanted to create a place.
- People could try his innovative food at the place.

➡ _____

_____

**17** 위 글의 밑줄 친 ⓐ와 바꿔 쓸 수 있는 것을 고르시오.

① utilized        ② accustomed
③ served         ④ applied
⑤ spent

**18** 위 글의 제목으로 알맞은 것을 고르시오.

① Why Is da Vinci Famous?
② How to Become a Cook
③ What to do as a Cook
④ Jack of All Trades: Leonardo da Vinci
⑤ Unachieved Dream of da Vinci

**[19~22]** 다음 글을 읽고 물음에 답하시오.

In the early 1480s, da Vinci began to work for Ludovico Sforza in Milan. He was given many different roles, such as a musician, a painter, and an engineer. He was also put in charge of the kitchen. He was happy to be given another chance to pursue his passion for cooking. Da Vinci did not stop ___ⓐ___ cooking creative dishes. He wanted to cook much more quickly and easily. Thus, he invented new machines for his kitchen. He created machines that could crush vegetables and pull spaghetti. He even made a device that could scare frogs away from the water tank. Surely, they were all very innovative, but (A)most of them were too big or too difficult to use.

출제율 90%

**19** 위 글의 빈칸 ⓐ에 알맞은 말을 쓰시오.

➡ _____

출제율 100%

**20** Which question can be answered after reading the passage?

① Who was Ludovico Sforza in Milan?
② What did da Vinci ask Ludovico Sforza to work for?
③ Why did da Vinci want to cook more differently?
④ Why did da Vinci invent new machines for his kitchen?
⑤ How could the device scare frogs away from the water tank?

출제율 95%

**21** 다음 문장에서 위 글의 내용과 다른 부분을 찾아서 고치시오.

Da Vinci was happy to have another chance to pursue his passion for painting.

_____ ➡ _____

출제율 90%

**22** 밑줄 친 (A)를 that을 이용하여 바꿔 쓰시오.

➡ _____
_____

[01~03] 다음 대화를 읽고 물음에 답하시오.

> M: Hello, ma'am. How can I help you?
>
> W: I bought this phone only a week ago, but it sometimes _____(A)_____.
>
> M: Oh, I see. May I have a look at it? (Pause) We're sorry for the ___(B)___. It'll take a few hours to fix it.
>
> W: (C)I don't like the phone. I'd like a new one.
>
> M: Of course. I just need to fill out this form.

**01** 다음 customer service report를 참고하여 빈칸 (A)를 알맞게 채우시오.

**CUSTOMER SERVICE REPORT**

| (1) Product | ☐ TV  ✓ Phone  ☐ Refrigerator |
|---|---|
| (2) Problem | ☐ It doesn't turn on.  ✓ It turns off by itself. |
| (3) Service needed | ☐ Fix broken parts.  ✓ Provide a new one. |

➡ _____

**02** 다음 영영풀이에 해당하는 말을 빈칸 (B)에 쓰시오.

> problems caused by something which annoy or affect you

➡ _____

**03** 위 대화의 밑줄 친 (C)와 같은 뜻의 말을 'satisfied'를 이용하여 쓰시오.

➡ _____

**04** 다음 주어진 문장의 밑줄 친 부분을 다시 쓰고자 한다. 빈칸에 알맞은 관계부사를 써 넣으시오.

(1) The exhausted employee needs a place to rest <u>in which</u> she can refresh her mind.
   ➡ The exhausted employee needs a place to rest _____ she can refresh her mind.

(2) Lunar New Year's Day is the day <u>on which</u> people gather and eat together.
   ➡ Lunar New Year's Day is the day _____ people gather and eat together.

(3) The police are trying to find out <u>the way in which</u> he escaped from the heavily guarded prison.
   ➡ The police are trying to find out _____ he escaped from the heavily guarded prison.

(4) No one knew the reason <u>for which</u> Brian cried while performing on his concert stage.
   ➡ No one knew the reason _____ Brian cried while performing on his concert stage.

(5) His funeral will be held next Friday <u>on which</u> all of his children will gather together.
   ➡ His funeral will be held next Friday _____ all of his children will gather together.

**05** 다음 〈보기〉에 주어진 단어들을 한 번씩만 사용해서 글의 흐름에 알맞게 빈칸을 채우시오.

> ┤ 보기 ├
>
> Thus, However, For example, In addition, In other words

(1) Da Vinci constantly made unique and creative dishes. _____, he was an experimental cook.

(2) Da Vinci wanted to be a successful cook. _____, people did not think of him as a cook.

(3) Da Vinci designed a device to crush vegetables. _____, he invented a machine to pull pasta out.

(4) Da Vinci was interested in cooking. _____, he thought long about what food to put on "*the Last Supper*" table.

(5) Da Vinci is known for his talents in various areas. _____, he is a painter, architect, mathematician and musician.

[06~08] 다음 글을 읽고 물음에 답하시오.

Leonardo da Vinci is known as one of the greatest painters of all time. He was also a great inventor, scientist, and musician. Very few people, however, know that da Vinci was also a creative cook.

ⓐIn 1473, twenty-years-old da Vinci worked as a cook at a restaurant in Florence, Italy. When he took charge of the kitchen, da Vinci changed the menu completely. He made simple but artistic dishes like fish with a few carrot slices. Some dishes were even decorated with flowers. Customers, however, were unhappy because they were used to dishes with big servings of meat.  (A)  , da Vinci lost his job.

A few years later, da Vinci opened a restaurant with his friend Sandro Botticelli. He wanted to create a place where people could try his innovative food. They put up a beautifully painted sign and made a uniquely written menu. Da Vinci believed that people would soon appreciate his creative cooking. Unfortunately, that never happened.

**06** 위 글의 빈칸 (A)에 들어갈 알맞은 말을 3 단어의 영어로 쓰시오.

➡ _____

**07** 위 글의 밑줄 친 ⓐ에서 어법상 <u>어색한</u> 것을 찾아 바르게 고치시오.

_____ ➡ _____

**08** Why did da Vinci lose his job?

➡ _____

## 창의사고력 서술형 문제

**01** 다음 그림을 보고 〈보기〉의 표현을 이용하여 다음 대화의 빈칸에 알맞은 말을 쓰시오.

**보기**

(1) drawing / color
(2) steak / rare

A: I'm not satisfied with this _____.
B: Why not?
A: _____.

**02** 다음 그림을 보고 〈보기〉의 단어들을 활용하여, 자유롭게 관계부사가 들어간 문장을 2개 만드시오. (단, 꼭 써야 할 단어는 포함해야 한다.)

(1)　　　　　(2)　　　　　(3)

**보기**

선행사: the place, the day, how / 꼭 써야 할 단어: eat(또는 not eat), the apple

(1) _____
(2) _____
(3) _____

**03** 다음 내용을 바탕으로 20년 뒤 자신의 꿈이 이루어졌다고 가정하고 쓴 자서전의 빈칸을 채우시오.

2030 made a small statue using technology, 2031 entered Korea Technical High School, 2034 entered Korea Art College, 2040 held my first exhibition, an artist who uses technology

My name is Kim Jieun. I am (A)_____ who uses technology. There was a special moment when I decided what I wanted to be. Back in 2030, I made a small statue (B)_____. It was a great chance to learn about (B)_____ for arts. Thus, I decided to go to a (C)_____ high school. After I graduated from high school, I entered Korea Art College and learned more about arts and technology. This year, I held (D)_____. I am very satisfied with my life.

# 단원별 모의고사

**01** 다음 짝지어진 단어의 관계가 같도록 빈칸에 알맞은 말을 쓰시오. (철자 p로 시작하여 쓸 것.)

> surely – certainly : supply – _____

**02** 주어진 영어 설명에 맞게 문장의 빈칸에 알맞은 말을 쓰시오.

> The car was completely _____ed under the truck.

> <영어설명> to press something so hard that it breaks or is damaged

➡ _____

**03** 다음 빈칸에 알맞은 말로 짝지어진 것을 고르시오.

> • We _____ our happiness for the rest of our lives.
> • I've never heard him _____ about anything.

① determine – provide
② decorate – appreciate
③ decorate – complain
④ pursue – complain
⑤ pursue – provide

**04** 다음 문장에 공통으로 들어갈 말은?

> • She was put in charge _____ the matter.
> • He is the greatest speaker _____ all time.

① by      ② with      ③ from
④ to      ⑤ of

**05** 우리말에 맞게 빈칸에 알맞은 말을 철자 t로 시작하여 쓰시오.

> 그 박물관은 연중 내내 매일 문을 연다.
> ➡ The museum is open daily _____ the year.

➡ _____

**06** 다음 영영풀이를 참고하여 빈칸에 알맞은 말을 쓰시오.

> to repair something that is broken or not working properly

> Can you organize someone to come over and _____ it?

➡ _____

**[07~09]** 다음 대화를 읽고 물음에 답하시오.

B: Mom, I want to go to an arts high school. I want to become an actor.
W: What? I thought you were interested in science.
B: I was but not anymore. I want to become a movie star.
W: Are you sure you want to be an actor?
B: Yes, ⓐI'll learn how to act. ⓑI promise I'll do my best.

**07** 위 대화의 밑줄 친 ⓐ를 'should'를 이용하여 바꿔 쓰시오.

➡ _____

**08** 위 대화의 밑줄 친 ⓑ를 'sure'를 이용하여 바꿔 쓰시오.

➡ _____

**09** Why does the boy want to go to an arts high school? Answer with the words "It's because."

➡ _____

**[10~12]** 다음 대화를 읽고 물음에 답하시오.

M: Hello, ma'am. How can I help you?

W: I bought this phone only a week ago, but it sometimes turns off by itself. (①)

M: Oh, I see. (②) (*Pause*) We're sorry for the inconvenience. It'll take a few hours to fix it.

W: I'm not satisfied with the phone. (③) I'd like a new one. (④)

M: Of course. I just need to fill out this form. (⑤)

**10** 위 대화의 (①)~(⑤) 중에서 주어진 문장이 들어가기에 가장 적절한 곳은?

| May I have a look at it? |
|---|

①        ②        ③        ④        ⑤

**11** What is the problem of the phone the woman bought?

➡ _____

**12** If the woman had her phone repaired, how long would it take to repair it?

➡ _____

**[13~14]** 다음 주어진 두 개의 문장을 같은 내용의 하나의 문장으로 바르게 옮긴 것은?

**13**

| Sam didn't have breakfast. However, he didn't feel hungry. |
|---|

① If he had breakfast, Sam wouldn't feel hungry.

② Since he didn't have breakfast, Sam felt hungry.

③ Though he didn't have breakfast, Sam didn't feel hungry.

④ As he didn't have breakfast, Sam didn't feel hungry.

⑤ Before he didn't have breakfast, Sam didn't feel hungry.

**14**

| The students had close contact with a patient in the PC cafe. Thus, they were infected with the virus. |
|---|

① Although the students had close contact with a patient in the PC cafe, they were infected with the virus.

② Since the students didn't have close contact with a patient in the PC cafe, they were infected with the virus.

③ As the students had close contact with a patient in the PC cafe, they were not infected with the virus.

④ Because the students had close contact with a patient in the PC cafe, they were infected with the virus.

⑤ Whereas the students had close contact with a patient in the PC cafe, they were infected with the virus.

**15** 다음 각 문장의 밑줄 친 '전치사+관계대명사'를 관계부사로 바꿀 때 어법상 어색한 것은?

① Paris is the city <u>in which</u> many artists come to live.
  → Paris is the city <u>where</u> many artists come to live.

② Donald will never forget the moment <u>at which</u> he saw the killer.
  → Donald will never forget the moment <u>when</u> he saw the killer.

③ She will tell you the reason <u>for which</u> you failed the test.
  → She will tell you the reason <u>why</u> you failed the test.

④ That's the way <u>in which</u> Paul persuaded the customer companies.
  → That's the way <u>how</u> Paul persuaded the customer companies.

⑤ This is the restaurant <u>in which</u> we had Bulgogi last month.
  → This is the restaurant <u>where</u> we had Bulgogi last month.

**16** 다음 각 문장의 밑줄 친 관계부사를 관계대명사를 이용해서 전환한 문장으로 옳지 <u>않은</u> 것은?

① Hongkong is the city <u>where</u> Henry was born.
  → Hongkong is the city which Henry was born in.

② Do you know the reason <u>why</u> Jerome didn't come?
  → Do you know the reason for which Jerome didn't come?

③ Teach me <u>how</u> the machine works.
  → Teach me the way in which the machine works.

④ The accident happened on the day <u>when</u> the president came back.
  → The accident happened on the day which the president came back in.

⑤ All of us saw the building <u>where</u> your mother works.
  → All of us saw the building which your mother works in.

**17** 다음 각 그림을 보고, 주어진 어구를 알맞게 배열하되, 반드시 However나 Thus 중 하나로 시작하는 문장을 만드시오.

(1)

➡ The hedgehog just wanted to get along with the dog. _____
_____. (painful, so, that, the dog, it, ran away, was)

(2)

➡ Today is the day when Sumi's parents are on duty for lunch. _____
_____.
(side dishes, Sumi, a lot of, asked for)

**[18~19]** 다음 글을 읽고 물음에 답하시오.

Leonardo da Vinci is known as one of the greatest painters of all time. He was also a great inventor, scientist, and musician. Very few people, however, know that da Vinci was also a creative cook.

In 1473, twenty-year-old da Vinci worked as a cook at a restaurant in Florence, Italy. When he took charge of the kitchen, da Vinci changed the menu completely. He made simple but artistic dishes like fish with a few carrot slices. Some dishes were even decorated with flowers. Customers, however, were unhappy because they were used to dishes with big servings of meat. As a result, da Vinci lost his job.

**18** 위 글에 언급된 다빈치의 직업이 <u>아닌</u> 것은?

① 화가　　② 발명가　　③ 조각가
④ 음악가　　⑤ 요리사

**19** When he took charge of the kitchen, what did da Vinci do with his dishes? Answer with 6 words.

➡ _____

**[20~22]** 다음 글을 읽고 물음에 답하시오.

My name is Kim Jieun. I am an artist who uses technology. There was a special moment ____ⓐ____ I decided what I wanted to be. (①) Back in 2030, I made a small statue using technology. (②) It was a great chance to learn about using technology for arts. (③) After I graduated from high school, I entered Korea Art College and learned more about arts and technology. (④) This year, I held my first exhibition. (⑤) I am very satisfied with my life.

**20** 위 글의 빈칸 ⓐ에 알맞은 것을 고르시오.

① what　　② why　　③ how
④ where　　⑤ when

**21** 위 글의 흐름으로 보아, 주어진 문장이 들어가기에 가장 적절한 곳은?

Thus, I decided to go to a technical high school.

①　　　②　　　③　　　④　　　⑤

**22** According to the passage, which is NOT true?

① Jieun is an artist who uses technology.
② Jieun's special moment was in 2030.
③ Jieun had a great chance to learn about using technology for arts.
④ Jieun decided to leave Korea Art College.
⑤ Jieun is very satisfied with her life.

# Lesson 7

# Wit and Wisdom

### 의사소통 기능

- 이해 확인하기
  Do you mean we should not judge others by their looks?

- 바람 · 소원 표현하기
  I wish I could sing like Jiho.

### 언어 형식

- 소유격 관계대명사 whose
  Among them was a man **whose** name was Raja Birbal.

- 가정법 과거
  **If** I **were** you, I **would give** him sweets.

# Words & Expressions

## Key Words

- **among**[əmʌ́ŋ] 전 ~ 중에, ~의 사이에
- **break**[breik] 동 깨지다, 부러뜨리다
- **certainly**[sə́:rtnli] 부 틀림없이, 분명히
- **correct**[kərékt] 형 맞는, 정확한
- **court**[kɔːrt] 명 대궐, 궁궐
- **emperor**[émpərər] 명 황제
- **exactly**[igzǽktli] 부 정확하게
- **exam**[igzǽm] 명 시험
- **expression**[ikspréʃən] 명 표현
- **favor**[féivər] 명 청, 부탁
- **gift**[gift] 명 선물
- **honesty**[ánisti] 명 정직
- **indeed**[indíːd] 부 정말, 확실히
- **journey**[dʒə́ːrni] 명 여행, 여정
- **leave**[liːv] 동 떠나다
- **match**[mætʃ] 명 경기, 시합, 성냥
- **must**[məst] 조 (틀림없이) ~일 것이다
- **mystery**[místəri] 명 수수께끼, 미스터리
- **narrow**[nǽrou] 형 좁은
- **offer**[ɔ́ːfər] 동 내놓다, 제공하다
- **official**[əfíʃəl] 명 고위 공무원, 관리

- **over**[óuvər] 전 (다른 사람·사물이 덮이도록) ~ 위에
- **past**[pæst] 명 과거
- **policy**[páləsi] 명 정책
- **potful**[pátful] 명 한 항아리[냄비]의 양
- **precious**[préʃəs] 형 귀중한, 값비싼
- **present**[préznt] 명 현재, 지금
- **pull**[pul] 동 끌다, 당기다, 끌어당기다
- **pumpkin**[pʌ́mpkin] 명 호박
- **punish**[pʌ́niʃ] 동 처벌하다, 벌주다
- **quick**[kwik] 형 빠른
- **really**[ríːəli] 부 정말로
- **return**[ritə́ːrn] 동 되돌려주다
- **speechless**[spíːtʃlis] 형 (화나거나 놀라서) 말을 못 하는
- **strange**[streindʒ] 형 이상한
- **sweet**[swiːt] 명 사탕, 단것 형 단, 달콤한
- **thus**[ðʌs] 부 그러므로
- **wisdom**[wízdəm] 명 지혜, 슬기, 현명함
- **wise**[waiz] 형 지혜로운, 현명한, 슬기로운
- **wit**[wit] 명 기지, 재치
- **worm**[wəːrm] 명 (땅속에 사는) 벌레

## Key Expressions

- **a number of** 많은
- **a potful of** 한 냄비의, 한 항아리의
- **be careful not to** ~하지 않도록 조심하다
- **be famous for** ~로 유명하다
- **be good at** ~을 잘하다
- **Break a leg!** 행운을 빌어!
- **come up with** ~을 찾아내다, ~을 떠올리다
- **focus on** ~에 주력하다, 집중하다
- **for oneself** 혼자서, 스스로
- **get up** 일어나다

- **hand in** ~을 제출하다
- **in one's place** ~의 처지에서, ~의 상황에서
- **It's better late than never.** 안 하는 것보다는 늦어도 하는 것이 낫다.
- **make sense** 타당하다, 말이 되다
- **over again** 다시 한 번
- **thanks to** ~ 덕분에
- **That's why ~.** 그것이 ~하는 이유이다.
- **the other** (둘 중) 다른 하나의
- **Time flies.** 시간이 쏜살같다.
- **without+동사-ing** ~하지 않고

## Word Power

※ 서로 비슷한 뜻을 가진 어휘

- ☐ **certainly** 틀림없이 – **surely** 확실히
- ☐ **correct** 맞는, 정확한 – **accurate** 정확한
- ☐ **court** 대궐, 궁궐 – **palace** 궁전
- ☐ **emperor** 황제 – **monarch** 군주
- ☐ **exactly** 정확하게 – **correctly** 정확하게
- ☐ **gift** 선물 – **present** 선물

- ☐ **indeed** 정말, 확실히 – **truly** 정말로
- ☐ **journey** 여행, 여정 – **travel** 여행
- ☐ **offer** 내놓다, 제공하다 – **provide** 제공하다
- ☐ **precious** 귀중한 – **valuable** 귀중한
- ☐ **quick** 빠른 – **swift** 신속한

※ 서로 반대되는 뜻을 가진 어휘

- ☐ **correct** 맞는, 정확한 ↔ **incorrect** 정확하지 않은
- ☐ **exactly** 정확하게 ↔ **inexactly** 부정확하게
- ☐ **honesty** 정직 ↔ **dishonesty** 불성실
- ☐ **leave** 떠나다 ↔ **arrive** 도착하다
- ☐ **narrow** 좁은 ↔ **wide** 넓은

- ☐ **over** ~ 위에 ↔ **under** ~ 아래에
- ☐ **precious** 귀중한 ↔ **worthless** 가치 없는
- ☐ **pull** 끌다 ↔ **push** 밀다
- ☐ **punish** 처벌하다 ↔ **praise** 칭찬하다
- ☐ **quick** 빠른 ↔ **slow** 느린

※ 접미사 -less

- ☐ **care** + **less** – **careless** 부주의한
- ☐ **hope** + **less** – **hopeless** 절망적인
- ☐ **use** + **less** – **useless** 쓸모없는
- ☐ **speech** + **less** – **speechless** 말문이 막히는
- ☐ **worth** + **less** – **worthless** 가치 없는
- ☐ **power** + **less** – **powerless** 힘없는

- ☐ **meaning** + **less** – **meaningless** 무의미한
- ☐ **value** + **less** – **valueless** 가치 없는
- ☐ **end** + **less** – **endless** 끝없는
- ☐ **penny** + **less** – **penniless** 돈이 없는
- *cf.* **price** + **less** – **priceless** 매우 소중한

※ Word Partner: out과 함께 쓰는 동사

- ☐ **take out** 가지고 나가다
- ☐ **check out** 확인하다
- ☐ **find out** 찾아내다
- ☐ **turn out** 판명되다, 밝혀지다

- ☐ **work out** 운동하다, 잘 풀리다
- ☐ **hang out** 많은 시간을 보내다
- ☐ **figure out** 알아내다

## English Dictionary

- ☐ **court** 대궐, 궁궐
  → the place where a king or queen lives and works
  왕이나 여왕이 살며 일하는 장소

- ☐ **emperor** 황제
  → the man who is the ruler of an empire
  제국의 통치자인 남자

- ☐ **journey** 여행, 여정
  → an occasion when you travel from one place to another
  한 장소에서 다른 장소로 여행하는 일

- ☐ **leave** 떠나다
  → to go away from a place or a person
  한 장소나 사람에게서 멀어져 가다

- ☐ **match** 경기, 시합
  → an organized sport event between two teams or people
  두 팀이나 사람 사이에 조직되어 있는 스포츠 행사

- ☐ **narrow** 좁은
  → measuring only a small distance from one side to the other; not wide
  한 쪽에서 다른 쪽까지 극히 작은 거리로 측정되는; 넓지 않은

- ☐ **official** 고위 공무원, 관리
  → someone who is in a position of authority in an organization
  어떤 조직에서 권력 있는 직책에 있는 사람

- ☐ **pumpkin** 호박
  → a lagre round vegetable with thick orange skin
  주황색 껍질이 두껍고 둥글고 큰 채소

**01** 다음 짝지어진 단어의 관계가 같도록 빈칸에 알맞은 말은?

> wit – humor : palace – _____

① emperor    ② course    ③ pot
④ official    ⑤ court

**02** 주어진 영어 설명에 맞게 문장의 빈칸에 알맞은 말을 쓰시오.

> He was a White House _____ during the Bush presidency.

> <영어 설명> someone who is in a position of authority in an organization

➡ _____

**03** 밑줄 친 부분의 의미로 알맞지 <u>않은</u> 것을 고르시오.

① Try to put yourself <u>in my place</u> and think how you would feel. (나의 입장에)
② It doesn't <u>make sense</u> for the government to tax certain foods. (타당하다, 말이 되다)
③ What can you <u>come up with</u> from his poem? (떠올리다)
④ There were quite <u>a number of</u> people in the park. (~의 수)
⑤ If you don't <u>focus on</u> the money but on doing a good job, the money will come. (~에 집중하다)

**04** 다음 빈칸에 들어갈 알맞은 말을 고르시오.

> In this job you need to exhibit the _____ of Solomon.

① wisdom    ② punish    ③ favor
④ expression  ⑤ pumpkin

**05** 다음 <보기>의 단어를 사용하여 자연스러운 문장을 만들 수 <u>없는</u> 것은?

> ┤ 보기 ├
> punish  speechless  correct  certainly

① I will _____ go there again.
② Laura was _____ with surprise.
③ You have to wait a day or two to get your _____ balance.
④ My parents used to _____ me by not letting me watch TV.
⑤ A cold spring will _____ a natural check on the number of insects.

**06** 다음 빈칸에 알맞은 말로 바르게 짝지어진 것을 고르시오.

> • This novel is full of the author's _____.
> • The early bird catches the _____.

① wit – warm    ② wit – worm
③ clever – warm   ④ clever – worm
⑤ intelligence – fever

**01** 다음 영영풀이에 알맞은 어휘를 〈보기〉에서 찾아 쓰시오.

┌─ 보기 ─┐
court   match   pumpkin   journey
└────────┘

(1) the place where a king or queen lives and works

➡ _____

(2) an occasion when you travel from one place to another

➡ _____

(3) an organized sport event between two teams or people

➡ _____

(4) a large round vegetable with thick orange skin

➡ _____

**02** 다음 짝지어진 두 단어의 관계가 같도록 빈칸에 알맞은 말을 쓰시오.

(1) care : careless = value : _____

(2) punish : punishment = wise : _____

**03** 다음 우리말에 맞도록 빈칸에 알맞은 한 단어를 쓰시오.

(1) 오늘 상영시간표 확인했어?

➡ Did you _____ out today's movie schedule?

(2) 그 소식을 듣고 나는 잠시 말을 못 했다.

➡ The news struck me _____ for a while.

(3) 쓰기를 멈추고 시험지를 제출하세요.

➡ Stop writing and _____ in your papers.

(4) 누군가를 이해할 수 없을 때에는 그의 입장에 처했다고 생각해 보라.

➡ When you can't understand someone, just try to put yourself in his _____.

**04** 우리말에 맞게 한 단어를 추가하여 주어진 단어를 알맞게 배열하시오.

(1) 난 쌍둥이 한 명을 다른 한 명과 구분할 수가 없다. (I, twin, one, can't, tell, the, from)

➡ _____

(2) 시민들은 길거리로 지갑을 가지고 나가도 안전함을 느낀다. (citizens, streets, wallets, secure, the, feel, their, out, on)

➡ _____
_____

(3) 나는 내 인격의 완전한 표현을 위해 자유를 원한다. (I, personality, freedom, the, want, full, my, of, for)

➡ _____

(4) 각 연습 문제는 각기 다른 문법 사항에 집중한다. (exercise, point, grammar, focuses, different, a, each)

➡ _____
_____

# Conversation

## 1 이해 확인하기

**Do you mean we should not judge others by their looks?**
사람을 겉모습으로 판단해선 안 된다는 뜻이야?

- 'Do you mean ~?'은 '~라는 말이니?'라는 뜻으로 자신이 이해한 의미가 상대가 의도한 것인지를 확인하는 말이다. 'You're saying ~?(~라고 말하는 거니?)', 'I think you mean ~(나는 네가 ~을 의미한다고 생각해.)'와 같은 표현도 자신이 이해한 의미를 상대에게 확인하는 표현이다.

- 'Do you know what I mean?(내가 무슨 말 하는지 알겠어?)'는 자신이 한 말을 상대가 이해했는지를 확인하기 위하여 묻는 말이다. 'Do you understand what I am saying?(내가 무슨 말 하는지 이해하겠어?)', 'Do you follow me?(내 말 이해해?)', 'Do you get it?(이해해?)', 'Are you with me?(내 말 알겠니?)'도 마찬가지로 상대의 이해를 확인하는 말이다.

- 'Can you explain that?(그걸 설명해 줄 수 있니?)'는 상대의 말을 알아듣지 못했을 때 설명을 요청하는 말이다. 'Could you give me more information?', 'Can you explain more in detail?', 'Could you be more specific?', 'Can you explain it to me?' 등도 마찬가지로 상대의 설명을 요청하는 말이다.

### 이해 확인하기

- Do you mean ~? ~라는 말이니?
- You're saying ~? ~라고 말하는 거니?
- I think you mean ~. 나는 네가 ~을 의미한다고 생각해.

### 이해 점검하기

- Do you know/see what I mean? 내가 무슨 말 하는지 알겠어?
- Do you understand what I am saying? 내가 무슨 말 하는지 이해하겠어?
- Do you follow me? 내 말 이해해?
- Are you with me? 내 말 알겠니?

### 핵심 Check

1. 괄호 안에 주어진 어휘를 이용하여 밑줄 친 우리말을 영작하시오.

   G: You look worried. Is something wrong?

   B: I had to hand in my science report by yesterday, but I didn't.

   G: It's better late than never.

   B: 늦었더라도 내는 게 낫다는 뜻이야? (mean, hand, even though)

   G: Yes, exactly. You should always finish what you've started.

   ➡ _____

**② 바람·소원 표현하기**

**I wish I could sing like Jiho.** 지호처럼 노래할 수 있으면 좋겠어.

- 'I wish I could ~.'는 '~라면 좋겠어.'의 뜻으로 바람이나 소원을 표현하는 말이다. '~라면 …할 텐데.'의 의미로 소원을 나타내는 말은 'If I were ~, I would/could ~.'이고 '나는 ~하기를 원한다.'는 'I want to ~.'이다. '~하기를 기대한다.'라고 할 때는 'I look forward to -ing.'라고 하고 'I expect to ~.'도 역시 기대를 나타내는 말이다.

- 소망이나 바람을 나타낼 때 사용하는 표현 'I wish I could ~'는 'I wish+가정법 과거'의 형태를 사용하여 '내가 ~할 수 있다면 좋을 텐데.'라는 뜻이다. 뒤에 나오는 가정법 과거는 동사의 과거형으로 나타내고, be동사는 주로 were를 쓴다. 이 표현은 어떤 일을 할 수 있으면 좋겠지만, 실제로 지금은 그렇게 할 수 없는 현재의 일에 대하여 말하는 사람의 소원을 나타내는 문장이다.

- 앞으로 일어날 일이나 하고 싶은 일에 대한 기대를 표현할 때는 '~을 기대한다.'라는 의미로 'I look forward to ~.'의 표현을 사용한다. 여기서 to는 전치사이므로 뒤에 명사나 동명사가 와야 한다. '~을 너무 하고 싶다.'의 뜻으로 'I can't wait for ~.', 'I can't wait to ~.'라고 하기도 한다.

- 강한 소원, 기대를 나타낼 때는 '열망하다'라는 의미의 동사 long을 써서 'I'm longing to+동사원형', 'I'm longing for+명사'라고 하거나 형용사 eager(열망하는)를 써서 'I'm eager to+동사원형', 'I'm eager for+명사'의 형태로 나타내기도 한다.

### 바람·소원 표현하기

- I wish 주어+과거 동사 ~. ~할 수 있으면 좋을 텐데.
- If I were ~, I would … 내가 ~라면 …할 텐데.
- I want to ~. 나는 ~하기를 원한다.
- I look forward to -ing…. ~하기를 기대한다.
- I hope to ~. ~하기를 희망한다.
- I'd like to ~. ~하고 싶다.
- I expect to 동사원형 ~. ~하기를 기대한다.

### 핵심 Check

**2.** 괄호 안에 주어진 어휘를 이용하여 밑줄 친 우리말을 영작하시오.

**B:** Wow, you really dance well.

**G:** Thanks. I love dancing. Everyone in my family is good at dancing.

**B:** Really? Your parents dance well, too?

**G:** Yes. They're also good singers.

**B:** What a family! <u>나도 너처럼 춤을 출 수 있으면 좋겠어.</u> (wish, like)

➡ _____

### Listen & Speak 1 A-1

G: You ❶look tired this morning.

B: I got up very early ❷to study for the exam.

G: ❸Good for you. The early bird catches the worm.

B: No. The early bird ❹gets tired quickly.

G: ❺Do you mean you don't like to get up early?

B: Yes, that's exactly ❻what I mean.

G: 오늘 아침 너 피곤해 보인다.
B: 시험 공부 하려고 아주 일찍 일어났거든.
G: 잘했어. 일찍 일어나는 새가 벌레를 잡는 법이지.
B: 아니. 일찍 일어나는 새가 빨리 지쳐.
G: 일찍 일어나는 게 싫다는 말이야?
B: 응, 정확히 그런 뜻이야.

❶ look+형용사: ～하게 보이다
❷ 부사적 용법 중에서 '목적(～하기 위해서)'으로 쓰였다.
❸ Good for you.: 잘했다. cf. be good for: ～에 좋다
❹ get+형용사: ～하게 되다
❺ 'Do you mean ～?'은 이해를 확인하기 위해 쓰는 표현이다.
❻ what은 선행사를 포함하는 관계대명사이다.

**Check(√) True or False**

(1) The girl looks tired this morning.　　　　　　T ☐  F ☐

(2) The boy doesn't like to get up early.　　　　　T ☐  F ☐

### Listen & Speak 1 A-2

G: I have to sing at the school's English pop song contest.

B: Wow. ❶Break a leg!

G: What? ❷Do you mean I have to break ❸one of my legs?

B: No, ❹it's an expression ❺meaning ❻I hope you do well.

G: 나는 학교의 영어 팝송 부르기 대회에서 노래를 해야 해.
B: 우와. 행운을 빌어!
G: 뭐? 내가 내 다리 한 쪽을 부러뜨려야 한다는 말이야?
B: 아니. 네가 잘하길 빈다는 뜻의 표현이야.

❶ Break a leg!: 행운을 빌어!
❷ 'Do you mean ～?'은 이해를 확인하기 위해 쓰는 표현이다.
❸ one of+복수 명사: ～ 중의 하나
❹ it은 'Break a leg!'을 가리키는 말이다.
❺ meaning은 현재분사로 an expression을 뒤에서 수식하고 있다.
❻ hope 다음에 목적절을 이끄는 접속사 that이 생략되어 있다.

**Check(√) True or False**

(3) The boy knows the expression, 'Break a leg!'　　T ☐  F ☐

(4) The girl has to break one of her legs.　　　　　T ☐  F ☐

### Listen & Speak 2 A-1

B: Wow, you really dance well.

G: Thanks. I love dancing. Everyone in my family ❶is good at dancing.

B: Really? Your parents dance well, too?

G: Yes. They're also good singers.

B: ❷What a family! ❸I wish I could dance like you.

❶ Everyone은 단수로 받는다. be good at: ∼을 잘하다
❷ 감탄문으로 '굉장한 가족이다!' 정도의 뜻이다.
❸ 'I wish ∼' 가정법 과거로 현재 사실과 반대되는 바람이나 소원을 말할 때 쓰는 표현이며 '∼라면 좋을 텐데' 정도의 뜻이다. 'I'm sorry I can't dance like you.'로 바꿔 쓸 수 있다.

### Listen & Speak 2 A-2

B: Hello, everyone! Time flies. I can't believe it's time ❶to say goodbye. ❷Thanks to my teachers and friends, I was really happy here. ❸I wish I could go back to my first year and live these years over again, but it's time ❹to start a new journey to high school. I hope I can see you again. Thank you.

❶ time을 수식하는 형용사적 용법의 부정사이다.
❷ thanks to: ∼ 덕분에
❸ 'I wish ∼' 가정법 과거로 'I'm sorry I can't go back to ∼.'로 바꿔 쓸 수 있다.
❹ time을 수식하는 형용사적 용법의 부정사이다.

### Communicate A

Anna: What's wrong? You don't ❶look so good.

Suho: I'm still thinking about our soccer match last week.

Anna: ❷Do you mean the game you lost last week?

Suho: Yes. ❸I wish I could forget about it, but I can't.

Anna: Well, you should always live for today.

Suho: Do you mean I should forget the past and ❹focus on the present?

Anna: Yes, exactly. People say, "Yesterday is history, tomorrow is a mystery, and today is a gift. ❺That's why it's called the present."

Suho: Now I see. You know so many great expressions. You're ❻as wise as my grandma.

❶ look+형용사: ∼하게 보이다
❷ 'Do you mean ∼?'은 이해를 확인하기 위해 쓰는 표현이다.
❸ 'I wish ∼' 가정법 과거로 'I'm sorry I can't forget about it.'으로 바꿔 쓸 수 있다.
❹ focus on: ∼에 집중하다
❺ That's why ∼: 그것이 ∼한 이유이다.
❻ 'as ∼ as'는 동등 비교를 나타내는 표현이다.

### Progress Check 1

G: You look worried. ❶Is something wrong?

B: I had to hand in my science report by yesterday, but I didn't.

G: It's better late than never.

B: ❷Do you mean it's better to ❸hand it in even though it's late?

G: Yes, exactly. You should always finish ❹what you've started.

❶ 'thing'으로 끝나는 부정대명사는 형용사가 뒤에서 수식한다.
❷ 'Do you mean ∼?'은 이해를 확인하기 위해 쓰는 표현이다.
❸ '타동사+부사'로 이루어진 구동사의 경우 목적어가 인칭대명사이면 반드시 '타동사+대명사 목적어+부사'의 순서로 쓴다.
❹ what은 선행사를 포함하는 관계대명사이다.

### Progress Check 2

B: Wow, you play the guitar so well.

G: Thanks. I love playing the guitar. I learned ❶it from my dad.

B: Really? Does your father play the guitar, too?

G: Yes. He was in a famous band.

B: ❷What a family! I wish I could play the guitar like you.

❶ it은 'playing the guitar'를 가리킨다.
❷ 감탄문으로 '굉장한 가족이다!' 정도의 뜻이다.

### Progress Check 3

M: You broke your friend's phone, and you don't know ❶what to do. Another friend says to you, "Honesty is the best policy." You don't know ❷what that means exactly.

❶ 'what to do'는 '의문사+to부정사'로 know의 목적어 역할을 하고 있다.
❷ 'what that means exactly'는 간접의문문으로 know의 목적어로 쓰이고 있다.

● 다음 우리말과 일치하도록 빈칸에 알맞은 말을 쓰시오.

### Listen & Speak 1 A-1

G: You _____ _____ this morning.

B: I got up very early _____ _____ for the exam.

G: _____ _____ you. The early bird catches the worm.

B: No. The early bird _____ _____ quickly.

G: _____ _____ _____ you don't like to get up early?

B: Yes, that's exactly _____ _____ _____ .

### Listen & Speak 1 A-2

G: I _____ _____ sing at the school's English pop song contest.

B: Wow. Break _____ _____ !

G: What? _____ _____ _____ I have to break _____ of my _____ ?

B: No, it's an expression _____ I hope _____ _____ _____ .

### Listen & Speak 2 A-1

B: Wow, you really dance well.

G: Thanks. I love dancing. Everyone in my family _____ _____ _____ dancing.

B: Really? Your parents dance well, _____ ?

G: Yes. They're also _____ _____ .

B: _____ _____ family! _____ _____ _____ _____ _____ dance like you.

### Listen & Speak 2 A-2

B: Hello, everyone! Time flies. I _____ _____ it's time _____ _____ goodbye. _____ _____ my teachers and friends, I was really happy here. _____ _____ _____ _____ go back to my first year and live these years over again, but it's time _____ _____ a new journey to high school. I hope I can see you again. Thank you.

**해석**

G: 오늘 아침 너 피곤해 보인다.
B: 시험 공부를 하려고 아주 일찍 일어났거든.
G: 잘했어. 일찍 일어나는 새가 벌레를 잡는 법이지.
B: 아니. 일찍 일어나는 새가 빨리 지쳐.
G: 일찍 일어나는 게 싫다는 말이야?
B: 응, 정확히 그런 뜻이야.

G: 나는 학교의 영어 팝송 부르기 대회에서 노래를 해야 해.
B: 우와. 행운을 빌어!
G: 뭐? 내가 내 다리 한 쪽을 부러뜨려야 한다는 말이야?
B: 아니, 네가 잘하길 빈다는 뜻의 표현이야.

B: 우와, 너 춤 정말 잘 춘다.
G: 고마워. 나 춤추는 거 정말 좋아해. 우리 가족 모두가 춤을 잘 춰.
B: 정말? 너희 부모님도 춤을 잘 추시니?
G: 맞아. 노래도 잘하셔.
B: 굉장한 가족이다! 나도 너처럼 춤을 출 수 있으면 좋겠어.

B: 안녕, 모두들! 시간이 참 빠르네요. 이제 작별 인사를 해야 할 시간이라는 게 믿어지지 않아요. 선생님들과 친구들 덕분에, 이곳에서 정말 행복했어요. 첫 해로 돌아가서 이 해들을 다시 지낼 수 있다면 좋겠지만, 이제는 고등학교로 새로운 여행을 떠나야 할 시간이에요. 여러분을 다시 볼 수 있다면 좋겠어요. 고맙습니다.

### Communicate A

**Anna:** What's wrong? You don't _____ so _____.

**Suho:** I'm still thinking about our soccer match last week.

**Anna:** _____ _____ _____ the game you lost last week?

**Suho:** Yes. _____ _____ _____ _____ forget about it, but I can't.

**Anna:** Well, you should always _____ _____ _____.

**Suho:** _____ _____ _____ I should forget the past and _____ _____ the present?

**Anna:** Yes, exactly. People say, "Yesterday is history, tomorrow is a mystery, and today is a gift. That's _____ it's _____ the present."

**Suho:** Now I see. You know so many great expressions. You're _____ _____ _____ my grandma.

### Progress Check 1

**G:** You _____ _____. Is something _____?

**B:** I had to _____ _____ my science report by yesterday, but I didn't.

**G:** It's _____ _____ _____ _____.

**B:** _____ _____ _____ it's better to _____ _____ _____ even though it's late?

**G:** Yes, exactly. You should always finish _____ you've started.

### Progress Check 2

**B:** Wow, you _____ _____ _____ so well.

**G:** Thanks. I love playing the guitar. I learned _____ from my dad.

**B:** Really? Does your father play the guitar, _____?

**G:** Yes. He was _____ a famous band.

**B:** _____ _____ family! _____ _____ I _____ play the guitar like you.

### Progress Check 3

**M:** You broke your friend's phone, and you don't know _____ _____ _____. _____ friend says to you, "Honesty is the best policy." You don't know _____ _____ _____ exactly.

Conversation **177**

**01** 다음 빈칸 (A)에 알맞은 문장을 고르시오.

> G: You look tired this morning.
> B: I got up very early to study for the exam.
> G: Good for you. The early bird catches the worm.
> B: No. The early bird gets tired quickly.
> G: Do you mean you don't like to get up early?
> B: ＿＿＿＿＿＿＿＿ (A) ＿＿＿＿＿＿＿＿

① Yes, I wish I could get up early.
② Yes, that's exactly what I mean.
③ No, I think I'm not satisfied with getting up early.
④ No, I think it's a little boring.
⑤ No, I mean I'm lazy.

**02** 밑줄 친 우리말을 주어진 단어를 이용하여 영작하시오.

> G: I have to sing at the school's English pop song contest.
> B: Wow. Break a leg!
> G: What? 내가 내 다리 한 쪽을 부러뜨려야 한다는 말이야?
>    (mean, break, one, leg, 11 단어)
> B: No, it's an expression meaning I hope you do well.

➡ ＿＿＿＿＿＿＿＿＿＿＿＿＿＿＿＿＿＿＿

**03** 주어진 문장 다음의 대화가 자연스럽게 연결되도록 (A)~(D)를 순서대로 적절하게 배열하시오.

> G: You look worried. Is something wrong?
> (A) Yes, exactly. You should always finish what you've started.
> (B) It's better late than never.
> (C) I had to hand in my science report by yesterday, but I didn't.
> (D) Do you mean it's better to hand it in even though it's late?

➡ ＿＿＿＿＿＿＿＿＿＿＿＿＿＿＿

**01** 다음 중 짝지어진 대화가 <u>어색한</u> 것은?

① A: Wow, you really dance well.

B: Thanks. I love dancing. Everyone in my family is good at dancing.

② A: I'm still thinking about our soccer match last week.

B: Do you mean the game you lost last week?

③ A: Do you mean I have to break one of my legs?

B: Break a leg!

④ A: I love playing the guitar. I learned it from my dad.

B: Really? Does your father play the guitar, too?

⑤ A: Your parents dance well, too?

B: Yes. They're also good singers.

A: What a family! I wish I could dance like you.

[02~04] 다음 대화를 읽고 물음에 답하시오.

G: I have to sing at the school's English pop song contest.

B: Wow. _____(A)_____

G: What? (a)You're saying I have to break one of my legs?

B: No, it's an expression _____(B)_____ I hope you do well.

 빈칸 (A)에 알맞은 말을 고르시오.

① Break a leg!

② Great English pop song contest.

③ What a nice school!

④ Good job.

⑤ Congratulations!

**03** 위 대화의 빈칸 (B)에 들어갈 말로 알맞은 것을 고르시오.

① mean    ② means    ③ meant

④ to mean    ⑤ meaning

서답형

**04** 위 대화의 밑줄 친 (a)와 같은 의미가 되도록 'mean'을 이용하여 다시 쓰시오.

➡ _____

[05~07] 다음 글을 읽고 물음에 답하시오.

B: Hello, everyone! (a)시간이 참 빠르네요. (①) Thanks to my teachers and friends, I was really happy here. (②) I wish _____(A)_____ my first year and live these years over again, but it's time to start a new journey to high school. (③) I hope I can see you again. (④) Thank you. (⑤)

**05** 위 글의 빈칸 (A)에 들어갈 말로 알맞은 것은?

① I hope to go back to

② I can go back to

③ I can't go back to

④ I couldn't go back to

⑤ I could go back to

 위 글의 (①)~(⑤) 중에서 주어진 문장이 들어가기에 적절한 곳은?

| I can't believe it's time to say goodbye. |
| --- |

①     ②     ③     ④     ⑤

**07** 밑줄 친 (a)의 우리말에 맞게 두 단어로 영작하시오.

➡ _____

**08** 다음 대화의 밑줄 친 부분의 의도로 알맞은 것은?

> G: You look worried. Is something wrong?
> B: I had to hand in my science report by yesterday, but I didn't.
> G: It's better late than never.
> B: Do you mean it's better to hand it in even though it's late?
> G: Yes, exactly. You should always finish what you've started.

① 불만 묻기　　② 희망 묻기
③ 이해 확인하기　　④ 경험 묻기
⑤ 바람·소원 표현하기

**09** 주어진 문장 사이의 대화가 자연스럽게 연결되도록 (A)~(D)를 순서대로 적절하게 배열하시오.

> G: You look tired this morning.

> (A) No. The early bird gets tired quickly.
> (B) I got up very early to study for the exam.
> (C) Good for you. The early bird catches the worm.
> (D) Do you mean you don't like to get up early?

> B: Yes, that's exactly what I mean.

➡ _____

[10~12] 다음 대화를 읽고 물음에 답하시오.

> Anna: What's wrong? You don't look so good.
> Suho: I'm still thinking about our soccer match last week.
> Anna: Do you mean the game you lost last week?
> Suho: Yes. I wish I could forget about it, but I can't.
> Anna: Well, you should always live for today.
> Suho: _____(A)_____ the past and focus on the present?
> Anna: Yes, exactly. People say, "Yesterday is history, tomorrow is a mystery, and today is a gift. That's ___(B)___ it's called the present."
> Suho: Now I see. You know so many great expressions. You're as wise as my grandma.

**10** 위 대화의 빈칸 (A)에 알맞은 말은?

① Do you think I already forgot
② Do you want me to remember
③ Do you mean I should forget
④ Do you know why I should forget
⑤ Do you think I'd better remember

**11** 위 대화의 빈칸 (B)에 알맞은 말을 한 단어로 쓰시오.

➡ _____

**12** 위 대화를 읽고 대답할 수 없는 것은?

① Why doesn't Suho look so good?
② Is Suho still thinking about his soccer match last week?
③ What does Suho wish?
④ Why does Anna live for today?
⑤ Does Anna know so many great expressions?

[01~03] 다음 대화를 읽고 물음에 답하시오.

Anna: What's wrong? You don't look so good.

Suho: I'm still thinking about our soccer match last week.

Anna: Do you mean the game you lost last week?

Suho: Yes. _____ (A) _____ but I can't.

Anna: Well, you should always live for today.

Suho: Do you mean I should forget the past and focus on the present?

Anna: Yes, exactly. People say, "Yesterday is history, tomorrow is a mystery, and today is a gift. That's why it's called the present."

Suho: Now I see. You know so many great expressions. (a)<u>넌 우리 할머니만큼 현명해.</u> (wise, my grandma.)

**01** 위 대화의 빈칸 (A)에 'I'm sorry I can't forget about it.'의 뜻을 갖는 문장을 wish를 포함하는 가정법으로 쓰시오.

➡ _____

**02** 괄호 안에 주어진 어휘를 이용하여 밑줄 친 우리말 (a)에 맞게 6 단어로 쓰시오.

➡ _____

**03** Why is today called the present? Use the word 'because'.

➡ _____

_____

[04~05] 다음 대화를 읽고 물음에 답하시오.

B: Wow, you play the guitar so well.

G: Thanks. I love playing the guitar. I learned it from my dad.

B: Really? Does your father play the guitar, too? _____ (A) _____

G: Yes. He was in a famous band.

B: What a family!

**04** 위 대화의 빈칸 (A)에 '기타를 칠 수 있기를 바라는' 말을 7 단어로 쓰시오.

➡ _____

**05** From whom did the girl learn how to play the guitar?

➡ _____

**06** 다음 대화에서 어법상 어색한 것을 찾아 바르게 고치시오. (2개)

G: You look worried. Is something wrong?

B: I had to hand in my science report by yesterday, but I didn't.

G: It's better late than never.

B: Do you mean it's better to hand in it even though it's late?

G: Yes, exactly. You should always finish that you've started.

(1) _____ ➡ _____

(2) _____ ➡ _____

# Grammar

교과서

## ① 소유격 관계대명사 whose

- Among them was a man **whose** name was Raja Birbal.
  그들 중에는 Raja Birbal이라는 이름의 한 남자가 있었다.

- Birbal came back with two pots **whose** necks were really narrow.
  Birbal은 목이 매우 좁은 항아리 두 개를 가지고 돌아왔다.

■ 관계대명사의 소유격은 선행사가 그 뒤에 나오는 문장에서 소유격 형태로 등장할 때, 두 문장을 하나로 이어 주어 '접속사'와 '대명사의 소유격'의 역할을 한다.

- I know a man. **His** daughter is an artist.
  = I know a man **and his** daughter is an artist.
  = I know a man **whose** daughter is an artist. 나는 딸이 화가인 한 남자를 안다.
- This is the house. **Its** roof is painted sky blue.
  = This is the house **whose** roof is painted sky blue. 이게 지붕 색이 스카이블루인 집이다.

■ 소유격을 대신하기 때문에 whose 뒤에 명사가 오고, 구조는 완전한 문장처럼 보인다. 그렇지만, whose 뒤에 오는 명사가 관사가 없다는 사실을 생각하면 완전한 문장은 아니다.

- The lawyer met a lady. Her son stole a car.
  = The lawyer met a lady **whose** <u>son</u> <u>stole</u> <u>a car</u>. 그 변호사는 아들이 차를 훔친 숙녀를 만났다.
                                      주어 동사 목적어

■ 관계대명사의 소유격은 선행사에 상관없이 whose를 쓸 수 있으나, 선행사가 사물일 경우에는 of which 로 바꿔 쓸 수 있다. (of which가 받는 명사 앞에는 정관사 the를 써야 하고, 선행사가 사람일 경우에는 of which를 쓸 수 없다.)

- They want to buy <u>the cars</u>. **Their** <u>engines</u> are in good condition.
  = They want to buy <u>the cars</u> **and their** <u>engines</u> are in good condition.
  = They want to buy <u>the cars</u> **whose** <u>engines</u> are in good condition.
  = They want to buy <u>the cars</u> **of which** <u>the engines</u> are in good condition.
  = They want to buy <u>the cars</u> <u>the engines</u> **of which** are in good condition.

### 핵심 Check

1. 괄호 안에서 알맞은 말을 고르시오.

  (1) Minju has a friend (whose / whom) mom is Vietnamese.

  (2) This is the house (which / of which) the door is painted black.

## ② 가정법 과거: 'If+주어+동사의 과거형 ~, 주어+would/could+동사원형 …'

- If I **were** you, I **would give** him sweets. 내가 당신이라면 그에게 사탕을 줄 텐데.
- It **would be** great if there **were** a man as wise as Birbal in our country.
  우리나라에도 비르발처럼 현명한 자가 있다면 정말 좋을 텐데.

■ 가정법 과거: '만약 ~라면 …할 텐데'의 뜻으로, 현재 사실을 반대로 가정하거나 실현 가능성이 없는 일에 대해서 가정할 때 쓰며, 'If+주어+동사 과거형 ~, 주어+would/could+동사원형 …'의 형태로 나타낸다.
  - If I **have** money, I **will buy** a new shirt. 내게 돈이 있다면, 새로운 셔츠를 살 것이다. (조건문, 사실)
  - If I **had** money, I **would buy** a new shirt. 내게 돈이 있다면, 새로운 셔츠를 살 텐데.(가정법 과거, 현재 사실의 반대 가정)
    = As I don't have money, I won't buy a new shirt. 내게 돈이 없기 때문에, 나는 새로운 셔츠를 사지 않을 것이다.
  - If she **were** my teacher, I **would follow** her. 그녀가 나의 선생님이라면, 그녀를 따라갈 텐데.

■ 'I wish' 가정법은 현재 사실에 반대되는 소망을 나타낸다.
  - I wish I **were** as wise as Birbal. 나도 Birbal만큼 지혜롭다면 좋을 텐데
    = In fact, I'm not as wise as Birbal.

■ 가정법 과거완료는 이미 일어난 과거 사실을 반대로 가정하는데 사용하며, 'If+주어+had+과거분사 ~, 주어+would/could+have+과거분사 …'의 형태로 나타낸다.
  - If the companies **had accepted** my suggestion, they **would** not **have failed**.
    그 기업들이 내 제안을 받아들였더라면, 그들은 망하지 않았을 텐데.

■ 가정법의 다양한 표현들로 직설법의 의미를 나타낼 수 있다.
  - As he is short, he cannot touch the ceiling. 그는 작기 때문에, 천장에 손이 닿을 수 없다. (직설법)
    → If he **were** not short, he **could touch** the ceiling. 그가 작지 않으면, 천장에 손이 닿을 수 있을 텐데. (가정법)
    → **Were** he not short, he **could touch** the ceiling. (If를 생략, 도치)

■ 다음은 주의할 가정법의 표현들이다.
  - **If it were not for** the sun, we **could** not **live** at all. 태양이 없다면 우리는 전혀 살 수 없을 텐데.
    → **Without** the sun, we **could** not **live** at all. (without 표현)
    → **Were it not for** the sun, we **could** not **live** at all. (If 생략, 도치)

### 핵심 Check

**2.** 다음 우리말에 맞게 괄호 안의 단어를 바르게 배열하시오.

(1) 내가 개라면, 하루 종일 잘 텐데. (a dog, sleep, long, if, would, all day, I, I, were)

➡ _____

(2) 그녀가 뉴욕에 산다면, 햄버거만 먹을 텐데. (lived, would, hamburgers, only, eat, in, if, she, she, New York)

➡ _____

**01** 다음 밑줄 친 부분 중 어법상 바르지 않은 것은?

① I have a friend whose puppy is all black.

② We saw the house whose roof was covered with grass.

③ Sarah went to the cinema whose the movie was playing.

④ Thomas met a girl whose father was a police officer.

⑤ We needed a table whose legs are a bit long.

**02** 다음 각 가정법 문장에서 어법상 어색한 단어를 한 개씩만 찾아 고치시오.

(1) If it is not raining, Susan would walk her dog.

_____ ➡ _____

(2) If I finished homework, I will go to the playground.

_____ ➡ _____

(3) If Andy has much money, he would buy a new car.

_____ ➡ _____

(4) I will go to the future if I had a time machine.

_____ ➡ _____

**03** 다음 두 문장을 관계대명사를 이용하여 하나의 문장으로 만드시오.

Cathy heard of a man. His wife wrote novels.

➡ _____

**04** 다음 빈칸에 들어갈 말로 알맞은 것은?

If Minju _____ his number, she would make a phone call to him.

① know          ② knows          ③ has known
④ knew          ⑤ had known

**01** 다음 문장의 밑줄 친 단어들 중 어법상 어색한 단어는?

> A lady ①of which hair ②was blond ③ was waiting ④for you ⑤at the cafe.

①    ②    ③    ④    ⑤

**02** 다음 중 어법상 어색한 문장은?

① If he were a good pitcher, we would win this game.
② If I knew the correct answer, I would tell him immediately.
③ If it were not for your help, we would not be able to fix our bikes.
④ If I were in Tokyo, I wouldn't be sure I would be OK from the disease.
⑤ If my father were very rich, he'll buy me any car I wanted.

**서답형**
[03~06] 다음 우리말과 일치하도록 괄호 안에 주어진 단어들을 바르게 배열하시오.

**03**
> Oliver는 색이 빨간 자전거를 갖고 있다.
> (a bike, is, Oliver, red, whose, has, color)

➡ _____

**04**
> 내가 그녀라면, 포기하지 않을 텐데.
> (give up, she, I, I, not, if, would, were)

➡ _____

**05**
> 나는 Bob처럼 그림을 잘 그리고 싶다.
> (wish, could, Bob, like, draw, I, I, well)

➡ _____

**06**
> 그들은 풍경이 아름다운 집을 구입할 것이다.
> (the scenery, buy, a house, are, they, of which, beautiful, going, is, to)

➡ _____

   _____

**07** 다음 중 빈칸 ⓐ~ⓕ에 같은 단어가 들어가는 것끼리 바르게 짝지어진 것은?

> • The team rescued a boy ⓐ_____ boat was hit by a big wave.
> • Birbal brought two pots ⓑ_____ the necks were really narrow.
> • They gave the prize to the singer ⓒ _____ performance was very excellent.
> • They were looking for the house ⓓ _____ the rooms were wide enough to raise cats.
> • My mother worked at a company ⓔ _____ goal was to contribute to the society.
> • This was the park ⓕ_____ the girl lost her watch.

① ⓐ, ⓒ, ⓓ      ② ⓐ, ⓒ, ⓔ
③ ⓒ, ⓔ, ⓕ      ④ ⓒ, ⓓ, ⓕ
⑤ ⓑ, ⓓ, ⓔ

[08~09] 다음 중 밑줄 친 부분의 쓰임이 나머지와 <u>다른</u> 것은?

**08** ① I wish I <u>could</u> speak Chinese.
② If she got good grades, she <u>could</u> go to the amusement park.
③ If he were rich, he <u>could</u> buy me the luxury car.
④ I <u>could</u> not help laughing at him yesterday evening.
⑤ If I had a passport, I <u>could</u> go to L.A. to watch the game.

**09** ① Do you like the cat <u>whose</u> hair is short?
② Shanon is the girl <u>whose</u> singing skill is at the highest level.
③ Do you remember the politician <u>whose</u> speech was so impressive?
④ We wondered <u>whose</u> book the thief stole.
⑤ I can't eat the pizza <u>whose</u> taste changed.

**10** 다음 중 같은 뜻을 가진 문장끼리 짝지어진 것은?

① My mom can't write a letter to my brother as she doesn't know his address.
= My mom couldn't write a letter to my brother if she didn't know his address.
② It rained, so we stayed home.
= If it rained, we wouldn't stay home.
③ Bobby doesn't work hard, so he can't make enough money he wants.
= If Bobby worked hard, he could make enough money he wants.
④ Tom didn't have a car, so he wouldn't drive.
= If Tom had a car, he would drive.
⑤ My uncle doesn't have a smartphone, so he wants to get one.
= My uncle would get a smartphone if he wanted to have one.

**11** 다음 중 어법상 옳은 문장은?

① Amy has a book of which cover is torn away.
② Mr. Parker invited me to the event whose organizer is unknown.
③ Laura is a good mom whose the kids respect her.
④ The young man of which the name is Peter came to see you.
⑤ The fish swam to the pond water of which is very dirty.

**12** 다음 중 어법상 <u>어색한</u> 것은?

① If I could be awarded the prize, my kids would be proud of me.
② If Mike had put on the glasses, he would have noticed her.
③ If Sujin got up earlier this morning, she wouldn't be late for school.
④ If Angelina missed the bus, she would not have been late for school.
⑤ If the girls told the truth to her, she would be surprised at what he did for her.

**13** 다음 짝지어진 두 문장의 의미가 같지 <u>않은</u> 것은?

① If Paul didn't run fast, he couldn't catch the first train.
= As Paul runs fast, he can catch the first train.

② If David told lies more often, I would not believe him.
= As David doesn't tell lies more often, I believe him.

③ I wish Kelly were a great singer.
= I'm sorry that she was not a great singer.

④ If my friends studied harder, they could get good grades.
= As my friends don't study harder, they can't get good grades.

⑤ I wish I could play the drums.
= I am sorry that I can't play the drums.

**[14~15]** 다음 주어진 두 문장을 관계대명사를 사용해서 하나의 문장으로 바르게 고친 것을 고르시오.

**14**
- The boy seemed to be embarrassed.
- His guitar was broken.

① The boy the guitar of which was broken seemed to be embarrassed.

② The boy whose the guitar was broken seemed to be embarrassed.

③ The boy who the guitar of his was broken seemed to be embarrassed.

④ The boy whose guitar was broken seemed to be embarrassed.

⑤ The boy whom the guitar was broken seemed to be embarrassed.

**15**
- More help is needed for small businesses.
- Their sales were damaged most during the crisis of Corona virus.

① More help is needed for small businesses the sales of whom were damaged most during the crisis of Corona virus.

② Small businesses whose help is needed were damaged most during the crisis of Corona virus.

③ More help is needed for small businesses of which sales were damaged most during the crisis of Corona virus.

④ Small businesses' sales were damaged most who are needed more help during the crisis of Corona virus.

⑤ More help is needed for small businesses whose sales were damaged most during the crisis of Corona virus.

**16** 다음 우리말을 영작할 때, 어법상 옳지 <u>않은</u> 문장을 고르시오.

물이 없다면, 지구에 생명체가 살 수 없을 것이다.

① If there were no water, life on Earth would not be able to live.

② If it were not for water, life on Earth would not be able to live.

③ Were it not for water, life on Earth would not be able to live.

④ If there is no water, life on Earth would not be able to live.

⑤ Without water, life on Earth would not be able to live.

**01** 다음 우리말과 일치하도록 괄호 안에 주어진 단어들을 빈칸에 알맞게 배열하시오.

(1) 내가 당신이라면, 당신의 머리카락을 잡아 당긴 사람에게 사탕을 줄 것이다. (would, pulled, to, sweets, who, were, I, you, the person, give)

➡ If I _____

_____ your hair.

(2) 우리나라에도 Birbal처럼 현명한 자가 있다면 정말 좋을 텐데. (if, as, would, were, great, wise, a man, be, there)

➡ It _____

as Birbal in our country.

(3) 그는 목이 매우 좁은 항아리 두 개를 들고 돌아왔다. (necks, narrow, whose, pots, were, two, really)

➡ He came back with _____

_____.

(4) 그들 중에는 Raja Birbal이라는 이름의 한 남자가 있었다. (was, whose, was, name, them, a man)

➡ Among _____

Raja Birbal.

**02** 다음 〈보기〉의 문장과 같은 뜻이 되도록 괄호 안에 주어진 조건에 맞게 빈칸을 채우시오.

┌── 보기 ├──

Without his wisdom, we could be in trouble with Persia.

(1) _____ his wisdom, we could be in trouble with Persia. (it, be동사 활용, 5 단어)

(2) _____ his wisdom, we could be in trouble with Persia. (it, be동사 활용, 4 단어)

(3) _____ his wisdom, we could be in trouble with Persia. (2 단어)

(4) _____ not be in trouble with Persia. (직설법, there, 접속사 as 활용, 7 단어)

**03** 다음 주어진 문장과 뜻이 같도록 빈칸을 알맞게 채우시오. (총 5 단어)

As the lady doesn't exercise regularly, she can't stay healthy.

➡ If the lady _____

_____ healthy.

**04** 다음 각 문장에서 어법상 어색한 단어를 한 개씩만 찾아 모두 고치시오.

(1) Amy has a book whose the pages are missing.

(2) My uncle ordered a table legs of which are very long.

(3) I played badminton after school with a friend who name is Tom.

(4) I would give sweets to the person whose pulled your hair.

(5) There is an officer who job is to check all the baggage at the airport.

(6) Grace bought a house which the roof was covered with grass.

➡ _____

_____

_____

[05~06] 다음 그림을 보고, 우리말에 맞게 괄호 안의 단어를 배열하여 빈칸을 채우시오.

**05**

다리가 네 개인 귀여운 몬스터가 나를 향해 손을 흔들었다.

➡ A cute monster the _____ me.

(wave, four, legs, which, at, of, are, 총 7 단어, 어형 변화 가능)

**06**

그녀의 눈이 피로한 한 소녀가 따뜻한 천으로 마사지를 하는 중이다.

➡ A girl _____ cloth.

(massage, is, with, whose, tired, warm, eyes, are, a / 총 9 단어, 어형 변화 가능)

**07** 다음 우리말을 괄호 안에 주어진 단어들을 사용하여 영작하시오. (필요시 단어를 추가할 수 있으나, 변형은 하지 말 것.)

(1) 나는 어머니가 매우 유명한 마술사인 친구가 있다. (magician, very, a friend, have, whose)

➡ _____

(2) 이것은 표지가 흑백인 잡지이다. (which, black and white, magazine, cover of)

➡ _____

(3) 내 남동생은 그의 영화를 당신이 본 배우이다. (an actor, film, watched, whose, little brother)

➡ _____

**08** 다음 각 가정법 문장에서 어법상 어색한 부분을 모두 찾아 바르게 고치시오.

(1) If I am the boss of the company, I would give every employee one month holidays.
(2) I wish I am as wise as Birbal.
(3) If you are in my situation, you would understand the decision.
(4) If I had a car, I can visit my aunt in Incheon more often.
(5) If it were not for the effort of the medical staff, we will not survive the disease.
(6) If there were no tests at school, I will be happy.
(7) Mary wouldn't be late for the meeting yesterday if she had not missed the bus.

➡ _____

Grammar **189**

# Reading

## Tales of Birbal

Akbar, the third Mogul emperor, had a number of wise officials at his court. Among them was a man whose name was Raja Birbal. He was famous for his quick wit and was very wise with his words. Thus, the emperor always liked to have Birbal near him.

### Sweet Punishment

To test his officials' wisdom, Akbar often asked them strange questions. One day, he came up with an interesting question.

**Akbar:** Someone pulled a hair from my head today. What should I do to him?

**Official 1:** He should be punished, of course.

**Official 2:** Yes, punish him!

Akbar turned to Birbal.

**Akbar:** What would you do if you were in my place, Birbal?

**Birbal:** If I were you, I would give him sweets.

**Official 3:** What's he talking about?

**Official 4:** Birbal's crazy!

**Akbar:** What made you say so?

**Birbal:** The person who pulled your hair must be your grandson. No one else could do such a thing.

**Akbar:** You are indeed correct, Birbal. I'm so glad to have someone as wise as you near me.

---

| emperor 황제 |
| a number of 많은 |
| wise 지혜로운, 현명한, 슬기로운 |
| official 고위 공무원, 관리 |
| court 대궐, 궁궐 |
| among ~ 중에, ~의 사이에 |
| wit 기지, 재치 |
| wisdom 지혜, 슬기, 현명함 |
| strange 이상한 |
| come up with 찾아내다, 떠올리다 |
| pull 끌다, 당기다, 끌어당기다 |
| punish 처벌하다, 벌주다 |

---

### 확인문제

● 다음 문장이 본문의 내용과 일치하면 T, 일치하지 않으면 F를 쓰시오.

1  Birbal was the third Mogul emperor. ☐

2  Akbar often asked his officials strange questions. ☐

3  Birbal thought that the officials were crazy. ☐

4  Akbar was glad to have Birbal near him. ☐

**A Potful of Wisdom**

One day, the king of Persia sent an official with a strange favor.

**Persian Official:** I hear you have a lot of wise men in your country. I've been asked by my king to bring him a potful of wisdom. <sub>현재완료 수동태</sub>

**Official 5:** That makes no sense! How can we put wisdom in a pot?

**Akbar:** Can you bring him a potful of wisdom, Birbal?

**Birbal:** It won't be a problem.

**Birbal:** Could you please wait a few weeks?

**Persian Official:** Of course! Take as much time as you need.
<sub>동등 비교</sub>

A few weeks later, Birbal came back with two pots whose necks were really narrow. He offered one to the Persian official.
<sub>a few+복수 명사</sub> <sub>소유격 관계대명사</sub>

**Birbal:** You can take this pot of wisdom to your king. Please ask him to return the pot to us after he takes the wisdom out of it.

**Birbal:** The pot is very precious, so please be careful not to break it. We only have two pots of wisdom.

The Persian official looked inside the pot and became speechless.
He thanked Birbal and left for his country.

**Persian Official:** It would be great if there were a man as wise as Birbal in our country.
<sub>가정법 과거</sub> <sub>동등 비교</sub>

After the Persian official left, Akbar asked Birbal what was inside the pot.

**Birbal:** Here is the other pot. You can see for yourself.
<sub>두 개 중에서 나머지 하나를 지칭</sub> <sub>직접 보다</sub> <sub>간접의문문(의문사+주어+동사)</sub>

Akbar looked inside the other pot and found a pumpkin just as big as the pot.

**Akbar:** I see! The pumpkin can't be taken out without breaking the pot. How did you do it?

**Birbal:** I put the pots over pumpkin flowers and waited until the pumpkins grew as big as the pots.
<sub>꼭 항아리만큼 큰 호박을 항아리 안에 넣은 것을 말함</sub> <sub>동등 비교</sub>

**Akbar:** Hahaha! This certainly is a potful of wisdom!

---

a potful of 한 냄비만큼의, 한 항아리만큼의
favor 청, 부탁
make sense 타당하다, 말이 되다
narrow 좁은
offer 내놓다, 제공하다
precious 귀중한, 값비싼
speechless (화나거나 놀라서) 말을 못하는
the other (둘 중) 다른 하나의
pumpkin 호박
without+동사-ing ~하지 않고
over (다른 사람·사물이 덮이도록) ~ 위에
certainly 틀림없이, 분명히

---

**확인문제**

● 다음 문장이 본문의 내용과 일치하면 T, 일치하지 않으면 F를 쓰시오.

1 A Persian Official was asked to bring his king a potful of wisdom. ☐

2 The Persian official looked at Birbal and became speechless. ☐

3 The pumpkin could be taken out without breaking the pot. ☐

● 우리말을 참고하여 빈칸에 알맞은 말을 쓰시오.

**1** _____ of Birbal

**2** Akbar, the third Mogul emperor, had _____ _____ _____ wise officials at his _____.

**3** Among them _____ a man _____ _____ was Raja Birbal.

**4** He was famous _____ his quick wit and was very wise _____ his words.

**5** _____, the emperor always liked _____ _____ Birbal _____ him.

**6** Sweet _____

**7** _____ _____ his officials' wisdom, Akbar often _____ _____ _____ _____.

**8** One day, he _____ _____ _____ an interesting question.

**9** Akbar: Someone pulled _____ _____ from my head today. What _____ _____ _____ _____ _____ him?

**10** Official 1: He should _____ _____, of course.

**11** Official 2: Yes, _____ him!

**12** Akbar _____ _____ Birbal.

**13** Akbar: What _____ you _____ _____ you _____ _____ _____ _____, Birbal?

**14** Birbal: _____ I _____ _____, I _____ _____ him sweets.

**15** Official 3: What's he _____ _____?

**16** Official 4: Birbal's _____!

**17** Akbar: _____ _____ _____ say so?

**18** Birbal: The person _____ pulled your hair _____ your grandson. No one _____ could do _____ _____ _____.

**19** Akbar: You are indeed correct, Birbal. I'm _____ glad _____ someone _____ _____ _____ you near me.

---

**1** 비르발 이야기

**2** 악바르는 무굴 제국의 제3대 황제로, 자신의 궁정에 많은 현명한 신하들이 있었다.

**3** 그 중 라자 비르발이라는 이름의 한 사람이 있었다.

**4** 그는 재빠른 재치로 유명했으며 말이 매우 지혜로웠다.

**5** 그래서, 황제는 언제나 비르발을 곁에 두기를 원했다.

**6** 달콤한 처벌

**7** 신하들의 지혜를 시험해 보기 위해, 악바르는 종종 그들에게 이상한 질문을 했다.

**8** 어느 날, 황제는 재미있는 질문이 생각났다.

**9** 악바르: 오늘 어떤 이가 내 머리에서 머리카락을 잡아당겼소. 이 자에게 무엇을 해야 하겠소?

**10** 신하 1: 당연히 처벌해야 합니다.

**11** 신하 2: 예, 그를 처벌하소서!

**12** 악바르가 비르발에게 돌아섰다.

**13** 악바르: 그대가 내 입장이라면 무엇을 하겠소, 비르발?

**14** 비르발: 소신이 폐하라면, 그에게 사탕을 주겠습니다.

**15** 신하 3: 저 사람은 무슨 말을 하는 건가?

**16** 신하 4: 비르발이 정신이 나갔어!

**17** 악바르: 왜 그렇게 말했소?

**18** 비르발: 폐하의 머리카락을 잡아당긴 사람은 폐하의 손자임이 분명합니다. 다른 그 누구도 그런 짓을 할 수 없지요.

**19** 악바르: 과연 그대의 말이 맞소, 비르발. 그대처럼 현명한 자를 옆에 두어 정말 기쁘오.

**20** A _____ of _____

**21** One day, the king of Persia sent an official _____ _____ _____.

**22** Persian Official: I hear you have _____ _____ wise men in your country. _____ _____ by my king _____ _____ him _____ _____ wisdom.

**23** Official 5: That _____ _____ _____! How can we _____ wisdom _____ a pot?

**24** Akbar: Can you bring him _____ _____ _____ _____ wisdom, Birbal?

**25** Birbal: It _____ _____ a problem.

**26** Birbal: Could you please wait _____ _____ weeks?

**27** Persian Official: Of course! Take _____ _____ _____ you need.

**28** _____ _____ weeks later, Birbal came back with two pots _____ necks were really narrow. He offered _____ to the Persian official.

**29** Birbal: You can _____ this pot of wisdom to your king. Please ask him _____ _____ the pot to us after he takes the wisdom _____ _____ _____ _____.

**30** Birbal: The pot is very precious, so please be careful _____ _____ _____ it. We only have two pots of wisdom.

**31** The Persian official looked inside the pot and became _____.

**32** He thanked Birbal and _____ _____ his country.

**33** Persian Official: It _____ _____ great _____ _____ a man _____ _____ _____ _____ Birbal in our country.

**34** After the Persian official left, Akbar asked Birbal _____ _____ inside the pot.

**35** Birbal: Here is _____ _____ pot. You can see _____ _____.

**36** Akbar looked inside _____ _____ pot and found a pumpkin just _____ _____ _____ the pot.

**37** Akbar: I see! The pumpkin _____ _____ _____ out _____ _____ the pot. How did you do it?

**38** Birbal: I put the pots _____ pumpkin flowers and waited until the pumpkins grew _____ _____ _____ the pots.

**39** Akbar: Hahaha! This certainly is _____ _____ wisdom!

---

**20** 한 항아리만큼의 지혜

**21** 어느 날, 페르시아의 왕이 이상한 요청과 함께 신하를 보냈다.

**22** 페르시아의 신하: 폐하의 나라에 현명한 자들이 많다고 들었습니다. 저는 저의 왕으로부터 한 항아리의 지혜를 왕께 가지고 오라는 명을 받았습니다.

**23** 신하 5: 저건 말이 안 되오! 어떻게 지혜를 항아리에 넣을 수 있단 말이오?

**24** 악바르: 그에게 지혜 한 항아리를 가져다줄 수 있겠소, 비르발?

**25** 비르발: 문제될 것이 없사옵니다.

**26** 비르발: 몇 주만 기다려 주시겠습니까?

**27** 페르시아의 신하: 물론이오! 필요한 만큼 얼마든지 시간을 가지시오.

**28** 몇 주 후, 비르발은 목이 매우 좁은 두 항아리를 들고 돌아왔다. 그는 하나를 페르시아의 신하에게 줬다.

**29** 비르발: 이 지혜의 항아리를 그대의 왕께 가져다 드리십시오. 왕께서 이 항아리에서 지혜를 꺼내신 후에는 항아리를 우리에게 돌려달라 전해 주십시오.

**30** 비르발: 그 항아리는 매우 귀중한 것이니, 그것을 깨지 않도록 조심해 주십시오. 우리는 오직 두 개의 지혜의 항아리만 갖고 있습니다.

**31** 페르시아 신하는 항아리 안을 들여다보곤 말을 잃었다.

**32** 그는 비르발에게 감사를 표한 뒤 그의 나라로 떠났다.

**33** 페르시아의 신하: 우리 나라에도 비르발처럼 현명한 자가 있다면 정말 좋을 텐데.

**34** 페르시아의 신하가 떠난 뒤, 악바르는 비르발에게 항아리 속에 무엇이 있었는지를 물었다.

**35** 비르발: 여기 또 다른 항아리가 있습니다. 직접 살펴보시지요.

**36** 악바르는 또 다른 항아리 안을 보고 꼭 항아리만큼 큰 호박을 발견했다.

**37** 악바르: 그렇군! 항아리를 깨지 않고는 호박을 꺼낼 수가 없구려! 어떻게 한 것이오?

**38** 비르발: 항아리를 호박꽃에 덮어 놓은 후 호박이 항아리만큼 클 때까지 기다렸습니다.

**39** 악바르: 하하하! 이건 정말로 지혜의 항아리구려!

● 우리말을 참고하여 본문을 영작하시오.

**1** 비르발 이야기
➡ _____

**2** 악바르는 무굴 제국의 제3대 황제로, 자신의 궁정에 많은 현명한 신하들이 있었다.
➡ _____

**3** 그 중 라자 비르발이라는 이름의 한 사람이 있었다.
➡ _____

**4** 그는 재빠른 재치로 유명했으며 말이 매우 지혜로웠다.
➡ _____

**5** 그래서, 황제는 언제나 비르발을 곁에 두기를 원했다.
➡ _____

**6** 달콤한 처벌
➡ _____

**7** 신하들의 지혜를 시험해 보기 위해, 악바르는 종종 그들에게 이상한 질문을 했다.
➡ _____

**8** 어느 날, 황제는 재미있는 질문이 생각났다.
➡ _____

**9** 악바르: 오늘 어떤 이가 내 머리에서 머리카락을 잡아당겼소. 이 자에게 무엇을 해야 하겠소?
➡ _____

**10** 신하 1: 당연히 처벌해야 합니다.
➡ _____

**11** 신하 2: 예, 그를 처벌하소서!
➡ _____

**12** 악바르가 비르발에게 돌아섰다.
➡ _____

**13** 악바르: 그대가 내 입장이라면 무엇을 하겠소, 비르발?
➡ _____

**14** 비르발: 소신이 폐하라면, 그에게 사탕을 주겠습니다.
➡ _____

**15** 신하 3: 저 사람은 무슨 말을 하는 건가?
➡ _____

**16** 신하 4: 비르발이 정신이 나갔어!
➡ _____

**17** 악바르: 왜 그렇게 말했소?
➡ _____

**18** 비르발: 폐하의 머리카락을 잡아당긴 사람은 폐하의 손자임이 분명합니다. 다른 그 누구도 그런 짓을 할 수 없지요.
➡ _____

**19** 악바르: 과연 그대의 말이 맞소, 비르발. 그대처럼 현명한 자를 옆에 두어 정말 기쁘오.
➡ _____

**20** 한 항아리만큼의 지혜
➡

**21** 어느 날, 페르시아의 왕이 이상한 요청과 함께 신하를 보냈다.
➡

**22** 페르시아의 신하: 폐하의 나라에 현명한 자들이 많다고 들었습니다. 저는 저의 왕으로부터 한 항아리의 지혜를 왕께 가지고 오라는 명을 받았습니다.
➡

**23** 신하 5: 저건 말이 안 되오! 어떻게 지혜를 항아리에 넣을 수 있단 말이오?
➡

**24** 악바르: 그에게 지혜 한 항아리를 가져다줄 수 있겠소, 비르발?
➡

**25** 비르발: 문제될 것이 없사옵니다.
➡

**26** 몇 주만 기다려 주시겠습니까?
➡

**27** 페르시아의 신하: 물론이오! 필요한 만큼 얼마든지 시간을 가지시오.
➡

**28** 몇 주 후, 비르발은 목이 매우 좁은 두 항아리를 들고 돌아왔다. 그는 하나를 페르시아의 신하에게 줬다.
➡

**29** 비르발: 이 지혜의 항아리를 그대의 왕께 가져다 드리십시오. 왕께서 이 항아리에서 지혜를 꺼내신 후에는 항아리를 우리에게 돌려달라 전해 주십시오.
➡

**30** 비르발: 그 항아리는 매우 귀중한 것이니, 그것을 깨지 않도록 조심해 주십시오. 우리는 오직 두 개의 지혜의 항아리만 갖고 있습니다.
➡

**31** 페르시아 신하는 항아리 안을 들여다보곤 말을 잃었다.
➡

**32** 그는 비르발에게 감사를 표한 뒤 그의 나라로 떠났다.
➡

**33** 페르시아의 신하: 우리 나라에도 비르발처럼 현명한 자가 있다면 정말 좋을 텐데.
➡

**34** 페르시아의 신하가 떠난 뒤, 악바르는 비르발에게 항아리 속에 무엇이 있었는지를 물었다.
➡

**35** 비르발: 여기 또 다른 항아리가 있습니다. 직접 살펴보시지요.
➡

**36** 악바르는 또 다른 항아리 안을 보고 꼭 항아리만큼 큰 호박을 발견했다.
➡

**37** 악바르: 그렇군! 항아리를 깨지 않고는 호박을 꺼낼 수가 없구려! 어떻게 한 것이오?
➡

**38** 비르발: 항아리를 호박꽃에 덮어 놓은 후 호박이 항아리만큼 클 때까지 기다렸습니다.
➡

**39** 악바르: 하하하! 이건 정말로 지혜의 항아리구려!
➡

**[01~03]** 다음 글을 읽고 물음에 답하시오.

Akbar, the third Mogul emperor, had a number of wise officials at his court. Among them was a man whose name was Raja Birbal. He was famous for his quick wit and was very ⓐwise with his words. Thus, the emperor always liked to have Birbal near him.

**Sweet Punishment**

To ⓑtest his officials' wisdom, Akbar often asked them strange questions. One day, he came up with an ⓒinteresting question.

Akbar: Someone pulled a hair from my head today. What should I do to him?

Official 1: He should be punished, of course.

Official 2: Yes, punish him!

Akbar turned to Birbal.

Akbar: What would you do if you were in my place, Birbal?

Birbal: If I were you, I would give him sweets.

Official 3: What's he talking about?

Official 4: Birbal's ___(A)___ !

Akbar: What made you say so?

Birbal: The person who pulled your hair ⓓshould be your grandson. No one else could do such a thing.

Akbar: You are indeed correct, Birbal. I'm so ⓔglad to have someone as wise as you near me.

**01** 위 글의 빈칸 (A)에 들어갈 알맞은 말을 고르시오.

① reasonable     ② crazy
③ sensible       ④ fair
⑤ logical

**02** 위 글의 밑줄 친 ⓐ~ⓔ 중 잘못 쓰인 것을 고르시오.

① ⓐ     ② ⓑ     ③ ⓒ     ④ ⓓ     ⑤ ⓔ

**03** According to the passage, which is NOT true?

① Akbar was the third Mogul emperor.
② Raja Birbal was famous for his quick wit and was very wise with his words.
③ One day, Akbar said that someone had pulled a hair from his head.
④ Birbal said that he would give sweets to the man who had pulled his hair.
⑤ Officials asked Akbar to praise the man who had pulled his hair.

**[04~06]** 다음 글을 읽고 물음에 답하시오.

One day, ①the king of Persia sent an official with a strange favor.

Persian Official: I hear you have ⓐa lot of wise men in your country. I've been asked by my king to bring ②him a potful of wisdom.

Official 5: That makes no sense! How can we put wisdom in a pot?

Akbar: Can you bring ③him a potful of wisdom, Birbal?

Birbal: It won't be a problem.

Birbal: Could you please wait a few weeks?

Persian Official: Of course! Take as much time as you need.

A few weeks later, Birbal came back with two pots ___(A)___ necks were really narrow. ④He offered one to the Persian official.

Birbal: You can take this pot of wisdom to your king. Please ask ⑤him to return the pot to us after he takes the wisdom out of it.

**04** 위 글의 빈칸 (A)에 들어갈 알맞은 말을 고르시오.

① what  ② who  ③ whose
④ which  ⑤ that

**05** 위 글의 밑줄 친 ⓐa lot of 대신 쓸 수 없는 것을 고르시오.

① a deal of  ② lots of
③ a number of  ④ many
⑤ plenty of

**06** 위 글의 밑줄 친 ①~⑤ 중에서 가리키는 대상이 다른 것을 고르시오.

①  ②  ③  ④  ⑤

[07~09] 다음 글을 읽고 물음에 답하시오.

Birbal: The pot is very precious, so please be careful not to break it. We only have two pots of wisdom.
　The Persian official looked inside the pot and became ___ⓐ___.
　He thanked Birbal and left for his country.
Persian Official: It would be great if there were a man as wise as Birbal in our country.
　After the Persian official left, Akbar asked Birbal what was inside the pot.
Birbal: Here is the other pot. (①)
　Akbar looked inside the other pot and found a pumpkin just as big as the pot.
Akbar: I see! (②) ⓑThe pumpkin can't take out without breaking the pot. How did you do it? (③)
Birbal: I put the pots over pumpkin flowers and waited until the pumpkins grew as big as the pots. (④)
Akbar: Hahaha! (⑤) This certainly is a potful of wisdom!

**07** 주어진 영영풀이를 참고하여 빈칸 ⓐ에 철자 s로 시작하는 단어를 쓰시오.

temporarily unable to speak

➡ _____

**08** 위 글의 흐름으로 보아, 주어진 문장이 들어가기에 가장 적절한 곳은?

You can see for yourself.

①  ②  ③  ④  ⑤

**09** 위 글의 밑줄 친 ⓑ에서 어색한 것을 찾아 바르게 고치시오.

_____ ➡ _____

[10~13] 다음 글을 읽고 물음에 답하시오.

　To test his officials' wisdom, Akbar often asked them strange questions. One day, he ⓐcame up with an interesting question.
Akbar: Someone pulled a hair from my head today. What should I do to him?
Official 1: He should be punished, of course.
Official 2: Yes, punish him!
　Akbar turned to Birbal.
Akbar: What would you do if you were in my place, Birbal?
Birbal: If I (A)[am / were] you, I would give him sweets.
Official 3: What's he talking about?
Official 4: Birbal's crazy!
Akbar: ⓑ왜 그렇게 말했소?
Birbal: The person (B)[which / who] pulled your hair must be your grandson. No one else could do such a thing.
Akbar: You are indeed correct, Birbal. I'm so glad to have someone as (C)[wise / wiser] as you near me.

서답형

**10** 위 글의 괄호 (A)~(C)에서 어법상 알맞은 낱말을 골라 쓰시오.

➡ (A) _____ (B) _____ (C) _____

**11** Which question CANNOT be answered after reading the passage?

① Why did Akbar often ask strange questions of his officials?

② Did Official 1,2,3,4 answer correctly?

③ Why did Akbar's grandson pull his hair?

④ Who pulled Akbar's hair?

⑤ Why was Akbar glad?

**12** 위 글의 밑줄 친 ⓐcame up with와 다른 의미로 쓰인 것을 고르시오.

① I can't come up with any creative ideas.

② I must come up with an excuse.

③ I hope you can come up with a better idea than this.

④ How long does it take for you to come up with a song?

⑤ How soon can you come up with the money?

서답형

**13** 위 글의 밑줄 친 ⓑ의 우리말을 make를 이용하여 5 단어로 영작하시오.

➡ _____

[14~16] 다음 글을 읽고 물음에 답하시오.

One day, the king of Persia sent an official with a strange favor.

**Persian Official:** I hear you have a lot of wise men in your country. I've been asked by my king ⓐto bring him a potful of wisdom.

**Official 5:** That makes no sense! How can we put wisdom in a pot?

**Akbar:** Can you bring him a potful of wisdom, Birbal?

**Birbal:** _____ (A) _____

**Birbal:** Could you please wait a few weeks?

**Persian Official:** Of course! Take as __(B)__ as you need.

**14** 위 글의 빈칸 (A)에 들어갈 말로 적절한 것은?

① How can I do that?

② It won't be a problem.

③ Why do you think I can do it?

④ Don't ask me such a question.

⑤ It can't be done.

**15** 위 글의 빈칸 (B)에 들어갈 말로 알맞은 것은?

① much time      ② more time

③ less time      ④ few time

⑤ little time

**16** 〈보기〉에서 밑줄 친 ⓐto bring과 문법적 쓰임이 같은 것의 개수를 고르시오.

┌─ 보기 ─┐

① Don't forget to bring your books with you.

② I didn't know how much to bring.

③ We went there to bring the equipment.

④ It is the first step to bring you success.

⑤ It is better not to bring the matter up.

① 1개   ② 2개   ③ 3개   ④ 4개   ⑤ 5개

[17~21] 다음 글을 읽고 물음에 답하시오.

A few weeks later, Birbal came back with two pots whose necks were really narrow. He offered one to the Persian official.

**Birbal:** You can take this pot of wisdom to your king. Please ask him to return the pot to us after he takes the wisdom out of it.

**Birbal:** The pot is very precious, so please be careful not to break it. We only have two pots of wisdom.

The Persian official looked inside the pot and became speechless.

He thanked Birbal and left _____ⓐ_____ his country.

**Persian Official:** (A)우리 나라에도 비르발처럼 현명한 자가 있다면 정말 좋을 텐데.

After the Persian official left, Akbar asked Birbal what was inside the pot.

**Birbal:** Here is _____ⓑ_____ pot. You can see for yourself.

Akbar looked inside _____ⓑ_____ pot and found a pumpkin just as big as the pot.

**Akbar:** I see! The pumpkin can't be taken out without breaking the pot. How did you do it?

**Birbal:** I put the pots over pumpkin flowers and waited until the pumpkins grew as big as the pots.

**Akbar:** Hahaha! This certainly is a potful of wisdom!

**17** 다음 중 위 글의 빈칸 ⓐ에 들어갈 말과 같은 말이 들어가는 것은?

① Everyone is worried _____ their food.

② A boy needs a father he can look up _____.

③ I always think of you _____ one of my family.

④ She was tired _____ hearing about their trip to India.

⑤ She moved back home to care _____ her elderly parents.

**18** 위 글의 빈칸 ⓑ에 공통으로 들어갈 말로 알맞은 것은?

① other        ② the another    ③ others
④ the other    ⑤ the others

**서답형**

**19** What did Birbal ask the Persian official to do? (Two things.)

➡ _____

_____

**서답형**

**20** 위 글의 밑줄 친 (A)의 우리말에 맞게 주어진 어휘를 알맞게 배열하여 영작하시오.

> Birbal, in our country, it, a man, if, be, were, would, wise, great, there, as, as

➡ _____

_____

**중요**

**21** According to the passage, which is NOT true?

① The Persian official became speechless when he took a look at the inside of the pot.

② The Persian official wished to have a wise man like Birbal.

③ Birbal asked the Persian official to be careful not to break the pot as they had only one.

④ The pumpkin couldn't be taken out without breaking the pot.

⑤ Birbal put the pots over pumpkin flowers and waited until the pumpkins grew as big as the pots.

**[01~03]** 다음 글을 읽고 물음에 답하시오.

Akbar, the third Mogul emperor, had a number of wise officials at his court. Among them was a man whose name was Raja Birbal. He was famous for his quick wit and was very wise with his words. Thus, the emperor always liked to have Birbal near him.

**Sweet Punishment**

To test his officials' wisdom, Akbar often asked them strange questions. One day, he came up with an interesting question.

**Akbar:** Someone pulled a hair from my head today. What should I do to him?

**Official 1:** He should be punished, of course.

**Official 2:** Yes, punish him!

Akbar turned to Birbal.

**Akbar:** What would you do if you were ⓐ내 입장이라면, Birbal?

**Birbal:** ⓑ소신이 폐하라면, 그에게 사탕을 주겠습니다. (I, you, were, give sweets)

**Official 3:** What's he talking about?

**Official 4:** Birbal's crazy!

**Akbar:** What made you say so?

**Birbal:** The person who pulled your hair <u>must</u> be your grandson. No one else could do such a thing.

**Akbar:** You are indeed correct, Birbal. I'm so glad to have someone as wise as you near me.

**01** 밑줄 친 ⓐ의 우리말에 맞게 place를 이용하여 세 단어를 쓰시오.

➡ _____

**02** 밑줄 친 ⓑ의 우리말에 맞게 주어진 어휘를 이용하여 9 단어로 영작하시오.

➡ _____

**03** Who pulled Akbar's hair? Answer in English with 5 words.

➡ _____

**[04~06]** 다음 글을 읽고 물음에 답하시오.

One day, the king of Persia sent an official with a strange favor.

**Persian Official:** I hear you have a lot of wise men in your country. I've been asked by my king to bring him a potful of wisdom.

**Official 5:** ⓐThat makes no sense!
_____(A)_____

**Akbar:** Can you bring him a potful of wisdom, Birbal?

**Birbal:** It won't be a problem.

**Birbal:** Could you please wait a few weeks?

**Persian Official:** Of course! Take as much time as you need.

**04** 위 글의 빈칸 (A)에 'We can't put wisdom in a pot.'이라는 의미의 말을 how를 이용한 의문문으로 쓰시오.

➡ _____

**05** 위 글의 밑줄 친 ⓐThat이 가리키는 것을 20자 내외의 우리 말로 쓰시오.

➡ _____

**06** What was the Persian official asked to do by his king?

➡ _____

[07~10] 다음 글을 읽고 물음에 답하시오.

A few weeks later, Birbal came back with two pots whose necks were really narrow. He offered one to the Persian official.

**Birbal:** You can take this pot of wisdom to your king. Please ask him ____ⓐ____ the pot to us after he takes the wisdom out of it.

**Birbal:** The pot is very precious, so please be careful not to break it. We only have two pots of wisdom.

The Persian official looked inside the pot and became speechless.

He thanked Birbal and left for his country.

**Persian Official:** ⓑIt would be great if there were a man as wise as Birbal in our country.

After the Persian official left, Akbar asked Birbal what was inside the pot.

**Birbal:** Here is the other pot. You can see for yourself.

Akbar looked inside the other pot and found a pumpkin just as big as the pot.

**Akbar:** I see! The pumpkin can't be taken out without breaking the pot. How did you do it?

**Birbal:** I put the pots over pumpkin flowers and waited until the pumpkins grew as big as the pots.

**Akbar:** Hahaha! This certainly is a potful of wisdom!

**07** 빈칸 ⓐ에 return을 알맞은 형태로 쓰시오.

➡ _____

**08** 위 글의 밑줄 친 ⓑ를 as를 이용하여 고쳐 쓰시오.

➡ _____
_____

**09** What was inside the pot when Akbar looked inside the other pot?

➡ _____

**10** 위 글의 내용과 일치하도록 다음 빈칸 (A)와 (B)에 알맞은 단어를 쓰시오.

Birbal offered the Persian official a pot which (A)_____ _____ was in. When the Persian official looked inside the pot, he (B)_____ _____.

[11~13] 다음 글을 읽고 물음에 답하시오.

**Tales of Birbal**

Akbar, the third Mogul emperor, had a number of wise officials at his court. ⓐ그 중 Raja Birbal이라는 이름의 한 사람이 있었다.(Among으로 시작, name) He was famous for his quick wit and was very wise with his words. ___(A)___, the emperor always liked to have Birbal near him.

**11** 위 글의 빈칸 (A)에 알맞은 말을 한 단어로 쓰시오.

➡ _____

 **12** 위 글의 밑줄 친 ⓐ의 우리말을 주어진 어휘를 이용하여 10 단어로 영작하시오.

➡ _____
_____

**13** What was Birbal famous for?

➡ _____

## Link

**A Shorter Line**

One day, Emperor Akbar drew a line on the ground and asked his officials.

**Akbar:** Make this line shorter without touching it.
전치사 뒤에 동명사

**Official 1:** Without touching it?
= the line that Emperor Akbar drew

**Official 2:** How can we do that?
= make the line shorter without touching it

Birbal smiled.

**Birbal:** That's too easy.
부사(너무)

Birbal drew a longer line next to the line that Akbar had drawn.
주격 관계대명사    대과거

**Birbal:** Your line is now shorter than mine.
= my line

**Akbar:** You did it, Birbal!

**Official 3:** I wish I were as wise as Birbal.
가정법        동등 비교

구문해설  • **next to:** ~ 옆에  • **wise:** 현명한

## Write

Dear Jaeha,

Time flies. I cannot believe that it is time to say goodbye. I still remember the
형용사적 용법
time when we went camping together. I really liked the movie we watched that
관계부사(= at which)                              목적격 관계대명사 that 또는 which 생략
night. I also loved playing basketball with you after school. I really want to
= to play
thank you for teaching me basketball skills. If I could turn back time, I would
전치사 뒤에 나온 동명사                              가정법 과거 = As I can't turn back time. I won't ~.
spend more time with you. I hope we keep in touch even after we graduate.

Best,

Jake

구문해설  • **go ~ing:** ~하러 가다  • **thank A for B:** B에 대하여 A에게 감사하다
• **spend time with A:** A와 시간을 보내다  • **graduate:** 졸업하다

## Culture Project

When my brother failed his driving test seven times, he was very disappointed.
감정(과거분사)
Kento, his friend from Japan, said to him, "If I were you, I wouldn't give up.
동격                        가정법 과거
Fall seven times, stand up eight." It's a Japanese saying that means "Do not
주격 관계대명사+동사 (meaning으로 전환 가능)
give up." My brother tried again and finally passed.
과거시제 병렬구조

구문해설  • **saying:** 격언, 속담  • **finally:** 마침내

해석

**더 짧은 선**

어느 날, 악바르 황제는 땅에 선을 그린 뒤 그의 신하들에게 물었다.

악바르: 이 선을 건드리지 않은 채 더 짧게 만들어 보게.

신하 1: 건드리지 않고 말씀입니까?

신하 2: 어떻게 그렇게 할 수 있습니까?

비르발은 미소를 지었다.

비르발: 너무 쉽군요.

비르발은 악바르가 그린 선 옆에 더 긴 선을 그렸다.

비르발: 폐하의 선이 이제 제 선보다 짧습니다.

악바르: 그대가 해냈소, 비르발!

신하 3: 제가 비르발만큼 지혜롭다면 좋겠군요.

재하에게,

시간 정말 빠르다. 작별 인사를 해야 할 시간이라는 게 믿어지지 않아. 아직도 우리가 함께 캠핑을 갔던 때가 생각나. 우리가 그날 밤에 봤던 영화를 정말 좋아했는데. 너와 방과 후에 농구를 하는 것도 정말로 좋아했어. 농구 기술들을 가르쳐 줘서 정말로 고맙다고 말하고 싶어. 시간을 되돌아갈 수 있다면. 너와 함께 더 많은 시간을 보낼 거야. 우리가 졸업한 뒤에도 계속 연락을 하면 좋겠다.

Jake가.

내 오빠가 운전 면허 시험에서 일곱 번 떨어졌을 때, 그는 매우 실망했습니다. 일본에서 온 그의 친구 Kento는 그에게, "내가 너라면, 포기하지 않을 거야. 일곱 번 넘어져도 여덟 번 일어나야지."하고 말했습니다. 이것은 "포기하지 마라."라는 뜻의 일본 격언입니다. 오빠는 다시 도전해 마침내 통과했습니다.

## Words & Expressions

**01** 〈보기〉의 밑줄 친 어휘와 같은 의미로 쓰인 것을 고르시오.

> ┤ 보기 ├
> Akbar, the third Mogul emperor, had a number of wise officials at his court.

① They often performed for the royal court.
② Prisoners are taken to court under police escort.
③ They marked out a tennis court on the lawn.
④ You must court an opportunity.
⑤ The court judged him guilty.

**02** 다음 영영풀이에 해당하는 단어를 주어진 철자로 시작하여 빈칸에 쓰고, 알맞은 것을 골라 문장을 완성하시오.

> • h_____ : the quality of being honest
> • w_____ : the ability to use your experience and knowledge in order to make sensible decisions or judgments

(1) She is a woman of great _____.
(2) Where is there dignity unless there is _____?

**03** 다음 빈칸에 〈영영풀이〉에 해당하는 어휘를 주어진 철자로 시작하여 쓰시오.

> Would you do me a f_____?

> <영영풀이> something that you do for someone in order to help them or be kind to them

➡ _____

**04** 괄호 안에 주어진 어휘를 이용하여 빈칸에 알맞게 쓰시오.

> • Even things that appear _____ have their use. (worth)
> • A number of _____ works of art were stolen from the gallery. (price)

**05** 다음 문장에 공통으로 들어갈 말을 고르시오.

> • Phone them up and find _____ when they are coming.
> • The report turned _____ to be false information.
> • I can't figure _____ how to do this.

① from        ② with        ③ out
④ to          ⑤ of

**Conversation**

**[06~07]** 다음 대화를 읽고 물음에 답하시오.

B: Wow, you play the guitar so well.
(A) (a)굉장한 가족이다! I wish I could play the guitar like you.
(B) Really? Does your father play the guitar, too?
(C) Yes. He was in a famous band.
(D) Thanks. I love playing the guitar. I learned it from my dad.

**06** 주어진 문장에 이어질 대화의 순서로 알맞은 것은?

① (B) – (A) – (C) – (D)
② (C) – (B) – (A) – (D)
③ (C) – (B) – (D) – (A)
④ (D) – (B) – (A) – (C)
⑤ (D) – (B) – (C) – (A)

**08** 다음 중 짝지어진 대화가 <u>어색한</u> 것은?

① A: Don't judge a book by its cover.
   B: Do you mean we should not judge others by their looks?
② A: The early bird catches the worm.
   B: No. The early bird gets tired quickly.
③ A: People say, "Yesterday is history, tomorrow is a mystery, and today is a gift. That's why it's called the present."
   B: Now I see. You know so many great expressions. You're as wise as my grandma.
④ A: You look worried. Is something wrong?
   B: I handed in my science report in time.
⑤ A: Do you mean everyone has a chance for success?
   B: Yes, that's what I mean.

**[09~11]** 다음 대화를 읽고 물음에 답하시오.

B: Wow, you really dance well.
G: Thanks. I love dancing. Everyone in my family (A)[is / are] good at dancing.
B: Really? Your parents dance well, (B)[either / too]?
G: Yes. They're also good singers.
B: What a family! I (C)[want / wish] I could dance like you.

**07** 위 대화의 밑줄 친 (a)의 우리말을 3 단어로 영작하시오.

➡ _____

**09** 위 대화의 괄호 (A)~(C)에서 알맞은 말을 고르시오.

➡ (A) _____ (B) _____ (C) _____

**10** What does everyone in the girl's family do well?

➡ _____

**11** What does the boy wish?

➡ _____

**12** 다음 주어진 두 문장을 관계대명사를 사용해서 하나의 문장으로 바르게 고친 것을 고르시오.

> • Sammy has a rabbit.
> • The rabbit's tail is very short.

① Sammy has a rabbit which tail is very short.
② Sammy has a rabbit whose tail is very short.
③ Sammy has a rabbit of which tail is very short.
④ Sammy has a rabbit that tail is very short.
⑤ Sammy has a rabbit which of the tail is very short.

**13** 다음 중 밑줄 친 부분의 쓰임이 〈보기〉와 같은 것은?

> ┤ 보기 ├
> I couldn't finish it if it were not for your help.

① Janet will ask me if Seohyun is in good condition.
② They wonder if Charles is at home.
③ Our country would be in trouble if there were no wise men.
④ Carol used to wonder if God exists.
⑤ We don't know if the soccer finals will be canceled because of the weather.

**14** 다음 주어진 문장을 가정법으로 바르게 고친 것은?

> As my daughters didn't return the books to the library, I had to pay the late fee.

① If my daughters returned the books to the library, I wouldn't have to pay the late fee.
② If my daughters returned the books to the library, I would have had to pay the late fee.
③ If my daughters had returned the books to the library, I wouldn't have to pay the late fee.
④ If my daughters had returned the books to the library, I wouldn't have had to pay the late fee.
⑤ If my daughters had returned the books to the library, I would have had to pay the late fee.

**15** 다음 〈보기〉와 같이 직설법 문장을 가정법으로 고치시오.

> ┌─── 보기 ───┐
> As I am not rich, I can't buy the bike.
> → If I were rich, I could buy the bike.

(1) As I am not Birbal, I can't answer the difficult question of the king.

➡ _____

_____

(2) As Bentley doesn't wear a skirt, he won't look like a girl.

➡ _____

(3) As there is no kettle, I can't boil and drink my tea.

➡ _____

(4) As Michelle has the glasses, it is easy for her to read the books.

➡ _____

_____

[16~17] 다음 우리말에 맞게 영작한 것을 고르시오.

**16**

> Teddy는 아버지가 완고한 여자 친구와 결혼하려고 결심했다.

① Teddy decided to marry the girl friend whose father was strict.
② Teddy decided to marry the girl friend who was her father strict.
③ Teddy decided to marry the girl friend of whom father was strict.
④ Teddy decided to marry the girl friend with whose father being strict.
⑤ Teddy decided to marry the girl friend the father of whom was strict.

**17**

> 비가 충분히 온다면 가뭄 걱정을 덜 수 있을 텐데.

① If it didn't rain enough, we could ease our concern for drought.
② If it had rained enough, we could have eased our concern for drought.
③ Had it rained enough, we could ease our concern for drought.
④ Did it rain enough, we can ease our concern for drought.
⑤ If it rained enough, we could ease our concern for drought.

**18** 다음 문장의 빈칸 (A)~(C)에 들어갈 말로 가장 적절한 것은?

> • If I (A)_____ a boyfriend, I would not eat alone.
> • If it were not for the thick trees, the bitter wind (B)_____ blow the house to pieces.
> • If the waiting time (C)_____ over, I will take part in the battle.

| | (A) | (B) | (C) |
|---|---|---|---|
| ① | have | will | will be |
| ② | have | would | were |
| ③ | had | could | were |
| ④ | had | would | is |
| ⑤ | have had | will | is |

**Reading**

**[19~21]** 다음 글을 읽고 물음에 답하시오.

_____(A)_____

To test his officials' wisdom, Akbar often asked them strange questions. One day, he came up with an interesting question.

Akbar: Someone pulled a hair from my head today. What should I do to him?

Official 1: He should be punished, of course.

Official 2: Yes, punish him!

Akbar turned to Birbal.

Akbar: (B)그대가 내 입장이라면 무엇을 하겠소, Birbal?

Birbal: If I were you, I would give him sweets.

Official 3: ⓐWhat's he talking about?

Official 4: ⓑBirbal's crazy!

Akbar: What made you say so?

Birbal: The person who pulled your hair must be your grandson. No one else could do such a thing.

Akbar: You are indeed correct, Birbal. I'm so glad to have someone as wise as you near me.

**19** 위 글의 빈칸 (A)에 제목으로 알맞은 것을 고르시오.

① Whom to Blame
② Sweet Punishment
③ How to Test Wisdom
④ Harsh Punishment
⑤ Crazy Birbal

**20** 위 글의 밑줄 친 (B)의 우리말에 맞게 주어진 어휘를 이용하여 10 단어로 영작하시오.

place, would, if, in

➡ _____

**21** 밑줄 친 ⓐ와 ⓑ가 의미하는 것을 sense를 이용하여 4 단어의 영어로 쓰시오.

➡ _____

**[22~24]** 다음 글을 읽고 물음에 답하시오.

**A Potful of Wisdom**

One day, the king of Persia sent an official with a strange ⓐfavor.

Persian Official: I hear you have ①a deal of wise men in your country. I've been asked by my king to bring him a potful of wisdom.

Official 5: That makes ②sense! How can we put wisdom in a pot?

Akbar: Can you bring him a potful of wisdom, Birbal?

Birbal: It won't be a ③matter.

Birbal: Could you please wait ④a little weeks?

Persian Official: Of course! Take as ⑤many time as you need.

**22** 위 글의 밑줄 친 ⓐfavor와 같은 의미로 쓰인 것을 고르시오.

① Could you do me a favor and pick up Sam from school today?
② Many countries favor a presidential system of government.
③ I offer you my heartfelt thanks for your favor.
④ The ladies received compacts as favors at the banquet.
⑤ He escaped under favor of night.

**23** 위 글의 밑줄 친 ①~⑤에서 흐름상 어색하지 <u>않은</u> 것을 고르시오.

   ①      ②      ③      ④      ⑤

**24** According to the passage, which is NOT true?

① The Persian official came with a strange favor.

② The king of Persia told the Persian official to bring him a potful of wisdom.

③ Official 5 thought that putting wisdom in a pot was impossible.

④ Birbal thought he could bring the Persian official a potful of wisdom.

⑤ The Persian official allowed little time to take.

[25~27] 다음 글을 읽고 물음에 답하시오.

Dear Jaeha,

  Time flies. I cannot believe that it is time to say goodbye. I still remember the time when we went camping together. I really liked the movie we watched that night. I also loved

playing basketball with you after school. I really want to thank you for teaching me basketball skills. (A)시간을 되돌아갈 수 있다면, 너와 함께 더 많은 시간을 보낼 거야.(turn back, time, spend) I hope we _____ⓐ_____ even after we graduate.

                      Best,

                      Jake

**25** 주어진 영영풀이에 해당하는 표현을 빈칸 ⓐ에 touch를 포함하여 3 단어로 써 넣으시오.

> communicate with somebody regularly

➡ _____

**26** 위 글의 밑줄 친 (A)의 우리말에 맞게 괄호 안에 주어진 어휘를 이용하여 13 단어로 영작하시오.

➡ _____

_____

**27** What does Jake still remember?

➡ _____

_____

## 출제율 95%

**01** 다음 중 짝지어진 단어의 관계가 나머지와 <u>다른</u> 것은?

① hopeful – hopeless
② valueless – priceless
③ valuable – precious
④ powerful – powerless
⑤ useful – useless

## 출제율 100%

**02** 밑줄 친 부분의 의미로 알맞지 <u>않은</u> 것은?

① This is your last chance to enter the <u>correct</u> password. (맞는, 정확한)
② The restaurant <u>offers</u> traditional home cooking. (내놓다, 제공하다)
③ Parents should <u>punish</u> their children in a proper way. (칭찬하다)
④ He wanted to become the <u>emperor</u> of Rome. (황제)
⑤ I've been asked by my king to bring him <u>a potful of</u> wisdom. (한 항아리만큼의)

## 출제율 95%

**03** 다음 밑줄 친 단어와 바꿔 쓸 수 있는 것은?

> <u>Priceless</u> antiques were destroyed in the fire.

① Worthless        ② Valueless
③ Useless          ④ Cheap
⑤ Invaluable

## 출제율 95%

**04** 다음 주어진 우리말에 맞게 빈칸을 채우시오. (철자가 주어진 경우 주어진 철자로 시작할 것)

(1) 그것을 다시 하는 것은 이해가 안 된다.
➡ It doesn't make _____ to do it again.

(2) 경험은 지혜의 아버지이고 기억의 어머니이다.
➡ Experience is the father of _____ and the mother of memory.

(3) 그 상점은 매월 무료 선물을 제공한다.
➡ The store p_____ a free gift every month.

**[05~07]** 다음 대화를 읽고 물음에 답하시오.

Anna: What's wrong? You don't look so good.
Suho: I'm still thinking about our soccer match last week.
Anna: Do you mean the game you lost last week?
Suho: Yes. I wish I could forget about it, but I can't.
Anna: Well, (A)넌 항상 오늘을 위해 살아야 해.
Suho: Do you mean I should forget the past and focus on the present?
Anna: (①) People say, "Yesterday is history, tomorrow is a mystery, and today is a gift. (②) That's why it's called the present."
Suho: Now I see. (③) You know so many great expressions. (④) You're as wise as my grandma. (⑤)

## 출제율 95%

**05** 위 대화의 (①)~(⑤) 중에서 주어진 글이 들어가기에 가장 적절한 곳은?

> Yes, exactly.

①        ②        ③        ④        ⑤

**06** 위 대화의 밑줄 친 우리말 (A)에 맞게 should를 이용하여 6 단어로 영작하시오.

➡ _____

**07** When did Suho lose his soccer match?

➡ _____

[08~10] 다음 대화를 읽고 물음에 답하시오.

G: You look worried. Is something wrong?
B: I had to hand in my science report by yesterday, but I didn't.
G: _____(A)_____
B: Do you mean it's better to hand it in __(B)__ it's late?
G: Yes, exactly. You should always finish what you've started.

**08** 위 대화의 빈칸 (A)에 알맞은 말을 고르시오.

① Don't judge a book by its cover.
② It's better late than never.
③ Haste makes waste.
④ Honesty is the best policy.
⑤ Prevention is better than cure.

**09** 위 대화의 빈칸 (B)에 알맞은 말을 고르시오.

① if          ② whether          ③ that
④ when          ⑤ even though

**10** 위 대화의 내용과 일치하지 않는 것은?

① The boy looks worried.
② The boy didn't hand in his science report yesterday.
③ The girl thinks it's better for the boy to hand in the report though it's late.
④ The girl thinks we should always finish what we've started.
⑤ The boy will hand in his science report.

**11** 다음 각 문장의 빈칸에 들어갈 알맞은 말을 〈보기〉에서 기호를 골라 괄호 안에 써 넣으시오.

┌─── 보기 ───┐
ⓐ who ⓑ whose ⓒ which ⓓ of which
└──────────┘

(1) We're going to buy a house _____ garden is beautiful. (　)
(2) We're going to buy a house _____ the garden is beautiful. (　)
(3) Dorothy met a tin man _____ heart was gone. (　)
(4) Brian is the one _____ car is orange red. (　)
(5) Brian is the one _____ has an orange red colored car. (　)
(6) I have to finish the project _____ the purpose is to market the new items. (　)
(7) I have to finish the project _____ has the purpose of marketing the new items. (　)
(8) I saw a building _____ wall is very high. (　)
(9) I saw a wall on _____ the ivy is growing. (　)

**12** 다음 가정법 문장들 중 어법상 올바른 것을 고르면?

① The president would feel proud of them if they win the final match.
② What would you do if another war occurrs?
③ She will be puzzled if you left her.
④ What would the king do if Birbal brought the pot of wisdom?
⑤ If the official from Persia look inside the pot, he would be speechless.

**13** 다음 중 어법상 올바른 것을 고르시오.

① Naomi has a son whose the job is to write novels.
② Yuna bought the shoes colors of which are bright red and ocean blue.
③ The police arrested the artist the works of whom were all fake.
④ The reporter was covering the hospital whose the doctors are famous for cancer surgery.
⑤ While in college, Brad majored in Latin the grammar of which was too complex.

**[14~16]** 다음에 주어진 두 문장을 합쳐서 가정법의 한 문장으로 영작하되, 주어진 단어로 시작하시오.

**14**
• Mike wants to call her but he can't.
• He doesn't know her phone number.

➡ If _____

_____.

**15**
• Tom didn't catch the school bus this morning.
• He was late for school again.

➡ If _____

_____.

**16**
• In fact, I'm not as wise as Birbal.
• I want to be as wise as Birbal.

➡ I _____.

**17** 다음 중 어법상 올바른 문장의 개수는?

ⓐ The house whose roof was damaged has now been repaired.
ⓑ The trees of which branches are covered with snow are beautiful.
ⓒ They talked with a woman of whom husband was killed in an accident.
ⓓ The man whose dog I took care of is in New York.
ⓔ It is a novel the author of which is unknown.
ⓕ The prize will go to the team whose performance the judges like best.
ⓖ It is a movie whose the title she has never heard of.
ⓗ Those are firefighters whose job is to put out fires.

① 1개          ② 2개          ③ 3개
④ 4개          ⑤ 5개

**[18~21]** 다음 글을 읽고 물음에 답하시오.

> (A)
>
> One day, Emperor Akbar drew a line on the ground and asked his officials.
>
> Akbar: Make this line shorter without touching it.
>
> Official 1: Without touching it?
>
> Official 2: _____ (B) _____
>
> Birbal smiled.
>
> Birbal: That's too easy.
>
> Birbal drew a longer line next to the line that Akbar ⓐhad drawn.
>
> Birbal: Your line is now shorter than ⓑmine.
>
> Akbar: You did it, Birbal!
>
> Official 3: I wish I were as wise as Birbal.

**18** 위 글의 빈칸 (A)에 들어갈 알맞은 말을 고르시오.

① Great Idea
② A Shorter Line
③ Who Is Wise?
④ Drawing Without Touching
⑤ How Wonderful!

**19** 위 글의 빈칸 (B)에 'We can't do that.'이라는 의미의 말을 how를 이용한 의문문으로 쓰시오.

➡ _____

**20** 위 글의 밑줄 친 ⓐ와 같은 용법으로 쓰인 것을 고르시오.

① I could find the destination easily because of the map he had drawn.
② She had drawn the same picture twice.
③ Akbar had just drawn the line.
④ Terry had drawn pictures for 10 years.
⑤ Merriam had drawn the picture since that morning.

**21** 위 글의 밑줄 친 ⓑmine을 두 단어로 바꿔 쓰시오.

➡ _____

**[22~24]** 다음 글을 읽고 물음에 답하시오.

> Dear Sumin,
>
>   Time flies. (①) I cannot believe that it is time to say goodbye. (②) I still remember the time when we had a party at my house. (③) I really liked talking with you about our worries and dreams all night long. (④) I really want to thank you for teaching me badminton skills. _____ ⓐ _____ (⑤) I hope we remain best friends even after we graduate.
>
>                                        Best,
>                                        Minji

**22** 위 글의 빈칸 ⓐ에 다음 문장을 if를 이용하여 바꿔 쓰시오.

> Since I cannot turn back time, I will not do more things together with you.

➡ _____
_____

**23** 위 글의 흐름으로 보아, 주어진 문장이 들어가기에 가장 적절한 곳은?

> I also loved playing badminton with you after school.

①      ②      ③      ④      ⑤

**24** What cannot Minji believe?

➡ _____
_____

[01~03] 다음 대화를 읽고 물음에 답하시오.

G: You look tired this morning.
B: I got up very early to study for the exam.
G: Good for you. The early bird catches the warm.
B: No. The early bird gets tired quickly.
G: (A)Do you mean you don't like to get up early?
B: Yes, that's exactly what I mean.

**01** 위 대화에서 <u>어색한</u> 어휘를 하나 찾아 바르게 고치시오.

_____ ➡ _____

**02** Why does the boy look tired?

➡ _____

**03** 위 대화의 밑줄 친 (A)를 'saying'을 이용하여 바꿔 쓰시오.

➡ _____
_____

**04** 다음 〈보기〉에 주어진 단어들을 활용하여, 그림에 맞는 우리말과 일치하도록 어법상 알맞은 형태로 바꿔 영작하시오. (사용하지 않는 단어는 없어야 하며, 영작 시 줄임말 불가.)

┌─ 보기 ─┐
Mina, families, cooking, grow longer, pay attention to, under 12, a lot of, lie, burn the food, more, visit, whose kids
└────────┘

• 미나가 요리에 더 신경을 쓴다면, 음식을 태우지 않을 텐데.
• 네가 거짓말을 하지 않았다면, 코가 더 길어지지 않았을 텐데.
• 아이들이 12살 이하인 많은 가족들이 동물원을 방문했다.

(1)

➡ _____
_____

(2)

➡ _____
_____

(3)

➡ _____
_____

[05~06] 다음 글을 읽고 물음에 답하시오.

A few weeks later, _____(A)_____. He offered one to the Persian official.

Birbal: You can take this pot of wisdom to your king. Please ask him to return the pot to us after he takes the wisdom out of it.

Birbal: The pot is very precious, so please be careful not to break it. We only have two pots of wisdom.

The Persian official looked inside the pot and became speechless.

He thanked Birbal and left for his country.

Persian Official: It would be great if there were a man as wise as Birbal in our country.

After the Persian official left, Akbar asked Birbal what was inside the pot.

Birbal: Here is the other pot. You can see for yourself.

Akbar looked inside the other pot and found a pumpkin just as big as the pot.

Akbar: I see! The pumpkin can't be taken out without breaking the pot. How did you do it?

Birbal: I put the pots over pumpkin flowers and waited until the pumpkins grew as big as the pots.

Akbar: Hahaha! (B)This certainly is a potful of wisdom!

**05** 위 글의 빈칸 (A)에 다음의 두 문장을 한 문장으로 바꿔 써 넣으시오.(whose를 이용할 것)

> • Birbal came back with two pots.
> • Their necks were really narrow.

➡ _____

_____

**06** What was offered to the Persian official by Birbal?

➡ _____

_____

[07~09] 다음 글을 읽고 물음에 답하시오.

**A Shorter Line**

One day, Emperor Akbar drew a line on the ground and asked his officials.

Akbar: Make this line shorter without touching it.

Official 1: Without touching it?

Official 2: How can we do that?

Birbal smiled.

Birbal: ⓐThat's too easy.

Birbal drew a longer line next to the line that Akbar had drawn.

Birbal: Your line is now shorter than mine.

Akbar: You did it, Birbal!

Official 3: ⓑ제가 비르발만큼 지혜롭다면 좋겠군요. (wish, wise)

**07** 위 글의 밑줄 친 ⓐThat이 가리키는 것을 우리말로 쓰시오.

➡ _____

**08** 위 글의 밑줄 친 ⓑ의 우리말에 맞게 주어진 어휘를 이용하여 영작하시오.

➡ _____

**09** 본문의 내용과 일치하도록 다음 빈칸 (A)와 (B)에 알맞은 단어를 쓰시오.

> When Akbar drew a line on the ground and asked his officials to make the line shorter (A)_____ _____ _____, Birbal made the line shorter by drawing (B)_____ _____ _____ next to the line that Akbar had drawn.

**01** 다음 각 그림들을 보고, 〈보기〉와 같이 소유격 관계대명사가 들어가는 문장을 2개 이상 영작하시오.

┤ 보기 ├

Snow White rejected the witch whose apple didn't look yummy.

**02** (A)의 어구를 이용하여 〈보기〉와 같이 다음 대화의 빈칸에 알맞은 말을 쓰시오.

┤ 보기 ├

You're good at singing.
I wish I could sing well like you.

You're good at _____.
I wish _____.

(A) draw / play soccer / dance / speak English

**03** 다음 〈보기〉의 속담을 바탕으로 만든 글의 빈칸을 주어진 어휘를 이용하여 알맞게 채우시오.

┤ 보기 ├

Fall seven times, stand up eight.

disappointed, give up, try

When my brother failed his driving test (A)_____, he was very (B)_____.
Kento, his friend from Japan, said to him, "If I were you, I wouldn't (C)_____.
Fall seven times, stand up (D)_____." It's a Japanese saying that means "Do not give up." My brother (E)_____ again and finally passed.

**01** 다음 짝지어진 단어의 관계가 같도록 빈칸에 알맞은 말을 쓰시오.

> precious – valuable : gift – _____

**[02~03]** 다음 주어진 영어 설명에 맞게 문장의 빈칸에 알맞은 말을 쓰시오.

**02**
> The _____ Theodosius ordered the temple to be closed.

> <영어 설명> the man who is the ruler of an empire

➡ _____

**03**
> Would you be so kind as to lock the door when you _____?

> <영어 설명> to go away from a place or a person

➡ _____

**04** 우리말과 일치하도록 주어진 단어를 배열하여 영작하시오.

(1) 왕은 그의 궁궐에서 많은 시간을 보냈다.
   (the king, time, court, lot, spent, a, his, at, of)
   ➡ _____

(2) 그의 부모님은 거짓말을 했다고 그를 벌 주셨다.
   (lying, his, him, parents, punished, for)
   ➡ _____

(3) 그녀의 책들은 재치와 지혜로 가득 차 있다.
   (her, books, and, full, of, her, wit, are, wisdom)
   ➡ _____

**05** 다음 빈칸에 알맞은 말로 짝지어진 것을 고르시오.

> • You can never wipe out the _____.
> • _____ your chair near the table.

① place – Push
② future – Push
③ future – Invent
④ past – Shake
⑤ past – Pull

**[06~08]** 다음 대화를 읽고 물음에 답하시오.

> B: Wow, you play the guitar so well.
> G: Thanks. I love ⓐplaying the guitar. I learned it from my dad.
> B: Really? Does your father play the guitar, too?
> G: Yes. He was in a ___(A)___ band.
> B: What a family! (B)I wish I could play the guitar like you.

**06** 다음 영영풀이에 해당하는 어휘를 빈칸 (A)에 쓰시오.

> being very well known

➡ _____

**07** 위 대화의 밑줄 친 (B)의 의도로 알맞은 것은?

① 걱정하기          ② 의향 말하기
③ 이해 확인하기     ④ 조언 구하기
⑤ 바람·소원 표현하기

**08** 다음 문장의 밑줄 친 부분이 위 대화의 밑줄 친 ⓐ와 문법적 쓰임이 같은 것은?

① How are you <u>feeling</u> now?

② No, it's an expression <u>meaning</u> I hope you do well.

③ Who is the man <u>standing</u> by the door?

④ Did you finish <u>talking</u> about your wishes?

⑤ I wish I could have a <u>flying</u> car.

**[09~10]** 다음 대화를 읽고 물음에 답하시오.

G: I have to sing at the school's English pop song contest.

B: Wow. (A)<u>Break a leg!</u>

G: What? Do you mean I have to break one of my legs?

B: No, (B)<u>네가 잘하기를 바란다는 뜻의 표현이야.</u> (do well, expression, it's, hope, mean).

**09** 밑줄 친 (A) 대신 쓸 수 있는 말을 고르시오.

① I'll keep my fingers crossed!

② Shake a leg!

③ Don't make a long face!

④ Don't let the cat out of the bag!

⑤ I wish I could have a green thumb!

**10** 밑줄 친 우리말 (B)를 주어진 어휘를 이용하여 9 단어로 영작하시오.

➡ _____

**[11~13]** 다음 대화를 읽고 물음에 답하시오.

Anna: What's wrong? You don't look so ① well.

Suho: I'm still thinking about our soccer match last week.

Anna: Do you mean the game you lost last week?

Suho: Yes. I wish I ②could forget about it, but I can't.

Anna: Well, you should always live for today.

Suho: Do you mean I should forget the past and focus ③on the present?

Anna: Yes, exactly. People say, "Yesterday is history, tomorrow is a mystery, and today is a gift. That's ④why it's called the present."

Suho: Now I see. You know so many great expressions. You're as ⑤wise as my grandma.

**11** What is the problem with Suho? Answer with 10 words.

➡ _____

_____

**12** 위 대화의 내용과 일치하도록 다음 문장의 빈칸에 알맞은 말을 쓰시오.

Anna wants Suho to forget the (A)_____
and live for (B)_____.

**13** 위 대화의 밑줄 친 ①~⑤에서 어색한 것은?

①     ②     ③     ④     ⑤

**14** 다음 중 〈보기〉의 문장과 의미가 가장 가까운 것을 고르시오.

> ┤ 보기 ├
>
> If Brian were in good condition, he would make twice as many buzzer beaters as any other players.

① As Brian was in good condition, he made twice as many buzzer beaters as any other players.

② As Brian was not in good condition, he didn't make twice as many buzzer beaters as any other players.

③ As Brian is not in good condition, he didn't make twice as many buzzer beaters as any other players.

④ As Brian is not in good condition, he doesn't make twice as many buzzer beaters as any other players.

⑤ Though Brian were not in good condition, he made twice as many buzzer beaters as any other players.

**15** 다음 중 밑줄 친 whose의 쓰임이 나머지와 다른 하나는?

① My friend wants to marry the girl whose father is very rich.

② The author whose latest book sold well will speak in front of the politicians.

③ Is there any movie at your cinema whose title we have heard of?

④ Would you let me know whose pencil Samantha borrowed yesterday?

⑤ The old gentleman whose hobby is playing online shooting games is Yena's grandfather.

**[16~17]** 다음 각 문장과 가장 가까운 의미가 되도록, 가정법을 이용하여 괄호 안에 주어진 단어를 빈칸에 알맞게 배열해 넣으시오.

**16**

> It is bad that there is no man as wise as Birbal in our country.

➡ It ＿＿＿＿＿＿＿＿＿＿＿＿＿＿＿

＿＿＿＿＿＿＿＿＿＿＿＿＿＿＿.

(if, great, a man, our, were, country, be, there, would, as wise as, in, Birbal)

**17**

> You have to break the pot to take out the pumpkin.

➡ Without ＿＿＿＿＿＿＿＿＿＿＿

＿＿＿＿＿＿＿＿＿＿＿＿＿＿＿.

(could, the pot, taken out, not, breaking, the pumpkin, be)

**18** 다음 밑줄 친 부분 중 어법상 어색한 것을 모두 고르시오.

① Eagles have special eyelids of which move sideways.

② The people whose village my team visited last year were so kind and honest.

③ They raised pandas whose eating habits differed from other bear species.

④ Anna told me about the statue of which the sculptor was my father.

⑤ Greg is the professor the opinion of whom is respected by many students.

**19** 다음 중 내용상 〈보기〉의 밑줄 친 부분과 바꿔 쓸 때 의미가 다른 것은?

> ┤ 보기 ├
>
> If the athlete were not so short, he could join the national team for Olympics.

① Were the athlete not so short,

② Without the problem of the athlete's height,

③ If it were not for the problem of the athlete's height,

④ Had it not been for the athlete's height,

⑤ Were it not for the problem of the athlete's height,

[20~21] 다음 주어진 두 문장을 관계대명사를 사용해서 하나의 문장으로 만드시오.

**20**

> • The student is studying foreign languages very hard.
> • Her goal is to become a diplomat.

➡ The student _____

_____ .

**21**

> • The lady's purse was stolen outside the department store.
> • The police came to question her.

➡ The police _____

_____ .

[22~25] 다음 글을 읽고 물음에 답하시오.

_____ⓐ_____ weeks later, Birbal came back with two pots ①whose necks were really narrow. He offered one to the Persian official.

Birbal: You can take this pot of wisdom to your king. Please ask him to return the pot to us after he takes the wisdom out of it.

Birbal: The pot is very precious, so please be careful ②to not break it. We only have two pots of wisdom.

The Persian official looked inside the pot and became speechless.

He thanked Birbal and left for his country.

Persian Official: It would be great if there ③are a man as wise as Birbal in our country.

After the Persian official left, Akbar asked Birbal ④what was inside the pot.

Birbal: Here is ⑤the other pot. You can see for yourself.

Akbar looked inside the other pot and found a pumpkin just as big as the pot.

Akbar: I see! The pumpkin can't be taken out without breaking the pot. How did you do ⓑit?

Birbal: I put the pots over pumpkin flowers and waited until the pumpkins grew as big as the pots.

Akbar: Hahaha! (A)This certainly is a potful of wisdom!

**22** 위 글의 빈칸 ⓐ에 들어갈 말로 알맞은 것은?

① Few      ② A few

③ A lot      ④ Little

⑤ A little

**23** 위 글의 밑줄 친 ⓑ가 가리키는 것을 25자 내외의 우리말로 쓰시오.

➡ _____

**24** 위 글에서 악바르가 밑줄 친 (A)처럼 말한 이유를 알 수 있는 두 문장을 본문에서 찾아 쓰시오.

(1) _____

_____

(2) _____

_____

**25** 위 글의 밑줄 친 ①~⑤에서 어법상 어색한 것을 두 개 골라 바르게 고치고 그 이유를 밝히시오.

➡ _____

이유 _____

_____

**[26~28]** 다음 글을 읽고 물음에 답하시오.

**A Shorter Line**

One day, Emperor Akbar drew a line on the ground and asked his officials.

Akbar: Make this line shorter without touching it.

Official 1: Without touching (A)it?

Official 2: How can we do that?

Birbal smiled.

Birbal: That's too easy.

Birbal drew a ___ⓐ___ line next to the line that Akbar ___ⓑ___.

Birbal: Your line is now shorter than mine.

Akbar: You did it, Birbal!

Official 3: I wish I were as wise as Birbal.

**26** 위 글의 빈칸 ⓐ에 들어갈 말로 알맞은 것을 고르시오.

① equal　　② curved　　③ flat

④ longer　　⑤ shorter

**27** 위 글의 빈칸 ⓑ에 draw를 어법에 맞게 시간의 차가 드러나도록 쓰시오.

➡ _____

**28** 위 글의 밑줄 친 (A)가 가리키는 것을 6 단어의 영어로 쓰시오.

➡ _____

# INSIGHT
## on the textbook

교과서 파헤치기

※ 다음 영어를 우리말로 쓰시오.

| | | |
|---|---|---|
| 01 | greenhouse | |
| 02 | harvest | |
| 03 | ad(= advertisement) | |
| 04 | exhibition | |
| 05 | underwater | |
| 06 | marine | |
| 07 | nationwide | |
| 08 | overseas | |
| 09 | promote | |
| 10 | bridge | |
| 11 | community | |
| 12 | moved | |
| 13 | heritage | |
| 14 | environment | |
| 15 | seafood | |
| 16 | several | |
| 17 | breadwinner | |
| 18 | female | |
| 19 | volcanic | |
| 20 | worldwide | |
| 21 | complete | |

| | | |
|---|---|---|
| 22 | breathe | |
| 23 | destroy | |
| 24 | waterfall | |
| 25 | trail | |
| 26 | intangible | |
| 27 | jellyfish | |
| 28 | press | |
| 29 | underground | |
| 30 | suitable | |
| 31 | audience | |
| 32 | overwork | |
| 33 | path | |
| 34 | realize | |
| 35 | wish for | |
| 36 | happen to | |
| 37 | walk along | |
| 38 | a couple of | |
| 39 | get into | |
| 40 | be suitable for | |
| 41 | give a talk | |
| 42 | a little bit | |
| 43 | be good for | |

※ 다음 우리말을 영어로 쓰시오.

| | | | | |
|---|---|---|---|---|
| 01 | 폭포 | | 22 | 수중의, 물속에서 |
| 02 | 광고 | | 23 | 해파리 |
| 03 | 경로, 길 | | 24 | 해양의, 바다의 |
| 04 | 과로하다 | | 25 | 수확하다 |
| 05 | 교량, 다리 | | 26 | 청중 |
| 06 | 좁은 길 | | 27 | 유산 |
| 07 | 지하의 | | 28 | 호흡하다 |
| 08 | 세계적으로 | | 29 | 전국적인 |
| 09 | 화산의, 화산 작용에 의한 | | 30 | 해외의 |
| 10 | 온실 | | 31 | 깨닫다, 인식하다 |
| 11 | 파괴하다 | | 32 | 단단히, 꽉 |
| 12 | 전시회, 박람회 | | 33 | (북 등을 치는) 소리, (심장의) 고동 |
| 13 | 홍보하다, 촉진하다 | | 34 | 풍년 |
| 14 | 완성[완료]하다 | | 35 | 휴가가다 |
| 15 | 몇몇의 | | 36 | ~에 들어가다 |
| 16 | 생계를 책임지는 사람, 가장 | | 37 | 우연히 ~하다 |
| 17 | 적합한, 적절한 | | 38 | ~을 따라 걷다 |
| 18 | 여성의 | | 39 | ~에 유익하다 |
| 19 | 누르다; 언론, 기자 | | 40 | 계속해서 ~하다 |
| 20 | 지역 공동체 | | 41 | 힘을 북돋아 주다, 격려하다 |
| 21 | 무형의, 만질 수 없는 | | 42 | 거들어 주다, 돕다 |
| | | | 43 | 발표하다 |

※ 다음 영영풀이에 알맞은 단어를 <보기>에서 골라 쓴 후, 우리말 뜻을 쓰시오.

1 _____ : to gather a crop: _____

2 _____ : under the surface of the ground: _____

3 _____ : to finish making or doing something: _____

4 _____ : one of a series of regular movements or hitting actions: _____

5 _____ : a place where a stream or river falls from a high place: _____

6 _____ : right or appropriate for a particular purpose or occasion: _____

7 _____ : to take air into your lungs and send it out again: _____

8 _____ : the people who live in the same area, town, etc.: _____

9 _____ : the traditional beliefs, values, customs of a family, country, or society: _____

10 _____ : having value but not existing physically: _____

11 _____ : to or in a foreign country that is across the sea: _____

12 _____ : fish and shellfish that live in the ocean and are used for food: _____

13 _____ : to damage something so badly that it no longer exists, works, etc.: _____

14 _____ : a picture, set of words, or a short film, intended to persuade people to buy: _____

15 _____ : a structure built over something such as a river so that people or vehicles can get across: _____

16 _____ : the member of a family who earns the money to support the others: _____

보기

| | | | |
|---|---|---|---|
| destroy | breadwinner | community | suitable |
| intangible | overseas | harvest | seafood |
| bridge | complete | waterfall | ad |
| heritage | breathe | beat | underground |

Step1

※ 다음 우리말과 일치하도록 빈칸에 알맞은 말을 쓰시오.

해석

### Listen & Speak 1 A-1

G: Wow, _____ _____ the _____ in this _____. I wonder
_____ _____ _____ _____ _____.

B: That's Gwangandaegyo in Busan.

G: _____ _____ you _____ that?

B: I _____ _____ _____ my family _____ _____.

G: 와, 이 광고에 나오는 다리 좀 봐. 어디에서 찍은 사진인지 궁금하네.
B: 부산의 광안대교야.
G: 그걸 어떻게 아니?
B: 작년 여름에 우리 가족들과 그곳에 갔었거든.

### Listen & Speak 1 A-2

B: _____ _____ there. _____ _____ _____ there are so
many people _____ _____ _____.

G: They're _____ _____ _____ _____ the new bakery there.

B: Why? Is it _____?

G: Yes. It was _____ a TV program.

B: Really? We _____ _____ their bread _____.

G: Sure.

B: 저기 좀 봐. 왜 저렇게 많은 사람들이 줄을 서서 기다리고 있는지 궁금하네.
G: 새로 생긴 제과점에 들어가려고 기다리고 있는 거야.
B: 왜? 유명한 곳이야?
G: 맞아. TV 프로그램에 나왔어.
B: 정말? 그럼 우리 저곳의 빵을 먹어 봐야겠다.
G: 그래.

### Listen & Speak 2 A-1

W: Excuse me, _____ _____ _____ _____ an audio guide.

M: _____ you _____.

W: Could you _____ _____ _____ _____ _____ _____?

M: Sure. _____ this button, and it'll tell you _____ _____
_____.

W: 실례합니다, 음성 가이드를 대여하고 싶은데요.
M: 여기 있습니다.
W: 어떻게 사용하는지 설명해 주실 수 있나요?
M: 물론이죠. 이 버튼을 누르면, 무엇을 해야 할지 말해 줄 겁니다.

### Listen & Speak 2 A-2

B: _____ you _____ _____ this summer?

G: I'm _____ _____ Jejudo to _____ _____ the Jeju Olle
Trail.

B: The Jeju Olle Trail? _____ _____ _____ _____ _____
_____?

G: It's a _____ _____ _____ _____ Jejudo.

B: Oh, I see. I hope you _____ _____ _____!

B: 이번 여름에 어디 갈 거야?
G: 제주 올레길을 따라 걸으러 제주도에 갈 거야.
B: 제주 올레길? 그게 무엇인지 설명해 줄래?
G: 제주도 둘레에 있는 긴 하이킹 코스야.
B: 오, 그렇구나. 즐거운 여행이 되길 바랄게!

### Communication A

**Jaden:** Do you hear that? _____ _____ _____ that music is _____ _____.

**Yuri:** I think it's coming from _____ _____. Do you want to go and _____ _____ _____?

**Jaden:** Yes, I love that _____ _____. Is it _____ Korean music?

**Yuri:** Yes, it's _____ nongak. It's _____ _____ _____ band music.

**Jaden:** Nongak? _____ _____ _____ _____ _____ _____ more about it?

**Yuri:** It's _____ used to _____ _____ farmers and _____ _____ a _____ _____.

**Jaden:** I see. Look! Some people _____ _____ _____ the _____.

**Yuri:** Yes, that's a big _____ _____ nongak. Dancing together _____ the music.

**Jaden:** _____ _____ them.

**Yuri:** Sure. _____ _____?

### Progree Check 1

**W:** Look over there. _____ _____ _____ _____ _____ _____ _____ _____ _____ on the road.

**M:** _____ _____ people are _____ _____ _____ this weekend.

**W:** Really? Then, _____ _____ _____ go somewhere, _____?

**M:** O.K.

### Progree Check 2

**B:** _____ me, I'd like to use a _____ _____.

**W:** O.K. You can use this machine.

**B:** Could you explain _____ _____ _____ _____ _____?

**W:** Sure. _____ the button for _____ _____, and then _____ the start button.

**B:** Thank you.

---

**Jaden:** 저거 들리니? 저 음악이 어디서 오는 것인지 궁금하네.
**유리:** 저기서 나오는 것 같은데. 가서 확인해 볼래?
**Jaden:** 그래, 저 강한 비트가 마음에 들어. 그게 한국의 전통 음악이니?
**유리:** 맞아, 농악이라고 해. 공동체 악단 음악의 한 종류야.
**Jaden:** 농악? 그것에 대해 좀 더 설명해 줄래?
**유리:** 그건 전통적으로 농부들의 힘을 북돋아 주고 풍년을 기원하기 위해 사용되었어.
**Jaden:** 그렇구나. 봐! 몇몇 사람들이 리듬에 맞춰 춤추고 있어.
**유리:** 그래, 그게 농악의 큰 부분이야. 함께 춤추는 것이 음악을 완성하지.
**Jaden:** 저들과 함께 하자.
**유리:** 물론이야. 왜 안 되겠어?

**W:** 저기 좀 봐요. 도로에 왜 저렇게 차가 많은지 궁금하네요.
**M:** 많은 사람들이 이번 주말에 휴가를 가거든요.
**W:** 정말로요? 그럼, 우리도 어디 가는 게 어떤가요?
**M:** 좋아요.

**B:** 실례합니다, 복사기를 좀 쓰고 싶은데요.
**W:** 알겠어요. 이 기계를 써도 돼요.
**B:** 어떻게 양면 복사를 하는지 설명해 주실 수 있나요?
**W:** 물론이죠. 양면 복사 버튼을 누르고, 시작 버튼을 누르세요.
**B:** 감사합니다.

※ 다음 우리말에 맞도록 대화를 영어로 쓰시오.

## Listen & Speak 1 A-1

G: _____

B: _____

G: _____

B: _____

해석

G: 와, 이 광고에 나오는 다리 좀 봐. 어디에서 찍은 사진인지 궁금하네.
B: 부산의 광안대교야.
G: 그걸 어떻게 아니?
B: 작년 여름에 우리 가족들과 그곳에 갔었거든.

## Listen & Speak 1 A-2

B: _____

G: _____

B: _____

G: _____

B: _____

G: _____

B: 저기 좀 봐. 왜 저렇게 많은 사람들이 줄을 서서 기다리고 있는지 궁금하네.
G: 새로 생긴 제과점에 들어가려고 기다리고 있는 거야.
B: 왜? 유명한 곳이야?
G: 맞아. TV 프로그램에 나왔어.
B: 정말? 그럼 우리 저곳의 빵을 먹어 봐야겠다.
G: 그래.

## Listen & Speak 2 A-1

W: _____

M: _____

W: _____

M: _____

W: 실례합니다. 음성 가이드를 대여하고 싶은데요.
M: 여기 있습니다.
W: 어떻게 사용하는지 설명해 주실 수 있나요?
M: 물론이죠. 이 버튼을 누르면, 무엇을 해야 할지 말해 줄 겁니다.

## Listen & Speak 2 A-2

B: _____

G: _____

B: _____

G: _____

B: _____

B: 이번 여름에 어디 갈 거야?
G: 제주 올레길을 따라 걸으러 제주도에 갈 거야.
B: 제주 올레길? 그게 무엇인지 설명해 줄래?
G: 제주도 둘레에 있는 긴 하이킹 코스야.
B: 오, 그렇구나. 즐거운 여행이 되길 바랄게!

## Communication A

Jaden: _____

Yuri: _____

Jaden: _____

Yuri: _____

Jaden: _____

Yuri: _____

Jaden: _____

Yuri: _____

Jaden: _____

Yuri: _____

Jaden: 저거 들리니? 저 음악이 어디서 오는 것인지 궁금하네.

유리: 저기서 나오는 것 같은데. 가서 확인해 볼래?

Jaden: 그래. 저 강한 비트가 마음에 들어. 그게 한국의 전통 음악이니?

유리: 맞아, 농악이라고 해. 공동체 악단 음악의 한 종류야.

Jaden: 농악? 그것에 대해 좀 더 설명해 줄래?

유리: 그건 전통적으로 농부들의 힘을 북돋아 주고 풍년을 기원하기 위해 사용되었어.

Jaden: 그렇구나. 봐! 몇몇 사람들이 리듬에 맞춰 춤추고 있어.

유리: 그래, 그게 농악의 큰 부분이야. 함께 춤추는 것이 음악을 완성하지.

Jaden: 저들과 함께 하자.

유리: 물론이야. 왜 안 되겠어?

## Progree Check 1

W: _____

M: _____

W: _____

M: _____

W: 저기 좀 봐요. 도로에 왜 저렇게 차가 많은지 궁금하네요.

M: 많은 사람들이 이번 주말에 휴가를 가거든요.

W: 정말로요? 그럼, 우리도 어디 가는 게 어떤가요?

M: 좋아요.

## Progree Check 2

B: _____

W: _____

B: _____

W: _____

B: _____

B: 실례합니다, 복사기를 좀 쓰고 싶은데요.

W: 알겠어요. 이 기계를 써도 돼요.

B: 어떻게 양면 복사를 하는지 설명해 주실 수 있나요?

W: 물론이죠. 양면 복사 버튼을 누르고, 시작 버튼을 누르세요.

B: 감사합니다.

※ 다음 우리말과 일치하도록 빈칸에 알맞은 것을 골라 쓰시오.

**1** _____, _____ _____ of Korea
　　A. Divers　　　B. Female　　　C. Haenyeo

**2** For the past _____ years, the _____ photographer Zin Kim has _____ the culture of Jeju haenyeo _____.
　　A. promoted　　B. several　　C. worldwide　　D. underwater

**3** Haenyeo are Korean _____ divers who _____ seafood _____ any _____ devices.
　　A. without　　B. female　　C. breathing　　D. harvest

**4** Their culture _____ UNESCO's _____ Cultural _____ in 2016.
　　A. Heritage　　B. Intangible　　C. made　　D. list

**5** At her studio _____ week, Zin Kim was _____ about her _____ of _____ pictures of haenyeo.
　　A. interviewed　　B. taking　　C. last　　D. experience

**6** Q. How did you _____ _____ _____ photos of haenyeo?
　　A. interested　　B. in　　C. become　　D. taking

**7** _____ _____, I _____ _____ take pictures of a haenyeo.
　　A. happened　　B. day　　C. to　　D. one

**8** I _____ _____ _____ that she was enjoying her job.
　　A. to　　B. was　　C. find　　D. surprised

**9** _____ then, I had only _____ black-and-white photos of haenyeo who _____ very _____.
　　A. looked　　B. until　　C. tired　　D. seen

**10** However, she _____ even after she had _____ in the water for _____ five hours.
　　A. over　　B. kept　　C. been　　D. laughing

**11** I _____ then that I _____ _____ pictures of haenyeo.
　　A. should　　B. realized　　C. take

**12** Q. You take beautiful pictures of them, but _____ _____ _____ take pictures of haenyeo?
　　A. to　　B. isn't　　C. difficult　　D. it

**13** _____ first, they didn't understand _____ _____ to take their pictures.
　　A. wanted　　B. why　　C. I　　D. at

**14** They didn't think they _____ _____ their _____.
　　A. pretty　　B. wetsuits　　C. looked　　D. in

**15** _____, I said to them, "You're _____ _____.
　　A. very　　B. so　　C. special

**16** I want to _____ your _____ the _____."
　　A. to　　B. show　　C. culture　　D. world

**17** They _____ _____ to me _____.
　　A. up　　B. opened　　C. then

**18** Of course, I also promised them that I would _____ _____ _____ in my pictures.
　　A. them　　B. beautiful　　C. make　　D. look

---

**1** 해녀, 한국의 여성 잠수부

**2** 지난 몇 년 동안, 수중 사진작가 Zin Kim은 제주 해녀 문화를 전 세계에 홍보해 왔다.

**3** 해녀는 어떤 호흡 장치도 사용하지 않고 해산물을 채취하는 한국의 여성 잠수부들이다.

**4** 그들의 문화는 2016년에 유네스코 무형문화유산에 등재되었다.

**5** 지난주 그녀의 작업실에서, Zin Kim과 해녀의 사진을 찍는 그녀의 경험에 대해 인터뷰를 했다.

**6** Q. 어떻게 해녀의 사진을 찍는 것에 관심을 가지게 되었나요?

**7** 어느 날, 저는 우연히 한 해녀의 사진을 찍게 되었어요.

**8** 저는 그녀가 자신의 일을 즐겁게 하는 것을 보고 놀랐습니다.

**9** 그때까지, 저는 흑백 사진 속의 아주 지친 모습의 해녀만 봐 왔죠.

**10** 하지만, 그녀는 다섯 시간이 넘도록 물속에 있은 후에도 계속 웃었어요.

**11** 저는 그때 해녀의 사진을 찍어야겠다고 깨달았어요.

**12** Q. 작가님은 아름다운 해녀 사진들을 찍으시는데, 그들의 사진을 찍는 것이 어렵진 않으신가요?

**13** 처음에, 그들은 제가 왜 자신들의 사진을 찍으려고 하는지 이해하지 못했어요.

**14** 그들은 잠수복을 입은 자신들의 모습이 예뻐 보인다고 생각하지 않았으니까요.

**15** 그래서, 제가 그들에게 말했죠, "여러분들은 아주 특별해요.

**16** 저는 여러분의 문화를 세계에 알리고 싶어요."

**17** 그들은 그때 제게 마음을 열었어요.

**18** 물론, 저 또한 그들에게 제 사진 속에서 그들을 아름답게 보이도록 하겠다고 약속했지요.

**19** Q. Could you _____ _____ _____ haenyeo?
A. more          B. tell          C. about          D. us

**20** What's _____ _____ _____ them?
A. special          B. about          C. so

**21** I _____ _____ _____ three _____ .
A. things          B. tell          C. you          D. can

**22** First, haenyeo are a _____ of _____ _____ .
A. strong          B. symbol          C. women

**23** Jejudo, which is a _____ island, is not _____ for _____ ,
so many haenyeo have become the _____ for their families.
A. suitable          B. breadwinners          C. farming          D. volcanic

**24** Second, haenyeo _____ their _____ communities and help
_____ _____ .
A. each          B. form          C. other          D. own

**25** For _____ , _____ haenyeo train _____ haenyeo.
A. example          B. less-experienced          C. more-experienced

**26** Third, because they _____ in the water _____ any _____
devices, haenyeo can't _____ a lot of seafood.
A. without          B. stay          C. catch          D. breathing

**27** This is _____ _____ the _____ .
A. good          B. environment          C. for          D. underwater

**28** Catching too much _____ life at one _____ in one _____
can _____ the ocean.
A. destroy          B. marine          C. place          D. time

**29** Q. Lastly, please tell us _____ you're _____ to _____ in
the _____ .
A. what          B. future          C. planning          D. do

**30** I once _____ an overseas _____ with a couple of haenyeo to
give a _____ about their _____ .
A. talk          B. attended          C. lives          D. exhibition

**31** When I _____ my talk, one of the haenyeo _____ my
_____ _____ .
A. held          B. tightly          C. finished          D. hand

**32** She _____ _____ me, "Thank you _____ _____ .
A. much          B. so          C. to          D. said

**33** I've never known in my whole life that I was _____ _____
_____ ."
A. special          B. a          C. person          D. such

**34** She was _____ _____ _____ .
A. with          B. crying          C. happiness

**35** Everyone in the audience _____ _____ _____ .
A. deeply          B. was          C. moved

**36** I can _____ _____ that _____ , so I'll _____ to take
pictures of haenyeo.
A. continue          B. forget          C. never          D. moment

**37** I want to tell _____ _____ _____ _____ them to many
more people in the world.
A. beautiful          B. about          C. more          D. stories

**19** Q. 해녀에 대해서 더 말씀해 주시겠어요?

**20** 그들은 무엇이 그렇게 특별한가요?

**21** 세 가지를 말씀 드릴게요.

**22** 첫 번째로, 해녀들은 강인한 여성의 상징이에요.

**23** 제주도는 화산섬이고, 이는 농사에 적합하지 않아서 많은 해녀들이 가족들의 생계비를 버는 가장이 되어 왔어요.

**24** 둘째로, 해녀들은 그들 자신의 공동체를 조직하고 서로 도와요.

**25** 예를 들어, 경험이 더 많은 해녀들이 경험이 적은 해녀들을 훈련시키지요.

**26** 세 번째로, 어떤 호흡 장치도 사용하지 않고 물속에 머물기 때문에, 해녀는 많은 해산물을 채취할 수가 없어요.

**27** 이것은 수중 환경에 좋은 것이지요.

**28** 한 번에 한 장소에서 너무 많은 해양생물을 채취하는 것은 바다를 파괴할 수 있으니까요.

**29** Q. 마지막으로, 앞으로 계획하고 있는 것에 대해 말씀해 주세요.

**30** 예전에 두 명의 해녀들과 함께 그들의 삶에 대해 이야기하기 위해 해외에서 열리는 박람회에 참가한 적이 있어요.

**31** 제가 연설을 마쳤을 때, 해녀 중 한 분이 제 손을 꼭 잡았어요.

**32** 그분이 말했죠, "너무 고마워.

**33** 내 평생 내가 이렇게 특별한 사람이라는 걸 미처 알지 못했어."

**34** 그녀는 행복해서 울고 있었어요.

**35** 청중들 모두가 깊은 감동을 받았어요.

**36** 전 그 순간을 절대 잊을 수가 없기 때문에 해녀의 사진을 계속해서 찍을 거예요.

**37** 저는 그들에 대한 더 많은 아름다운 이야기들을 세계의 더 많은 사람들에게 알려 주고 싶어요.

Step2

※ 다음 우리말과 일치하도록 빈칸에 알맞은 말을 쓰시오.

**1** Haenyeo, _____ _____ of Korea

**2** For the past several years, the _____ _____ Zin Kim _____ _____ the culture of Jeju haenyeo _____.

**3** Haenyeo are Korean _____ _____ who harvest seafood _____ _____ _____ _____.

**4** Their culture _____ _____ _____ _____ _____ _____ _____ in 2016.

**5** At her studio last week, Zin Kim _____ _____ about her _____ _____ _____ _____ of haenyeo.

**6** Q. How did you _____ _____ _____ _____ _____ photos of haenyeo?

**7** _____ _____, I _____ _____ take pictures of a haenyeo.

**8** I _____ _____ _____ _____ that she _____ _____ her job.

**9** _____ _____, I _____ _____ black-and-white photos of haenyeo who _____ _____ _____.

**10** However, she _____ _____ even after she had been in the water _____ _____ _____ _____.

**11** I _____ then that I _____ _____ _____ _____ of haenyeo.

**12** Q. You take beautiful pictures of them, but _____ _____ _____ _____ _____ _____ of haenyeo?

**13** _____ _____, they didn't understand _____ _____ to take their pictures.

**14** They didn't think they _____ _____ _____ _____.

**15** So, I said to them, "You're _____ _____.

**16** I want to _____ your culture _____ the world."

**17** They _____ _____ to me _____.

**18** _____ _____, I also promised them that I would _____ _____ look _____ in my pictures.

1 해녀, 한국의 여성 잠수부
2 지난 몇 년 동안, 수중 사진작가 Zin Kim은 제주 해녀 문화를 전 세계에 홍보해 왔다.
3 해녀는 어떤 호흡 장치도 사용하지 않고 해산물을 채취하는 한국의 여성 잠수부들이다.
4 그들의 문화는 2016년에 유네스코 무형문화유산에 등재되었다.
5 지난주 그녀의 작업실에서, Zin Kim과 해녀의 사진을 찍는 그녀의 경험에 대해 인터뷰를 했다.
6 Q. 어떻게 해녀의 사진을 찍는 것에 관심을 가지게 되었나요?
7 어느 날, 저는 우연히 한 해녀의 사진을 찍게 되었어요.
8 저는 그녀가 자신의 일을 즐겁게 하는 것을 보고 놀랐습니다.
9 그때까지, 저는 흑백 사진 속의 아주 지친 모습의 해녀만 봐 왔죠.
10 하지만, 그녀는 다섯 시간이 넘도록 물속에 있은 후에도 계속 웃었어요.
11 저는 그때 해녀의 사진을 찍어야겠다고 깨달았어요.
12 Q. 작가님은 아름다운 해녀 사진들을 찍으시는데, 그들의 사진을 찍는 것이 어렵진 않으신가요?
13 처음에, 그들은 제가 왜 자신들의 사진을 찍으려고 하는지 이해하지 못했어요.
14 그들은 잠수복을 입은 자신들의 모습이 예뻐 보인다고 생각하지 않았으니까요.
15 그래서, 제가 그들에게 말했죠. "여러분들은 아주 특별해요.
16 저는 여러분의 문화를 세계에 알리고 싶어요."
17 그들은 그때 제게 마음을 열었어요.
18 물론, 저 또한 그들에게 제 사진 속에서 그들을 아름답게 보이도록 하겠다고 약속했지요.

**19** Q. Could you tell us _____ _____ haenyeo?

**20** What's _____ _____ about them?

**21** I _____ _____ _____ three things.

**22** First, haenyeo are a _____ _____ _____ _____.

**23** Jejudo, _____ is a volcanic island, _____ _____ _____ _____ farming, so many haenyeo _____ _____ _____ _____ their families.

**24** Second, haenyeo _____ their _____ and help _____ _____.

**25** For example, _____ haenyeo train _____ haenyeo.

**26** Third, _____ they stay in the water _____ any _____ _____, haenyeo _____ _____ a lot of seafood.

**27** This _____ _____ _____ _____ the _____ _____.

**28** _____ too much marine life _____ _____ _____ _____ _____ _____ _____ the ocean.

**29** Q. Lastly, please tell us _____ you're _____ _____ _____ in the future.

**30** I once _____ an _____ _____ _____ with a couple of haenyeo to _____ _____ _____ about their lives.

**31** When I finished my talk, one of the haenyeo _____ _____ _____.

**32** She said to me, "Thank you _____ _____.

**33** I've never known in my _____ _____ that I was _____ _____ _____."

**34** She was _____ _____ _____.

**35** Everyone in the audience _____ _____ _____.

**36** I _____ _____ _____ that moment, so I'll _____ _____ pictures of haenyeo.

**37** I want to tell _____ _____ _____ _____ _____ _____ to many more people in the world.

**19** Q. 해녀에 대해서 더 말씀해 주시겠어요?

**20** 그들은 무엇이 그렇게 특별한가요?

**21** 세 가지를 말씀 드릴게요.

**22** 첫 번째로, 해녀들은 강인한 여성의 상징이에요.

**23** 제주도는 화산섬이고, 이는 농사에 적합하지 않아서 많은 해녀들이 가족들의 생계비를 버는 가장이 되어 왔어요.

**24** 둘째로, 해녀들은 그들 자신의 공동체를 조직하고 서로 도와요.

**25** 예를 들어, 경험이 더 많은 해녀들이 경험이 적은 해녀들을 훈련시키지요.

**26** 세 번째로, 어떤 호흡 장치도 사용하지 않고 물속에 머물기 때문에, 해녀는 많은 해산물을 채취할 수가 없어요.

**27** 이것은 수중 환경에 좋은 것이지요.

**28** 한 번에 한 장소에서 너무 많은 해양생물을 채취하는 것은 바다를 파괴할 수 있으니까요.

**29** Q. 마지막으로, 앞으로 계획하고 있는 것에 대해 말씀해 주세요.

**30** 예전에 두 명의 해녀들과 함께 그들의 삶에 대해 이야기하기 위해 해외에서 열리는 박람회에 참가한 적이 있어요.

**31** 제가 연설을 마쳤을 때, 해녀 중 한 분이 제 손을 꼭 잡았어요.

**32** 그분이 말했죠. "너무 고마워.

**33** 내 평생 내가 이렇게 특별한 사람이라는 걸 미처 알지 못했어."

**34** 그녀는 행복해서 울고 있었어요.

**35** 청중들 모두가 깊은 감동을 받았어요.

**36** 전 그 순간을 절대 잊을 수가 없기 때문에 해녀의 사진을 계속해서 찍을 거예요.

**37** 저는 그들에 대한 더 많은 아름다운 이야기들을 세계의 더 많은 사람들에게 알려 주고 싶어요.

※ 다음 문장을 우리말로 쓰시오.

**1** Haenyeo, Female Divers of Korea
➡ _____

**2** For the past several years, the underwater photographer Zin Kim has promoted the culture of Jeju haenyeo worldwide.
➡ _____

**3** Haenyeo are Korean female divers who harvest seafood without any breathing devices.
➡ _____

**4** Their culture made UNESCO's Intangible Cultural Heritage list in 2016.
➡ _____

**5** At her studio last week, Zin Kim was interviewed about her experience of taking pictures of haenyeo.
➡ _____

**6** Q. How did you become interested in taking photos of haenyeo?
➡ _____

**7** One day, I happened to take pictures of a haenyeo.
➡ _____

**8** I was surprised to find that she was enjoying her job.
➡ _____

**9** Until then, I had only seen black-and-white photos of haenyeo who looked very tired.
➡ _____

**10** However, she kept laughing even after she had been in the water for over five hours.
➡ _____

**11** I realized then that I should take pictures of haenyeo.
➡ _____

**12** Q. You take beautiful pictures of them, but isn't it difficult to take pictures of haenyeo?
➡ _____

**13** At first, they didn't understand why I wanted to take their pictures.
➡ _____

**14** They didn't think they looked pretty in their wetsuits.
➡ _____

**15** So, I said to them, "You're very special.
➡ _____

**16** I want to show your culture to the world."
➡ _____

**17** They opened up to me then.
➡ _____

**18** Of course, I also promised them that I would make them look beautiful in my pictures.
➡ _____

**19** Q. Could you tell us more about haenyeo?w
➡ _____

**20** What's so special about them?

➡ _____

**21** I can tell you three things.

➡ _____

**22** First, haenyeo are a symbol of strong women.

➡ _____

**23** Jejudo, which is a volcanic island, is not suitable for farming, so many haenyeo have become the breadwinners for their families.

➡ _____

**24** Second, haenyeo form their own communities and help each other.

➡ _____

**25** For example, more-experienced haenyeo train less-experienced haenyeo.

➡ _____

**26** Third, because they stay in the water without any breathing devices, haenyeo can't catch a lot of seafood.

➡ _____

**27** This is good for the underwater environment.

➡ _____

**28** Catching too much marine life at one time in one place can destroy the ocean.

➡ _____

**29** Q. Lastly, please tell us what you're planning to do in the future.

➡ _____

**30** I once attended an overseas exhibition with a couple of haenyeo to give a talk about their lives.

➡ _____

**31** When I finished my talk, one of the haenyeo held my hand tightly.

➡ _____

**32** She said to me, "Thank you so much.

➡ _____

**33** I've never known in my whole life that I was such a special person."

➡ _____

**34** She was crying with happiness.

➡ _____

**35** Everyone in the audience was deeply moved.

➡ _____

**36** I can never forget that moment, so I'll continue to take pictures of haenyeo.

➡ _____

**37** I want to tell more beautiful stories about them to many more people in the world.

➡ _____

※ 다음 괄호 안의 단어들을 우리말에 맞도록 바르게 배열하시오.

**1** (Female / Haenyeo, / of / Divers / Korea)
➡ _____

**2** (the / for / past / years, / several / underwater / the / Zin / photographer / Kim / promoted / has / culture / the / Jeju / of / worldwide. / haenyeo)
➡ _____
_____

**3** (are / haenyeo / Korean / divers / female / harvest / who / without / seafood / breathing / any / devices.)
➡ _____
_____

**4** (culture / their / UNESCO's / made / Cultural / Intangible / Heritage / in / list / 2016.)
➡ _____

**5** (her / at / last / studio / week, / Kim / Zin / interviewed / was / her / about / of / experience / taking / of / pictures / haenyeo.)
➡ _____
_____

**6** (Q. / did / how / become / you / in / interested / photos / taking / haenyeo? / of)
➡ _____

**7** (day, / one / happened / I / take / to / of / pictures / haenyeo. / a)
➡ _____

**8** (was / I / to / surprised / find / she / that / enjoying / was / job. / her)
➡ _____

**9** (then, / until / had / I / seen / only / photos / black-and-white / haenyeo / of / looked / who / tired. / very)
➡ _____
_____

**10** (she / however, / laughing / kept / after / even / she / been / had / the / in / water / over / for / hours. / five)
➡ _____
_____

**11** (realized / I / that / then / should / I / pictures / take / haenyeo. / of)
➡ _____

**12** (Q. / take / you / pictures / beautiful / them, / of / isn't / but / difficult / it / take / to / of / pictures / haenyeo?)
➡ _____
_____

**1** 해녀, 한국의 여성 잠수부

**2** 지난 몇 년 동안, 수중 사진작가 Zin Kim은 제주 해녀 문화를 전 세계에 홍보해 왔다.

**3** 해녀는 어떤 호흡 장치도 사용하지 않고 해산물을 채취하는 한국의 여성 잠수부들이다.

**4** 그들의 문화는 2016년에 유네스코 무형문화유산에 등재되었다.

**5** 지난주 그녀의 작업실에서, Zin Kim과 해녀의 사진을 찍는 그녀의 경험에 대해 인터뷰를 했다.

**6** Q. 어떻게 해녀의 사진을 찍는 것에 관심을 가지게 되었나요?

**7** 어느 날, 저는 우연히 한 해녀의 사진을 찍게 되었어요.

**8** 저는 그녀가 자신의 일을 즐겁게 하는 것을 보고 놀랐습니다.

**9** 그때까지, 저는 흑백 사진 속의 아주 지친 모습의 해녀만 봐 왔죠.

**10** 하지만, 그녀는 다섯 시간이 넘도록 물속에 있은 후에도 계속 웃었어요.

**11** 저는 그때 해녀의 사진을 찍어야겠다고 깨달았어요.

**12** Q. 작가님은 아름다운 해녀 사진들을 찍으시는데, 그들의 사진을 찍는 것이 어렵진 않으신가요?

**13** (first, / at / didn't / they / why / understand / wanted / I / take / to / pictures. / their)

➡ _____

**14** (didn't / they / they / think / pretty / looked / their / in / wetsuits.)

➡ _____

**15** (I / so, / said / them, / to / very / "you're / special.)

➡ _____

**16** (want / I / show / to / culture / your / the / to / world.")

➡ _____

**17** (opened / they / to / up / then. / me)

➡ _____

**18** (course, / of / also / I / them / promised / I / that / make / would / look / them / in / beautiful / pictures. / my)

➡ _____

**19** (Q. / you / could / us / tell / about / more / haenyeo?)

➡ _____

**20** (so / what's / about / special / them?)

➡ _____

**21** (can / I / you / tell / things. / three)

➡ _____

**22** (haenyeo / first, / a / are / of / symbol / women. / strong)

➡ _____

**23** (which / Jejudo, / is / volcanic / a / island, / not / is / for / suitable / farming, / many / so / have / haenyeo / the / become / breadwinners / their / for / families.)

➡ _____

**24** (haenyeo / second, / their / form / communities / own / and / each / help / other.)

➡ _____

**25** (example, / for / haenyeo / more-experienced / less-experienced / train / haenyeo.)

➡ _____

**13** 처음에, 그들은 제가 왜 자신들의 사진을 찍으려고 하는지 이해하지 못했어요.

**14** 그들은 잠수복을 입은 자신들의 모습이 예뻐 보인다고 생각하지 않았으니까요.

**15** 그래서, 제가 그들에게 말했죠. "여러분들은 아주 특별해요.

**16** 저는 여러분의 문화를 세계에 알리고 싶어요."

**17** 그들은 그때 제게 마음을 열었어요.

**18** 물론, 저 또한 그들에게 제 사진 속에서 그들을 아름답게 보이도록 하겠다고 약속했지요.

**19** Q. 해녀에 대해서 더 말씀해 주시겠어요?

**20** 그들은 무엇이 그렇게 특별한가요?

**21** 세 가지를 말씀 드릴게요.

**22** 첫 번째로, 해녀들은 강인한 여성의 상징이에요.

**23** 제주도는 화산섬이고, 이는 농사에 적합하지 않아서 많은 해녀들이 가족들의 생계비를 버는 가장이 되어 왔어요.

**24** 둘째로, 해녀들은 그들 자신의 공동체를 조직하고 서로 도와요.

**25** 예를 들어, 경험이 더 많은 해녀들이 경험이 적은 해녀들을 훈련시키지요.

**26** (because / third, / stay / they / the / in / without / water / breathing / any / devices, / can't / haenyeo / a / catch / of / lot / seafood.)

➡ _____

_____

**27** (is / this / for / good / underwater / the / environment.)

➡ _____

**28** (too / catching / much / life / marine / one / at / time / one / in / place / destroy / can / ocean. / the)

➡ _____

_____

**29** (Q. / please / lastly, / us / tell / you're / what / to / planning / do / the / in / future.)

➡ _____

_____

**30** (once / I / an / attneded / overseas / with / exhibition / a / of / couple / haenyeo / a / give / to / talk / their / lives. / about)

➡ _____

_____

**31** (I / when / my / finished / talk, / of / one / haenyeo / the / my / held / tightly. / hand)

➡ _____

**32** (said / she / me, / to / you / "thank / much. / so)

➡ _____

**33** (never / I've / in / known / whole / my / that / life / was / I / a / such / person." / special)

➡ _____

**34** (was / she / with / crying / happiness.)

➡ _____

**35** (in / everyone / audience / the / was / moved. / deeply)

➡ _____

**36** (can / I / forget / never / moment, / that / I'll / so / to / continue / take / of / haenyeo / pictures)

➡ _____

_____

**37** (want / I / to / more / tell / stories / beautiful / about / to / them / more / many / people / the / in / world.)

➡ _____

_____

**26** 세 번째로, 어떤 호흡 장치도 사용하지 않고 물속에 머물기 때문에, 해녀는 많은 해산물을 채취할 수가 없어요.

**27** 이것은 수중 환경에 좋은 것이지요.

**28** 한 번에 한 장소에서 너무 많은 해양생물을 채취하는 것은 바다를 파괴할 수 있으니까요.

**29** Q. 마지막으로, 앞으로 계획하고 있는 것에 대해 말씀해 주세요.

**30** 예전에 두 명의 해녀들과 함께 그들의 삶에 대해 이야기하기 위해 해외에서 열리는 박람회에 참가한 적이 있어요.

**31** 제가 연설을 마쳤을 때, 해녀 중한 분이 제 손을 꼭 잡았어요.

**32** 그분이 말했죠, "너무 고마워.

**33** 내 평생 내가 이렇게 특별한 사람이라는 걸 미처 알지 못했어."

**34** 그녀는 행복해서 울고 있었어요.

**35** 청중들 모두가 깊은 감동을 받았어요.

**36** 전 그 순간을 절대 잊을 수가 없기 때문에 해녀의 사진을 계속해서 찍을 거예요.

**37** 저는 그들에 대한 더 많은 아름다운 이야기들을 세계의 더 많은 사람들에게 알려 주고 싶어요.

※ **다음 우리말을 영어로 쓰시오.**

**1**  해녀, 한국의 여성 잠수부
➡ _____

**2**  지난 몇 년 동안, 수중 사진작가 Zin Kim은 제주 해녀 문화를 전 세계에 홍보해 왔다.
➡ _____
_____

**3**  해녀는 어떤 호흡 장치도 사용하지 않고 해산물을 채취하는 한국의 여성 잠수부들이다.
➡ _____

**4**  그들의 문화는 2016년에 유네스코 무형문화유산에 등재되었다.
➡ _____

**5**  지난주 그녀의 작업실에서, Zin Kim과 해녀의 사진을 찍는 그녀의 경험에 대해 인터뷰를 했다.
➡ _____

**6**  Q. 어떻게 해녀의 사진을 찍는 것에 관심을 가지게 되었나요?
➡ _____

**7**  어느 날, 저는 우연히 한 해녀의 사진을 찍게 되었어요.
➡ _____

**8**  저는 그녀가 자신의 일을 즐겁게 하는 것을 보고 놀랐습니다.
➡ _____

**9**  그때까지, 저는 흑백 사진 속의 아주 지친 모습의 해녀만 봐 왔죠.
➡ _____

**10**  하지만, 그녀는 다섯 시간이 넘도록 물속에 있은 후에도 계속 웃었어요.
➡ _____

**11**  저는 그때 해녀의 사진을 찍어야겠다고 깨달았어요.
➡ _____

**12**  Q. 작가님은 아름다운 해녀 사진들을 찍으시는데, 그들의 사진을 찍는 것이 어렵진 않으신가요?
➡ _____

**13**  처음에, 그들은 제가 왜 자신들의 사진을 찍으려고 하는지 이해하지 못했어요.
➡ _____

**14**  그들은 잠수복을 입은 자신들의 모습이 예뻐 보인다고 생각하지 않았으니까요.
➡ _____

**15**  그래서, 제가 그들에게 말했죠, "여러분들은 아주 특별해요.
➡ _____

**16**  저는 여러분의 문화를 세계에 알리고 싶어요."
➡ _____

**17**  그들은 그때 제게 마음을 열었어요.
➡ _____

**18**  물론, 저 또한 그들에게 제 사진 속에서 그들을 아름답게 보이도록 하겠다고 약속했지요.
➡ _____

**19**  Q. 해녀에 대해서 더 말씀해 주시겠어요?
➡ _____

**20** 그들은 무엇이 그렇게 특별한가요?

➡ _____

**21** 세 가지를 말씀 드릴게요.

➡ _____

**22** 첫 번째로, 해녀들은 강인한 여성의 상징이에요.

➡ _____

**23** 제주도는 화산섬이고, 이는 농사에 적합하지 않아서 많은 해녀들이 가족들의 생계비를 버는 가장이 되어 왔어요.

➡ _____

**24** 둘째로, 해녀들은 그들 자신의 공동체를 조직하고 서로 도와요.

➡ _____

**25** 예를 들어, 경험이 더 많은 해녀들이 경험이 적은 해녀들을 훈련시키지요.

➡ _____

**26** 세 번째로, 어떤 호흡 장치도 사용하지 않고 물속에 머물기 때문에, 해녀는 많은 해산물을 채취할 수가 없어요.

➡ _____

**27** 이것은 수중 환경에 좋은 것이지요.

➡ _____

**28** 한 번에 한 장소에서 너무 많은 해양생물을 채취하는 것은 바다를 파괴할 수 있으니까요.

➡ _____

**29** Q. 마지막으로, 앞으로 계획하고 있는 것에 대해 말씀해 주세요.

➡ _____

**30** 예전에 두 명의 해녀들과 함께 그들의 삶에 대해 이야기하기 위해 해외에서 열리는 박람회에 참가한 적이 있어요.

➡ _____

**31** 제가 연설을 마쳤을 때, 해녀 중 한 분이 제 손을 꼭 잡았어요.

➡ _____

**32** 그분이 말했죠. "너무 고마워.

➡ _____

**33** 내 평생 내가 이렇게 특별한 사람이라는 걸 미처 알지 못했어."

➡ _____

**34** 그녀는 행복해서 울고 있었어요.

➡ _____

**35** 청중들 모두가 깊은 감동을 받았어요.

➡ _____

**36** 전 그 순간을 절대 잊을 수가 없기 때문에 해녀의 사진을 계속해서 찍을 거예요.

➡ _____

**37** 저는 그들에 대한 더 많은 아름다운 이야기들을 세계의 더 많은 사람들에게 알려 주고 싶어요.

➡ _____

※ 다음 우리말과 일치하도록 빈칸에 알맞은 말을 쓰시오.

## Communicate – B Talk and Play

1. A: I wonder _____ _____ _____ .

2. B: They're _____ _____ .

3. A: Could you _____ _____ _____ them?

4. B: They're _____ _____ _____ _____ .

1. A: 나는 이것들이 무엇인지 궁금해.
2. B: 그것들은 송편이라고 불려.
3. A: 이것에 대해 좀 더 설명해 줄래?
4. B: 그것들은 전통적인 한국 떡이야.

## After You Read A

1. A _____ _____ _____ Haenyeo

2. Zin Kim, _____ _____ _____ , _____ _____ the culture of Jeju haenyeo _____ .

3. She _____ _____ _____ _____ of them _____ _____ _____ a haenyeo _____ _____ _____ her job.

4. _____ was not _____ _____ their pictures _____ _____ .

5. _____ , when she told them _____ she wanted to show _____ _____ _____ _____ _____ , the haenyeo _____ _____ _____ .

6. _____ _____ _____ , she _____ _____ _____ about the lives of haenyeo.

7. After her speech, _____ _____ the haenyeo _____ _____ _____ .

8. Zin Kim said that she _____ _____ _____ _____ pictures of haenyeo.

1. 해녀를 사랑하는 사진작가
2. 수중 사진작가 김진은 전 세계에 제주의 해녀 문화를 홍보해 왔다.
3. 그녀는 자신의 일을 즐기고 있었던 한 해녀를 만났을 때, 그들의 사진을 찍기로 결심했다.
4. 처음에는 그들의 사진을 찍는 것이 쉽지 않았다.
5. 그러나, 그녀가 세상 사람들에게 그들의 문화를 보여주고 싶다고 그들에게 말했을 때, 마침내 해녀들은 마음을 열었다.
6. 한 해외 전시회에서 그녀는 해녀들의 삶에 대해 강연했다.
7. 그녀의 연설이 끝나자 해녀들 중 한 사람은 기쁨의 눈물을 흘렸다.
8. 김진은 앞으로도 해녀들의 사진 찍는 일을 계속할 것이라고 말했다.

## Write

1. Kim Minho is a barista. He _____ _____ _____ _____ _____ _____ .

2. He _____ _____ _____ after he _____ _____ _____ _____ _____ _____ for coffee.

3. _____ _____ _____ _____ his job is _____ _____ _____ hot milk and _____ his customers _____ it.

4. He is _____ _____ _____ his own coffee shop.

1. 김민호는 바리스타이다. 그의 직업은 커피 음료를 만드는 것이다.
2. 그는 커피에 대한 그의 열정을 발견한 후에 바리스타가 되었다.
3. 그의 직업에서 그가 가장 좋아하는 부분은 뜨거운 우유로 커피를 장식하고 그의 손님들이 그것을 즐기는 것을 보는 것이다.
4. 그는 자신의 커피점을 열 계획이다.

※ 다음 우리말을 영어로 쓰시오.

**Communicate – B Talk and Play**

1. A: 나는 이것들이 무엇인지 궁금해.
   ➡ _____

2. B: 그것들은 송편이라고 불려.
   ➡ _____

3. A: 이것에 대해 좀 더 설명해 줄래?
   ➡ _____

4. B: 그것들은 전통적인 한국 떡이야.
   ➡ _____

**After You Read A**

1. 해녀를 사랑하는 사진작가
   ➡ _____

2. 수중 사진작가 김진은 전 세계에 제주의 해녀 문화를 홍보해 왔다.
   ➡ _____

3. 그녀는 자신의 일을 즐기고 있었던 한 해녀를 만났을 때, 그들의 사진을 찍기로 결심했다.
   ➡ _____

4. 처음에는 그들의 사진을 찍는 것이 쉽지 않았다.
   ➡ _____

5. 그러나, 그녀가 세상 사람들에게 그들의 문화를 보여주고 싶다고 그들에게 말했을 때, 마침내 해녀들은 마음을 열었다.
   ➡ _____
   _____

6. 한 해외 전시회에서 그녀는 해녀들의 삶에 대해 강연했다.
   ➡ _____

7. 그녀의 연설이 끝나자 해녀들 중 한 사람은 기쁨의 눈물을 흘렸다.
   ➡ _____

8. 김진은 앞으로도 해녀들의 사진 찍는 일을 계속할 것이라고 말했다.
   ➡ _____

**Write**

1. 김민호는 바리스타이다. 그의 직업은 커피 음료를 만드는 것이다.
   ➡ _____

2. 그는 커피에 대한 그의 열정을 발견한 후에 바리스타가 되었다.
   ➡ _____

3. 그의 직업에서 그가 가장 좋아하는 부분은 뜨거운 우유로 커피를 장식하고 그의 손님들이 그것을 즐기는 것을 보는 것이다.
   ➡ _____

4. 그는 자신의 커피점을 열 계획이다.
   ➡ _____

※ 다음 영어를 우리말로 쓰시오.

01 seafood _____

02 anxious _____

03 competition _____

04 enemy _____

05 relax _____

06 graduate _____

07 actually _____

08 helpless _____

09 professional _____

10 instead _____

11 judge _____

12 stranger _____

13 lucky _____

14 relieved _____

15 famously _____

16 prepare _____

17 mind _____

18 nervous _____

19 confident _____

20 behavior _____

21 unique _____

22 psychologist _____

23 carefully _____

24 political _____

25 supporter _____

26 apart _____

27 chew _____

28 presentation _____

29 solution _____

30 convenient _____

31 rare _____

32 rival _____

33 stressful _____

34 psychology _____

35 get off _____

36 make a presentation _____

37 stop by _____

38 not ~ at all _____

39 by oneself _____

40 come up with _____

41 make a reservation _____

42 turn A into B _____

43 not only A but also B _____

※ 다음 우리말을 영어로 쓰시오.

| | | |
|---|---|---|
| 01 | 졸업하다 | |
| 02 | 행동 | |
| 03 | 자신감 있는 | |
| 04 | 해결책 | |
| 05 | 결심하다 | |
| 06 | 적 | |
| 07 | (음식을) 씹다 | |
| 08 | 유명하게 | |
| 09 | 전문적인 | |
| 10 | 실제로 | |
| 11 | 심리학자 | |
| 12 | 드문, 희귀한 | |
| 13 | 스트레스가 많은 | |
| 14 | 휴식을 취하다 | |
| 15 | 지원자 | |
| 16 | 해산물, 해물 | |
| 17 | 정치적인 | |
| 18 | 안도하는 | |
| 19 | 무력한 | |
| 20 | 조심스럽게 | |
| 21 | 심리학 | |
| 22 | 경쟁, 대회 | |
| 23 | 대신에 | |
| 24 | 이어달리기 | |
| 25 | 발표 | |
| 26 | 판단하다 | |
| 27 | 편리한 | |
| 28 | 경쟁자 | |
| 29 | 낯선 사람 | |
| 30 | 독특한 | |
| 31 | 행운인, 운이 좋은 | |
| 32 | 준비하다 | |
| 33 | 빌려주다 | |
| 34 | 추측하다 | |
| 35 | ~에 따르면 | |
| 36 | A를 B로 바꾸다 | |
| 37 | 발표하다 | |
| 38 | A뿐만 아니라 B도 | |
| 39 | 혼자서 | |
| 40 | (해답 등을) 찾아내다, 내놓다 | |
| 41 | 결코 ~가 아닌 | |
| 42 | 예약하다 | |
| 43 | 더 이상 ~가 아닌 | |

※ 다음 영영풀이에 알맞은 단어를 <보기>에서 골라 쓴 후, 우리말 뜻을 쓰시오.

1 _____ : not common: _____

2 _____ : to cook something using dry heat, in an oven: _____

3 _____ : someone who hates you and wants to harm you: _____

4 _____ : someone that you do not know: _____

5 _____ : to bite food several times before swallowing it: _____

6 _____ : someone who supports a particular person, group, or plan: _____

7 _____ : unable to look after yourself or to do anything to help yourself: _____

8 _____ : useful to you because it saves you time: _____

9 _____ : to complete your education at a college, school, etc.: _____

10 _____ : an event at which you describe or explain a new product or idea:

_____

11 _____ : feeling happy because you are no longer worried about something:

_____

12 _____ : the study of the mind and how it influences people's behavior:

_____

13 _____ : to let someone borrow money or something that belongs to you for a

short time: _____

14 _____ : to rest or do something that is enjoyable, especially after you have been

working: _____

15 _____ : sure that something will happen in the way that you want or expect:

_____

16 _____ : a person, group, or organization that you compete with in sport, business,

a fight, etc. : _____

| 보기 | | | |
|---|---|---|---|
| rival | chew | helpless | convenient |
| graduate | lend | stranger | rare |
| relax | relieved | psychology | presentation |
| supporter | confident | bake | enemy |

※ 다음 우리말과 일치하도록 빈칸에 알맞은 말을 쓰시오.

## Listen & Speak 1 A-1

G: What _____ _____ your shoes? _____ they new?

B: Yes, but my dog _____ them. He does it _____ _____ _____. I'm _____ _____ him.

G: He was probably _____. _____ _____ _____ _____ _____ him more often?

B: O.K., I will. I _____ he will _____ _____ my shoes.

G: 신발이 왜 그래? 새것 아니었어?
B: 맞는데, 내 개가 씹어 버렸어. 항상 그렇게 해. 그 개가 걱정돼.
G: 아마 심심했었을 거야. 개와 더 자주 놀아 주는 게 어때?
B: 알겠어, 그럴게. 그 개가 내 신발 씹는 걸 그만두면 좋겠네.

## Listen & Speak 1 A-2

B: You look a bit _____.

G: I'm _____ _____ my _____ _____ this Saturday.

B: Don't _____. You're such a good swimmer. Just _____ and _____ yourself!

G: Thanks. I feel _____ _____ now.

B: 너 좀 긴장한 것 같아 보이는데.
G: 이번 토요일에 있는 수영 대회가 걱정돼.
B: 걱정 마. 너는 수영을 아주 잘 하잖아. 그냥 긴장을 풀고 즐겨!
G: 고마워. 기분이 훨씬 괜찮아졌어.

## Listen & Speak 2 A-1

B: Mom, _____ _____ are we going to _____ _____ tomorrow morning?

W: _____ 8 a.m. I'm going to _____ _____ for her before we go.

B: Then, should I _____ _____ _____ to help you?

W: You _____ _____ _____. Your dad will help me.

B: O.K, then. Good night, Mom!

B: 엄마, 우리 내일 아침 몇 시에 할머니 댁에 가나요?
W: 8시쯤에. 가기 전에 할머니를 위해 쿠키를 구울 거란다.
B: 그럼, 제가 일찍 일어나서 도와드릴까요?
W: 그럴 필요 없단다. 아빠가 도와주실 거야.
B: 알겠어요, 그럼. 안녕히 주무세요, 엄마!

## Listen & Speak 2 A-2

W: _____ _____ _____ that new Mexican restaurant tomorrow?

M: _____ not? I'll _____ the restaurant to _____ _____ _____ for us.

W: You _____ _____ _____ call them. You can do it _____.

M: Oh, I see. _____ _____!

W: 우리 내일 새로 생긴 멕시코 레스토랑에 가 볼까요?
M: 좋죠! 레스토랑에 전화해서 예약해 둘게요.
W: 전화할 필요 없어요. 온라인으로 할 수 있거든요.
M: 오, 그렇군요. 정말 편리하네요!

## Communicate A

**Yuri:** Hi, Jaden. Sports Day is next Friday. I _____ _____!

**Jaden:** Really? I'm _____ _____ about it.

**Yuri:** Why? _____ you _____ _____ sports?

**Jaden:** Yes, I am, but I'm _____ about the 800-meter _____.

**Yuri:** _____ do you _____?

**Jaden:** I'm the _____ _____. _____ _____ our team loses _____ _____ me?

**Yuri:** I think you're _____ _____ _____ _____ _____ yourself.

**Jaden:** Really? Don't you think I should _____ every day?

**Yuri:** No, you _____ _____ _____ _____ that. It's just a school race. It's not about _____ or _____.

**Jaden:** I guess you're _____, Yuri. I'm _____ to have a friend _____ you.

유리: 안녕, Jaden. 운동회가 다음 주 금요일이야. 너무 기다려져!
Jaden: 정말? 난 사실 걱정돼.
유리: 왜? 너 운동 잘하지 않아?
Jaden: 응, 그렇긴 하지만, 800미터 릴레이가 걱정돼.
유리: 무슨 뜻이니?
Jaden: 내가 마지막 주자거든. 나 때문에 우리 팀이 지면 어쩌지?
유리: 넌 네 스스로에게 너무 많은 압박을 주고 있는 것 같아.
Jaden: 그래? 내가 매일 연습해야 한다고 생각하지 않니?
유리: 아니, 그럴 필요 없어. 그냥 학교 경기일 뿐인걸. 이기고 지고에 관한 게 아냐.
Jaden: 네 말이 맞는 것 같다, 유리야. 너 같은 친구를 둬서 다행이야.

## Progress Check 1

**B:** You look a bit _____.

**G:** Well, I'm _____ _____ my _____ in _____ _____.

**B:** Don't worry. You've _____ _____ _____. You'll _____ a great _____.

**G:** Thanks. I _____ _____ _____ now.

B: 너 좀 긴장한 것 같다.
G: 그게, 역사 수업 시간에 내가 할 발표가 걱정돼.
B: 걱정 마. 많이 준비했잖아. 잘할 거야.
G: 고마워. 기분이 훨씬 나아졌어.

## Progress Check 2

**M:** Shall we have _____ _____ for dinner?

**W:** Sure. I'll _____ _____ the store _____ _____ _____ home.

**M:** _____ _____ _____ _____ _____ do that. We already have _____ we _____.

**W:** Oh, I see. Then, I'll be _____ _____ _____ 6 to _____ you _____.

M: 우리 저녁으로 해물 스파게티를 먹을까요?
W: 좋아요. 집에 오는 길에 가게에 들를게요.
M: 그럴 필요 없어요. 필요한 건 이미 가지고 있거든요.
W: 오, 그렇군요. 그럼, 6시까지 돌아와서 요리하는 걸 도울게요.

# 대화문 Test

※ 다음 우리말에 맞도록 대화를 영어로 쓰시오.

### Listen & Speak 1 A-1

G: _____

B: _____

G: _____

B: _____

G: 신발이 왜 그래? 새것 아니었어?
B: 맞는데, 내 개가 씹어 버렸어. 항상 그렇게 해. 그 개가 걱정돼.
G: 아마 심심했었을 거야. 개와 더 자주 놀아 주는 게 어때?
B: 알겠어, 그럴게. 그 개가 내 신발 씹는 걸 그만두면 좋겠네.

### Listen & Speak 1 A-2

B: _____

G: _____

B: _____

G: _____

B: 너 좀 긴장한 것 같아 보이는데.
G: 이번 토요일에 있는 수영 대회가 걱정돼.
B: 걱정 마. 너는 수영을 아주 잘 하잖아. 그냥 긴장을 풀고 즐겨!
G: 고마워. 기분이 훨씬 괜찮아졌어.

### Listen & Speak 2 A-1

B: _____

W: _____

B: _____

W: _____

B: _____

B: 엄마, 우리 내일 아침 몇 시에 할머니 댁에 가나요?
W: 8시쯤에. 가기 전에 할머니를 위해 쿠키를 구울 거란다.
B: 그럼, 제가 일찍 일어나서 도와드릴까요?
W: 그럴 필요 없단다. 아빠가 도와주실 거야.
B: 알겠어요, 그럼. 안녕히 주무세요, 엄마!

### Listen & Speak 2 A-2

W: _____

M: _____

W: _____

M: _____

W: 우리 내일 새로 생긴 멕시코 레스토랑에 가 볼까요?
M: 좋죠! 레스토랑에 전화해서 예약해 둘게요.
W: 전화할 필요 없어요. 온라인으로 할 수 있거든요.
M: 오, 그렇군요. 정말 편리하네요!

## Communicate A

Yuri: _____

Jaden: _____

Yuri: _____

Jaden: _____

Yuri: _____

Jaden: _____

Yuri: _____

Jaden: _____

Yuri: _____
_____

Jaden: _____

유리: 안녕, Jaden. 운동회가 다음 주 금요일이야. 너무 기다려져!

Jaden: 정말? 난 사실 걱정돼.

유리: 왜? 너 운동 잘하지 않아?

Jaden: 응, 그렇긴 하지만, 800미터 릴레이가 걱정돼.

유리: 무슨 뜻이니?

Jaden: 내가 마지막 주자거든. 나 때문에 우리 팀이 지면 어쩌지?

유리: 넌 네 스스로에게 너무 많은 압박을 주고 있는 것 같아.

Jaden: 그래? 내가 매일 연습해야 한다고 생각하지 않니?

유리: 아니, 그럴 필요 없어. 그냥 학교 경기일 뿐인걸. 이기고 지고에 관한 게 아냐.

Jaden: 네 말이 맞는 것 같다, 유리야. 너 같은 친구를 둬서 다행이야.

## Progress Check 1

B: _____

G: _____

B: _____

G: _____

B: 너 좀 긴장한 것 같다.

G: 그게, 역사 수업 시간에 내가 할 발표가 걱정돼.

B: 걱정 마. 많이 준비했잖아. 잘할 거야.

G: 고마워. 기분이 훨씬 나아졌어.

## Progress Check 2

M: _____

W: _____

M: _____

W: _____

M: 우리 저녁으로 해물 스파게티를 먹을까요?

W: 좋아요. 집에 오는 길에 가게에 들를게요.

M: 그럴 필요 없어요. 필요한 건 이미 가지고 있거든요.

W: 오, 그렇군요. 그럼, 6시까지 돌아와서 요리하는 걸 도울게요.

※ 다음 우리말과 일치하도록 빈칸에 알맞은 것을 골라 쓰시오.

**1** ＿＿＿＿＿＿＿＿ Your ＿＿＿＿＿＿＿＿
 A. Answers   B. Questions  C. Psychology

**2** Do you ＿＿＿＿＿ you ＿＿＿＿＿ a ＿＿＿＿＿ problem?
 A. unique    B. have     C. think

**3** ＿＿＿＿＿ are that ＿＿＿＿＿ ＿＿＿＿＿ people have the ＿＿＿＿＿ problem.
 A. same    B. chances   C. other    D. many

**4** Psychology is the study of the ＿＿＿＿＿ ＿＿＿＿＿ and ＿＿＿＿＿,
so it can help you find a ＿＿＿＿＿ to your problem.
 A. behavior   B. solution   C. mind    D. human

**5** How do I ＿＿＿＿＿ ＿＿＿＿＿ ＿＿＿＿＿?
 A. less     B. become   C. nervous

**6** It was five minutes before Jisu's big ＿＿＿＿＿ in ＿＿＿＿＿ of the ＿＿＿＿＿.
 A. class    B. presentation C. whole   D. front

**7** ＿＿＿＿＿ ＿＿＿＿＿, Jisu was ＿＿＿＿＿ ＿＿＿＿＿ her notes in her chair.
 A. carefully   B. feeling   C. studying  D. nervous

**8** Then, her teacher ＿＿＿＿＿ and told her to ＿＿＿＿＿ like Wonder Woman.
 A. over    B. came    C. tall    D. stand

**9** After ＿＿＿＿＿ ＿＿＿＿＿ for a few minutes, Jisu did ＿＿＿＿＿ feel nervous ＿＿＿＿＿.
 A. anymore   B. tall    C. not    D. standing

**10** ＿＿＿＿＿, she was ＿＿＿＿＿ that she would make a great ＿＿＿＿＿.
 A. fact    B. presentation C. in    D. confident

**11** ＿＿＿＿＿ to Amy Cuddy, a famous psychologist, we can become more confident just by ＿＿＿＿＿ ＿＿＿＿＿ for two minutes before ＿＿＿＿＿ events.
 A. stressful   B. standing  C. according  D. tall

**12** Our ＿＿＿＿＿ change our ＿＿＿＿＿, and our minds can ＿＿＿＿＿ our ＿＿＿＿＿.
 A. behavior   B. bodies   C. minds   D. change

**13** Do you ＿＿＿＿＿ ＿＿＿＿＿ ＿＿＿＿＿ ＿＿＿＿＿?
 A. confident   B. to     C. feel    D. want

**14** Stand ＿＿＿＿＿ your feet ＿＿＿＿＿, and ＿＿＿＿＿ your hands ＿＿＿＿＿ your hips.
 A. place    B. apart    C. with    D. on

**15** You will ＿＿＿＿＿ only feel ＿＿＿＿＿ about yourself ＿＿＿＿＿ also look ＿＿＿＿＿ to other people.
 A. but     B. not     C. confident  D. sure

**16** Who can ＿＿＿＿＿ me ＿＿＿＿＿ ＿＿＿＿＿?
 A. feel     B. help     C. better

**17** When he ＿＿＿＿＿ high school next year, Taeho wants to ＿＿＿＿＿ a ＿＿＿＿＿ farmer.
 A. from    B. professional C. graduates  D. become

**18** ＿＿＿＿＿, he ＿＿＿＿＿ ＿＿＿＿＿ ＿＿＿＿＿ anyone about it.
 A. never    B. however  C. told    D. has

---

1 심리학이 당신의 물음에 답하다

2 여러분은 당신만의 유일무이한 고민을 가지고 있다고 생각하는가?

3 아마 많은 다른 사람들이 여러분과 똑같은 고민을 가지고 있을 것이다.

4 심리학은 인간의 마음과 행동에 관한 연구이며, 따라서 여러분이 문제에 대한 해결책을 찾는데 도움을 줄 수 있다.

5 어떻게 하면 긴장을 덜 할 수 있나요?

6 지수가 반 전체 앞에서 발표를 하기 5분 전이었다.

7 지수는 긴장이 되어, 의자에 앉아 자신의 필기를 열심히 들여다보고 있었다.

8 그때 선생님이 다가와서는 원더우먼처럼 꼿꼿이 서 있어 보라고 말했다.

9 그렇게 몇 분을 우뚝 선 후에, 지수는 더 이상 긴장되지 않았다.

10 사실, 그녀는 발표를 멋지게 할 수 있을 것이라는 자신감이 생겼다.

11 유명한 심리학자인 Amy Cuddy에 의하면, 우리는 스트레스를 받는 상황 이전에 2분 정도 꼿꼿이 서 있는 것만으로도 자신감이 더 생길 수 있다고 한다.

12 우리의 몸은 마음을 바꾸고, 마음은 우리의 행동을 바꿀 수 있다.

13 자신감이 생기기를 원하는가?

14 양발을 벌리고, 허리께에 손을 올려 보아라.

15 자신에 대한 확신이 생길 뿐만 아니라 다른 사람이 보기에도 자신감에 차 보인다.

16 누가 내 기분을 낫게 해 줄 수 있나요?

17 내년에 고등학교를 졸업한 이후에 태호는 전문적인 농부가 되고 싶어 한다.

18 하지만, 누구에게도 그것에 대해 한 번도 말하지 않았다.

**19** He is _____ _____ his parents or his friends _____ not _____.
A. understand    B. worried    C. will    D. that

**20** _____ to _____ his mind, Taeho decided to take a day trip on a train _____ _____.
A. himself    B. wanting    C. by    D. clear

**21** On the train, he told a _____ _____ _____ _____ him about his problem.
A. sitting    B. complete    C. beside    D. stranger

**22** He had no idea _____ _____ _____ _____.
A. he    B. why    C. it    D. did

**23** However, he _____ _____ _____ when he got _____ the train.
A. off    B. much    C. felt    D. better

**24** _____ _____, we often tell _____ about our problems just _____ Taeho.
A. enough    B. strangely    C. like    D. strangers

**25** That is _____ we do not have to worry about _____ or _____ them again.
A. being    B. because    C. seeing    D. judged

**26** If you have a problem that you cannot _____ your family or friends, _____ _____ to a stranger.
A. with    B. talking    C. share    D. try

**27** You will _____ _____ _____.
A. much    B. feel    C. better

**28** How do I _____ a _____ _____ a friend?
A. rival    B. turn    C. into

**29** Benjamin Franklin once had a _____ rival who did _____ like him _____.
A. not    B. political    C. all    D. at

**30** Franklin wanted to become _____ _____ him, so he _____ _____ with a plan.
A. came    B. friends    C. with    D. up

**31** His _____ had a _____ _____.
A. rival    B. rare    C. book

**32** Franklin asked his rival _____ _____ him the book _____ a _____ days.
A. few    B. lend    C. for    D. to

**33** When Franklin _____ the book, he _____ him _____.
A. thanked    B. returned    C. deeply

**34** _____ that day, his rival became not _____ a political _____ but _____ a good friend.
A. only    B. also    C. since    D. supporter

**35** Franklin _____ said, "_____ who do you one _____ will want to do _____."
A. favor    B. famously    C. more    D. enemies

**36** If you want to _____ a rival _____ a friend, don't do your _____ a _____.
A. into    B. rival    C. turn    D. favor

**37** _____, ask your _____ to _____ you a _____.
A. rival    B. favor    C. instead    D. do

---

**19** 그는 부모님이나 친구들이 이해하지 못할까 걱정이 된다.

**20** 마음을 정리하기 위해서, 태호는 혼자 하루 기차 여행을 떠나기로 결심했다.

**21** 기차에서, 그는 옆에 앉은 전혀 모르는 사람에게 자신의 고민에 대해서 말했다.

**22** 그는 자신이 왜 그랬는지 알 수 없었다.

**23** 그러나, 기차에서 내릴 때 기분이 훨씬 좋아졌다.

**24** 정말 이상하게도, 우리는 태호처럼 우리의 문제에 대해 낯선 사람에게 말할 때가 있다.

**25** 그것은 우리가 평가받거나 그 사람을 다시 볼 것이라는 걱정을 할 필요가 없기 때문이다.

**26** 만약 가족이나 친구들과도 나눌 수 없는 고민이 있다면, 낯선 이에게 말해 보아라.

**27** 기분이 훨씬 나아질 것이다.

**28** 라이벌을 어떻게 친구로 만들 수 있을까요?

**29** Benjamin Franklin에게는 한때 그를 전혀 좋아하지 않는 정치적 경쟁자가 있었다.

**30** Franklin은 그와 친구가 되고 싶어서, 계획을 세웠다.

**31** 그의 경쟁자는 희귀한 책을 가지고 있었다.

**32** Franklin은 그의 정적에게 그 책을 며칠 동안 빌려달라고 부탁했다.

**33** Franklin이 그 책을 돌려줄 때, 그는 그에게 진심으로 감사를 표했다.

**34** 그날 이후로, 그의 경쟁자는 정치적인 후원자뿐만 아니라 좋은 친구가 되었다.

**35** Franklin은 "당신을 한 번 도운 적은 더 돕고 싶어 하게 된다."라는 유명한 말을 했다.

**36** 여러분이 경쟁자를 친구로 만들고 싶다면, 경쟁자의 부탁을 들어주지 마라.

**37** 대신, 경쟁자에게 부탁을 해 보아라.

※ 다음 우리말과 일치하도록 빈칸에 알맞은 것을 골라 쓰시오.

**1** _____ Your _____

**2** Do you think you have a _____ _____ ?

**3** _____ _____ that many other people have the same problem.

**4** Psychology is the study of the _____ _____ and _____, _____ it can _____ you _____ a solution _____ your problem.

**5** How do I _____ _____ _____ ?

**6** It was five minutes before Jisu's _____ _____ in _____ of the _____ _____.

**7** _____ _____, Jisu was _____ _____ her notes in her chair.

**8** Then, her teacher _____ _____ and told her _____ _____ _____ Wonder Woman.

**9** After _____ _____ for _____ _____ minutes, Jisu did _____ feel nervous _____.

**10** _____ _____, she was _____ _____ she would _____ a great _____.

**11** _____ _____ Amy Cuddy, a famous psychologist, we can _____ more confident just _____ _____ _____ _____ two minutes before _____ _____.

**12** Our _____ change our _____, and our _____ can change our _____.

**13** Do you want to _____ _____ ?

**14** Stand with your _____ _____, and _____ your hands _____ your hips.

**15** You will _____ _____ _____ _____ about yourself _____ _____ to _____ _____.

**16** Who can help me _____ _____ ?

**17** When he _____ _____ high school _____ _____, Taeho wants to become a _____ farmer.

**18** _____, he _____ _____ _____ anyone about it.

**1** 심리학이 당신의 물음에 답하다

**2** 여러분은 당신만의 유일무이한 고민을 가지고 있다고 생각하는가?

**3** 아마 많은 다른 사람들이 여러분과 똑같은 고민을 가지고 있을 것이다.

**4** 심리학은 인간의 마음과 행동에 관한 연구이며, 따라서 여러분이 문제에 대한 해결책을 찾는 데 도움을 줄 수 있다.

**5** 어떻게 하면 긴장을 덜 할 수 있나요?

**6** 지수가 반 전체 앞에서 발표를 하기 5분 전이었다.

**7** 지수는 긴장이 되어, 의자에 앉아 자신의 필기를 열심히 들여다보고 있었다.

**8** 그때 선생님이 다가와서는 원더우먼처럼 꼿꼿이 서 있어 보라고 말했다.

**9** 그렇게 몇 분을 우뚝 선 후에, 지수는 더 이상 긴장되지 않았다.

**10** 사실, 그녀는 발표를 멋있게 할 수 있을 것이라는 자신감이 생겼다.

**11** 유명한 심리학자인 Amy Cuddy에 의하면, 우리는 스트레스를 받는 상황 이전에 2분 정도 꼿꼿이 서 있는 것만으로도 자신감이 더 생길 수 있다고 한다.

**12** 우리의 몸은 마음을 바꾸고, 마음은 우리의 행동을 바꿀 수 있다.

**13** 자신감이 생기기를 원하는가?

**14** 양발을 벌리고, 허리께에 손을 올려 보아라.

**15** 자신에 대한 확신이 생길 뿐만 아니라 다른 사람이 보기에도 자신감에 차 보인다.

**16** 누가 내 기분을 낫게 해 줄 수 있나요?

**17** 내년에 고등학교를 졸업한 이후에 태호는 전문적인 농부가 되고 싶어 한다.

**18** 하지만, 누구에게도 그것에 대해 한 번도 말하지 않았다.

**19** He is _____ _____ his parents or his friends _____ _____ _____.

**20** _____ to _____ _____ _____, Taeho _____ _____ _____ a day trip on a train _____ _____.

**21** On the train, he told a _____ stranger _____ _____ him about his problem.

**22** He had no idea _____ _____ _____ _____.

**23** _____, he _____ _____ _____ when he _____ _____ the train.

**24** _____ _____, we _____ _____ _____ about our problems just like Taeho.

**25** That is _____ we do _____ _____ _____ worry about _____ _____ or _____ them again.

**26** If you have a problem _____ you cannot _____ _____ your family or friends, try _____ to a _____.

**27** You will _____ _____ _____.

**28** How do I _____ a _____ _____ a friend?

**29** Benjamin Franklin once had a _____ _____ _____ did _____ like him _____ _____.

**30** Franklin wanted to _____ _____ _____ him, so he _____ _____ _____ a plan.

**31** His rival had a _____ book.

**32** Franklin asked his rival _____ _____ him the book for _____ _____ _____.

**33** When Franklin returned the book, he thanked him _____.

**34** _____ that day, his rival became _____ _____ a political supporter _____ _____ a good friend.

**35** Franklin _____ said, "Enemies _____ _____ _____ _____ will want to do more."

**36** If you want to _____ a rival _____ a friend, don't _____ _____ _____ _____.

**37** _____, ask your rival _____ _____ you a _____.

---

**19** 그는 부모님이나 친구들이 이해하지 못할까 걱정이 된다.

**20** 마음을 정리하기 위해서, 태호는 혼자 하루 기차 여행을 떠나기로 결심했다.

**21** 기차에서, 그는 옆에 앉은 전혀 모르는 사람에게 자신의 고민에 대해서 말했다.

**22** 그는 자신이 왜 그랬는지 알 수 없었다.

**23** 그러나, 기차에서 내릴 때 기분이 훨씬 좋아졌다.

**24** 정말 이상하게도, 우리는 태호처럼 우리의 문제에 대해 낯선 사람에게 말할 때가 있다.

**25** 그것은 우리가 평가받거나 그 사람을 다시 볼 것이라는 걱정을 할 필요가 없기 때문이다.

**26** 만약 가족이나 친구들과도 나눌 수 없는 고민이 있다면, 낯선 이에게 말해 보아라.

**27** 기분이 훨씬 나아질 것이다.

**28** 라이벌을 어떻게 친구로 만들 수 있을까요?

**29** Benjamin Franklin에게는 한때 그를 전혀 좋아하지 않는 정치적 경쟁자가 있었다.

**30** Franklin은 그와 친구가 되고 싶어서, 계획을 세웠다.

**31** 그의 경쟁자는 희귀한 책을 가지고 있었다.

**32** Franklin은 그의 정적에게 그 책을 며칠 동안 빌려달라고 부탁했다.

**33** Franklin이 그 책을 돌려줄 때, 그는 그에게 진심으로 감사를 표했다.

**34** 그날 이후로, 그의 경쟁자는 정치적인 후원자뿐만 아니라 좋은 친구가 되었다.

**35** Franklin은 "당신을 한 번 도운 적은 더 돕고 싶어 하게 된다."라는 유명한 말을 했다.

**36** 여러분이 경쟁자를 친구로 만들고 싶다면, 경쟁자의 부탁을 들어주지 마라.

**37** 대신, 경쟁자에게 부탁을 해 보아라.

※ 다음 문장을 우리말로 쓰시오.

**1** Psychology Answers Your Questions
➡ _____

**2** Do you think you have a unique problem?
➡ _____

**3** Chances are that many other people have the same problem.
➡ _____

**4** Psychology is the study of the human mind and behavior, so it can help you find a solution to your problem.
➡ _____

**5** How do I become less nervous?
➡ _____

**6** It was five minutes before Jisu's big presentation in front of the whole class.
➡ _____

**7** Feeling nervous, Jisu was carefully studying her notes in her chair.
➡ _____

**8** Then, her teacher came over and told her to stand tall like Wonder Woman.
➡ _____

**9** After standing tall for a few minutes, Jisu did not feel nervous anymore.
➡ _____

**10** In fact, she was confident that she would make a great presentation.
➡ _____

**11** According to Amy Cuddy, a famous psychologist, we can become more confident just by standing tall for two minutes before stressful events.
➡ _____
_____

**12** Our bodies change our minds, and our minds can change our behavior.
➡ _____

**13** Do you want to feel confident?
➡ _____

**14** Stand with your feet apart, and place your hands on your hips.
➡ _____

**15** You will not only feel sure about yourself but also look confident to other people.
➡ _____

**16** Who can help me feel better?
➡ _____

**17** When he graduates from high school next year, Taeho wants to become a professional farmer.
➡ _____

**18** However, he has never told anyone about it.
➡ _____

**19** He is worried that his parents or his friends will not understand.
➡ _____

**20** Wanting to clear his mind, Taeho decided to take a day trip on a train by himself.
➡ _____

**21** On the train, he told a complete stranger sitting beside him about his problem.
➡ _____

**22** He had no idea why he did it.
➡ _____

**23** However, he felt much better when he got off the train.
➡ _____

**24** Strangely enough, we often tell strangers about our problems just like Taeho.
➡ _____

**25** That is because we do not have to worry about being judged or seeing them again.
➡ _____

**26** If you have a problem that you cannot share with your family or friends, try talking to a stranger.
➡ _____

**27** You will feel much better.
➡ _____

**28** How do I turn a rival into a friend?
➡ _____

**29** Benjamin Franklin once had a political rival who did not like him at all.
➡ _____

**30** Franklin wanted to become friends with him, so he came up with a plan.
➡ _____

**31** His rival had a rare book.
➡ _____

**32** Franklin asked his rival to lend him the book for a few days.
➡ _____

**33** When Franklin returned the book, he thanked him deeply.
➡ _____

**34** Since that day, his rival became not only a political supporter but also a good friend.
➡ _____

**35** Franklin famously said, "Enemies who do you one favor will want to do more."
➡ _____

**36** If you want to turn a rival into a friend, don't do your rival a favor.
➡ _____

**37** Instead, ask your rival to do you a favor.
➡ _____

※ 다음 괄호 안의 단어들을 우리말에 맞도록 바르게 배열하시오.

**1** (Answers / Psychology / Questions / Your)
➡ _____

**2** (you / do / you / think / a / have / problem? / unique)
➡ _____

**3** (are / chances / many / that / people / other / the / have / problem. / same)
➡ _____

**4** (is / psychology / the / of / study / the / mind / human / and / so / behavior, / it / help / can / you / a / find / to / solution / problem. / your)
➡ _____

**5** (do / how / become / I / nervous? / less)
➡ _____

**6** (was / it / minutes / five / Jisu's / before / presentation / big / front / in / the / of / class. / whole)
➡ _____

**7** (nervous, / feeling / was / Jisu / carefully / her / studying / notes / her / in / chair.)
➡ _____

**8** (her / then, / teacher / over / came / and / her / told / to / tall / stand / Wonder / like / Woman.)
➡ _____

**9** (standing / after / for / tall / few / a / minutes, / did / Jisu / feel / not / anymore. / nervous)
➡ _____

**10** (fact, / in / was / she / that / confident / would / she / a / make / presentation. / great)
➡ _____

**11** (to / according / Cuddy, / Amy / a / psychologist, / famous / can / we / more / become / just / confident / by / tall / standing / two / for / before / minutes / events. / stressful)
➡ _____

**12** (bodies / our / change / minds, / our / and / minds / our / change / can / behavior. / our)
➡ _____

**13** (you / do / to / want / confident? / feel)
➡ _____

**14** (with / stand / feet / your / apart, / place / and / hands / your / on / hips. / your)
➡ _____

**15** (will / you / only / not / sure / feel / yourself / about / also / but / confident / look / other / to / people.)
➡ _____

**16** (can / who / me / help / better? / feel)
➡ _____

**17** (he / when / graduates / high / from / school / year, / next / wants / Taeho / to / a / become / farmer. / professional)
➡ _____

**18** (he / however, / never / has / anyone / told / it. / about)
➡ _____

1 심리학이 당신의 물음에 답하다

2 여러분은 당신만의 유일무이한 고민을 가지고 있다고 생각하는가?

3 아마 많은 다른 사람들이 여러분과 똑같은 고민을 가지고 있을 것이다.

4 심리학은 인간의 마음과 행동에 관한 연구이며, 따라서 여러분이 문제에 대한 해결책을 찾는 데 도움을 줄 수 있다.

5 어떻게 하면 긴장을 덜 할 수 있나요?

6 지수가 반 전체 앞에서 발표를 하기 5분 전이었다.

7 지수는 긴장이 되어, 의자에 앉아 자신의 필기를 열심히 들여다보고 있었다.

8 그때 선생님이 다가와서는 원더 우먼처럼 꼿꼿이 서 있어 보라고 말했다.

9 그렇게 몇 분을 우뚝 선 후에, 지수는 더 이상 긴장되지 않았다.

10 사실, 그녀는 발표를 멋있게 할 수 있을 것이라는 자신감이 생겼다.

11 유명한 심리학자인 Amy Cuddy에 의하면, 우리는 스트레스를 받는 상황 이전에 2분 정도 꼿꼿이 서 있는 것만으로도 자신감이 더 생길 수 있다고 한다.

12 우리의 몸은 마음을 바꾸고, 마음은 우리의 행동을 바꿀 수 있다.

13 자신감이 생기기를 원하는가?

14 양발을 벌리고, 허리께에 손을 올려 보아라.

15 자신에 대한 확신이 생길 뿐만 아니라 다른 사람이 보기에도 자신감에 차 보인다.

16 누가 내 기분을 낫게 해 줄 수 있나요?

17 내년에 고등학교를 졸업한 이후에 태호는 전문적인 농부가 되고 싶어 한다.

18 하지만, 누구에게도 그것에 대해 한 번도 말하지 않았다.

**19** (is / he / that / worried / parents / his / or / friends / his / not / will / understand.)
➡ _____

**20** (to / wanting / his / clear / mind, / decided / Taeho / take / to / day / a / trip / a / on / train / himself. / by)
➡ _____

**21** (the / on / train, / told / he / complete / a / stranger / beside / sitting / about / him / problem. / his)
➡ _____

**22** (had / he / idea / no / he / why / it. / did)
➡ _____

**23** (he / however, / felt / better / much / he / when / off / got / train. / the)
➡ _____

**24** (enough, / strangely / often / we / strangers / tell / our / about / problems / like / Taeho. / just)
➡ _____

**25** (is / that / we / because / not / do / to / have / worry / being / about / or / judged / them / seeing / again.)
➡ _____

**26** (you / if / a / have / problem / you / that / share / cannot / with / family / your / friends, / or / talking / try / a / to / stranger.)
➡ _____

**27** (will / you / much / feel / better.)
➡ _____

**28** (do / how / turn / I / into / rival / friend? / a)
➡ _____

**29** (Franklin / Benjamin / had / once / a / rival / political / did / who / like / not / at / him / all.)
➡ _____

**30** (wanted / Franklin / become / to / with / friends / him, / he / so / up / came / a / with / plan.)
➡ _____

**31** (rival / his / a / had / book. / rare)
➡ _____

**32** (asked / Franklin / rival / his / lend / to / the / him / for / book / few / a / days.)
➡ _____

**33** (Franklin / when / the / returned / book, / thanked / he / deeply. / him)
➡ _____

**34** (that / since / day, / rival / his / not / became / only / political / a / but / supporter / a / also / friend. / good)
➡ _____

**35** (Franklin / said, / famously / who / "enemies / you / do / favor / one / want / will / do / to / more.")
➡ _____

**36** (you / if / to / want / turn / rival / a / into / friend, / a / do / don't / rival / your / favor. / a)
➡ _____

**37** (ask / instead, / rival / your / do / to / you / favor. / a)
➡ _____

**19** 그는 부모님이나 친구들이 이해하지 못할까 걱정이 된다.

**20** 마음을 정리하기 위해서, 태호는 혼자 하루 기차 여행을 떠나기로 결심했다.

**21** 기차에서, 그는 옆에 앉은 전혀 모르는 사람에게 자신의 고민에 대해서 말했다.

**22** 그는 자신이 왜 그랬는지 알 수 없었다.

**23** 그러나, 기차에서 내릴 때 기분이 훨씬 좋아졌다.

**24** 정말 이상하게도, 우리는 태호처럼 우리의 문제에 대해 낯선 사람에게 말할 때가 있다.

**25** 그것은 우리가 평가받거나 그 사람을 다시 볼 것이라는 걱정을 할 필요가 없기 때문이다.

**26** 만약 가족이나 친구들과도 나눌 수 없는 고민이 있다면, 낯선 이에게 말해 보아라.

**27** 기분이 훨씬 나아질 것이다.

**28** 라이벌을 어떻게 친구로 만들 수 있을까요?

**29** Benjamin Franklin에게는 한때 그를 전혀 좋아하지 않는 정치적 경쟁자가 있었다.

**30** Franklin은 그와 친구가 되고 싶어서, 계획을 세웠다.

**31** 그의 경쟁자는 희귀한 책을 가지고 있었다.

**32** Franklin은 그의 정적에게 그 책을 며칠 동안 빌려달라고 부탁했다.

**33** Franklin이 그 책을 돌려줄 때, 그는 그에게 진심으로 감사를 표했다.

**34** 그날 이후로, 그의 경쟁자는 정치적인 후원자뿐만 아니라 좋은 친구가 되었다.

**35** Franklin은 "당신을 한 번 도운 적은 더 돕고 싶어 하게 된다."라는 유명한 말을 했다.

**36** 여러분이 경쟁자를 친구로 만들고 싶다면, 경쟁자의 부탁을 들어주지 마라.

**37** 대신, 경쟁자에게 부탁을 해 보아라.

※ 다음 우리말을 영어로 쓰시오.

**1** 심리학이 당신의 물음에 답하다

➡ _____

**2** 여러분은 당신만의 유일무이한 고민을 가지고 있다고 생각하는가?

➡ _____

**3** 아마 많은 다른 사람들이 여러분과 똑같은 고민을 가지고 있을 것이다.

➡ _____

**4** 심리학은 인간의 마음과 행동에 관한 연구이며, 따라서 여러분이 문제에 대한 해결책을 찾는 데 도움을 줄 수 있다.

➡ _____

_____

**5** 어떻게 하면 긴장을 덜 할 수 있나요?

➡ _____

**6** 지수가 반 전체 앞에서 발표를 하기 5분 전이었다.

➡ _____

**7** 지수는 긴장이 되어, 의자에 앉아 자신의 필기를 열심히 들여다보고 있었다.

➡ _____

**8** 그때 선생님이 다가와서는 원더우먼처럼 꼿꼿이 서 있어 보라고 말했다.

➡ _____

**9** 그렇게 몇 분을 우뚝 선 후에, 지수는 더 이상 긴장되지 않았다.

➡ _____

**10** 사실, 그녀는 발표를 멋있게 할 수 있을 것이라는 자신감이 생겼다.

➡ _____

**11** 유명한 심리학자인 Amy Cuddy에 의하면, 우리는 스트레스를 받는 상황 이전에 2분 정도 꼿꼿이 서 있는 것만으로도 자신감이 더 생길 수 있다고 한다.

➡ _____

_____

**12** 우리의 몸은 마음을 바꾸고, 마음은 우리의 행동을 바꿀 수 있다.

➡ _____

**13** 자신감이 생기기를 원하는가?

➡ _____

**14** 양발을 벌리고, 허리께에 손을 올려 보아라.

➡ _____

**15** 자신에 대한 확신이 생길 뿐만 아니라 다른 사람이 보기에도 자신감에 차 보인다.

➡ _____

**16** 누가 내 기분을 낮게 해 줄 수 있나요?

➡ _____

**17** 내년에 고등학교를 졸업한 이후에 태호는 전문적인 농부가 되고 싶어 한다.

➡ _____

**18** 하지만, 누구에게도 그것에 대해 한 번도 말하지 않았다.

➡ _____

**19** 그는 부모님이나 친구들이 이해하지 못할까 걱정이 된다.

➡ _____

**20** 마음을 정리하기 위해서, 태호는 혼자 하루 기차 여행을 떠나기로 결심했다.

➡ _____

**21** 기차에서, 그는 옆에 앉은 전혀 모르는 사람에게 자신의 고민에 대해서 말했다.

➡ _____

**22** 그는 자신이 왜 그랬는지 알 수 없었다.

➡ _____

**23** 그러나, 기차에서 내릴 때 기분이 훨씬 좋아졌다.

➡ _____

**24** 정말 이상하게도, 우리는 태호처럼 우리의 문제에 대해 낯선 사람에게 말할 때가 있다.

➡ _____

**25** 그것은 우리가 평가받거나 그 사람을 다시 볼 것이라는 걱정을 할 필요가 없기 때문이다.

➡ _____

**26** 만약 가족이나 친구들과도 나눌 수 없는 고민이 있다면, 낯선 이에게 말해 보아라.

➡ _____

**27** 기분이 훨씬 나아질 것이다.

➡ _____

**28** 라이벌을 어떻게 친구로 만들 수 있을까요?

➡ _____

**29** Benjamin Franklin에게는 한때 그를 전혀 좋아하지 않는 정치적 경쟁자가 있었다.

➡ _____

**30** Franklin은 그와 친구가 되고 싶어서, 계획을 세웠다.

➡ _____

**31** 그의 경쟁자는 희귀한 책을 가지고 있었다.

➡ _____

**32** Franklin은 그의 정적에게 그 책을 며칠 동안 빌려달라고 부탁했다.

➡ _____

**33** Franklin이 그 책을 돌려줄 때, 그는 그에게 진심으로 감사를 표했다.

➡ _____

**34** 그날 이후로, 그의 경쟁자는 정치적인 후원자뿐만 아니라 좋은 친구가 되었다.

➡ _____

**35** Franklin은 "당신을 한 번 도운 적은 더 돕고 싶어 하게 된다."라는 유명한 말을 했다.

➡ _____

**36** 여러분이 경쟁자를 친구로 만들고 싶다면, 경쟁자의 부탁을 들어주지 마라.

➡ _____

**37** 대신, 경쟁자에게 부탁을 해 보아라.

➡ _____

※ 다음 우리말과 일치하도록 빈칸에 알맞은 말을 쓰시오.

## Listen & Speak 2 - Think and Talk

1. A: What _____ I _____ _____ _____ on Stress-Free Day?

2. B: You _____ _____ _____ _____ the classroom.

3. C: You _____ _____ _____ _____ _____ _____ _____ 8:30.

## Link

1. _____ _____ do you _____ _____ _____?

2. _____ _____ _____ the answer to this question, we _____ _____ _____ about confidence.

3. Thirty students _____ _____ _____. The _____ was nine.

4. Eighteen students _____ _____ _____ _____ _____ _____.

5. _____, sixty percent of the students _____ _____ _____ _____ _____.

## Write

1. _____ _____ _____ in my life

2. The _____ _____ _____ _____ _____ _____ was when my grandmother _____ _____ five years _____.

3. When I was _____, she _____ _____ _____ me _____ _____ the time.

4. _____ _____ _____ _____, I _____ _____ and _____.

5. _____ _____, I _____ my grandmother's diary.

6. She _____ _____ _____ _____ _____ about her memories _____ _____ _____ that I would lead a happy life.

7. _____ _____ _____, I _____ _____ that I should _____ _____ _____ just _____ _____ _____.

※ **다음 우리말을 영어로 쓰시오.**

**Listen & Speak 2 - Think and Talk**

1. A: 스트레스가 없는 날에 무엇을 할 필요가 없을까?

➡ _____

2. B: 너는 교실 청소를 할 필요가 없어.

➡ _____

3. C: 너는 8:30분까지 학교에 올 필요가 없어.

➡ _____

**Link**

1. 당신은 스스로에 대해 얼마나 확신이 있나요?

➡ _____

2. 질문에 대한 답을 찾고 싶어, 우리는 자신감에 대한 검사지를 만들었습니다.

➡ _____

3. 30명의 학생들이 검사를 했습니다. 평균적인 점수는 9점이었습니다.

➡ _____

4. 18명의 학생들이 평균 점수를 넘었습니다.

➡ _____

5. 따라서, 학생들의 60%가 그들 스스로에 대해 꽤 자신감을 갖고 있습니다.

➡ _____

**Write**

1. 내 삶에서 가장 힘들었던 순간

➡ _____

2. 내 삶에서 가장 힘들었던 순간은 5년 전 할머니께서 돌아가셨을 때였다.

➡ _____

3. 내가 더 어렸을 때, 그녀는 대부분의 시간 동안 나를 돌봐 주셨다.

➡ _____

4. 그녀가 곁에 없어서, 나는 슬프고 외로웠다.

➡ _____

5. 어느 날, 나는 할머니의 일기장을 발견했다.

➡ _____

6. 그녀는 그녀의 기억에 대해 많이 적었을 뿐만 아니라, 내가 행복한 삶을 살기를 바랐다.

➡ _____

7. 이 경험을 통해, 나는 그녀가 원했던 것처럼 행복해지려고 노력해야 한다는 것을 배웠다.

➡ _____

※ 다음 영어를 우리말로 쓰시오.

| 01 | uniquely | | 22 | honestly |
| 02 | check | | 23 | complain |
| 03 | crush | | 24 | passion |
| 04 | unfortunately | | 25 | finish |
| 05 | surely | | 26 | pay |
| 06 | appreciate | | 27 | innovative |
| 07 | fantastic | | 28 | throughout |
| 08 | fix | | 29 | provide |
| 09 | grand | | 30 | form |
| 10 | happen | | 31 | slice |
| 11 | completely | | 32 | fresh |
| 12 | inconvenience | | 33 | gladly |
| 13 | pursue | | 34 | successful |
| 14 | customer | | 35 | fill out |
| 15 | inventor | | 36 | scare away |
| 16 | reason | | 37 | now that |
| 17 | creative | | 38 | as a result |
| 18 | role | | 39 | of all time |
| 19 | real | | 40 | put up |
| 20 | rare | | 41 | be used to |
| 21 | satisfied | | 42 | do one's best |
| | | | 43 | take charge of |

※ 다음 우리말을 영어로 쓰시오.

| | |
|---|---|
| 01 열정, 흥미 | |
| 02 진가를 알아보다, 고마워하다 | |
| 03 계산서 | |
| 04 ~ 동안 내내 | |
| 05 덜 익은, 살짝 익힌 | |
| 06 지불하다, 지급하다 | |
| 07 수리하다 | |
| 08 서류 | |
| 09 확실히, 분명히 | |
| 10 불편, 애로 | |
| 11 완전하게 | |
| 12 기꺼이 | |
| 13 추구하다, 추진하다 | |
| 14 이유 | |
| 15 역할, 배역 | |
| 16 일어나다 | |
| 17 불평하다 | |
| 18 장식하다, 꾸미다 | |
| 19 환상적인 | |
| 20 식사 | |
| 21 신선한 | |

| | |
|---|---|
| 22 솔직하게, 솔직히 | |
| 23 창의적인, 창조적인 | |
| 24 으깨다 | |
| 25 획기적인 | |
| 26 한 조각, 일부 | |
| 27 성공적인 | |
| 28 불행하게도 | |
| 29 웅장한, 위대한 | |
| 30 고객, 소비자 | |
| 31 독특하게 | |
| 32 만찬, 저녁 식사 | |
| 33 제공하다 | |
| 34 만족한 | |
| 35 ~에 익숙하다 | |
| 36 작성하다 | |
| 37 더 이상 아니다 | |
| 38 결과적으로 | |
| 39 역대, 지금껏 | |
| 40 최선을 다하다 | |
| 41 ~할 마음이 나다 | |
| 42 내붙이다, 게시하다 | |
| 43 겁주어 쫓아내다 | |

※ 다음 영영풀이에 알맞은 단어를 <보기>에서 골라 쓴 후, 우리말 뜻을 쓰시오.

1 _____ : the character played by an actor: _____

2 _____ : cooked a short time; still red inside: _____

3 _____ : the foods eaten or prepared for eating at one time: _____

4 _____ : to supply something that is wanted or needed: _____

5 _____ : an informal meal that people eat in the evening: _____

6 _____ : during the whole period of time of something: _____

7 _____ : a bill for the food and drinks that are served in a restaurant: _____

8 _____ : to like something because one recognizes its good qualities: _____

9 _____ : to press something so hard that it breaks or is damaged: _____

10 _____ : someone who buys goods or services from a shop, company, etc.: _____

11 _____ : to make something look more nice by putting something pretty on it: _____

12 _____ : to repair something that is broken or not working properly: _____

13 _____ : an official document with spaces where you write information: _____

14 _____ : a person who has invented something or whose job is inventing things: _____

15 _____ : to say that you are annoyed, not satisfied, or unhappy about something or someone: _____

16 _____ : to make efforts to achieve a particular aim or result, often over a long period of time: _____

| 보기 | | | |
|---|---|---|---|
| complain | inventor | meal | throughout |
| crush | decorate | check | rare |
| pursue | form | provide | role |
| fix | customer | supper | appreciate |

※ 다음 우리말과 일치하도록 빈칸에 알맞은 말을 쓰시오.

### Listen & Speak 1 A-1

**B:** Wow! Did you _____ this?

**G:** I _____ . Do you like _____ ?

**B:** Yes, the bread and the milk _____ _____ _____ . I _____ _____ _____ _____ _____ the bread.

**G:** Thanks, but _____ _____ _____ it. It's not _____ .

**B:** I don't think _____ . I think it's a _____ _____ .

**B:** 우와! 이거 네가 그린 거야?
**G:** 내가 그렸어. 마음에 들어?
**B:** 응, 빵이랑 우유가 정말 진짜 같아. 빵을 한 입 먹고 싶어지는데.
**G:** 고마워, 하지만 이건 만족스럽진 않아. 독창적이지 않아.
**B:** 난 그렇게 생각 안 해. 정말 멋진 그림인 것 같아.

### Listen & Speak 1 A-2

**M:** Hello, ma'am. _____ _____ I _____ you?

**W:** I _____ this phone _____ _____ _____ _____ _____ , but it _____ _____ _____ _____ _____ .

**M:** Oh, I see. May I _____ _____ _____ _____ _____ it? (*Pause*) We're sorry for the _____ . It'll _____ a _____ _____ _____ it.

**W:** _____ _____ _____ _____ _____ the phone. I'd _____ a new _____ .

**M:** Of _____ . I just need to _____ _____ this _____ .

**M:** 안녕하세요, 고객님. 무엇을 도와드릴까요?
**W:** 이 휴대전화를 겨우 일주일 전에 샀는데, 가끔 저절로 꺼져요.
**M:** 오, 그렇군요. 제가 좀 봐도 될까요? 불편을 드려 죄송합니다. 고치는 데 몇 시간 정도 걸릴 거예요.
**W:** 그 휴대전화가 만족스럽지 않아요. 새것을 원해요.
**M:** 물론이죠. 이 서류만 작성하면 됩니다.

### Listen & Speak 2 A-1

**G:** Wow, I like this blueberry jam. Where _____ you _____ it?

**B:** I made it _____ .

**G:** Really? This is _____ _____ _____ _____ _____ I've ever had. You _____ _____ _____ .

**B:** Do you think people _____ want _____ _____ this?

**G:** Of course. _____ _____ _____ _____ your first customer.

**G:** 우와, 이 블루베리 잼 마음에 든다. 어디서 샀어?
**B:** 직접 만든 거야.
**G:** 정말? 내가 지금껏 먹어본 잼 중에 제일 좋아. 팔아도 되겠어.
**B:** 사람들이 이걸 사길 원할 거라고 생각해?
**G:** 물론이지. 내가 너의 첫 손님이 되겠다고 약속할게.

### Listen & Speak 2 A-2

**B:** Mom, I want to go to an arts high school. I want to become an actor.

**W:** What? I _____ you _____ _____ _____ science.

**B:** I was but _____ _____ . I _____ _____ _____ a movie star.

**W:** _____ you _____ you want to be an actor?

**B:** Yes, I'll learn _____ _____ _____ . _____ _____ _____ _____ _____ _____ .

**B:** 엄마, 저 예술 고등학교에 가고 싶어요. 배우가 되고 싶어요.
**W:** 뭐라고? 네가 과학에 관심이 있다고 생각했는데.
**B:** 그랬었는데 더는 아니에요. 저는 영화배우가 되고 싶어요.
**W:** 배우가 되고 싶은 게 확실하니?
**B:** 네, 연기하는 방법을 배울 거예요. 최선을 다하겠다고 약속할게요.

### Communicate A

**Man:** Are you enjoying _____ _____ ?

**Woman:** Well, the bread was _____, and the salad was _____.

**Man:** How _____ your steak?

**Woman:** Honestly, _____ _____ _____ _____ the steak. It's too _____ for me.

**Man:** I'm sorry. _____ you _____ me _____ _____ you _____ _____ ?

**Woman:** That's O.K. I need to _____ _____. Let me just _____ the _____, please.

**Man:** I'm really sorry. You _____ _____ _____ the steak.

**Woman:** O.K. Thanks.

**Man:** _____ _____ _____ _____ you _____ a better _____ next time you visit.

남자: 식사가 마음에 드십니까?
여자: 음, 빵은 괜찮았고, 샐러드도 신선했어요.
남자: 스테이크는 어떠세요?
여자: 솔직히, 스테이크는 만족스럽지 않아요. 제겐 너무 덜 익었어요.
남자: 죄송합니다. 다른 것으로 가져다 드릴까요?
여자: 괜찮아요. 가봐야 해서요. 그냥 계산서 좀 갖다주세요.
남자: 정말 죄송합니다. 스테이크 값은 지불하지 않으셔도 됩니다.
여자: 알겠습니다. 감사해요.
남자: 다음에 방문하실 때는 더 좋은 경험을 드릴 것을 약속드릴게요.

### Progress Check 1

**M:** Hello, ma'am. _____ _____ _____ help you?

**W:** I _____ this hat _____ a gift yesterday, but _____ _____ _____ _____ the color.

**M:** Oh, I see. We have this hat _____ _____ _____.

**W:** Do you have _____ _____ _____ ?

**M:** Yes, we _____. I'll _____ _____ for you.

**W:** Thanks.

M: 안녕하세요, 고객님. 무엇을 도와드릴까요?
W: 어제 이 모자를 선물 받았는데, 색상이 마음에 들지 않아요.
M: 오, 그렇군요. 이 모자로 다른 색상도 있습니다.
W: 파란 것도 있나요?
M: 네, 있습니다. 하나 가져다 드릴게요.
W: 고맙습니다.

### Progress Check 2

**B:** Mom, I want to _____ cooking _____.

**W:** What? I thought you were _____ _____ sports.

**B:** I was but _____ _____. I want to become a _____.

**W:** Are you sure? Cooking is _____ _____.

**B:** Don't _____. _____ _____ _____ _____ my best.

**W:** O.K., _____.

B: 엄마, 저 요리 수업을 듣고 싶어요.
W: 뭐? 네가 스포츠에 관심이 있다고 생각했는데.
B: 그랬는데 더는 아니에요. 저는 요리사가 되고 싶어요.
W: 정말이니? 요리는 힘든 일이란다.
B: 걱정하지 마세요. 최선을 다하겠다고 약속할게요.
W: 그래, 그럼.

### Progress Check 3

**G:** Dad, I want to watch a movie _____ TV now.

**M:** _____ you _____ your homework?

**G:** No, but _____ _____ _____ _____ it after I watch TV.

G: 아빠, 저 지금 TV에서 영화를 보고 싶어요.
M: 숙제는 끝냈니?
G: 아니요, 하지만 TV를 보고 나서 끝낼 것을 약속드릴게요.

※ 다음 우리말에 맞도록 대화를 영어로 쓰시오.

### Listen & Speak 1 A-1

B: _____

G: _____

B: _____

G: _____

B: _____

B: 우와! 이거 네가 그린 거야?
G: 내가 그렸어. 마음에 들어?
B: 응, 빵이랑 우유가 정말 진짜 같아. 빵을 한 입 먹고 싶어지는데.
G: 고마워. 하지만 이건 만족스럽진 않아. 독창적이지 않아.
B: 난 그렇게 생각 안 해. 정말 멋진 그림인 것 같아.

### Listen & Speak 1 A-2

M: _____

W: _____

M: _____

_____

W: _____

M: _____

M: 안녕하세요, 고객님. 무엇을 도와드릴까요?
W: 이 휴대전화를 겨우 일주일 전에 샀는데, 가끔 저절로 꺼져요.
M: 오, 그렇군요. 제가 좀 봐도 될까요? 불편을 드려 죄송합니다. 고치는 데 몇 시간 정도 걸릴 거예요.
W: 그 휴대전화가 만족스럽지 않아요. 새것을 원해요.
M: 물론이죠. 이 서류만 작성하면 됩니다.

### Listen & Speak 2 A-1

G: _____

B: _____

G: _____

B: _____

G: _____

G: 우와, 이 블루베리 잼 마음에 든다. 어디서 샀어?
B: 직접 만든 거야.
G: 정말? 내가 지금껏 먹어본 잼 중에 제일 좋아. 팔아도 되겠어.
B: 사람들이 이걸 사길 원할 거라고 생각해?
G: 물론이지. 내가 너의 첫 손님이 되겠다고 약속할게.

### Listen & Speak 2 A-2

B: _____

W: _____

B: _____

W: _____

B: _____

B: 엄마, 저 예술 고등학교에 가고 싶어요. 배우가 되고 싶어요.
W: 뭐라고? 네가 과학에 관심이 있다고 생각했는데.
B: 그랬었는데 더는 아니에요. 저는 영화 배우가 되고 싶어요.
W: 배우가 되고 싶은 게 확실하니?
B: 네, 연기하는 방법을 배울 거예요. 최선을 다하겠다고 약속할게요.

## Communicate A

Man: _____

Woman: _____

Man: _____

Woman: _____

Man: _____

Woman: _____

Man: _____

Woman: _____

Man: _____

남자: 식사가 마음에 드십니까?

여자: 음, 빵은 괜찮았고, 샐러드도 신선했어요.

남자: 스테이크는 어떠세요?

여자: 솔직히, 스테이크는 만족스럽지 않아요. 제겐 너무 덜 익었어요.

남자: 죄송합니다. 다른 것으로 가져다 드릴까요?

여자: 괜찮아요. 가봐야 해서요. 그냥 계산서 좀 갖다주세요.

남자: 정말 죄송합니다. 스테이크 값은 지불하지 않으셔도 됩니다.

여자: 알겠습니다. 감사해요.

남자: 다음에 방문하실 때는 더 좋은 경험을 드릴 것을 약속드릴게요.

## Progress Check 1

M: _____

W: _____

M: _____

W: _____

M: _____

W: _____

M: 안녕하세요, 고객님. 무엇을 도와드릴까요?

W: 어제 이 모자를 선물 받았는데, 색상이 마음에 들지 않아요.

M: 오, 그렇군요. 이 모자로 다른 색상도 있습니다.

W: 파란 것도 있나요?

M: 네, 있습니다. 하나 가져다 드릴게요.

W: 고맙습니다.

## Progress Check 2

B: _____

W: _____

B: _____

W: _____

B: _____

W: _____

B: 엄마, 저 요리 수업을 듣고 싶어요.

W: 뭐? 네가 스포츠에 관심이 있다고 생각했는데.

B: 그랬는데 더는 아니에요. 저는 요리사가 되고 싶어요.

W: 정말이니? 요리는 힘든 일이란다.

B: 걱정하지 마세요. 최선을 다하겠다고 약속할게요.

W: 그래, 그럼.

## Progress Check 3

G: _____

M: _____

G: _____

G: 아빠, 저 지금 TV에서 영화를 보고 싶어요.

M: 숙제는 끝냈니?

G: 아니요, 하지만 TV를 보고 나서 끝낼 것을 약속드릴게요.

※ 다음 우리말과 일치하도록 빈칸에 알맞은 것을 골라 쓰시오.

**1** Da _____ _____ _____
A. Cook        B. the        C. Vinci

**2** Leonardo da Vinci is _____ _____ one of the _____ painters of all _____.
A. time      B. known      C. greatest      D. as

**3** He was _____ a great _____, scientist, and _____.
A. inventor      B. musician      C. also

**4** Very _____ people, _____, know _____ da Vinci was also a _____ cook.
A. creative      B. however      C. few      D. that

**5** _____ 1473, twenty-year-old da Vinci _____ a cook _____ a restaurant in Florence, Italy.
A. as      B. in      C. worked      D. at

**6** When he _____ _____ of the kitchen, da Vinci _____ the menu _____.
A. changed      B. charge      C. completely      D. took

**7** He made _____ but _____ dishes _____ fish with a few carrot _____.
A. slices      B. simple      C. like      D. artistic

**8** Some _____ were _____ _____ _____ flowers.
A. decorated      B. dishes      C. with      D. even

**9** Customers, however, were unhappy _____ they were _____ to dishes _____ big _____ of meat.
A. servings      B. used      C. with      D. because

**10** _____ a _____, da Vinci _____ his _____.
A. lost      B. as      C. job      D. result

**11** A _____ years _____, da Vinci _____ a restaurant _____ his friend Sandro Botticelli.
A. opened      B. later      C. few      D. with

**12** He wanted to _____ a place _____ people could _____ his _____ food.
A. innovative      B. create      C. try      D. where

**13** They _____ _____ a beautifully painted sign and made a _____ _____ menu.
A. uniquely      B. up      C. written      D. put

**14** Da Vinci _____ that people would soon _____ his _____.
A. appreciate      B. believed      C. cooking      D. creative

**15** _____, that _____ _____.
A. happened      B. unfortunately      C. never

1 요리사 다빈치

2 레오나르도 다빈치는 역대 가장 위대한 화가들 중의 한 명으로 알려져 있다.

3 그는 또한 위대한 발명가, 과학자, 그리고 음악가였다.

4 하지만, 극히 소수의 사람만이 또한 그가 창의적인 요리사였다는 것을 안다.

5 1473년, 스무 살의 레오나르도 다빈치는 이탈리아 플로렌스에 있는 음식점에서 요리사로 일했다.

6 그가 부엌을 책임지게 되었을 때, 다빈치는 메뉴를 완전히 바꿔 버렸다.

7 그는 약간의 당근 조각을 곁들인 생선과 같이 간단하지만 예술적인 음식을 만들었다.

8 몇몇 음식들은 심지어 꽃으로 장식되었다.

9 하지만, 손님들은 많은 양의 고기 요리에 익숙했었기 때문에 불만족스러워했다.

10 그 결과, 다빈치는 그의 직업을 잃었다.

11 몇 년 후, 다빈치는 그의 친구인 산드로 보티첼리와 함께 음식점을 열었다.

12 그는 사람들이 그의 획기적인 음식을 먹어 볼 수 있는 장소로 만들기를 원했다.

13 그들은 아름답게 그려진 간판을 내걸었고 독특하게 써진 메뉴를 만들었다.

14 다빈치는 사람들이 곧 그의 창의적인 요리의 진가를 알아볼 것이라고 믿었다.

15 불행히도, 그런 일은 결코 일어나지 않았다.

**16** _____ the _____ 1480s, da Vinci began to _____ Ludovico Sforza in Milan.

A. work        B. early        C. for        D. in

**17** He was given many _____ _____, _____ a musician, a painter, and an engineer.

A. as        B. different        C. such        D. roles

**18** He was also _____ _____ _____ the kitchen.

A. of        B. put        C. charge        D. in

**19** He was happy to be given _____ _____ to _____ his _____ for cooking.

A. pursue        B. passion        C. chance        D. another

**20** Da Vinci did not _____ _____ _____ _____ dishes.

A. creative        B. stop        C. cooking        D. at

**21** He wanted to cook _____ _____ _____ and _____.

A. easily        B. more        C. much        D. quickly

**22** _____, he _____ new _____ for his kitchen.

A. machines        B. invented        C. thus

**23** He _____ machines that could _____ _____ and _____ spaghetti.

A. crush        B. created        C. pull        D. vegetables

**24** He even made a _____ that could _____ frogs _____ the water tank.

A. from        B. scare        C. device        D. away

**25** Surely, they were all very _____, but _____ of them were too big or _____ difficult _____ use.

A. too        B. innovative        C. most        D. to

**26** In 1495, Sforza asked da Vinci to make a _____ painting, which was _____ the last supper of Jesus, on the _____ of a church in Milan.

A. based        B. wall        C. grand        D. on

**27** Da Vinci gladly _____ on the project _____ he had always _____ in food.

A. interested        B. took        C. been        D. because

**28** He _____ a lot of time cooking all _____ of food to decide _____ to _____ on the table in his picture.

A. kinds        B. what        C. spent        D. put

**29** "Da Vinci has _____ his time in the kitchen for _____ a year. That's the _____ why he hasn't finished the painting yet," _____ the people from the church to Sforza.

A. over        B. complained        C. reason        D. wasted

**30** _____ da Vinci never became a _____ cook, he showed great _____ in cooking _____ his life.

A. throughout        B. successful        C. interest        D. although

**31** He was _____ _____ a great painter _____ _____ a creative cook.

A. also        B. not        C. but        D. only

**32** Now _____ you know all about his _____ passion for cooking, you will never look at *The Last Supper* the _____ _____.

A. same        B. secret        C. that        D. way

---

**16** 1480년대 초반에, 다빈치는 밀라노에서 루도비코 스포르차를 위해 일하기 시작했다.

**17** 그는 음악가, 화가, 그리고 공학자와 같은 많은 역할들을 부여받았다.

**18** 그는 또한 주방을 책임지게 되었다.

**19** 그는 요리를 향한 그의 열정을 추구할 또 다른 기회를 얻게 되어 행복했다.

**20** 다빈치는 창의적인 요리를 만드는 것에 멈추지 않았다.

**21** 그는 훨씬 더 빠르고 쉽게 요리하고 싶어했다.

**22** 따라서, 그는 그의 주방에서 사용할 새로운 기계들을 발명하였다.

**23** 그는 채소를 으깨고 스파게티를 뽑는 기계들을 만들었다.

**24** 그는 심지어 개구리를 겁주어 물탱크에서 쫓아낼 수 있는 기구도 만들었다.

**25** 확실히 그것들은 모두 매우 획기적이었지만, 그것들 중 대부분은 사용하기에 너무 크거나 너무 어려웠다.

**26** 1495년, 스포르차는 다빈치에게 웅장한 그림을 밀라노에 있는 교회의 벽에 그려 달라고 부탁했는데, 그것은 예수의 최후의 만찬을 바탕으로 한 것이었다.

**27** 다빈치는 기꺼이 그 작업을 맡았는데, 그가 항상 음식에 흥미를 가졌기 때문이었다.

**28** 그는 그림 속 식탁 위에 어떤 음식을 올릴지 결정하기 위해 모든 종류의 음식을 요리하느라 많은 시간을 썼다.

**29** "다빈치는 1년 넘게 부엌에서 시간을 낭비해 오고 있습니다. 그것이 그가 아직도 그림을 끝내지 못한 이유입니다."라고 교회 사람들이 스포르차에게 불평을 했다.

**30** 다빈치는 결코 성공적인 요리사는 되지 못했지만 그는 그의 생애 내내 요리에 대한 큰 흥미를 보여 주었다.

**31** 그는 훌륭한 화가일 뿐만 아니라 창의적인 요리사였다.

**32** 이제 여러분은 요리에 대한 그의 비밀스런 열정을 모두 알게 되었기 때문에 〈최후의 만찬〉을 절대 같은 식으로는 보지 않을 것이다.

※ 다음 우리말과 일치하도록 빈칸에 알맞은 것을 골라 쓰시오.

**1** Da Vinci ＿＿＿＿＿ ＿＿＿＿＿

**2** Leonardo da Vinci ＿＿＿＿ ＿＿＿＿ ＿＿＿ one of the ＿＿＿＿
＿＿＿＿ ＿＿＿＿ ＿＿＿＿ ＿＿＿＿.

**3** He was ＿＿＿＿ a great ＿＿＿＿, ＿＿＿＿, and musician.

**4** Very ＿＿＿＿ people, ＿＿＿＿, know that da Vinci was also a
＿＿＿＿ ＿＿＿＿.

**5** In 1473, ＿＿＿＿＿ da Vinci worked ＿＿＿＿ ＿＿＿＿
＿＿＿＿ at a restaurant in Florence, Italy.

**6** When he ＿＿＿＿ ＿＿＿＿ ＿＿＿＿ the kitchen, da Vinci
＿＿＿＿ the menu ＿＿＿＿.

**7** He made simple ＿＿＿＿ artistic dishes ＿＿＿＿ fish with
＿＿＿＿ ＿＿＿＿ ＿＿＿＿.

**8** Some dishes ＿＿＿＿ ＿＿＿＿ ＿＿＿＿ ＿＿＿＿ flowers.

**9** Customers, ＿＿＿＿, were unhappy because they ＿＿＿＿
＿＿＿＿ dishes ＿＿＿＿ big ＿＿＿＿ of meat.

**10** ＿＿＿＿ ＿＿＿＿ ＿＿＿＿, da Vinci lost his job.

**11** ＿＿＿＿ ＿＿＿＿ years ＿＿＿＿, da Vinci opened a restaurant
with his friend Sandro Botticelli.

**12** He wanted ＿＿＿＿ ＿＿＿＿ a place ＿＿＿＿ people could try
his ＿＿＿＿ food.

**13** They ＿＿＿＿ ＿＿＿＿ a ＿＿＿＿ ＿＿＿＿ sign and made a
＿＿＿＿ ＿＿＿＿ menu.

**14** Da Vinci believed that people ＿＿＿＿ soon ＿＿＿＿ his ＿＿＿＿
cooking.

**15** ＿＿＿＿, that never ＿＿＿＿.

**1** 요리사 다빈치

**2** 레오나르도 다빈치는 역대 가장 위대한 화가들 중의 한 명으로 알려져 있다.

**3** 그는 또한 위대한 발명가, 과학자, 그리고 음악가였다.

**4** 하지만, 극히 소수의 사람들만이 또한 그가 창의적인 요리사였다는 것을 안다.

**5** 1473년, 스무 살의 레오나르도 다빈치는 이탈리아 플로렌스에 있는 음식점에서 요리사로 일했다.

**6** 그가 부엌을 책임지게 되었을 때, 다빈치는 메뉴를 완전히 바꿔 버렸다.

**7** 그는 약간의 당근 조각을 곁들인 생선과 같이 간단하지만 예술적인 음식을 만들었다.

**8** 몇몇 음식들은 심지어 꽃으로 장식되었다.

**9** 하지만, 손님들은 많은 양의 고기 요리에 익숙했었기 때문에 불만족스러워했다.

**10** 그 결과, 다빈치는 그의 직업을 잃었다.

**11** 몇 년 후, 다빈치는 그의 친구인 산드로 보티첼리와 함께 음식점을 열었다.

**12** 그는 사람들이 그의 획기적인 음식을 먹어 볼 수 있는 장소로 만들기를 원했다.

**13** 그들은 아름답게 그려진 간판을 내걸었고 독특하게 쓰인 메뉴를 만들었다.

**14** 다빈치는 사람들이 곧 그의 창의적인 요리의 진가를 알아볼 것이라고 믿었다.

**15** 불행히도, 그런 일은 결코 일어나지 않았다.

**16** In the _____ 1480s, da Vinci began _____ _____ for Ludovico Sforza in Milan.

**17** He _____ _____ many different _____, _____ _____ a musician, a painter, and an engineer.

**18** He _____ also _____ _____ _____ _____ the kitchen.

**19** He was happy _____ _____ _____ _____ chance _____ _____ his _____ for cooking.

**20** Da Vinci did not _____ _____ cooking creative dishes.

**21** He wanted to cook _____ _____ quickly and easily.

**22** _____, he _____ new machines for his kitchen.

**23** He created machines _____ could _____ vegetables and pull spaghetti.

**24** He even made a device _____ could _____ frogs _____ _____ the water tank.

**25** Surely, they were all very innovative, but most of them _____ _____ big or _____ difficult _____ _____.

**26** In 1495, Sforza asked da Vinci _____ _____ a grand painting, _____ _____ _____ _____ the last supper of Jesus, on the wall of a church in Milan.

**27** Da Vinci gladly _____ _____ the project because he _____ always _____ _____ _____ food.

**28** He spent _____ _____ _____ time _____ all kinds of food to decide _____ _____ _____ on the table in his picture.

**29** "Da Vinci has wasted his time in the kitchen _____ _____ a year. That's the reason _____ he hasn't finished the painting yet," complained the people from the church _____ Sforza.

**30** _____ da Vinci never became a successful cook, he showed great _____ _____ cooking _____ his life.

**31** He was _____ _____ a great painter _____ _____ a _____ _____.

**32** _____ _____ you know all about his _____ for cooking, you will never look at _The Last Supper_ _____ _____ _____.

**16** 1480년대 초반에, 다빈치는 밀라노에서 루도비코 스포르차를 위해 일하기 시작했다.

**17** 그는 음악가, 화가, 그리고 공학자와 같은 많은 역할들을 부여받았다.

**18** 그는 또한 주방을 책임지게 되었다.

**19** 그는 요리를 향한 그의 열정을 추구할 또 다른 기회를 얻게 되어 행복했다.

**20** 다빈치는 창의적인 요리를 만드는 것에 멈추지 않았다.

**21** 그는 훨씬 더 빠르고 쉽게 요리하고 싶어했다.

**22** 따라서, 그는 그의 주방에서 사용할 새로운 기계들을 발명하였다.

**23** 그는 채소를 으깨고 스파게티를 뽑는 기계들을 만들었다.

**24** 그는 심지어 개구리를 겁주어 물탱크에서 쫓아낼 수 있는 기구도 만들었다.

**25** 확실히 그것들은 모두 매우 획기적이었지만, 그것들 중 대부분은 사용하기에 너무 크거나 너무 어려웠다.

**26** 1495년, 스포르차는 다빈치에게 웅장한 그림을 밀라노에 있는 교회의 벽에 그려 달라고 부탁했는데, 그것은 예수의 최후의 만찬을 바탕으로 한 것이었다.

**27** 다빈치는 기꺼이 그 작업을 맡았는데, 그가 항상 음식에 흥미를 가졌기 때문이었다.

**28** 그는 그림 속 식탁 위에 어떤 음식을 올릴지 결정하기 위해 모든 종류의 음식을 요리하느라 많은 시간을 썼다.

**29** "다빈치는 1년 넘게 부엌에서 시간을 낭비해 오고 있습니다. 그것이 그가 아직도 그림을 끝내지 못한 이유입니다."라고 교회 사람들이 스포르차에게 불평을 했다.

**30** 다빈치는 결코 성공적인 요리사는 되지 못했지만 그는 그의 생애 내내 요리에 대한 큰 흥미를 보여 주었다.

**31** 그는 훌륭한 화가일 뿐만 아니라 창의적인 요리사였다.

**32** 이제 여러분은 요리에 대한 그의 비밀스런 열정을 모두 알게 되었기 때문에 〈최후의 만찬〉을 절대 같은 식으로는 보지 않을 것이다.

※ 다음 문장을 우리말로 쓰시오.

**1** Da Vinci the Cook

➡ _____

**2** Leonardo da Vinci is known as one of the greatest painters of all time.

➡ _____

**3** He was also a great inventor, scientist, and musician.

➡ _____

**4** Very few people, however, know that da Vinci was also a creative cook.

➡ _____

**5** In 1473, twenty-year-old da Vinci worked as a cook at a restaurant in Florence, Italy.

➡ _____

**6** When he took charge of the kitchen, da Vinci changed the menu completely.

➡ _____

**7** He made simple but artistic dishes like fish with a few carrot slices.

➡ _____

**8** Some dishes were even decorated with flowers.

➡ _____

**9** Customers, however, were unhappy because they were used to dishes with big servings of meat.

➡ _____

**10** As a result, da Vinci lost his job.

➡ _____

**11** A few years later, da Vinci opened a restaurant with his friend Sandro Botticelli.

➡ _____

**12** He wanted to create a place where people could try his innovative food.

➡ _____

**13** They put up a beautifully painted sign and made a uniquely written menu.

➡ _____

**14** Da Vinci believed that people would soon appreciate his creative cooking.

➡ _____

**15** Unfortunately, that never happened.

➡ _____

**16** In the early 1480s, da Vinci began to work for Ludovico Sforza in Milan.

➡ _____

**17** He was given many different roles, such as a musician, a painter, and an engineer.

➡ _____

**18** He was also put in charge of the kitchen.

➡ _____

**19** He was happy to be given another chance to pursue his passion for cooking.

➡ _____

**20** Da Vinci did not stop at cooking creative dishes.

➡ _____

**21** He wanted to cook much more quickly and easily.

➡ _____

**22** Thus, he invented new machines for his kitchen.

➡ _____

**23** He created machines that could crush vegetables and pull spaghetti.

➡ _____

**24** He even made a device that could scare frogs away from the water tank.

➡ _____

**25** Surely, they were all very innovative, but most of them were too big or too difficult to use.

➡ _____

**26** In 1495, Sforza asked da Vinci to make a grand painting, which was based on the last supper of Jesus, on the wall of a church in Milan.

➡ _____

_____

**27** Da Vinci gladly took on the project because he had always been interested in food.

➡ _____

**28** He spent a lot of time cooking all kinds of food to decide what to put on the table in his picture.

➡ _____

**29** "Da Vinci has wasted his time in the kitchen for over a year. That's the reason why he hasn't finished the painting yet," complained the people from the church to Sforza.

➡ _____

_____

**30** Although da Vinci never became a successful cook, he showed great interest in cooking throughout his life.

➡ _____

**31** He was not only a great painter but also a creative cook.

➡ _____

**32** Now that you know all about his secret passion for cooking, you will never look at *The Last Supper* the same way.

➡ _____

_____

※ 다음 괄호 안의 단어들을 우리말에 맞도록 바르게 배열하시오.

**1** (Vinci / Da / Cook / the)

➡ _____

**2** (da / Leonardo / Vinci / known / is / one / as / the / of / painters / greatest / all / of / time.)

➡ _____

**3** (was / he / also / a / inventor, / great / musician. / and / scientist,)

➡ _____

**4** (few / very / people, / know / however, / that / Vinci / da / also / was / a / cook. / creative)

➡ _____

**5** (1473, / in / twenty-year-old / da / worked / Vinci / a / as / cook / a / at / restaurant / in / Italy. / Florence,)

➡ _____
_____

**6** (he / when / took / of / charge / kitchen, / the / Vinci / da / the / changed / completely. / menu)

➡ _____
_____

**7** (made / he / simple / artistic / but / like / dishes / with / fish / few / a / slices. / carrot)

➡ _____
_____

**8** (dishes / some / even / were / with / decorated / flowers.)

➡ _____

**9** (however, / customers, / unhappy / were / they / because / were / used / dishes / to / big / with / of / servings / meat.)

➡ _____
_____

**10** (a / as / result, / Vinci / da / his / lost / job.)

➡ _____

**11** (few / a / later, / years / Vinci / da / a / opened / restaurant / his / with / Sandro / friend / Botticelli.)

➡ _____
_____

**1** 요리사 다빈치

**2** 레오나르도 다빈치는 역대 가장 위대한 화가들 중의 한 명으로 알려져 있다.

**3** 그는 또한 위대한 발명가, 과학자, 그리고 음악가였다.

**4** 하지만, 극히 소수의 사람들만이 또한 그가 창의적인 요리사였다는 것을 안다.

**5** 1473년, 스무 살의 레오나르도 다빈치는 이탈리아 플로렌스에 있는 음식점에서 요리사로 일했다.

**6** 그가 부엌을 책임지게 되었을 때, 다빈치는 메뉴를 완전히 바꿔 버렸다.

**7** 그는 약간의 당근 조각을 곁들인 생선과 같이 간단하지만 예술적인 음식을 만들었다.

**8** 몇몇 음식들은 심지어 꽃으로 장식되었다.

**9** 하지만, 손님들은 많은 양의 고기 요리에 익숙했었기 때문에 불만족스러워했다.

**10** 그 결과, 다빈치는 그의 직업을 잃었다.

**11** 몇 년 후, 다빈치는 그의 친구인 산드로 보티첼리와 함께 음식점을 열었다.

**12** (wanted / he / create / to / place / a / where / could / people / his / try / food. / innovative)

➡ _____

_____

**13** (put / they / up / beautifully / a / painted / and / sign / made / uniquely / a / menu. / written)

➡ _____

_____

**14** (Vinci / da / believed / people / that / soon / would / appreciate / creative / his / cooking.)

➡ _____

_____

**15** (that / unfortunately, / happened. / never)

➡ _____

**16** (the / in / 1480s, / early / Vinci / da / to / began / for / work / Sforza / Ludovico / Milan. / in)

➡ _____

**17** (was / he / many / given / roles, / different / as / such / musician, / a / painter, / a / and / engineer. / an)

➡ _____

_____

**18** (was / he / put / also / charge / in / the / of / kitchen.)

➡ _____

**19** (was / he / to / happy / given / be / chance / another / pursue / to / passion / his / cooking. / for)

➡ _____

_____

**20** (Vinci / da / not / did / at / stop / creative / cooking / dishes.)

➡ _____

**21** (wanted / he / cook / to / more / much / easily. / and / quickly)

➡ _____

**12** 그는 사람들이 그의 획기적인 음식을 먹어 볼 수 있는 장소로 만들기를 원했다.

**13** 그들은 아름답게 그려진 간판을 내걸었고 독특하게 써진 메뉴를 만들었다.

**14** 다빈치는 사람들이 곧 그의 창의적인 요리의 진가를 알아볼 것이라고 믿었다.

**15** 불행히도, 그런 일은 결코 일어나지 않았다.

**16** 1480년대 초반에, 다빈치는 밀라노에서 루도비코 스포르차를 위해 일하기 시작했다.

**17** 그는 음악가, 화가, 그리고 공학자와 같은 많은 역할들을 부여받았다.

**18** 그는 또한 주방을 책임지게 되었다.

**19** 그는 요리를 향한 그의 열정을 추구할 또 다른 기회를 얻게 되어 행복했다.

**20** 다빈치는 창의적인 요리를 만드는 것에 멈추지 않았다.

**21** 그는 훨씬 더 빠르고 쉽게 요리하고 싶어했다.

**22** (he / thus, / iinvented / machines / new / his / for / kitchen.)
➡ _____

**23** (created / he / that / machines / crush / could / vegetables / pull / and / spaghetti.)
➡ _____

**24** (even / he / a / made / that / device / scare / could / away / frogs / the / from / tank. / water)
➡ _____

**25** (they / surely, / were / very / all / innovative, / of / but / most / them / too / were / big / too / or / difficult / use. / to)
➡ _____
_____

**26** (1495, / in / asked / Sforza / Vinci / da / make / to / grand / a / painting, / was / which / on / based / the / supper / last / Jesus, / of / the / on / wall / a / of / in / church / Milan.)
➡ _____
_____

**27** (Vinci / da / took / gladly / the / on / because / project / had / he / been / always / interested / food. / in)
➡ _____
_____

**28** (spent / he / lot / a / of / cooking / time / all / of / kinds / to / food / what / decide / to / on / put / table / the / his / in / picture.)
➡ _____

**29** (Vinci / "da / wasted / has / time / his / the / in / for / kitchen / over / year. / a // the / that's / why / reason / hasn't / he / the / finished / yet," / painting / `complained / people / the / from / church / the / Sforza. / to)
➡ _____
_____
_____

**30** (da / although / Vinci / became / never / a / cook, / successful / showed / he / interest / great / cooking / in / his / throughout / life.)
➡ _____
_____

**31** (was / he / only / not / great / a / but / painter / also / creative / a / cook.)
➡ _____

**32** (that / now / know / you / about / all / secret / his / for / passion / cooking, / will / you / look / never / *The* / at / *Supper* / *Last* / same / the / way.)
➡ _____
_____

---

**22** 따라서, 그는 그의 주방에서 사용할 새로운 기계들을 발명하였다.

**23** 그는 채소를 으깨고 스파게티를 뽑는 기계들을 만들었다.

**24** 그는 심지어 개구리를 겁주어 물탱크에서 쫓아낼 수 있는 기구도 만들었다.

**25** 확실히 그것들은 모두 매우 획기적이었지만, 그것들 중 대부분은 사용하기에 너무 크거나 너무 어려웠다.

**26** 1495년, 스포르차는 다빈치에게 웅장한 그림을 밀라노에 있는 교회의 벽에 그려 달라고 부탁했는데, 그것은 예수의 최후의 만찬을 바탕으로 한 것이었다.

**27** 다빈치는 기꺼이 그 작업을 맡았는데, 그가 항상 음식에 흥미를 가졌기 때문이었다.

**28** 그는 그림 속 식탁 위에 어떤 음식을 올릴지 결정하기 위해 모든 종류의 음식을 요리하느라 많은 시간을 썼다.

**29** "다빈치는 1년 넘게 부엌에서 시간을 낭비해 오고 있습니다. 그것이 그가 아직도 그림을 끝내지 못한 이유입니다."라고 교회 사람들이 스포르차에게 불평을 했다.

**30** 다빈치는 결코 성공적인 요리사는 되지 못했지만 그는 그의 생애 내내 요리에 대한 큰 흥미를 보여 주었다.

**31** 그는 훌륭한 화가일 뿐만 아니라 창의적인 요리사였다.

**32** 이제 여러분은 요리에 대한 그의 비밀스런 열정을 모두 알게 되었기 때문에 〈최후의 만찬〉을 절대 같은 식으로는 보지 않을 것이다.

※ 다음 우리말을 영어로 쓰시오.

**1**  요리사 다빈치
➡ _____

**2**  레오나르도 다빈치는 역대 가장 위대한 화가들 중의 한 명으로 알려져 있다.
➡ _____

**3**  그는 또한 위대한 발명가, 과학자, 그리고 음악가였다.
➡ _____

**4**  하지만, 극히 소수의 사람들만이 또한 그가 창의적인 요리사였다는 것을 안다.
➡ _____

**5**  1473년, 스무 살의 레오나르도 다빈치는 이탈리아 플로렌스에 있는 음식점에서 요리사로 일했다.
➡ _____

**6**  그가 부엌을 책임지게 되었을 때, 다빈치는 메뉴를 완전히 바꿔 버렸다.
➡ _____

**7**  그는 약간의 당근 조각을 곁들인 생선과 같이 간단하지만 예술적인 음식을 만들었다.
➡ _____

**8**  몇몇 음식들은 심지어 꽃으로 장식되었다.
➡ _____

**9**  하지만, 손님들은 많은 양의 고기 요리에 익숙했었기 때문에 불만족스러워했다.
➡ _____

**10**  그 결과, 다빈치는 그의 직업을 잃었다.
➡ _____

**11**  몇 년 후, 다빈치는 그의 친구인 산드로 보티첼리와 함께 음식점을 열었다.
➡ _____

**12**  그는 사람들이 그의 획기적인 음식을 먹어 볼 수 있는 장소로 만들기를 원했다.
➡ _____

**13**  그들은 아름답게 그려진 간판을 내걸었고 독특하게 써진 메뉴를 만들었다.
➡ _____

**14**  다빈치는 사람들이 곧 그의 창의적인 요리의 진가를 알아볼 것이라고 믿었다.
➡ _____

**15**  불행히도, 그런 일은 결코 일어나지 않았다.
➡ _____

**16**  1480년대 초반에, 다빈치는 밀라노에서 루도비코 스포르차를 위해 일하기 시작했다.
➡ _____

**17**  그는 음악가, 화가, 그리고 공학자와 같은 많은 역할들을 부여받았다.
➡ _____

**18** 그는 또한 주방을 책임지게 되었다.

➡ _____

**19** 그는 요리를 향한 그의 열정을 추구할 또 다른 기회를 얻게 되어 행복했다.

➡ _____

**20** 다빈치는 창의적인 요리를 만드는 것에 멈추지 않았다.

➡ _____

**21** 그는 훨씬 더 빠르고 쉽게 요리하고 싶어했다.

➡ _____

**22** 따라서, 그는 그의 주방에서 사용할 새로운 기계들을 발명하였다.

➡ _____

**23** 그는 채소를 으깨고 스파게티를 뽑는 기계들을 만들었다.

➡ _____

**24** 그는 심지어 개구리를 겁주어 물탱크에서 쫓아낼 수 있는 기구도 만들었다.

➡ _____

**25** 확실히 그것들은 모두 매우 획기적이었지만, 그것들 중 대부분은 사용하기에 너무 크거나 너무 어려웠다.

➡ _____

**26** 1495년, 스포르차는 다빈치에게 웅장한 그림을 밀라노에 있는 교회의 벽에 그려 달라고 부탁했는데, 그것은 예수의 최후의 만찬을 바탕으로 한 것이었다.

➡ _____

_____

**27** 다빈치는 기꺼이 그 작업을 맡았는데, 그가 항상 음식에 흥미를 가졌기 때문이었다.

➡ _____

**28** 그는 그림 속 식탁 위에 어떤 음식을 올릴지 결정하기 위해 모든 종류의 음식을 요리하느라 많은 시간을 썼다.

➡ _____

**29** "다빈치는 1년 넘게 부엌에서 시간을 낭비해 오고 있습니다. 그것이 그가 아직도 그림을 끝내지 못한 이유입니다."라고 교회 사람들이 스포르차에게 불평을 했다.

➡ _____

_____

**30** 다빈치는 결코 성공적인 요리사는 되지 못했지만 그는 그의 생애 내내 요리에 대한 큰 흥미를 보여 주었다.

➡ _____

_____

**31** 그는 훌륭한 화가일 뿐만 아니라 창의적인 요리사였다.

➡ _____

**32** 이제 여러분은 요리에 대한 그의 비밀스런 열정을 모두 알게 되었기 때문에 〈최후의 만찬〉을 절대 같은 식으로는 보지 않을 것이다.

➡ _____

_____

※ 다음 우리말과 일치하도록 빈칸에 알맞은 말을 쓰시오.

### Write

1. My name is Kim Jieun. I am _____ _____ _____ _____ _____.

2. There was a _____ _____ when I _____ _____ _____ _____ to be.

3. _____ _____ 2030, I made a _____ _____ _____ _____.

4. It was a _____ _____ _____ _____ about _____ _____ for arts.

5. Thus, I _____ _____ go to a _____ _____ _____.

6. _____ I _____ _____ high school, I _____ Korea Art College and _____ more about _____ and _____.

7. _____ _____, I _____ my first _____.

8. I _____ very _____ _____ my life.

1. 내 이름은 김지은이다. 나는 기술을 사용하는 예술가다.
2. 내가 예술가가 되기로 결심했을 때 특별한 순간이 있었다.
3. 2030년에, 나는 기술을 사용해 작은 동상을 만들었다.
4. 그것은 예술을 위한 기술을 배우는 데에 아주 좋은 기회였다.
5. 따라서, 나는 기술 고등학교에 진학하기로 결심했다.
6. 고등학교를 졸업한 뒤, 나는 한국 예술 대학에 입학해서 예술과 기술에 대해 더 배웠다.
7. 올해, 나는 내 첫 전시회를 열었다.
8. 나는 내 인생에 매우 만족한다.

### Link

1. Some people think creativity is _____ _____ _____ _____ when they _____ _____ _____.

2. They like to _____ _____ _____ new ideas and _____ _____ _____.

3. Thus, they want to _____ _____ _____ _____ _____ they can _____ _____ _____.

1. 어떤 사람들은 직업을 선택할 때 고려해야 할 가장 중요한 것은 창의력이라고 생각한다.
2. 그들은 새로운 아이디어를 떠올리고 새로운 것들을 구상하기를 좋아한다.
3. 따라서, 그들은 그들의 창의력을 발휘할 수 있는 곳에서 일하기를 원한다.

### Watch and Think Share

1. Winston Churchill _____ _____ _____ _____ the Prime Minister of the United Kingdom _____ World War II.

2. Very _____ _____, _____, know that he was also a _____, a _____, and a _____.

3. He even _____ the _____ _____ _____ _____ in 1953.

1. Winston Churchill은 제 2차 세계대전 중 영국의 수상이었던 것으로 알려져 있다.
2. 하지만, 극소수의 사람들은 그가 또한 사학자이며, 화가이자, 작가임을 알고 있다.
3. 심지어 그는 1953년에 노벨 문학상을 수상하기도 했다.

※ 다음 우리말을 영어로 쓰시오.

### Write

1. 내 이름은 김지은이다. 나는 기술을 사용하는 예술가다.

   ➡ _____

2. 내가 예술가가 되기로 결심했을 때 특별한 순간이 있었다.

   ➡ _____

3. 2030년에, 나는 기술을 사용해 작은 동상을 만들었다.

   ➡ _____

4. 그것은 예술을 위한 기술을 배우는 데에 아주 좋은 기회였다.

   ➡ _____

5. 따라서, 나는 기술 고등학교에 진학하기로 결심했다.

   ➡ _____

6. 고등학교를 졸업한 뒤, 나는 한국 예술 대학에 입학해서 예술과 기술에 대해 더 배웠다.

   ➡ _____

   _____

7. 올해, 나는 내 첫 전시회를 열었다.

   ➡ _____

8. 나는 내 인생에 매우 만족한다.

   ➡ _____

### Link

1. 어떤 사람들은 직업을 선택할 때 고려해야 할 가장 중요한 것은 창의력이라고 생각한다.

   ➡ _____

2. 그들은 새로운 아이디어를 떠올리고 새로운 것들을 구상하기를 좋아한다.

   ➡ _____

3. 따라서, 그들은 그들의 창의력을 발휘할 수 있는 곳에서 일하기를 원한다.

   ➡ _____

### Watch and Think Share

1. Winston Churchill은 제 2차 세계대전 중 영국의 수상이었던 것으로 알려져 있다.

   ➡ _____

2. 하지만, 극소수의 사람들은 그가 또한 사학자이며, 화가이자, 작가임을 알고 있다.

   ➡ _____

3. 심지어 그는 1953년에 노벨 문학상을 수상하기도 했다.

   ➡ _____

※ 다음 영어를 우리말로 쓰시오.

01 precious

02 correct

03 exactly

04 official

05 potful

06 honesty

07 indeed

08 among

09 break

10 journey

11 strange

12 match

13 wise

14 wit

15 narrow

16 offer

17 court

18 emperor

19 worm

20 policy

21 sweet

22 punish

23 pumpkin

24 return

25 expression

26 favor

27 speechless

28 thus

29 wisdom

30 present

31 certainly

32 must

33 pull

34 exam

35 for oneself

36 hand in

37 come up with

38 thanks to

39 focus on

40 in one's place

41 make sense

42 be famous for

43 a potful of

※ 다음 우리말을 영어로 쓰시오.

| | | |
|---|---|---|
| 01 | 지혜로운, 현명한 | |
| 02 | 표현 | |
| 03 | 청, 부탁 | |
| 04 | ~ 중에, ~의 사이에 | |
| 05 | 틀림없이, 분명히 | |
| 06 | 선물 | |
| 07 | 정직 | |
| 08 | 처벌하다, 벌주다 | |
| 09 | 좁은 | |
| 10 | 귀중한, 값비싼 | |
| 11 | 맞는, 정확한 | |
| 12 | 현재, 지금 | |
| 13 | 고위 공무원, 관리 | |
| 14 | 이상한 | |
| 15 | 정말, 확실히 | |
| 16 | 정책 | |
| 17 | 여행, 여정 | |
| 18 | (땅속에 사는) 벌레 | |
| 19 | 경기, 시합 | |
| 20 | 호박 | |
| 21 | 깨지다, 부러뜨리다 | |

| | | |
|---|---|---|
| 22 | 황제 | |
| 23 | 대궐, 궁궐 | |
| 24 | (화나거나 놀라서) 말을 못 하는 | |
| 25 | 시험 | |
| 26 | 기지, 재치 | |
| 27 | 과거 | |
| 28 | 정확하게 | |
| 29 | 되돌려주다 | |
| 30 | 사탕, 단것 | |
| 31 | 그러므로 | |
| 32 | 지혜, 슬기, 현명함 | |
| 33 | 한 항아리의 양 | |
| 34 | 내놓다, 제공하다 | |
| 35 | 제출하다 | |
| 36 | ~에 주력하다, 집중하다 | |
| 37 | 다시 한 번 | |
| 38 | ~의 처지에서, ~의 상황에서 | |
| 39 | 혼자서, 스스로 | |
| 40 | ~을 찾아내다, ~을 떠올리다 | |
| 41 | ~로 유명하다 | |
| 42 | ~ 덕분에 | |
| 43 | 타당하다, 말이 되다 | |

※ 다음 영영풀이에 알맞은 단어를 <보기>에서 골라 쓴 후, 우리말 뜻을 쓰시오.

1 _____ : the quality of being honest: _____

2 _____ : existing or happening now: _____

3 _____ : rare and worth a lot of money: _____

4 _____ : to go away from a place or a person: _____

5 _____ : the man who is the ruler of an empire: _____

6 _____ : accurate or true, without any mistakes: _____

7 _____ : the place where a king or queen lives and works: _____

8 _____ : a large round vegetable with thick orange skin: _____

9 _____ : an occasion when you travel from one place to another: _____

10 _____ : an organized sport event between two teams or people: _____

11 _____ : a long, thin creature with a soft body and no bones or legs: _____

12 _____ : measuring only a small distance from one side to the other, not wide: _____

13 _____ : someone who is in a position of authority in an organization: _____

14 _____ : a thing that you give to somebody, especially on a special occasion or to say thank you: _____

15 _____ : to make somebody suffer because they have broken the law or done something wrong: _____

16 _____ : not able to speak, especially because you are extremely angry or surprised: _____

보기

| | | | |
|---|---|---|---|
| precious | honesty | worm | match |
| speechless | gift | pumpkin | emperor |
| leave | present | narrow | journey |
| official | punish | correct | court |

※ 다음 우리말과 일치하도록 빈칸에 알맞은 말을 쓰시오.

### Listen & Speak 1 A-1

G: You _____ _____ this morning.

B: I _____ _____ very early _____ _____ for the exam.

G: _____ _____ you. The _____ _____ catches the _____.

B: No. The early bird _____ _____ quickly.

G: _____ _____ _____ you don't like to get up early?

B: Yes, that's _____ _____ _____ _____.

G: 오늘 아침 너 피곤해 보인다.
B: 시험 공부를 하려고 아주 일찍 일어났거든.
G: 잘했어. 일찍 일어나는 새가 벌레를 잡는 법이지.
B: 아니. 일찍 일어나는 새가 빨리 지쳐.
G: 일찍 일어나는 게 싫다는 말이야?
B: 응, 정확히 그런 뜻이야.

### Listen & Speak 1 A-2

G: I _____ _____ sing at the school's English pop song contest.

B: Wow. Break _____ _____!

G: What? _____ _____ _____ I have to _____ _____ of my _____?

B: No, it's an _____ _____ I hope _____ _____ _____.

G: 나는 학교의 영어 팝송 부르기 대회에서 노래를 해야 해.
B: 우와. 행운을 빌어!
G: 뭐? 내가 내 다리 한 쪽을 부러뜨려야 한다는 말이야?
B: 아니, 네가 잘하길 빈다는 뜻의 표현이야.

### Listen & Speak 2 A-1

B: Wow, you really _____ _____.

G: Thanks. I love dancing. _____ in my family _____ _____ _____ dancing.

B: Really? Your parents dance well, _____?

G: Yes. They're also _____ _____.

B: _____ _____ family! _____ _____ _____ _____ _____ dance _____ you.

B: 우와, 너 춤 정말 잘 춘다.
G: 고마워. 나 춤추는 거 정말 좋아해. 우리 가족 모두가 춤을 잘 춰.
B: 정말? 너희 부모님도 춤을 잘 추시니?
G: 맞아. 노래도 잘하셔.
B: 굉장한 가족이다! 나도 너처럼 춤을 출 수 있으면 좋겠어.

### Listen & Speak 2 A-2

B: Hello, everyone! Time flies. I _____ _____ it's time _____ _____ goodbye. _____ _____ my teachers and friends, I was really happy here. _____ _____ _____ _____ go _____ _____ my first year and live these years over again, but it's time _____ _____ a _____ _____ to high school. I hope I can see you again. Thank you.

B: 안녕, 모두들! 시간이 참 빠르네요. 이제 작별 인사를 해야 할 시간이라는 게 믿어지지 않아요. 선생님들과 친구들 덕분에, 이곳에서 정말 행복했어요. 첫 해로 돌아가서 이 해들을 다시 지낼 수 있다면 좋겠지만, 이제는 고등학교로 새로운 여행을 떠나야 할 시간이에요. 여러분을 다시 볼 수 있다면 좋겠어요. 고맙습니다.

### Communicate A

**Anna:** What's _____? You don't _____ so _____.

**Suho:** I'm still _____ _____ our soccer match last week.

**Anna:** _____ _____ _____ the game you _____ last week?

**Suho:** Yes. _____ _____ _____ _____ forget about it, but I can't.

**Anna:** Well, you should always _____ _____ _____.

**Suho:** _____ _____ _____ I should forget the past and _____ _____ the present?

**Anna:** Yes, _____. People say, "Yesterday is history, tomorrow is a mystery, and today is a _____. That's _____ it's _____ the present."

**Suho:** Now I see. You know so many great _____. You're _____ _____ _____ my grandma.

### Progress Check 1

**G:** You _____ _____. Is something _____?

**B:** I had to _____ _____ my science report _____ yesterday, but I didn't.

**G:** It's _____ _____ _____ _____ _____.

**B:** _____ _____ _____ it's better to _____ _____ _____ _____ _____ it's _____?

**G:** Yes, exactly. You should always finish _____ you've started.

### Progress Check 2

**B:** Wow, you _____ _____ _____ so well.

**G:** Thanks. I love playing the guitar. I learned _____ from my dad.

**B:** Really? Does your father play the guitar, _____?

**G:** Yes. He was _____ a famous band.

**B:** _____ _____ family! _____ _____ I _____ play the guitar _____ you.

### Progress Check 3

**M:** You _____ your friend's phone, and you don't know _____ _____ _____. _____ friend says to you, "_____ is the best _____." You don't know _____ _____ _____ exactly.

---

Anna: 무슨 일 있니? 별로 좋아 보이질 않네.

수호: 지난주 우리의 축구 시합을 여전히 생각하고 있어.

Anna: 지난주에 진 게임 말이니?

수호: 응. 그걸 잊을 수 있음 좋겠는데, 못하겠네.

Anna: 음, 넌 항상 오늘을 살아야 해.

수호: 과거는 잊고 현재에 집중해야 한다는 뜻이니?

Anna: 그래, 바로 그거야. 사람들이 "어제는 역사, 내일은 미스터리, 그리고 오늘은 선물이다. 그게 바로 오늘을 선물이라 부르는 이유."라고 하잖아.

수호: 그렇구나. 넌 정말 좋은 표현들을 많이 알고 있구나. 넌 우리 할머니만큼 현명해.

G: 걱정이 있는 것 같아 보인다. 무슨 문제 있니?

B: 어제까지 과학 보고서를 냈어야 했는데, 내지 않았어.

G: 늦더라도 안 하는 것보다는 낫지.

B: 늦었더라도 내는 게 낫다는 뜻이야?

G: 맞아, 정확해. 언제나 시작을 했으면 끝을 봐야지.

B: 우와, 너 기타 정말 잘 친다.

G: 고마워. 나 기타 치는 거 정말 좋아해. 아버지께 배웠어.

B: 정말? 너희 아버지도 기타를 치시니?

G: 응. 유명한 밴드에 계셨어.

B: 굉장한 가족이다! 나도 너처럼 기타를 칠 수 있다면 좋겠어.

M: 여러분은 친구의 휴대전화를 부수었고, 어떻게 해야 할지 모릅니다. 다른 친구가 여러분에게, "정직이 최선의 방책이야."라고 말합니다. 여러분은 그것이 정확히 무슨 뜻인지 모릅니다.

※ 다음 우리말에 맞도록 대화를 영어로 쓰시오.

## Listen & Speak 1 A-1

G: _____

B: _____

G: _____

B: _____

G: _____

B: _____

G: 오늘 아침 너 피곤해 보인다.
B: 시험 공부를 하려고 아주 일찍 일어났거든.
G: 잘했어. 일찍 일어나는 새가 벌레를 잡는 법이지.
B: 아니. 일찍 일어나는 새가 빨리 지쳐.
G: 일찍 일어나는 게 싫다는 말이야?
B: 응, 정확히 그런 뜻이야.

## Listen & Speak 1 A-2

G: _____

B: _____

G: _____

B: _____

G: 나는 학교의 영어 팝송 부르기 대회에서 노래를 해야 해.
B: 우와. 행운을 빌어!
G: 뭐? 내가 내 다리 한 쪽을 부러뜨려야 한다는 말이야?
B: 아니, 네가 잘하길 빈다는 뜻의 표현이야.

## Listen & Speak 2 A-1

B: _____

G: _____

B: _____

G: _____

B: _____

B: 우와, 너 춤 정말 잘 춘다.
G: 고마워. 나 춤추는 거 정말 좋아해. 우리 가족 모두가 춤을 잘 춰.
B: 정말? 너희 부모님도 춤을 잘 추시니?
G: 맞아. 노래도 잘하셔.
B: 굉장한 가족이다! 나도 너처럼 춤을 출 수 있으면 좋겠어.

## Listen & Speak 2 A-2

B: _____

_____

_____

_____

B: 안녕, 모두들! 시간이 참 빠르네요. 이제 작별 인사를 해야 할 시간이라는 게 믿어지지 않아요. 선생님들과 친구들 덕분에, 이곳에서 정말 행복했어요. 첫 해로 돌아가서 이 해들을 다시 지낼 수 있다면 좋겠지만, 이제는 고등학교로 새로운 여행을 떠나야 할 시간이에요. 여러분을 다시 볼 수 있다면 좋겠어요. 고맙습니다.

## Communicate A

Anna: _____

Suho: _____

Anna: _____

Suho: _____

Anna: _____

Suho: _____

Anna: _____
_____

Suho: _____
_____

Anna: 무슨 일 있니? 별로 좋아 보이질 않네.

수호: 지난주 우리의 축구 시합을 여전히 생각하고 있어.

Anna: 지난주에 진 게임 말이니?

수호: 응. 그걸 잊을 수 있음 좋겠는데, 못하겠네.

Anna: 음, 넌 항상 오늘을 살아야 해.

수호: 과거는 잊고 현재에 집중해야 한다는 뜻이니?

Anna: 그래, 바로 그거야. 사람들이 "어제는 역사, 내일은 미스터리, 그리고 오늘은 선물이다. 그게 바로 오늘을 선물이라 부르는 이유."라고 하잖아.

수호: 그렇구나. 넌 정말 좋은 표현들을 많이 알고 있구나. 넌 우리 할머니만큼 현명해.

## Progress Check 1

G: _____

B: _____

G: _____

B: _____

G: _____

G: 걱정이 있는 것 같아 보인다. 무슨 문제 있니?

B: 어제까지 과학 보고서를 냈어야 했는데, 내지 않았어.

G: 늦더라도 안 하는 것보다는 낫지.

B: 늦었더라도 내는 게 낫다는 뜻이야?

G: 맞아, 정확해. 언제나 시작을 했으면 끝을 봐야지.

## Progress Check 2

B: _____

G: _____

B: _____

G: _____

B: _____

B: 우와, 너 기타 정말 잘 친다.

G: 고마워. 나 기타 치는 거 정말 좋아해. 아버지께 배웠어.

B: 정말? 너희 아버지도 기타를 치시니?

G: 응. 유명한 밴드에 계셨어.

B: 굉장한 가족이다! 나도 너처럼 기타를 칠 수 있다면 좋겠어.

## Progress Check 3

M: _____
_____
_____

M: 여러분은 친구의 휴대전화를 부수었고, 어떻게 해야 할지 모릅니다. 다른 친구가 여러분에게, "정직이 최선의 방책이야."라고 말합니다. 여러분은 그것이 정확히 무슨 뜻인지 모릅니다.

※ 다음 우리말과 일치하도록 빈칸에 알맞은 것을 골라 쓰시오.

**1** _____ _____ Birbal

　　A. of　　　　　　　B. tales

**2** Akbar, the third Mogul _____, had a _____ of wise _____ at his _____.

　　A. court　　　B. emperor　　　C. officials　　　D. number

**3** _____ them was a man _____ _____ was Raja Birbal.

　　A. whose　　　B. among　　　C. name

**4** He was _____ _____ his quick wit and was very wise _____ his _____.

　　A. for　　　B. with　　　C. words　　　D. famous

**5** _____, the _____ always liked to _____ Birbal _____ him.

　　A. near　　　B. thus　　　C. have　　　D. emperor

**6** _____ _____

　　A. Punishment　　　B. Sweet

**7** To _____ his officials' _____, Akbar often _____ them _____ questions.

　　A. wisdom　　　B. strange　　　C. test　　　D. asked

**8** _____ day, he _____ _____ _____ an interesting question.

　　A. up　　　B. one　　　C. with　　　D. came

**9** Akbar: Someone _____ a _____ from my _____ today. What _____ I do to him?

　　A. should　　　B. pulled　　　C. head　　　D. hair

**10** Official 1: He should _____ _____, of _____.

　　A. course　　　B. punished　　　C. be

**11** Official 2: Yes, _____ _____!

　　A. him　　　B. punish

**12** Akbar _____ _____ Birbal.

　　A. to　　　B. turned

**13** Akbar: What _____ you _____ if you _____ in my _____, Birbal?

　　A. were　　　B. would　　　C. place　　　D. do

**14** Birbal: _____ I _____ you, I _____ _____ him sweets.

　　A. give　　　B. were　　　C. if　　　D. would

**15** Official 3: What's he _____ _____?

　　A. about　　　B. talking

**16** Official 4: _____ _____!

　　A. crazy　　　B. Birbal's

---

**1** 비르발 이야기

**2** 악바르는 무굴 제국의 제3대 황제로, 자신의 궁정에 많은 현명한 신하들이 있었다.

**3** 그 중 라자 비르발이라는 이름의 한 사람이 있었다.

**4** 그는 재빠른 재치로 유명했으며 말이 매우 지혜로웠다.

**5** 그래서, 황제는 언제나 비르발을 곁에 두기를 원했다.

**6** 달콤한 처벌

**7** 신하들의 지혜를 시험해 보기 위해, 악바르는 종종 그들에게 이상한 질문을 했다.

**8** 어느 날, 황제는 재미있는 질문이 생각났다.

**9** 악바르: 오늘 어떤 이가 내 머리에서 머리카락을 잡아당겼소. 이 자에게 무엇을 해야 하겠소?

**10** 신하 1: 당연히 처벌해야 합니다.

**11** 신하 2: 예, 그를 처벌하소서!

**12** 악바르가 비르발에게 돌아섰다.

**13** 악바르: 그대가 내 입장이라면 무엇을 하겠소, 비르발?

**14** 비르발: 소신이 폐하라면, 그에게 사탕을 주겠습니다.

**15** 신하 3: 저 사람은 무슨 말을 하는 건가?

**16** 신하 4: 비르발이 정신이 나갔어!

**17** Akbar: _____ _____ you _____ _____ ?

A. made      B. so      C. what      D. say

**18** Birbal: The person who pulled your hair _____ _____ your grandson. No one _____ could do _____ a thing.

A. such      B. be      C. else      D. must

**19** Akbar: You are indeed _____, Birbal. I'm _____ glad to have someone as _____ as you _____ me.

A. wise      B. correct      C. near      D. so

**20** A _____ of _____

A. Wisdom      B. Potful

**21** One day, the king of Persia _____ an official _____ a _____ _____.

A. favor      B. sent      C. with      D. strange

**22** Persian Official: I hear you have a lot of wise men in your country. I've _____ _____ by my king to _____ him a _____ of wisdom.

A. bring      B. asked      C. potful      D. been

**23** Official 5: That _____ no _____! How can we _____ wisdom _____ a pot?

A. put      B. makes      C. in      D. sense

**24** Akbar: Can you _____ him a _____ of _____, Birbal?

A. wisdom      B. bring      C. potful

**25** Birbal: It _____ _____ a _____.

A. be      B. won't      C. problem

**26** Birbal: Could you please _____ _____ _____ _____ ?

A. a      B. wait      C. weeks      D. few

**27** Persian Official: Of course! Take as _____ _____ _____ you _____.

A. time      B. as      C. much      D. need

**28** A _____ weeks later, Birbal came _____ with two pots _____ necks were really _____. He offered one to the Persian official.

A. narrow      B. back      C. few      D. whose

**29** Birbal: You can _____ this pot of wisdom to your king. Please ask him to _____ the pot to us _____ he takes the wisdom _____ of it.

A. return      B. out      C. take      D. after

**17** 악바르: 왜 그렇게 말했소?

**18** 비르발: 폐하의 머리카락을 잡아당긴 사람은 폐하의 손자임이 분명합니다. 다른 그 누구도 그런 짓을 할 수 없지요.

**19** 악바르: 과연 그대의 말이 맞소, 비르발. 그대처럼 현명한 자를 옆에 두어 정말 기쁘오.

**20** 한 항아리만큼의 지혜

**21** 어느 날, 페르시아의 왕이 이상한 요청과 함께 신하를 보냈다.

**22** 페르시아의 신하: 폐하의 나라에 현명한 자들이 많다고 들었습니다. 저는 저의 왕으로부터 한 항아리의 지혜를 왕께 가지고 오라는 명을 받았습니다.

**23** 신하 5: 저건 말이 안 되오! 어떻게 지혜를 항아리에 넣을 수 있단 말이오?

**24** 악바르: 그에게 지혜 한 항아리를 가져다줄 수 있겠소, 비르발?

**25** 비르발: 문제될 것이 없사옵니다.

**26** 비르발: 몇 주만 기다려 주시겠습니까?

**27** 페르시아의 신하: 물론이오! 필요한 만큼 얼마든지 시간을 가지시오.

**28** 몇 주 후, 비르발은 목이 매우 좁은 두 항아리를 들고 돌아왔다. 그는 하나를 페르시아의 신하에게 줬다.

**29** 비르발: 이 지혜의 항아리를 그대의 왕께 가져다 드리십시오. 왕께서 이 항아리에서 지혜를 꺼내신 후에는 항아리를 우리에게 돌려달라 전해 주십시오.

**30** Birbal: The pot is very _____, so please be _____ not to _____ it. We only have two pots of _____.

    A. break        B. precious        C. wisdom        D. careful

**31** The Persian _____ looked _____ the pot and _____ _____.

    A. inside        B. speechless        C. official        D. became

**32** He _____ Birbal and _____ _____ his _____.

    A. for        B. thanked        C. country        D. left

**33** Persian Official: It would _____ great _____ there _____ a man _____ wise as Birbal in our country.

    A. be        B. as        C. if        D. were

**34** _____ the Persian official _____, Akbar asked Birbal _____ was _____ the pot.

    A. what        B. left        C. inside        D. after

**35** Birbal: Here is _____ _____ pot. You can see _____ _____.

    A. for        B. other        C. yourself        D. the

**36** Akbar looked inside the _____ pot and _____ a pumpkin just as _____ _____ the pot.

    A. big        B. as        C. other        D. found

**37** Akbar: I see! The pumpkin can't _____ _____ out _____ _____ the pot. How did you do it?

    A. breaking        B. be        C. without        D. taken

**38** Birbal: I _____ the pots _____ pumpkin flowers and waited _____ the pumpkins _____ as big as the pots.

    A. until        B. over        C. grew        D. put

**39** Akbar: Hahaha! This _____ is a _____ _____ _____!

    A. wisdom        B. certainly        C. of        D. potful

**30** 비르발: 그 항아리는 매우 귀중한 것이니, 그것을 깨지 않도록 조심해 주십시오. 우리는 오직 두 개의 지혜의 항아리만 갖고 있습니다.

**31** 페르시아 신하는 항아리 안을 들여다보곤 말을 잃었다.

**32** 그는 비르발에게 감사를 표한 뒤 그의 나라로 떠났다.

**33** 페르시아의 신하: 우리 나라에도 비르발처럼 현명한 자가 있다면 정말 좋을 텐데.

**34** 페르시아의 신하가 떠난 뒤, 악바르는 비르발에게 항아리 속에 무엇이 있었는지를 물었다.

**35** 비르발: 여기 또 다른 항아리가 있습니다. 직접 살펴보시지요.

**36** 악바르는 또 다른 항아리 안을 보고 꼭 항아리만큼 큰 호박을 발견했다.

**37** 악바르: 그렇군! 항아리를 깨지 않고는 호박을 꺼낼 수가 없구려! 어떻게 한 것이오?

**38** 비르발: 항아리를 호박꽃에 덮어 놓은 후 호박이 항아리만큼 클 때까지 기다렸습니다.

**39** 악바르: 하하하! 이건 정말로 지혜의 항아리구려!

※ 다음 우리말과 일치하도록 빈칸에 알맞은 것을 골라 쓰시오.

1 ＿＿＿＿ ＿＿＿＿ Birbal

2 Akbar, the third Mogul emperor, had ＿＿＿ ＿＿＿ ＿＿＿ ＿＿＿ at his ＿＿＿.

3 ＿＿＿ them ＿＿＿ a man ＿＿＿ ＿＿＿ was Raja Birbal.

4 He was famous ＿＿＿ his quick ＿＿＿ and was very wise ＿＿＿ his words.

5 ＿＿＿, the ＿＿＿ always liked ＿＿＿ ＿＿＿ Birbal ＿＿＿ him.

6 Sweet ＿＿＿

7 ＿＿＿ ＿＿＿ his ＿＿＿ ＿＿＿, Akbar often ＿＿＿ ＿＿＿ ＿＿＿ ＿＿＿.

8 One day, he ＿＿＿ ＿＿＿ ＿＿＿ an interesting question.

9 Akbar: Someone pulled ＿＿＿ ＿＿＿ from my head today. What ＿＿＿ ＿＿＿ ＿＿＿ ＿＿＿ him?

10 Official 1: He should ＿＿＿ ＿＿＿, of ＿＿＿.

11 Official 2: Yes, ＿＿＿ him!

12 Akbar ＿＿＿ ＿＿＿ Birbal.

13 Akbar: What ＿＿＿ you ＿＿＿ you ＿＿＿ ＿＿＿ ＿＿＿ ＿＿＿, Birbal?

14 Birbal: ＿＿＿ I ＿＿＿ ＿＿＿, I ＿＿＿ ＿＿＿ him ＿＿＿.

15 Official 3: What's he ＿＿＿ ＿＿＿?

16 Official 4: Birbal's ＿＿＿!

17 Akbar: ＿＿＿ ＿＿＿ ＿＿＿ say so?

18 Birbal: The person ＿＿＿ pulled your hair ＿＿＿ ＿＿＿ your grandson. No one ＿＿＿ could do ＿＿＿ ＿＿＿.

19 Akbar: You are ＿＿＿ ＿＿＿, Birbal. I'm ＿＿＿ glad ＿＿＿ ＿＿＿ someone ＿＿＿ ＿＿＿ ＿＿＿ you near me.

1 비르발 이야기
2 악바르는 무굴 제국의 제3대 황제로, 자신의 궁정에 많은 현명한 신하들이 있었다.
3 그 중 라자 비르발이라는 이름의 한 사람이 있었다.
4 그는 재빠른 재치로 유명했으며 말이 매우 지혜로웠다.
5 그래서, 황제는 언제나 비르발을 곁에 두기를 원했다.
6 달콤한 처벌
7 신하들의 지혜를 시험해 보기 위해, 악바르는 종종 그들에게 이상한 질문을 했다.
8 어느 날, 황제는 재미있는 질문이 생각났다.
9 악바르: 오늘 어떤 이가 내 머리에서 머리카락을 잡아당겼소. 이 자에게 무엇을 해야 하겠소?
10 신하 1: 당연히 처벌해야 합니다.
11 신하 2: 예, 그를 처벌하소서!
12 악바르가 비르발에게 돌아섰다.
13 악바르: 그대가 내 입장이라면 무엇을 하겠소, 비르발?
14 비르발: 소신이 폐하라면, 그에게 사탕을 주겠습니다.
15 신하 3: 저 사람은 무슨 말을 하는 건가?
16 신하 4: 비르발이 정신이 나갔어!
17 악바르: 왜 그렇게 말했소?
18 비르발: 폐하의 머리카락을 잡아당긴 사람은 폐하의 손자임이 분명합니다. 다른 그 누구도 그런 짓을 할 수 없지요.
19 악바르: 과연 그대의 말이 맞소, 비르발. 그대처럼 현명한 자를 옆에 두어 정말 기쁘오.

**20** A _____ of _____

**21** One day, the king of Persia sent an official _____ _____
_____ _____.

**22** Persian Official: I hear you have _____ _____
wise men in your country. _____ _____
by my king _____ _____ him _____ _____
_____ _____.

**23** Official 5: That _____ _____! How can we _____
wisdom _____ _____ _____?

**24** Akbar: Can you bring him _____ _____ wisdom,
Birbal?

**25** Birbal: It _____ _____ a problem.

**26** Birbal: Could you please wait _____ _____ _____?

**27** Persian Official: Of course! Take _____ _____
_____ you need.

**28** _____ _____ weeks later, Birbal came back with two pots
_____ necks were really _____. He offered _____ to the
Persian _____.

**29** Birbal: You can _____ this pot of wisdom to your king. Please
ask him _____ _____ the pot to us after he takes the
wisdom _____ _____ _____.

**30** Birbal: The pot is very precious, so please be careful _____
_____ _____ it. We only have two pots of wisdom.

**31** The Persian official looked inside the pot and became _____.

**32** He _____ Birbal and _____ _____ his country.

**33** Persian Official: It _____ _____ great _____
_____ a man _____ _____ _____ Birbal in our
country.

**34** _____ the Persian official _____, Akbar asked Birbal
_____ _____ inside the pot.

**35** Birbal: Here is _____ _____ pot. You can see _____
_____.

**36** Akbar looked inside _____ _____ pot and found a
pumpkin just _____ _____ _____ the pot.

**37** Akbar: I see! The pumpkin _____ _____ _____ out
_____ _____ the pot. How did you do it?

**38** Birbal: I put the pots _____ pumpkin flowers and waited
_____ the pumpkins grew _____ _____
the pots.

**39** Akbar: Hahaha! This _____ is _____ _____
_____!

**20** 한 항아리만큼의 지혜
**21** 어느 날, 페르시아의 왕이 이상한 요청과 함께 신하를 보냈다.
**22** 페르시아의 신하: 폐하의 나라에 현명한 자들이 많다고 들었습니다. 저는 저의 왕으로부터 한 항아리의 지혜를 왕께 가지고 오라는 명을 받았습니다.
**23** 신하 5: 저건 말이 안 되오! 어떻게 지혜를 항아리에 넣을 수 있단 말이오?
**24** 악바르: 그에게 지혜 한 항아리를 가져다줄 수 있겠소, 비르발?
**25** 비르발: 문제될 것이 없사옵니다.
**26** 비르발: 몇 주만 기다려 주시겠습니까?
**27** 페르시아의 신하: 물론이오! 필요한 만큼 얼마든지 시간을 가지시오.
**28** 몇 주 후, 비르발은 목이 매우 좁은 두 항아리를 들고 돌아왔다. 그는 하나를 페르시아의 신하에게 줬다.
**29** 비르발: 이 지혜의 항아리를 그대의 왕께 가져다 드리십시오. 왕께서 이 항아리에서 지혜를 꺼내신 후에는 항아리를 우리에게 돌려달라 전해 주십시오.
**30** 비르발: 그 항아리는 매우 귀중한 것이니, 그것을 깨지 않도록 조심해 주십시오. 우리는 오직 두 개의 지혜의 항아리만 갖고 있습니다.
**31** 페르시아 신하는 항아리 안을 들여다보곤 말을 잃었다.
**32** 그는 비르발에게 감사를 표한 뒤 그의 나라로 떠났다.
**33** 페르시아의 신하: 우리 나라에도 비르발처럼 현명한 자가 있다면 정말 좋을 텐데.
**34** 페르시아의 신하가 떠난 뒤, 악바르는 비르발에게 항아리 속에 무엇이 있었는지를 물었다.
**35** 비르발: 여기 또 다른 항아리가 있습니다. 직접 살펴보시지요.
**36** 악바르는 또 다른 항아리 안을 보고 꼭 항아리만큼 큰 호박을 발견했다.
**37** 악바르: 그렇군! 항아리를 깨지 않고는 호박을 꺼낼 수가 없구려! 어떻게 한 것이오?
**38** 비르발: 항아리를 호박꽃에 덮어 놓은 후 호박이 항아리만큼 클 때까지 기다렸습니다.
**39** 악바르: 하하하! 이건 정말로 지혜의 항아리구려!

※ 다음 문장을 우리말로 쓰시오.

**1** Tales of Birbal
➡ _____

**2** Akbar, the third Mogul emperor, had a number of wise officials at his court.
➡ _____

**3** Among them was a man whose name was Raja Birbal.
➡ _____

**4** He was famous for his quick wit and was very wise with his words.
➡ _____

**5** Thus, the emperor always liked to have Birbal near him.
➡ _____

**6** Sweet Punishment
➡ _____

**7** To test his officials' wisdom, Akbar often asked them strange questions.
➡ _____

**8** One day, he came up with an interesting question.
➡ _____

**9** Akbar: Someone pulled a hair from my head today. What should I do to him?
➡ _____

**10** Official 1: He should be punished, of course.
➡ _____

**11** Official 2: Yes, punish him!
➡ _____

**12** Akbar turned to Birbal.
➡ _____

**13** Akbar: What would you do if you were in my place, Birbal?
➡ _____

**14** Birbal: If I were you, I would give him sweets.
➡ _____

**15** Official 3: What's he talking about?
➡ _____

**16** Official 4: Birbal's crazy!
➡ _____

**17** Akbar: What made you say so?
➡ _____

**18** Birbal: The person who pulled your hair must be your grandson. No one else could do such a thing.
➡ _____

**19** Akbar: You are indeed correct, Birbal. I'm so glad to have someone as wise as you near me.
➡ _____

**20** ▶ A Potful of Wisdom
➡ _____

**21** ▶ One day, the king of Persia sent an official with a strange favor.
➡ _____

**22** ▶ Persian Official: I hear you have a lot of wise men in your country. I've been asked by my king to bring him a potful of wisdom.
➡ _____

**23** ▶ Official 5: That makes no sense! How can we put wisdom in a pot?
➡ _____

**24** ▶ Akbar: Can you bring him a potful of wisdom, Birbal?
➡ _____

**25** ▶ Birbal: It won't be a problem.
➡ _____

**26** ▶ Could you please wait a few weeks?
➡ _____

**27** ▶ Persian Official: Of course! Take as much time as you need.
➡ _____

**28** ▶ A few weeks later, Birbal came back with two pots whose necks were really narrow. He offered one to the Persian official.
➡ _____

**29** ▶ Birbal: You can take this pot of wisdom to your king. Please ask him to return the pot to us after he takes the wisdom out of it.
➡ _____

**30** ▶ Birbal: The pot is very precious, so please be careful not to break it. We only have two pots of wisdom.
➡ _____

**31** ▶ The Persian official looked inside the pot and became speechless.
➡ _____

**32** ▶ He thanked Birbal and left for his country.
➡ _____

**33** ▶ Persian Official: It would be great if there were a man as wise as Birbal in our country.
➡ _____

**34** ▶ After the Persian official left, Akbar asked Birbal what was inside the pot.
➡ _____

**35** ▶ Birbal: Here is the other pot. You can see for yourself.
➡ _____

**36** ▶ Akbar looked inside the other pot and found a pumpkin just as big as the pot.
➡ _____

**37** ▶ Akbar: I see! The pumpkin can't be taken out without breaking the pot. How did you do it?
➡ _____

**38** ▶ Birbal: I put the pots over pumpkin flowers and waited until the pumpkins grew as big as the pots.
➡ _____

**39** ▶ Akbar: Hahaha! This certainly is a potful of wisdom!
➡ _____

※ 다음 괄호 안의 단어들을 우리말에 맞도록 바르게 배열하시오.

**1** (of / Birbal / Tales)
➡ _____

**2** (the / Akbar, / Mogul / third / emperor, / a / had / of / number / wise / at / officials / court. / his)
➡ _____
_____

**3** (them / among / a / was / man / name / whose / was / Birbal. / Raja)
➡ _____

**4** (was / he / for / famous / quick / his / and / wit / was / wise / very / his / with / words.)
➡ _____

**5** (the / thus, / always / emperor / to / liked / Birbal / have / him. / near)
➡ _____

**6** (Punishment / Sweet)
➡ _____

**7** (test / to / officials' / his / Akbar / wisdom, / asked / often / strange / them / questions.)
➡ _____

**8** (day, / one / came / he / with / up / interesting / an / question.)
➡ _____

**9** (Akbar: / pulled / someone / a / from / hair / head / my / today. // should / what / do / I / him? / to)
➡ _____
_____

**10** (Official 1: / should / he / punished, / be / course. / of)
➡ _____

**11** (Official 2: / punish / yes, / him!)
➡ _____

**12** (turned / Akbar / Birbal. / to)
➡ _____

**13** (Akbar: / would / what / do / you / if / were / you / in / Bribal? / place,)
➡ _____

**14** (Birbal: / I / if / you, / were / would / I / him / give / sweets.)
➡ _____

**15** (Official 3: / he / what's / about? / talking)
➡ _____

**16** (Official 3: / crazy! / Birbal's)
➡ _____

1 비르발 이야기

2 악바르는 무굴 제국의 제3대 황제로, 자신의 궁정에 많은 현명한 신하들이 있었다.

3 그 중 라자 비르발이라는 이름의 한 사람이 있었다.

4 그는 재빠른 재치로 유명했으며 말이 매우 지혜로웠다.

5 그래서, 황제는 언제나 비르발을 곁에 두기를 원했다.

6 달콤한 처벌

7 신하들의 지혜를 시험해 보기 위해, 악바르는 종종 그들에게 이상한 질문을 했다.

8 어느 날, 황제는 재미있는 질문이 생각났다.

9 악바르: 오늘 어떤 이가 내 머리에서 머리카락을 잡아당겼소. 이 자에게 무엇을 해야 하겠소?

10 신하 1: 당연히 처벌해야 합니다.

11 신하 2: 예, 그를 처벌하소서!

12 악바르가 비르발에게 돌아섰다.

13 악바르: 그대가 내 입장이라면 무엇을 하겠소, 비르발?

14 비르발: 소신이 폐하라면, 그에게 사탕을 주겠습니다.

15 신하 3: 저 사람은 무슨 말을 하는 건가?

16 신하 4: 비르발이 정신이 나갔어!

**17** (Akbar: / made / what / say / you / so?)
➡ _____

**18** (Birbal: / person / the / pulled / who / hair / your / be / must / grandson. / your // one / no / could / else / such / do / thing. / a)
➡ _____

**19** (Akbar: / are / you / indeed / Birbal. / correct, // I'm / glad / so / to / someone / have / as / as / wise / you / me. / near)
➡ _____

**20** (Potful / A / Wisdom / of)
➡ _____

**21** (day, / one / king / the / Persia / of / an / sent / official / a / with / favor. / strange)
➡ _____

**22** (Persian Official: / hear / I / have / you / a / of / lot / wise / in / men / country. / your // I've / asked / been / my / by / king / bring / to / him / potful / a / wisdom. / of)
➡ _____

**23** (Official 5: / makes / that / sense! / no // how / we / can / wisdom / put / in / pot? / a)
➡ _____

**24** (Akbar: / you / can / him / bring / a / of / potful / Birbal? / wisdom,)
➡ _____

**25** (Birbal: / won't / it / a / be / problem.)
➡ _____

**26** (Birbal: / you / could / please / a / wait / weeks? / few)
➡ _____

**27** (Persian Official: / course! / of // take / much / as / time / you / as / need.)
➡ _____

**28** (few / a / later, / weeks / came / Birbal / with / back / pots / two / necks / whose / really / were / narrow. // offered / he / to / one / the / official. / Persian)
➡ _____

**29** (Birbal: / can / you / take / pot / this / of / to / wisdom / king. / your // ask / please / to / him / the / return / pot / us / to / he / after / takes / wisdom / the / out / it. / of)
➡ _____

---

**17** 악바르: 왜 그렇게 말했소?

**18** 비르발: 폐하의 머리카락을 잡아당긴 사람은 폐하의 손자임이 분명합니다. 다른 그 누구도 그런 짓을 할 수 없지요.

**19** 악바르: 과연 그대의 말이 맞소, 비르발. 그대처럼 현명한 자를 옆에 두어 정말 기쁘오.

**20** 한 항아리만큼의 지혜

**21** 어느 날, 페르시아의 왕이 이상한 요청과 함께 신하를 보냈다.

**22** 페르시아의 신하: 폐하의 나라에 현명한 자들이 많다고 들었습니다. 저는 저의 왕으로부터 한 항아리의 지혜를 왕께 가지고 오라는 명을 받았습니다.

**23** 신하 5: 저건 말이 안 되오! 어떻게 지혜를 항아리에 넣을 수 있단 말이오?

**24** 악바르: 그에게 지혜 한 항아리를 가져다줄 수 있겠소, 비르발?

**25** 비르발: 문제될 것이 없사옵니다.

**26** 비르발: 몇 주만 기다려 주시겠습니까?

**27** 페르시아의 신하: 물론이오! 필요한 만큼 얼마든지 시간을 가지시오.

**28** 몇 주 후, 비르발은 목이 매우 좁은 두 항아리를 들고 돌아왔다. 그는 하나를 페르시아의 신하에게 줬다.

**29** 비르발: 이 지혜의 항아리를 그대의 왕께 가져다 드리십시오. 왕께서 이 항아리에서 지혜를 꺼내신 후에는 항아리를 우리에게 돌려달라 전해 주십시오.

**30** (Birbal: / pot / the / is / precious, / very / please / so / careful / be / to / not / it. / break // we / have / only / pots / two / wisdom. / of)

➡ _____

_____

**31** (Persian / the / looked / official / the / inside / pot / and / speechless. / became)

➡ _____

**32** (thanked / he / and / Birbal / left / his / for / country.)

➡ _____

**33** (Persian Official: / would / it / be / if / great / were / there / man / a / as / as / wise / in / Birbal / country. / our)

➡ _____

_____

**34** (the / after / offical / Persian / left, / asked / Akbar / what / Birbal / was / the / inside / pot.)

➡ _____

**35** (Birbal: / is / here / other / the / pot. // can / you / see / yourself. / for)

➡ _____

**36** (looked / Akbar / the / inside / pot / other / and / a / found / just / pumpkin / as / big / the / as / pot.)

➡ _____

_____

**37** (Akbar: / see! / I // the / can't / pumpkin / taken / be / without / out / breaking / pot. / the // did / how / do / you / it?)

➡ _____

_____

**38** (Birbal: / put / I / pots / the / pumpkin / over / flowers / and / until / waited / pumpkins / the / as / grew / big / the / as / pots.)

➡ _____

_____

**39** (Akbar: / hahaha! // certainly / this / a / is / of / potful / wisdom!)

➡ _____

**30** 비르발: 그 항아리는 매우 귀중한 것이니, 그것을 깨지 않도록 조심해 주십시오. 우리는 오직 두 개의 지혜의 항아리만 갖고 있습니다.

**31** 페르시아 신하는 항아리 안을 들여다보곤 말을 잃었다.

**32** 그는 비르발에게 감사를 표한 뒤 그의 나라로 떠났다.

**33** 페르시아의 신하: 우리 나라에도 비르발처럼 현명한 자가 있다면 정말 좋을 텐데.

**34** 페르시아의 신하가 떠난 뒤, 악바르는 비르발에게 항아리 속에 무엇이 있었는지를 물었다.

**35** 비르발: 여기 또 다른 항아리가 있습니다. 직접 살펴보시지요.

**36** 악바르는 또 다른 항아리 안을 보고 꼭 항아리만큼 큰 호박을 발견했다.

**37** 악바르: 그렇군! 항아리를 깨지 않고는 호박을 꺼낼 수가 없구려! 어떻게 한 것이오?

**38** 비르발: 항아리를 호박꽃에 덮어 놓은 후 호박이 항아리만큼 클 때까지 기다렸습니다.

**39** 악바르: 하하하! 이건 정말로 지혜의 항아리구려!

※ 다음 우리말을 영어로 쓰시오.

**1** 비르발 이야기
➡ _____

**2** 악바르는 무굴 제국의 제3대 황제로, 자신의 궁정에 많은 현명한 신하들이 있었다.
➡ _____

**3** 그 중 라자 비르발이라는 이름의 한 사람이 있었다.
➡ _____

**4** 그는 재빠른 재치로 유명했으며 말이 매우 지혜로웠다.
➡ _____

**5** 그래서, 황제는 언제나 비르발을 곁에 두기를 원했다.
➡ _____

**6** 달콤한 처벌
➡ _____

**7** 신하들의 지혜를 시험해 보기 위해, 악바르는 종종 그들에게 이상한 질문을 했다.
➡ _____

**8** 어느 날, 황제는 재미있는 질문이 생각났다.
➡ _____

**9** 악바르: 오늘 어떤 이가 내 머리에서 머리카락을 잡아당겼소. 이 자에게 무엇을 해야 하겠소?
➡ _____

**10** 신하 1: 당연히 처벌해야 합니다.
➡ _____

**11** 신하 2: 예, 그를 처벌하소서!
➡ _____

**12** 악바르가 비르발에게 돌아섰다.
➡ _____

**13** 악바르: 그대가 내 입장이라면 무엇을 하겠소, 비르발?
➡ _____

**14** 비르발: 소신이 폐하라면, 그에게 사탕을 주겠습니다.
➡ _____

**15** 신하 3: 저 사람은 무슨 말을 하는 건가?
➡ _____

**16** 신하 4: 비르발이 정신이 나갔어!
➡ _____

**17** 악바르: 왜 그렇게 말했소?
➡ _____

**18** 비르발: 폐하의 머리카락을 잡아당긴 사람은 폐하의 손자임이 분명합니다. 다른 그 누구도 그런 짓을 할 수 없지요.
➡ _____

**19** 악바르: 과연 그대의 말이 맞소, 비르발. 그대처럼 현명한 자를 옆에 두어 정말 기쁘오.
➡ _____

**20** 한 항아리만큼의 지혜
➡ _____

**21** 어느 날, 페르시아의 왕이 이상한 요청과 함께 신하를 보냈다.
➡ _____

**22** 페르시아의 신하: 폐하의 나라에 현명한 자들이 많다고 들었습니다. 저는 저의 왕으로부터 한 항아리의 지혜를 왕께 가지고 오라는 명을 받았습니다.
➡ _____
_____

**23** 신하 5: 저건 말이 안 되오! 어떻게 지혜를 항아리에 넣을 수 있단 말이오?
➡ _____

**24** 악바르: 그에게 지혜 한 항아리를 가져다줄 수 있겠소, 비르발?
➡ _____

**25** 비르발: 문제될 것이 없사옵니다.
➡ _____

**26** 비르발: 몇 주만 기다려 주시겠습니까?
➡ _____

**27** 페르시아의 신하: 물론이오! 필요한 만큼 얼마든지 시간을 가지시오.
➡ _____

**28** 몇 주 후, 비르발은 목이 매우 좁은 두 항아리를 들고 돌아왔다. 그는 하나를 페르시아의 신하에게 줬다.
➡ _____

**29** 비르발: 이 지혜의 항아리를 그대의 왕께 가져다 드리십시오. 왕께서 이 항아리에서 지혜를 꺼내신 후에는 항아리를 우리에게 돌려달라 전해 주십시오.
➡ _____

**30** 비르발: 그 항아리는 매우 귀중한 것이니, 그것을 깨지 않도록 조심해 주십시오. 우리는 오직 두 개의 지혜의 항아리만 갖고 있습니다.
➡ _____
_____

**31** 페르시아 신하는 항아리 안을 들여다보곤 말을 잃었다.
➡ _____

**32** 그는 비르발에게 감사를 표한 뒤 그의 나라로 떠났다.
➡ _____

**33** 페르시아의 신하: 우리 나라에도 비르발처럼 현명한 자가 있다면 정말 좋을 텐데.
➡ _____

**34** 페르시아의 신하가 떠난 뒤, 악바르는 비르발에게 항아리 속에 무엇이 있었는지를 물었다.
➡ _____

**35** 비르발: 여기 또 다른 항아리가 있습니다. 직접 살펴보시지요.
➡ _____

**36** 악바르는 또 다른 항아리 안을 보고 꼭 항아리만큼 큰 호박을 발견했다.
➡ _____

**37** 악바르: 그렇군! 항아리를 깨지 않고는 호박을 꺼낼 수가 없구려! 어떻게 한 것이오?
➡ _____

**38** 비르발: 항아리를 호박꽃에 덮어 놓은 후 호박이 항아리만큼 클 때까지 기다렸습니다.
➡ _____

**39** 악바르: 하하하! 이건 정말로 지혜의 항아리구려!
➡ _____

※ 다음 우리말과 일치하도록 빈칸에 알맞은 말을 쓰시오.

## Link

1. A _____ _____

2. One day, Emperor Akbar _____ _____ _____ on the ground and _____ _____ _____.

3. Akbar: _____ this line _____ _____ _____ it.

4. Official 1: _____ _____ it?

5. Official 2: _____ can we do _____?

6. Birbal _____.

7. Birbal: That's _____ _____.

8. Birbal drew a longer line _____ _____ the line _____ Akbar _____ _____.

9. Birbal: Your line is now _____ _____ _____.

10. Akbar: You _____ _____, Birbal!

11. Official 3: I _____ I _____ _____ _____ _____ Birbal.

## Write

1. _____ Jaeha,

2. Time _____. I cannot believe that it is time _____ _____ _____.

3. I still remember _____ _____ _____ _____ camping together.

4. I really liked _____ _____ _____ _____ that night.

5. I also loved _____ _____ _____ you _____ _____.

6. I really want to thank you _____ _____ _____ _____.

7. If I _____ _____ _____ _____ _____, I _____ more time with you.

8. I hope we _____ _____ _____ even after we _____.

9. _____, Jake

## Culture Project

1. _____ my brother _____ his driving test _____ _____, he was very _____.

2. Kento, his friend _____ Japan, _____ _____ him, "_____ _____ _____ you, I _____ _____ _____ _____."

3. _____ seven times, _____ _____ eight."

4. It's a _____ _____ that means "_____ _____ _____ _____."

5. My brother _____ _____ and _____ _____.

1. 더 짧은 선
2. 어느 날, 악바르 황제는 땅에 선을 그린 뒤 그의 신하들에게 물었다.
3. 악바르: 이 선을 건드리지 않은 채 더 짧게 만들어 보게.
4. 신하 1: 건드리지 않고 말씀입니까?
5. 신하 2: 어떻게 그렇게 할 수 있습니까?
6. 비르발은 미소를 지었다.
7. 비르발: 너무 쉽군요.
8. 비르발은 악바르가 그린 선 옆에 더 긴 선을 그렸다.
9. 비르발: 폐하의 선이 이제 제 선보다 짧습니다.
10. 악바르: 그대가 해냈소, 비르발!
11. 신하 3: 제가 비르발만큼 지혜롭다면 좋겠군요.

1. 재하에게,
2. 시간 정말 빠르다. 작별 인사를 해야 할 시간이라는 게 믿어지지 않아.
3. 아직도 우리가 함께 캠핑을 갔던 때가 생각나.
4. 우리가 그날 밤에 봤던 영화를 정말 좋아했는데.
5. 너와 방과 후에 농구를 하는 것도 정말로 좋아했어.
6 농구 기술들을 가르쳐 줘서 정말로 고맙다고 하고 싶어.
7. 시간을 되돌갈 수 있다면, 너와 함께 더 많은 시간을 보낼 거야.
8. 우리가 졸업한 뒤에도 계속 연락을 하면 좋겠다.
9. Jake가.

※ 다음 우리말을 영어로 쓰시오.

**Link**

1. 더 짧은 선
➡ _____

2. 어느 날, 악바르 황제는 땅에 선을 그린 뒤 그의 신하들에게 물었다.
➡ _____

3. 악바르: 이 선을 건드리지 않은 채 더 짧게 만들어 보게.
➡ _____

4. 신하 1: 건드리지 않고 말씀입니까?
➡ _____

5. 신하 2: 어떻게 그렇게 할 수 있습니까?
➡ _____

6. 비르발은 미소를 지었다.
➡ _____

7. 비르발: 너무 쉽군요.
➡ _____

8. 비르발은 악바르가 그린 선 옆에 더 긴 선을 그렸다.
➡ _____

9. 비르발: 폐하의 선이 이제 제 선보다 짧습니다.
➡ _____

10. 악바르: 그대가 해냈소, 비르발!
➡ _____

11. 신하 3: 제가 비르발만큼 지혜롭다면 좋겠군요.
➡ _____

**Write**

1. 재하에게,
➡ _____

2. 시간 정말 빠르다. 작별 인사를 해야 할 시간이라는 게 믿어지지 않아.
➡ _____

3. 아직도 우리가 함께 캠핑을 갔던 때가 생각나.
➡ _____

4. 우리가 그날 밤에 봤던 영화를 정말 좋아했는데.
➡ _____

5. 너와 방과 후에 농구를 하는 것도 정말로 좋아했어.
➡ _____

6. 농구 기술들을 가르쳐 줘서 정말로 고맙다고 하고 싶어.
➡ _____

7. 시간을 되돌아갈 수 있다면, 너와 함께 더 많은 시간을 보낼 거야.
➡ _____

8. 우리가 졸업한 뒤에도 계속 연락을 하면 좋겠다.
➡ _____

9. Jake가.
➡ _____

**Culture Project**

1. 내 오빠가 운전 면허 시험에서 일곱 번 떨어졌을 때, 그는 매우 실망했습니다.
➡ _____

2. 일본에서 온 그의 친구 Kento는 그에게, "내가 너였다면, 포기하지 않을 거야.
➡ _____

3. 일곱 번 넘어져도 여덟 번 일어나야지."하고 말했습니다.
➡ _____

4. 이것은 "포기하지 마라."라는 뜻의 일본 격언입니다.
➡ _____

5. 오빠는 다시 도전해 마침내 통과했습니다.
➡ _____

MEMO

MEMO

# MEMO

영어 기출 문제집

적중100

2학기

# 정답 및 해설

미래 | 최연희

중 3

적중100

# This Is Korea

01 lend      02 ⑤      03 ⑤

04 (1) (w)etsuit   (2) (w)orldwide   (3) ad   (4) bridge

05 (1) is good for   (2) wish for   (3) Cheer up
     (4) walk along   (5) get into

06 ②

01 주어진 단어는 반의어 관계이다. lend: 빌려주다, borrow: 빌리다

02 '가치가 있지만 물리적으로 존재하지는 않는'을 의미하는 말은 intangible(무형의)이다.

03 experience: 경험

04 wetsuit: 잠수복, worldwide: 세계적으로, ad: 광고, bridge: 다리

05 cheer up: 격려하다, wish for: 기원하다, get into: ~에 들어가다, be good for: ~에 유익하다, walk along: ~을 따라 걷다

06 주어진 문장에서 press는 '누르다'를 의미하며 이와 같은 의미로 쓰인 것은 ②번이다. 나머지는 모두 '신문, 언론'을 뜻한다.

서술형 시험대비      p.09

01 past

02 (1) (p)ath   (2) community   (3) (p)romote
     (4) jellyfish

03 (1) We had a good harvest last year.
     (2) Money does not always bring happiness.
     (3) Our national heritage was destroyed by the fire.

04 (1) We walked along the street for an hour.
     (2) This book is suitable for elementary school
        students.
     (3) Let's make double-sided copies to save paper.

05 (1) promote   (2) realize   (3) several
     (4) underwater   (5) volcanic

01 주어진 단어는 반의어 관계이다. future: 미래, past: 과거

02 path: 길, community: 지역 공동체, promote: 홍보하다, jellyfish: 해파리

03 good harvest: 풍년, happiness: 행복, heritage: 유산

04 walk along: ~을 따라 걷다, be suitable for: ~에 적절하다, make double-sided copies: 양면 복사를 하다

05 realize: 깨닫다, promote: 홍보하다, underwater: 물속의, 수중의, volcanic: 화산의, several: 몇몇의

교과서
## Conversation

핵심 Check      p.10~11

1 I wonder where the photo was taken.

2 (C) → (B) → (A)

교과서 대화문 익히기

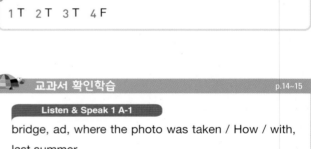

Check(√) True or False      p.12

1 T   2 T   3 T   4 F

교과서 확인학습      p.14~15

**Listen & Speak 1 A-1**

bridge, ad, where the photo was taken / How / with, last summer

**Listen & Speak 1 A-2**

I wonder why, waiting in line / get into / famous / on / try

**Listen & Speak 2 A-1**

I'd like to borrow / explain how to use it / Press, what to do

**Listen & Speak 2 A-2**

somewhere / walk along / Could you explain / long hiking path / enjoy your trip

**Communicate A**

I wonder where / check it out / strong beat, traditional / community / Could you explain / traditionally, cheer up, good harvest / rhythm / completes / Why not

**Progress Check 1**

I wonder why there are so many cars / going on vacation / why don't we

copy machine / how to make double-sided copies /
Press, press

---

**시험대비 기본평가** p.16

01 I wonder where the photo was taken.
02 How do you know that?
03 Could you tell me what that is?  04 ⑤

01 간접의문문 어순으로 '의문사+주어+동사'의 어순이 알맞다.
04 Tom이 구체적으로 제주 올레길에 대한 설명을 요청한 것으로
   보아 Tom이 이미 올레길에 대해 잘 알고 있다는 설명은 일치하
   지 않는다.

---

**시험대비 실력평가** p.17~18

01 (E) → (C) → (B) → (D) → (A)  02 ⑤
03 ⓑ → was taken  04 ⑤  05 ⑤
06 ⑤  07 (C) → (B) → (D) → (E) → (A)
08 ④
09 Dancing together completes the music.
10 ⑤

01 (E) 궁금함에 대한 대답 → (C) 유명한지 질문→ (B) 대답 및
   이유 설명 → (D) 제안 → (A) 동의
02 ⑤번을 제외한 나머지는 모두 설명을 요청하는 표현이다.
03 사진이 찍혔으므로 수동태가 알맞다.
04 소녀가 다리 사진을 찍고 싶다는 내용은 대화를 통해 알 수 없다.
05 (A)는 진행을 나타내는 현재분사 waiting, (B) get into: 들어
   가다, get out: 나가다, (C) TV에 나왔음을 나타내는 on이 적
   절하다.
06 Brian과 수진은 줄을 서 있는 사람들을 보고 있다.
07 (C) 하고 싶은 일 부탁 → (B) 허락 → (D) 양면 복사 방법 질
   문 → (E) 대답 → (A) 감사 표현
08 궁금함을 나타내는 표현으로 ④번으로 바꾸어 쓸 수 있다.
09 complete: 완성하다
10 궁금한 것을 알고 싶다는 말에 노력에 감사하다는 대답은 어색
   하다.

---

**서술형 시험대비** p.19

01 Could you explain how to use it?
02 She gets to know what she should do.
03 (A) waiting in line  (B) the new bakery
   (C) get into  (D) it was on a TV program

---

04 (1) band  (2) strong  (3) farmers  (4) harvest
05 They are going to join some people dancing to
   the rhythm.

02 버튼을 누르면 여자는 무엇을 해야 하는지 알 수 있다.
03 Brian과 Sujin은 새로 생긴 제과점 앞에 줄을 서 있는 많은 사
   람들을 보았다. 사람들은 그곳에 들어가고 싶어 했다. 새로 생긴
   제과점은 매우 인기가 있었다. 왜냐하면 TV 프로그램에 나왔었
   기 때문이다. Brian과 Sujin은 함께 그곳의 빵을 먹어보고 싶
   어 했다.
05 Jaden과 유리는 대화 후 춤추는 사람들과 함께 할 것이다.

---

교과서
# Grammar

**핵심 Check** p.20~21

1 (1) had  (2) visited
2 (1) will she make → she will make
  (2) was Sarah → Sarah was

---

**시험대비 기본평가** p.22

01 ⑤  02 ③  03 ④
04 (1) asked how she became interested
   (2) tell us what is so special

01 기준이 되는 시점이 과거이고, 그 이전에 일어난 동작이므로 과
   거완료시제를 찾는다.
02 의문사가 없는 의문문의 간접의문문은 if 또는 whether가 접속
   사 역할을 한다.
03 ① '지금까지'이므로 현재완료시제로 써야 한다. had lived →
   has lived, ② has → had ③ had found → found, ⑤ 과거
   시점 이전에 일어난 일이므로 had gone이 적절하다.
04 간접의문문을 만들 때, 의문사는 접속사 역할을 하고 '의문사+주
   어+동사'의 어순이 된다. 시제와 수에 유의하여, 동사를 적절히
   쓴다. 의문사가 주어일 때는 순서가 바뀌지 않는 것도 주의한다.

---

**시험대비 실력평가** p.23~25

01 ③  02 ⑤  03 ④  04 ④
05 ⑤  06 had been → has been  07 ⑤
08 ⑤  09 ②  10 ④  11 ③
12 ⑤

13 many customers  had spent quite a long time lining up in order to eat pork cutlet

14 Why do you think the temples are famous?

15 (1) asked his sister why people could not fly  in the sky

(2) told his friend that he had touched a hive  that morning

01 ③ 과거시점(Lucy asked) 이전에 발생한 일이다. has broken → had broken이 적절하다.

02 간접의문문의 어순은 '의문사+주어+동사'이다. 원래의 의문문 'What is that?'에서 What은 주어로 쓰인 것이 아님에 유의하여 'what that is' 어순으로 배열한 정답을 찾는다.

03 '의문사+be+there+주어'는 간접의문문이 될 때, '의문사+there+be+주어'의 어순이 된다.

04 ① had read → has read ② 'San Francisco로 이사를 하기 전에 New York에서 살았다'는 문장이므로 'William lived[had lived] in New York before he moved to San Francisco.'가 적절하다. ③ '민수가 보고서를 완성해야 한다고 요구'한 것이므로 had completed → (should) complete ⑤ had not eaten → have not eaten

05 ① what so special is → what is so special ② do I like → I like ③ Do you imagine how old → How old do you imagine ④ what is your favorite food → what your favorite food is

06 과거의 특정 시점 이전에 발생한 일을 과거완료시제로 표현해야 한다. 종속절이 'since+과거시제'이므로, 주절은 과거완료가 아니라 현재완료시제로 표현하는 것이 적절하다.

07 간접의문문의 접속사 역할을 하는 who가 주어로 사용되었으므로, 어순을 바꿀 필요가 없다. 'who took away her kids' toys' 원래 어순 그대로 쓰는 것이 적절하다.

08 <보기>의 had found는 과거완료시제 중 '완료' 용법으로 쓰였다. ①, ③, ④는 '계속', ②는 '경험' 용법이다.

09 <보기> if는 조건의 '부사절' 접속사이며, ②도 그렇다. 나머지는 모두 '의문사 없는 간접의문문을 이끄는 접속사'이다.

10 본동사가 think일 때, 간접의문문의 의문사는 문두로 보내고 어순은 '주어+동사' 순으로 한다.

11 ① 내용상 '내가 사준 것'이 '그녀가 목걸이를 잃어버린 것'보다 먼저이기 때문에 'Cecilia lost the necklace which I had bought for her.'가 적절하다. ② had melted → melted ④ have → had ⑤ has → had

12 ① Do you think where → Where do you think ② what did your action mean → what your action meant ③ did anyone see → anyone saw ④ how the writer of these books old → how old the writer of these books is

13 과거완료시제(had spent)와, 'spend+시간+V-ing'를 활용하

14 간접의문문을 활용하는 문제이다. 생각 동사 think, believe, imagine 등이 주절에 올 때, 간접의문문의 의문사를 문두로 보내는 것에 유의한다.

15 (1) 의문사 why를 간접의문문으로 활용한 문장이다. '지호는 누나에게 왜 사람이 하늘을 날 수 없는지 물어봤다.' (2) 과거완료시제를 이용하여, 어구를 배열하는 문장이다. 'Pooh는 그의 친구에게 그 날 아침에 벌집을 건드렸었다고 말했다.'

### 🦉 서술형 시험대비

p.26~27

01 (1) collected many Korean treasures that some French had stolen before

(2) wonders how she can promote the haenyeo worldwide

(3) he found someone had broken into his house

(4) Can you guess where the photographer took

02 (1) how they could get to the meeting on time

(2) which boy the girl next to Jane chose at the blind date

(3) if(또는 whether) Shrek hasn't learned German yet

(4) where Alex found the baby tiger

(5) the new employee looks

03 had only seen black-and-white photos of haenyeo who

04 (1) Can you tell me where the magician was when he disappeared?

(2) Does the young student know how far the hotel is?

(3) Do you know if[whether] I could take pictures of haenyeo?

(4) They didn't understand why the girl wanted to take their pictures.

(5) Tell me what Zin Kim promised the haenyeo.

(6) I wonder why Jejudo isn't suitable for farming.

05 The haenyeo had not thought that she was pretty until the photographer took her picture twelve years ago.

06 (1) Tom wondered how haenyeo could stay in the water for so long without any breathing devices.

(2) They are studying how catching too much marine life can destroy the ocean.

(3) The witch asked the mirror who the most beautiful woman in the world was.

(4) The mother goat did not know when the babies opened the door to the wolf.

**4** 정답 및 해설

01 (1), (3) 과거의 특정 시점 이전에 일어난 일은 '과거완료시제'로 쓰는 것에 유의한다. (2), (4) '간접의문문'의 어순은 '의문사+주어+동사'이다. 특히, (4)번에서 guess라는 생각 동사가 오지만, yes나 no로 대답이 가능한 의문문의 경우 의문사가 앞으로 가지 않는 것에 유의한다.

02 '간접의문문'의 어순은 '의문사+주어+동사'이다. 어순이 바뀔 때는 수와 시제에 유의해야 한다. (5)번에서 think와 같은 생각 동사가 있을 때는 의문사가 문두로 와야 한다.

03 only see를 과거완료시제로 표현하면 had only seen이다. 빈칸 뒤의 looked가 동사이므로 주어 역할의 관계대명사 who를 마지막에 쓴다.

04 (1) was the magician → the magician was (2) how the hotel is far → how far the hotel is (3) could I → if(또는 whether) I could (4) did the girl want → the girl wanted (5) did Zin Kim promise → Zin Kim promised (6) why is Jejudo not → why Jejudo isn't

05 과거의 어느 특정 시점을 기준으로 그 전의 동작은 과거완료시제로 표현한다. 12년 전에 사진작가가 사진을 찍기까지는 자신을 예쁘다고 생각하지 않았으므로, 부정의 과거완료시제를 사용해서 표현하면, 'had not thought that she was pretty'가 적절하다.

06 주어진 단어들 중 동사의 수와 시제에 유의하여, 간접의문문의 어순과 내용에 알맞게 적절한 문장을 영작한다.

## Reading

### 확인문제      p.28

1 T   2 F   3 F   4 T   5 F

### 확인문제      p.29

1 T   2 F   3 T   4 F   5 T

### 교과서 확인학습 A      p.30~31

01 Female Divers
02 underwater photographer, has promoted
03 without any breathing devices
04 made UNESCO's Intangible Cultural Heritage list
05 was interviewed
06 become interested in
07 happened to
08 was surprised to find
09 looked very tired
10 kept laughing
11 should take
12 isn't it difficult

---

13 why I wanted
14 in their wetsuits
15 very special
16 show, to
17 opened up
18 make them, beautiful
19 more about
20 so special
21 can tell you
22 strong women
23 is not suitable for, the breadwinners for
24 form, each other
25 more-experienced, less-experienced
26 without, can't catch
27 is good for
28 at one time in one place
29 planning to do
30 attended, give a talk
31 held my hand
32 so much
33 such a special person
34 with happiness
35 was deeply moved
36 can never forget
37 more beautiful stories about them

### 교과서 확인학습 B      p.32~33

1 Haenyeo, Female Divers of Korea
2 For the past several years, the underwater photographer Zin Kim has promoted the culture of Jeju haenyeo worldwide.
3 Haenyeo are Korean female divers who harvest seafood without any breathing devices.
4 Their culture made UNESCO's Intangible Cultural Heritage list in 2016.
5 At her studio last week, Zin Kim was interviewed about her experience of taking pictures of haenyeo.
6 Q. How did you become interested in taking photos of haenyeo?
7 One day, I happened to take pictures of a haenyeo.
8 I was surprised to find that she was enjoying her job.
9 Until then, I had only seen black-and-white photos of haenyeo who looked very tired.
10 However, she kept laughing even after she had been in the water for over five hours.
11 I realized then that I should take pictures of haenyeo.
12 Q. You take beautiful pictures of them, but isn't it difficult to take pictures of haenyeo?
13 At first, they didn't understand why I wanted to take their pictures.
14 They didn't think they looked pretty in their wetsuits.

15 So, I said to them, "You're very special.

16 I want to show your culture to the world."

17 They opened up to me then.

18 Of course, I also promised them that I would make them look beautiful in my pictures.

19 Q. Could you tell us more about haenyeo?

20 What's so special about them?

21 I can tell you three things.

22 First, haenyeo are a symbol of strong women.

23 Jejudo, which is a volcanic island, is not suitable for farming, so many haenyeo have become the breadwinners for their families.

24 Second, haenyeo form their own communities and help each other.

25 For example, more-experienced haenyeo train less-experienced haenyeo.

26 Third, because they stay in the water without any breathing devices, haenyeo can't catch a lot of seafood.

27 This is good for the underwater environment.

28 Catching too much marine life at one time in one place can destroy the ocean.

29 Q. Lastly, please tell us what you're planning to do in the future.

30 I once attended an overseas exhibition with a couple of haenyeo to give a talk about their lives.

31 When I finished my talk, one of the haenyeo held my hand tightly.

32 She said to me, "Thank you so much.

33 I've never known in my whole life that I was such a special person."

34 She was crying with happiness.

35 Everyone in the audience was deeply moved.

36 I can never forget that moment, so I'll continue to take pictures of haenyeo.

37 I want to tell more beautiful stories about them to many more people in the world.

## 시험대비 실력평가
p.34~37

01 ②, ④   02 ⑤   03 ④   04 ③

05 laughing   06 ④   07 ⑤   08 ②

09 they didn't understand why I wanted to take their pictures

10 (A) attended   (B) such   (C) so

11 ⑤   12 ④   13 ②, ③

14 breadwinners   15 that → which

16 because they stay in the water without any breathing devices, haenyeo can't catch a lot of seafood

17 ②   18 ③   19 ①

20 looking → look   21 ④   22 ③

23 suitable → not suitable 또는 unsuitable

24 ①, ⑤   25 to catch

01 주격 관계대명사 who와 that이 적절하다.

02 ⓑ와 ⑤: ~이 되다, ~의 지위를 얻다; ~으로 승진[승격]하다, 존스는 5년 만에 교수가 되었다. ① 만들다[제작/제조하다], ② (~로 하여금 …하게) 만들다[하게], ③ 선출[임명/지명]하다, ④ (억지로 무엇을 하게) 만들다[시키다]

03 해녀는 어떤 호흡 장치도 '사용하지 않고' 해산물을 채취하는 한국의 여성 잠수부들이다.

04 대답에서 해녀의 사진을 찍는 것에 관심을 가지게 된 이유를 설명하고 있으므로, 빈칸에 들어갈 질문으로는 ③번 '어떻게 해녀의 사진을 찍는 것에 관심을 가지게 되었나요?'가 적절하다.

05 keep -ing: 계속 ~하다

06 (B)와 ②: 계속 용법, ①, ④: 완료 용법, ③: 결과 용법, ⑤: 경험 용법

07 주어진 문장의 then에 주목한다. 그들이 '그때' 제게 마음을 열었다고 했을 때의 '그때'는 ⑤번 앞 문장에서 말한 "여러분들은 아주 특별해요. 저는 여러분의 문화를 세계에 알리고 싶어요."라고 말한 때를 가리키므로 ⑤번이 적절하다.

08 이 글은 '글쓴이가 해녀들을 설득하여 그들의 사진을 찍게 된 과정'을 설명하는 글이므로, 제목으로는 ②번 '와! 해녀들은 내가 사진을 통해 그들의 문화를 알리도록 허락해 주었어!'가 적절하다.

09 why는 의문문의 문두에 쓰이는 의문사이지만 간접의문문에서는 문장 안에 쓰인다. 이때는 보통 주어가 동사 앞에 와서 '의문사+주어+동사'의 순서로 쓰인다.

10 (A) 박람회에 '참가한' 적이 있다고 해야 하므로 attended가 옳다. attend to: ~을 돌보다, 시중들다, (B) 'such+a+형용사+명사'의 순서로 써야 하므로 such가 옳다. 'so+형용사+a+명사', (C) '그 순간을 절대 잊을 수가 없기 때문에 해녀의 사진을 계속해서 찍을 것'이라고 해야 하므로 so가 옳다.

11 중반부의 'She was crying with happiness. Everyone in the audience was deeply moved.'를 통해 'touching'을 찾을 수 있다. touching: 감동적인, ① 혼란스러운, ② 재미있는, 흥미로운, ③ 우울하게 만드는, 우울한, ④ 지루한

12 Zin Kim이 얼마나 오랫동안 해녀들의 사진을 찍어 왔는지는 대답할 수 없다. ① With a couple of haenyeo. ② To give a talk about haenyeo's lives. ③ She said, "Thank you so much. I've never known in my whole life that I was such a special person." ⑤ She wants to tell more

beautiful stories about haenyeo.

13 ⓐ와 ②, ③: 경험 용법, ① 완료 용법, ④ 완료 용법, ⑤ 계속 용법

14 필수적인 것들을 위해 가족이 필요한 돈을 버는 사람들, breadwinner: (집안의) 생계비를 버는 사람, 가장

15 관계대명사 that은 계속적 용법으로 쓸 수 없으므로 which로 바꾸는 것이 적절하다.

16 앞 문장의 내용을 가리킨다.

17 이 글은 '해녀에 대해 무엇이 특별한지'를 설명하는 글이므로, 주제로는 ②번 '해녀에 대한 특별한 점들'이 적절하다. ① subject: (그림·사진 등의) 대상[소재]

18 ⓐ in: '착용'을 나타내는 전치사, ⓑ show는 3형식으로 고칠 때 전치사 to를 사용한다.

19 ①은 Zin Kim을 가리키고, 나머지는 다 '해녀들'을 가리킨다.

20 사역동사 make의 목적격보어이므로 동사원형으로 고치는 것이 적절하다.

21 전반부의 'they didn't understand why I wanted to take their pictures'를 통해 'puzzled'를, 중반부의 'They opened up to me then.'을 통해 'consenting'을 찾을 수 있다. puzzled: 어리둥절해하는, 얼떨떨한, consenting: 동의[승낙]하는, ① nervous: 초조한, ② delighted: 아주 기뻐하는, upset: 속상한, ③ agreeing: 동의하는, ⑤ confused: 혼란스러워 하는, disappointed: 실망한

22 앞의 내용의 예가 나오고 있으므로 For example이 가장 적절하다. ① 그러므로, ④ 게다가, ⑤ 그 결과

23 제주도는 화산섬이라서 농사에 '적합하지 않다'로 고치는 것이 적절하다.

24 (B)와 ②, ③, ④: 동명사(목적, 용도), ①, ⑤: 현재분사(동작의 진행)

25 to부정사를 진주어로 하여 고치는 것이 적절하다.

### 서술형 시험대비
p.38~39

01 by chance (또는 by accident )

02 have → had

03 (A) enjoying   (B) laughing

04 (A) For   (B) any   (C) Intangible

05 Haenyeo 또는 haenyeo

06 two thousand (and) sixteen 또는 twenty sixteen

07 marine

08 (A) breathing devices   (B) can't catch

09 (1) 해녀들은 강인한 여성의 상징이다.
   (2) 해녀들은 그들 자신의 공동체를 조직하고 서로 돕는다.
   (3) 어떤 호흡 장치도 사용하지 않고 물속에 머물기 때문에, 해녀는 많은 해산물을 채취할 수가 없다.

10 what you're planning to do in the future

11 me                 12 touched

13 (A) take pictures    (B) more beautiful stories

01 by chance = by accident = accidentally: 우연히, 뜻밖에, happen to do it = do it by chance[by accident]: 우연히 ~하다

02 Until then이 있으므로 과거완료로 고치는 것이 적절하다.

03 Zin Kim이 우연히 한 해녀의 사진을 찍게 되었을 때, 그녀는 자신의 직업을 '즐겼고 '다섯 시간이 넘도록 물속에 있은 후에도 계속 '웃었다'. Zin Kim은 그것에 놀라서 해녀의 사진을 찍어야겠다고 결심했다.

04 (A) '지난 몇 년 동안'이라고 해야 하므로 For가 옳다. during 은 뒤에 기간을 나타내는 명사를 써서, 특정 기간 중의 어느 한 시점을 가리키고, for는 'how long?'에 대한 답을 나타낸다. (B) 부정의 뜻을 가지는 without이 있으므로 any가 옳다. (C) '무형문화유산'이라고 해야 하므로 Intangible이 옳다. tangible: 유형의

05 haenyeo를 복수로 취급했고, 한 명의 해녀는 a haenyeo라고 하는 것이 적절하다.

06 2001년부터 2009년까지는 two thousand (and) ~로 읽는 것이 적절하다.

07 바다 혹은 바다에서 사는 동식물들과 관련된, marine: 바다의, 해양의

08 해녀는 어떤 '호흡 장치'도 사용하지 않고 물속에 머물러서, 많은 해산물을 '채취할 수가 없기' 때문이다.

09 인터뷰 질문에 대한 답 세 가지를 쓰는 것이 적절하다.

10 간접의문문의 순서(의문사+주어+동사)로 쓰는 것이 적절하다.

11 소유격+신체의 일부를 나타내는 명사 = 목적격+전치사+the+ 신체의 일부를 나타내는 명사

12 moved = touched: 감동한

13 Zin Kim은 해녀 중 한 분이 그녀에게 감사를 표했던 순간을 절대 잊을 수가 없기 때문에 해녀의 '사진을 계속해서 찍을' 것이다. 그녀는 그들에 대한 '더 많은 아름다운 이야기들을' 세계의 더 많은 사람들에게 알려 주고 싶어 한다.

### 영역별 핵심문제
p.41~46

01 happiness          02 ②          03 ⑤

04 (1) go on (a) vacation   (2) a couple of
   (3) cheer up   (4) Give, a call

05 (1) overwork   (2) greenhouse   (3) breathe
   (4) device   (5) heritage

06 He wants to make double-sided copies.

07 He will press the button for double-sided copies.

08 ③          09 ⑤          10 ⓐ → check it out

7

11 beat　　12 ⑤　　　　13 had eaten

14 ①, ②　　15 ③, ④

16 (1) thinking about which university he should go
to

　　(2) wondering when the rain will stop

17 (1) had pulled　(2) was killed

　　(3) had already gone　(4) had been

　　(5) had seen　(6) appeared

18 (1) what time the store opens

　　(2) how we can contact the store manager

　　(3) where the store is located

　　(4) if[whether] there is any subway station near the
store

19 (1) ⓑ　(2) ⓒ　(3) ⓐ　(4) ⓒ　(5) ⓐ　(6) ⓓ　(7) ⓑ

　　(8) ⓓ

20 (1) Vanessa had cleaned the windows and (had)
washed the dishes

　　(2) Sally had given the dog some food and (had)
watered the plant

21 (1) why she had to learn how to cook in another
country

　　(2) if there are any seats left on the plane

22 ③　　　　23 ①, ④　　24 ⑤　　　25 ②

26 ③　　　　27 ⑤　　　　28 ④　　　29 ②

---

01 주어진 단어는 형용사와 명사의 관계이다.

02 '가족을 부양하려고 돈을 버는 가족 구성원'을 나타내는 말은
breadwinner(생계를 책임지는 사람, 가장)이다.

03 path: 오솔길, 작은 길

04 go on (a) vacation: 휴가가다, a couple of: 두 서너 개의,
cheer up: 힘을 북돋아 주다, 격려하다, give (someone) a
call: 전화를 걸다

05 heritage: 유산, greenhouse: 온실, device: 장치, breathe:
호흡하다, overwork: 과로

06 Jack은 양면 복사를 하고 싶다.

07 Jack은 시작 버튼을 누르기 전에 양면 복사 버튼을 누를 것이
다.

08 주어진 문장은 구체적인 설명을 요청하는 것이므로 이어지는 문
장에서 구체적인 제주 올레길에 대한 설명이 이어지는 (C)에 들
어가는 것이 적절하다.

09 Tom이 제주도에서 무엇을 하고 싶은지는 대화를 통해 알 수 없
다.

10 '동사+부사'로 이루어진 구동사의 목적어가 인칭대명사일 때 목
적어가 동사 바로 뒤에 위치한다.

11 '일련의 규칙적인 움직임 또는 치는 동작 중의 하나'를 가리키는
말은 beat(소리)이다.

12 유리는 함께 춤추는 것이 음악을 완성한다고 설명한다.

13 대학 졸업 전에 처음 치즈 퐁듀를 먹었다고 했으므로, 과거완료
시제이다. before와 같이 명백한 전후 관계를 알 수 있는 접속
사가 있을 때는 과거시제로 써도 괜찮다. 그러나 빈칸이 두 개이
므로 과거완료시제를 쓰는 것이 적절하다.

14 ① where the monsters are from ② why 뒤에는 완전한
문장 구조가 와야 한다. in 뒤에 특정한 명사를 덧붙이거나 why
대신 의문대명사 who, which, what 등을 써야 한다.

15 간접의문문에서는 '의문사+주어+동사' 구조를 잘 이해하고,
think 동사 등의 예외에 주의해야 한다. ③ when did he
leave → when he left ④ Do you think when → When
do you think

16 (1) 준호는 어느 대학에 갈지 생각 중이다. (2) 예은이는 비가
언제 그칠지 궁금해 하고 있다.

17 (1), (3), (4), (5) 과거의 어느 특정 시점을 기준으로 그 이전에
시작된 일은 과거완료시제로 표현한다. (2) '역사적 사실'은 주
절의 동사 시제와 상관없이 과거시제를 쓴다. (6) when은 '시
점'을 표현하기 때문에 의문문 또는 간접의문문에서 완료시제로
표현할 수 없다.

18 의문문이 간접의문문이 될 때는 '의문사+주어+동사'의 어순이
된다. 의문사가 없을 경우 if 또는 whether를 써서 접속사 역할
을 하도록 한다.

19 과거완료시제는 완료, 경험, 결과, 계속 등의 용법으로 구분할
수 있으며, 해석을 정확하게 하는 것이 중요하다.

20 우리말에 맞게 과거완료시제를 사용하여 쓴다.

21 (1) 간접의문문의 어순은 '의문사+주어+동사'이다. (2) '의문사
가 없는 간접의문문'은 if또는 whether가 접속사 역할을 한다.

22 ⓐ be suitable for: ~에 적합하다, ⓑ the breadwinners
for their families: 가족들의 생계비를 버는 가장

23 ⓒ와 ①, ④: 동명사, ②, ③, ⑤ : 현재분사

24 어떤 호흡 장치도 사용하지 않고 물속에 머물기 때문에, 해녀는
한 번에 많은 해산물을 채취할 수가 '없다.'

25 ⓐ와 ②: 감동시키다, ① (몸 등을) 움직이다, ③ (집, 근무지
등을) 옮기다[이사하다], ④ (차·배 따위가) 나아가다, 전진하
다, ⑤ (안건 등을) 제안[제출]하다

26 이 글은 'Zin Kim이 앞으로 계획하고 있는 것'을 설명하는 글
이므로, 주제로는 ③번 'Zin Kim의 앞으로의 계획'이 적절하
다.

27 앞에 나오는 내용과 상반되는 내용이 뒤에 이어지므로
However가 가장 적절하다. ① 즉[말하자면], ② 게다가, 더욱
이, ③ 따라서, 그러므로

28 위 글은 '기사문'이다. ① (책·연극·영화 등에 대한) 논평[비평],
감상문, ② 독후감, ⑤ 자서전

29 Zin Kim이 어떻게 해녀들의 사진을 찍었는지는 대답할 수 없
다. ① She is an underwater photographer. ③ When
she met a haenyeo who was enjoying her job. ④ No.
⑤ Haenyeo's culture.

01 ①　　　　02 (D) → (C) → (A) → (B)　　　03 ②

04 ⑤

05 She wants to borrow an audio guide.

06 She should press the button.

07 I wonder why there are so many cars on the road.

08 how about going somewhere, too?

09 (D) → (B) → (A) → (C)

10 Could you explain how to make double-sided copies?

11 ⑤　　　　　　12 ①

13 (1) After Susan had learned the importance of recycling, she promised her teacher not to throw away used batteries.

(2) Before Sunwoo lay in his room all day long, he had sprained his ankle during the basketball game.

14 ⓐ when the shopping mall closes

ⓒ what kind of movie she was watching

ⓓ what she usually does on Sundays

ⓕ what time the show begins

15 ④, ⑤

16 how much he weighed, he had already gained, had often eaten

17 ④　　　　　18 ④　　　　　19 ③

20 She had only seen black-and-white photos of haenyeo who looked very tired.

21 ⑤　　　　22 ②　　　　23 ①　　　　24 ④

25 ②　　　　26 for　　　　27 barista

28 It's decorating coffee with hot milk and watching his customers enjoying it.

01 give a presentation: 발표하다, give a hand: 돕다, give a call: 전화를 걸다

02 (D) 궁금한 점 말하기 → (C) 궁금한 점에 대한 답변 → (A) 제안 → (B) 수락

03 농악을 소개하는 문장으로 그것은 한국의 전통 음악인지 묻는 대답으로 적절하므로 (B)가 적절하다.

04 대화를 통해 어떤 종류의 춤이 음악을 완성하는지 알 수 없다.

05 여자는 음성 가이드를 빌리고 싶다.

06 여자는 음성 가이드를 사용하기 위해 버튼을 눌러야 한다.

08 'Why don't we ~?'는 '~하는 게 어때?'라고 제안하는 표현으로 'How about ~?'으로 바꾸어 쓸 수 있다.

09 (D) 궁금한 것 말하기 → (B) 궁금한 것에 대한 설명 → (A) 어떻게 알게 되었는지 질문 → (C) 대답

10 double-sided: 양면의

11 Jack은 양면 복사 버튼을 먼저 누르고 시작 버튼을 눌러야 한

다.

12 'Do you suppose?'와 'What music is Paul listening to?'를 한 문장으로 합칠 때 간접의문문의 의문사를 문두로 보내고 '주어+동사'의 어순으로 정리하면 ①과 같다.

13 과거의 특정 시점을 기준으로 전에 일어난 동작이나 상태를 과거완료로 표현한다. before나 after와 같이 '명확한 전후 관계'를 알 수 있는 경우 과거완료를 쓰지 않아도 되지만, 문제의 조건에 맞게 과거완료를 사용하도록 한다.

14 간접의문문의 어순은 '의문사+주어+동사'이다. 시제와 인칭에 맞게 동사의 형태에 유의한다.

15 과거 이전에 발생한 일은 과거완료시제로 표현한다. ① '그의 가족은 Brian이 전날 열심히 일했지만 결국 병원에 실려갔다는 사실을 우연히 알게 되었다' has worked → had worked ② '우리가 경기장에 도착했을 때, 전반전이 벌써 시작되었다'는 The first half of the match had already started when we arrived at the stadium.이 적절하다. ③ '대부분의 아시아인들은 봉감독이 칸 영화제에서 대상을 수상한 것을 자랑스럽게 느꼈다.' has won → had won 또는 felt → feel로 고쳐도 된다.

16 '불독은 몸무게가 얼마나 될지 알고 싶었다. 그는 저울에 오르기 전에 이미 살이 쪘다는 사실을 알게 되어 놀랐다. 그는 자기 전에 간식을 자주 먹었던 것을 후회했다.'

17 간접의문문 앞에 think, believe, imagine, guess 등 생각, 추측 등의 동사가 있을 때는 의문사를 문두로 보낸다. How old do you guess she is?가 적절하다.

18 앞에 나오는 내용과 상반되는 내용이 뒤에 이어지므로 however가 가장 적절하다. ① 게다가, ③ 즉, ⑤ 그러므로

19 이 글은 '어떻게 Zin Kim이 해녀의 사진을 찍는 것에 관심을 가지게 되었는지'를 설명하는 글이므로, 주제로는 ③번 'Zin Kim이 해녀의 사진을 찍는 것에 관심을 가지게 된 이유'가 적절하다.

20 Zin Kim이 우연히 한 해녀의 사진을 찍었을 때까지, '그녀는 흑백 사진 속의 아주 지친 모습의 해녀만 봐 왔다.'

21 ⓐ와 ⑤: 가주어, ① 가목적어, ② 비인칭 주어, ③ 'It is … that'의 구문으로 문장의 주어·목적어·부사어구를 강조하는 대명사, ④ 그것(앞에 이미 언급되었거나 현재 이야기되고 있는 사물·동물을 가리킴)

22 처음에, 해녀들은 왜 Zin Kim이 자신들의 사진을 찍으려고 하는지 이해하지 못했다.

23 주어진 문장의 my talk에 주목한다. ①번 앞 문장의 a talk를 받고 있으므로 ①번이 적절하다.

24 lastly = finally: (여러 개를 언급할 때) 마지막으로, ① 결국, 마침내, ② 즉시, ③ 극도로, 극히, ⑤ 마침내[드디어]

25 ⓐ와 ①, ③, ④: 부사적 용법, ②: 형용사적 용법, ⑤: 명사적 용법

26 ⓐ for a living: 밥벌이로, 생계 수단으로, ⓑ passion for: ~

에 대한 열정

27 barista: 바리스타, 커피 내리는 사람

28 '뜨거운 우유로 커피를 장식하고 그의 손님들이 그것을 즐기는 것을 보는 것'이다.

하므로 for가 옳다. be good at: ~을 잘하다, be good for: ~에 좋다, (C) 한 번에 한 장소에서 너무 많은 해양생물을 채취하는 것은 바다를 '파괴할 수 있다'고 해야 하므로 destroy가 옳다. protect: ~을 보호하다

11 '경험이 적은 해녀들'은 '경험이 더 많은 해녀들'에 의해 훈련을 받는다.

12 '어떤 호흡 장치도 사용하지 않고 물속에 머물기' 때문이다.

 **서술형 실전문제**　　　　　　p.52~53

01 They are waiting to get into the new bakery.

02 Because it was on a TV program.

03 He wants to try the new bakery's bread.

04 ① The film director was tired because he spoke[had spoken] in front of so many people.

05 ④ Where do you think the police officer caught the thief?

06 (1) Because Mary had learned taekwondo before, she fought off a strange man's attack.

　　(2) Until Kevin saw a video of himself being a heavy drinker, he had never thought of quitting drinking.

07 prettily → pretty

08 I would make them look beautiful in my pictures.

09 (A) very special　(B) show their culture

10 (A) without　(B) for　(C) destroy

11 (A) Less-experienced　(B) more-experienced

12 Because they stay in the water without any breathing devices.

01 많은 사람들이 새로 생긴 제과점에 들어가려고 줄을 서서 기다리고 있다.

02 새로 생긴 제과점이 TV에 나왔었기 때문이다.

03 Brian은 새로 생긴 제과점의 빵을 먹어 보고 싶어 한다.

04 영화감독이 피곤한 것은 너무나 많은 사람들 앞에서 연설했기 때문이다. 피곤한 상황이 과거완료가 되어서는 전후 관계가 뒤바뀌므로 적절하지 않다.

05 간접의문문 앞에 think, believe, imagine, guess 등 생각, 추측 등의 동사가 있을 때 의문사가 문두에 와야 한다.

06 (1) 'Mary는 전에 태권도를 배웠기 때문에 낯선 남자의 공격을 물리쳤다' (2) 'Kevin이 본인의 주정뱅이 모습을 보기 전에는 술을 끊는 것을 생각해 본 적이 없었다.'

07 감각동사 looked의 보어로 형용사를 써야 하므로 pretty로 고치는 것이 적절하다.

08 사역동사 make+목적어+목적격보어(동사원형)의 순서로 쓰는 것이 적절하다.

09 해녀들은 '아주 특별하고', 세계에 '그들의 문화를 알리고' 싶었기 때문이다.

10 (A) 어떤 호흡 장치도 '사용하지 않고'라고 해야 하므로 without이 옳다. (B) 이것은 수중 환경에 '좋은' 것이라고 해야

 **창의사고력 서술형문제**　　　　　　p.54

|모범답안|

01 (A) strong beat　(B) where the music came from

　(C) nongak　(D) community band music

　(E) cheer up farmers and wish for a good harvest

02 (1) He wants to know when I fed the puppy.

　(2) Did you check whether the plant is dried?

　(3) Tell me where I should empty the waste bin.

01 거리를 걷다가, 나는 강한 비트가 있는 음악을 들었다. 나는 음악이 어디서 오는 것인지 알고 싶었다. 유리와 나는 그것이 농악이라고 불리는 한국의 전통 음악이라는 것을 알게 되었다. 유리는 그것이 공동체 악단 음악의 한 종류로 전통적으로 농부들의 힘을 북돋아 주고 풍년을 기원하기 위해 사용되었다고 설명했다. 나는 몇몇 사람들이 리듬에 맞춰 춤을 추는 것이 인상 깊었다. 왜냐하면 함께 춤추는 것이 음악을 완성했기 때문이다. 유리와 나는 함께 했고 음악을 완성했다.

**단원별 모의고사**　　　　　　p.55~58

01 ①　　　　　02 ①

03 (1) I want to be a photographer.

　(2) She was the most suitable candidate.

　(3) He held my hand tightly.

　(4) I'd like to borrow the novel.

04 ⑤

05 He visited Gwangandaegyo in Busan (with his family).

06 I wonder why there are so many people waiting in line.

07 ⑤　　　　08 (C) → (D) → (E) → (A) → (B)

09 Because lots of people are going on vacation this weekend.

10 She suggested going somewhere.

11 ⑤　　12 ②　　13 ④　　14 ⑤

15 if the woman had really　put(또는 really had put) the fish

01 '사람들이 사도록 설득하려고 의도된 사진, 어구 또는 짧은 영상'을 가리키는 말은 advertisement(광고)이다.

02 주어진 문장에서 beat는 '리듬, 비트'를 가리키며 이와 같은 의미로 쓰인 것은 ①번이다. ②번은 '이기다', 나머지는 모두 '때리다, 두드리다'를 뜻한다.

03 photographer: 사진작가, suitable: 적절한, tightly: 단단히, 꽉, novel: 소설, borrow: 빌리다

04 ⑤번을 제외하고는 궁금한 점을 묻는 표현이다.

05 소년은 (그의 가족들과) 부산에 있는 광안대교를 방문했다.

07 위 대화를 통해 새로 생긴 제과점이 언제 TV에 방영되었는지는 알 수 없다.

08 (C) 이번 여름 계획 질문 → (D) 계획 설명 → (E) 올레길에 대한 설명 요청 → (A) 올레길에 대한 설명 → (B) 바람 표현

09 길 위에 많은 차들이 있는 것은 많은 사람들이 이번 주말에 휴가를 가려고 하기 때문이다.

10 Emma는 어딘가 갈 것을 제안했다.

11 궁금한 것을 묻는 질문에 이해가 가지 않는다는 말은 어색하다.

12 간접의문문의 어순은 '의문사+주어+동사'이다. 의문사를 문두로 보낼 이유가 없다.

13 그가 바이러스에 감염된 것은 그 질병의 중심지에서 3개월간 체류했던 것 때문이며, 과거보다 더 앞선 시점의 일이다. 과거완료 시제를 활용하는 것이 적절하다.

14 모두 '명사절로 사용된 간접의문문'인데, ⑤번만 '관계대명사가 이끄는 형용사절'로 쓰였다.

15 James는 그 여자가 붕어빵에 정말로 붕어를 넣었는지 궁금했다. 부사 really는 'had+p.p'의 중간에 와도 좋고, had 앞에 위치해도 괜찮다.

16 (A) Yori는 WeTube에서 그녀의 첫 비디오가 2만 개의 조회수를 얻었을 때 콘텐츠 창작자가 되었다. (B) 그녀가 자신의 직업에서 가장 좋아하는 부분은 한국 음식의 어떤 점이 특별한지 세계의 많은 사람들과 공유하는 것이다.

17 ⓐ와 ①, ③: 부사적 용법, ②, ⑤: 명사적 용법, ④: 형용사적 용법

18 Zin Kim이 우연히 한 해녀의 사진을 찍기 전에 그녀는 '흑백 사진 속의' 아주 지친 모습의 해녀만 봐 왔다.

19 이 글은 '해녀에 대해 무엇이 특별한지'를 설명하는 글이므로, 빈칸에 들어갈 질문으로는 ①번 '그들은 무엇이 그렇게 특별한가요?'가 적절하다. ④ hold one's breath: 숨을 참다

20 주어진 문장의 This에 주목한다. ④번 앞 문장의 내용을 받고 있으므로 ④번이 적절하다.

21 '되어 왔어요'를 현재완료 시제로 쓰는 것이 적절하다.

22 twenty thousands로 읽지 않도록 조심해야 한다.

23 what 다음의 동사가 is이므로, the things which[that]는 적절하지 않다.

24 Yori가 WeTube의 그녀의 첫 번째 동영상에 대해 언제 20,000 뷰를 돌파했는지는 알 수 없다. ① She is a content creator about traditional Korean food. ② By getting 20,000 views on her first video clip on WeTube. ④ It is sharing what is special about Korean food with many people around the world. ⑤ She is planning to write a cookbook on Korean food.

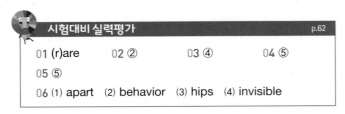

## Lesson 5
# A Journey into Your Mind

### 시험대비 실력평가                              p.62

01 (r)are    02 ②    03 ④    04 ⑤
05 ⑤
06 (1) apart  (2) behavior  (3) hips  (4) invisible

01 주어진 단어는 반의어 관계이다. common: 흔한, rare: 드문, 귀한

02 사람의 마음과 그것이 행동에 영향을 미치는 방식을 연구하는 학문을 가리키는 말은 psychology(심리학)이다.

03 confident: 자신감 있는

04 주어진 문장에서 judge는 '판단하다'를 의미한다. ① 심사위원을 하다 ② 판사 ③ 추정하다 ④ 재판하다 ⑤ 판단하다

05 come back: 돌아오다, come up with: 떠올리다, come over: (장소에) 들르다

06 apart: 떨어진, behavior: 행동, hip: 엉덩이, 허리께, invisible: 눈에 보이지 않는

### 서술형 시험대비                              p.63

01 careful 또는 careless
02 (1) Chances are that  (2) Strangely enough
   (3) stand tall  (4) by myself
03 (1) I want to become a professional psychologist.
   (2) Children get bored easily.
   (3) My dog often chews my shoes.
   (4) Believe in yourself, and be confident.
04 (1) judge  (2) law  (3) loudly  (4) rivals  (5) seat
05 (1) His drawing skills are almost professional.
   (2) What if she forgets to make a reservation?
   (3) I decided to take a walk to clear my mind.
   (4) Stand with your feet apart and your hands
       facing upwards.

01 주어진 단어는 명사와 형용사와의 관계를 나타낸다. careful: 주의 깊은, careless: 부주의한

02 chances are that: 아마 ~일 것이다, strangely enough: 매우 이상하게도, stand tall: 당당해 보이다, by oneself: 혼자서

03 professional: 전문적인, psychologist: 심리학자, bored: 지루해하는, chew: 씹다, confident: 자신감 있는

04 rival: 경쟁자, seat: 좌석, judge: 판단하다, loudly: 큰 소리

로, law: 법

05 professional: 전문적인, What if ~?: ~하면 어쩌지?, clear one's mind: 마음을 가다듬다 with one's feet apart: 양발을 벌린 채로

### 교과서
## Conversation

### 핵심 Check                              p.64~65

1 I'm worried about him.
2 No, you don't have to. / No, you don't need to.
3 (C) → (A) → (B)

### 교과서 대화문 익히기

### Check(√) True or False                    p.66

1 T  2 F  3 T  4 F

### 교과서 확인학습                            p.68~69

**Listen & Speak 1 A-1**
happened to / chewed, all the time, worried about / bored . Why don't you / hope, chewing

**Listen & Speak 1 A-2**
nervous / swimming competition / worry, relax, enjoy / better

**Listen & Speak 2 A-1**
what time / bake cookies / get up / don't have to

**Listen & Speak 2 A-2**
Shall we try / Why, make a reservation / don't have to, online / convenient

**Communicate A**
wait / worried / good at / relay / What, mean / last runner, What if / putting too much pressure on / practice / don't have to do / winning, losing / right, lucky

**Progress Check 1**
nervous / presentation, history / prepared, do, job / feel much better

**Progress Check 2**
seafood spaghetti / stop by, on the way / You don't have to, what / back, help, cook

01 ⓔ → chewing　　　　02 ②

03 She's worried about her swimming competition this Saturday.

04 He advises her to relax and enjoy herself.

01 stop+to부정사: ~하기 위해 멈추다, stop+~ing: ~하던 것을 멈추다. 개가 신발을 씹는 걸 그만두길 바란다는 내용이 이어져야 하므로 chewing이 적절하다.

02 Brian은 항상 개가 신발을 씹는다고 이야기했다.

03 소녀는 이번 주 토요일에 있는 수영대회에 대해 걱정한다.

04 소년은 소녀에게 긴장을 풀고 즐길 것을 조언한다.

01 ①, ③

02 How about playing with him more often?

03 ⑤　　　　04 ⑤　　　　05 ①

06 (E) → (C) → (B) → (D) → (A)

07 She suggests trying that new Mexican restaurant tomorrow.

08 Because he can do it online.

09 ②　　　　10 ⑤　　　　11 ⑤

01 걱정을 나타내는 표현으로 ①, ③번과 바꾸어 쓸 수 있다.

02 Why don't you ~? = How about ~ing?: ~하는 게 어때?

03 Brian이 언제 신발을 샀는지는 알 수 없다.

04 이어지는 대화에서 걱정하는 모습이 나타나므로 nervous가 적절하다.

05 수영대회에 대해 걱정했지만 기분이 나아졌으므로 ①번이 적절하다. relieved: 안도된, 안심한, lonely: 외로운

06 (E) 몇 시에 출발할지 질문 → (C) 대답 및 계획 설명 → (B) 일찍 일어나야 하는지 질문 → (D) 대답 → (A) 반응 및 인사

07 Emily는 새로운 멕시코 레스토랑에 가볼 것을 제안한다.

08 레스토랑 예약은 온라인으로 할 수 있기 때문에 Tom은 레스토랑에 전화할 필요가 없다.

09 (A) be concerned about: ~에 대해 걱정하다 (B) because+주어+동사, because of+명사(대명사), (C) 주어와 목적어가 일치하므로 재귀대명사 yourself가 적절하다.

10 대화를 통해 누가 800미터 릴레이에 첫 번째 주자인지는 알 수 없다.

11 영어 수업 시간에 할 발표에 긴장하고 있다는 말에 감사하다는 말은 어색하다.

01 (B) → (D) → (C) → (A)

02 He's going to go to his grandma's place.

03 She is going to bake cookies for her.

04 She doesn't need his help because his dad will help her.

05 (A) last runner
(B) my team might lose because of me
(C) much pressure　(D) I should practice
(E) winning or losing

01 (B) 긴장되어 보임을 언급 → (D) 걱정 표현 → (C) 격려 → (A) 감사 표현

02 Jack은 내일 할머니 댁에 갈 것이다.

03 엄마는 할머니를 위해 쿠키를 구울 것이다.

04 엄마는 아빠가 그녀를 도와줄 것이기 때문에 Jack의 도움이 필요하지 않다.

05 오늘 나는 운동회에 대해 매우 걱정했다. 나는 800미터 릴레이의 마지막 주자로 선정되었다. 모든 학급 친구들은 내가 잘할 수 있을 것이라고 믿었다. 하지만 나는 매우 부담이 되었다. 나는 만약 나 때문에 팀이 지게 될까봐 걱정되었다. 나는 이것에 대해 유리에게 이야기를 했고 그녀는 내가 스스로에게 너무 많은 부담을 주고 있다고 말했다. 사실, 나는 내가 매일 연습을 해야 할지 말지 생각 중이었다. 유리는 내게 하지 말라고 했다. 왜냐하면 이것은 단지 학교 경기일 뿐이며 이기고 지는 것에 관한 것이 아니기 때문이었다. 나는 그녀로 인해 많이 용기를 북돋게 되었으며 정말로 그녀에게 고마웠다.

교과서

 Grammar

1 (1) Feeling　(2) coming

2 (1) teach → teaches　(2) are → is

01 ⑤　　　　02 ③　　　　03 ④

04 (1) he listened to music　(2) she felt lonely
(3) Though[Although] he is small and weak

01 상관접속사 not only와 but also 뒤에는 문법적으로 같은 것이 들어가야 한다.

02 부사절을 분사구문으로 바꿀 때, 주어가 같으면 주어를 생략하

고 분사를 쓴다. ④의 완료분사구문은 종속절의 시제가 주절의 시제보다 앞설 때 써야 한다.

**03** ④ 상관접속사 not only와 but also 뒤에는 문법적으로 같은 것이 들어가야 한다. 동사 writes가 오면, but also 뒤에도 dances가 와야 한다.

**04** 분사구문은 분사를 활용하여 부사절을 부사구로 줄인 표현이다. 대개 양보, 동시동작, 이유, 시간, 조건 등의 부사절이며, 절과 구의 전환시 동사의 시제 등에 유의해야 한다. (3)은 내용상 양보이므로 Though 외에도 Although, Even though 등의 접속사가 가능하다.

---

**시험대비 실력평가** p.77~79

| 01 ① | 02 ⑤ | 03 ④ | 04 ③ |
|---|---|---|---|
| 05 ⑤ | 06 Exhausting → Exhausted | | |
| 07 ② | 08 ① | 09 ② | 10 ④ |
| 11 ③ | 12 ⑤ | | |

**13** Having been built of wood and dry grass
**14** Not wanting to be late for the meeting
**15** (1) standing tall like Wonder Woman for a few minutes
(2) not only late for school but also hit by

---

**01** ① not only ~ but also에서는 but also 뒤의 명사에 동사의 수를 일치시킨다. have → has가 적절하다.

**02** 'with+목적어+분사' 구문은 '목적어의 능/수동' 여부가 중요하다. 눈이 '감겨진 것'이므로 closed가 적절하다.

**03** 부사절로 영작하면, 'Though he had bullied many people, Tom lived well off.'이다. 분사구문 Having bullied에 의미를 명확하게 하기 위해 접속사 Though를 추가한 문장이 ④이다.

**04** ① both는 복수 주어(is → are) ② 'not only A but also B'는 B가 주어(have → has) ④ neither ~ nor는 부정문과 함께 쓸 수 없다(don't have → have 또는 neither ~ nor → either ~ or) ⑤ not only가 문두에 오면 주어와 동사를 도치시킨다.(I am → am I)

**05** ① speak → speaks ② know → knows ③ is → are ④ she likes to go → where she likes to go

**06** '고된 일로 지친 것'(수동)이므로 Being이 생략된 과거분사 형태가 문두에 오는 것이 적절하다.

**07** ② Both A and B는 복수 동사를 써야 한다. listens → listen이 적절하다.

**08** <보기>와 ①은 '양보' 의미의 분사구문이다.

**09** <보기>는 'Josh 뿐만 아니라 Mina도 음주 뿐 아니라 흡연을 좋아하지 않는다.'라는 뜻이다. ① 'Josh와 Mina 둘 다 흡연이 아닌 음주를 좋아한다.' ③ 'Josh 또는 Mina 둘 중 하나는 흡연

---

도 음주도 좋아하지 않는다.' ④ 문법적 오류 ⑤ 'Josh와 Mina 둘 다 흡연이 아닌 음주를 싫어한다.'

**10** 완료분사구문과 양보 의미의 부사구가 쓰였으므로, 접속사는 Though, 시제는 came이 적절하다.

**11** ① and also → but also ② likes → like ④ the passengers were → were the passengers ⑤ only → not only

**12** ① or → and ② nor → or ③ wonder → wonders ④ know → knows

**13** 종속절의 시제가 앞서 있고, 수동태이므로 완료분사구문의 수동형인 'Having been p.p.'를 활용하여 알맞게 배열한다.

**14** 분사구문의 부정은 분사 앞에 not이나 never를 쓴다.

**15** (1) '몇 분간 원더우먼처럼 꼿꼿이 서 있고 나서, 지수는 더 이상 긴장되지 않았다.' (2) 'Jenny는 학교에 늦었을 뿐만 아니라 도로에서 물벼락까지 맞았다.' *splash: 물이 튐

---

**서술형 시험대비** p.80~81

**01** (1) Wanting to clear his mind
(2) not only feel sure about yourself but also look confident
(3) Wanting to turn a rival into a friend

**02** (1) When he graduates from high school next year
(2) Though I was sick all day long
(3) If you have a problem that you cannot share with your family or friends
(4) While he listened to the radio
(5) Because we do not have to worry about being judged

**03** (1) Having no friends at school,
(2) She not only helped me but also became a good friend.
(3) Asking for help, you can make friends.

**04** (1) Minju's mom is not only a good doctor but also a great cook.
(2) Harry not only speaks Spanish but also dances well.
(3) Seohyun is not only beautiful but also very kind.
(4) Not only Frank but also his parents are nice.

**05** (1) study → studies  (2) is → are  (3) is → are
(4) stress → stressful  (5) is → are

**06** (1) that its food is not only delicious[healthy] but also healthy[delicious]
(2) Having picked a huge carrot, the farmer donated it

---

01 (1), (3)은 분사구문을 활용하는 문제이다. 의미에 맞게 단어를 배열하도록 한다. *clear one's mind: 마음을 정리하다 *do one a favor: A에게 부탁을 들어주다[호의를 베풀다] (2)는 'not only A but also B' 구문이다.

02 문제에 쓰인 분사구문은 각각 시간, 양보, 조건, 동시동작, 이유 등의 의미로 쓰였다. (1) 내년에 고등학교를 졸업할 때, Tammy는 전문적인 농부가 되고 싶어 한다.(동사 시제를 현재형으로 쓰는 것에 유의할 것) (2) 비록 하루 종일 아팠지만, 나는 그 힘든 프로젝트를 완수할 수 있었다. (3) 가족이나 친구들과 나눌 수 없는 문제가 있다면, 낯선 이에게 얘기를 걸어보라. (4) 라디오를 들으면서, Henry는 자신의 기타들을 닦았다. (5) 우리가 평가받을 것에 대해 걱정할 필요가 없기 때문에, 우리는 종종 낯선 사람에게 우리 문제를 말한다.

03 (1) not ~ any를 no로 바꾸면, 'As I had no friends at school'이 된다. 분사구문으로 전환하면 'Having no friends at school'이다. (3) 부사절을 활용하면, 'If you ask for help'이며, 분사구문으로 바꾸면 'Asking for help'가 된다.

04 (1) 민주의 엄마는 좋은 의사일 뿐만 아니라 훌륭한 요리사이다. (2) Harry는 스페인어를 말할 뿐 아니라 춤도 잘 춘다. (3) 서현이는 예쁠 뿐만 아니라 매우 친절하다. (4) Frank뿐만 아니라 그의 부모님 또한 착하다.

05 (1) 그녀는 모든 시험에서 만점을 받아야 한다고 생각할 뿐만 아니라, 잠도 안 자고 공부한다. (2) Both는 항상 복수 동사가 온다. (3) either A or B는 동사와 가까운 주어에 수를 일치시킨다. (4) 'not only A but also B'는 등위접속사이므로 문법적으로 같은 것을 써야 한다. stress는 명사이므로, 형용사형으로 고치는 것이 적절하다. (5) but also 뒤의 주어에 일치시킨다. the islands가 복수이다.

06 (1) 이 식당의 음식은 맛있을 뿐만 아니라 건강에 좋다.(건강에 좋을 뿐만 아니라 맛있다) healthy와 delicious는 서로 자리가 바뀌어도 좋다. (2) 거대한 당근을 수확했기 때문에, 그 농부는 그것을 원님에게 기부했다.

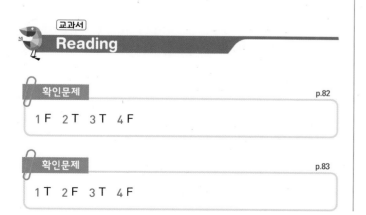

**교과서**
## Reading

| 확인문제 | p.82 |
| --- | --- |

1 F  2 T  3 T  4 F

| 확인문제 | p.83 |
| --- | --- |

1 T  2 F  3 T  4 F

---

### 교과서 확인학습 A
p.84~85

01 Psychology  　　　02 unique
03 Chances are
04 human mind, behavior, so, find, to
05 become less
06 big presentation, whole class
07 Feeling, carefully studying
08 came over, to stand tall
09 standing tall, not, anymore
10 In fact, confident that, make
11 become, by standing tall, stressful events
12 bodies, minds, minds, behavior
13 feel confident  　　　14 apart, place, on
15 not only feel sure, but also look confident
16 feel
17 graduates from, professional
18 However, has never told
19 worried that, will not understand
20 Wanting, clear his mind, to take, by himself
21 complete, sitting  　　　22 why he did it
23 However, felt much better  　24 Strangely enough
25 because, being judged, seeing
26 that, share with, talking  　27 feel much
28 turn, rival into  　　　29 who, not, at all
30 become friends with, came up with
31 rare  　　　32 to lend, a few days
33 deeply
34 Since, not only, but also
35 who do you one favor
36 turn, into, do your rival a favor
37 Instead, to do

---

### 교과서 확인학습 B
p.86~87

1 Psychology Answers Your Questions
2 Do you think you have a unique problem?
3 Chances are that many other people have the same problem.
4 Psychology is the study of the human mind and behavior, so it can help you find a solution to your problem.
5 How do I become less nervous?
6 It was five minutes before Jisu's big presentation in front of the whole class.
7 Feeling nervous, Jisu was carefully studying her notes in her chair.

8 Then, her teacher came over and told her to stand tall like Wonder Woman.

9 After standing tall for a few minutes, Jisu did not feel nervous anymore.

10 In fact, she was confident that she would make a great presentation.

11 According to Amy Cuddy, a famous psychologist, we can become more confident just by standing tall for two minutes before stressful events.

12 Our bodies change our minds, and our minds can change our behavior.

13 Do you want to feel confident?

14 Stand with your feet apart, and place your hands on your hips.

15 You will not only feel sure about yourself but also look confident to other people.

16 Who can help me feel better?

17 When he graduates from high school next year, Taeho wants to become a professional farmer.

18 However, he has never told anyone about it.

19 He is worried that his parents or his friends will not understand.

20 Wanting to clear his mind, Taeho decided to take a day trip on a train by himself.

21 On the train, he told a complete stranger sitting beside him about his problem.

22 He had no idea why he did it.

23 However, he felt much better when he got off the train.

24 Strangely enough, we often tell strangers about our problems just like Taeho.

25 That is because we do not have to worry about being judged or seeing them again.

26 If you have a problem that you cannot share with your family or friends, try talking to a stranger.

27 You will feel much better.

28 How do I turn a rival into a friend?

29 Benjamin Franklin once had a political rival who did not like him at all.

30 Franklin wanted to become friends with him, so he came up with a plan.

31 His rival had a rare book.

32 Franklin asked his rival to lend him the book for a few days.

33 When Franklin returned the book, he thanked him deeply.

34 Since that day, his rival became not only a political supporter but also a good friend.

35 Franklin famously said, "Enemies who do you one favor will want to do more."

36 If you want to turn a rival into a friend, don't do your rival a favor.

37 Instead, ask your rival to do you a favor.

---

### 시험대비 실력평가  p.88~91

01 ②   02 ③   03 ④   04 ①, ⑤
05 to do   06 ②   07 ①
08 by himself   09 why → because
10 (A) less   (B) confident   (C) apart
11 Chances   12 ⑤   13 ④
14 ②   15 ⑤
16 his rival became a good friend as well as a political supporter
17 professional   18 ④   19 ①
20 ③   21 ③   22 no more → anymore
23 ①, ④

01 이어지는 글의 내용이 긴장하고 있던 지수가 몇 분을 우뚝 선 후에, 더 이상 긴장되지 않았다는 것이므로 '어떻게 하면 긴장을 덜 할 수 있나요?'가 적절하다.

02 psychologist: 심리학자 psychology: 심리학

03 ④ 선생님은 지수에게 다가와서 원더우먼처럼 꼿꼿이 서 있어 보라고 말했다.

04 관계대명사 주격이 필요한 자리이므로 who나 that이 적절하다.

05 ask의 목적격보어로 to부정사가 적절하다.

06 ②번은 Franklin의 정치적 경쟁자를 가리키지만, 나머지는 모두 Franklin을 가리킨다.

07 주어진 문장의 However와 it에 주목한다. However로 앞 문장과 상반되는 내용이 나오며 it이 앞 문장의 내용을 가리키므로 ①번이 적절하다.

08 by oneself: 혼자

09 That is why: 그것이 ~한 이유이다(앞에는 원인이 나오고, 뒤에는 결과가 나옴), That is because: 그것은 ~ 때문이다(앞에는 결과가 나오고 뒤에는 원인이 나옴). 앞 문장의 원인이 이어지므로 That is because가 적절하다. 원인이냐 결과냐를 따지지 말고 해석으로 판단하는 것이 더 좋다.

10 (A) 지수가 원더우먼처럼 꼿꼿이 서 있고 난 후 더 이상 긴장되지 않았다고 했으므로 less가 적절하다. (B) Amy Cuddy를 들어 앞의 내용을 추가 설명하고 있으므로 confident가 적절하다. (C) 원더우먼처럼 꼿꼿이 서려면 양발을 '벌리고' 서야 하므로 apart가 적절하다.

11 Chances are that ~: 아마 ~일 것이다

12 ⓑ와 ⑤번은 분사구문으로 쓰인 현재분사이다. ① 목적격보어로 쓰인 현재분사, ② 진행형에 쓰인 현재분사, ③, ④ 동명사

13 왜 우리의 몸이 마음을 바꾸는지는 대답할 수 없다. ① Amy Cuddy is a famous psychologist. ② By standing tall for a few minutes. ③ She told her to stand tall. ⑤ She stood tall for a few minutes.

14 책을 빌리고 돌려줄 때 진심으로 감사를 표한 후, 경쟁자가 후원자뿐만 아니라 좋은 친구가 되었다는 내용이다.

15 뒤에 days라는 복수 명사가 나오므로 a few가 적절하다. little과 a little은 복수 명사와 함께 쓰이지 않는다.

16 not only A but also B = B as well as A

17 professional: 전문적인, 영영풀이: 전문가는 진보한 교육과 훈련을 요구하는 직업을 갖고 있다.

18 앞에 나오는 내용과 상반되는 내용이 뒤에 이어지므로 However가 가장 적절하다. ① Moreover: 게다가, 더욱이, ③ Therefore: 그러므로, ⑤ In addition: 게다가

19 (A)의 much는 비교급을 강조하는 말로 even, a lot, far, still 등으로 바꿔 쓸 수 있다.

20 ③ 위 글에서 'He had no idea why he did it.'이라고 말하고 있다. ① A professional farmer. ② He has never told anyone about it. ④ Because he wanted to clear his mind. ⑤ By telling a complete stranger about our problem.

21 '선생님이 말씀하신 대로 몇 분을 우뚝 선 후에, 지수는 더 이상 긴장되지 않았다.'고 했으므로 어떻게 하면 긴장을 '덜' 할 수 있나요?가 적절하다.

22 not ~ anymore = ~ no more. 앞에 not이 나와 있으므로 no more를 anymore로 고치는 것이 적절하다.

23 (B)와 ②, ③, ⑤: 동명사, ①, ④: 현재분사

서술형 시험대비     p.92~93

01 a complete stranger

02 Strangely enough

03 we often tell strangers about our problems just like Taeho

04 Because psychology is the study of the human mind and behavior.

05 We can get to be more confident just by standing tall for two minutes before stressful events.

06 Becaus[As, Since] she was feeling

07 with

08 deep → deeply

09 his rival became a good friend as well as a political supporter

10 (A) Wanting   (B) sitting   (C) being judged

11 Taeho wants to become a professional farmer

12 He had no idea why he did it.

13 (A) a complete stranger   (B) much better

01 태호가 옆에 앉은 전혀 모르는 사람에게 자신의 고민에 대해서 말한 후 기분이 훨씬 좋아졌다고 했다.

02 Strangely enough: 정말 이상하게도, 기이하게도

03 앞 문장의 내용을 가리킨다.

04 '심리학은 인간의 마음과 행동에 관한 연구이며, 따라서 여러분이 문제에 대한 해결책을 찾는 데 도움을 줄 수 있다.'라고 하고 있다

05 'Amy Cuddy에 의하면, 우리는 스트레스를 받는 상황 이전에 2분 정도 꼿꼿이 서 있는 것만으로도 자신감이 더 생길 수 있다고 한다.'라고 하고 있다

06 Feeling은 'Because[As, Since] she was feeling'을 분사구문으로 고친 것이다.

07 become friends with: ~와 친구가 되다 come up with: (해답 등을) 찾아내다, 내놓다

08 deep: (깊이가) 깊이, 깊게, deeply: ('매우'의 의미로) 깊이, 철저하게

09 not only A but also B = B as well as A

10 (A) 주어인 태호가 원하는 것이므로 능동의 뜻을 갖는 Wanting이 적절하다. (B) 문장의 동사로 told가 나와 있으므로 sitting이 적절하다. (C) 우리가 평가하는 것이 아니라 평가를 받는 것이므로 being judged가 적절하다.

11 ⓐ의 it은 앞 문장에서 언급된 '태호가 전문적인 농부가 되고 싶어 하는 것'을 가리킨다.

12 why he did it(의문사+주어+동사)의 순서로 쓰는 것이 적절하다. have no idea = do not know

13 태호는 전문적인 농부가 되고 싶어 하지만, 부모님이나 친구들이 이해하지 못할까봐 걱정이 된다. 혼자 하루 기차 여행을 하는 동안, 그는 전혀 모르는 사람에게 자신의 고민에 대해서 말했다. 그는 자신이 왜 그랬는지 알 수 없었다. 그러나, 기차에서 내릴 때 기분이 훨씬 좋아졌다.

영역별 핵심문제     p.95~99

01 successful      02 ①      03 ⑤

04 (1) (p)robably   (2) professional   (3) psychology   (4) (r)are

p.100~103

05 (1) make a presentation  (2) stop by  (3) stand tall
   (4) Chances are that  (5) get off
06 ①          07 ⓔ → help you cook[to cook]
08 ①          09 ②
10 I'm worried about my presentation in history class.
11 ⑤          12 (C) → (D) → (B) → (A)
13 His dog chewed them.
14 She advises him to play with him[his dog] more often.          15 ④
16 (1) Both the honeybee and the ladybug are in trouble
   (2) neither to go to college nor  to get a job
17 ②, ③
18 (1) likes  (2) dancing  (3) or  (4) is  (5) appears
19 ⑤          20 ②          21 ①          22 ④
23 ②          24 ②          25 ⑤          26 ⑤
27 ③          28 ③
29 He lent his rare book to Franklin.

01 주어진 단어는 명사와 형용사와의 관계를 나타낸다. successful: 성공적인, traditional: 전통적인

02 '대학, 학교 등에서 교육을 끝내다'를 가리키는 말은 graduate(졸업하다)이다.

03 apart: 떨어져

04 probably: 아마도, professional: 전문적인, psychology: 심리학, rare: 희귀한

05 chances are that: 아마 ~일 것이다, get off: 내리다, stop by: 들르다, stand tall: 당당해 보이다, make a presentation: 발표하다

06 by oneself: 혼자서, stop by: 들르다, by 6: 6시까지

07 help는 준사역동사로 원형부정사 또는 to부정사를 목적격 보어로 취할 수 있다.

08 stop by = drop by: 들르다

12 (C) 제안 → (D) 수락 → (B) 의무 부인하기 → (A) 반응

13 그의 개가 씹었다.

14 그녀는 Brian에게 개와 더 자주 놀아줄 것을 조언한다.

15 '큰 아파트에 혼자 살고 있는 것'과 '거의 외로움을 느끼지 않는 것'은 '역접' 관계이다. '양보' 접속사가 적절하다..

16 (1) 꿀벌과 무당벌레 둘 다 거미줄에서 곤경에 처했다. (2) 지호는 대학 진학도 취업도 하지 않기로 결정했다.

17 ② Both A and B로 고친다. ③ Either A or B로 고친다.

18 (1) 'not only A but also B'는 B에 동사의 수를 일치시킨다.
   (2) 'not only A but also B'는 문법적으로 같은 것을 받으며, 준동사도 그렇다. (3), (4) Either A는 or B와 함께 써서 'A 또는 B 둘 중 하나'를 가리키며, 동사와 가까운 주어에 일치시킨

다. (5) Not A but B는 B에 동사를 일치한다.

19 분사구문의 부정은 분사 앞에 not을 쓴다. 접속사를 쓸 경우, 접속사 뒤에 주어가 오면 분사구문은 쓸 수 없다.

20 분사구문에서의 비인칭 주어 It과 주절의 주어가 다르므로, 'It raining all day' 형태의 독립분사구문이 적절하다.

21 ⓐ a solution to A: A에 대한 해결책, to: [행위·동작·작용의 대상] ~에 대하여 ⓑ told의 목적격보어로 to부정사가 적절하다.

22 ② in fact: 사실(앞 문장에 나온 내용에 대해서 자세한 내용을 덧붙이거나 내용을 강조할 때 사용), ③ 게다가, 더욱이, ⑤ 그러므로

23 이 글은 '만약 가족이나 친구들과도 나눌 수 없는 고민이 있다면, 낯선 이에게 말해 보면 기분이 훨씬 나아질 것임'을 설명하고 있으므로, 주제로는 '고민이 있을 때 기분이 나아지는 법'이 적절하다.

24 밑줄 친 ⓐ는 내용상 이유를 나타내는 분사구문으로 보는 것이 적절하다. ⑤번으로 보면 이후의 진행과 연결이 어색하다.

25 '태호는 옆에 앉은 전혀 모르는 사람에게 자신의 고민에 대해서 말했다. 그는 자신이 왜 그랬는지 알 수 없었다.'라고 되어 있다.

26 앞의 내용에 대안을 제시하고 있으므로 '대신에'가 가장 적절하다. ③ Nonetheless: 그럼에도 불구하고

27 주어진 문장의 the book이 ③번 앞 문장의 a rare book을 받고 있으므로 ③번이 적절하다.

28 ① wicked: 사악한, ⑤ evil: 나쁜, 흉악한

29 Franklin의 정치적 경쟁자는 Franklin에게 그의 희귀한 책을 빌려 주었다.

**단원별 예상문제**  p.100~103

01 ⑤
02 (1) Don't put too much pressure on yourself.
   (2) Stand with your feet apart.
   (3) I'll call the restaurant and make a reservation.
03 He is going to cook seafood spaghetti (for dinner).
04 It's because Minsu and Emma already have what they need.
05 She will be back home by 6 to help him.
06 (C) → (D) → (A) → (B)          07 You don't have to.
08 ④          09 ⑤          10 ⑤          11 ②
12 ②, ⑤          13 ④          14 ④
15 (1) Using green energy vehicles
   (2) Anne not coming back
   (3) Not having been invited to the final match

16 ③        17 sixty

18 Because[As/Since] we wanted to find the answer to this question,

19 unique

20 Chances are that many other people have the same problem.

21 ③

22 Her teacher advised Jisu to stand tall like Wonder Woman.

23 ⑤

01 '당신을 싫어하면서 당신에게 해를 끼치고 싶어 하는 사람'을 가리키는 말은 enemy(적)이다.

02 put too much pressure on: ~에게 너무 많은 부담을 주다, with your feet apart: 양발을 벌린 채로, make a reservation: 예약하다

03 민수는 저녁으로 해물 스파게티를 요리할 것이다.

04 민수와 Emma는 이미 필요한 것을 갖고 있기 때문에 가게에 들를 필요가 없다.

05 Emma는 6시까지 민수를 도우러 집에 돌아올 것이다.

06 (C) 신발에 생긴 일에 대해 질문 → (D) 설명 및 걱정 표현 → (A) 제안 → (B) 수용 및 바람 표현

07 don't have to: ~할 필요 없다

08 ④ Jack의 엄마는 내일 아침에 쿠키를 구울 것이다.

09 주어진 문장은 매일 연습을 해야 한다고 생각하는가에 대한 질문에 대한 대답으로 알맞으므로 (E)가 적절하다.

10 유리는 Jaden이 매일 연습을 할 필요가 없다고 이야기한다.

11 수영대회는 이번 주 토요일이다.

12 ① Opened → Opening ③ Worked → Working ④ Knowing not → Not knowing

13 but also 뒤에 형용사 generous가 있으므로, 부사 truly(진심으로, 진정으로)는 적절하지 않다.

14 not only 뒤에 과거동사가 나왔으므로, 과거시제 동사가 아닌 것을 찾는다. ④ proud는 형용사이다.

15 부사절을 분사구문으로 만들 때, 일반적으로 접속사를 생략한 후 주어가 같으면 주어도 생략하고, 동사를 V-ing 형태로 바꾸는데 Being은 보통 생략한다. 주절보다 시제가 앞서면 Having been 형태가 되고, 부정문에서 not은 분사 앞에 쓰는 것이 적절하다.

16 'not only A but also B'가 주어 자리에 있을 때는 but also 뒤의 B에 동사를 일치시킨다. 주어가 their mom이므로 동사는 likes가 적절하다.

17 30명의 학생들 중에서 18명의 학생들이 평균 점수를 넘었으므

로 60%이다.

18 이유를 나타내는 부사절로 고치는 것이 적절하다.

19 unique: 유일무이한, 독특한

20 chances are that ~: 아마 ~일 것이다

21 주어진 문장의 After에 주목한다. ③번 앞 문장에서 '선생님이 다가와서는 원더우먼처럼 꼿꼿이 서 있어 보라고 말했'으므로 ③번이 적절하다.

22 지수의 선생님은 지수에게 원더우먼처럼 꼿꼿이 서 있어 보라고 했다.

23 not only A but also B = not only A but B = not simply A but (also) B = not just A but (also) B = not merely A but (also) B cf. not A but B: A가 아니라 B

## 서술형 실전문제     p.104~105

01 She is looking forward to Sports Day.

02 He is worried that his team may[might] lose because of him.

03 Because she thinks that the 800-meter relay is just a school race and it's not about winning or losing.

04 (1) Walking down the street
   (2) Not knowing what her father meant
   (3) There being any seats left on the plane
   (4) Wanting to clear her mind

05 either / Neither, nor, Not only, but also / both, and

06 Because[As/Since] I didn't have her around

07 Not only did she write a lot about her memories

08 필자는 할머니가 원했던 것처럼 행복해지려고 노력해야 한다는 것을 배웠다.

09 nose

10 (A) getting hotter   (B) rises

11 (A) lying   (B) Not only do they   (C) as if (D) rises

01 유리는 운동회를 기대하고 있다.

02 Jaden은 800미터의 마지막 주자로서 그의 팀이 자기 때문에 질까봐 걱정한다.

03 유리는 800미터 릴레이는 학교 경기일 뿐이며 이기고 지고에 관한 것이 아니라고 생각한다.

04 주어진 어휘에 접속사들이 없으므로, 분사구문을 배열하는 문제이다. 각각 (1) 시간, (2) 양보, (3) 조건, (4) 이유 등의 부사절

을 분사구문으로 만든 것이며, (3)의 경우 주절과 종속절의 주어
가 다르기 때문에, 유도부사 There 등을 문두에 써야 한다.

05 지나가 지훈에게 엄마의 생일을 묻자, 지훈은 11월 10일인지,
12일인지라고 대답해서 지나를 답답하게 한다. 지나는 아빠뿐
만 아니라, 동생도 엄마에게 관심이 없다고 말하고, 미안한 지훈
이는 어떻게 할지를 묻는다.

06 이유를 나타내는 부사절로 고치는 것이 적절하다.

07 부정어구(not only)로 문장이 시작되면 의문문 형식으로 도치
가 이루어진다.

08 본문의 마지막 부분의 내용을 쓰는 것이 적절하다.

09 Pinocchio Effect(피노키오 효과)를 설명하는 대화로 마지막
부분에서 '코가 더 뜨거워지고 눈 주위의 체온이 올라가는 것처
럼 느낀다'라고 하고 있으므로 nose가 적절하다.

10 코가 더 뜨거워지고 눈 주위의 체온이 올라가는 것처럼 느끼기
때문이다.

11 (A) '거짓말하다'라는 의미의 자동사 lie가 쓰일 자리이므로 현
재분사 lying이 적절하다. (B) 부정어구(not only)로 문장이
시작되면 의문문 형식으로 도치가 이루어지므로 Not only do
they가 적절하다. (C) even if: (비록) ~일지라도, (설사) ~이
라고 할지라도, as if: 마치 ~인 것처럼, 흡사 ~와도 같이 (D)
체온이 올라간다는 뜻의 자동사 rises가 적절하다. raise는 타동
사로 '~을 올리다, 끌어올리다'라는 뜻이다.

---

### 창의사고력 서술형 문제　　　　　p.106

|모범답안|

01 (A) Grandma's place　(B) bake cookies
(C) My dad

02 (A) has just moved to a new school　(B) lonely
(C) Having nobody to talk to
(D) showed me her notes but also started to talk
about herself
(E) helps you make new friends

01 나는 내일 할머니 댁을 방문하는 것을 기대하고 있다. 우리는 내
일 8시쯤에 떠날 것이다. 엄마는 할머니를 위해 쿠키를 만들 계
획이다. 아빠는 엄마를 아침 일찍 도와주실 것이다. 나는 할머니
를 뵙는 것이 몹시 기대된다.

---

### 단원별 모의고사　　　　　p.107~111

01 (1) came up with　(2) (c)ame over　(3) came back

---

02 (1) text message　(2) anxious　(3) unique
(4) prepare　(5) mind　(6) competition

03 (1) Are you interested in the political issue?
(2) You don't have to prepare your speech every
day.
(3) I'm not worried about our presentation at all.

04 ⑤

05 She is concerned about her presentation in
history class.

06 It's because she's prepared a lot.

07 ⑤　　　　08 make a reservation　　09 ②

10 (B) → (C) → (D) → (A)　　　　11 ④

12 (A) nervous　(B) her swimming competition
(C) this Saturday
(D) just relax and enjoy yourself

13 ③　　　　14 ④　　　　15 ④

16 Both Minju[Sam] and Sam[Minju] are interested
in joining a club

17 ⑤

18 ④ Having seen him before, Julie decided to
make friends with Charles.

19 ⑤ Neither the president nor his secretaries want
to know the basic causes of the problem.

20 ② Having, ③ classmates
이유: ② 주어인 I가 친구가 없는 것이므로 능동의 의미로
쓰여야 한다. ③ 'one of+복수 명사'로 쓰인다.

21 ①　　　　22 ③　　　　23 ②

24 He took a day trip on a train by himself to clear
his mind.

25 ②

---

01 come up with: ~을 떠올리다, come over: (장소에) 들르다,
come back: 돌아오다

02 competition: 경쟁 text message: 문자 메시지, prepare: 준
비하다, mind: 마음, 생각, anxious: 걱정하는, unique: 독특
한

03 political: 정치적인, prepare: 준비하다, be worried about:
~에 대해 걱정하다, not ~ at all: 전혀 ~ 아닌

04 가족이 걱정된다는 말에 서로 이야기할 필요가 없다는 대답은
어색하다.

05 소녀는 역사 시간에 할 발표에 대해 걱정한다.

06 소년은 소녀가 준비를 많이 했기 때문에 잘할 것이라고 생각

까 걱정이 된다.'라고 하고 있으므로 ②번이 어색하다.

**07** 엄마가 쿠키를 굽기 위해 내일 몇 시에 일어날지는 대화를 통해 알 수 없다.

**10** (B) 긴장한 것 같아 보인다고 이야기함 → (C) 걱정 표현하기 → (D) 격려 → (A) 감사 표현

**11** (A) be worried about: ~에 대해 걱정하다, (B) 감정을 나타내므로 과거분사 bored, (C) stop+~ing: ~하던 것을 멈추다, stop+to부정사: ~하기 위해 멈추다

**12** 소녀는 긴장돼 보였다. 그녀는 수영대회 때문에 매우 걱정이 되었다. 대회는 이번 주 토요일에 열릴 것이다. 소년은 그녀가 수영을 잘한다는 것을 알기 때문에 긴장을 풀고 즐기라고 말하며 그녀를 격려했다. 소년 덕분에 소녀는 안도감을 느꼈다.

**13** 'not only V-ed but also V-ed' 형태로 영작하는 것이 적절하다. look은 2형식 동사로서 형용사 보어 confident를 받는다. ④의 경우, feel과 Jisu의 위치를 바꾼다면, 정답이 될 수 있다.

**14** 'not only A but also B' 구문이 주어가 아닌, 문장을 꾸미는 형태에서 Not only가 문두로 나오면, 주어와 동사는 '도치'되므로 정답은 ④가 적절하다.

**15** '날씨가 춥지만 맑았다'는 내용과, '우리가 소풍을 갔다'는 내용은 '양보' 접속사 though로 표현하기에 어색하다. '이유'를 나타내는 Because 또는 As 등이 적절하다.

**16** Minju와 Sam 둘 모두 동아리에 가입해서 봉사활동을 하는 것에 관심이 있다.

**17** ①, ③, ④ '주절과 종속절의 주어가 다르므로, 분사구문의 주어를 쓴다.' ① Watching → Babe watching, ② 주절과 종속절의 주어가 같으면, 주어를 생략한다. She going → Going, ③ Cutting → You cutting, ④ Being → It being

**18** 분사구문에서 부사절의 주어와, 주절의 주어가 같을 때 분사구문에 주어를 쓰지 않는다. 내용상 '전에 그를 본 적이 있기 때문에, Julie는 Charles와 친구가 되기로 했다'는 것이므로, Julie와 she는 동일 인물이다.

**19** 'Neither A nor B'는 동사와 가까운 주어에 수를 일치시킨다. secretaries가 복수이므로 wants → want가 적절하다.

**21** 도와달라고 부탁했을 때 도와주었을 뿐만 아니라 좋은 친구가 되었다고 했으므로 ①번이 적절하다.

**22** 'Having no friends at school'이라고 하고 있다.

**23** 이 글은 '모르는 사람에게 자신의 고민에 대해서 말한 후 기분이 좋아졌다.'는 글이므로, 빈칸에 들어갈 말로는 ②번 '누가 내 기분을 낫게 해 줄 수 있나요?'가 적절하다.

**25** ②번 다음 문장에서 '그는 부모님이나 친구들이 이해하지 못할

# Find Your Passion

01 ⑤     02 pursue     03 ④     04 ①

05 ③     06 ②

01 동의어 관계이다. check: 계산서, bill: 계산서, decide: 결정하다, determine: 결정하다

02 '종종 오랜 시간에 걸쳐, 어떤 특정 목표나 결과를 달성하기 위해 노력하다'는 'pursue(추구하다, 추진하다)'가 적절하다. 더 이상 논의할 필요가 없다.

03 ① promise: 약속하다, 다짐하다. 내가 뭘 할 수 있을지 보기는 하겠지만 아무것도 약속할 수는 없어요. ② fix: 수리하다. 전화를 수리하도록 기술자를 보낸대요. ③ slice: 한 조각, 일부. 나는 보통 매일 아침 빵 한 조각을 먹는다. ④ decorate: 장식하다, 꾸미다. 배우들의 사진이 그 레스토랑의 벽을 장식하고 있다. ⑤ provide: 제공하다. 교사들은 아동들에게 본뜰 수 있는 모델을 제시한다.

04 passion: 열정, 흥미 / 너만의 열정을 찾고 너의 꿈을 따라가라.

05 ① scare away: 겁주어 쫓아내다. 그들은 겁을 주어 그 곰들을 간신히 쫓았다. ② fill out: 작성하다. 이 양식들 좀 작성해 주세요. ③ be used to (동)명사: ~에 익숙하다. 저는 한 손으로 쟁반을 나르는 것에 익숙하지 못했어요. be used to 동사원형: ~에 사용되다 ④ take on: 떠맡다. 저는 새로운 책무를 맡을 준비가 안 되어 있는 것 같습니다. ⑤ take classes: 수업을 듣다. 이 수업을 들으려면 컴퓨터를 사용할 수 있어야 한다.

06 take charge of: ~의 책임을 지다, ~을 떠맡다. 네가 그 회사를 맡게 될 거야. of all time: 역대, 지금껏. 내 생각에는 그가 역대 최고의 코미디언 중 한 명인 것 같다. To my thinking: 내 생각에는

01 (1) complain    (2) customer

     (3) appreciate    (4) form

02 (1) complaint    (2) unnatural

03 (1) innovative    (2) decorate

     (3) device    (4) role

04 (1) I have a passion for fashion.

     (2) The new restaurant put up a bright and colorful sign.

(3) Thank you for your understanding and we apologize for any inconvenience.

(4) Now that it's winter, I'm going to go skiing every weekend.

01 (1) complain: 불평하다 / 무엇이나 누군가에 대해 짜증나거나 불만족스럽거나 불쾌하다고 말하다 (2) customer: 고객, 소비자 / 상점, 회사 등으로부터 상품이나 서비스를 구입하는 사람 (3) appreciate: 진가를 알아보다 / 어떤 것의 좋은 점을 인정하여 그것을 좋아하다 (4) form: 서류 / 당신이 정보를 적을 여백을 가진 공식적인 문서

02 (1) '동사 – 명사'의 관계이다. decide: 결정하다 – decision: 결정, complain: 불평하다 – complaint: 불평 (2) '반의어' 관계이다. completely: 완전하게 – incompletely: 불완전하게, natural: 자연스러운 – unnatural: 자연스럽지 않은

03 (1) innovative: 획기적인 (2) decorate: 장식하다 (3) device: 장치, 기구 (4) role: 역할 the main role: 주인공

04 (1) passion: 열정, passion을 추가한다. (2) put up: 세우다, 내붙이다, put을 추가한다. (3) inconvenience: 불편, 애로, thank A for B ~의 형태로 쓰이므로 for를 추가한다. (4) now that: ~이기 때문에, ~이므로, now that으로 접속사 역할을 하도록 that을 추가한다. go ~ing: ~하러 가다

1 I'm not satisfied with the phone.

2 I promise I'll do my best.

1 F    2 T    3 F    4 T

did, it / look so real, feel like having a bite of / I'm not satisfied with, unique / so, fantastic drawing

**Listen & Speak 1 A-2**

How can, help / only a week ago, sometimes turns off by itself / have a look at, inconvenience, take, few hours to / I'm not satisfied with, one / fill out, form

**Listen & Speak 2 A-1**

myself / better than any other jam / it / would / I promise I'll be

**Listen & Speak 2 A-2**

were interested in / not anymore, want to / Are, sure / how to act, I promise I'll do

**Communicate A**

your meal / good, fresh / about / I'm not satisfied with, rare / to bring, another one / be going, have, check / won't have to / I promise we'll provide, with

**Progress Check 1**

How can I / got, as, I'm not satisfied with / in / one in blue / do, get one

**Progress Check 2**

take, classes / interested in / not anymore / worry, I promise I'll do / then

**Progress Check 3**

on / Have, finished / I promise I'll finish

 **시험대비 기본평가**     p.124

01 ②　　　02 I promise I'll be your first customer.
03 (C) – (B) – (A) – (D)

01 뒤에 나오는 'It's not unique.'로 보아 ②번이 가장 적절하다. 'I'm not satisfied with it'은 불만족을 표현하는 말이다.

02 'I promise I'll be your first customer.'는 다짐을 말할 때 쓰는 표현이다. promise 뒤에는 구체적인 내용을 명사절을 써서 나타내며, "I promise to be your first customer."로 바꿔 쓸 수 있다.

03 '무엇을 도와드릴까요?'라는 주어진 글에 이어서 (C)에서 불만을 말하고, (B)에서 사과하며 '고치는 데 몇 시간 정도 걸릴 거예요.'라며 고쳐 주겠다고 하자, (A)에서 '새것을 원한다'는 말에, (D)에서 '물론.'이라며 '서류만 작성하면 된다.'고 말하는 순서가 적절하다.

**시험대비 실력평가**     p.125~126

01 ④　　　02 ①　　　03 Yes, we do.
04 Do you have one in blue?　　　05 ⑤
06 ⑤　　　07 not anymore
08 (C) – (B) – (A) – (D)　　09 ④　　10 one

---

11 ②　　　12 next time you visit　　　13 ⑤

01 'not anymore'로 보아 A와 B를 서로 바꾸는 것이 적절하다.

02 다음에 '다른 색상도 있습니다.'라는 말로 보아 색상이 가장 적절하다.

03 뒤에 이어서 남자가 'I'll get one for you.'라고 하고 있으므로 가지고 있다고 했음을 알 수 있다.

04 hat을 대신해서 쓰인 부정대명사 one을 이용하여 one in blue로 영작한다.

05 마지막의 one은 'a hat'을 대신하는 부정대명사이다.

06 빈칸 앞에서 '배우가 되고 싶은 게 확실하니?'라는 질문에 '네, 연기하는 방법을 배울 거예요.'라고 답하고 있으므로 '최선을 다하겠다고 약속할게요.'라는 말이 자연스럽다.

07 not anymore: 더 이상 ~ 아니다, 이젠 ~ 않다

08 손님을 맞이하는 주어진 글에 이어, (C)에서 마음에 들지 않는 색상에 대한 불만족을 말하고, (B)에서 다른 색상도 있음을 설명하고, (A)에서 원하는 색상을 말하고, (D)에서 있다며 하나 가져다 드리겠다고 한 후, 고맙다는 말로 마무리한다.

09 뒤에서 'It's too rare for me.'라고 하는 것으로 보아 불만족을 말하는 것이 적절하다.

10 steak를 대신하는 부정대명사 one이 적절하다.

11 남자가 스테이크를 항상 덜 익은 상태로 제공하는지는 대화를 통해 알 수 없다.

12 'next time'을 하나의 접속사처럼 생각한다.

13 밑줄 친 문장은 다짐을 말할 때 쓰는 표현이다.

 **서술형 시험대비**     p.127

01 (D) → (B) → (C) → (A)
02 You won't have to pay for the steak.
03 Because the steak was too rare for her. 또는 The woman isn't satisfied with the steak because it was too rare for her.
04 I'm not satisfied with the phone.
05 by itself
06 (1) I was. → I did.
　(2) feel like to have → feel like having

01 빵과 샐러드에 대해 언급한 문장에 이어서, 스테이크는 어땠는지 묻는 (D)가 나오고, 스테이크에 대해 불만족을 언급하는 (B)가 나오고, 사과하며 다른 것으로 가져다 드릴지를 묻는 (C)가 나오고, 괜찮다며 가봐야 한다는 (A)로 이어지는 순서가 적절하다.

02 'not have to(~할 필요 없다)'와 'pay for(지불하다)'를 이용한다. 주어의 의지를 나타내는 will과 'not have to'를 'won't

have to'로 쓴다.

03 남자의 '스테이크는 어떠세요?'라는 질문에 여자가 '솔직히, 스테이크는 만족스럽지 않아요. 제겐 너무 덜 익었어요.'라고 하고 있다.

04 'be not satisfied with ~'는 불만족을 나타내는 표현이다.

05 by itself: 스스로, 저절로

06 (1) 일반동사 draw를 받는 대동사이므로 was가 아니라 did로 써야 한다. (2) feel like -ing: ~하고 싶다

---

## 교과서 Grammar

### 핵심 Check
p.128~129

1 (1) why  (2) when

2 (1) However  (2) Thus

---

### 시험대비 기본평가
p.130

01 ③          02 (1) in which, where

(2) for which, why          03 ②

04 (1) However  (2) Thus  (3) however

   (4) However  (5) Thus

01 콘서트가 취소된 것과 가수와 팬들이 실망한 것은 인과 관계이다.

02 '전치사+관계대명사'는 관계부사로 표현할 수도 있다. 선행사가 장소일 때 where, 선행사가 이유일 때는 why를 쓴다.

03 관계부사가 오면 뒤의 문장은 완전한 절의 형태여야 한다. 문미에 전치사 in이 남아 있으므로, 관계부사 where가 아닌 관계대명사 which로 고치는 것이 적절하다.

04 접속부사는 앞뒤 문장의 내용을 연결하는 역할을 한다. however는 '대조, 반대' 등의 '역접'을, thus는 '결과, 결론' 등의 '순접'을 의미한다. 해석을 통해 내용의 자연스러운 연결, 또는 반대 연결을 판단하여 어떤 종류의 접속부사로 문맥을 연결할지 결정하는 것이 중요하다.

---

### 시험대비 실력평가
p.131~133

01 ③       02 ④       03 ②       04 ⑤

05 ①       06 (1) For example  (2) Moreover

(3) Similarly  (4) However  (5) However  07 ⑤

08 ③       09 ⑤       10 ③       11 where

12 when    13 mother was born in the year when

World War II broke out    14 why the subway has

---

not arrived for 30 minutes  15 ③

16 (1) couldn't understand about the way his mother cut them straight

   (2) to hear how I could be rich

---

01 선행사 the way와 관계부사 how는 함께 쓸 수 없다. 둘 중 하나를 삭제하면 옳은 문장이 된다.

02 William은 그 공원 옆에서 3년 동안 살았다. (그래서 → 그러나) 한 번도 그곳을 가 본 적이 없다. Thus를 However로 바꾸는 것이 적절하다.

03 그 영화는 실망스러웠다. (그러므로 → 그렇지만), 배우들의 연기는 훌륭했다. Therefore를 However로 바꾸는 것이 적절하다.

04 선행사가 the time이므로 '관계부사' when 또는 '전치사+관계대명사' at which 등으로 연결해서 표현 가능하다.

05 선행사가 the reason일 때, '전치사+관계대명사'로 받을 때는 for which를, '관계부사'로 받을 때는 why를 쓰는 것이 적절하며, the reason과 why 둘 중 하나만 쓰는 것도 가능하다. ④에는 which 앞에 the reason이 필요하다.

06 (1) Shakespeare가 단어들을 만들어 낸 사례들 (2) 추운데다가 바람까지 세차게 불었다. (3) 아들은 아버지를, 마찬가지로 딸은 엄마를 따른다. (4) 소극적인 성격이지만, 불쌍한 사람들을 위해서는 적극적인 Lily. (5) 세계 경제가 불황이라서 사람들이 실직하게 되었다.

07 ① However → Thus ② Thus → However ③ However → Thus ④ Thus → However

08 ① Thus → However ② However → Thus ④ However → Thus ⑤ Thus → However

09 선행사가 the reason일 때, '전치사+관계대명사' 표현은 'for which'가 적절하며, 관계부사 why는 the reason과 함께 써도 되고, 생략도 가능하다.

10 선행사가 the way일 때, 관계부사 how는 같이 쓰지 않으며, 관계부사 앞에 전치사 in을 쓰지도 않는다.

12 두 문장을 연결해 주는 빈칸 뒤에 완전한 문장이 오고, 선행사가 장소일 때는 관계부사 where를, 선행사가 시간일 때는 관계부사 when을 쓰는 것이 적절하다.

13 시간을 나타내는 선행사 the year 뒤에 관계부사 when을 쓴다.

14 이유는 the reason인데 관계부사 why와 함께 쓸 수도 있고, 둘 중 하나를 생략해도 된다. 보기에 the reason이 없으므로, why를 이용하여 알맞게 단어를 배열한다.

15 <보기>는 'Dahyun이 피자 다섯 조각과 햄버거 두 개를 먹었지만 여전히 배가 고프다.'라는 뜻이다. ③ '~에도 불구하고'의 양보 의미를 가진 접속사 Though로 표현된 문장이 가장 가까운 뜻이다.

16 (1) 석봉은 자신의 형편없는 글씨들을 보며, 어떻게 그의 어머니가 그것들을 똑바로 썰었는지 이해할 수 없었다. (2) 내 친구들은 내가 어떻게 부자가 될 수 있었는지 듣고 놀랐다.

01 However

02 (1) However, customers were unhappy because they were used to

(2) Thus, he invented new machines for his kitchen.

(3) However, your mind can change your behavior as well.

(4) Thus, she decided to take a day trip by herself.

03 (1) They found a special cave where their ancestors spent the winter.

(2) The singer told me how she could be world famous.

(3) My favorite season is spring when I can see the life coming back.

(4) Please tell your mom the reason why you hid the the letter from Grace.

(5) That is the soccer stadium where the Korean national team beat Brazil.

(6) I remember the day when my first daughter was born.

04 (1) the restaurant where she made a hamburger

(2) a charity box where a girl putsome money

(3) the cafe where we talked over teaand coffee

(4) a laptop where she wrote a marketing report

05 (A) However   (B) However

(C) However   (D) Thus

06 ④ Thus → However, ⑥ However → Thus

07 the summer vacation when she played in the pool with

02 (1), (3)은 '역접' 관계이므로 접속부사 However를, (2), (4) 는 '순접' 관계이므로 접속부사 Thus를 쓰는 것이 적절하다. 그 외의 단어 배열은 의미와 어법에 알맞게 한다. *be used to: ~ 에 익숙하다 *clear one's mind: 마음을 정리하다

03 (1) 그들은 그들의 조상이 겨울을 보냈던 특별한 동굴을 찾았 다. (2) 그 가수는 어떻게 그녀가 세계적으로 유명하게 되었는지 를 내게 말해줬다. (3) 내가 가장 좋아하는 계절은 생명이 되돌 아오는 것을 볼 수 있는 봄이다. (4) 제발 너의 엄마에게 왜 네가 Grace에게서 온 편지를 숨겼는지 그 이유를 말해라. (5) 저곳 이 한국 국가대표팀이 브라질을 이겼던 축구 경기장이다. (6) 나 는 나의 첫째 딸이 태어난 날을 기억한다.

04 (1) 그녀가 햄버거를 만든 식당에서 한 남자에게 영수증이 건 네졌다. (2) 한 소녀가 돈을 넣는 자선 상자가 있었다. (3) 이 곳은 우리가 차와 커피를 마시며 얘기를 나눴던 카페였다. (4) Brenda는 그녀가 마케팅 보고서를 기록하는 노트북 한 대를 가 져왔다.

05 (A)~(C)는 모두 '역접'이다. 교과서의 원문에는 (A)에는

Unfortunately가, (B)에는 But이, (C)에는 접속사 Although를 이용한 표현이었다. (D)는 내용상 순접이고, Thus가 적절하다.

06 내용상 ④는 '역접'이므로 However를, ⑥은 '순접'이므로 Thus를 쓰는 것이 적절하다.

07 민주는 사촌들과 수영장에서 물놀이를 했던 여름방학을 결코 잊 을 수 없었다.

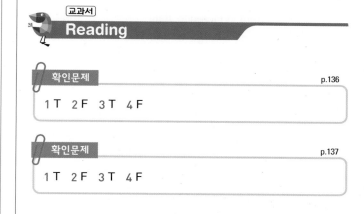

### Reading

1 T   2 F   3 T   4 F

1 T   2 F   3 T   4 F

01 the Cook

02 is known as, painters of all time

03 also

04 few, however, creative

05 twenty-year-old, as

06 took charge of, completely   07 but, like, a few

08 were even decorated with

09 however, were used to, servings

10 As a result      11 A few

12 where, innovative

13 beautifully painted, uniquely written

14 would, appreciate, creative   15 happened

16 to work

17 was given, such as

18 was, put in charge of

19 to be given another, to pursue

20 stop at      21 much more

22 Thus      23 that

24 that, scare, away from   25 were too, too, to

26 to make, which was based on

27 took on, had, been

28 a lot of, cooking, what to put

29 for over, why, to

30 Although, throughout

31 not only, but also

32 Now that, the same way

25

1 Da Vinci the Cook

2 Leonardo da Vinci is known as one of the greatest painters of all time.

3 He was also a great inventor, scientist, and musician.

4 Very few people, however, know that da Vinci was also a creative cook.

5 In 1473, twenty-year-old da Vinci worked as a cook at a restaurant in Florence, Italy.

6 When he took charge of the kitchen, da Vinci changed the menu completely.

7 He made simple but artistic dishes like fish with a few carrot slices.

8 Some dishes were even decorated with flowers.

9 Customers, however, were unhappy because they were used to dishes with big servings of meat.

10 As a result, da Vinci lost his job.

11 A few years later, da Vinci opened a restaurant with his friend Sandro Botticelli.

12 He wanted to create a place where people could try his innovative food.

13 They put up a beautifully painted sign and made a uniquely written menu.

14 Da Vinci believed that people would soon appreciate his creative cooking.

15 Unfortunately, that never happened.

16 In the early 1480s, da Vinci began to work for Ludovico Sforza in Milan.

17 He was given many different roles, such as a musician, a painter, and an engineer.

18 He was also put in charge of the kitchen.

19 He was happy to be given another chance to pursue his passion for cooking.

20 Da Vinci did not stop at cooking creative dishes.

21 He wanted to cook much more quickly and easily.

22 Thus, he invented new machines for his kitchen.

23 He created machines that could crush vegetables and pull spaghetti.

24 He even made a device that could scare frogs away from the water tank.

25 Surely, they were all very innovative, but most of them were too big or too difficult to use.

26 In 1495, Sforza asked da Vinci to make a grand painting, which was based on the last supper of Jesus, on the wall of a church in Milan.

27 Da Vinci gladly took on the project because he had always been interested in food.

28 He spent a lot of time cooking all kinds of food to decide what to put on the table in his picture.

29 "Da Vinci has wasted his time in the kitchen for over a year. That's the reason why he hasn't finished the painting yet," complained the people from the church to Sforza.

30 Although da Vinci never became a successful cook, he showed great interest in cooking throughout his life.

31 He was not only a great painter but also a creative cook.

32 Now that you know all about his secret passion for cooking, you will never look at The Last Supper the same way.

01 ②    02 appreciate    03 ④    04 ③
05 ①    06 to use    07 ⑤
08 Now that    09 ③
10 (A) painters (B) a few (C) lost
11 ④    12 ②    13 ⑤
14 Da Vinci not only cooked creative dishes but also wanted to cook much more quickly and easily.
15 that could scare frogs away from the water tank
16 ②    17 ④
18 He spent a lot of time cooking all kinds of food to decide what to put on the table in his picture.
19 ①    20 pursue    21 ③    22 ①

01 이어지는 글에서 다빈치가 '음식점에서 요리사로 일했다'고 하고 있으므로 '창의적인 요리사'가 적절하다.

02 appreciate: ~의 진가를 인정하다 <영영풀이: 그것의 좋은 특성 때문에 그것을 좋아하다>

03 '손님들은 많은 양의 고기 요리에 익숙했기 때문에 불만족스러워했다. 그 결과, 다빈치는 그의 직업을 잃었다.'라고 하고 있다.

04 ⓐ for: [획득·추구·기대의 대상] ~을 얻기 위해[위한], ⓒ away from: ~에서 떠나서

05 앞 문장의 내용에 대한 결과가 이어지고 있으므로 Thus가 적절하다.

06 too ~ to ...: …하기에 너무 ~한, 너무 ~해서 …할 수 없다

07 (C)의 the project가 주어진 글의 a grand painting을 가리키므로 제일 먼저 오고 (B)에서 어떤 음식을 올릴지 결정하기 위해 모든 종류의 음식을 요리하느라 많은 시간을 쓰고 (A)에서 (B)의 시간 낭비에 대해 불평하는 것이 적절하다.

08 now that: ~이기 때문에, ~이므로

09 앞에서 '다빈치는 1년 넘게 부엌에서 시간을 낭비해 오고 있습니다.'라고 하고 있으므로 **complained**가 적절하다. complain: 불평하다, commend: 칭찬하다

10 (A) 'one of+최상급+복수 명사'의 형태로 쓰므로 **painters**가 적절하다. (B) 'a few+셀 수 있는 명사 복수, a little+셀 수 없는 명사 단수'이므로 **a few**가 적절하다. (C) '손님들은 많은 양의 고기 요리에 익숙했었기 때문에 불만족스러워했다.'고 했으므로 **lost**가 적절하다.

11 da Vinci가 얼마나 오래 요리사로 일했는지는 대답할 수 없다. ① No. ② A cook. ③ He changed the menu completely. ⑤ Customers didn't like the dishes that da Vinci made.

12 ① 두통은 스트레스의 징후일 수 있다. ② 많은 건물 간판이 영어로 쓰여 있다. ③ 그가 엄지손가락을 세우는 몸짓을 해 보였다. ④ 그는 나더러 뜰에 들어오라고 손짓했다. ⑤ 사람이 살고 있는 흔적이 없다.

13 ① common: 일반적인, 평범한 ② routine: 판에 박힌 ③ plain: 평이한 ④ traditional: 전통적인 ⑤ innovative: 혁신적인

14 '다빈치는 창의적인 요리를 만드는 것에 멈추지 않았다. 그는 훨씬 더 빠르고 쉽게 요리하고 싶어했다.'는 것은 '다빈치는 창의적인 요리를 만드는 것뿐만 아니라 훨씬 더 빠르고 쉽게 요리하고 싶어했다.'고 쓸 수 있으므로 'not only A but also B' 구문을 이용한다.

15 scare A away from B: A를 겁주어 B로부터 멀어지도록 하다, that은 주격 관계대명사이다.

16 뒤에서 '"그것이 그가 아직도 그림을 끝내지 못한 이유입니다."라고 교회 사람들이 스포르차에게 불평을 했다.'라고 하고 있으므로 **wasted**가 적절하다.

17 주절의 내용과 상반되는 내용이므로 **Although**가 가장 적절하다.

18 spend+시간+~ing: ~하는 데 시간을 보내다, '의문사+to부정사(to put)'가 decide의 목적어가 되도록 배열한다.

19 다빈치가 스포르차에게 무엇을 하도록 요청했는지는 알 수 없다. ② It was based on the last supper of Jesus. ③ Because he had always been interested in food. ④ Da Vinci spend a lot of time cooking all kinds of food to decide what to put on the table in his picture. ⑤ Because we know all about da Vinci's secret passion for cooking.

20 pursue: 추구하다 <영영풀이: 종종 오랜 기간에 걸쳐 특정한 목적이나 결과를 달성하기 위해 노력하다>

21 (B)에서 also로 주어진 글의 내용에 추가되고 있으므로 제일 먼저 오고 (C)에서 Thus로 (B)의 내용에 대한 결과가 나오므로 (B) 다음에 (C)가 이어지고 (A)의 they가 (C)의 machines

를 가리키므로 (C) 다음에 (A)가 나오는 것이 적절하다.

22 위 글에서는 과학자로서의 역할에 대해서는 언급하고 있지 않다.

01 It's because customers were not satisfied with his creative dishes.

02 He wanted to create a place where people could try his innovative food.

03 people would soon appreciate his creative cooking

04 He invented new machines for his kitchen.

05 the other → another

06 new machines for his kitchen

07 and it

08 He was a creative cook as well as a great painter.

09 decide what to put on the table in his picture

10 however

11 (A) completely (B) unhappy (C) appreciate

12 da Vinci, Sandro Botticelli

01 손님들이 그의 창의적인 요리에 불만족스러워했기 때문이었다.

02 a place를 선행사로 하는 관계부사 where를 이용하여 영작한다.

03 앞 문장의 내용을 가리킨다.

04 '그는 훨씬 더 빠르고 쉽게 요리하고 싶어했다. 따라서, 그는 그의 주방에서 사용할 새로운 기계들을 발명하였다.'라고 하고 있다

05 the other는 '두 개 중의 나머지 하나'를 일컬을 때 쓰므로 '또 다른 하나'를 말할 때 쓰는 another로 고치는 것이 적절하다.

06 '그의 주방에서 사용할 새로운 기계들'을 가리킨다.

07 계속적 용법의 관계대명사 = 접속사+대명사

08 not only A but also B = B as well as A

09 '그는 그림 속 식탁 위에 어떤 음식을 올릴지 결정하기 위해 모든 종류의 음식을 요리하느라 많은 시간을 썼다.'라고 하고 있다.

10 앞 문장의 내용과 상반되는 내용이며 문장의 중간에 콤마(,)로 삽입되어 있는 형식으로 쓰였으므로 however가 적절하다.

11 (A) 형용사로 쓰일 경우 수식하는 명사나 보어로서의 역할이 없으므로 동사 changed를 수식하는 completely가 적절하다.
(B) 이어서 'As a result, da Vinci lost his job.'라는 것으로 보아 unhappy가 적절하다. (C) 이어서 'Unfortunately, that never happened.'라는 것으로 보아 appreciate가 적절하다. depreciate는 '평가 절하하다, 가치[평가]를 떨어뜨리다'라는 뜻이다.

12 다빈치와 그의 친구인 산드로 보티첼리를 가리킨다.

27

01 ①      02 decorate    03 unusual, Unfortunately

04 (r)eason, (r)are (1) reason    (2) rare

05 purchase    06 put      07 ③

08 I promise I'll be your first customer.      09 ③

10 ②      11 ④      12 ③      13 ④

14 (1) However  (2) However  (3) Thus

     (4) However  (5) Thus  (6) Thus

15 (1) how da Vinci made his creative cooking

     (2) when I can have a delicious meal with my

       friends

16 ③      17 ①      18 ④      19 ④

20 ②      21 ③

22 He changed the menu completely.

23 such as    24 that[which]

25 most of them were too big or too difficult to use

26 ④      27 ①

28 It was based on the last supper of Jesus.

29 ①          30 where they can use their creativity

01 <보기>와 ①은 '계산서'의 뜻으로 쓰였다. ① 계산서 좀 갖다 주시겠어요? ② 그들은 공항에서 보안 점검을 실시했다. ③ 제가 이 카드를 잘 작성했는지 봐주시겠습니까? ④ 이 수표를 현금으로 바꾸고 싶습니다. ⑤ 자동차는 생산 라인에서 나올 때 점검을 받는다.

02 '어떤 예쁜 것을 올려놓아 어떤 것을 더 매력적으로 보이게 만들다'라는 의미로 'decorate(장식하다, 꾸미다)'가 적절하다.

03 (1) 형용사 usual에 un을 붙여 반의어가 된 어휘이다. unusual: 흔치 않은. 거대한 소행성이 지구에 너무 가까이 접근하는 것은 흔치 않은 일이다. (2) 문장 구성상 부사가 적절하다. unfortunately: 불행하게도. 형용사 fortunate에 un을 붙여 반대의 뜻을 갖는 형용사가 되고 거기에 ly를 붙여 부사가 된 어휘이다. 불행히도, 저는 그 회의에 참석할 수 없을 거예요.

04 (1) reason: 이유. 누군가가 어떤 것을 하기로 결정한 이유, 또는 일어난 어떤 것에 대한 원인이나 설명. 그렇게 늦은 것에 대한 이유가 있니? (2) rare: 덜 익은, 살짝 익힌. 잠깐 요리된; 속이 아직 붉은. 우리 아버지는 속이 약간 분홍빛이 도는 덜 익은 고기를 좋아하신다.

05 반의어 관계이다. rare: 덜 익은, well-done: 잘 익은, sell: 팔다, purchase: 구입하다

06 • put ... in charge of ~: …에게 ~의 책임을 맡기다 / 그들은 그에게 그 공원을 책임지게 했다. • put up: 내붙이다, 게시하다 / 그는 "반려동물 출입 금지"라는 팻말을 내걸었다. • put out: (불을) 끄다 / 소방차들이 화재를 진화하기 위해 도착했다. • put on: 입다 / 내게 네가 입을 수 있는 스웨터가 있어.

07 '배우가 되고 싶다'는 말에 '최선을 다하겠다고 약속한다'는 것은

08 'I promise ~'는 다짐을 말할 때 쓰는 표현으로 promise 뒤에는 구체적인 내용을 명사절을 써서 나타낸다.

09 (C)의 it이 주어진 글의 this blueberry를 가리키므로 가장 먼저 나오고, (B)에서 'Really?'로 (C)에서 한 말에 대해 놀라움을 나타내고, (A)에서 (B)에서 말한 '팔아도 되겠다'는 말에 대해 '사람들이 이걸 살 거라고 생각하는지' 묻고, (D)에서 '물론'이라는 말로 답하는 순서가 적절하다.

10 'I made it myself.(직접 만든 거야.)'라고 하고 있다.

11 '큰 아파트에 혼자 살고 있는 것'과 '거의 외로움을 느끼지 않는 것'은 '역접' 관계이다. '역접'의 접속부사 Nevertheless가 쓰인 문장이 적절하다.

12 which를 where로 바꾸거나 which 앞이나 stayed 다음에 in이 있어야 한다.

13 'space or building in which'에서 which 뒤의 절이 불완전하므로 in which를 which로 바꾸어야 한다.

15 (1) 사람들은 다빈치가 어떻게 그의 창의적인 요리를 만드는지 관심이 없었다. (2) 학교에서, 나는 친구들과 맛있는 식사를 할 수 있는 점심시간이 제일 좋다.

16 선행사 the way와 관계부사 how는 함께 쓸 수 없다.

17 관계부사 where 뒤에는 완전한 절의 구조가 와야 하는데, 전치사 in이 있으므로 where를 which로 고치는 것이 적절하다.

18 시간을 나타내는 선행사 뒤에 관계부사를 찾는 문제이다. ①은 부사절 접속사 ②, ③, ⑤는 의문사로 사용되었다.

19 '그의 설명이 명확하지 않아서 이해를 못했다'는 것은 '순접'의 인과 관계이다. Since, As, Because 등의 접속사를 이용해서 한 문장으로 만드는 것이 적절하다.

20 '(a) few+셀 수 있는 명사 복수, (a) little+셀 수 없는 명사 단수'이며 'few와 little'은 '부정'의 의미이고 'a few와 a little'은 '긍정'의 의미이므로 few가 적절하다. however로 앞부분과 상반되고 있음을 확인한다.

21 주어진 문장의 however에 주목한다. however로 앞 문장과 상반되는 내용이 나오므로 ③번이 적절하다. 또한 ③번 다음 문장에서 As a result로 주어진 문장의 결과가 나오고 있음에도 유의한다.

22 When he took charge of the kitchen, da Vinci changed the menu completely.

23 like = such as: ~와 같은

24 주격 관계대명사가 필요한 자리이다. 선행사가 사물이므로 that이나 which가 적절하다.

25 'too ~ to ...(…하기에 너무 ~한, 너무 ~해서 … 할 수 없다)' 구문을 이용한다. most of them: 그것들 중 대부분

26 '선행사로 the reason이 나와 있으므로 관계부사 why가 적절하다.

**27** 주어진 문장의 the project가 ①번 앞 문장에서 언급한 '웅장한 그림을 밀라노에 있는 교회의 벽에 그리는 것'을 말하고 있으므로 ①번이 적절하다.

**28** '그것은 예수의 최후의 만찬을 바탕으로 한 것이었다.'라고 하고 있다.

**29** ⓐ와 ①: 형용사적 용법 ②, ⑤ 부사적 용법 ③, ④ 명사적 용법

**30** 관계부사 where를 이용하여 'they can use their creativity'가 선행사 a place를 수식하도록 한다.

---

### 단원별 예상문제

01 ③　　　　02 ⑤　　　　03 charge
04 (1) of all (t)ime　(2) (u)sed to　(3) (u)nique
05 ②　　　　06 ⑤
07 I feel like having a bite of the bread.　08 ①
09 She asks the man to let her just have the check.
10 ①　　　　11 (1) however　(2) Thus　(3) Thus
(4) However　(5) Thus　　12 ③　　　　13 the reason why he hadn't finished the painting earlier
14 (1) Jamaica is a country where international reggae festivals take place every summer.
(2) Show your brother how you solved the puzzle in such a short time.
(3) Everyone but me knows the day when I will be transferred to Jeju island.
(4) Katherine won't tell her teacher the reason why she ran out of the classroom.
15 where people have to line up all night to eat pizza
16 He wanted to create a place where people could try his innovative food.
17 ②　　　　18 ⑤　　　　19 at　　　　20 ④
21 painting → cooking
22 most of them were so big or so difficult that people couldn't use them

**01** ③번은 동의어 관계이다. 나머지는 모두 반의어 관계이다. check: 계산서, bill: 계산서 ① inconvenience: 불편, convenience: 편리함 ② sell: 팔다, purchase: 구매하다 ④ satisfied: 만족한, dissatisfied: 불만족한 ⑤ creative: 창의적인, uncreative: 창의적이지 않은

**02** ① appreciate: 진가를 알아보다, 고마워하다 / 무엇이든 문제가 있으면 알려주면 고맙겠습니다. ② feel like -ing: ~할 마음이 나다 / 정말 더 이상 일하고 싶지 않아요. ③ not ~ anymore: 더 이상 ~ 아니다 / 그곳은 더 이상 조용한 섬이 아니야. ④ have a bite of: 한 입 베어 물다 / 이 버거를 한 입 먹

어보고 싶지 않나요? ⑤ now that: ~이기 때문에, ~이므로 / 이제라도 내가 알았으니 너를 챙겨 줄게.

**03** • put ~ in charge of: ~에게 …의 책임을 맡기다 / 나는 사무실 책임자를 맡게 되었다. • take charge of: ~의 책임을 지다, ~을 떠맡다 / 아버지가 돌아가신 후 그가 농장을 책임지게[떠맡게] 되었다.

**04** (1) of all time: 역대, 지금껏 (2) be used to 동명사: ~하는 것에 익숙하다 (3) unique: 독특한, 고유의, 특유의

**05** look+형용사: ~처럼[하게] 보이다 really를 real로 고쳐야 한다.

**06** 소녀가 독창적이지 않다고 할 뿐 무엇이 독창적인지는 알 수 없다.

**07** feel like ~ing: ~하고 싶다

**08** ①을 제외한 모두는 불만족을 표현하고 있다. pitiful: 동정적인, 처량한

**09** 여자는 'Let me just have the check, please.'라고 말하고 있다.

**10** 여자는 '빵은 괜찮았고, 샐러드는 신선했어요.'라고 하고 있다.

**11** (1) 레오나르도 다빈치는 역대 가장 위대한 화가들 중의 한 명이자 위대한 발명가, 과학자, 그리고 음악가로 알려졌다. 하지만, 극히 소수의 사람들만이 그가 창의적인 요리사였다는 것을 안다. (2) 다빈치의 창의적인 음식을 본 손님들은 많은 양의 고기 요리에 익숙했기 때문에 불만족스러워했다. 그래서, 다빈치는 그의 직업을 잃었다. (3) 다빈치는 창의적인 요리를 더 빠르고 더 쉽게 요리하고 싶어 했다. 따라서, 그는 채소를 으깨고 스파게티를 뽑을 수 있는 새로운 기계들을 발명했다. (4) 다빈치는 살아 있을 때, 결코 성공적인 요리사는 되지 못했다. 그러나, 그는 그의 생애 내내 요리에 대한 큰 흥미를 보여 주었다. (5) 나는 다빈치의 요리에 대한 비밀스런 열정에 대해 배웠다. 그러므로, 나는 결코 예전과 같은 방식으로 '최후의 만찬'을 바라보지 않을 것이라고 생각한다.

**12** ③은 '의문사+to부정사' 형태의 what이 적절하다. ① 계속적 용법의 관계대명사 which, ② 인과 관계를 나타내는 접속사 because. ④ 선행사 the reason, ⑤ 부사 yet이다.

**13** 사람들은 다빈치가 너무 많은 시간을 음식에 낭비했고 그것이 그가 그림을 더 일찍 끝내지 못한 이유라고 불평했다.

**14** 각각의 선행사에 맞게 관계부사를 쓰되, the way는 how와 같이 쓸 수 없으므로, (2)에서 선행사 없이 관계부사가 이끄는 절만 쓰는 것에 유의한다.

**15** 저기가 사람들이 피자를 먹으러 밤새 줄을 서는 그 유명한 식당이다.

**16** a place를 선행사로 하는 관계부사 where를 이용하여 한 문장으로 바꾼다.

**17** be[get] used to+명사 = be[get] accustomed to+명사: ~

에 익숙하다[익숙해지다]

18 이 글은 '다빈치가 창의적인 요리사였지만 요리사로서 성공하지는 못했다'는 내용이므로, 제목으로는 '다빈치의 이루지 못한 꿈'이 적절하다. Jack of all trades: 팔방미인

19 stop at cooking: 요리를 만드는 것에 멈추지 않다, stop cooking: 요리하는 것을 멈추다. 요리를 멈춘 것이 아니라 요리를 만드는 것에 멈추지 않고 그 이상을 했다는 의미가 적절하다.

20 ④ Because da Vinci wanted to cook much more quickly and easily. 나머지는 모두 대답할 수 없다.

21 '그는 요리를 향한 그의 열정을 추구할 또 다른 기회를 얻게 되어 행복했다.'라고 하고 있다.

22 'too ~ to … = so ~ that 주어 can't …'. use의 주어로 일반 사람을 나타내는 people을 쓰는 것이 적절하다.

01 turns off by itself
02 inconvenience
03 I'm not satisfied with the phone.
04 (1) where (2) when (3) how (4) why (5) when
05 (1) In other words (2) However (3) In addition
   (4) Thus (5) For example
06 As a result
07 twenty-years-old → twenty-year-old
08 Because customers were unhappy with his dishes.

02 '당신을 귀찮게 하거나 악영향을 주는 어떤 것에 의해 일어나는 문제들'은 'inconvenience(불편, 애로)'이다.

03 'I don't like ~', 'I'm not satisfied with ~'는 모두 불만족을 표현하는 말이다.

04 각각의 선행사가 (1) 장소, (2) 시간, (3) 방법, (4) 이유, (5) 시간 등이다.

05 (1) 다빈치는 늘 독특하고 창의적인 음식을 만들었다. 즉, 그는 실험적 요리사였다. (2) 다빈치는 성공적인 요리사가 되고 싶었다. 그러나, 사람들은 그를 요리사로 여기지 않았다. (3) 다빈치는 채소를 으깨는 장치를 고안했다. 게다가, 그는 파스타를 뽑아내는 기계를 발명했다. (4) 다빈치는 요리에 관심이 있었다. 그래서 그는 <최후의 만찬> 테이블에 무슨 음식을 놓을지 오래 생각했다. (5) 다빈치는 다양한 분야에서 그의 재능으로 알려졌다. 예를 들어, 그는 화가이자, 건축가, 수학자, 그리고 음악가이다.

06 앞 문장에 대한 결과가 이어지고 있으므로 As a result가 적절하다.

07 twenty-year-old처럼 하이픈(-)으로 연결되어 뒤에 나오는 명사를 수식하는 경우 형용사처럼 쓰이는 것이므로 복수형 years라고 하지 않는다.

08 '다빈치는 기꺼이 그 작업을 맡았는데, 그가 항상 음식에 흥미를 가졌기 때문이었다.'라고 하고 있다.

|모범답안|

01 (1) drawing, I don't like the color.
   (2) steak, It's too rare.
02 (1) This is not the place where I eat the apple.
   (2) This is the day when I don't eat the apple.
   (3) The witch asked the mirror how she could make Snow White eat the apple.
02 (A) an artist (B) using technology (C) technical
   (D) my first exhibition

02 보기의 단어들을 적절히 조합하여 그림과 어법에 맞게 영작한 답이면 된다.

01 provide    02 crush    03 ④    04 ⑤
05 throughout      06 fix
07 I'll learn how I should act.
08 I will make sure that I'll do my best.
09 It's because he wants to become an actor.
10 ②      11 It sometimes turns off by itself.
12 It would take a few hours.      13 ③
14 ④      15 ④      16 ④
17 (1) However, it was so painful that the dog ran away.
   (2) Thus, Sumi asked for a lot of side dishes.
18 ③      19 He made simple but artistic dishes.
20 ⑤      21 ③      22 ④

01 surely: 확실히 – certainly: 확실하게, supply 제공하다 – provide 제공하다

02 '어떤 것을 세게 눌러서 깨지거나 손상되게 하다'는 'crush(으깨다, 쭈그러뜨리다)'가 적절하다. 그 승용차는 트럭에 깔려 완전히 쭈그러졌다.

03 • 우리는 평생 행복을 추구한다. • 나는 그가 불평하는 것을 들어본 적이 없다. pursue: 추구하다, 추진하다. complain: 불평하

다, determine: 결정하다, provide: 제공하다, decorate: 장식하다

04 put ~ in charge of: ~에게 …의 책임을 맡기다, of all time: 역대, 지금껏

05 throughout: ~ 동안 내내

06 fix: 수리하다. 망가지거나 제대로 작동하지 않는 것을 수리하다. 수리할 사람을 보내 주시겠습니까?

07 의문사+to부정사 = 의문사+주어+should+동사원형

08 'I promise ~'와 'I will make sure that ~'은 모두 다짐을 말하는 표현으로 쓸 수 있다.

09 소년은 'I want to go to an arts high school. I want to become an actor.'라고 하고 있다.

10 '제가 좀 봐도 될까요?'라는 뜻의 주어진 문장은 ②번 다음 문장인 '불편을 드려 죄송합니다. 고치는 데 몇 시간 정도 걸릴 거예요.'의 앞에 들어가는 것이 자연스럽다.

11 'I bought this phone only a week ago, but it sometimes turns off by itself.'라고 하고 있다.

12 'It'll take a few hours to fix it.'이라고 하고 있다.

13 'Sam이 아침식사를 하지 않은 것'과 '배고픔을 느끼지 않는 것'은 '역접' 관계로서 '접속부사' however가 쓰였다. 이것을 한 문장으로 바꾸면, '역접'의 '접속사' Though를 활용한 ③번 문장이 가장 적절하다.

14 '학생들이 환자와 PC방에서 밀접한 접촉을 가진 것'이 원인이고, '그들이 바이러스에 감염된 것'이 결과이므로, '순접'의 '인과 관계'를 나타내는 접속사 Because, As, Since 등으로 한 문장을 만드는 것이 적절하다. ②와 ③은 보기의 문장과 내용이 조금 바뀌었으므로, 유의하도록 한다.

15 선행사가 the way일 때, how는 같이 사용하지 않는다.

16 '선행사'가 the day일 때, 전치사는 in이 아니라, on을 쓰는 것이 적절하다.

17 (1) 고슴도치는 그저 그 개와 잘 지내고 싶었을 뿐이었다. 그렇지만, 너무 아파서 그 개는 도망을 갔다. (2) 오늘은 수미의 부모님이 급식 당번을 하는 날이다. 그래서, 수미는 반찬을 많이 달라고 했다.

18 '조각가'가 아니라 '과학자'로 소개하고 있다.

19 '그가 부엌을 책임지게 되었을 때, 다빈치는 메뉴를 완전히 바꿔 버렸다. 그는 약간의 당근 조각을 곁들인 생선과 같이 단순하지만 예술적인 음식을 만들었다.'라고 하고 있다.

20 a special moment(시간)를 선행사로 하는 관계부사 when이 적절하다.

21 주어진 문장의 Thus가 ③번 앞 문장에서 언급하고 있는 내용의 결과를 이끌고 있으므로 ③번이 적절하다.

22 'I entered Korea Art College.'라고 언급되었다.

## Lesson 7

# Wit and Wisdom

01 유의어 관계이다. wit: 기지, 재치, humor: 유머, 해학, palace: 궁전, court: 대궐, 궁궐

02 '어떤 조직에서 권력 있는 직책에 있는 사람'은 'official(고위 공무원, 관리)'이 적절하다. 그는 부시 대통령 재임 시절 백악관 공무원이었다.

03 ① in one's place: ~의 입장에, ~의 상황에. 당신이 내 입장이 되면 어떤 기분이 들지 생각해 보세요. ② make sense: 타당하다, 말이 되다. 정부가 특정 음식에 세금을 부과한다는 것은 말이 안 돼. ③ come up with: 찾아내다, 떠올리다. 그의 시를 보고 무엇이 떠오르니? ④ a number of: 많은. 공원에는 꽤 많은 사람들이 있었습니다. the number of: ~의 수 ⑤ focus on: ~에 집중하다. 돈보다 일을 잘하는 데 집중하다 보면 돈은 저절로 들어온다.

04 wisdom: 지혜, 슬기, 현명함, 이 직업에서는 솔로몬의 지혜를 발휘할 필요가 있다.

05 ① certainly: 틀림없이, 분명히. 나는 분명히 그곳에 다시 갈 것이다. ② speechless: (화나거나 놀라서) 말을 못 하는. Laura는 놀라서 아무 말도 못했다. ③ correct: 맞는, 정확한. 정확한 잔액을 확인하려면 하루나 이틀 정도 기다려야 한다. ④ punish: 처벌하다, 벌주다. 우리 부모님은 내게 TV를 못 보게 하는 것으로 벌을 주고는 하셨다. ⑤ provide (필요품을) 주다, 공급[지급]하다. 봄 날씨가 추우면 해충의 수가 자연스럽게 억제될 것이다.

06 wit: 기지, 재치. 이 소설은 작가의 재치가 넘친다. worm: 벌레. 일찍 일어나는 새가 벌레를 잡는다.

01 (1) court   (2) journey   (3) match   (4) pumpkin

02 (1) valueless   (2) wisdom

03 (1) check   (2) speechless   (3) hand   (4) place

04 (1) I can't tell one twin from the other.
(2) Citizens feel secure taking out their wallets on the streets.
(3) I want freedom for the full expression of my personality.

(4) Each exercise focuses on a different grammar point.

01 (1) court: 대궐, 궁궐, 왕이나 여왕이 살며 일하는 장소 (2) journey: 여행, 여정, 한 장소에서 다른 장소로 여행하는 일 (3) match: 경기, 시합, 두 팀이나 사람 사이에 조직되어 있는 스포츠 행사 (4) pumpkin: 주황색 껍질이 두껍고 둥글고 큰 채소

02 (1) '명사+less'로 형용사가 되는 어휘들이다. care: 주의, 조심 – careless: 부주의한, value: 가치 – valueless: 가치 없는 (2) '동사 - 명사' 관계이다. punish: 처벌하다 – punishment: 처벌, wise: 지혜로운, 현명한 – wisdom: 지혜

03 (1) check out: 확인하다 (2) speechless: (화나거나 놀라서) 말을 못 하는 (3) hand in: 제출하다 (4) in one's place: ~의 입장에

04 (1) the other: (둘 중) 다른 하나. other를 추가한다. (2) take out: 가지고 나가다. take를 추가한다. (3) expression: 표현. expression을 추가한다. (4) focus on: ~에 집중하다. on을 추가한다.

### 교과서
## Conversation

1 Do you mean it's better to hand it in even though it's late?
2 I wish I could dance like you.

### 교과서 대화문 익히기

1 F   2 T   3 T   4 F

### 교과서 확인학습

**Listen & Speak 1 A-1**

look tired / to study / Good for / gets tired / Do you mean / what I mean

**Listen & Speak 1 A-2**

have to / a leg / Do you mean, one, legs / meaning, you do well

is good at / too / good singers / What a, I wish I
could

can't believe, to say, Thanks to, I wish I could, to
start

look, good / Do you mean / I wish I could / live for
today / Do you mean, focus on / why, called / as
wise as

look worried, wrong / hand in / better late than
never / Do you mean, hand it in / what

play the guitar / it / too / in / What a, I wish, could

what to do, Another, what that means

## 시험대비 기본평가     p.178

01 ②

02 Do you mean I have to break one of my legs?

03 (C) – (B) – (D) – (A)

01 앞에서 '일찍 일어나는 새가 빨리 지쳐.'라고 하는 것으로 보아
'일찍 일어나는 게 싫다'는 뜻으로 ②번이 가장 적절하다.

02 'Do you mean ~?'은 이해를 확인하기 위해 쓰는 표현이다.
'one of+복수 명사'는 '~ 중의 하나'라는 의미이다.

03 주어진 '무슨 문제 있니?'라는 질문에 (C)에서 '과학 보고서
를 냈어야 했는데, 내지 않았다'고 문제를 언급하고, (D)에서
'Do you mean ~?'으로 (B)에서 말한 'It's better late than
never.'에 대해 '이해를 확인'하는 질문을 하고 있으므로, (B)
다음에 (D)가 이어지고, (A)에서 (D)의 질문에 대한 답을 하고
있으므로 (D) 다음에 (A)가 이어지는 순서가 적절하다.

## 시험대비 실력평가     p.179~180

01 ③      02 ①      03 ⑤

04 Do you mean I have to break one of my legs?

05 ⑤      06 ①      07 Time flies.

08 ③      09 (B) – (C) – (A) – (D)      10 ③

11 why      12 ④

01 '내가 내 다리 한 쪽을 부러뜨려야 한다는 말이야?'에 '행운을 빌
어!'로 답하는 것은 어색하다. A와 B 서로 바꾸는 것이 적절
하다.

02 뒤에서 '내 다리 한 쪽을 부러뜨려야 한다는 말이야?'라는 말로
보아 'Break a leg!'이 가장 적절하다.

03 an expression을 뒤에서 수식하는 현재분사 meaning이 적절
하다.

04 'Do you mean ~?'은 이해를 확인하는 표현이다.

05 빈칸에는 'I wish ~' 가정법이 들어가야 하는데 현재 사실과 반
대되는 바람이나 소원을 말하는 것이 문맥에 맞으므로 가정법
과거로 쓰는 것이 자연스러우므로 'I could go back to'가 적
절하다.

06 '시간이 참 빠르다'고 한 후 '작별 인사를 해야 할 시간이라는 게
믿어지지 않는다'고 하면서 '선생님들과 친구들 덕분에, 이곳에
서 정말 행복했다'고 하는 것이 자연스럽다.

07 Time flies: 세월은 유수와 같다, 시간이 쏜살같다.

08 밑줄 친 문장은 이해를 확인할 때 쓰는 표현이다.

09 좀 피곤해 보인다는 주어진 문장에 이어, (B)에서 '아주 일찍 일
어났다'고 이유를 설명하고, (C)에서 일찍 일어난 것에 대해 잘
했다고 말하자, (A)에서 반론을 제시하고, (D)에서 그 말에 대
한 이해를 확인하는 질문을 한 후, '그렇다'는 말로 마무리하는
순서가 자연스럽다.

10 뒤에서 'Yes, exactly.'라고 하는 것으로 보아 이해를 확인하는
것이 적절하다.

11 That's why ~: 그것이 ~한 이유이다.

12 Anna가 왜 오늘을 위해 사는지는 대화를 통해 알 수 없다.

## 서술형 시험대비     p.181

01 I wish I could forget about it

02 You're as wise as my grandma.

03 It's because today is a gift. 또는 Today is called
the present because today is a gift.

04 I wish I could play the guitar.

05 She learned how to play the guitar from her dad.

06 (1) hand in it → hand it in

    (2) finish that → finish what

01 'I wish ~' 가정법 과거로 현재 사실과 반대되는 바람이나 소원
을 말할 때 쓰는 표현이며 '~하면 좋을 텐데' 정도의 뜻이다.

02 as ~ as 동등 비교를 쓴다.

03 "어제는 역사, 내일은 미스터리, 그리고 오늘은 현재이다. 그게
바로 오늘을 선물이라 부르는 이유."라고 하고 있다.

04 'I wish+가정법 과거'는 현재 사실과 반대되는 바람이나 소원을
말할 때 쓰는 표현이다.

05 소녀는 '아버지께 배웠어.'라고 하고 있다.

06 (1) 목적어가 인칭대명사이므로 '타동사+인칭대명사 목적어+
부사'의 순서로 써야 한다. (2) finish와 started의 목적어 역할

을 할 수 있는 what이 적절하다.

## 교과서 Grammar

### 핵심 Check
p.182~183

1 (1) whose  (2) of which
2 (1) If I were a dog, I would sleep all day long.
 (2) If she lived in New York, she would eat only hamburgers.

### 시험대비 기본평가
p.184

01 ③

02 (1) is → were[was]  (2) will → would
 (3) has → had  (4) will → would

03 Cathy heard of a man whose wife wrote novels.

04 ④

01 내용상 '영화관의 영화'가 아니라, '영화관에서 영화가 상영되고 있었다'는 것이므로, 장소의 선행사 뒤에 관계부사 where를 쓰는 것이 적절하다. 소유격 whose 뒤에 정관사 the가 오는 것도 어법상 어색하다.

02 문제에서 모든 문장이 가정법 문장이라고 했고, 모든 문장의 구조는 '가정법 과거' 형태이므로, 조건절의 동사를 과거로, 주절의 조동사도 과거형으로 고치는 것이 적절하다. (1)은 현대 영어에서 was도 가능하다.

03 두 문장의 공통되는 명사 중 소유격 부분을 관계대명사 소유격으로 전환하여, 하나의 문장으로 영작한다.

04 주절에 조동사의 과거형이 나왔으므로, 가정법 문장이다. If절에 know의 과거동사를 쓰면 되고, 현재완료시제로는 가정법을 쓰지 않는다.

### 시험대비 실력평가
p.185~187

01 ①     02 ⑤

03 Oliver has a bike whose color is red.

04 If I were she, I would not give up.

05 I wish I could draw well like Bob.

06 They are going to buy a house of which the scenery is beautiful.

07 ②     08 ④     09 ④     10 ③
11 ②     12 ④     13 ③     14 ④
15 ⑤     16 ④

01 '금발머리 아가씨가 전망 좋은 카페에서 당신을 기다리고 있었다.'는 문장이다. 사람이 선행사인 경우 소유격 관계대명사는 whose만 가능하다.

02 가정법 문장이라면 he'll을 he would로, 직설법 문장이라면 were를 is로 쓰는 것이 적절하다.

03 관계대명사의 소유격이 있으므로 선행사 a bike 뒤에 whose color를 배열하는 것이 적절하다.

04 가정법 과거 시제의 문장이다. If I were she로 시작하고 주절에 조동사의 과거형 would를 쓴다. 구어체에서는 If I were her를 많이 쓴다.

05 가정법 중에서 I wish 가정법이 사용된 문장이다. 직설법으로는 'Bob처럼 그림을 잘 그리지 못한다'는 내용이므로, I wish절에 동사의 과거시제를 가정법과 마찬가지로 쓴다.

06 집을 구입할 것이고, 그 집의 풍경이 아름답다는 내용이므로, 관계대명사의 소유격을 써야 하는데, of which가 나왔다. of which 뒤에 the scenery를 쓰는 것에 유의하여 배열한다. of which the scenery 대신 the scenery of which도 가능하다.

07 ⓐ, ⓒ, ⓔ는 whose, ⓑ, ⓓ는 of which, ⓕ는 in which 또는 where를 써야 한다. 사람이 선행사일 때 소유격 관계대명사는 whose만 쓰며, 사물이 선행사일 때는 whose와 of which 둘 다 가능하지만 of which를 쓸 때는 뒤에 정관사가 온다.

08 ④를 제외한 나머지는 모두 가정법의 주절에서 실현 불가능한 가정 상황에서의 '가능'을 나타내는 조동사이다. ④에 쓰인 could는 can의 과거시제 역할로 사용되었다.

09 ④는 의문사의 소유격으로 쓰였다. 앞에 선행사가 없는 것이 특징이다. 그 외에는 모두 선행사 뒤에 쓰인 관계대명사의 소유격 whose이다.

10 ①은 가정법 과거가 현재 사실의 반대인데, 가정법과 직설법 모두 not이 있다. ②와 ④는 직설법과 같은 뜻이 되려면, 가정법 과거완료시제가 필요하다. ⑤는 직설법으로는, '스마트폰이 없어서 한 대 갖고 싶어 한다'는 내용인데, 가정법으로는 '갖고자 한다면 얻을 수 있다'는 내용으로 같은 뜻이 아니다.

11 ② '주최자가 알려지지 않은 행사'라는 의미로서, 선행사 the event 뒤에 소유격이 적절히 쓰였다. ① of which cover → whose cover 또는 of which the cover, ③ the → 삭제, ④ of which the name → whose name, ⑤ water of which → the water of which 또는 whose water

12 주절은 가정법 과거완료 문장이고, If절은 가정법 과거 시제 형태인데, 해석을 해보면 '버스를 놓친다면, 지각하지 않았을 것이다'가 되어, 의미상으로도 부적절하다. 가정법 과거 시제를 활용하여, 알맞게 고쳐본다면, 'If Angelina missed the bus, she would be late for school.'이 된다.

13 'I wish 가정법 과거'는 직설법 현재 시제의 반대 의미이므로, was not을 is not으로 고치는 것이 적절하다.

14 '그의 기타가 부서진 그 소년이 당혹스러워 보였다.'라는 문장이다. 관계대명사의 소유격 whose를 사용해서 하나의 문장으로

만드는 것이 적절하며, of which는 선행사가 사람인 경우에는 쓰지 않는다. whose 뒤에 정관사 the를 함께 쓸 수 없다.

15 '코로나 바이러스 위기 때 매출 피해가 가장 컸던 소기업들에 대한 도움이 더 필요하다.'라는 문장이다. 관계대명사의 소유격 whose를 사용해서 하나의 문장으로 만드는 것이 적절하며, of which를 이용할 때는 of which 뒤에 정관사 the를 쓴다. whose 뒤에 정관사 the를 함께 쓰지 않는다. ④의 경우, who are needed보다는 who need로 하면, 의미는 비슷해지나 문제가 요구하는 범위를 많이 벗어난다.

16 '~가 없다면'이라는 가정법 표현은 'If there were no ~'로 나타내며, without 또는 'If it were not for ~'로 대체할 수 있다. 'If it were not for'는 if를 생략해서 'Were it not for ~'로 표현 가능하다.

### 서술형 시험대비  p.188~189

01 (1) were you, I would give sweets to the person who pulled
(2) would be great if there were a man as wise
(3) two pots whose neckswere really narrow
(4) them was a man whose name was

02 (1) If it were not for
(2) Were it not for
(3) But for
(4) As there is his wisdom, we can

03 exercised regularly, she could stay

04 (1) the → 삭제  (2) legs → the legs
(3) who → whose  (4) whose → who
(5) who → whose  (6) which → of which

05 legs of which are four waved at

06 whose eyes are tired is massaging with a warm

07 (1) I have a friend whose mother is a very famous magician.
(2) This is the magazine the cover of which is black and white.
(3) My little brother is an actor whose film you watched.

08 (1) am → were  (2) am → were[was]
(3) are → were  (4) can → could
(5) will → would  (6) will → would
(7) be → have been

01 가정법과 '가주어-진주어' 구문, 소유격 관계대명사 whose 등에 유의하여, 주어진 단어들을 적절히 배열한다.

02 '그의 지혜가 없다면, Persia와 문제가 생길 수도 있다.'는 내용으로 직설법으로 표현하면, '그의 지혜가 있기 때문에, Persia와 문제가 생길 리 없다.'가 된다. 가정법 과거를 전제로, 'Without

= But for = If it were not for = Were it not for = If there were no'를 기억해 두는 것이 좋다.

03 '그 숙녀가 규칙적으로 운동을 하지 않기 때문에 건강이 좋지 않다.'라는 직설법 문장을 가정법으로 표현하면, '그 숙녀가 규칙적으로 운동을 하면, 건강이 좋을 것이다.'가 된다. If절에는 과거동사, 주절에는 조동사의 과거형에 유의하여 영작한다.

04 어법상 어색한 단어를 하나만 찾아야 하므로, 관계대명사의 소유격을 쓰는 여러 가지 상황에서 하나의 오류만을 찾아 적절하게 고치도록 한다. (4)는 소유격이 아니라 주격 관계대명사를 써야 하는 것에 유의한다.

05 선행사는 monster이고, 바로 뒤에 정관사 the가 있으므로, 관계대명사 소유격 whose를 쓸 수 없다. the legs of which 표현을 떠올리는 것이 중요하다. 과거 시제이므로 waved의 어형 변화에도 유의한다.

06 그녀의 눈이 피로해진 것은 'her eyes are tired'라고 표현한다. 소유격 관계대명사 whose를 활용하여, 'whose eyes are tired'까지 표현하고, 진행형이므로 massage를 massaging으로 표현하는 것에 유의한다.

07 (1), (3)은 선행사가 사람이므로 관계대명사 whose를 쓴다. (2)는 'This is the magazine of which the cover is black and white.'로도 영작이 가능하지만, 주어진 단어에 cover of가 있으므로, the cover of which로 표현하는 것에 유의한다.

08 문제에서 각 문장이 가정법이라고 했으므로, (1), (2), (3) if절의 be동사 또는 I wish 뒤에 오는 be동사를 were로 바꾸는 것이 적절하다 (4), (5), (6) 가정법 과거 문장의 주절에는 조동사의 과거형을 쓴다. (7) 내용상 시제가 '가정법 과거완료'이므로, 주절에 '조동사+have+p.p.'가 와야 한다.

### 교과서 Reading

#### 확인문제  p.190
1 F  2 T  3 F  4 T

#### 확인문제  p.191
1 T  2 F  3 F

### 교과서 확인학습 A  p.192~193

01 Tales
02 a number of, court
03 was, whose name
04 for, with
05 Thus, to have, near
06 Punishment

07 To test, asked them strange questions

08 came up with

09 a hair, should I do to　　10 be punished

11 punish　　12 turned to

13 would, do if, were in my place

14 If, were you, would give　　15 talking about

16 crazy　　17 What made you

18 who, must be, else, such a thing

19 so, to have, as wise as　　20 Potful, Wisdom

21 with a strange favor

22 a lot of, I've been asked, to bring, a potful of

23 makes no sense, put, in　　24 a potful of

25 won't be　　26 a few

27 as much time as　　28 A few, whose, one

29 take, to return, out of it　　30 not to break

31 speechless　　32 left for

33 would be, if there were, as wise as

34 what was

35 the other, for yourself　　36 the other, as big as

37 can't be taken, without breaking

38 over, as big as　　39 a potful of

---

## 교과서 확인학습 B

p.194~195

1 Tales of Birbal

2 Akbar, the third Mogul emperor, had a number of wise officials at his court.

3 Among them was a man whose name was Raja Birbal.

4 He was famous for his quick wit and was very wise with his words.

5 Thus, the emperor always liked to have Birbal near him.

6 Sweet Punishment

7 To test his officials' wisdom, Akbar often asked them strange questions.

8 One day, he came up with an interesting question.

9 Akbar: Someone pulled a hair from my head today. What should I do to him?

10 Official 1: He should be punished, of course.

11 Official 2: Yes, punish him!

12 Akbar turned to Birbal.

13 Akbar: What would you do if you were in my place, Birbal?

14 Birbal: If I were you, I would give him sweets.

15 Official 3: What's he talking about?

16 Official 4: Birbal's crazy!

17 Akbar: What made you say so?

18 Birbal: The person who pulled your hair must be your grandson. No one else could do such a thing.

19 Akbar: You are indeed correct, Birbal. I'm so glad to have someone as wise as you near me.

20 A Potful of Wisdom

21 One day, the king of Persia sent an official with a strange favor.

22 Persian Official: I hear you have a lot of wise men in your country. I've been asked by my king to bring him a potful of wisdom.

23 Official 5: That makes no sense! How can we put wisdom in a pot?

24 Akbar: Can you bring him a potful of wisdom, Birbal?

25 Birbal: It won't be a problem.

26 Could you please wait a few weeks?

27 Persian Official: Of course! Take as much time as you need.

28 A few weeks later, Birbal came back with two pots whose necks were really narrow. He offered one to the Persian official.

29 Birbal: You can take this pot of wisdom to your king. Please ask him to return the pot to us after he takes the wisdom out of it.

30 Birbal: The pot is very precious, so please be careful not to break it. We only have two pots of wisdom.

31 The Persian official looked inside the pot and became speechless.

32 He thanked Birbal and left for his country.

33 Persian Official: It would be great if there were a man as wise as Birbal in our country.

34 After the Persian official left, Akbar asked Birbal what was inside the pot.

35 Birbal: Here is the other pot. You can see for yourself.

36 Akbar looked inside the other pot and found a pumpkin just as big as the pot.

37 Akbar: I see! The pumpkin can't be taken out without breaking the pot. How did you do it?

38 Birbal: I put the pots over pumpkin flowers and waited until the pumpkins grew as big as the pots.

39 Akbar: Hahaha! This certainly is a potful of wisdom!

01 ②　　02 ④　　03 ⑤　　04 ③
05 ①　　06 ④　　07 speechless
08 ①　　09 can't take out → can't be taken out
10 (A) were (B) who (C) wise　　11 ③
12 ⑤　　13 What made you say so? 14 ②
15 ①　　16 ③　　17 ⑤　　18 ④
19 Birbal asked him to ask his king to return the pot and be careful not to break it.
20 It would be great if there were a man as wise as Birbal in our country.
21 ③

01 '황제의 머리카락을 잡아당긴 사람에게 사탕을 주라'고 했으므로 보통 사람들의 생각으로는 '정신이 나갔다'고 하는 것이 적절하다. ① reasonable: 분별 있는, 사리를 아는 ③ sensible: 분별 있는, 사리를 아는 ④ fair: 공정한, 올바른 ⑤ logical: 논리적인

02 여기서는 '~해야만 한다'는 뜻의 should가 아니라 '~임에 틀림 없다'는 뜻의 must가 적절하다.

03 신들은 '처벌해야 한다'고 말했다. punish: 처벌하다, praise: 칭찬하다

04 뒤에 명사가 나오며 완전한 절이 이어지므로 소유격 관계대명사 whose가 적절하다.

05 'a lot of'는 many와 much 둘 다로 쓰일 수 있지만 뒤에 복수 명사인 men이 나오는 것으로 보아 many로 쓰인 것이다. 'a deal of'는 much의 뜻으로만 쓰인다.

06 ④번은 Birbal을 가리키지만, 나머지는 모두 the king of Persia를 가리킨다.

07 일시적으로 말할 수 없는, speechless: (충격 따위로) 말이 안 나오는

08 주어진 문장의 for yourself(직접)에 주목한다. ①번 앞에서 '또 다른 항아리가 있습니다.'라고 한 후 이어지는 문장에서 Akbar가 '또 다른 항아리 안을 보고 꼭 항아리만큼 큰 호박을 발견했다.'라고 하고 있으므로 ①번이 적절하다.

09 호박이 무엇을 꺼내는 '능동'이 아니라 꺼내지는 '수동'이 적절하므로 조동사가 있는 문장의 수동태로 '조동사+be+p.p.' 형태로 고쳐야 한다.

10 (A) 가정법 과거의 문장이므로 were가 적절하다. 구어체에서는 was를 쓰기도 한다. (B) 선행사가 The person으로 사람이므로 who가 적절하다. (C) 'as ~ as' 구문에서는 원급을 사용하므로 wise가 적절하다.

11 악바르의 손자가 왜 그의 머리를 당겼는지는 대답할 수 없다. ① To test their wisdom. ② No. ④ His Grandson. ⑤ He was glad to have someone as wise as Birbal near him.

12 ① 난 창의적인 생각들이 떠오르지 않아. ② 저는 무언가 핑계를 만들어야만 합니다. ③ 당신이 이것보다 더 좋은 아이디어를 제안해줬으면 좋겠어요. ④ 노래 한 곡 쓰는 데 시간이 얼마나 걸리나요? ⑤ 그 돈을 얼마나 빨리 마련해 주실 수 있으세요?

13 사역동사 make를 이용하여 'made+목적어+동사원형'의 형태로 쓴다.

14 뒤에서 '몇 주만 기다려 주시겠습니까?'라고 하고 있으므로 '문제될 것이 없사옵니다.'가 가장 적절하다.

15 'as ~ as' 구문에서는 원급을 사용하므로 much time이 적절하다. time이 셀 수 없는 명사이므로 much가 수식하도록 한다.

16 ⓐ와 ①, ②, ⑤: 명사적 용법 ③: 부사적 용법, ④: 형용사적 용법

17 ⓑ leave for: ~로 (향해서) 떠나다 ① be worried about: ~에 대해 걱정하다 ② look up to: ~을 존경하다 ③ think of A as B: A를 B로 여기다 ④ be tired of: ~에 싫증나다 ⑤ care for: 좋아하다, 돌보다

18 두 개 중의 처음 하나는 one으로 쓰고 나머지 두 번째 하나는 the other로 쓴다.

19 '왕께서 이 항아리에서 지혜를 꺼내신 후에는 항아리를 우리에게 돌려달라 전해 주십시오.', '그 항아리는 매우 귀중한 것이니, 그것을 깨지 않도록 조심해 주십시오.'라고 하고 있다.

20 현재 사실과 반대되는 말을 가정하는 가정법 과거(If+주어+동사의 과거형, 주어+조동사의 과거형+동사원형)를 이용하여 배열한다.

21 '우리는 오직 두 개의 지혜의 항아리만 갖고 있습니다.'라고 말하고 있다.

01 in my place
02 If I were you, I would give him sweets.
03 His grandson pulled Akbar's hair.
04 How can we put wisdom in a pot?
05 **한 항아리만큼의 지혜를 자신의 왕께 가지고 가는 것**
06 He was asked to bring a potful of wisdom by his king.
07 to return
08 It is not great as there is not a man as wise as Birbal in our country.
09 There was a pumpkin as big as the pot.
10 (A) a pumpkin　(B) became speechless
11 Thus
12 Among them was a man whose name was Raja Birbal.
13 He was famous for his quick wit.

01 in one's place: ~의 처지에서, ~의 입장에서

02 현재 사실과 반대되는 말을 가정하는 가정법 과거(If+주어+동사의 과거형, 주어+조동사의 과거형+동사원형)를 이용한다.

03 마지막 문장에서 '과연 그대의 말이 맞소, 비르발.'이라고 하고 있다.

04 '지혜를 항아리에 넣을 수 없다.'라는 평서문을 같은 뜻의 의문문으로 바꾸면 '어떻게 지혜를 항아리에 넣을 수 있는가?'라고 할 수 있다. 이러한 의문문을 수사의문문이라고 한다.

05 앞 문장에서 '저의 왕으로부터 한 항아리만큼의 지혜를 왕께 가지고 오라는 명을 받았습니다.'라고 하고 있다.

06 '저는 저의 왕으로부터 한 항아리만큼의 지혜를 왕께 가지고 오라는 명을 받았습니다.'라고 하고 있다.

07 ask의 목적격 보어로 to부정사가 적절하다.

08 가정법 과거(If+주어+동사의 과거형, 주어+조동사의 과거형+동사원형)는 현재 사실과 반대되는 말을 가정하는 것으로 as나 because, since 등을 이용하여 같은 뜻의 말로 바꿔 쓸 수 있다.

09 '악바르는 또 다른 항아리 안을 보고 꼭 항아리만큼 큰 호박을 발견했다.'라고 하고 있다.

10 비르발은 호박이 들어 있는 항아리를 페르시아의 신하에게 주었고 그가 항아리 안을 들여다보고는 말을 잃었다.

11 앞 문장의 내용에 대한 결과가 이어지고 있으므로 Thus가 적절하다.

12 앞 문장과의 연결성을 높이기 위해서 전치사구가 앞으로 이동하면서 다음에 나오는 주어와 동사의 어순도 바뀌어 '동사+주어'가 되었다. a man을 수식하는 소유격 관계대명사 whose를 이용한다. 소유격 관계대명사는 그 다음에 명사가 이어지며 완전한 절을 이끈다. among them: 그들 중에

13 '그는 재빠른 재치로 유명했으며'라고 하고 있다.

### 영역별 핵심문제
p.203~208

01 ①　　02 (h)onesty, (w)isdom (1) wisdom
(2) honesty　03 favor　04 worthless, priceless
05 ③　　06 ⑤　　07 What a family!
08 ④　　09 (A) is (B) too (C) wish
10 Everyone in her family dances well.
11 He wishes he could dance like the girl.
12 ②　　13 ③　　14 ④
15 (1) If I were Birbal, I could answer the difficult question of the king.
　(2) If Bentley wore a skirt, he would look like a girl.
　(3) If there were a kettle, I could boil and drink my tea.

(4) If Michelle didn't have the glasses, it would not be easy for her to read the books.
16 ①　　17 ⑤　　18 ④　　19 ②
20 What would you do if you were in my place
21 It doesn't make sense. 또는 That makes no sense.
22 ①　　23 ③　　24 ⑤
25 keep in touch
26 If I could turn back time, I would spend more time with you.
27 He still remembers the time when Jaeha and he went camping together.

01 <보기>와 ①: 대궐, 궁궐 ① 그들은 종종 궁궐에서 공연을 했다. ② 죄수들은 경찰의 호위 하에 법원으로 이송된다. ③ 그들은 잔디밭에 테니스 코트를 그렸다. ④ 너는 기회를 얻도록 노력해야 한다. ⑤ 법정은 그에게 유죄 판결을 내렸다.

02 (1) wisdom: 지혜, 슬기, 현명함. 그녀는 아주 지혜로운 여성이다. (2) honesty: 정직, 정직이 없다면 존엄성은 어디에 있는가?

03 '누군가를 돕기 위해 또는 그에게 친절하기 위해 당신이 해주는 어떤 것'이라는 의미로 'favor(청, 부탁)'가 적절하다. 부탁 좀 들어주시겠어요?

04 (1) worthless: 가치 없는. worth에 less를 붙여 형용사가 된 어휘이다. 하잘것없어 보이는 물건도 다 쓸모가 있다. (2) priceless: 매우 소중한. price에 less를 붙여 형용사가 된 어휘인데 '너무 소중해서 값을 매길 수 없는, 그래서 매우 소중한'이라는 뜻이다. 많은 소중한 예술 작품들이 갤러리에서 도난당했다.

05 • find out: 찾아내다, 알아보다. 그들에게 전화해서 언제 올 건지 알아봐. • turn out: 판명되다, 밝혀지다. 그 보도는 틀린 보도로 판명되었다. • figure out: 알아내다. 난 이걸 어떻게 하는 건지 알 수가 없어.

06 기타를 정말 잘 친다는 칭찬의 말에 이어, 고맙다며 아버지께 배웠다고 말하고(D), 아버지도 기타를 치시는지 추가 질문하자(B), 유명한 밴드에 계셨다고 답하고(C), 너처럼 기타를 칠 수 있다면 좋겠다고 바람을 말하는(A) 문장으로 이어지는 것이 적절하다.

07 'What+a+명사'의 순서로 감탄문이다.

08 무슨 문제 있느냐는 질문에 '과학 보고서를 제때에 냈다.'고 대답하는 것은 어색하다.

09 (A) Everyone이 주어이므로 is, (B) 긍정문이므로 too (C) 뒤에 있는 조동사의 과거형 could로 보아 가정법으로 쓰이는 wish가 적절하다.

10 소녀는 'Everyone in my family is good at dancing.'이라고 하고 있다.

11 소년은 'I wish I could dance like you.'라고 하고 있다.

12 'Sammy는 꼬리가 매우 짧은 토끼를 갖고 있다'는 문장이다. 관계대명사의 소유격 whose를 사용해서 하나의 문장으로 만드는 것이 적절하다.

13 <보기>의 if는 가정법 과거를 이끄는 종속접속사로 쓰였다. ③ 외에 나머지는 모두 간접의문문의 명사절을 이끄는 접속사로서 '~인지'라는 뜻이다.

14 '과거시제의 직설법 문장'을 가정법으로 고치면 '가정법 과거완료'가 된다. If절에 'had+p.p.', 주절에 '조동사 과거+have+p.p.'를 쓰되, 직설법과 반대되도록 not을 쓴다. 'I wouldn't have had to pay the late fee'는 '연체료를 내야만 하지 않았을 텐데'라는 뜻이다.

15 직설법 현재 문장을 가정법으로 바꿀 때, 종속절에는 동사의 과거형을, 주절에는 '조동사의 과거형+동사원형'을 쓰는 것에 유의하여, 문장을 전환한다. (4)에서 'it is easy'는 가정법으로 바꾸면 조동사 would를 활용하고, 내용이 반대가 되므로 'it would not be easy'로 바뀌는 것에 유의한다.

16 관계대명사의 소유격을 활용한 문장을 찾는다.

17 가정법 과거에 맞게 동사의 과거형을 쓰되, 이 예문의 경우 비인칭 주어 it과 동사 rained를 사용하는 것에 유의한다.

18 (A)와 (B)는 가정법 과거 형태의 문장들이다. If절에는 동사의 과거형을, 주절에는 조동사의 과거형을 쓰는 것이 적절하다. (C)는 주절에 will이 있으므로, 직설법 현재 is가 적절하다.

19 황제의 머리카락을 잡아당긴 손자에게 사탕을 주겠다는 이야기로 '달콤한 처벌'이 적절하다. ④ Harsh: 모진, 가혹한

20 가정법 과거(If+주어+동사의 과거형, 주어+조동사의 과거형+동사원형)로 쓴다. in one's place: ~의 처지에서, ~의 입장에서

21 황제의 머리에서 머리카락을 잡아당긴 사람에게 사탕을 주겠다는 비르발의 말에 '그건 말이 안 된다.'는 의미로 말한 것임을 유추할 수 있다.

22 ⓐ와 ①: 요청, 부탁, ② (시스템, 계획, 방식 등을) 선호하다, ③ 호의, ④ (호의·친절·애정을 나타내는) 선물, 기념품, ⑤ 도움, 조력

23 각각 ① a lot of, ② no sense, ④ a few, ⑤ much가 적절하다. ③ matter: (관심·고찰의) 문제

24 '필요한 만큼 얼마든지 시간을 가지시오.'라고 하고 있다.

25 keep in touch: (~와 편지·전화로) 연락하고 지내다[연락하다]

26 현재 사실과 반대되는 말을 가정하는 가정법 과거(If+주어+동사의 과거형, 주어+조동사의 과거형+동사원형)로 쓴다.

27 '우리가 함께 캠핑을 갔던 때가 생각나.'라고 하고 있다.

---

단원별 예상문제     p.209~212

01 ③    02 ③    03 ⑤

04 (1) sense   (2) wisdom   (3) (p)rovides    05 ①

06 you should always live for today

07 He lost his soccer match last week.    08 ②

09 ⑤    10 ⑤

11 (1) ⓑ (2) ⓓ (3) ⓑ (4) ⓑ (5) ⓐ (6) ⓓ (7) ⓒ (8) ⓑ (9) ⓒ

12 ④    13 ⑤

14 Mike knew her phone number, he could call her

15 Tom had caught the school bus this morning, he would not have been late for school again

16 wish I were[was] as wise as Birbal

17 ⑤    18 ②    19 How can we do that?

20 ①    21 my line

22 If I could turn back time, I would do more things together with you.

23 ④

24 She[Minji] cannot believe (that) it is time to say goodbye.

---

01 ③번은 동의어 관계이다. 나머지는 모두 반의어 관계이다. valuable: 귀중한, precious: 귀중한 ① hopeful: 희망이 있는, hopeless: 희망 없는 ② valueless: 가치가 없는, priceless: 대단히 귀중한 ④ powerful: 유력한, powerless: 무력한 ⑤ useful: 쓸모 있는, useless: 쓸모 없는

02 ① correct: 맞는, 정확한. 정확한 암호를 입력할 수 있는 마지막 기회입니다. ② offer: 내놓다, 제공하다. 그 식당에서는 전통 가정식 요리를 제공한다. ③ punish: 처벌하다. 부모들은 적절한 방법으로 아이들을 벌주어야 한다. ④ emperor: 황제. 그는 로마의 황제가 되기를 원했다. ⑤ a potful of: 한 항아리만큼의. 저는 저의 왕으로부터 한 항아리만큼의 지혜를 왕께 가지고 오라는 명을 받았습니다.

03 priceless: 값을 매길 수 없는, 대단히 귀중한. 그 화재로 대단히 귀중한 골동품들이 소실되었다. ① 가치 없는 ② 가치 없는 ③ 소용없는, 쓸모 없는 ④ 값이 싼 ⑤ 값을 헤아릴 수 없는

04 (1) make sense: 이해가 되다, 타당하다 (2) wisdom: 지혜 (3) provide: 제공하다

05 ①번 뒤에 이어지는 내용으로 보아 주어진 문장은 ①번 앞 문장의 질문에 대한 답으로 적절하다.

06 live for today: 오늘을 위해 살다

07 Anna의 '지난주에 진 게임 말이니?'라는 물음에, 수호가 '응.'이라고 대답하고 있다.

08 뒤에서 '늦었더라도 내는 게 낫다는 뜻이야?'라고 하고 있으므로

'It's better late than never.(늦더라도 안 하는 것보다는 낫지.)'가 적절하다.

09 빈칸을 중심으로 앞과 뒤의 내용이 상반되므로 양보절을 이끄는 even though가 가장 적절하다.

10 소년이 과학 보고서를 낼 것인지는 대화에 나와 있지 않다.

11 (1), (3), (4), (8)은 소유격 관계대명사 whose가 적절하다. (2), (6)은 내용상 소유격이 필요한데, 정관사 the가 있으므로 of which를 쓴다. (5), (7)은 주격 관계대명사이며, (9)는 전치사 on의 목적어 자리에 쓰는 관계대명사이다.

12 가정법 과거 문장들이다. ① win → won ② occurrs → occurred ③ will → would ⑤ look → looked

13 관계대명사의 소유격을 응용한 문장들이다. ① the 생략 ② colors → the colors ③ the works of whom → whose works ④ the doctors → doctors 또는 whose → of which *fake: 가짜인

14 직설법에서 '그녀에게 전화하고 싶지만 할 수 없고, 그녀의 번호를 모른다.'라고 했으므로, 가정법 과거 시제 '전화번호를 안다면 그녀에게 전화할 수 있을 텐데.'라고 표현하는 것이 적절하다.

15 직설법에서 '스쿨 버스를 놓쳐서 오늘 아침에 또 지각했다.'라고 했으므로, 가정법 과거완료 시제 '스쿨 버스를 탔다면, 다시 지각하지 않았을 텐데.'라고 표현하는 것이 적절하다. if절에는 had caught를, 주절에는 조동사 과거형 would 뒤에 not have been을 쓰는 것에 유의한다.

16 직설법에서 'Birbal만큼 지혜롭지 않은데, Birbal처럼 지혜롭고 싶다.'고 했으므로, 가정법으로는 'Birbal처럼 지혜로우면 좋을 텐데'를 표현하는 I wish 가정법이 적절하다.

17 옳은 문장은 ⓐ, ⓓ, ⓔ, ⓕ, ⓗ 5개이다. ⓑ of which branches → whose branches 또는 of which the branches, ⓒ of whom → whose, ⓖ whose the title → whose title 또는 of which the title

18 황제가 그린 선보다 더 '긴' 선을 그림으로써 황제가 그린 선을 건드리지 않고 더 짧게 만들었다는 내용의 글이므로 '더 짧은 선'이 적절하다.

19 '그것을 할 수 없다.'라는 평서문을 같은 뜻의 의문문으로 바꾸면 '어떻게 그것을 할 수 있는가?'라고 할 수 있다. 이렇게 부정의 뜻을 갖는 평서문을 긍정의 의문문으로 쓸 수 있고 이러한 의문문을 수사의문문이라고 한다.

20 ⓐ와 ①: 대과거 용법 ② 경험 용법 ③ 완료 용법 ④, ⑤ 계속 용법

21 위 글의 소유대명사 mine은 'my line'을 의미한다.

22 현재 사실과 반대되는 말을 가정하는 가정법 과거(If+주어+동사의 과거형, 주어+조동사의 과거형+동사원형)로 바꿔 쓴다.

23 주어진 문장의 also에 주목한다. ④번 앞 문장의 내용에 추가되고 있으므로 ④번이 적절하다.

24 '작별 인사를 해야 할 시간이라는 게 믿어지지 않아.'라고 하고 있다.

### 서술형 실전문제 p.213~214

01 warm → worm

02 Because he got up very early to study for the exam.

03 Are you saying (that) you don't like to get up early?

04 (1) If Mina paid more attention to cooking, she would not burn the food.
  (2) If you had not lied, your nose would not have grown longer.
  (3) A lot of families whose kids are under 12 visited the zoo.

05 Birbal came back with two pots whose necks were really narrow.

06 One[A 또는 The] pot whose neck was really narrow was offered to the Persian official by Birbal.

07 악바르 황제가 그린 선을 건드리지 않은 채 더 짧게 만드는 것

08 I wish I were[was] as wise as Birbal.

09 (A) without touching it  (B) a longer line

01 warm: 따뜻한, worm: 벌레

02 소녀의 '피곤해 보인다.'는 말에 소년이 '시험 공부 하려고 아주 일찍 일어났거든.'이라고 하고 있다.

03 'Do you mean ~?'은 이해를 확인하는 표현으로 'Are you saying ~?'으로 바꿔서 말할 수 있다.

04 (1) 그림에서 이미 불타고 있으므로, 현재 사실의 반대를 가정하는 가정법 과거 문장이다. If절에 과거동사 paid attention을 쓰되, more를 삽입하는 것에 유의한다. (2) 과거 사실에 대한 반대 가정이므로, 가정법 과거완료 문장을 사용하는 것이 적절하다. 'would not have p.p.' 형태에 유의한다. (3) 관계대명사의 소유격을 사용하는 문장이다.

05 소유격 관계대명사 whose를 이용하여 'Their necks'를 'whose necks'로 바꿔 한 문장으로 만든다.

06 '비르발은 목이 매우 좁은 두 항아리를 들고 돌아왔다. 그는 하나를 페르시아의 신하에게 줬다.'라고 하고 있다.

07 '악바르 황제가 그린 선을 건드리지 않은 채 더 짧게 만드는 것'

을 가리킨다.

08 'I wish+가정법'과 동등 비교 'as ~ as' 구문을 이용한다.

09 악바르 황제가 땅에 선을 그린 뒤 그의 신하들에게 그 선을 '건드리지 않은 채' 더 짧게 만들어 보라고 했을 때, 비르발은 악바르가 그린 선 옆에 '더 긴 선'을 그림으로써 그 선을 짧게 만들었다.

## 창의사고력 서술형 문제
p.215

|모범답안|

01 (1) The evil queen whose apples didn't work was angry at the mirror.

(2) Snow White whose appetite was gone rejected the apples.

(3) The witch whose plan failed was angry.

02 (1) You're good at drawing. I wish I could draw well like you.

(2) You're good at playing soccer. I wish I could play soccer well like you.

(3) You're good at dancing. I wish I could dance well like you.

(4) You're good at speaking English. I wish I could speak English well like you.

03 (A) seven times   (B) disappointed   (C) give up
(D) eight   (E) tried

01 *reject: 거부하다 *appetite: 입맛

## 단원별 모의고사
p.216~220

01 present   02 emperor   03 leave

04 (1) The king spent a lot of time at his court.

(2) His parents punished him for lying.

(3) Her books are full of her wit and wisdom.

05 ⑤   06 famous   07 ⑤   08 ④

09 ①   10 it's an expression meaning I hope you do well   11 He can't forget about the game he lost last week.   12 (A) past (B) today

13 ①   14 ④   15 ④   16 would be great if there were a man as wise as Birbal in our country   17 breaking the pot, the pumpkin could not be taken out   18 ①, ⑤   19 ④

20 whose goal is to become a diplomat is studying foreign languages very hard

21 came to question the lady whose purse was stolen outside the department store

22 ②   23 목이 매우 좁은 항아리에 꼭 항아리만큼 큰 호박을 넣은 것

24 (1) Please ask him to return the pot to us after he takes the wisdom out of it.

(2) The pumpkin can't be taken out without breaking the pot.

25 ②not to break, ③were / ② to부정사의 부정은 not 이나 never를 to부정사 앞에 쓴다. ③ 가정법 과거이므로 be동사의 과거형 were를 써야 한다.

26 ④   27 had drawn

28 the line that Emperor Akbar drew

01 precious: 귀중한, 값비싼 – valuable: 귀중한, gift: 선물 – present: 선물

02 '제국의 통치자인 남자'는 'emperor(황제)'가 적절하다.

03 '어떤 장소나 사람에게서 멀어져 가다'는 'leave(떠나다)'가 적절하다. 떠나실 때 문 좀 잠가 주시겠어요?

04 court: 궁정, 궁궐, punish: 벌을 주다, wit: 기지, 재치, wisdom: 지혜

05 past: 과거, pull: 끌다, 당기다, 끌어당기다 • 결코 과거를 지워버릴 수는 없다. • 의자를 식탁 가까이로 당겨 와. place: 장소, 입장, push: 밀다, future: 미래, invent: 발명하다, shake: 흔들다

06 '매우 잘 알려진'을 나타내는 말은 'famous'이다.

07 밑줄 친 문장은 바람·소원을 나타낼 때 쓰는 표현이다.

08 ⓐ와 ④: 동명사, 나머지는 모두 현재분사이다.

09 ① 행운을 빌어! ② 서둘러! ③ 슬퍼하지 마! ④ 무심코 비밀을 누설하지 마! ⑤ 원예의 재능이 있다면 좋을 텐데!

10 mean을 현재분사 meaning으로 바꿔 an expression을 수식하도록 영작한다.

11 수호는 지난주에 진 축구 시합을 잊을 수 있으면 좋겠다고 했다.

12 Anna는 수호가 과거는 잊고 오늘을 살기를 원한다.

13 'look+형용사'가 되어야 하는데 well이 형용사로 쓰이면 '건강한'이라는 뜻으로 어색하므로 well을 good으로 고치는 것이 적절하다.

14 주어진 문장은 'Brian이 컨디션이 좋다면, 다른 선수들보다 두 배의 버저비터를 해낼 텐데.'라는 가정법 과거 문장이다. 직설법으로는 반대의 현재시제이므로, As가 이끄는 종속절과 주절에 모두 현재시제가 있는 ④가 정답이다. 'Brian이 컨디션이 좋지

41

41

않아서, 다른 선수들보다 두 배의 버저비터를 성공하지 않는다.'

15 ④의 whose는 의문형용사이다. 나머지는 모두 관계대명사의 소유격이다.

16 주어진 문장은 '우리나라에 Birbal과 같은 지혜로운 사람이 아무도 없어 안 좋다.'는 내용이다. 가정법을 활용하면 '우리나라에 Birbal같은 지혜로운 사람이 있다면 좋을 텐데.'가 된다.

17 주어진 문장은 '호박을 꺼내려면 항아리를 깨야 한다.'는 내용이다. 가정법을 이용해서 표현하면, '항아리를 깨지 않으면, 호박이 꺼내질 수 없을 텐데.'가 된다.

18 ① 주격 관계대명사의 자리이다 of which를 of가 없는 which 또는 that으로 바꾸는 것이 적절하다. ⑤ 선행사가 the professor로 사람일 때, 소유격 관계대명사는 whose만 가능하다. the opinion of whom을 whose opinion으로 바꾸는 것이 적절하다.

19 '그 선수가 너무 작지 않으면, 올림픽 국가 대표팀에 선발될 것이다'라는 문장이며, '그의 키 문제가 아니라면'과 같은 표현으로 대체할 수 있다. If it were not for = Were it not for = Without ④ 'Had it not been for'는 'If it had not been for'에서 if를 생략하고 도치된 표현으로서 가정법 과거완료시제에 사용하므로, 적절하지 않다.

20 내용상 '목표가 외교관인 그 학생은 외국어들을 매우 열심히 공부하고 있다.'는 내용이다. student가 선행사이므로, 사람을 선행사로 하는 소유격 관계대명사 whose를 이용하여, 두 문장을 연결하는 것이 적절하다. *diplomat: 외교관

21 내용상 '지갑을 도둑맞은 여성에게 경찰이 질문하러 왔다'는 내용이다. lady가 선행사이므로, 사람을 선행사로, 소유격 관계대명사 whose를 활용한다.

22 뒤에 weeks라는 복수 명사가 나오므로 A few가 적절하다. little과 a little은 복수 명사와 함께 쓰이지 않는다.

24 비르발이 '항아리에서 지혜를 꺼내신 후에는 항아리를 우리에게 돌려달라'고 했는데 악바르가 보니 '항아리를 깨지 않고는 호박을 꺼낼 수가 없기' 때문이다.

26 악바르 황제가 그린 선보다 더 '긴' 선을 그림으로써 황제가 그린 선을 더 짧게 만들었다고 하는 것이 적절하다.

27 악바르 황제가 그린 것이 비르발이 그린 것보다 앞선 시제이므로 과거완료로 나타내는 것이 적절하다.

28 '악바르 황제가 그린 선'을 가리킨다.

# 교과서 파헤치기

**Lesson 4**

8 community, 지역 공동체   9 heritage, 유산
10 intangible, 무형의, 만질 수 없는   11 overseas, 해외의
12 seafood, 해산물   13 destroy, 파괴하다   14 ad, 광고
15 bridge, 다리   16 breadwinner, 생계를 책임지는 사람, 가장

## 단어 TEST Step 1                    p.02

| | | |
|---|---|---|
| 01 온실 | 02 수확하다 | 03 광고 |
| 04 전시회, 박람회 | 05 수중의, 물속에서 | 06 해양의, 바다의 |
| 07 전국적인 | 08 해외의 | |
| 09 홍보하다, 촉진하다 | | 10 교량, 다리 |
| 11 지역 공동체 | 12 감동받은 | 13 유산 |
| 14 환경 | 15 해산물 | 16 몇몇의 |
| 17 생계를 책임지는 사람, 가장 | | 18 여성의 |
| 19 화산의, 화산 작용에 의한 | | 20 세계적으로 |
| 21 완성[완료]하다 | 22 호흡하다 | 23 파괴하다 |
| 24 폭포 | 25 좁은 길 | |
| 26 무형의, 만질 수 없는 | | 27 해파리 |
| 28 누르다; 언론, 기자 | 29 지하의 | 30 적합한, 적절한 |
| 31 청중 | 32 과로하다 | 33 경로, 길 |
| 34 깨닫다, 인식하다 | 35 ~을 기원하다 | 36 우연히 ~하다 |
| 37 ~을 따라 걷다 | 38 두 서너 개의 | 39 ~에 들어가다 |
| 40 ~에 적절하다 | 41 강의하다, 연설하다 | |
| 42 조금, 약간 | 43 ~에 유익하다 | |

## 단어 TEST Step 2                    p.03

| | | |
|---|---|---|
| 01 waterfall | 02 ad(=advertisement) | |
| 03 path | 04 overwork | 05 bridge |
| 06 trail | 07 underground | 08 worldwide |
| 09 volcanic | 10 greenhouse | 11 destroy |
| 12 exhibition | 13 promote | 14 complete |
| 15 several | 16 breadwinner | 17 suitable |
| 18 female | 19 press | 20 community |
| 21 intangible | 22 underwater | 23 jellyfish |
| 24 marine | 25 harvest | 26 audience |
| 27 heritage | 28 breathe | 29 nationwide |
| 30 overseas | 31 realize | 32 tightly |
| 33 beat | 34 good harvest | 35 go on vacation |
| 36 get into | 37 happen to | 38 walk along |
| 39 be good for | 40 keep -ing | 41 cheer up |
| 42 give (someone) a hand | | |
| 43 give a presentation | | |

## 단어 TEST Step 3                    p.04

1 harvest, 수확하다   2 underground, 지하의
3 complete, 완성[완료]하다   4 beat, (북 등을 치는) 소리
5 waterfall, 폭포   6 suitable, 적합한   7 breathe, 호흡하다

## 대화문 TEST Step 1                    p.05~06

**Listen & Speak 1 A-1**

look at, bridge, ad, where the photo was taken /
How do, know / went there with, last summer

**Listen & Speak 1 A-2**

Look over I wonder why, waiting in line / waiting to
get into / famous / on / should try, then

**Listen & Speak 2 A-1**

I'd like to borrow / Here, are / explain how to use it /
Press, what to do

**Listen & Speak 2 A-2**

Are, going somewhere / going to, walk along / Could
you explain what that is / long hiking path around /
enjoy your trip

**Communicate A**

I wonder where, coming from / over there, check it
out / strong beat, traditional / called, a kind of
community / Could you explain a little bit /
traditionally, cheer up, wish for. good harvest / are
dancing to, rhythm / part of, completes / Let's join /
Why not

**Progress Check 1**

I wonder why there are so many cars / Lots of, going
on vacation / why don't we, too

**Progress Check 2**

Excuse, copy machine / how to make double-sided
copies / Press, double-sided copies, press

## 대화문 TEST Step 2                    p.07~08

**Listen & Speak 1 A-1**

G: Wow, look at the bridge in this ad. I wonder where
   the photo was taken.

B: That's Gwangandaegyo in Busan.

G: How do you know that?

B: I went there with my family last summer.

**Listen & Speak 1 A-2**

B: Look over there. I wonder why there are so many
   people waiting in line.

G: They're waiting to get into the new bakery there.

B: Why? Is it famous?

G: Yes. It was on a TV program.

B: Really? We should try their bread then.

G: Sure.

**Listen & Speak 2 A-1**

W: Excuse me, I'd like to borrow an audio guide.

M: Here you are.

W: Could you explain how to use it?

M: Sure. Press this button, and it'll tell you what to do.

**Listen & Speak 2 A-2**

B: Are you going somewhere this summer?

G: I'm going to Jejudo to walk along the Jeju Olle Trail.

B: The Jeju Olle Trail? Could you explain what that is?

G: It's a long hiking path around Jejudo.

B: Oh, I see. I hope you enjoy your trip!

**Communicate A**

Jaden: Do you hear that? I wonder where that music is coming from.

Yuri: I think it's coming from over there. Do you want to go and check it out?

Jaden: Yes, I love that strong beat. Is it traditional Korean music?

Yuri: Yes, it's called nongak. It's a kind of community band music.

Jaden: Nongak? Could you explain a little bit more about it?

Yuri: It's traditionally used to cheer up farmers and wish for a good harvest.

Jaden: I see. Look! Some people are dancing to the rhythm.

Yuri: Yes, that's a big part of nongak. Dancing together completes the music.

Jaden: Let's join them.

Yuri: Sure. Why not?

**Progress Check 1**

W: Look over there. I wonder why there are so many cars on the road.

M: Lots of people are going on vacation this weekend.

W: Really? Then, why don't we go somewhere, too?

M: O.K.

**Progress Check 2**

B: Excuse me, I'd like to use a copy machine.

W: O.K. You can use this machine.

B: Could you explain how to make double-sided copies?

W: Sure. Press the button for double-sided copies, and then press the start button.

B: Thank you.

**본문 TEST** Step 1      p.09~10

01 Haenyeo, Female Divers

02 several, underwater, promoted, worldwide

03 female, harvest, without, breathing

04 made, Intangible, Heritage list

05 last, interviewed, experience, taking

06 become interested in taking

07 One day, happened to    08 was surprised to find

09 Until, seen, looked, tired

10 kept laughing, been, over

11 realized, should take    12 isn't it difficult to

13 At, why I wanted

14 looked pretty in, wetsuits

15 So, very special

16 show, culture to, world

17 opened up, then

18 make them look beautiful

19 tell us more about    20 so special about

21 can tell you, things

22 symbol, strong women

23 volcanic, suitable, farming, breadwinners

24 form, own, each other

25 example, more-experienced, less-experienced

26 stay, without, breathing, catch

27 good for, underwater environment

28 marine, time, destory, place

29 what, planning, do, future

30 attended, exhibition, talk, lives

31 finished, held, hand tightly

32 said to, so much

33 such a special person

34 crying with happiness

35 was deeply moved

36 never forget, moment, continue

37 more beautiful stories about

01 Female Divers

02 underwater photographer, has promoted, worldwide

03 female divers, without any breathing devices

04 made UNESCO's Intangible Cultural Heritage list

05 was interviewed, experience of taking picutres

06 become interested in taking

07 One day, happened to

08 was surprised to find, was enjoying

09 Until then, had only seen, looked very tired

10 kept laughing, for over five hours

11 realized, should take pictures

12 isn't it difficult to take pictures

13 At first, why I wanted

14 looked pretty in their wetsuits

15 very special          16 show, to

17 opened up, then

18 Of course, make them, beautiful

19 more about          20 so special

21 can tell you

22 symbol of strong women

23 which, is not suitable for, have become the breadwinners for

24 form, own communities, each other

25 more-experienced, less-experienced

26 because, without, breathing devices, can't catch

27 is good for, underwater environment

28 Catching, at one time in one place can destory

29 what, planning to do

30 attended, overseas exhibition, give a talk

31 held my hand tightly

32 so much

33 whole life, such a special person

34 crying with happiness

35 was deeply moved

36 can never forget, continue to take

37 more beautiful stories about them

1 해녀, 한국의 여성 잠수부

2 지난 몇 년 동안, 수중 사진작가 Zin Kim은 제주 해녀 문화를 전 세계에 홍보해 왔다.

3 해녀는 어떤 호흡 장치도 사용하지 않고 해산물을 채취하는 한국의 여성 잠수부들이다.

4 그들의 문화는 2016년에 유네스코 무형문화유산에 등재되었다.

5 지난주 그녀의 작업실에서, Zin Kim과 해녀의 사진을 찍는 그녀의 경험에 대해 인터뷰를 했다.

6 Q. 어떻게 해녀의 사진을 찍는 것에 관심을 가지게 되었나요?

7 어느 날, 저는 우연히 한 해녀의 사진을 찍게 되었어요.

8 저는 그녀가 자신의 일을 즐겁게 하는 것을 보고 놀랐습니다.

9 그때까지, 저는 흑백 사진 속의 아주 지친 모습의 해녀만 봐 왔죠.

10 하지만, 그녀는 다섯 시간이 넘도록 물속에 있은 후에도 계속 웃었어요.

11 저는 그때 해녀의 사진을 찍어야겠다고 깨달았어요.

12 Q. 작가님은 아름다운 해녀 사진들을 찍으시는데, 그들의 사진을 찍는 것이 어렵진 않으신가요?

13 처음에, 그들은 제가 왜 자신들의 사진을 찍으려고 하는지 이해하지 못했어요.

14 그들은 잠수복을 입은 자신들의 모습이 예뻐 보인다고 생각하지 않았으니까요.

15 그래서, 제가 그들에게 말했죠, "여러분들은 아주 특별해요.

16 저는 여러분의 문화를 세계에 알리고 싶어요."

17 그들은 그때 제게 마음을 열었어요.

18 물론, 저 또한 그들에게 제 사진 속에서 그들을 아름답게 보이도록 하겠다고 약속했지요.

19 Q. 해녀에 대해서 더 말씀해 주시겠어요?

20 그들은 무엇이 그렇게 특별한가요?

21 세 가지를 말씀 드릴게요.

22 첫 번째로, 해녀들은 강인한 여성의 상징이에요.

23 제주도는 화산섬이고, 이는 농사에 적합하지 않아서 많은 해녀들이 가족들의 생계비를 버는 가장이 되어 왔어요.

24 둘째로, 해녀들은 그들 자신의 공동체를 조직하고 서로 도와요.

25 예를 들어, 경험이 더 많은 해녀들이 경험이 적은 해녀들을 훈련시키지요.

26 세 번째로, 어떤 호흡 장치도 사용하지 않고 물속에 머물기 때문에, 해녀는 많은 해산물을 채취할 수가 없어요.

27 이것은 수중 환경에 좋은 것이지요.

28 한 번에 한 장소에서 너무 많은 해양생물을 채취하는 것은 바다를 파괴할 수 있으니까요.

29 Q. 마지막으로, 앞으로 계획하고 있는 것에 대해 말씀해 주세요.

30 예전에 두 명의 해녀들과 함께 그들의 삶에 대해 이야기하기 위해 해외에서 열리는 박람회에 참가한 적이 있어요.

31 제가 연설을 마쳤을 때, 해녀 중 한 분이 제 손을 꼭 잡았어요.

32 그분이 말했죠, "너무 고마워.

33 내 평생 내가 이렇게 특별한 사람이라는 걸 미처 알지 못했어."

34 그녀는 행복해서 울고 있었어요.

35 청중들 모두가 깊은 감동을 받았어요.

36 전 그 순간을 절대 잊을 수가 없기 때문에 해녀의 사진을 계속해서 찍을 거예요.

37 저는 그들에 대한 더 많은 아름다운 이야기들을 세계의 더 많은 사람들에게 알려 주고 싶어요.

1 Haenyeo, Female Divers of Korea

2 For the past several years, the underwater photographer Zin Kim has promoted the culture of Jeju haenyeo worldwide.

3 Haenyeo are Korean female divers who harvest seafood without any breathing devices.

4 Their culture made UNESCO's Intangible Cultural Heritage list in 2016.

5 At her studio last week, Zin Kim was interviewed about her experience of taking pictures of haenyeo.

6 Q. How did you become interested in taking photos of haenyeo?

7 One day, I happened to take pictures of a haenyeo.

8 I was surprised to find that she was enjoying her job.

9 Until then, I had only seen black-and-white photos of haenyeo who looked very tired.

10 However, she kept laughing even after she had been in the water for over five hours.

11 I realized then that I should take pictures of haenyeo.

12 Q. You take beautiful pictures of them, but isn't it difficult to take pictures of haenyeo?

13 At first, they didn't understand why I wanted to take their pictures.

14 They didn't think they looked pretty in their wetsuits.

15 So, I said to them, "You're very special.

16 I want to show your culture to the world."

17 They opened up to me then.

18 Of course, I also promised them that I would make them look beautiful in my pictures.

19 Q. Could you tell us more about haenyeo?

20 What's so special about them?

21 I can tell you three things.

22 First, haenyeo are a symbol of strong women.

23 Jejudo, which is a volcanic island, is not suitable for farming, so many haenyeo have become the breadwinners for their families.

24 Second, haenyeo form their own communities and help each other.

25 For example, more-experienced haenyeo train less-experienced haenyeo.

26 Third, because they stay in the water without any breathing devices, haenyeo can't catch a lot of seafood.

27 This is good for the underwater environment.

28 Catching too much marine life at one time in one place can destroy the ocean.

29 Q. Lastly, please tell us what you're planning to do in the future.

30 I once attended an overseas exhibition with a couple of haenyeo to give a talk about their lives.

31 When I finished my talk, one of the haenyeo held my hand tightly.

32 She said to me, "Thank you so much.

33 I've never known in my whole life that I was such a special person."

34 She was crying with happiness.

35 Everyone in the audience was deeply moved.

36 I can never forget that moment, so I'll continue to take pictures of haenyeo.

37 I want to tell more beautiful stories about them to many more people in the world.

**Communicate – B Talk and Play**

1. what these are
2. called songpyeon
3. explain more about
4. traditional Korean rice cakes

**After You Read A**

1. Photographer Who Loves
2. an underwater photographer, has promoted, worldwide
3. decided to take pictures, when she met, who was enjoying
4. It, easy taking, at first
5. However, that, their culture to the world, finally opened their minds
6. At an overseas exhibition, gave a talk
7. one of, was crying with happiness
8. would continue to take

**Write**

1. makes coffee drinks for a living
2. became a barista, had found out about his passion
3. His favorite part of, decorating coffee with, watching, enjoying
4. planning to open

## Communicate – B Talk and Play

1. A: I wonder what these are.

2. B: They're called songpyeon.

3. A: Could you explain more about them?

4. B: They're traditional Korean rice cakes.

## After You Read A

1. A Photographer Who Loves Haenyeo

2. Zin Kim, an underwater photographer, has promoted the culture of Jeju haenyeo worldwide.

3. She decided to take pictures of them when she met a haenyeo who was enjoying her job.

4. It was not easy taking their pictures at first.

5. However, when she told them that she wanted to show their culture to the world, the haenyeo finally opened their minds.

6. At an overseas exhibition, she gave a talk about the lives of haenyeo.

7. After her speech, one of the haenyeo was crying with happiness.

8. Zin Kim said that she would continue to take pictures of haenyeo.

## Write

1. Kim Minho is a barista. He makes coffee drinks for a living.

2. He became a barista after he had found out about his passion for coffee.

3. His favorite part of his job is decorating coffee with hot milk and watching his customers enjoying it.

4. He is planning to open his own coffee shop.

Lesson 5

| 01 해산물, 해물 | 02 불안해하는 | 03 경쟁, 대회 |
| 04 적 | 05 휴식을 취하다 | 06 졸업하다 |
| 07 실제로 | 08 무력한 | 09 전문적인 |
| 10 대신에 | 11 판단하다 | 12 낯선 사람 |
| 13 행운인, 운이 좋은 | 14 안도하는 | 15 유명하게 |
| 16 준비하다 | 17 마음, 정신 | 18 불안해하는 |
| 19 자신감 있는 | 20 행동 | 21 독특한 |
| 22 심리학자 | 23 조심스럽게 | 24 정치적인 |
| 25 지원자 | 26 (거리 · 공간 · 시간상으로) 떨어져 | |
| 27 (음식을) 씹다 | 28 발표 | 29 해결책 |
| 30 편리한 | 31 드문, 희귀한 | 32 경쟁자 |
| 33 스트레스가 많은 | 34 심리학 | 35 내리다 |
| 36 발표하다 | 37 ~에 이르다 | 38 결코 ~가 아닌 |
| 39 혼자서 | 40 (해답 등을) 찾아내다, 내놓다 | |
| 41 예약하다 | 42 A를 B로 바꾸다 | 43 A뿐만 아니라 B도 |

| 01 graduate | 02 behavior | 03 confident |
| 04 solution | 05 decide | 06 enemy |
| 07 chew | 08 famously | 09 professional |
| 10 actually | 11 psychologist | 12 rare |
| 13 stressful | 14 relax | 15 supporter |
| 16 seafood | 17 political | 18 relieved |
| 19 helpless | 20 carefully | 21 psychology |
| 22 competition | 23 instead | 24 relay |
| 25 presentation | 26 judge | 27 convenient |
| 28 rival | 29 stranger | 30 unique |
| 31 lucky | 32 prepare | 33 lend |
| 34 guess | 35 according to | 36 turn A into B |
| 37 make a presentation | | |
| 38 not only A but also B | | 39 by oneself |
| 40 come up with | 41 not ~ at all | |
| 42 make a reservation | | 43 not ~ anymore |

1 rare, 드문, 희귀한   2 bake, 굽다   3 enemy, 적
4 stranger, 낯선 사람   5 chew, (음식을) 씹다
6 supporter, 지원자   7 helpless, 무력한
8 convenient, 편리한   9 graduate, 졸업하다
10 presentation, 발표   11 relieved, 안도하는
12 psychology, 심리학   13 lend, 빌려주다
14 relax, 휴식을 취하다   15 confident, 자신감 있는
16 rival, 경쟁자

### Listen & Speak 1 A-1

happened to, Aren't / chewed, all the time, worried about / bored, Why don't you play with / hope, stop chewing

### Listen & Speak 1 A-2

nervous / worried about, swimming competition / worry, relax, enjoy / much better

### Listen & Speak 2 A-1

what time, Grandma's place / About, bake cookies / get up early / don't have to

### Listen & Speak 2 A-2

Shall we try / Why, call, make a reservation / don't have to, online / How convenient

### Communicate A

can't wait / actually worried / Aren't, good at / worried, relay / What, mean / last runner, What if, because of / putting too much pressure on / practice / don't have to do / winning, losing / right, lucky, like

### Progress Check 1

nervous / worried about, presentation, history class / prepared a lot, do, job / feel much better

### Progress Check 2

seafood spaghetti / stop by, on the way / You don't have to, what, need / back home by, help, cook

### Listen & Speak 1 A-1

G: What happened to your shoes? Aren't they new?
B: Yes, but my dog chewed them. He does it all the time. I'm worried about him.
G: He was probably bored. Why don't you play with him more often?
B: O.K., I will. I hope he will stop chewing my shoes.

### Listen & Speak 1 A-2

B: You look a bit nervous.
G: I'm worried about my swimming competition this Saturday.
B: Don't worry. You're such a good swimmer. Just relax and enjoy yourself!
G: Thanks. I feel much better now.

### Listen & Speak 2 A-1

B: Mom, what time are we going to Grandma's place tomorrow morning?
W: About 8 a.m. I'm going to bake cookies for her before we go.
B: Then, should I get up early to help you?
W: You don't have to. Your dad will help me.
B: O.K, then. Good night, Mom!

### Listen & Speak 2 A-2

W: Shall we try that new Mexican restaurant tomorrow?
M: Why not? I'll call the restaurant to make a reservation for us.
W: You don't have to call them. You can do it online.
M: Oh, I see. How convenient!

### Communicate A

Yuri: Hi, Jaden. Sports Day is next Friday. I can't wait!
Jaden: Really? I'm actually worried about it.
Yuri: Why? Aren't you good at sports?
Jaden: Yes, I am, but I'm worried about the 800-meter relay.
Yuri: What do you mean?
Jaden: I'm the last runner. What if our team loses because of me?
Yuri: I think you're putting too much pressure on yourself.
Jaden: Really? Don't you think I should practice every day?
Yuri: No, you don't have to do that. It's just a school race. It's not about winning or losing.
Jaden: I guess you're right , Yuri. I'm lucky to have a friend like you.

### Progress Check 1

B: You look a bit nervous.
G: Well, I'm worried about my presentation in history class.
B: Don't worry. You've prepared a lot. You'll do a great job.
G: Thanks. I feel much better now.

M: Shall we have seafood spaghetti for dinner?

W: Sure. I'll stop by the store on the way home.

M: You don't have to do that. We already have what we need.

W: Oh, I see. Then, I'll be back home by 6 to help you cook.

## 본문 TEST Step 1 p.29~30

01 Psychology Answers, Questions

02 think, have, unique

03 Chances, many other, same

04 human mind, behavior, solution

05 become less nervous

06 presentation, front, whole class

07 Feeling nervous, carefully studying

08 came over, stand tall

09 standing tall, not, anymore

10 In fact, confident, presentation

11 According, standing tall, stressful

12 bodies, minds, change, behavior

13 want to feel confident

14 with, apart, place, on

15 not, sure, but, confident

16 help, feel better

17 graduates from, become, professional

18 However, has never told

19 worried that, will, understand

20 Wanting, clear, by himself

21 complete stranger sitting beside

22 why he did it

23 felt much better, off

24 Strangely enough, strangers, like

25 because, being judged, seeing

26 share with, try talking    27 feel much better

28 turn, rival into    29 political, not, at all

30 friends with, came up    31 rival, rare book

32 to lend, for, few

33 returned, thanked, deeply

34 Since, only, supporter, also

35 famously, Enemies, favor, more

36 turn, into, rival, favor

37 Instead, rival, do, favor

## 본문 TEST Step 2 p.31~32

01 Psychology Answers, Questions

02 unique problem

03 Chances are

04 human mind, behavior, so, help, find, to

05 become less nervous

06 big presentation, front, whole class

07 Feeling nervous, carefully studying

08 came over, to stand tall like

09 standing tall, a few, not, anymore

10 In fact, confident that, make, presentation

11 According to, become, by standing tall for, stressful events

12 bodies, minds, minds, behavior

13 feel confident

14 feet apart, place, on

15 not only feel sure, but also look confident, other people

16 feel better

17 graduates from, next year, professional

18 However, has never told

19 worried that, will not understand

20 Wanting, clear his mind, decided to take, by himself

21 complete, sitting beside    22 why he did it

23 However, felt much better, got off

24 Strangely enough, often tell strangers

25 because, not have to, being judged, seeing

26 that, share with, talking, stranger

27 feel much better    28 turn, rival into

29 political rival who, not, at all

30 become friends with, came up with

31 rare

32 to lend, a few days    33 deeply

34 Since, not only, but also

35 famously, who do you one favor

36 turn, into, do your rival a favor

37 Instead, to do, favor

## 본문 TEST Step 3 p.33~34

1 심리학이 당신의 물음에 답하다

2 여러분은 당신만의 유일무이한 고민을 가지고 있다고 생각하는가?

3 아마 많은 다른 사람들이 여러분과 똑같은 고민을 가지고 있을 것이다.

4 심리학은 인간의 마음과 행동에 관한 연구이며, 따라서 여러분이 문제에 대한 해결책을 찾는 데 도움을 줄 수 있다.

5 어떻게 하면 긴장을 덜 할 수 있나요?

6 지수가 반 전체 앞에서 발표를 하기 5분 전이었다.

7 지수는 긴장이 되어, 의자에 앉아 자신의 필기를 열심히 들여다보고 있었다.

8 그때 선생님이 다가와서는 원더우먼처럼 꼿꼿이 서 있어 보라고 말했다.

9 그렇게 몇 분을 우뚝 선 후에, 지수는 더 이상 긴장되지 않았다.

10 사실, 그녀는 발표를 멋있게 할 수 있을 것이라는 자신감이 생겼다.

11 유명한 심리학자인 Amy Cuddy에 의하면, 우리는 스트레스를 받는 상황 이전에 2분 정도 꼿꼿이 서 있는 것만으로도 자신감이 더 생길 수 있다고 한다.

12 우리의 몸은 마음을 바꾸고, 마음은 우리의 행동을 바꿀 수 있다.

13 자신감이 생기기를 원하는가?

14 양발을 벌리고, 허리께에 손을 올려 보아라.

15 자신에 대한 확신이 생길 뿐만 아니라 다른 사람이 보기에도 자신감에 차 보인다.

16 누가 내 기분을 낫게 해 줄 수 있나요?

17 내년에 고등학교를 졸업한 이후에 태호는 전문적인 농부가 되고 싶어 한다.

18 하지만, 누구에게도 그것에 대해 한 번도 말하지 않았다.

19 그는 부모님이나 친구들이 이해하지 못할까 걱정이 된다.

20 마음을 정리하기 위해서, 태호는 혼자 하루 기차 여행을 떠나기로 결심했다.

21 기차에서, 그는 옆에 앉은 전혀 모르는 사람에게 자신의 고민에 대해서 말했다.

22 그는 자신이 왜 그랬는지 알 수 없었다.

23 그러나, 기차에서 내릴 때 기분이 훨씬 좋아졌다.

24 정말 이상하게도, 우리는 태호처럼 우리의 문제에 대해 낯선 사람에게 말할 때가 있다.

25 그것은 우리가 평가받거나 그 사람을 다시 볼 것이라는 걱정을 할 필요가 없기 때문이다.

26 만약 가족이나 친구들과도 나눌 수 없는 고민이 있다면, 낯선 이에게 말해 보아라.

27 기분이 훨씬 나아질 것이다.

28 라이벌을 어떻게 친구로 만들 수 있을까요?

29 Benjamin Franklin에게는 한때 그를 전혀 좋아하지 않는 정치적 경쟁자가 있었다.

30 Franklin은 그와 친구가 되고 싶어서, 계획을 세웠다.

31 그의 경쟁자는 희귀한 책을 가지고 있었다.

32 Franklin은 그의 정적에게 그 책을 며칠 동안 빌려달라고 부탁했다.

33 Franklin이 그 책을 돌려줄 때, 그는 그에게 진심으로 감사를 표했다.

34 그날 이후로, 그의 경쟁자는 정치적인 후원자뿐만 아니라 좋은 친구가 되었다.

35 Franklin은 "당신을 한 번 도운 적은 더 돕고 싶어 하게 된다."

라는 유명한 말을 했다.

36 여러분이 경쟁자를 친구로 만들고 싶다면, 경쟁자의 부탁을 들어주지 마라.

37 대신, 경쟁자에게 부탁을 해 보아라.

1 Psychology Answers Your Questions

2 Do you think you have a unique problem?

3 Chances are that many other people have the same problem.

4 Psychology is the study of the human mind and behavior, so it can help you find a solution to your problem.

5 How do I become less nervous?

6 It was five minutes before Jisu's big presentation in front of the whole class.

7 Feeling nervous, Jisu was carefully studying her notes in her chair.

8 Then, her teacher came over and told her to stand tall like Wonder Woman.

9 After standing tall for a few minutes, Jisu did not feel nervous anymore.

10 In fact, she was confident that she would make a great presentation.

11 According to Amy Cuddy, a famous psychologist, we can become more confident just by standing tall for two minutes before stressful events.

12 Our bodies change our minds, and our minds can change our behavior.

13 Do you want to feel confident?

14 Stand with your feet apart, and place your hands on your hips.

15 You will not only feel sure about yourself but also look confident to other people.

16 Who can help me feel better?

17 When he graduates from high school next year, Taeho wants to become a professional farmer.

18 However, he has never told anyone about it.

19 He is worried that his parents or his friends will not understand.

20 Wanting to clear his mind, Taeho decided to take a day trip on a train by himself.

21 On the train, he told a complete stranger sitting beside him about his problem.

22 He had no idea why he did it.

23 However, he felt much better when he got off the train.

24 Strangely enough, we often tell strangers about our problems just like Taeho.

25 That is because we do not have to worry about being judged or seeing them again.

26 If you have a problem that you cannot share with your family or friends, try talking to a stranger.

27 You will feel much better.

28 How do I turn a rival into a friend?

29 Benjamin Franklin once had a political rival who did not like him at all.

30 Franklin wanted to become friends with him, so he came up with a plan.

31 His rival had a rare book.

32 Franklin asked his rival to lend him the book for a few days.

33 When Franklin returned the book, he thanked him deeply.

34 Since that day, his rival became not only a political supporter but also a good friend.

35 Franklin famously said, "Enemies who do you one favor will want to do more."

36 If you want to turn a rival into a friend, don't do your rival a favor.

37 Instead, ask your rival to do you a favor.

---

**Listen & Speak 2 - Think and Talk**

1. A: What don't I have to do on Stress-Free Day?

2. B: You don't have to clean the classroom.

3. C: You don't have to come to school by 8:30.

**Link**

1. How confident do you feel about yourself?

2. Wanting to find the answer to this question, we created a test about confidence.

3. Thirty students took the test. The average score was nine.

4. Eighteen students scored above the average score.

5. Thus, sixty percent of the students felt quite confident about themselves.

**Write**

1. The hardest time in my life

2. The hardest time in my life was when my grandmother passed away five years ago.

3. When I was younger, she took care of me most of the time.

4. Not having her around, I felt sad and lonely.

5. One day, I found my grandmother's diary.

6. She not only wrote a lot about her memories but also wished that I would lead a happy life.

7. From this experience, I have learned that I should try to be happy just as she wished.

---

**Listen & Speak 2 - Think and Talk**

1. don't, have to do

2. don't have to clean

3. don't have to come to school by

**Link**

1. How confident, feel about yourself

2. Wanting to find, created a test

3. took the test, average score

4. scored above the average score

5. Thus, felt quite confident about themselves

**Write**

1. The hardest time

2. hardest time in my life, passed away, ago

3. younger, took care of, most of

4. Not having her around, nfelt sad, lonely

5. One day, found

6. not only wrote a lot, but also wished

7. From this experience, have learned, try to be happy, as she wished

## 단어 TEST Step 1　　　　　　　　p.41

| | | |
|---|---|---|
| 01 독특하게 | 02 계산서 | 03 으깨다 |
| 04 불행하게도 | 05 확실히, 분명히 | |
| 06 진가를 알아보다, 고마워하다 | | 07 환상적인 |
| 08 수리하다 | 09 웅장한, 위대한 | 10 일어나다 |
| 11 완전하게 | 12 불편, 애로 | 13 추구하다, 추진하다 |
| 14 고객, 소비자 | 15 발명가 | 16 이유 |
| 17 창의적인, 창조적인 | | 18 역할, 배역 |
| 19 사실적인 | 20 덜 익은, 살짝 익힌 | 21 만족한 |
| 22 솔직하게, 솔직히 | 23 불평하다 | 24 열정, 흥미 |
| 25 끝마치다 | 26 지불하다, 지급하다 | |
| 27 획기적인 | 28 ~ 동안 내내 | 29 제공하다 |
| 30 서류 | 31 한 조각, 일부 | 32 신선한 |
| 33 기꺼이 | 34 성공적인 | 35 작성하다 |
| 36 겁주어 쫓아내다 | 37 ~이기 때문에, ~이므로 | |
| 38 결과적으로 | 39 역대, 지금껏 | 40 내붙이다, 게시하다 |
| 41 ~에 익숙하다 | 42 최선을 다하다 | |
| 43 ~의 책임을 지다, ~을 떠맡다 | | |

## 단어 TEST Step 2　　　　　　　　p.42

| | | |
|---|---|---|
| 01 passion | 02 appreciate | 03 check |
| 04 throughout | 05 rare | 06 pay |
| 07 fix | 08 form | 09 surely |
| 10 inconvenience | 11 completely | 12 gladly |
| 13 pursue | 14 reason | 15 role |
| 16 happen | 17 complain | 18 decorate |
| 19 fantastic | 20 meal | 21 fresh |
| 22 honestly | 23 creative | 24 crush |
| 25 innovative | 26 slice | 27 successful |
| 28 unfortunately | 29 grand | 30 customer |
| 31 uniquely | 32 supper | 33 provide |
| 34 satisfied | 35 be used to | 36 fill out |
| 37 not anymore | 38 as a result | 39 of all time |
| 40 do one's best | 41 feel like -ing | 42 put up |
| 43 scare away | | |

## 단어 TEST Step 3　　　　　　　　p.43

1 role, 역할, 배역　 2 rare, 덜 익은, 살짝 익힌

3 meal, 식사　 4 provide, 제공하다

5 supper, 만찬, 저녁 식사　 6 throughout, ~동안 내내

7 check, 계산서　 8 appreciate, 진가를 알아보다

9 crush, 으깨다　 10 customer, 고객, 소비자

11 decorate, 장식하다, 꾸미다　 12 fix, 수리하다

13 form, 서류　 14 inventor, 발명가

15 complain, 불평하다　 16 pursue, 추구하다, 추진하다

## 대화문 TEST Step 1　　　　　　　　p.44~45

**Listen & Speak 1 A-1**

draw, did, it / look so real, feel like having a bite of / I'm not satisfied with, unique / so, fantastic drawing

**Listen & Speak 1 A-2**

How can, help / bought, only a week ago, sometimes turns off by itself / have a look at, inconvenience, take, few hours to fix / I'm not satisfied with, like, one / course, fill out, form

**Listen & Speak 2 A-1**

did, buy / myself / better than any other jam / should sell it / would, to buy / I promise I'll be

**Listen & Speak 2 A-2**

thought, were interested in / not anymore, want to become / Are, sure / how to act, I promise I'll do my best

**Communicate A**

your meal / good, fresh / about / I'm not satisfied with, rare / Would, like, to bring, another one / be going, have, check / won't have to pay for / I promise we'll provide, with, experience

**Progress Check 1**

How can I / got, as, I'm not satisfied with / in different colors / one in blue / do, get one

**Progress Check 2**

take, classes / interested in / not anymore, chef / hard work / worry, I promise I'll do / then

**Progress Check 3**

on / Have, finished / I promise I'll finish

## 대화문 TEST Step 2　　　　　　　　p.46~47

**Listen & Speak 1 A-1**

B: Wow! Did you draw this?

G: I did. Do you like it?

B: Yes, the bread and the milk look so real. I feel like having a bite of the bread.

G: Thanks, but I'm not satisfied with it. It's not unique.

B: I don't think so. I think it's a fantastic drawing.

## Listen & Speak 1 A-2

M: Hello, ma'am. How can I help you?

W: I bought this phone only a week ago, but it sometimes turns off by itself.

M: Oh, I see. May I have a look at it? (Pause) We're sorry for the inconvenience. It'll take a few hours to fix it.

W: I'm not satisfied with the phone. I'd like a new one.

M: Of course. I just need to fill out this form.

## Listen & Speak 2 A-1

G: Wow, I like this blueberry jam. Where did you buy it?

B: I made it myself.

G: Really? This is better than any other jam I've ever had. You should sell it.

B: Do you think people would want to buy this?

G: Of course. I promise I'll be your first customer.

## Listen & Speak 2 A-2

B: Mom, I want to go to an arts high school. I want to become an actor.

W: What? I thought you were interested in science.

B: I was but not anymore. I want to become a movie star.

W: Are you sure you want to be an actor?

B: Yes, I'll learn how to act. I promise I'll do my best.

## Communicate A

Man: Are you enjoying your meal?

Woman: Well, the bread was good, and the salad was fresh.

Man: How about your steak?

Woman: Honestly, I'm not satisfied with the steak. It's too rare for me.

Man: I'm sorry. Would you like me to bring you another one?

Woman: That's O.K. I need to be going. Let me just have the check, please.

Man: I'm really sorry. You won't have to pay for the steak.

Woman: O.K. Thanks.

Man: I promise we'll provide you with a better experience next time you visit.

## Progress Check 1

M: Hello, ma'am. How can I help you?

W: I got this hat as a gift yesterday, but I'm not satisfied with the color.

M: Oh, I see. We have this hat in different colors.

W: Do you have one in blue?

M: Yes, we do. I'll get one for you.

W: Thanks.

## Progress Check 2

B: Mom, I want to take cooking classes.

W: What? I thought you were interested in sports.

B: I was but not anymore. I want to become a chef.

W: Are you sure? Cooking is hard work.

B: Don't worry. I promise I'll do my best.

W: O.K., then.

## Progress Check 3

G: Dad, I want to watch a movie on TV now.

M: Have you finished your homework?

G: No, but I promise I'll finish it after I watch TV.

## 본문 TEST Step 1                    p.48~49

01 Vinci the Cook

02 known as, greatest, time

03 also, inventor, musician

04 few, however, that, creative

05 In, worked as, at

06 took charge, changed, completely

07 simple, artistic, like, slices

08 dishes, even decorated with

09 because, used, with, servings

10 As, result, lost, job

11 few, later, opened, with

12 create, where, try, innovative

13 put up, uniquely written

14 believed, appreciate, creative cooking

15 Unfortunately, never happened

16 In, early, work for

17 different roles, such as

18 put in charge of

19 another chance, pursue, passion

20 stop at cooking creative

21 much more quickly, easily

22 Thus, invented, machines

23 created, crush vegetables, pull

24 device, scare, away from

25 innovative, most, too, to

26 grand, based on, wall

27 took, because, been interested

28 spent, kinds, what, put

29 wasted, over, reason, complained

30 Although, successful, interest, throughout

31 not only, but also

32 that, secret, same way

53

01 the Cook

02 is known as, greatest painters of all time

03 also, inventor, scientist

04 few, however, creative cook

05 twenty-year-old, as a cook

06 took charge of, changed, completely

07 but, like, a few carrot slices

08 were even decorated with

09 however, were used to, with, servings

10 As a result      11 A few, later

12 to create, where, innovative

13 put up, beautifully painted, uniquely written

14 would, appreciate, creative

15 Unfortunately, happened      16 early, to work

17 was given, roles, such as

18 was, put in charge of

19 to be given another, to pursue, passion

20 stop at      21 much more

22 Thus, invented      23 that, crush

24 that, scare, away from

25 were too, too, to use

26 to make, which was based on

27 took on, had, been interested in

28 a lot of, cooking, what to put

29 for over, why, to

30 Although, interest in, throughout

31 not only, but also, creative cook

32 Now that, secret passion, the same way

1 요리사 다빈치

2 레오나르도 다빈치는 역대 가장 위대한 화가들 중의 한 명으로 알려져 있다.

3 그는 또한 위대한 발명가, 과학자, 그리고 음악가였다.

4 하지만, 극히 소수의 사람들만이 또한 그가 창의적인 요리사였다는 것을 안다.

5 1473년, 스무 살의 레오나르도 다빈치는 이탈리아 플로렌스에 있는 음식점에서 요리사로 일했다.

6 그가 부엌을 책임지게 되었을 때, 다빈치는 메뉴를 완전히 바꿔 버렸다.

7 그는 약간의 당근 조각을 곁들인 생선과 같이 간단하지만 예술적인 음식을 만들었다.

8 몇몇 음식들은 심지어 꽃으로 장식되었다.

9 하지만, 손님들은 많은 양의 고기 요리에 익숙했었기 때문에 불만족스러워했다.

10 그 결과, 다빈치는 그의 직업을 잃었다.

11 몇 년 후, 다빈치는 그의 친구인 산드로 보티첼리와 함께 음식점을 열었다.

12 그는 사람들이 그의 획기적인 음식을 먹어 볼 수 있는 장소로 만들기를 원했다.

13 그들은 아름답게 그려진 간판을 내걸었고 독특하게 써진 메뉴를 만들었다.

14 다빈치는 사람들이 곧 그의 창의적인 요리의 진가를 알아볼 것이라고 믿었다.

15 불행히도, 그런 일은 결코 일어나지 않았다.

16 1480년대 초반에, 다빈치는 밀라노에서 루도비코 스포르차를 위해 일하기 시작했다.

17 그는 음악가, 화가, 그리고 공학자와 같은 많은 역할들을 부여받았다.

18 그는 또한 주방을 책임지게 되었다.

19 그는 요리를 향한 그의 열정을 추구할 또 다른 기회를 얻게 되어 행복했다.

20 다빈치는 창의적인 요리를 만드는 것에 멈추지 않았다.

21 그는 훨씬 더 빠르고 쉽게 요리하고 싶어했다.

22 따라서, 그는 그의 주방에서 사용할 새로운 기계들을 발명하였다.

23 그는 채소를 으깨고 스파게티를 뽑는 기계들을 만들었다.

24 그는 심지어 개구리를 겁주어 물탱크에서 쫓아낼 수 있는 기구도 만들었다.

25 확실히 그것들은 모두 매우 획기적이었지만, 그것들 중 대부분은 사용하기에 너무 크거나 너무 어려웠다.

26 1495년, 스포르차는 다빈치에게 웅장한 그림을 밀라노에 있는 교회의 벽에 그려 달라고 부탁했는데, 그것은 예수의 최후의 만찬을 바탕으로 한 것이었다.

27 다빈치는 기꺼이 그 작업을 맡았는데, 그가 항상 음식에 흥미를 가졌기 때문이었다.

28 그는 그림 속 식탁 위에 어떤 음식을 올릴지 결정하기 위해 모든 종류의 음식을 요리하느라 많은 시간을 썼다.

29 "다빈치는 1년 넘게 부엌에서 시간을 낭비해 오고 있습니다. 그것이 그가 아직도 그림을 끝내지 못한 이유입니다."라고 교회 사람들이 스포르차에게 불평을 했다.

30 다빈치는 결코 성공적인 요리사는 되지 못했지만 그는 그의 생애 내내 요리에 대한 큰 흥미를 보여 주었다.

31 그는 훌륭한 화가일 뿐만 아니라 창의적인 요리사였다.

32 이제 여러분은 요리에 대한 그의 비밀스런 열정을 모두 알게 되었기 때문에 〈최후의 만찬〉을 절대 같은 식으로는 보지 않을 것이다.

1 Da Vinci the Cook

2 Leonardo da Vinci is known as one of the greatest painters of all time.

3 He was also a great inventor, scientist, and musician.

4 Very few people, however, know that da Vinci was also a creative cook.

5 In 1473, twenty-year-old da Vinci worked as a cook at a restaurant in Florence, Italy.

6 When he took charge of the kitchen, da Vinci changed the menu completely.

7 He made simple but artistic dishes like fish with a few carrot slices.

8 Some dishes were even decorated with flowers.

9 Customers, however, were unhappy because they were used to dishes with big servings of meat.

10 As a result, da Vinci lost his job.

11 A few years later, da Vinci opened a restaurant with his friend Sandro Botticelli.

12 He wanted to create a place where people could try his innovative food.

13 They put up a beautifully painted sign and made a uniquely written menu.

14 Da Vinci believed that people would soon appreciate his creative cooking.

15 Unfortunately, that never happened.

16 In the early 1480s, da Vinci began to work for Ludovico Sforza in Milan.

17 He was given many different roles, such as a musician, a painter, and an engineer.

18 He was also put in charge of the kitchen.

19 He was happy to be given another chance to pursue his passion for cooking.

20 Da Vinci did not stop at cooking creative dishes.

21 He wanted to cook much more quickly and easily.

22 Thus, he invented new machines for his kitchen.

23 He created machines that could crush vegetables and pull spaghetti.

24 He even made a device that could scare frogs away from the water tank.

25 Surely, they were all very innovative, but most of them were too big or too difficult to use.

26 In 1495, Sforza asked da Vinci to make a grand painting, which was based on the last supper of Jesus, on the wall of a church in Milan.

27 Da Vinci gladly took on the project because he had always been interested in food.

28 He spent a lot of time cooking all kinds of food to decide what to put on the table in his picture.

29 "Da Vinci has wasted his time in the kitchen for over a year. That's the reason why he hasn't finished the painting yet," complained the people from the church to Sforza.

30 Although da Vinci never became a successful cook, he showed great interest in cooking throughout his life.

31 He was not only a great painter but also a creative cook.

32 Now that you know all about his secret passion for cooking, you will never look at *The Last Supper* the same way.

**Write**

1. an artist who uses technology

2. special moment, decided what I wanted

3. Back in, small statue using technology

4. great chance to learn, using technology

5. decided to, technical high school

6. After, graduated from, entered, learned, arts, technology

7. This year, held, exhibition

8. am, satisfied with

**Link**

1. the most important thing to consider, choose their career

2. come up with, design new things

3. work at a place where, use their creativity

**Watch and Think Share**

1. is known for using, during

2. few people, however, historian, painter, writer

3. won, Nobel Prize in Literature

**Write**

1. My name is Kim Jieun. I am an artist who uses technology.

2. There was a special moment when I decided what I wanted to be.

3. Back in 2030, I made a small statue using technology.

55

4. It was a great chance to learn about using technology for arts.

5. Thus, I decided to go to a technical high school.

6. After I graduated from high school, I entered Korea Art College and learned more about arts and technology.

7. This year, I held my first exhibition.

8. I am very satisfied with my life.

**Link**

1. Some people think creativity is the most important thing to consider when they choose their career.

2. They like to come up with new ideas and design new things.

3. Thus, they want to work at a place where they can use their creativity.

**Watch and Think Share**

1. Winston Churchill is known for using the Prime Minister of the United Kingdom during World War II.

2. Very few people, however, know that he was also a historian, a painter, and a writer.

3. He even won the Nobel Prize in Literature in 1953.

## 단어 TEST Step 1 p.61

01 귀중한, 값비싼　02 맞는, 정확한　03 정확하게
04 고위 공무원, 관리 05 한 항아리[냄비]의 양
06 정직　07 정말, 확실히　08 ~중에, ~의 사이에
09 깨지다, 부러뜨리다　10 여행, 여정
11 이상한　12 경기, 시합
13 지혜로운, 현명한, 슬기로운　14 기지, 재치
15 좁은　16 내놓다, 제공하다　17 대궐, 궁궐
18 황제　19 (땅속에 사는) 벌레 20 정책
21 사탕, 단것; 단, 달콤한　22 처벌하다, 벌주다
23 호박　24 되돌려주다　25 표현
26 청, 부탁　27 (화나거나 놀라서) 말을 못 하는
28 그러므로　29 지혜, 슬기, 현명함 30 현재, 지금
31 틀림없이, 분명히　32 (틀림없이) ~일 것이다
33 끌다, 당기다, 끌어당기다　34 시험
35 혼자서, 스스로　36 ~을 제출하다
37 ~을 찾아내다, ~을 떠올리다　38 ~ 덕분에
39 ~에 주력하다, 집중하다
40 ~의 처지에서, ~의 상황에서　41 타당하다, 말이 되다
42 ~로 유명하다　43 한 냄비의, 한 항아리의

## 단어 TEST Step 2 p.62

01 wise　02 expression　03 favor
04 among　05 certainly　06 gift
07 honesty　08 punish　09 narrow
10 precious　11 correct　12 present
13 official　14 strange　15 indeed
16 policy　17 journey　18 worm
19 match　20 pumpkin　21 break
22 emperor　23 court　24 speechless
25 exam　26 wit　27 past
28 exactly　29 return　30 sweet
31 thus　32 wisdom　33 potful
34 offer　35 hand in　36 focus on
37 over again　38 in one's place 39 for oneself
40 come up with 41 be famous for 42 thanks to
43 make sense

## 단어 TEST Step 3 p.63

1 honesty, 정직　2 present, 현재, 지금
3 precious, 귀중한, 값비싼　4 leave, 떠나다

5 emperor, 황제   6 correct, 맞는, 정확한

7 court, 대궐, 궁궐   8 pumpkin, 호박

9 journey, 여행, 여정   10 match, 경기, 시합

11 worm, 벌레   12 narrow, 좁은

13 official, 고위 공무원, 관리   14 gift, 선물

15 punish, 처벌하다, 벌주다

16 speechless, (화나거나 놀라서) 말을 못 하는

## 대화문 TEST Step 1 p.64~65

### Listen & Speak 1 A-1

look tired / got up, to study / Good for, early bird, worm / gets tired / Do you mean / exactly what I mean

### Listen & Speak 1 A-2

have to / a leg / Do you mean, break one, legs / expression meaning, you do well

### Listen & Speak 2 A-1

dance well / Everyone, is good at / too / good singers / What a, I wish I could, like

### Listen & Speak 2 A-2

can't believe, to say, Thanks to, I wish I could, back to, to start, new journey

### Communicate A

wrong, look, good / thinking about / Do you mean, lost / I wish I could / live for today / Do you mean, focus on / exactly, gift, why, called / expressions, as wise as

### Progress Check 1

look worried, wrong / hand in, by / better late than never / Do you mean, hand it in even though, late / what

### Progress Check 2

play the guitar / it / too / in / What a, I wish, could, like

### Progress Check 3

broke, what to do, Another, Honesty, policy, what that means

## 대화문 TEST Step 2 p.66~67

### Listen & Speak 1 A-1

G: You look tired this morning.

B: I got up very early to study for the exam.

G: Good for you. The early bird catches the worm.

B: No. The early bird gets tired quickly.

G: Do you mean you don't like to get up early?

B: Yes, that's exactly what I mean.

### Listen & Speak 1 A-2

G: I have to sing at the school's English pop song contest.

B: Wow. Break a leg!

G: What? Do you mean I have to break one of my legs?

B: No, it's an expression meaning I hope you do well.

### Listen & Speak 2 A-1

B: Wow, you really dance well.

G: Thanks. I love dancing. Everyone in my family is good at dancing.

B: Really? Your parents dance well, too?

G: Yes. They're also good singers.

B: What a family! I wish I could dance like you.

### Listen & Speak 2 A-2

B: Hello, everyone! Time flies. I can't believe it's time to say goodbye. Thanks to my teachers and friends, I was really happy here. I wish I could go back to my first year and live these years over again, but it's time to start a new journey to high school. I hope I can see you again. Thank you.

### Communicate A

Anna: What's wrong? You don't look so good.

Suho: I'm still thinking about our soccer match last week.

Anna: Do you mean the game you lost last week?

Suho: Yes. I wish I could forget about it, but I can't.

Anna: Well, you should always live for today.

Suho: Do you mean I should forget the past and focus on the present?

Anna: Yes, exactly. People say, "Yesterday is history, tomorrow is a mystery, and today is a gift. That's why it's called the present."

Suho: Now I see. You know so many great expressions. You're as wise as my grandma.

### Progress Check 1

G: You look worried. Is something wrong?

B: I had to hand in my science report by yesterday, but I didn't.

G: It's better late than never.

B: Do you mean it's better to hand it in even though it's late?

G: Yes, exactly. You should always finish what you've started.

### Progress Check 2

B: Wow, you play the guitar so well.

57

G: Thanks. I love playing the guitar. I learned it from my dad.

B: Really? Does your father play the guitar, too?

G: Yes. He was in a famous band.

B: What a family! I wish I could play the guitar like you.

**Progress Check 3**

M: You broke your friend's phone, and you don't know what to do. Another friend says to you, "Honesty is the best policy." You don't know what that means exactly.

---

**본문 TEST** Step 1                                    p.68~70

01 Tales of

02 emperor, number, officials, court

03 Among, whose name

04 famous for, with, words

05 Thus, emoeror, have, near

06 Sweet Punishment

07 test, wisdom, asked, strange

08 One, came up with

09 pulled, hair, head, should

10 be punished, course          11 punish him

12 turned to

13 would, do, were, place

14 If, were you, would give      15 talking about

16 Birbal's crazy

17 What made, say so             18 must be, else, such

19 correct, so, wise, near       20 Potful, Wisdom

21 sent, with, strange favor

22 been asked, bring, potful

23 makes, sense, put, in

24 bring, potful, wisdom         25 won't be, problem

26 wait a few weeks             27 much time as, need

28 few, back, whose, narrow

29 take, return, after, out

30 precious, careful, break, wisdom

31 official, inside, became speechless

32 thanked, left for, country    33 be, if, were, as

34 After, left, what, inside

35 the other, for yourself

36 other, found, big as

37 be taken, without breaking

38 put, over, until, grew

39 certainly, potful of wisdom

---

**본문 TEST** Step 2                                    p.71~72

01 Tales of

02 a number of wise officials, court

03 Among, was, whose name  04 for, wit, with

05 Thus, emperor, to have, near

06 Punishment

07 To test, officials' wisdom, asked them strange questions

08 came up with

09 a hair, should I do to

10 be punished, course          11 punish

12 turned to

13 would, do if, were in my place

14 If, were you, would give      15 talking about

16 crazy                         17 What made you

18 who, must be, else, such a thing

19 indeed correct, so, to have, as wise as

20 Potful, Wisdorn

21 with a strange favor

22 a lot of, I've been asked, to bring, a potful of wisdom

23 makes no sense, put, in a pot

24 a potful of                   25 won't be

26 a few weeks                   27 as much time as

28 A few, whose, narrow, one, official

29 take, to return, out of it    30 not to break

31 speechless                    32 thanked, left for

33 would be, if there were, as wise as

34 After, left, what was

35 the other, for yourself       36 the other, as big as

37 can't be taken, without breaking

38 over, until, as big as

39 certainly, a potful of wisdom

---

**본문 TEST** Step 3                                    p.73~74

1 비르발 이야기

2 악바르는 무굴 제국의 제3대 황제로, 자신의 궁정에 많은 현명한 신하들이 있었다.

3 그 중 라자 비르발이라는 이름의 한 사람이 있었다.

4 그는 재빠른 재치로 유명했으며 말이 매우 지혜로웠다.

5 그래서, 황제는 언제나 비르발을 곁에 두기를 원했다.

6 달콤한 처벌

7 신하들의 지혜를 시험해 보기 위해, 악바르는 종종 그들에게 이상한 질문을 했다.

8 어느 날, 황제는 재미있는 질문이 생각났다.

9 악바르: 오늘 어떤 이가 내 머리에서 머리카락을 잡아당겼소. 이

---

자에게 무엇을 해야 하겠소?

10 신하 1: 당연히 처벌해야 합니다.

11 신하 2: 예, 그를 처벌하소서!

12 악바르가 비르발에게 돌아섰다.

13 악바르: 그대가 내 입장이라면 무엇을 하겠소, 비르발?

14 비르발: 소신이 폐하라면, 그에게 사탕을 주겠습니다.

15 신하 3: 저 사람은 무슨 말을 하는 건가?

16 신하 4: 비르발이 정신이 나갔어!

17 악바르: 왜 그렇게 말했소?

18 비르발: 폐하의 머리카락을 잡아당긴 사람은 폐하의 손자임이 분명합니다. 다른 그 누구도 그런 짓을 할 수 없지요.

19 악바르: 과연 그대의 말이 맞소, 비르발. 그대처럼 현명한 자를 옆에 두어 정말 기쁘오.

20 한 항아리만큼의 지혜

21 어느 날, 페르시아의 왕이 이상한 요청과 함께 신하를 보냈다.

22 페르시아의 신하: 폐하의 나라에 현명한 자들이 많다고 들었습니다. 저는 저의 왕으로부터 한 항아리의 지혜를 왕께 가지고 오라는 명을 받았습니다.

23 신하 5: 저건 말이 안 되오! 어떻게 지혜를 항아리에 넣을 수 있단 말이오?

24 악바르: 그에게 지혜 한 항아리를 가져다줄 수 있겠소, 비르발?

25 비르발: 문제될 것이 없사옵니다.

26 몇 주만 기다려 주시겠습니까?

27 페르시아의 신하: 물론이오! 필요한 만큼 얼마든지 시간을 가지시오.

28 몇 주 후, 비르발은 목이 매우 좁은 두 항아리를 들고 돌아왔다. 그는 하나를 페르시아의 신하에게 줬다.

29 비르발: 이 지혜의 항아리를 그대의 왕께 가져다 드리십시오. 왕께서 이 항아리에서 지혜를 꺼내신 후에는 항아리를 우리에게 돌려달라 전해 주십시오.

30 비르발: 그 항아리는 매우 귀중한 것이니, 그것을 깨지 않도록 조심해 주십시오. 우리는 오직 두 개의 지혜의 항아리만 갖고 있습니다.

31 페르시아 신하는 항아리 안을 들여다보곤 말을 잃었다.

32 그는 비르발에게 감사를 표한 뒤 그의 나라로 떠났다.

33 페르시아의 신하: 우리 나라에도 비르발처럼 현명한 자가 있다면 정말 좋을 텐데.

34 페르시아의 신하가 떠난 뒤, 악바르는 비르발에게 항아리 속에 무엇이 있었는지를 물었다.

35 비르발: 여기 또 다른 항아리가 있습니다. 직접 살펴보시지요.

36 악바르는 또 다른 항아리 안을 보고 꼭 항아리만큼 큰 호박을 발견했다.

37 악바르: 그렇군! 항아리를 깨지 않고는 호박을 꺼낼 수가 없구려! 어떻게 한 것이오?

38 비르발: 항아리를 호박꽃에 덮어 놓은 후 호박이 항아리만큼 클 때까지 기다렸습니다.

39 악바르: 하하하! 이건 정말로 지혜의 항아리구려!

1 Tales of Birbal

2 Akbar, the third Mogul emperor, had a number of wise officials at his court.

3 Among them was a man whose name was Raja Birbal.

4 He was famous for his quick wit and was very wise with his words.

5 Thus, the emperor always liked to have Birbal near him.

6 Sweet Punishment

7 To test his officials' wisdom, Akbar often asked them strange questions.

8 One day, he came up with an interesting question.

9 Akbar: Someone pulled a hair from my head today. What should I do to him?

10 Official 1: He should be punished, of course.

11 Official 2: Yes, punish him!

12 Akbar turned to Birbal.

13 Akbar: What would you do if you were in my place, Birbal?

14 Birbal: If I were you, I would give him sweets.

15 Official 3: What's he talking about?

16 Official 4: Birbal's crazy!

17 Akbar: What made you say so?

18 Birbal: The person who pulled your hair must be your grandson. No one else could do such a thing.

19 Akbar: You are indeed correct, Birbal. I'm so glad to have someone as wise as you near me.

20 A Potful of Wisdom

21 One day, the king of Persia sent an official with a strange favor.

22 Persian Official: I hear you have a lot of wise men in your country. I've been asked by my king to bring him a potful of wisdom.

23 Official 5: That makes no sense! How can we put wisdom in a pot?

24 Akbar: Can you bring him a potful of wisdom, Birbal?

25 Birbal: It won't be a problem.

26 Birbal: Could you please wait a few weeks?

27 Persian Official: Of course! Take as much time as you need.

28 A few weeks later, Birbal came back with two pots whose necks were really narrow. He offered one to the Persian official.

29 Birbal: You can take this pot of wisdom to your

king. Please ask him to return the pot to us after he takes the wisdom out of it.

30 Birbal: The pot is very precious, so please be careful not to break it. We only have two pots of wisdom.

31 The Persian official looked inside the pot and became speechless.

32 He thanked Birbal and left for his country.

33 Persian Official: It would be great if there were a man as wise as Birbal in our country.

34 After the Persian official left, Akbar asked Birbal what was inside the pot.

35 Birbal: Here is the other pot. You can see for yourself.

36 Akbar looked inside the other pot and found a pumpkin just as big as the pot.

37 Akbar: I see! The pumpkin can't be taken out without breaking the pot. How did you do it?

38 Birbal: I put the pots over pumpkin flowers and waited until the pumpkins grew as big as the pots.

39 Akbar: Hahaha! This certainly is a potful of wisdom!

## 구석구석지문 TEST Step 1　　　　　p.80

### Link
1. Shorter Line
2. drew a line, asked his officials
3. Make, shorter without touching
4. Without touching
5. How, that
6. smiled
7. too easy
8. next to, that, had drawn
9. shorter than mine
10. did it
11. wish, were as wise as

### Write
1. Dear
2. flies, to say goodbye
3. the time when we went
4. the movie we watched
5. playing basketball with, after school
6. for teaching me basketball skills
7. could turn back time, would spend
8. keep in touch, graduate

9. Best

### Culture Project
1. When, failed, seven times, disappointed
2. from, said to, If I were, wouldn't give up
3. Fall, stand up
4. Japanese saying, Do not give up
5. tried again, finally passed

## 구석구석지문 TEST Step 2　　　　　p.81

### Link
1. A Shorter Line
2. One day, Emperor Akbar drew a line on the ground and asked his officials.
3. Akbar: Make this line shorter without touching it.
4. Official 1: Without touching it?
5. Official 2: How can we do that?
6. Birbal smiled.
7. Birbal: That's too easy.
8. Birbal drew a longer line next to the line that Akbar had drawn.
9. Birbal: Your line is now shorter than mine.
10. Akbar: You dud it, Birbal!
11. Official 3: I wish I were as wise as Birbal.

### Write
1. Dear Jaeha,
2. Time flies. I cannot believe that it is time to say goodbye.
3. I still remember the time when we went camping together.
4. I really liked the movie we watched that night.
5. I also loved playing basketball with you after school.
6. I really want to thank you for teaching me basketball skills.
7. If I could turn back time, I would spend more time with you.
8. I hope we keep in touch even after we graduate.
9. Best, Jake

### Culture Project
1. When my brother failed his driving test seven times, he was very disappointed.
2. Kento, his friend from Japan, said to him, "If I were you, I wouldn't give up.
3. Fall seven times, stand up eight."
4. It's a Japanese saying that means "Do not give up."
5. My brother tried again and finally passed.

문항수 : 선택형(26문항) 서술형(3문항)　　20 ． ． ．

| 반 | |
| --- | --- |
| 이름 | |
| 점수 | |

◎ 선택형 문항의 답안은 컴퓨터용 수정 싸인펜을 사용하여 OMR 답안지에 바르게 표기하시오.
◎ 서술형 문제는 답을 답안지에 반드시 검정 볼펜으로 쓰시오.
◎ 총 29문항 100점 만점입니다. 문항별 배점은 각 문항에 표시되어 있습니다.

[전북 ㅇㅇ중]

## 01 다음 빈칸에 공통으로 들어갈 가장 알맞은 단어는? (3점)

• Can you _____ me a hand? I need some help.
• Let's talk about it tomorrow. I'll _____ you a call.

① make ② give ③ take
④ get ⑤ have

[충북 ㅇㅇ중]

## 02 다음 밑줄 친 낱말이 어색한 것은? (3점)

① Deep breathing will <u>consider</u> you relax.
② The <u>interviewer</u> asked me about my future plans.
③ We learn many things from <u>past</u> mistakes.
④ The number of <u>audience</u> was more than a million.
⑤ She invited me to her photo <u>exhibition</u>.

[전북 ㅇㅇ중]

## 03 다음 대화의 빈칸에 가장 알맞은 표현은? (4점)

M: Do you hear that? _____
W: I think it's coming from over there. Do you want to go and check it out?
M: Yes, I love that strong beat. Is it traditional Korean music?
W: Yes, it's called nongak.

① How often do you play strong beats?
② Can you explain how to play that music?
③ I wonder where that music is coming from.
④ Are you going to wish for a good harvest?
⑤ Do you want to dance to the rhythm?

[경북 ㅇㅇ중]

## 04 다음 빈칸에 알맞은 말을 넣어 자연스러운 대화를 완성할 때, 들어갈 수 있는 표현을 아래 〈보기〉에서 모두 고른 것은? (3점)

A: Are you going somewhere this summer?
B: I'm going to Jejudo to walk along the Jeju Olle Trail.
A: The Jeju Olle Trail? _____
B: It's a long hiking path around Jejudo.
A: Oh, I see. I hope you enjoy your trip!

보기
ⓐ Could you explain what that is?
ⓑ How many times did you go there?
ⓒ Can you tell me more about it?
ⓓ I wonder where you go.
ⓔ Do you need more information about that?

① ⓐ ② ⓐ, ⓒ
③ ⓐ, ⓒ, ⓔ ④ ⓐ, ⓒ, ⓓ, ⓔ
⑤ ⓐ, ⓑ, ⓒ, ⓓ, ⓔ

[충북 ㅇㅇ중]

## 05 다음 대화의 우리말과 일치하도록 괄호 안의 단어를 사용하여 대화를 완성하시오. (3점)

A: Wow, look at the photo. Isn't it beautiful?
B: Yes. It's so wonderful. I wonder _____ _____. (the photo) (나는 네가 그 사진을 어디서 찍었는지 궁금해.)
A: That's Gwangandaegyo in Busan. I went there with my family last summer.

→ I wonder _____.

[6~7] 다음 대화를 읽고 물음에 답하시오.

> Jaden: Do you hear that? I wonder where that music is coming from.
> Yuri: I think it's coming from over there. Do you want to go and check it out?
> Jaden: Yes, I love that strong beat. Is it traditional Korean music?
> Yuri: Yes, it's called *nongak*. It's a kind of community band music.
> Jaden: *Nongak*? Could you explain a little bit more about it?
> Yuri: It's traditionally used to cheer up farmers and wish for a good harvest.
> Jaden: I see. Look! Some people are dancing to the rhythm.
> Yuri: Yes, that's a big part of *nongak*. Dancing together completes the music.
> Jaden: Let's join them.
> Yuri: Sure. Why not?

**06** 위 대화의 'nongak'에 대한 내용과 일치하지 않는 것은? (4점)

① It has a strong beat.

② People can't dance to it.

③ It is used to cheer up farmers.

④ People use it to wish a good harvest.

⑤ It is a kind of community band music.

**07** 위 대화 후 'Jaden'과 'Yuri'의 행동으로 가장 적절한 것은? (3점)

① 농악을 배우러 간다.

② 농악 연주가에 대해 조사하러 간다.

③ 농악에 따라 춤추는 사람들과 합류한다.

④ 농악에 대해 음악 선생님에게 물어본다.

⑤ 농악 소리가 나는 곳이 어딘지 찾아본다.

**08** 다음 대화에 대한 질문의 적절한 대답은? (3점)

> B: Look over there. I wonder why there are so many people waiting in line.
> G: They're waiting to get into the new bakery there.
> B: Why? Is it famous?
> G: Yes. It was on a TV program.
> B: Really? We should try their bread then.
> G: Sure.

> Question: What are they going to do after the dialog?
> → They will _____.

① watch TV

② get in line

③ bake bread together

④ visit another bakery

⑤ speak to other people there

**09** 다음 (A)~(D)를 자연스러운 대화가 되도록 바르게 배열한 것은? (3점)

> (A) Sure. Press this button, and it'll tell you what to do.
> (B) Here you are.
> (C) Excuse me. I'd like to borrow an audio guide.
> (D) Could you explain how to use it?

① (C)-(A)-(B)-(D)   ② (C)-(B)-(D)-(A)

③ (C)-(D)-(A)-(B)   ④ (D)-(A)-(C)-(B)

⑤ (D)-(B)-(A)-(C)

**10** 다음 문장에서 어색한 부분을 찾아 바르게 고쳐 올바른 문장으로 쓰시오. (3점)

> • Nobody knows why was Tom late.
> → Nobody knows _____.

→ _____

[11~12] 다음 대화를 읽고 물음에 답하시오.

> Jaden: Do you hear that? (A)나는 저 음악이 어디서 나오는지 궁금해.
>
> Yuri: I think it's coming from over there. Do you want to go and check it out?
>
> Jaden: Yes, I love that strong beat. Is it traditional Korean music?
>
> Yuri: Yes, it's called *nongak*. It's a kind of community band music.
>
> Jaden: *Nongak*? Could you explain a little bit more about it?
>
> Yuri: It's traditionally used to cheer up farmers and wish for a good harvest.
>
> Jaden: I see. Look! Some people are dancing to the rhythm.
>
> Yuri: Yes, that's a big part of *nongak*. Dancing together completes the music.
>
> Jaden: Wow! I want to learn more about *nongak*.

## 11 위 대화의 내용과 일치하는 것은? (3점)

① Jaden asks Yuri for more information about nongak.

② Yuri becomes interested in traditional Korean song.

③ Nongak is a community music used to pray for rain on the harvest day.

④ Dancing is not allowed while nongak band plays music.

⑤ Jaden and Yuri are going to enjoy the rhythm by dancing with the band.

## 12 위 대화의 (A)를 〈보기〉의 단어를 모두 사용하여 하나의 문장으로 영작할 경우 5번째에 오는 단어는? (4점)

> **보기**
>
> coming / wonder / that / music / from / I / where / is

① music   ② wonder   ③ that

④ where   ⑤ from

## 13 다음 〈보기〉를 참고하여 주어진 두 문장을 연결하여 한 문장으로 고쳐 쓰시오. (어법이 <u>어색한</u> 경우 부분점수 없음.) (6점)

> **보기**
>
> • I wonder. + When will he come?
> → I wonder when he will come.

> (A) Can you tell me? + What did you do?
> (B) Nobody knows. + Why was she late?

(A) _____

(B) _____

## 14 다음 중 어법상 <u>어색한</u> 문장은? (4점)

① I didn't understand why she wanted to take pictures of us.

② He asked me where I had eaten lunch.

③ They have visited the place many times before.

④ I have gone shopping at the market before I had dinner.

⑤ She was tired after she had played in the water for two hours.

## 15 다음 빈칸 (A)에 들어갈 가장 적절한 것은? (3점)

> • I wonder. + What did he buy yesterday?
> → I wonder (A)_____.

① what he buy yesterday

② what he bought yesterday

③ what did he buy yesterday

④ what he did bought yesterday

⑤ what did he bought yesterday

**[16~17]** 다음 글을 읽고 물음에 답하시오.

For the past several years, the underwater photographer Zin Kim has advertised the culture of Jeju haenyeo worldwide. ⓐHaenyeo are Korean female divers that harvests seafood without any breathing devices. Their culture made UNESCO's Intangible Cultural Heritage list in 2016. At her studio last week, ⓑZin Kim interviewed about her experience of taking pictures of haenyeo.

Q. *How did you become interested in taking photos of haenyeo?*
A. One day, I got a chance to take pictures of a haenyeo. ⓒI was surprised to find that she was enjoying her job. Until then, I had only seen black-and-white photos of haenyeo who looked very tired. However, ⓓshe had kept laughing even after she was in the water for over five hours. I realized then that I should take pictures of haenyeo.

Q. *Could you tell us more about haenyeo?*
A. Sure. Because they stay in the water without any breathing devices, haenyeo can't catch a lot of seafood. This is good for the underwater environment. ⓔIt can destroy the ocean catching too much marine life at one time in one place.

**16** 위 글의 ⓐ~ⓔ 중 어법상 맞는 것은? (4점)

① ⓐ　② ⓑ　③ ⓒ　④ ⓓ　⑤ ⓔ

**17** 위 글에서 답을 찾을 수 없는 질문은? (3점)

① What is the definition of haenyeo?

② Why does the way haenyeo work protect the ocean?

③ In which year was Jeju haenyeo's culture added to UNESCO's list?

④ What made Zin Kim interested in taking photos of haenyeo?

⑤ How do haenyeo keep catching seafood underwater without any breathing devices?

*definition: 정의, 뜻

**[18~20]** 다음 글을 읽고 물음에 답하시오.

(A) I'll tell you three things. First, haenyeo are a symbol of ⓐstrong women. (B) Jejudo, which is a volcanic island, is not ⓑsuitable for farming, so many haenyeo have become the breadwinners for their families. (C) Second, haenyeo ⓒform their own communities and help each other. For example, more-experienced haenyeo ⓓjoin less-experienced haenyeo. (D) Third, because they stay in the water without any breathing devices, haenyeo can't catch a lot of seafood. (E) Catching too much marine life at one time in one place can ⓔdestroy the ocean.

**18** 위 글의 밑줄 친 ⓐ~ⓔ 중, 흐름상 낱말의 쓰임이 적절하지 않은 것은? (3점)

① ⓐ　② ⓑ　③ ⓒ　④ ⓓ　⑤ ⓔ

**19** 위 글의 흐름으로 보아 (A)~(E) 중, 다음 문장이 들어가기에 가장 적절한 곳은? (4점)

> This is good for the underwater environment.

① (A)　② (B)　③ (C)　④ (D)　⑤ (E)

**20** 위 글은 어떤 질문에 대한 대답인가? (3점)

① What are you planning to do in the future?

② How long can haenyeo breathe underwater?

③ What's so special about haenyeo?

④ What has Zin Kim done for the past several years?

⑤ How can you protect marine life?

[21~23] 다음 글을 읽고 물음에 답하시오.

"Q: You take beautiful pictures of them, but isn't it (A)_____ to take pictures of haenyeo?"
At first, they didn't understand the reason that I wanted to take their pictures. They didn't think they looked pretty in their wetsuits. I said to them, "You are very special. I want to show your culture to the world." They opened up to me then. Of course, I also promised them that (a)내 사진 속에서 그들을 아름답게 보이도록 해주겠다고.
"Q: Could you tell us more about haenyeo? What's so special about them?"
I can tell you three things. First, haenyeo are a (B)_____ of strong women. Jejudo, which is a volcanic island, is not suitable for farming, so many haenyeo have become the breadwinners for their families. Second, haenyeo form their own communities and help each other. For example, more-experienced haenyeo train less-experienced haenyeo. Third, because they stay in the water without any breathing devices, haenyeo can't catch a lot of seafood. This is good for the underwater environment. Catching too much marine life at one time in one place can (C)_____ the ocean.

**21** 위 글의 내용과 일치하는 것은? (3점)

① 해녀들은 잠수복을 입은 자신의 모습이 예뻐 보인다고 생각했다.
② 제주도는 농사짓기 좋은 섬이다.
③ 해녀들은 서로 가르쳐 주기보다는 스스로 훈련하는 경우가 많다.
④ 해녀들은 숨쉬기 위한 장치를 달고 물속에 머문다.
⑤ 한 장소에서 한 번에 많은 해양생물을 잡는 것은 환경에 좋지 않을 수 있다.

**22** (a)를 영작한 것으로 옳은 것은? (3점)

① I would make them to look beautiful in my pictures.
② I would make them look beautiful in my pictures.
③ I would making them to look beautiful in my pictures.
④ I would be beautiful to look them in my pictures.
⑤ I would look beautiful to them in my pictures.

**23** 위 글의 (A), (B), (C)에 들어갈 문맥상 알맞은 어휘로 짝지어진 것은? (3점)

|  | (A) | (B) | (C) |
|---|---|---|---|
| ① | difficult | symbol | destroy |
| ② | difficult | symptom | develop |
| ③ | different | symbol | destroy |
| ④ | different | symbol | develop |
| ⑤ | different | symptom | develop |

**24** 다음 글의 흐름으로 보아, 주어진 문장이 위치할 가장 적절한 곳은? (4점)

When I finished my talk, one of the haenyeo held my hand tightly.

(A) I once attended an overseas exhibition with a couple of haenyeo to give a talk about their lives. (B) She said to me, "Thank you so much. (C) I've never known in my life that I was such a special person." (D) She was crying with happiness. Everyone in the audience was deeply moved. (E)

① (A)　② (B)　③ (C)　④ (D)　⑤ (E)

[25~27] 다음 글을 읽고 물음에 답하시오.

*Q: Could you tell us more about haenyeo? What's so special about them?*

I can tell you three things. First, haenyeo are a symbol of strong women. Jejudo, which is a volcanic island, is not ⓐsuitable for farming, so many haenyeo have become the ⓑbreadwinners for their families. Second, haenyeo form their own communities and help each other.

For example, more-experienced haenyeo train ⓒless-experienced haenyeo. Third, because they stay in the water without any breathing devices, haenyeo can't catch a lot of seafood. This is ⓓgood for the underwater environment. Catching too much marine life at one time in one place can ⓔconserve ocean life.

*Q. Lastly, please tell us what you're planning to do in the future.*

I once (A)[attended / attended to] an overseas exhibition with a couple of haenyeo to give a talk about their lives. When I finished my talk, one of the haenyeo held my hand tightly. She said to me, "Thank you so much. I've never known in my whole life (가)that I was such a special person." She was crying with (B)[sadness / happiness]. Everyone in the audience (C)[were / was] deeply moved. I can never forget that moments, so I'll continue to take pictures of haenyeo. I want to tell more beautiful stories about them to many more people in the world.

**25** 위 글에서 문맥상 (A), (B), (C)에 들어갈 말로 가장 적절하게 짝지어진 것은?  (4점)

|  | (A) | (B) | (C) |
|---|---|---|---|
| ① | attended | sadness | were |
| ② | attended | happiness | was |
| ③ | attended to | happiness | was |
| ④ | attended to | sadness | were |
| ⑤ | attended to | sadness | was |

**26** 위 글의 밑줄 친 ⓐ~ⓔ 중 문맥상 낱말의 쓰임이 적절하지 않은 것은?  (4점)

① ⓐ  ② ⓑ  ③ ⓒ  ④ ⓓ  ⑤ ⓔ

**27** 위 글의 밑줄 친 (가)와 쓰임이 같은 것은?  (3점)

① The book that is on the desk is mine.
② The dress that she is wearing is new.
③ He is the man that I met yesterday.
④ She thinks that he is a thief.
⑤ Have you found the keys that you lost?

[28~29] 다음 글을 읽고 물음에 답하시오.

For the past several years, the underwater photographer Zin Kim has promoted the culture of Jeju haenyeo worldwide. Haenyeo are Korean female divers who harvest seafood without any breathing devices. Their culture made UNESCO's _____ Cultural Heritage list in 2016. At her studio last week, Zin Kim was interviewed about her experience of taking pictures of haenyeo.

**28** What has Zin Kim promoted for the past several years?  (4점)

① 제주도의 해산물을 홍보해 왔다.
② 한국에 해녀 문화를 홍보해 왔다.
③ UNESCO의 장점에 대해 홍보해 왔다.
④ 전 세계에 해녀 문화를 홍보해 왔다.
⑤ 제주도의 해안 사진을 찍어 홍보해 왔다.

**29** 위 글의 빈칸에 들어가기에 가장 적절한 단어는?  (3점)

① Unimportant  ② Visible  ③ Touchable
④ Intangible  ⑤ Material

◎ 선택형 문항의 답안은 컴퓨터용 수정 싸인펜을 사용하여 OMR 답안지에 바르게 표기하시오.
◎ 서술형 문제는 답을 답안지에 반드시 검정 볼펜으로 쓰시오.
◎ 총 27문항 100점 만점입니다. 문항별 배점은 각 문항에 표시되어 있습니다.

[전북 ○○중]

**01** 다음 밑줄 친 부분을 잘못 해석한 것은?　(3점)

One day, I happened to take pictures of a haenyeo. I was surprised to find that she was enjoying her job. Until then, I only have seen black-and-white photos of haenyeo who looked very tired. However, she kept laughing even after she had been in the water for over five hours. I realized then that I should take pictures of haenyeo.

① happened to: 우연히 ~했다
② was surprised to: ~해서 놀랐다
③ black-and-white: 흑백의
④ kept laughing: 계속 웃었다
⑤ realized: 실행했다

[전북 ○○중]

**02** 상대방에게 도움을 청할 때 빈칸에 적합한 단어를 각각 순서대로 쓰시오.　(4점)

> • Could you (A)_____ me a (B)_____?

→ (A)_____ (B)_____

[wjs북 ○○중]

**03** 다음 (A)~(E)를 자연스러운 대화가 되도록 배열할 때, 세 번째로 오는 것은?　(4점)

(A) It's a long hiking path around Jejudo.
(B) I'm going to Jejudo to walk along the Jeju Olle Trail.
(C) Oh, I see. I hope you enjoy your trip!
(D) The Jeju Olle Trail? Could you explain what that is?
(E) Are you going somewhere this summer?

① (A)　② (B)　③ (C)　④ (D)　⑤ (E)

[rud북 ○○중]

**04** According to the following dialogue, which is NOT true about nongak?　(4점)

Jaden: Do you hear that? I wonder where that music is coming from.
Yuri: I think it's coming from over there. Do you want to go and check it out?
Jaden: Yes, I love that strong beat. Is it traditional Korean music?
Yuri: Yes, it's called nongak. It's a kind of community band music.
Jaden: Nongak? Could you explain a little bit about it?
Yuri: It's traditionally used to cheer up farmers and wish for a good harvest.
Jaden: I see. Look! Some people are dancing to the rhythm.
Yuri: Yes, that's a big part of nongak. Dancing together completes the music.
Jaden: Let's join them.
Yuri: Sure. Why not?

① It has a strong beat.
② It's a traditional Korean music.
③ It's used to wish for a good harvest.
④ It's a sort of community band music.
⑤ It's music just for viewing and enjoying quietly.

[대전 ○○중]

**05** 대화의 빈칸 (A)에 가장 적절한 것은?　(3점)

Andy: Wow, look at the bridge in this ad. I wonder (A)_____ the photo was taken.
Robert: That's Gwangandaegyo in Busan. I went there with my family last summer.

① how　　② when　　③ what
④ where　　⑤ which

**[6~7]** 다음 대화를 읽고 물음에 답하시오.

Jaden: Do you hear that? I wonder (A)_____ that music is coming from.

Yuri: I think it's coming from over there. Do you want to go and check it out?

Jaden: Yes, I love that strong beat. Is it traditional Korean music?

Yuri: Yes, it's called nongak. It's a kind of community band music.

Jaden: Nongak? Could you explain a little bit more about it?

Yuri: It's traditionally used to cheer up farmers and wish for a good harvest.

Jaden: I see. Look! Some people are dancing to the rhythm.

Yuri: Yes, that's a big part of nongak. Dancing together completes the music.

Jaden: Let's join them.

Yuri: Sure. Why not?

**06** 위 대화의 빈칸 (A)에 들어갈 알맞은 것은? (3점)

① where　　② when　　③ how
④ why　　⑤ what

**07** 위 대화의 내용과 일치하는 것은? (4점)

① 몇몇 사람들이 리듬에 맞춰 노래를 부르고 있다.
② Jaden은 농악에 관심이 없다.
③ 농악은 해녀들의 힘을 북돋운다.
④ 농악은 공동체 악단 음악의 한 종류이다.
⑤ 두 사람은 공연에 참여하고 싶어 하지 않다.

**08** 다음 (A)~(D)를 자연스러운 대화가 되도록 바르게 배열한 것은? (4점)

(A) I agree. I wonder how we can promote that place worldwide.

(B) How about posting an article introducing the cultural heritage of Ikseon-dong on SNS with pictures?

(C) I think Ikseon-dong is a great place to experience Korean cultures.

(D) In that picture, people will know this place shows the harmony of the old and new cultures of Korea.

① (C)-(A)-(B)-(D)　　② (B)-(C)-(A)-(D)
③ (B)-(D)-(C)-(A)　　④ (A)-(C)-(B)-(D)
⑤ (C)-(D)-(A)-(B)

**09** 다음 대화의 흐름상 빈칸에 들어갈 말로 가장 적절한 것은? (3점)

A: Look over there. _____
B: They're waiting to get into the new bakery there.
A: Why? Is it famous?
B: Yes. It was on a TV program.
A: Really? We should try their bread then.
B: Sure.

① I wonder why there is a new store.
② I wonder what they ate for lunch.
③ I wonder why you look upset today.
④ I wonder why there is a boy riding a bicycle.
⑤ I wonder why there are so many people waiting in line.

**10** 다음 우리말에 맞도록 주어진 단어들을 사용하여 올바른 문장으로 만드시오. (5점)

why / understand / the boy / is / angry / his mom / doesn't (그 소년은 자신의 엄마가 왜 화가 나는지 이해하지 못한다.)

→ _____

**[11∼12] 다음 글을 읽고 물음에 답하시오.**

A: Do you hear that? I wonder where that music is coming from.

B: I think it's coming from over there. Do you want to go and check it out?

A: Yes, I love that strong beat. Is it traditional Korean music?

B: Yes, it's called nongak. It's a kind of community band music.

A: Nongak? Could you explain a little bit more about it?

B: It's traditionally used to cheer up farmers and wish for a good harvest.

A: I see. Look! Some people are dancing to the rhythm.

B: Yes, that's a big part of nongak. Dancing together completes the music.

A: ⓐ_____

B: Sure. Why not?

**11** 위 대화로 알 수 있는 사실이 <u>아닌</u> 것은? (4점)

① A likes a strong beat music.

② B knows the traditional Korean music, nongak.

③ Chances are that A hears the nongak for the first time.

④ Nongak is used to cheer up farmers and wish for a good harvest.

⑤ A wants to know about nongak in detail and now he hears the explanation of nongak from the band.

**12** 위 대화의 빈칸 ⓐ에 들어갈 말로 알맞지 <u>않은</u> 것은? (4점)

① Would you mind joining them?

② Why don't we join them?

③ How about joining them?

④ Shall we join them?

⑤ Let's join them.

**13** 다음 중 어법상 올바른 것은? (4점)

① Peter had lost the key that I gave to him.

② My father has gone to China three times.

③ How long has she lived there when she got married?

④ Before John arrived at home, his family has already left.

⑤ Last weekend, Mina bought a new cell phone with the money she had saved.

**14** 다음 주어진 문장을 어법상 적절하게 영어로 옮긴 것은? (3점)

> • 내가 기차역에 도착했을 때 기차는 이미 떠났다.

① I had arrived at the station after the train left.

② The train had already left when I arrived at the station.

③ When the train left, I had already arrived at the station.

④ When I arrived at the station, the train has already left.

⑤ I arrived at the station before the train had already left.

**15** 한 문장으로 바꿔 쓸 때 알맞은 것은? (3점)

> • I wonder. + Why did she leave so early?

① I wonder why did she leave so early.

② I wonder why she leave so early.

③ I wonder why she left so early.

④ I wonder why she leaves so early.

⑤ I wonder why she did left so early.

**[16~18]** 다음 글을 읽고, 물음에 답하시오.

For the past several years, the underwater photographer Zin Kim has promoted the culture of Jeju haenyeo worldwide. Haenyeo are Korean female divers who harvest seafood without any breathing devices. Their culture made UNESCO's Intangible Cultural Heritage list in 2016. At her studio last week, Zin Kim was interviewed about her experience of taking pictures of haenyeo.

*Q. How did you become interested in taking photos of haenyeo?*
One day, I happened to take pictures of a haenyeo. (A) I was surprised to find that she was enjoying her job. (B) Until then, I had only seen black-and-white photos of haenyeo who looked very tired. ⓐ_____, she kept laughing even after she had been in the water for over five hours. (C) I realized then that I should take pictures of haenyeo.

*Q. You take beautiful pictures of them, but isn't it difficult to take pictures of haenyeo?*
At first, they didn't understand why I wanted to take their pictures. (D) So, I said to them, "You're very special. I want to show your culture to the world." They opened up to me then. (E) Of course, I also promised them that I would make them look beautiful in my pictures.

**16** 위 글을 읽고 답할 수 <u>없는</u> 질문은? (3점)

① What does Zin Kim do for a living?
② What did Zin Kim promise the haenyeo?
③ Why did Zin Kim become a photographer?
④ Why did Zin Kim want to take pictures of haenyeo?
⑤ What has Zin Kim promoted for the past several years?

**17** 빈칸 ⓐ에 들어갈 말로 알맞은 것은? (4점)

① So   ② Finally   ③ Also
④ However   ⑤ Therefore

**18** 위 글의 (A)~(E) 중 다음 문장이 들어가기에 가장 알맞은 곳은? (4점)

Because they didn't think they looked pretty in their wetsuits.

① (A)   ② (B)   ③ (C)   ④ (D)   ⑤ (E)

**19** 다음 글의 괄호 (A), (B), (C) 안에서 문법상 적절한 표현끼리 짝지은 것은? (4점)

*Q. Lastly, please tell us what you're planning to do in the future.*
I once attended an overseas exhibition with a couple of haenyeo to give a talk about their lives. When I finished my talk, one of the haenyeo held my hand tightly. She said to me, "Thank you so much. I've never (A)[know / known] in my whole life that I was such a special person." She was crying with happiness.
Everyone in the audience (B)[was / were] deeply moved. I can never forget that moment, so I'll continue (C)[to take / take] pictures of haenyeo. I want to tell more beautiful stories about them to many more people in the world.

| | (A) | (B) | (C) |
|---|---|---|---|
| ① | known | was | take |
| ② | know | was | take |
| ③ | known | was | to take |
| ④ | know | were | to take |
| ⑤ | known | were | to take |

[20~22] 다음 글을 읽고 물음에 답하시오.

@For the past several years, the underwater photographer Zin Kim has promoted the culture of Jeju haenyeo worldwide. Haenyeo are Korean female divers who harvest seafood without any breathing devices. ⓑTheir culture made UNESCO's Intangible Cultural Heritage list in 2016. At her studio last week, Zin Kim was interviewed about her experience of taking pictures of haenyeo.

Q: ⓒHow did you become interested in taking photos of haenyeo?
ⓓOne day, I happened to taking pictures of a haenyeo. I was surprised (A)to find that she was enjoying her job. Until then, I had only seen black-and-white photos of haenyeo who looked very tired. However, ⓔshe kept laughing even after she had been in the water for over five hours. I realized then that I should take pictures of haenyeo.

Q: You take beautiful pictures of them, but isn't it difficult to take pictures of haenyeo?
At first, they didn't understand why I wanted to take their pictures. They didn't think they looked pretty in their wetsuits. So, I said to them, "You're very special. I want to show your culture to the world." They opened up to me then. Of course, I also promised them that I would make them look beautiful in my pictures.

## 20 위 글의 내용과 일치하지 않는 것은? (4점)

① 해녀는 호흡 장치 없이 해산물을 채취한다.
② 해녀 문화는 2016년에 유네스코 무형문화유산에 등재되었다.
③ Zin Kim은 제주 해녀로 활동하고 있다.
④ 처음에 해녀들은 자신들의 잠수복 입은 모습이 예뻐 보이지 않는다고 생각했다.
⑤ 사진작가는 사진에서 해녀들의 모습이 아름답게 나오도록 노력할 것이다.

## 21 위 글의 밑줄 친 @~ⓔ 중 어법상 어색한 문장은? (4점)

① @    ② ⓑ    ③ ⓒ    ④ ⓓ    ⑤ ⓔ

## 22 위 글의 밑줄 친 (A)와 용법이 같은 것은? (3점)

① We continue to do various projects for saving animals.
② Isn't it difficult to take pictures of haenyeo?
③ I was very excited to meet my Korean fans again.
④ Do you have time to help me write my essay?
⑤ The meeting is to be held next Friday.

## 23 다음 글의 흐름으로 보아 주어진 문장이 들어가기에 가장 적절한 곳은? (4점)

For example, more-experienced haenyeo train less-experienced haenyeo.

Q: Could you tell us more about haenyeo? What's so special about them?
I can tell you three things. (A) First, haenyeo are a symbol of strong women. Jejudo, which is a volcanic island, is not suitable for farming, so many haenyeo have become the breadwinners for their families. (B) Second, haenyeo form their own communities and help each other. (C) Third, because they stay in the water without any breathing devices, haenyeo can't catch a lot of seafood. (D) This is good for the underwater environment. (E) Catching too much marine life at one time in one place can destroy the ocean.

① (A)    ② (B)    ③ (C)    ④ (D)    ⑤ (E)

[24~25] 다음 글을 읽고 물음에 답하시오.

*Q. (A)_____*
I can tell you three things. First, haenyeo are a symbol of strong women. Jejudo, which is a volcanic island, is not suitable for farming, so many haenyeo have become the breadwinners for their families. Second, haenyeo form their own communities and help each other. For example, more-experienced haenyeo train less-experienced haenyeo. Third, because they stay in the water without any breathing devices, haenyeo can't catch a lot of seafood. This is good for the underwater environment. Catching too much marine life at one time in one place can destroy the ocean.

*Q. Lastly, please tell us what you're planning to do in the future.*
I once attended an overseas exhibition with a couple of haenyeo to give a talk about their lives. When I finished my talk, one of the haenyeo held my hand tightly. She said to me, "Thank you so much. I've never known in my whole life that I was such a special person." ⓐShe was crying with happiness. Everyone in the audience was deeply moved. I can never forget that moment, so I'll continue to take pictures of haenyeo. I want to tell more beautiful stories about them to many more people in the world.

**24** 빈칸 (A)에 들어갈 가장 적절한 것은? (4점)

① What is special about haenyeo?

② What kind of seafood do you like?

③ How can you take pictures of haenyeo?

④ Why is Jejudo not suitable for farming?

⑤ Why can't haenyeo catch a lot of seafood?

**25** ⓐ에 담겨 있는 감정으로 적절한 것은? (3점)

① 슬픔　　② 후회　　③ 안도

④ 걱정　　⑤ 기쁨

[26~27] 다음 글을 읽고 물음에 답하시오.

*Q. How did you become interested in taking photos of haenyeo?*
One day, I happened to take pictures of a haenyeo. I was surprised to find that she was enjoying her job. Until then, I had only seen black-and-white photos of haenyeo who looked very tired. However, she kept laughing even after she had been in the water for over five hours. I realized then that (A)_____.

*Q. You take beautiful pictures of them, but isn't it difficult to take pictures of haenyeo?*
At first, they didn't understand why I wanted to take their pictures. They didn't think they looked pretty in their wetsuits. So, I said to them, "You're very special. I want to show your culture to the world." They opened up to me then. Of course, I also promised them that I would make them look beautiful in my pictures.

**26** 위 글의 빈칸 (A)에 들어갈 말로 가장 적절한 것은? (4점)

① it is very hard for haenyeo to hold their breath

② I took only black-and-white photos

③ I should take pictures of haenyeo

④ they are interested in staying in the water

⑤ the ocean is in danger because of the plastic waste

**27** 위 글의 내용과 일치하지 <u>않는</u> 것은? (4점)

① 처음에 해녀들은 작가를 이해하지 못했다.

② 해녀들은 잠수복을 입은 자신들의 모습이 예쁘지 않다고 생각했다.

③ 작가는 해녀의 문화를 세계에 알리고자 했다.

④ 해녀들은 작가의 말을 듣고 마음을 열었다.

⑤ 해녀들은 아름답게 보이도록 하겠다고 약속했다.

◎ 선택형 문항의 답안은 컴퓨터용 수정 싸인펜을 사용하여 OMR 답안지에 바르게 표기하시오.
◎ 서술형 문제는 답을 답안지에 반드시 검정 볼펜으로 쓰시오.
◎ 총 29문항 100점 만점입니다. 문항별 배점은 각 문항에 표시되어 있습니다.

[전북 ○○중]

**01** 다음 중 짝지어진 단어의 관계가 〈보기〉와 같은 것은?　(3점)

> 보기
>
> person : personal

① decide : decision
② reserve : reservation
③ visible : invisible
④ stress : stressful
⑤ graduate : graduation

[충북 ○○중]

**02** 다음 글의 빈칸에 들어갈 말로 적절한 것은?　(4점)

> Do you think you have a unique problem? _____ are that many other people have the same problem. (아마 다른 많은 사람들이 여러분과 똑같이 고민을 가지고 있을 것이다.) Psychology is the study of the human mind and behavior, so it can help you find a solution to your problem.

① Chances　② Maybe　③ Problems
④ There　⑤ Times

[전북 ○○중]

**03** 다음 대화를 읽고 (A)에 주어진 철자들을 올바른 순서로 쓰시오.　(3점)

> W: Shall we try that new Mexican restaurant tomorrow?
> M: Why not? I'll call the restaurant to make a reservation for us.
> W: You don't have to call them. You can do it online.
> M: Oh, I see. How (A)[t,v,n,c,n,n,e,e,o,i]!

→ _____

[충북 ○○중]

**04** 다음 대화의 내용과 일치하지 <u>않는</u> 것은?　(3점)

> Yuri: Hi, Jaden. Sports Day is next Friday. I can't wait!
> Jaden: Really? I'm actually worried about it.
> Yuri: Why? Aren't you good at sports?
> Jaden: Yes, I am, but I'm worried about the 800-meter relay.
> Yuri: What do you mean?
> Jaden: I'm the last runner. What if our team loses because of me?
> Yuri: I think you're putting too much pressure on yourself.
> Jaden: Really? Don't you think I should practice every day?
> Yuri: No, you don't have to do that. It's just a school race. It's not about winning or losing.
> Jaden: I guess you're right, Yuri. I'm lucky to have a friend like you.

① 체육대회는 다음 주에 열린다.
② Jaden은 운동을 잘한다.
③ Jaden은 릴레이 경주의 마지막 주자이다.
④ Yuri는 Jaden이 매일 달리기를 연습해야 한다고 생각한다.
⑤ Jaden은 Yuri의 생각에 동의한다.

[전북 ○○중]

**05** 다음 대화의 순서가 바르게 배열된 것은?　(3점)

> (A) Don't worry. You've prepared a lot. You'll do a great job.
> (B) Well. I'm concerned about my presentation in history class.
> (C) You look a bit nervous.
> (D) Thanks. I feel much better now.

① (A)-(C)-(B)-(D)　② (B)-(A)-(C)-(D)
③ (B)-(C)-(A)-(D)　④ (C)-(B)-(A)-(D)
⑤ (C)-(A)-(B)-(D)

**[6~7] 다음 대화를 읽고, 물음에 답하시오.**

> Yuri: Hi, Jaden. Sports Day is next Friday. I can't wait!
>
> Jaden: Really? I'm actually worried about it.
>
> Yuri: Why? Aren't you good (A)_____ sports?
>
> Jaden: Yes, I am, but I'm worried about the 800-meter relay.
>
> Yuri: What do you mean?
>
> Jaden: I'm the last runner. What if our team loses because of me?
>
> Yuri: I think you're putting too much pressure on yourself.
>
> Jaden: Really? Don't you think I should practice every day?
>
> Yuri: No, you don't have to do that. It's just a school race. It's not about winning or losing.
>
> Jaden: I guess you're right, Yuri. I'm lucky to have a friend (B)_____ you.

**06** 위 대화의 빈칸 (A)와 (B)에 들어갈 말이 순서대로 짝지어진 것은? (4점)

① in - at  ② in - for  ③ at - by
④ at - like  ⑤ at - with

**07** 위 대화의 내용과 일치하는 것은? (3점)

① Yuri is waiting for Sports Day.
② Jaden has nothing to worry about.
③ Jaden is the first runner of the relay.
④ Yuri thinks Jaden should practice every day.
⑤ Jaden is not putting pressure on himself.

**08** 다음 대화의 빈칸에 들어갈 말로 가장 적절한 것은? (3점)

> B: You look a bit nervous.
> G: I'm worried about my swimming competition this Saturday.
> B: Don't worry. You're such a good swimmer. _____
> G: Thanks. I feel much better now.

① I don't think you can do it.
② Just relax and enjoy yourself.
③ Just think about another career.
④ You will compete with best teams.
⑤ Swimming is a good exercise for you.

**09** 다음 대화를 읽고, 개가 쓴 요약문의 빈칸에 들어갈 단어를 조건에 맞게 쓰시오. (4점)

> G: What happened to your shoes? Aren't they new?
> B: Yes, but my dog chewed them. He does it all the time. I'm worried about him.
> G: He was probably bored. Why don't you play with him more often?
> B: OK, I will. I hope he will stop chewing my shoes.

 The dog: I chewed the boy's new shoes. He is worried about me because I chew his shoes all the time. The girl advised _____ _____ _____ with me more often. He hopes I will stop chewing his shoes.

→ _____ _____ _____

**10** 다음 두 문장의 뜻이 같도록 할 때 빈칸에 알맞은 것은? (3점)

> • Feeling tired, my mom went to bed early.
> = _____ my mom was tired, she went to bed early.

① While  ② Because  ③ After
④ If  ⑤ Although

**[11~12] 다음 대화를 읽고 물음에 답하시오.**

Yuri: Hi, Jaden. Sports Day is next Friday. I can't wait! (A)

Jaden: Really? I'm actually worried about it.

Yuri: Why? Aren't you good at sports? (B)

Jaden: Yes, I am, but I'm worried about the 800-meter relay.

Yuri: What do you mean? (C)

Jaden: I'm the last runner. (D)

Yuri: I think you're putting too much pressure on yourself. (E)

Jaden: Really? Don't you think I should practice every day?

Yuri: ⓐ_____ It's just a school race. It's not about winning or losing.

Jaden: I guess you're right, Yuri. I'm lucky to have a friend like you.

**11** 위 대화의 흐름으로 보아 주어진 문장이 들어가기에 가장 적절한 곳은? (4점)

> What if our team loses because of me?

① (A)　② (B)　③ (C)　④ (D)　⑤ (E)

**12** 위 대화의 빈칸 ⓐ에 들어갈 말로 가장 적절한 것은? (3점)

① Yes, you should do that.

② No, you must not practice.

③ No, you don't have to do that.

④ Yes, you need to be good at running.

⑤ No, you should not be the last runner.

**13** 다음 중 대화의 내용이 자연스럽지 <u>않은</u> 것은? (3점)

① A: Let's join the dancing farmers.

　B: Sure. Why not?

② A: This is a personal question.

　B: I see. Then I have to answer it.

③ A: Do you have any good ideas?

　B: Yes, I just came up with a great idea!

④ A: I'm worried about the science project.

　B: Don't worry! How about doing it together?

⑤ A: What are you planning to do in the future?

　B: I want to take more beautiful pictures of Haenyeo.

**14** 다음 중 어법상 옳은 문장은? (4점)

① She can read not only German but also speak.

② Mina not only dances well but also singing well.

③ These shoes are not only light but also very cheaply.

④ I not only finished my homework but also read a book.

⑤ Mr. Kim is not only a good teacher but being a good leader.

**15** 다음 밑줄 친 부분 중 어법상 <u>어색한</u> 것은? (3점)

① <u>Seeing</u> him, I felt very happy.

② <u>Being</u> lonely, she called her mother.

③ <u>Thought</u> her baby was asleep, she walked quietly.

④ <u>Having</u> a test tomorrow, Judy is studying now.

⑤ <u>Watching</u> TV, I fell asleep on the sofa.

[16~19] 다음 글을 읽고 물음에 답하시오.

When he becomes a college student next year, Taeho wants to become a farmer. However, he has never told anyone about it. He is worried that his parents or his friends will not understand. As he wanted to clear his mind, Taeho decided to take a day trip on a train by himself. On the train, he told a complete stranger sitting beside him about his problem.

After that, he felt much better when he got off the train. Strangely enough, we often tell strangers about our problems just like Taeho. Do you know why? Since we won't see the strangers again, we don't need to worry that they will judge us. If you have a problem that you cannot share with your family or friends, try talking to a stranger. You will feel much better.

Benjamin Franklin once had a political rival who did not like ⓐhim at all. Franklin wanted to become friends with ⓑhim, so ⓒhe thought of a plan. His rival had a rare book. Franklin asked his rival to lend ⓓhim the book for a few days. When Franklin returned the book, ⓔhe thanked his rival deeply. Since that day, (A)그의 경쟁자는 정치적인 후원자뿐만 아니라 좋은 친구가 되었다. Franklin famously said, "Enemies who do you one favor will want to do more." If you want to turn a rival into a friend, don't do your rival a favor. Instead, make your rival do you a favor.

**16** 위 글의 내용과 일치하지 <u>않는</u> 것은?  (4점)

① Taeho has not yet graduated from high school.

② Taeho went on a trip alone and met a stranger.

③ Taeho carefully listened to the advice he got from the stranger.

④ Franklin became a good friend with his enemy after Franklin showed deep appreciation to him.

⑤ Franklin borrowed a rare book from his rival and returned it.

**17** 위 글의 ⓐ~ⓔ 중 가리키는 대상이 <u>다른</u> 것은?  (3점)

① ⓐ    ② ⓑ    ③ ⓒ    ④ ⓓ    ⑤ ⓔ

**18** 위 글을 요약한 다음 글 중 <u>어색한</u> 것은?  (4점)

| | | |
|---|---|---|
| Problem | ⓐ You have a problem that might not be understood. | ⓑ You have a rival, and want to be a friend with him/her. |
| Solution | ⓒ Try sharing your concern with a stranger! | Ask a rival to do you a favor |
| Explanation | ⓓ As we don't meet them again, we have no worry about being judged. | ⓔ Enemies will want to do you a favor if you do them one favor. |

① ⓐ    ② ⓑ    ③ ⓒ    ④ ⓓ    ⑤ ⓔ

**19** 위 글의 밑줄 친 (A)를 영어로 옮길 때 옳은 것은?  (4점)

① his rival became not only a good friend but also a political supporter.

② his rival became not a political supporter but a good friend.

③ his rival became a good friend as well as a political supporter.

④ his rival became a political supporter as well as a good friend.

⑤ his rival became as well as political supporter and a good friend.

[20~22] 다음 글을 읽고 물음에 답하시오.

Benjamin Franklin once had a political rival who did not like him at all. Franklin wanted to become friends with him, so he came up with a plan. His rival had a rare book. Franklin asked his rival to lend him the book for a few days. When Franklin returned the book, he thanked him deeply. Since that day, his rival became (A)[a political / also / friend / not / a good / but / supporter / only]. Franklin famously said, "(B)_____" If you want to turn a rival into a friend, don't do your rival a favor. Instead, ask your rival to do you a favor.

**20** 위 글의 빈칸 (B)에 들어갈 표현으로 가장 적절한 것은? (3점)

① I want you to do me a favor.
② Enemies who do you one favor will want to do more.
③ Enemies will not do you a favor.
④ Give rivals a favor.
⑤ Rivals always know what my favorite thing is.

**21** 위 글을 읽고 대답할 수 없는 질문은? (4점)

① What was Benjamin Franklin's plan?
② What did Benjamin Franklin's rival have?
③ What was the name of Benjamin Franklin's rival?
④ What did Benjamin Franklin ask his rival to do?
⑤ What could you do if you want to turn a rival into a friend?

**22** 위 글의 (A)를 주어진 해석에 맞게 재배열하여 문장을 완성하시오. (4점)

> • 그날부터, 그의 경쟁자는 정치적 지지자뿐만 아니라 좋은 친구가 되었다.
> → Since that day, his rival became _____
> _____.

→ _____

[23~24] 다음 글을 읽고 물음에 답하시오.

When he graduates from high school next year, Taeho wants to become a professional farmer. However, he has never told anyone about it. He is worried that his parents or his friends will not understand. ⓐWant to clear his mind, Taeho decided to take a day trip on a train by himself. On the train, he told a complete stranger ⓑsitting beside him about his problem. He had no idea ⓒwhy he did it. However, he felt ⓓmuch better when he got off the train. Strangely enough, we often tell strangers about our problems just like Taeho. That is because we do not have to worry about being judged or ⓔseeing them again. If you have a problem that you cannot share with your family or friends, _____. You will feel better.

**23** 위 글의 밑줄 친 ⓐ~ⓔ 중 어법상 어색한 것은? (3점)

① ⓐ    ② ⓑ    ③ ⓒ    ④ ⓓ    ⑤ ⓔ

**24** 위 글의 빈칸에 문맥상 들어갈 가장 적절한 말은? (3점)

① make an effort to take a trip by yourself
② try not to meet your friends when you feel lonely
③ try to have a realistic job
④ try talking to a total stranger
⑤ try to talk with counselors about your problem

**[25~27]** 다음 글을 읽고 물음에 답하시오.

When he graduates from high school next year, Taeho wants to become a professional farmer. However, he ⓐhad never told anyone about it. He is worried that his parents or his friends will not understand. Because he wanted to clear his mind, Taeho decided to take a day trip on a train by himself. On the train, he told a complete stranger ⓑsat beside him about his problem. He had no idea why he did it. However, he felt ⓒmany better when he got off the train. ⓓEnough strangely, we often tell strangers about our problems just like Taeho. (A)That is because we do not have to worry about being _____ or seeing them again. If you have a problem that you cannot share with your family or friends, try ⓔtalking to a stranger. You will feel much better.

**25** 위 글의 내용과 일치하는 것은? (3점)

① 태호는 대학교를 졸업하면 농부가 되고 싶다.

② 태호의 친구들과 부모님들은 태호의 꿈을 이해하지 못했다.

③ 태호는 혼자서 버스를 타고 하루 동안 여행을 떠나기로 결심했다.

④ 태호는 모르는 사람에게 그의 문제에 관해 말하기를 망설였다.

⑤ 낯선 사람에게 자신의 문제에 관해 이야기하면 기분이 나아질 수 있다.

**26** 위 글의 ⓐ~ⓔ 중 어법상 옳은 것은? (4점)

① ⓐ　　② ⓑ　　③ ⓒ　　④ ⓓ　　⑤ ⓔ

**27** 위 글의 (A)의 해석을 참고하여 빈칸에 들어갈 어휘를 올바른 형태로 쓰시오. (3점)

> **해석**
> • 그것은 우리가 판단되거나 그 사람을 다시 볼 것이라는 걱정을 할 필요가 없기 때문이다.

(A) _____

**[28~29]** 다음 글을 읽고 물음에 답하시오.

It was five minutes before Jisu's big presentation in front of the whole class. Feeling nervous, Jisu was carefully studying her notes in her chair. (가)_____ According to Amy Cuddy, a famous psychologist, we can become more confident just by standing tall for two minutes before stressful events. Our bodies change our minds, and our minds can change our behavior. Do you want to feel confident? Stand with your feet apart, and place your hands on your hips. You will not only feel sure about yourself but also look confident to other people.

**28** 위 글의 빈칸 (가)에 들어갈 내용의 순서로 가장 적절한 것은? (4점)

> (A) In fact, she was confident that she would make a great presentation.
> (B) Then, her teacher came over and told her to stand tall like Wonder Woman.
> (C) After standing tall for a few minutes, Jisu did not feel nervous anymore.

① (A)-(B)-(C)　　　② (A)-(C)-(B)

③ (B)-(A)-(C)　　　④ (B)-(C)-(A)

⑤ (C)-(B)-(A)

**29** 위 글의 제목으로 가장 적절한 것은? (4점)

① How to Become Less Nervous

② The Importance of Looking Confident

③ The Advice on Getting a Good Result

④ Meeting with a Famous Psychologist

⑤ A Way to Positive Attitude in Presentation

# 3학년 영어 2학기 중간고사(5과) 2회

문항수 : 선택형(29문항) 서술형(2문항)

반
이
름

점수

20 .   .   .

◎ 선택형 문항의 답안은 컴퓨터용 수정 싸인펜을 사용하여 OMR 답안지에 바르게 표기하시오.
◎ 서술형 문제는 답을 답안지에 반드시 검정 볼펜으로 쓰시오.
◎ 총 31문항 100점 만점입니다. 문항별 배점은 각 문항에 표시되어 있습니다.

[전북 ㅇㅇ중]

## 01 다음 중 짝지어진 단어의 관계가 <u>어색한</u> 것은? (2점)

① profession - professional
② tradition - traditional
③ magic - magicful
④ use - useful
⑤ care - careful

[전북 ㅇㅇ중]

## 02 다음 〈보기〉에서 밑줄 친 단어와 의미상 비슷한 것은? (3점)

보기

Do you think you have a unique problem? <u>Chances are that</u> many other people have the same problem.

① Probably   ② Strangely   ③ Differently
④ Surprisingly ⑤ Interestingly

[경북 ㅇㅇ중]

## 03 다음 대화의 빈칸에 들어갈 표현으로 가장 적절한 것은? (3점)

A: What happened to your shoes? Aren't they new?
B: Yes, but my dog chewed them. He does it all the time. _____
A: He was probably bored. Why don't you play with him more often?
B: O.K., I will. I hope he will stop chewing my shoes.

① I'm happy with it.
② I'm satisfied with it.
③ I'm worried about him.
④ I promise it won't happen again.
⑤ You don't have to worry about him.

[전북 ㅇㅇ중]

## 04 다음 대화의 내용과 일치하는 것은? (3점)

Yuri:   Hi, Jaden. Sports Day is next Friday. I can't wait!
Jaden:  Really? I'm actually worried about it.
Yuri:   Why? Aren't you good at sports?
Jaden:  Yes, I am, but I'm worried about the 800-meter relay.
Yuri:   What do you mean?
Jaden:  I'm the last runner. What if our team loses because of me?
Yuri:   I think you're putting too much pressure on yourself.
Jaden:  Really? Don't you think I should practice every day?
Yuri:   No, you don't have to do that. It's just a school race. It's not about winning or losing.
Jaden:  I guess you're right, Yuri. I'm lucky to have a friend like you.

① Jaden isn't good at sports.
② Jaden's team lost the 800-meter relay because of him.
③ Yuri isn't looking forward to Sports Day.
④ Yuri is advising Jaden to practice every day.
⑤ Yuri thinks Jaden is under too much pressure to win the 800-meter relay.

[전북 ㅇㅇ중]

## 05 다음 주어진 문장 다음에 이어질 대화가 자연스럽게 되도록 (A)~(C)를 바르게 배열한 것은? (3점)

You look a bit nervous.
(A) Don't worry. You're such a good swimmer. Relax and enjoy yourself!
(B) Thanks. I feel much better now.
(C) I'm worried about my swimming competition this Saturday.

① (C)-(A)-(B)      ② (C)-(B)-(A)
③ (A)-(C)-(B)      ④ (B)-(C)-(A)
⑤ (A)-(B)-(C)

[6~8] 다음 대화를 읽고 물음에 답하시오.

> Yuri: Hi, Jaden. Sports Day is next Friday. I can't wait!
> Jaden: (A) Really? I'm actually worried about it.
> Yuri: Why? Aren't you good at sports?
> Jaden: Yes, I am, but I'm worried about the 800-meter relay.
> Yuri: What do you mean?
> Jaden: I'm the last runner. (B)
> Yuri: I think you're putting too much pressure on yourself.
> Jaden: (C) Really? Don't you think I should practice every day? (D)
> Yuri: No, you ⓐ_____ do that. It's a just a school race. It's not about winning or losing.
> Jaden: (E) I guess you're right, Yuri. I'm lucky to have a friend like you.

**06** 위 대화의 (A)~(E) 중 주어진 말이 들어갈 위치로 알맞은 것은? (3점)

> What if our team loses because of me?

① (A)　② (B)　③ (C)　④ (D)　⑤ (E)

**07** 위 대화의 빈칸 ⓐ에 들어갈 말로 가장 적절한 것은? (2점)

① can　　② must not　③ cannot
④ don't have to　　⑤ have to

**08** 위 대화의 내용과 일치하는 것은? (3점)

① Yuri is giving Jaden some advice.
② Jaden is excited about the 400-meter relay.
③ Yuri thinks Jaden is putting too much pressure on his teammates.
④ Yuri thinks Jaden should practice every day.
⑤ Sports Day is next Thursday.

[9~10] 다음 대화를 읽고 물음에 답하시오.

> Suho: Mom, what time are we going to Grandma's place tomorrow morning?
> Mom: About 8 a.m. I'm going to bake cookies for her before we go.
> Suho: Then, should I get up early to help you?
> Mom: _____ Your dad will help me.
> Suho: O.K., then. Good night, Mom!

**09** 위 대화의 빈칸에 들어갈 말로 적절한 것은? (3점)

① Of course.
② You should,
③ You don't have to.
④ You are going to do that.
⑤ You are wrong about me.

**10** What will Suho do tomorrow morning? (4점)

① He will get up early.
② He is going to help his mom.
③ He will buy some cookies at a bakery.
④ He is going to his grandma's place.
⑤ He is going to bake cookies for his grandma.

**11** 다음 대화의 순서가 바르게 배열된 것은? (3점)

> (A) Why not? I'll call the restaurant to make a reservation for us.
> (B) Shall we try that new Mexican restaurant tomorrow?
> (C) Oh, I see. How convenient!
> (D) You don't have to call them. You can do it online.

① (A)-(D)-(B)-(C)　② (C)-(B)-(A)-(D)
③ (C)-(A)-(B)-(D)　④ (B)-(C)-(A)-(D)
⑤ (B)-(A)-(D)-(C)

## 12 다음 대화의 ⓐ~ⓔ 중 흐름상 어색한 것은? (4점)

Yuri: Hi, Jaden. School's dance festival is next Friday. I can't wait to see your dance!

Jaden: Really? I'm afraid I'll make a mistake. ⓐDon't you think I should practice hard?

Yuri: No, you don't have to do that. ⓑYou're a good dancer.

Jaden: I'm too nervous. ⓒWhat if our dance team loses because of me?

Yuri: Don't get so nervous. ⓓThere's no need to put too much pressure on yourself.

Jaden: I guess you're right. ⓔI should practice much harder than now.

Yuri: There you go. Just relax and enjoy yourself as you said!

① ⓐ    ② ⓑ    ③ ⓒ    ④ ⓓ    ⑤ ⓔ

## 13 다음 대화의 빈칸에 들어갈 말로 알맞은 것은? (3점)

W: Shall we try that new Mexican restaurant tomorrow?

M: Why not? I'll call the restaurant to make a reservation for us.

W: _____ You can do it online.

M: Oh, I see. How convenient!

① You should call them.

② You don't have to call them.

③ You must call them.

④ You haven't called them.

⑤ You'd better call them.

## 14 다음 밑줄 친 부분이 어법상 어색한 것은? (4점)

① Watching TV, I fell asleep on the sofa.

② Inviting to the party, she did not come.

③ Not feeling well, he didn't go to school today.

④ After having lunch, I went out to walk my dog.

⑤ A black cloud appeared, covering the whole sky.

## 15 다음 중 어법상 맞는 것은? (3점)

① Not only she but also he are good at dancing.

② He not only sings well but also play the piano well.

③ She as well as you need to learn how to solve the problem.

④ I am concerned about not only punished but also being judged.

⑤ As she had no friends at the party, she felt not only lonely but also embarrassed.

## 16 다음 주어진 문장을 〈조건〉에 맞추어 접속사가 있는 문장으로 바꾸어 쓰시오. (5점)

조건
• 문장의 의미에 어울리는 접속사를 사용할 것. (단, as는 제외), 전체 문장을 옮겨 적을 것.

(1) Coming home late from school, he sent a text message to his dad.

→ _____

(2) Feeling lonely, she called her mother.

→ _____

**[17~21] 다음 글을 읽고, 물음에 답하시오.**

Do you think you have a unique problem? (A)Chances are that many other people have the same problem. Psychology is the study of the human mind and behavior, so it can help you find a solution to your problem.

How do I become less ⓐ_____?

It was five minutes before Jisu's big presentation in front of the whole class. Feeling nervous, Jisu was carefully studying her notes in her chair. Then, her teacher came over and told her to stand tall like Wonder Woman. After standing tall for a few minutes, Jisu did not feel nervous anymore. In fact, she was ⓑ_____ that she would make a great presentation. According to Amy Cuddy, a famous psychologist, we can become more ⓒ_____ just by standing tall for two minutes before stressful events. Our bodies change our minds, and our minds can change our behavior. Do you want to feel ⓓ_____? (B)Stand with your feet part, and place your hands on your hips. You will not only feel sure about yourself but also look ⓔ_____ to other people.

**17** 위 글의 빈칸 ⓐ~ⓔ에 들어갈 단어가 <u>다른</u> 것은? (3점)

① ⓐ　　② ⓑ　　③ ⓒ　　④ ⓓ　　⑤ ⓔ

**18** 위 글의 밑줄 친 (A)의 의미로 가장 알맞은 것은? (3점)

① 당신의 고민에 공감하는 사람은 없을 것이다.
② 고민이 없는 사람은 거의 없을 것이다.
③ 많은 사람이 같은 문제로 고민할 것이다.
④ 많은 사람이 고민으로부터 자유로워지기를 원할 것이다.
⑤ 사람들은 큰 고민거리가 생길 기회가 많을 것이다.

**19** 위 글의 전개 방법으로 가장 알맞은 것은? (4점)

① Watch and Play
② Cause and Effect
③ Problem and Solution
④ Write and Speak
⑤ Supporting ideas and Main idea

**20** 위 글에서 Amy Cuddy가 주장하는 바로 가장 적절한 것은? (3점)

① 생각을 바꾸면 감정을 바꿀 수 있다.
② 꼿꼿이 오래 서 있으면 건강이 좋아진다.
③ 인간만이 감정을 조절할 수 있다.
④ 일관된 생각을 가지면 확신을 얻을 수 있다.
⑤ 행동을 통해 감정을 조절할 수 있다.

**21** 위 글의 밑줄 친 (B)에서 <u>어색한</u> 부분을 찾아 바르게 고쳐 쓰시오. (4점)

→ (1) 어색한 것: _____
　 (2) 고친 것: _____

**22** 다음 빈칸에 들어갈 가장 알맞은 말은? (3점)

The hardest time in my life was my first grade in middle school. When my family moved to Gunsan, I had to go to a new school. Having no friends at school, I felt sad and lonely. One day, I asked one of my classmates to show me her notes. She not only helped me but also became a good friend. From this experience, I have learned that _____ is a good way to make friends.

① giving help
② asking for help
③ feeling sad and lonely
④ moving to another school
⑤ talking a lot about myself

Do you think you have a ⓐunique problem? Chances are (A)[that / which] many other people have the same problem. Psychology is the study of the human mind and behavior, so it can help you find a ⓑsolution to your problem.

How do I become less nervous?
It was five minutes before Jisu's big presentation in front of the whole class. (B)[Feel / Feeling] nervous, Jisu was carefully studying her notes in her chair. Then, her teacher came over and told her to stand tall like Wonder Woman. After standing tall for a few minutes, Jisu did not feel nervous anymore. In fact, she was confident that she would make a great presentation. According to Amy Cuddy, a famous ⓒpsychologist, we can become more confident just by standing tall for two minutes before ⓓrelaxing events. Our bodies change our minds, and our minds can change our behavior. Do you want to feel confident? Stand with your feet apart, and ⓔput your hands on your hips. You will not only feel sure about yourself but also (C)[look / looking] confident to other people.

**23** 위 글의 ⓐ~ⓔ 중, 문맥상 낱말의 쓰임이 적절하지 <u>않은</u> 것은?
(4점)

① ⓐ　　② ⓑ　　③ ⓒ　　④ ⓓ　　⑤ ⓔ

**24** 위 글의 내용과 일치하지 <u>않는</u> 것은?　　(3점)

① 심리학은 인간의 마음과 행동을 연구한다.
② 몇 분간 우뚝 선 후에, 지수는 더 이상 긴장하지 않았다.
③ 지수는 반 전체 앞에서의 발표를 앞두고 긴장하고 있었다.
④ 선생님이 지수에게 원더우먼처럼 꼿꼿이 서 있으라고 하셨다.
⑤ 지수는 긴장하지 않고 의자에 앉아 노트를 들여다보고 있었다.

**25** 위 글의 괄호 (A), (B), (C) 안에서 어법에 맞는 낱말로 가장 적절한 것은?　　(3점)

|  | (A) | (B) | (C) |
|---|---|---|---|
| ① | that | Feel | look |
| ② | that | Feeling | look |
| ③ | which | Feel | look |
| ④ | which | Feeling | looking |
| ⑤ | that | Feel | looking |

[26~27] 다음 글을 읽고 물음에 답하시오.

ⓐ<u>The hardest time in my life was my first grade in middle school.</u> ⓑ<u>When my family moved to Gunsan, I had to go to a new school.</u> ⓒ<u>Having no friends at school, I felt excited and pleasant.</u> ⓓ<u>One day, I asked one of my classmates to show me her notes.</u> ⓔ<u>She not only helped me but also became a good friend.</u>

**26** 위 글의 흐름상 자연스럽지 <u>않은</u> 문장은?　　(3점)

① ⓐ　　② ⓑ　　③ ⓒ　　④ ⓓ　　⑤ ⓔ

**27** 위 글을 읽고 답할 수 <u>없는</u> 것은?　　(3점)

① When was the hardest time in the writer's life?
② What happened to the writer then?
③ Did the writer have a lot of friends at the new school?
④ Who helped the writer?
⑤ How much did the writer spend on his or her new books?

**[28~29]** 다음 글을 읽고 물음에 답하시오.

It was five minutes before Jisu's big presentation in front of the whole class. Feeling nervous, Jisu was carefully studying her notes in her chair. Then, her teacher came over and told her to stand tall like Wonder Woman. After standing tall for a few minutes, Jisu did not feel nervous anymore. In fact, she was (A)[confidence / confident] that she would make a great presentation. According to Amy Cuddy, a famous psychologist, we can become more confident just by standing tall for two minutes before (B)[stressful / stress] events. Our bodies change our minds, and our minds can change our behavior. Do you want to feel confident? Stand with your feet apart, and place your hands on your hips. You will not only feel sure about yourself but also (C)[looking / look] confident to other people.

**28** 위 글의 제목으로 가장 적절한 것은? (3점)

① Who can make me feel pleased?

② How do I become less anxious?

③ What makes you feel nervous?

④ What can make me feel more nervous?

⑤ Why do I become more nervous?

**29** 위 글의 괄호 (A), (B), (C)에 들어갈 말로 적절하게 짝지어진 것은? (4점)

| | (A) | (B) | (C) |
|---|---|---|---|
| ① | confidence | stress | looking |
| ② | confidence | stressful | looking |
| ③ | confident | stressful | look |
| ④ | confident | stress | look |
| ⑤ | confident | stressful | looking |

**[30~31]** 다음 글을 읽고 물음에 답하시오.

When he graduates from high school next year, Taeho wants to become a professional farmer. However, he has never told anyone about it. He is worried that his parents or his friends will not understand. Wanting to clear his mind, Taeho decided to take a day trip on a train by himself. On the train, he told a complete stranger sitting beside him about his problem. He had no idea why he did it. However, he felt much better when he got off the train. Strangely enough, we often tell strangers about our problems just like Taeho. That is because we do not have to worry about being judged or seeing them again. If you have a problem that you cannot share with your family or friends, try talking to a stranger. You will feel much better.

**30** 위 글을 다음과 같이 요약했을 때 어색한 것은? (3점)

ⓐ Title: Who can help you feel better?
ⓑ Problem: You cannot tell anyone about your problem.
ⓒ Solution: Try to talk with your family or friends.
ⓓ Effect: You will feel much better.
ⓔ Explanation: You don't have to worry about being judged or seeing the stranger again.

① ⓐ    ② ⓑ    ③ ⓒ    ④ ⓓ    ⑤ ⓔ

**31** 위 글을 읽고 답할 수 없는 질문은? (3점)

① What does Taeho want to be after graduating from high school?

② What is Taeho worried about?

③ What did Taeho do to clear his mind?

④ Did Taeho's parents support his dream?

⑤ Why do we often tell strangers about our problems?

반

이름

점수

◎ 선택형 문항의 답안은 컴퓨터용 수정 싸인펜을 사용하여 OMR 답안지에 바르게 표기하시오.

◎ 서술형 문제는 답을 답안지에 반드시 검정 볼펜으로 쓰시오.

◎ 총 27문항 100점 만점입니다. 문항별 배점은 각 문항에 표시되어 있습니다.

[충북 ○○중]

**01** 다음 중 밑줄 친 어휘의 쓰임이 <u>잘못된</u> 것은?     (4점)

① Her explanation was <u>clear</u>, so I couldn't understand.

② It is <u>unusual</u> to have snow in October.

③ The customer was <u>unhappy</u> with the service. The waiter was very unkind.

④ You should <u>put on</u> a raincoat. It is raining outside.

⑤ They <u>put out</u> forest fires.

[충북 ○○중]

**02** 다음 문장의 영영풀이에 해당하는 단어는?     (3점)

happy because you have gotten what you wanted or needed

① honest     ② satisfied     ③ interested

④ jealous     ⑤ inconvenient

[전북 ○○중]

**03** 다음 대화에서 밑줄 친 ⓐ~ⓔ 중 가리키는 대상이 나머지 넷과 <u>다른</u> 것은?     (3점)

M: Hello, ma'am. How can I help you?

W: I bought this phone only a week ago, but ⓐ<u>it</u> sometimes turns off by ⓑ<u>itself</u>.

M: Oh, I see. May I have a look at ⓒ<u>it</u>? We're sorry for the inconvenience. ⓓ<u>It'll</u> take a few hours to fix ⓔ<u>it</u>.

W: I'd like a new one.

M: Of course. I just need to fill out this form.

① ⓐ     ② ⓑ     ③ ⓒ     ④ ⓓ     ⑤ ⓔ

[서울 양천구 ○○중]

**04** 다음 대화가 자연스럽게 이어지도록 ⓐ~ⓔ를 배열한 것은?     (4점)

A: Hey! What do you think of my drawing?

ⓐ Wow! It's great. Did you draw this?

ⓑ Thanks, but I'm not happy with the result. It's not unique.

ⓒ Yes. The bread and the milk look so real.

ⓓ Yes, I did. Do you like it?

ⓔ I don't think so. I think it's a fantastic drawing.

① ⓐ-ⓒ-ⓓ-ⓑ-ⓔ     ② ⓐ-ⓓ-ⓒ-ⓑ-ⓔ

③ ⓐ-ⓔ-ⓑ-ⓒ-ⓓ     ④ ⓔ-ⓑ-ⓐ-ⓓ-ⓒ

⑤ ⓔ-ⓒ-ⓐ-ⓑ-ⓓ

[전북 ○○중]

**05** 다음 대화를 통해 알 수 <u>없는</u> 것은?     (4점)

B: Mom, I want to go to an arts high school. I want to become an actor.

W: What? I thought you were interested in science.

B: I was but not anymore. I want to become a movie star.

W: Are you sure you want to be an actor?

B: Yes, I'll learn how to act. I promise I'll do my best.

① 남자아이의 장래 희망

② 엄마가 추천하는 공부 방법

③ 엄마가 생각했던 아들의 좋아하는 과목

④ 엄마를 설득하기 위한 아들의 약속

⑤ 남자아이가 가고 싶은 고등학교

[6~8] 다음 대화를 읽고 물음에 답하시오.

Man: Are you enjoying your meal?
Woman: Well, the bread was good, and the salad was fresh.
Man: How about your steak?
Woman: Honestly, I'm not satisfied with the steak. It's too rare for me.
Man: I'm sorry. Would you like me to bring you another one?
Woman: That's O.K. I need to be going. Let me just have the check, please.
Man: I'm really sorry. You won't have to pay for the steak.
Woman: O.K. Thanks.
Man: I promise we'll provide you with a better experience next time you visit.

**06** 위 대화가 이루어지는 장소로 가장 알맞은 것은? (3점)

① bakery  ② bookstore
③ coffee shop  ④ restaurant
⑤ grocery store

**07** 위 대화를 읽고, 다음 질문에 대한 답으로 가장 알맞은 것은? (4점)

Why is the woman not satisfied with the steak?

① It is not fresh.
② It is too expensive.
③ It is not big enough.
④ It is not rare enough.
⑤ It isn't cooked enough.

**08** According to the dialogue, which is NOT true? (4점)

① The woman won't pay for the steak.
② The man promised a better service next time.
③ The woman was satisfied with the bread and salad.
④ The woman didn't like the steak.
⑤ The woman wanted the man to bring her another steak.

**09** What does the girl promise to do? (4점)

G: Wow, I like this blueberry jam. Where did you buy it?
B: I made it myself.
G: Really? This is better than any other jam I've ever had. You should sell it.
B: Do you think people would want to buy this?
G: Of course. I promise I will be your first customer.

*G: Girl B: Boy

① buy the boy's jam
② promote the boy's jam
③ help the boy make jam
④ sell the boy's jam to her friends
⑤ plant the blueberry to make jam

**10** 다음 대화의 빈칸 (A)에 가장 적절한 것은? (3점)

Mr. Park: I'm not satisfied with this phone.
Ariana: Why?
Mr. Park: (A)_____

① It's very useful.
② It's not expensive.
③ It's too big and heavy.
④ It's uniquely designed.
⑤ It's in blue and I like blue.

[전북 ○○중]

**11** 다음 대화를 읽고, 괄호 안에 주어진 여자아이의 말을 영작하여 빈칸을 채우시오. (4점)

> B: Wow! Did you draw this?
> G: Yes, I did. Do you like it?
> B: Yes, the bread and milk look so real. I feel like having a bite of the bread.
> D: Thanks, but I _____ _____ _____ _____ it. (나는 그것에 만족하지 않아.) It's not unique.
> B: I don't think so. I think it's a fantastic drawing.

→ _____ _____ _____ _____

[경북 ○○중]

**12** 다음 중 밑줄 친 부분을 바르게 해석한 것은? (4점)

① I forgot to send an e-mail to my teacher. (보낼 것을 잊어버렸다)

② My parents tried to save money for a year. (시험 삼아 모았다)

③ They stopped to hold a surprising party for her. (여는 것을 멈췄다)

④ I regret playing with friends during the final exam. (놀게 되어 유감이다)

⑤ He must remember visiting Jeju island with his grandmother. (방문할 것을 기억하다)

[충북 ○○중]

**13** 다음 중 밑줄 친 부분이 문맥상 어색한 것은? (4점)

① He is an active person. His brother, however, is shy and quiet.

② I got up late and couldn't get to school on time. Nevertheless, I was late for the class.

③ It was hot yesterday. Moreover, it was very humid.

④ I don't really want to go to see a movie. Besides, it's too late!

⑤ I worked out a lot. As a consequence, I got a well-balanced body.

[대전 ○○중]

**14** 다음 중 어법상 적절한 것은? (3점)

① Tell me the way how I can cook well.

② Today is the day in which I was born.

③ I don't know why he was upset yesterday.

④ This park is when he goes jogging every day.

⑤ This is the house where I lived in last year.

[전북 ○○중]

**15** 다음 대화의 괄호 (A)~(C)에 들어갈 단어가 적절한 것끼리 묶인 것은? (4점)

> G: Wow, I like this blueberry jam. Where did you buy it?
> B: I made it (A)[myself / yourself].
> G: Really? This is better than any other jam I've ever (B)[have / had]. You should sell it.
> B: Do you think people would want to buy this?
> G: Of course. I promise I'll be your first (C)[seller / customer].

|   | (A) | (B) | (C) |
|---|-----|-----|-----|
| ① | myself | have | customer |
| ② | myself | had | seller |
| ③ | myself | had | customer |
| ④ | yourself | have | seller |
| ⑤ | yourself | have | customer |

[16~18] 다음 글을 읽고 물음에 답하시오.

Leonardo da Vinci ⓐ역대 가장 위대한 화가들 중의 한 명으로 알려져 있다. He was also a great inventor, scientist, and musician. Very few people, however, know that da Vinci was also a (A)_____.
In 1473, twenty-year-old da Vinci worked as a cook at a restaurant in Florence, Italy. ⓑ그가 부엌을 책임지게 되었을 때, da Vinci changed the menu completely. He made simple but artistic dishes like fish with a few carrot slices. ⓒ몇몇 음식들은 심지어 꽃으로 장식되었다. Customers, however, were unhappy ⓓ그들은 많은 양의 고기 요리에 익숙했었기 때문에. ㉠_____, da Vinci lost his job.
A few years later, da Vinci opened a restaurant with his friend Sandro Botticelli. He wanted to create ⓔ그의 획기적인 음식을 먹어 볼 수 있는 장소를. They put up a beautifully painted sign and made a uniquely written menu. Da Vinci believed that people would soon appreciate his creative cooking. ㉡_____, that never happened.

**16** 위 글의 흐름으로 보아 빈칸 (A)에 들어갈 적절한 것은? (3점)

① creative cook　　② great businessman
③ famous cook　　④ popular cook
⑤ unique customer

**17** 위 글의 ⓐ~ⓔ의 표현을 영어로 바르게 옮긴 것은? (4점)

① ⓐ - is known as one of the greatest painter of all time

② ⓑ - When he took charge in the kitchen

③ ⓒ - Some dishes even decorated with flowers.

④ ⓓ - because they were used to dishes with big servings of meat

⑤ ⓔ - when people could try his innovative food

**18** 위 글의 빈칸 ㉠과 ㉡에 들어갈 적절한 접속사는? (4점)

|  | ㉠ | ㉡ |
|---|---|---|
| ① | As a result | Unfortunately |
| ② | However | Unfortunately |
| ③ | But | Luckily |
| ④ | As a result | Fortunately |
| ⑤ | Thus | Fortunately |

**19** 다음 글의 흐름으로 보아, 주어진 문장이 들어갈 가장 적절한 곳은? (4점)

For example, he created machines that could crush vegetables and pull spaghetti.

In the early 1480s, da Vinci began to work for Ludovico Sforza in Milan. He was given many different roles, such as a musician, a painter, and an engineer. (A) He was also put in charge of the kitchen. (B) He was happy to be given another chance to pursue his passion for cooking. Da Vinci did not stop at cooking creative dishes. (C) He wanted to cook much more quickly and easily. So, he invented new machines for his kitchen. (D) Also, he made a device that could scare frogs away from the water tank. (E) Surely, they were all very innovative, but most of them were too big or too difficult to use.

① (A)　② (B)　③ (C)　④ (D)　⑤ (E)

**[20~21] 다음 글을 읽고 물음에 답하시오.**

In 1495, Sforza asked da Vinci to make a grand painting, which was based on the last supper of Jesus, on the wall of a church in Milan. Da Vinci ⓐgladly took on the project because he had always been interested in food. (가)그는 모든 종류의 음식을 요리하느라 많은 시간을 썼다 to decide what to put on the table in his picture. "Da Vinci has wasted his time in the kitchen for over a year. That's the ⓑreason why he hasn't finished the painting yet," complained the people from the church to Sforza.

Although da Vinci never became a successful cook, he showed great interest in cooking ⓒthroughout his life. He was not only a great painter but also a ⓓsuccessful cook. Now that you know all about his secret ⓔpassion for cooking, you will never look at *The Last Supper* the same way.

**20** 위 글의 밑줄 친 ⓐ~ⓔ 중, 문맥상 낱말의 쓰임이 <u>어색한</u> 것은? (3점)

① ⓐ ② ⓑ ③ ⓒ ④ ⓓ ⑤ ⓔ

**21** 위 글의 밑줄 친 (가)의 우리말과 의미가 일치하도록 다음 단어를 배열할 때, 7번째 들어갈 단어는? (4점)

> 보기
>
> spent / he / a / of / food / lot
> / time / kinds / cooking / all / of

→ ____ ____ ____ ____ ____ ____
( ____ ) ____ ____ ____ ____

\* 주어진 단어를 모두 한 번씩 사용.
대·소문자 구분 없음.

① spent ② of ③ food
④ time ⑤ cooking

**[22~23] 다음 글을 읽고 물음에 답하시오.**

In the early 1480s, da Vinci began to work for Ludovico Sforza in Milan. He was given many different roles, such as a musician, a painter, and an engineer. He was also put in charge of the kitchen. He was happy to be given another chance to pursue his passion for cooking. Da Vinci did not stop at cooking creative dishes. He wanted to cook much more quickly and easily. Thus, he invented new machines for his kitchen. He created machines that could crush vegetables and pull spaghetti. He even made a device that could scare frogs away from the water tank. Surely, they were all very innovative, but most of them were too big or too difficult to use.

**22** 위 글의 제목으로 적절한 것은? (4점)

① His Funny Cooking
② His Invention for Cooking
③ His Life as a Painter
④ The Successful Cooking Machines
⑤ His Strange Hobbies

**23** 위 글을 읽고 다음 질문에 답할 수 <u>없는</u> 것은? (4점)

① Who did da Vinci work for?
② Did da Vinci give up his cooking?
③ Did people like da Vinci's cooking?
④ Why did da Vinci make new machines for his kitchen?
⑤ Were the new machines invented by da Vinci easy to use?

[24~25] 다음 글을 읽고 물음에 답하시오.

One day, da Vinci opened a restaurant with his friend Sandro Botticelli. He wanted to create a place to show his innovative food. Da Vinci believed that people would soon appreciate his creative cooking. Unfortunately, that never happened.

In the early 1480s, da Vinci began to work for Ludovico Sforza in Milan. He was given many different roles like a musician, a painter, and an ⓐengineer. He was given a chance to ⓑpursue his ⓒpassion for cooking. Da Vinci did not stop at cooking creative food. He wanted to cook much more quickly and easily. So, he ⓓinvented new machines for his kitchen. He created machines that could crush vegetables and pull spaghetti. He even made a ⓔdevice that could scare frogs away from the water tank.

## 24 위 글의 내용과 일치하는 것은? (4점)

① Da Vinci and Sandro Botticelli's creative food made customers satisfied.

② Ludovico Sforza ordered Da Vinci to invent machines to cook easily and quickly.

③ Da Vinci created a machine which could crush vegetables to scare frogs.

④ Da Vinci had a passion for cooking and challenged many things.

⑤ Finally, in the 1480s, Da Vinci became famous for his creative cooking.

## 25 위 글의 밑줄 친 ⓐ~ⓔ의 단어가 의미상 어디에도 들어갈 수 없는 것은? (4점)

① He wished to _____ a medical career.

② Our national heritage was _____ by the fire.

③ A smart _____ like a tablet is now replacing a textbook.

④ Please send me a(n) _____ to fix my broken computer.

⑤ The team won the first place because of their _____.

[26~27] 다음 글을 읽고 물음에 답하시오.

In 1473, twenty-year-old da Vinci worked as a cook at a restaurant in Florence, Italy. (A) When he took charge of the kitchen, da Vinci changed the menu completely. (B) He made simple but artistic dishes like fish with a few carrot slices. (C) Some dishes were even decorated with flowers. (D) Customers, however, were unhappy because they ⓐ_____ dishes with big servings of meat. (E)

## 26 위 글의 (A)~(E) 중 다음 문장이 들어갈 곳은? (4점)

As a result, da Vinci lost his job.

① (A)    ② (B)    ③ (C)    ④ (D)    ⑤ (E)

## 27 위 글의 빈칸 ⓐ에 '익숙하다'라는 표현을 넣으려 할 때 가장 적절한 것은? (3점)

① used to          ② is used to

③ are used to      ④ was used to

⑤ were used to

# 3학년 영어 2학기 기말고사(6과) 2회

문항수 : 선택형(26문항) 서술형(3문항)    20 . . .

◎ 선택형 문항의 답안은 컴퓨터용 수정 싸인펜을 사용하여 OMR 답안지에 바르게 표기하시오.
◎ 서술형 문제는 답을 답안지에 반드시 검정 볼펜으로 쓰시오.
◎ 총 29문항 100점 만점입니다. 문항별 배점은 각 문항에 표시되어 있습니다.

[충북 ㅇㅇ중]

**01** 다음 중 반의어 관계가 잘못된 것은? (3점)

① convenient - unconvenient
② natural - unnatural
③ easy - uneasy
④ clear - unclear
⑤ usual - unusual

[전북 ㅇㅇ중]

**02** 다음 중 밑줄 친 표현이 문장의 흐름과 어울리지 <u>않는</u> 것은? (3점)

① I have a <u>passion</u> for fashion.
② This place is open <u>throughout</u> the year.
③ She was put in <u>charge</u> of the matter.
④ <u>Unfortunately</u>, I have no money with me.
⑤ It is hard to cook five <u>reasons</u> of food all at once.

[서울 양천구 ㅇㅇ중]

**03** 다음 ⓐ~ⓔ 중 대화의 흐름상 <u>어색한</u> 것은? (3점)

Man:       Are you enjoying your meal?
Woman: Well, the bread was good, and the salad was fresh.
Man:       How about your steak?
Woman: ⓐ<u>Honestly, it was really satisfying.</u> It's too rare for me.
Man:       I'm sorry you didn't like it. ⓑ<u>Would you like me to bring you another one?</u>
Woman: That's O.K. I need to be going. ⓒ<u>Let me just have the check, please.</u>
Man:       I'm really sorry. ⓓ<u>You won't have to pay for the steak.</u>

Woman: O.K. Thanks.
Man:       ⓔ<u>I'll make sure we provide you with a better experience next time you visit.</u>

① ⓐ    ② ⓑ    ③ ⓒ    ④ ⓓ    ⑤ ⓔ

[충북 ㅇㅇ중]

**04** 다음 대화의 내용과 일치하지 <u>않는</u> 것은? (4점)

B: Mom, I want to go to an arts high school. I want to become an actor.
W: What? I thought you were interested in science.
B: I was but not anymore. I want to become a movie star.
W: Are you sure you want to be an actor?
B: Yes, I'll learn how to act. I promise I'll do my best.

① The boy had an interest in science.
② The boy wants to learn how to act.
③ The boy hopes to become an actor.
④ The boy is still interested in science.
⑤ The boy promises to do his best.

[충북 ㅇㅇ중]

**05** 다음 문장이 자연스러운 대화가 되도록 (A)~(D)를 바르게 배열한 것은? (4점)

Wow, I like this blueberry jam. Where did you buy it?
(A) Really? This is better than any other jam I've ever had. You should sell it.
(B) Of course. I promise I'll be your first customer.
(C) Do you think people would want to buy this?
(D) I made it myself.

① (A)-(D)-(C)-(B)    ② (B)-(C)-(A)-(D)
③ (B)-(A)-(D)-(C)    ④ (D)-(A)-(C)-(B)
⑤ (D)-(C)-(B)-(A)

[6~7] 다음 대화를 읽고 물음에 답하시오.

M: Hello, ma'am. How can I help you?
W: I bought this phone only a week ago, but it sometimes turns off (A)_____ itself.
M: Oh, I see. May I have a look at it? (Pause) We're sorry for the inconvenience. It'll take a few hours to fix it.
W: I'm not satisfied with the phone. I'd like a new one.
M: Of course. I just need to fill out this form.
*M: Man W: Woman

**06** 위 대화의 빈칸 (A)에 들어갈 알맞은 말은? (3점)

① at    ② with    ③ in    ④ to    ⑤ by

**07** 위 대화의 내용에 답할 수 없는 질문을 고르면? (3점)

① Why did the woman buy the phone?
② When did the woman buy the phone?
③ What's the problem with the woman's phone?
④ Does the woman want a new phone?
⑤ How long will it take to fix the woman's phone?

[8~9] 다음 대화를 읽고 물음에 답하시오.

Man: Are you enjoying your meal?
Woman: Well, the bread was good, and the salad was fresh.
Man: How about your steak?
Woman: Honestly, I'm not satisfied with the steak. (A)
Man: I'm sorry. Would you like me to bring you another one? (B)

Woman: That's O.K. I need to be going. Let me just have the check, please. (C)
Man: I'm really sorry. You won't have to pay for the steak. (D)
Woman: O.K. Thanks. (E)
Man: I promise to provide you with a better service next time you visit.

**08** 위 대화의 (A)~(E) 중, 주어진 문장이 들어갈 위치로 가장 적절한 곳은? (3점)

It's too rare for me.

① (A)    ② (B)    ③ (C)    ④ (D)    ⑤ (E)

**09** 위 대화가 일어나는 장소로 알맞은 곳은? (3점)

① bakery           ② art museum
③ grocery store    ④ cooking class
⑤ restaurant

**10** 다음 (a)~(d)를 자연스러운 대화가 되도록 바르게 배열한 것은? (4점)

A: Mom, I want to go to an arts high school. I want to become an actor.
(a) I was but not anymore. I want to become a movie star.
(b) Are you sure you want to be an actor?
(c) Yes, I'll learn how to act. I promise I'll do my best.
(d) What? I thought you were interested in science.

① (a)-(d)-(b)-(c)          ② (b)-(c)-(a)-(d)
③ (b)-(a)-(c)-(d)          ④ (d)-(c)-(b)-(a)
⑤ (d)-(a)-(b)-(c)

## 11 다음 대화의 내용과 일치하지 <u>않는</u> 것은? (4점)

> Man: Are you enjoying your meal?
> Woman: Well, the bread was good, and the salad was fresh.
> Man: How about your steak?
> Woman: Honestly, I'm not happy with the steak. It's too rare for me.
> Man: I'm sorry. Would you like me to bring you another one?
> Woman: That's O.K. I need to be going. Let me just have the check, please.
> Man: I'm really sorry. You won't have to pay for the steak.
> Woman: O.K. Thanks.
> Man: I swear we'll provide you with a better experience next time you visit.

① 여성은 빵과 샐러드에 만족하고 있다.
② 스테이크는 여성에게 너무 질기다.
③ 여성은 계산서를 요구하고 있다.
④ 남성은 스테이크 값을 요구하지 않는다.
⑤ 남자는 다음 방문에 더 좋은 경험을 약속한다.

## 12 다음 중 어법상 올바르지 <u>않은</u> 문장 한 개를 찾아 〈조건〉에 맞게 바르게 고치시오. (4점)

> (A) This is the river in which I used to swim.
> (B) I remember the day on which I met him.
> (C) Tell me the way he solved the problem.
> (D) This is the house in that ghosts live.

조건
1. 대·소문자 및 철자에 유의할 것.
2. 반드시 관계부사를 사용하여 고칠 것.

→ _____

## 13 다음 중 어법상 올바른 문장은? (3점)

① That is the restaurant where they had lunch yesterday at the place.
② Tomorrow is the day when my friend is going back to her country tomorrow.
③ He doesn't know the reason why are people running.
④ I remember the day when we first met.
⑤ He knows the way how it works well.

## 14 다음 문장 (A), (B)에 들어갈 가장 알맞은 말은? (4점)

> • Mary did not study hard for the test, (A)_____ she failed.
> • Tom did not feel well, (B)_____, he went to school.

|  | (A) | (B) |
|---|---|---|
| ① | however | therefore |
| ② | thus | therefore |
| ③ | however | thus |
| ④ | otherwise | however |
| ⑤ | thus | however |

## 15 다음 빈칸에 들어갈 말이 차례로 바르게 짝지어진 것은? (3점)

> • The house _____ we're going to move is not far from here.
> • I'll never forget the day _____ I first met him.

① where - when
② which - which
③ where - which
④ which - when
⑤ which - whose

[16~18] 다음 글을 읽고 물음에 답하시오.

In 1495, Sforza asked da Vinci to make a grand painting, which was based on the last supper of Jesus, on the wall of a church in Milan. Da Vinci ⓐhappily took on the project _____ he had always been interested in food. He spent a lot of time cooking all kinds of food to decide what to put on the table in his picture. "Da Vinci has ⓑ saved his time in the kitchen for over a year. (A)그 것이 바로 그가 그 그림을 끝내지 못한 이유입니다," ⓒcomplained the people from the church to Sforza.

Even though da Vinci never became a successful cook, he showed a great ⓓlove in cooking throughout his life. He was not only a great ⓔ artist but also a creative cook. _____ you know all about his secret passion for cooking, you will never look at *The Last Supper* the same way.

**16** 위 글의 밑줄 친 ⓐ~ⓔ 중 문맥상 어울리지 <u>않는</u> 단어는? (3점)

① ⓐ    ② ⓑ    ③ ⓒ    ④ ⓓ    ⑤ ⓔ

**17** 위 글의 빈칸에 공통으로 들어갈 접속사를 두 단어로 쓰시오.
(대·소문자 구분 상관 없음.)　　　　　　　(4점)

→ _____

**18** 위 글의 밑줄 친 우리말 문장 (A)를 〈조건〉에 맞게 영작하시오.
　　　　　　　　　　　　　　　　　　　(4점)

> **조건**
> 1. 대·소문자 및 철자에 유의할 것.
> 2. 아래의 단어들을 재배열하여 영작할 것.
> (he / why / hasn't / the reason / the painting / that's / finished)

→ _____

[19~20] 다음 글을 읽고 물음에 답하시오.

Leonardo da Vinci ⓐis known as one of the greatest painters of all time. He was also a great inventor, scientist, and musician. ⓑVery few people, however, know that da Vinci was also a creative cook.

In 1473, twenty-year-old da Vinci worked (A)_____ a cook at a restaurant in Florence, Italy. When he took charge (B)_____ the kitchen, da Vinci changed the menu completely. He made simple but artistic dishes (C)_____ fish with a few carrot slices. Some dishes were even decorated (D)_____ flowers. Customers, however, were unhappy because they ⓒwere used to dishes with big servings of meat. ⓓAs a result, da Vinci lost his job.

A few years later, da Vinci opened a restaurant with his friend Sandro Botticelli. He wanted to create a place where people could try his innovative food. They put up ⓔa beautifully painted sign and made a uniquely written menu. Da Vinci believed that people would soon appreciate his creative cooking. Unfortunately, that never happened.

**19** 위 글의 밑줄 친 ⓐ~ⓔ를 문맥상 <u>잘못</u> 해석한 것은?　　(3점)

① ⓐis known as: ~로 알려져 있다
② ⓑVery few people: 극히 소수의 사람들
③ ⓒwere used to: ~하기 위해 사용되었다
④ ⓓAs a result: 그 결과로
⑤ ⓔa beautifully painted sign: 아름답게 그려진 간판

**20** 위 글의 빈칸 (A)~(D)에 들어갈 단어로 적절하지 <u>않은</u> 것은?
　　　　　　　　　　　　　　　　　　　(4점)

① of　　　② like　　　③ as
④ with　　⑤ to

**[21~22] 다음 글을 읽고 물음에 답하시오.**

In 1495, Sforza asked da Vinci to make a grand painting, which was based on the last supper of Jesus, on the wall of a church in Milan. Da Vinci gladly took on the project because he had always been interested in food. He spent a lot of time cooking all kinds of food to decide what to put on the table in his picture. "Da Vinci has wasted his time in the kitchen for over a year. That's the reason why he hasn't finished the painting yet," complained the people from the church to Sforza. Although da Vinci never became a successful cook, he showed great interest in cooking throughout his life. He was not only a great painter but also a (A)creative cook. Now that you know all about his secret passion for cooking, you will never look at *The Last Supper* the same way.

**21** 위 글을 읽고 답할 수 <u>없는</u> 질문은? (4점)

① What did Sforza ask da Vinci to make?
② What kind of foods can you find in *The Last Supper*?
③ Why did da Vinci gladly take on the project from Sforza?
④ When did Sforza ask da Vinci to make a grand painting?
⑤ Why did it take long time for da Vinci to finish the painting, *The Last Supper*?

**22** 위 글의 밑줄 친 (A)와 뜻이 가장 가까운 것은? (3점)

① ancient       ② pursue       ③ useless
④ talented       ⑤ innovative

**[23~24] 다음 글을 읽고 물음에 답하시오.**

(A) In the early 1480s, da Vinci began ⓐto work for Ludovico Sforza in Milan. He was given many different roles, such as a musician, a painter, and an engineer. (B) He was happy ⓑto be given another chance ⓒto pursue his passion for cooking. Da Vinci did not stop at cooking creative dishes. (C) He wanted ⓓto cook much more quickly and easily. Thus, he invented new machines for his kitchen. He created machines that could crush vegetables and pull spaghetti. (D) He even made a device that could scare frogs away from the water tank. Surely, they were all very innovative, but most of them were too big or too difficult ⓔto use. (E)

**23** 위 글의 (A)~(E) 중에서 다음 문장이 들어가기에 가장 적절한 것은? (4점)

He was also put in charge of the kitchen.

① (A)   ② (B)   ③ (C)   ④ (D)   ⑤ (E)

**24** 위 글의 ⓐ~ⓔ 중에서 to부정사가 다음 문장의 밑줄 친 부분과 동일하게 사용된 것은? (3점)

• I have many things <u>to do</u> today.

① ⓐ   ② ⓑ   ③ ⓒ   ④ ⓓ   ⑤ ⓔ

**25** 밑줄 친 ⓐ~ⓔ 중 글의 흐름상 <u>어색한</u> 것은? (3점)

My name is Kim Jieun. I am an artist ⓐwho uses technology. There was a special moment ⓑwhen I decided what I wanted to be. Back in 2030, I made a small statue using technology for arts. It was a great chance to learn about using technology for arts. ⓒThus, I decided to go to a technical high school. ⓓBefore graduating from high school, I entered Korea Art College and learned more about arts and technology. This year, I held my first exhibition. I am very ⓔsatisfied with my life.

① ⓐ   ② ⓑ   ③ ⓒ   ④ ⓓ   ⑤ ⓔ

[26~27] 다음 글을 읽고 물음에 답하시오.

In 1495, Sforza asked da Vinci to make a grand painting, which was based on the last supper of Jesus, on the wall of a church in Milan. Da Vinci gladly took on the project because he had always been (A)_____ in food. He spent a lot of time (B)_____ all kinds of food to decide what to put on the table in his picture. "Da Vinci has wasted his time in the kitchen for over a year. That's the reason why he hasn't finished the painting yet," (C)_____ the people from the church to Sforza.

Although da Vinci never became a successful cook, he showed great interest in cooking throughout his life. He was not only a great painter but also a creative cook. Now that you know all about his secret passion for cooking, you will never look at *The Last Supper* the same way.

**26** 위 글의 흐름으로 보아 (A)~(C)에 들어갈 적절한 표현은? (4점)

|   | (A) | (B) | (C) |
|---|---|---|---|
| ① | bored | making | appreciated |
| ② | interesting | to cook | complained |
| ③ | interested | cooking | complained |
| ④ | excited | to cook | appreciated |
| ⑤ | exciting | cooking | complained |

**27** 위 글의 내용과 일치하는 것은? (3점)

① 다빈치는 밀라노에 있는 교회의 벽에 그림을 그려 달라고 Sforza에게 부탁했다.
② 다빈치는 요리를 하고 싶어서 벽화 그림을 그리는 데 망설였다.
③ 다빈치는 부엌에서 요리를 해야 했으므로 그림을 완성하는 데 1년이 넘게 걸렸다.
④ 다빈치는 일생 동안 요리에 대한 흥미를 잃지 않아 성공한 요리사가 되었다.
⑤ 다빈치는 훌륭한 화가이며 창의적인 요리사였다.

[28~29] 다음 글을 읽고 물음에 답하시오.

In 1473, ⓐtwenty-years-old da Vinci worked as a cook at a restaurant in Florence, Italy. When he took charge of the kitchen, da Vinci changed the menu completely. He made simple but ⓑartistically dishes like fish with a few carrot slices. Some dishes were even decorated with flowers. Customers, (A)_____, were unhappy because they ⓒused to dishes with big servings of meat. (B)_____, da Vinci lost his job.

Several years later, da Vinci opened a restaurant with his friend Sandro Botticelli. He wanted to create a place in which people could try his innovative food. They put up a beautifully ⓓpainting sign and made a uniquely ⓔwritten menu. Da Vinci believed that people would soon appreciate his creative cooking. (C)_____, that never happened.

**28** 위 글의 밑줄 친 ⓐ~ⓔ 중에서 어법상 옳은 것은? (3점)

① ⓐ  ② ⓑ  ③ ⓒ  ④ ⓓ  ⑤ ⓔ

**29** 위 글의 빈칸 (A)~(C)에 들어갈 알맞은 연결사는? (4점)

|   | (A) | (B) | (C) |
|---|---|---|---|
| ① | however | Therefore | Fortunately |
| ② | thus | Therefore | Unfortunately |
| ③ | however | In addition | Unfortunately |
| ④ | thus | In addition | Fortunately |
| ⑤ | however | Therefore | Unfortunately |

◎ 선택형 문항의 답안은 컴퓨터용 수정 싸인펜을 사용하여 OMR 답안지에 바르게 표기하시오.

◎ 서술형 문제는 답을 답안지에 반드시 검정 볼펜으로 쓰시오.

◎ 총 29문항 100점 만점입니다. 문항별 배점은 각 문항에 표시되어 있습니다.

[전북 ○○중]

**01** 다음 단어 중 의미가 <u>어색한</u> 것은?  (3점)

① useless - 쓸모없는

② careless - 부주의한

③ homeless - 집이 없는

④ hopeless - 희망이 없는

⑤ speechless - 부자연스러운

[경북 ○○중]

**02** 다음 밑줄 친 낱말의 쓰임이 적절하지 <u>않은</u> 것은?  (4점)

① He was <u>unfortunate</u> to lose in the final match.

② She felt <u>uneasy</u> after moving to a new town.

③ It's difficult to look <u>unnatural</u> when you're feeling nervous.

④ I'm worried because I feel <u>uncertain</u> about choosing my high school.

⑤ The shop manager was <u>unkind</u> to customers, so he got a complaint about poor service.

[전북 ○○중]

**03** 다음 문장이 자연스러운 대화가 되도록 (A)~(D)를 바르게 배열한 것은?  (3점)

(A) What? Do you mean I have to break one of my legs?

(B) I have to sing at the school's Korean song contest.

(C) No, it's an expression meaning I hope you do well.

(D) Wow, break a leg!

① (B)-(D)-(A)-(C)  ② (B)-(C)-(A)-(D)

③ (A)-(D)-(B)-(C)  ④ (D)-(A)-(B)-(C)

⑤ (C)-(D)-(A)-(B)

[전북 ○○중]

[4~5] 다음 대화를 읽고 물음에 답하시오.

Anna: What's wrong? You don't look so good.

Suho: I'm still thinking about our soccer match last week.

Anna: Do you mean the game you lost last week?

Suho: Yes. I wish I could forget about it, but I can't.

Anna: People say, "Yesterday is history, tomorrow is a mystery, and today is a gift. That's why it's called ⓐthe present."

**04** 위 대화에서 Anna의 메시지로 가장 적절한 것은?  (4점)

① 절대 포기하지 말아라.

② 과거를 잊고 현재를 살아라.

③ 너를 위해 비싼 선물을 사라.

④ 다시는 같은 실수를 하지 말아라.

⑤ 너의 미래를 위한 큰 꿈을 가져라.

**05** 위 대화에서 밑줄 친 ⓐthe present의 2가지 의미를 우리말로 쓰시오.  (4점)

(1) _____  (2) _____

**06** 다음 대화의 빈칸 (A)에 가장 적절한 것은? (3점)

> G: I have to sing at the school's English pop song contest.
> B: Wow. Break a leg!
> G: Do you mean I have to break one of my legs?
> B: No, it's an expression meaning (A)_____.

① bad luck      ② thank you

③ good luck      ④ I love you

⑤ see you again

[7~8] 다음 대화를 읽고 물음에 답하시오.

> Anna: ⓐWhat's wrong? You don't look so good.
> Suho: I'm still thinking about our soccer match last week.
> Anna: Do you mean the game you lost last week?
> Suho: Yes. ⓑI wish I could forget about it, but I can't.
> Anna: Well, you should always live for today.
> Suho: ⓒDo you mean I should focus on the past?
> Anna: Yes, exactly. People say, "Yesterday is history, tomorrow is a mystery, and today is a gift ⓓThat's why it's called the present."
> Suho: Now I see. You know so many great expressions. ⓔYou're as wise as my grandma.

**07** 위 대화의 밑줄 친 ⓐ~ⓔ 중 흐름상 적절하지 않은 것은? (4점)

① ⓐ    ② ⓑ    ③ ⓒ    ④ ⓓ    ⑤ ⓔ

**08** What is Anna's message? (3점)

① Don't judge others by their looks.

② Have a big dream for your future.

③ Don't make the same mistake again.

④ Forget the past and live in the present.

⑤ It's important to try your best in the game.

**09** 다음 대화를 읽고 "일찍 일어나는 새가 벌레를 잡는다"라는 의미로 쓰인 한 문장을 찾아 쓰시오. (4점)

> Girl: You look tired this morning.
> Boy: I got up very early to study for the exam.
> Girl: Good for you. The early bird catches the worm.
> Boy: No. The early bird gets tired quickly.
> Girl: Do you mean you don't like to get up early?
> Boy: Yes, that's exactly what I mean.

→ _____

**10** 다음 대화의 빈칸 (A), (B)에 공통으로 들어갈 적절한 것은? (3점)

> Boy: Wow, you really dance well.
> Girl: Thanks. I love dancing. Everyone in my family is good at dancing.
> Boy: Really? Your parents (A)_____ well, too?
> Girl: Yes. They're also good singers.
> Boy: What a family! I wish I could (B)_____ like you.

① talk      ② walk      ③ sing

④ study      ⑤ dance

## 11 다음 문장을 자연스러운 대화가 되도록 순서를 바르게 나열한 것은? (3점)

> (A) Wow. Break a leg!
> (B) What? Do you mean I have to break one of my legs?
> (C) I have to sing at the school's English pop song contest.
> (D) No, it's an expression meaning I hope you do well.

① (B)-(A)-(D)-(C)　② (B)-(D)-(A)-(C)

③ (C)-(B)-(A)-(D)　④ (C)-(A)-(B)-(D)

⑤ (D)-(A)-(C)-(B)

## 12 다음 중 밑줄 친 관계대명사의 쓰임이 적절하지 않은 것은? (3점)

① I have a friend <u>whose</u> parents are from Japan.

② We helped someone <u>whose</u> leg was broken.

③ I need a table <u>which</u> is very long.

④ This is my new phone <u>which</u> design is very innovative.

⑤ He came back with two pots <u>which</u> were full of wisdom.

## 13 다음 주어진 문장을 어법상 적절하게 영어로 옮긴 것은? (3점)

> • 비가 오고 있지 않다면 우리는 산책할 수 있을 텐데.

① If it were raining, we could take a walk.

② If it were raining, we could not take a walk.

③ If it were not raining, we can take a walk.

④ If it were not raining, we could take a walk.

⑤ If it were not raining, we could not take a walk.

## 14 다음 중 해석이 <u>어색한</u> 문장은? (4점)

① The crown was set with precious jewels.
(그 왕관에는 값비싼 보석들이 박혀 있었다.)

② The magic carriage turned back into a pumpkin. (그 마법 마차가 호박으로 돌아왔다.)

③ The narrow roads are crowded with people.
(좁은 길들이 사람들로 붐빈다.)

④ The hotel offers excellent facilities for families. (그 호텔은 가족들을 위한 훌륭한 시설을 제공한다.)

⑤ I'm certainly never going there again.
(나는 아마도 거기에 다시 안 갈 거야.)

## 15 다음 〈보기〉의 문장을 '가정법 과거' 구문을 사용하여 밑줄 친 (A)의 우리말과 같도록 고쳐 쓰시오. (4점)

> 보기
> • It will be great if there are men as wise as Birbal.
> (A): <u>Birbal처럼 현명한 자들이 있다면 아주 좋을 텐데.</u>

→ _____

**[16~18]** 다음 글을 읽고 물음에 답하시오.

A Potful of Wisdom
*One day, the king of Persia @sent an official with a strange favor.*

Persian Official:  I hear you have a lot of wise men in your country. (A) I've been asked by my king to bring him a ⓑpotful of wisdom.

Official 5: (B) How can we put wisdom in a pot?

Akbar: (C) Can you bring him a potful of wisdom, Birbal?

Birbal: It won't be a ⓒproblem.

Birbal: (D) Could you please wait a few weeks?

Persian Official: (E) Of course! Take as much time as you need.

*A few weeks later, Birbal came back with two pots* (가)_____ *necks were really narrow. He offered one to the Persian official.*

Birbal: You can take this pot of wisdom to your king. Please ask him to ⓓreturn the pot to us after he takes the wisdom out of it.

Birbal: The pot is very ⓔuseless, so please be careful not to break it. We only have two pots of wisdom.

**16** 위 글의 (A)~(E) 중 다음 문장이 들어가기에 알맞은 곳은?
(4점)

> That makes no sense!

① (A)  ② (B)  ③ (C)  ④ (D)  ⑤ (E)

**17** 위 글의 밑줄 친 @~ⓔ 중 문맥상 쓰임이 <u>어색한</u> 것은? (3점)

① @  ② ⓑ  ③ ⓒ  ④ ⓓ  ⑤ ⓔ

**18** 위 글의 빈칸 (가)에 들어갈 말로 적절한 것은? (3점)

① where  ② who  ③ whose
④ that  ⑤ why

**[19~20]** 다음 글을 읽고 물음에 답하시오.

Akbar, the third Mogul emperor, had a number of wise officials at @his court. Among them (A)were a man (B)who name was Raja Birbal. He was famous for his quick wit and was very wise with ⓑhis words. Thus, the emperor always liked to have Birbal near ⓒhim. To test ⓓhis officials' wisdom, Akbar often asked them strange questions.
One day, ⓔhe came up with an (C)interested question.

Akbar: Someone pulled a hair from my head today. What should I do to him?

Official 1:  He should be (D)punished, of course.

Official 2: Yes, punish him!

**19** 위 글의 밑줄 친 @~ⓔ 중 가리키는 대상이 나머지 넷과 <u>다른</u> 것은? (3점)

① @  ② ⓑ  ③ ⓒ  ④ ⓓ  ⑤ ⓔ

**20** 위 글의 밑줄 친 (A)~(D) 중 어법상 올바르지 않은 것이 있다면 그 개수는 모두 몇 개인가? (4점)

① 0개  ② 1개  ③ 2개
④ 3개  ⑤ 4개

**[21~22]** 다음 글을 읽고 물음에 답하시오.

The next day, Akbar announced that he would send Birbal to heaven.

Birbal: I would be more than happy to go to heaven and keep your father company. How did you come up with this wonderful idea?

Akbar: Actually, it was my barber ⓐwho came up with the idea.

Birbal: I see. Please give me some time to prepare.

Birbal got ⓑa few trusty men to build a tunnel from the funeral grounds to his house. On the day of his burial, he escaped through the tunnel and ⓒhide in his house. For the next six months, he made sure not ⓓto cut his hair or shave his face.

Akbar: "Birbal, you're back! How's my father doing?"

Birbal: "Your father's doing very well. The only problem is that he can't get a haircut because there's no barber in heaven. That's the reason ⓔwhy my hair is so long."

**21** 위 글의 내용과 일치하는 것은? (4점)

① 악바르는 비르발을 천국으로 보내자는 생각을 떠올렸다.

② 비르발은 천국으로 가는 것을 두려워했다.

③ 비르발은 자신의 매장 날 터널을 통해 탈출했다.

④ 비르발은 악바르의 아버지가 천국에서 지루해 한다고 말했다.

⑤ 비르발은 악바르에게 돌아오기 전에 깔끔히 면도를 했다.

**22** 위 글의 ⓐ~ⓔ 중 어법상 올바르지 않은 것은? (4점)

① ⓐ    ② ⓑ    ③ ⓒ    ④ ⓓ    ⑤ ⓔ

**[23~24]** 다음 글을 읽고 물음에 답하시오.

Akbar, the third Mogul emperor, had ⓐa number of wise officials at his court. Among them (A)_____ a man whose name was Raja Birbal. He was famous for his quick wit and was very wise with his words. Thus, the emperor always liked to have Birbal near him.

**23** 밑줄 친 ⓐ와 바꿔 쓸 수 있는 것은? (3점)

① few    ② some    ③ many

④ much    ⑤ a few

**24** 빈칸 (A)에 적절한 것은? (3점)

① is    ② am    ③ are

④ was    ⑤ were

**25** 다음 글에서 지혜의 항아리 안에 들어 있었던 것은? (3점)

Akbar looked inside the other pot and found a pumpkin just as big as the pot.

Akbar: I see! The pumpkin can't be taken out without breaking the pot. How did you do it?

Birbal: I put the pots over pumpkin flowers and waited until the pumpkins grew as big as the pots.

Akbar: Hahaha! This certainly is a potful of wisdom!

① 호박    ② 오이    ③ 참외    ④ 수박    ⑤ 고구마

[26~28] 다음 글을 읽고 물음에 답하시오.

A few weeks later, Birbal came back with ⓐtwo pots whose necks were really narrow. He offered one to the Persian official.

Birbal: You can take this pot of wisdom to your king. Please ask him to return the pot to us after he takes the wisdom out of it. The pot is very precious, so please be careful ⓑto not break it. We only have two pots of wisdom.

The Persian official looked inside the pot and became speechless. He thanked Birbal and left for his country.

Persian Official: It would be great if ⓒthere were a man as wise as Birbal in our country.

After the Persian official left, Akbar asked Birbal what was inside the pot.

Birbal: Here is the other pot. You can see for yourself.

Akbar looked inside the other pot and found a pumpkin just as big as the pot.

Akbar: I see! The pumpkin can't be ⓓtaken out without breaking the pot. How did you do it?

Birbal: I put the pots over pumpkin flowers and waited until the pumpkins ⓔgrew as big as the pots.

Akbar: Hahaha! This certainly is a potful of wisdom!

## 26 위 글의 내용과 일치하는 것은? (4점)

① Birbal put pumpkin flowers over pots.

② Akbar was not satisfied with Birbal's solution.

③ Birbal told Akbar to look inside the other pot.

④ The persian official didn't think Birbal was wise.

⑤ The persian official left with two pots of wisdom.

## 27 위 글의 밑줄 친 ⓐ~ⓔ 중 어법상 옳지 않은 것은? (3점)

① ⓐ   ② ⓑ   ③ ⓒ   ④ ⓓ   ⑤ ⓔ

## 28 위 글에서 다음 빈칸에 적절한 단어를 찾아 쓰시오. (4점)

(A) Something that is _____ is valuable and important and should not be wasted or used without care.

(B) If you are _____, you are temporarily unable to speak, usually because something has shocked you.

→ (A) _____, (B) _____

## 29 다음 글을 읽고, 알맞은 전치사를 고르면? (3점)

Akbar, the third Mogul emperor, had a number of wise officials (A)_____ his court. Among them was a man and his name was Raja Birbal. He was famous (B)_____ his quick wit and was very wise (C)_____ his words. Thus, the emperor always liked to have Birbal near him.

| | (A) | (B) | (C) |
|---|---|---|---|
| ① | at | for | with |
| ② | at | for | of |
| ③ | at | from | with |
| ④ | in | from | of |
| ⑤ | in | for | with |

◎ 선택형 문항의 답안은 컴퓨터용 수정 싸인펜을 사용
하여 OMR 답안지에 바르게 표기하시오.
◎ 서술형 문제는 답을 답안지에 반드시 검정 볼펜으
로 쓰시오.
◎ 총 26문항 100점 만점입니다. 문항별 배점은 각
문항에 표시되어 있습니다.

[전북 ○○중]

**01** 다음 빈칸에 들어갈 말이 순서대로 짝지어진 것은?     (4점)

- Let's find _____ what happened there.
- It is _____ to have snow in April.

① at – natural      ② on – common

③ out – unusual    ④ from – natural

⑤ to – strange

[경북 ○○중]

**02** 다음 빈칸에 들어갈 단어로 적절하지 않은 것은?     (4점)

(A) He put _____ a beautiful sign saying, "enjoy your life."

(B) The firefighter tried to put _____ the fire.

(C) It's very cold outside. You'd better put _____ your coat.

(D) Because the cook will quit the job, my owner will put me in charge _____ the restaurant.

① off    ② on    ③ out    ④ up    ⑤ of

[전북 ○○중]

[3~4] 다음 대화를 읽고 물음에 답하시오.

Anna: What's wrong? You don't look so good.
Suho: I'm still thinking about our soccer match last week.
Anna: Do you mean the game you lost last week?
Suho: Yes. I wish I could forget about it, but I can't.

Anna: Well, you should always live for today.
Suho: Do you mean I should forget the past and focus on the present?
Anna: Yes, exactly. People say, "Yesterday is history, tomorrow is a mystery, and today is a gift. That's why it's called the _____."
Suho: Now I see. You know so many great expressions. You're as wise as my grandma.

**03** 위 대화를 읽고 알 수 없는 것은?     (3점)

① Suho의 표정이 좋지 않은 이유

② Suho가 바라는 것

③ Anna가 Suho에게 해 준 조언의 내용

④ 지난 주 Suho가 참여했던 축구 경기의 결과

⑤ Anna가 좋은 표현들을 많이 아는 이유

**04** 위 대화의 빈칸에 들어갈 적절한 한 단어를 대화 내용에서 찾아 쓰시오.     (4점)

→ _____

[경북 ○○중]

**05** 다음 (A)~(D)를 자연스러운 대화가 되도록 바르게 배열한 것은?     (4점)

A: Wow, you play the guitar very well.

(A) What a family! I wish I could play the guitar like you.

(B) Thanks. I love playing the guitar. I learned it from my sister.

(C) Yes, she is in her school band.

(D) Really? Does your sister play the guitar, too?

① (A)-(B)-(D)-(C)    ② (B)-(A)-(D)-(C)

③ (B)-(A)-(C)-(D)    ④ (B)-(D)-(C)-(A)

⑤ (D)-(C)-(A)-(B)

[6~7] 다음 대화를 읽고 물음에 답하시오.

> Anna: What's wrong? You don't look so good.
> Suho: I'm still thinking about our soccer match last week.
> Anna: Do you mean the game you lost last week?
> Suho: Yes. I ⓐ_____ I could forget about it, but I can't.
> Anna: Well, you should always live for today.
> Suho: Do you mean I should forget the past and focus on the present?
> Anna: Yes, exactly. People say, "Yesterday is (A)_____, tomorrow is a (B)_____, and today is (C)_____. That's why it's called the present."
> Suho: Now I see. You know so many great expressions. You're as wise as my grandma.

**06** 위 대화의 빈칸 (A)~(C)에 적절한 것은?  (4점)

|     | (A)       | (B)      | (C)      |
|-----|-----------|----------|----------|
| ①   | history   | mystery  | a gift   |
| ②   | history   | a gift   | mystery  |
| ③   | mystery   | history  | a gift   |
| ④   | mystery   | a gift   | history  |
| ⑤   | a gift    | mystery  | history  |

**07** 위 대화의 ⓐ에 가장 적절한 것은?  (3점)

① want  ② wish  ③ wonder
④ promise  ⑤ hope

**08** 다음 대화의 빈칸에 가장 적절한 표현은?  (4점)

> G: You look worried. Is something wrong?
> B: I had to hand in my science report by yesterday, But I didn't.
> G: _____
> B: Do you mean it's better to hand it in even though it's late?
> G: Yes, exactly. You should always finish what you've started.

① Heaven helps those who help themselves.
② If, at first, you don't succeed, try, try again.
③ The early bird catches the worm.
④ I'll keep my fingers crossed for you.
⑤ It's better late than never.

**09** 다음 대화가 어울리도록 ⓐ~ⓓ를 적절하게 연결한 것은? (4점)

> G: You look tired this morning.
> B: I got up very early to study for the exam.
> G: _____
> B: _____
> G: _____
> B: _____

> ⓐ No. The early bird gets tired quickly.
> ⓑ Yes, that's exactly what I mean.
> ⓒ Good for you. The early bird catches the worm.
> ⓓ Do you mean you don't like to get up early?

① ⓒ-ⓐ-ⓓ-ⓑ  ② ⓒ-ⓓ-ⓐ-ⓑ
③ ⓓ-ⓑ-ⓒ-ⓐ  ④ ⓓ-ⓐ-ⓒ-ⓑ
⑤ ⓐ-ⓑ-ⓒ-ⓓ

**10** 다음 문장을 가정법 과거를 활용하여 영어로 바꾸어 쓰시오. (7 words)  (5점)

> • 내가 너처럼 춤을 출 수 있으면 좋겠다.

→ _____

**11** 다음 대화의 빈칸에 들어갈 표현으로 가장 적절한 것은? (4점)

> A: _____
> B: Do you mean everyone has a chance at success?
> A: Yes, that's what I mean.

① Let's call it a day.

② Every dog has its day.

③ It's time to hit the sack.

④ It's time to hit the books.

⑤ A picture is worth a thousand words.

**12** 다음 중 빈칸에 들어갈 말이 나머지와 <u>다른</u> 것은? (3점)

① Lisa is the girl _____ likes to watch action movies.

② I helped someone _____ car broke down.

③ I met a boy _____ name was James.

④ I want to live in a house _____ garden is covered with flowers.

⑤ Look at the woman _____ dress looks beautiful.

**13** 다음 우리말과 일치하도록 빈칸에 알맞은 말을 쓰시오. (4점)

> • 황제는 늘 Birbal을 곁에 두고 싶어 했다.

→ The emperor always liked _____ _____ _____ _____ him.

**14** 다음 중 어법상 어색한 문장을 <u>모두</u> 고른 것은? (4점)

> ⓐ What you do, I'll support you.
> ⓑ What I really need is just a short break.
> ⓒ The cookies his mother made were delicious.
> ⓓ I want to meet you at the place which we met yesterday.
> ⓔ He didn't study hard. That's the reason why he failed the exam.
> ⓕ I saw a boy and a dog which were running along the street.

① ⓐ, ⓕ

② ⓐ, ⓓ, ⓕ

③ ⓑ, ⓒ, ⓕ

④ ⓐ, ⓒ, ⓓ, ⓕ

⑤ ⓒ, ⓓ, ⓔ, ⓕ

**15** 다음 Minho의 바람을 완성할 때 빈칸에 들어갈 말로 가장 적절한 것은? (4점)

If it _____ not raining now, I _____ my dog.

① be - will walk

② is - would walk

③ was - was walking

④ were - would have walked

⑤ were - would walk

**[16~18] 다음 글을 읽고 물음에 답하시오.**

*One day, the king of Persia sent an official with ⓐ a strange favor.*

Persian Official: I hear you have a lot of wise men in your country. I've been asked by my king to bring him a potful of wisdom.
Official 5: That makes no sense! How can we put wisdom in a pot?
Akbar: Can you bring him a potful of wisdom, Birbal?
Birbal: It won't be a problem.
Birbal: Could you please wait a few weeks?
Persian Official: Of course! Take as much time as you need.

*A few weeks later, Birbal came back with two pots whose necks were really narrow. He offered one to the Persian official.*

Birbal: You can take this pot of wisdom to your king. Please ask him ⓑ돌려주다 the pot to us after he takes the wisdom out of it.
Birbal: The pot is very precious, so please be careful not to break it. We only have two pots of wisdom.

*The Persian official looked inside the pot and became speechless. He thanked Birbal and left for his country.*

Persian Official: It would be great if there were a man as wise as Birbal in our country.

*After the Persian official left, Akbar asked Birbal what was inside the pot.*

Birbal: Here is the other pot. You can see for yourself.

*Akbar looked inside the other pot and found a pumpkin just as big as the pot.*

Akbar: I see! ⓒ항아리를 깨지 않고는 호박을 꺼낼 수가 없구려. How did you do it?
Birbal: I put the pots over pumpkin flowers and waited until the pumpkins grew as big as the pots.
Akbar: Hahaha! This certainly is a potful of wisdom!

**16** 위 글의 밑줄 친 ⓐ의 의미로 가장 적절한 것은? (4점)

① 페르시아 왕에게 지혜의 항아리를 가져가는 것
② 호박꽃을 항아리에 담아 오는 것
③ 지혜로운 신하를 페르시아로 보내는 것
④ 두 개의 항아리 중 입구가 좁은 것을 가져가는 것
⑤ 항아리를 깨지 않고 조심히 운반하는 것

**17** 위 글의 밑줄 친 ⓑ에 들어갈 형태로 가장 적절한 것은? (3점)

① return  ② returning  ③ to return
④ will return  ⑤ returned

**18** 위 글의 밑줄 친 ⓒ의 우리말과 의미가 일치하도록 다음 단어를 배열할 때, 6번째 들어갈 단어는? (5점)

> → The pumpkin ＿＿＿ ＿＿＿ ＿＿＿ ＿＿＿ ＿＿＿ ＿＿＿ ＿＿＿.
> (can't, pot, out, the, taken, breaking, be, without)
> ※ 주어진 단어를 모두 한 번씩 사용할 것.

① can't  ② out  ③ taken
④ breaking  ⑤ without

**[19~20] 다음 글을 읽고 물음에 답하시오.**

(A) Akbar, the third Mogul emperor, had a number of wise officials at his court. (가)Among them was a man whose name was Raja Birbal. He was famous for his quick wit and was very wise with his words. Thus, the emperor always liked to have Birbal near him.

Sweet Punishment
(나)To test his officials' wisdom, Akbar often asked them strange questions. One day, he came up with an interesting question.

Akbar: Someone pulled a hair from my head today. What should I do to him?
Official 1: (다)He should be punished, of course.
Official 2: Yes, punish him!

(B) Akbar turned to Birbal?
Akbar: What would you do if you were in my place, Birbal?
Birbal: If I were you, I would ⓐgive sweets him.
Official 3: What's he talking about?
Official 4: Birbal's crazy!
Akbar: What ⓑmade you to say so?
Birbal: The person ⓒwho pulled your hair must be your grandson. No one else could do such a thing.
Akbar: You are indeed correct, Birbal. I'm so glad ⓓhaving someone ⓔas wisely as you near me.

**19** 위 글의 (A)에서 밑줄 친 (가)~(다) 문장을 가장 적절하게 분석한 학생을 고르면? (4점)

① 연수: (가) - 형용사구가 문장의 앞으로 나오면서 주어와 동사의 도치가 일어났어.
② 효영: (가) - 가정법 과거의 문장이므로 3인칭 단수 주어에 맞는 be동사의 과거형 was가 쓰였어.
③ 혜민: (나) - to부정사가 동사의 목적을 나타내는 부사적 용법으로 쓰였어.
④ 준행: (나) - 복수 명사의 소유격을 표시하려면 officals'를 official's로 바꿔야 해.
⑤ 의성: (다) - 조동사 뒤에는 to부정사가 와야 하는데 수동태가 쓰였기 때문에 to를 생략했어.

**20** 위 글의 (B)에서 밑줄 친 ⓐ~ⓔ 중 문법적으로 옳은 것은? (4점)

① ⓐ   ② ⓑ   ③ ⓒ   ④ ⓓ   ⑤ ⓔ

**[21~22] 다음 글을 읽고 물음에 답하시오.**

Hello, everyone! Time flies. I can't believe it's time to say goodbye. Thanks to my teachers and friends, I was really happy here. I wish I could (A)_____ and live these years over again, but it's time to start a new journey to high school. I hope I can see you again. Thank you.

**21** 위 글의 빈칸 (A)에 들어갈 말로 가장 적절한 것은? (3점)

① say goodbye
② go to high school
③ fly in the sky
④ travel to a new place
⑤ go back to my first year

**22** What's the purpose of the above speech? (4점)

① to say goodbye
② to welcome new students
③ to keep his or her promise
④ to give advice to his or her friends
⑤ to explain how to study in high school

**[23~25] 다음 글을 읽고 물음에 답하시오.**

The Persian official looked inside the pot and became speechless. He thanked Birbal and left for his country.
Persian Official: It would be great if there (가)[is / were] a wise man like Birbal in our country. (A)

After the Persian official left, Akbar asked Birbal (나)[what / that] was inside the pot.
Birbal: Here is the other pot. You can see for yourself. (B)

Akbar looked inside the other pot and found a pumpkin just as big as the pot.
Akbar: I see! The pumpkin can't be taken out without (다)[breaking / break] the pot. (C)
Birbal: I put the pots over pumpkin flowers and waited until the pumpkins grew as big as the pots. (D)
Akbar: (E) Hahaha! This certainly is a potful of wisdom!

**23** 위 글에서 〈보기〉 문장이 들어갈 위치로 가장 적절한 것은?

(4점)

> **보기**
>
> How did you do it?

① (A)  ② (B)  ③ (C)  ④ (D)  ⑤ (E)

**24** 위 글의 (가)~(다)에 들어갈 말로 가장 적절한 것은? (4점)

| | (가) | (나) | (다) |
|---|---|---|---|
| ① | is | that | break |
| ② | were | what | breaking |
| ③ | were | that | break |
| ④ | is | what | break |
| ⑤ | were | that | breaking |

**25** 위 글의 내용과 일치하지 <u>않는</u> 것은? (3점)

① The Persian official was surprised when he looked inside the pot.
② The Persian official had a wise man like Birbal in his country.
③ The pumpkins grew inside the pots.
④ The pot contained a pumpkin as big as the pot itself.
⑤ Akbar was satisfied with the wisdom of Birbal.

**26** 다음 글의 내용과 일치하는 문장은? (4점)

Dear Jaeha,

Time flies. I cannot believe that it is time to say goodbye. I still remember the time when we went camping together. I really liked the movie we watched that night. I also loved to play basketball with you after school. I really want to thank you for teaching me basketball skills. I'm so sad because I don't have much time to be with you. I hope we keep in touch even after we graduate.

Best, Jake

① 재하와 제이크는 함께 캠핑을 간 적이 있다.
② 재하는 제이크와 함께 보았던 영화가 아주 좋았다.
③ 제이크는 재하에게 농구 기술을 가르쳐 주었다.
④ 재하는 졸업 후에 제이크에게 연락할 것이다.
⑤ 편지를 쓴 사람은 재하이다.

# 정답 및 해설

## Lesson 4 (중간) 1회

```
01 ②  02 ①  03 ③  04 ②
05 where you took the photo  06 ②  07 ③  08 ②  09 ②
10 why Tom was late  11 ①  12 ①
13 (A) Can you tell me what you did?
   (B) Nobody knows why she was late.
14 ④  15 ②  16 ③  17 ⑤  18 ④  19 ⑤  20 ③  21 ⑤
22 ②  23 ①  24 ②  25 ②  26 ⑤  27 ④  28 ④  29 ④
```

**01** give a hand: 돕다 give a call: 전화하다

**02** consider는 '고려하다'라는 뜻으로 make 정도로 바꿔야 한다.

**03** 'I think it's coming from over there.'라는 답으로 보아 궁금한 것을 물을 때 쓰는 'I wonder ~.' 표현의 ③번이 적절하다.

**04** 'It's a long hiking path around Jejudo.'라고 설명하고 있으므로 '설명'을 요청하는 표현이 적절하다.

**05** 궁금하다는 표현의 'I wonder'가 이미 있으므로 의문사가 where로 시작하여 간접의문문의 어순(의문사+주어+동사)으로 쓴다.

**06** 'Some people are dancing to the rhythm.'이라고 했다.

**07** Jaden이 'Let's join them.'이라고 하자 Yuri가 'Sure. Why not?'이라고 했다.

**08** 'We should try their bread then.'에 'Sure.'라고 했다.

**09** (C) 음성 가이드를 대여하고 싶다는 말에 (B) 여기 있다고 하고 (D) 사용법 설명을 요청하자 (A) 설명해 주는 순서이다.

**10** 간접의문문은 '의문사+주어+동사'의 어순이다.

**11** 'Could you explain a little bit more about it?'이라고 했다.

**12** 영작하면 'I wonder where that music is coming from.'이다.

**13** 간접의문문은 '의문사+주어+동사'의 어순이다.

**14** 과거보다 앞선 시제이므로 과거완료로 쓰는 것이 적절하다. have gone → had gone

**15** 간접의문문은 '의문사+주어+동사'의 어순이다.

**16** ⓐ harvests → harvest
ⓑ interviewed → was interviewed
ⓓ had kept → kept, was → had been
ⓔ 전체 → Catching ~ place can destroy the ocean.

**17** 어떻게 해녀들이 어떤 호흡 장치도 없이 물속에서 계속 해산물을 채취하는지는 알 수 없다.

**18** ⓓ는 join이 아니라 train 정도가 적절하다.

**19** This가 (E) 앞 문장의 내용을 가리키므로 (E)가 적절하다.

**20** 해녀의 특별한 점에 대해 답하는 내용이다.

**21** 'Catching too much marine life at one time in one place can destroy the ocean.'이라고 했다.

**22** 사역동사 make 다음에 '목적어+동사원형'이 나오도록 쓴다.

**23** (A) 해녀의 사진을 찍기 시작했을 때의 어려움을 토로하고 있다. (B) 해녀들이 가족들의 생계비를 버는 가장이 되어 왔다는 것으로 보아 강한 여성의 '상징'이 적절하다. (C) 한곳에서 한 번에 너무 많은 해산물을 채취하면 바다를 파괴할 수 있다.

**24** (B) 다음의 She가 주어진 문장의 'one of the haenyeo'이므로 (B)가 적절하다.

**25** (A) attend가 '참석하다'라는 뜻의 타동사로 쓰였다. (B) 앞에서 '특별한 사람'이라고 했으므로 happiness가 적절하다. (C) Everyone이 주어이므로 단수 was가 적절하다.

**26** ⓔ의 conserve는 '보호하다'라는 뜻으로 destroy가 적절하다.

**27** (가)와 ④는 접속사이고 나머지는 모두 관계대명사이다.

**28** 'Zin Kim has promoted the culture of Jeju haenyeo worldwide'라고 했다.

**29** intangible: 만질 수 없는, 만져서 알 수 없는, 무형의

## Lesson 4 (중간) 2회

```
01 ⑤  02 (A) give (B) hand 또는 (A) do (B) favor
03 ④  04 ⑤  05 ④  06 ①  07 ④  08 ①  09 ⑤
10 The boy doesn't understand why his mom is angry.
11 ⑤  12 ①  13 ⑤  14 ②  15 ⑤  16 ③  17 ④  18 ④
19 ③  20 ③  21 ④  22 ③  23 ③  24 ①  25 ⑤  26 ③
27 ⑤
```

**01** realize: 깨닫다, 인식하다

**02** give someone a hand: 도와주다 do someone a favor: 호의를 베풀다, 남의 부탁을 들어주다

**03** 순서대로 배열하면 (E)-(B)-(D)-(A)-(C)이다.

**04** '보고 즐기기만을 위한 음악'이라는 내용은 잘못되었다.

**05** 'That's Gwangandaegyo in Busan.'이라는 답으로 보아 '장소'를 물었음을 알 수 있다.

**06** 'it's coming from over there'라는 답으로 보아 '장소'를 물었음을 알 수 있다.

**07** 'It's a kind of community band music.'이라고 했다.

**08** (C) 익선동이 좋은 곳이라고 하자 (A) 동의하며 홍보 방법을 궁금해 하자 (B) SNS에 사진과 기사 게시를 제안하고 (D) 사진으로 사람들이 알게 될 것이라고 하는 순서가 적절하다.

**09** 'They're waiting ~'이라는 답으로 보아 ⑤번이 적절하다.

**10** 간접의문문의 어순, '의문사+주어+동사'에 주의한다.

**11** 'from the band'가 아니라 'from B'이다.

**12** 'mind'로 물으면 '부정'으로 답해야 '긍정'의 의미가 된다.

**13** ① had lost → lost, gave → had given

② gone → been

③ has she lived → had she lived

④ has → had

**14** 내가 도착한 것보다 기차가 떠난 것이 앞서므로 '내가 도착한 것'은 '과거'로, '기차가 떠난 것'은 '과거완료'로 쓴다.

**15** 간접의문문은 '의문사+주어+동사'의 어순이다.

**16** 왜 Zin Kim이 사진작가가 되었는지는 알 수 없다.

**17** 앞의 내용과 상반되는 내용이 이어지므로 'However'가 적절하다.

**18** Because로 (D) 앞 문장의 'why I wanted to take their pictures'에 대한 이유를 언급하므로 (D)가 적절하다.

**19** (A) 완료시제이므로 과거분사 known이, (B) Everyone이 주어이므로 단수 was가, (C) continue의 목적어로 to take가 적절하다.

**20** Zin Kim은 사진작가이다.

**21** happen to+동사원형: 우연히 ~하다

**22** (A)와 ③: 부사적 용법 ①, ②: 명사적 용법 ④, ⑤: 형용사적 용법

**23** 'For example'로 (C) 앞 문장의 예를 들고 있으므로 (C)가 적절하다.

**24** 대답으로 해녀의 특별한 점에 대해 언급하고 있다.

**25** 'with happiness'로 보아 '기쁨'이다.

**26** '어떻게 해녀의 사진을 찍는 것에 관심을 갖게 되었는지'에 대한 답이므로 ③번이 적절하다.

**27** 사진작가가 해녀들이 아름답게 보이도록 하겠다고 약속했다.


# Lesson 5 (중간)　　1회

| 01 ④ | 02 ① | 03 convenient | | 04 ④ | 05 ④ | 06 ④ |
|------|------|------|------|------|------|------|
| 07 ① | 08 ② | 09 him to play | | 10 ② | 11 ④ | 12 ③ |
| 13 ② | 14 ④ | 15 ③ | 16 ③ | 17 ② | 18 ⑤ | 19 ③ | 20 ② |
| 21 ③ | | | | | | |

22 not only a political supporter but also a good friend

| 23 ① | 24 ④ | 25 ⑤ | 26 ⑤ | 27 judged | | 28 ④ | 29 ① |

**01** <보기>와 ④: 명사-형용사 ①, ②, ⑤: 동사-명사 ③ 반의어

**02** Chances are that: 아마 ~일 것이다, ~할 가능성이 충분하다

**03** 전화로 예약할 필요 없이 온라인으로 된다고 했으므로 'convenient(편리한)'가 적절하다.

**04** Yuri는 'you don't have to do that'이라고 했다.

**05** (C) 긴장한 것 같다고 하자 (B) 발표가 걱정된다고 하고 (A) 걱정 말라며 잘할 거라고 하자 (D) 고맙다고 하는 순서이다.

**06** be good at: ~을 잘하다, like: ~ 같은

**07** 'I can't wait!'는 '너무 기다려져!'라는 뜻이다.

**08** 긴장하는 G에게 걱정 말라며 '긴장 풀고 즐기라'고 조언한다.

**09** advise의 목적격보어로 to부정사를 쓴다.

**10** '접속사+주어+동사'를 분사구문으로 바꾼 것이다. 분사구문이 '이유'의 부사절을 대신하는 경우이다.

**11** 주어진 문장은 '걱정'하는 내용이다. (D) 뒤에서 '스스로에게 너무 많은 압박을 주고 있는 것 같다'며 조언하는 말이 나오므로 (D)가 적절하다. What if ~? ~하면 어쩌지?

**12** 뒤에서 '그냥 학교 경기일 뿐'이라고 했으므로 '그럴 필요 없다'고 하는 것이 자연스럽다.

**13** '개인적인 질문'이라고 했는데 그럼 '대답해야만 한다'고 하는 것은 어색하다.

**14** 'not only A but also B'에서 A와 B에는 문법적으로 같은 성격의 어구가 와야 한다. ① → She can not only read but also speak German. ② singing → sings ③ cheaply → cheap ⑤ being → being 생략

**15** 'As she thought ~'를 분사구문으로 만든 것이므로 Thinking이 되어야 한다.

**16** 낯선 사람에게서 조언을 받았다는 내용은 없다.

**17** ⓑ는 'a political rival'이고 나머지는 'Franklin'이다.

**18** 'if you do them one favor'가 아닌 'if they do you one favor'가 본문의 내용이다.

**19** not only A but also B = B as well as A: A뿐만 아니라 B도

**20** 뒤에서 'If you want to turn a rival into a friend, don't do your rival a favor. Instead, ask your rival to do you a favor.'라고 했으므로 ②번이 적절하다.

**21** Franklin의 정치적 경쟁자의 이름은 알 수 없다.

**22** not only A but also B: A뿐만 아니라 B도

**23** 접속사 없이 두 개의 절이 연결되어 있으므로 Wanting으로 분사구문을 만들어야 한다.

**24** 전혀 모르는 사람에게 자신의 고민에 대해서 말한 후 기분이 훨씬 좋아졌다고 했으므로 ④번이 적절하다.

**25** 전혀 모르는 사람에게 자신의 고민에 대해서 말한 후 기분이 훨씬 좋아졌다고 했다.

**26** ⓐ had → has ⓑ sat → sitting ⓒ many → much ⓓ Enough strangely → Strangely enough

**27** '판단되거나'는 '수동'의 의미이므로 과거분사 형태가 적절하다.

**28** (B) 선생님이 다가와서 꼿꼿이 서 있어 보라고 말하고 (C) 몇 분을 우뚝 선 후에 더 이상 긴장되지 않았으며 (A) 자신감이 생겼다는 순서가 적절하다.

**29** '긴장을 덜 하게 되는 방법'에 대해 말하고 있다.

## Lesson 5 (중간) <sup>2회</sup>

**01** '명사 - 형용사'의 관계인데 magic은 그 자체로 명사와 형용사로 쓰이며 magical이 형용사형이다.

**02** chances are that: 아마 ~일 것이다, ~할 가능성이 충분하다

**03** '개가 신발을 씹어 버렸다고 하면서 항상 그렇게 한다'고 했으니 '걱정된다'는 말이 적절하다.

**04** Yuri는 'you're putting too much pressure on yourself'라고 했다.

**05** (C) 수영 대회가 걱정된다는 말에 (A) 걱정 말라고 조언하고 (B) 고마워하는 순서가 적절하다.

**06** 주어진 문장은 '걱정'하는 내용으로 (B) 뒤에서 '스스로에게 너무 많은 압박을 주고 있는 것 같다'고 했으므로 (B)가 적절하다.

**07** 뒤에서 'It's a just a school race.'라고 했으므로 ④번이 적절하다.

**08** 걱정하는 Jaden에게 Yuri가 조언하고 있는 대화이다.

**09** 뒤에서 '아빠가 도와주실 거'라고 했으므로 ③번이 적절하다.

**10** 'what time are we going to Grandma's place tomorrow morning?'이라고 묻자 'About 8 a.m.'이라고 답하고 있다.

**11** (B) 멕시코 레스토랑에 가 보겠느냐고 묻자 (A) 좋다며 전화해서 예약하겠다고 하고 (D) 온라인으로 할 수 있다고 하자 (C) 정말 편리하다고 하는 순서가 자연스럽다.

**12** '스스로에게 너무 많은 압박을 주고 있는 것 같다'는 말에 '네 말이 맞는 것 같다'라고 한 후, '지금보다 훨씬 더 열심히 연습하겠다'라고 말하는 것은 어색하다.

**13** '전화해서 예약하겠다'라는 말에 '온라인으로 할 수 있다'라고 했으므로 '전화할 필요 없다'라는 말이 적절하다. don't have to: ~할 필요 없다

**14** 파티에 초대된 것이므로 '수동'의 Invited가 적절하다.

**15** ① are → is ② play → plays ③ need → needs ④ punished → being punished

**16** 의미상 '이유'를 나타내는 부사절이 적절하다. 분사를 '접속사

(Because)+주어+동사'로 바꾼다.

**17** ⓐ에는 'nervous'가, 나머지는 'confident'가 들어가야 한다.

**18** chances are that: 아마 ~일 것이다, ~할 가능성이 충분하다

**19** 문제를 이야기하고 그에 대한 해결책을 제시하고 있다.

**20** '2분 정도 꼿꼿이 서 있는 것만으로도 자신감이 더 생길 수 있다'고 했으므로 ⑤번이 적절하다.

**21** part: 얼마만큼, 어느 정도 apart: 떨어져서, 떨어지게 하여

**22** 급우에게 부탁을 하고 그로 인해 좋은 친구가 되었다는 경험을 말하고 있다.

**23** '스트레스'를 받는 상황에서 '자신감'이 더 생길 수 있다고 하는 것이 자연스러우므로 relaxing이 아닌 stressful이 적절하다.

**24** 'Feeling nervous, Jisu was carefully studying her notes in her chair.'라고 했다.

**25** (A) chances are that: 아마 ~일 것이다 (B) 접속사가 없으므로 분사구문의 Feeling (C) not only feel과 같은 형태의 but also look이 적절하다.

**26** '친구가 없어서 신나고 즐거웠다'라고 하는 것은 어색하다.

**27** 새 책들에 얼마나 썼는지는 알 수 없다.

**28** 어떻게 하면 긴장을 덜 할 수 있는지에 관한 글이다.

**29** (A) be동사의 보어로 형용사 (B) 명사 events를 수식하는 형용사 (C) not only feel에 이어지는 but also look이 적절하다.

**30** 가족이나 친구에게 말한 것이 아니라 낯선 사람에게 말했다.

**31** 태호의 부모님이 그의 꿈을 지지했는지는 알 수 없다.

## Lesson 6 (기말) <sup>1회</sup>

**01** 뒤에서 '이해하지 못했다'라고 했으므로 clear를 unclear로 고쳐야 한다.

**02** '원했던 것이나 필요로 했던 것을 얻어서 행복한'을 의미하는 것은 'satisfied(만족한)'이다.

**03** ⓓ는 비인칭주어이지만 나머지는 모두 phone을 가리킨다.

**04** 내 그림에 대해 어떻게 생각하느냐는 질문에 ⓐ 멋있다며 상대방이 그렸는지 묻고 ⓓ 자기가 그렸다며 마음에 드는지 묻자 ⓒ 그렇다며 빵과 우유가 진짜처럼 보인다고 하고 ⓑ 고맙지만 독창적이지 않아서 별로 만족스럽지 않다고 하고 ⓔ 그렇게 생각 안 한다며 정말 멋진 그림인 것 같다고 하는 순서가 적절하다.

**05** '엄마가 추천하는 공부 방법'에 대한 언급은 나와 있지 않다.

**06** '빵, 샐러드, 스테이크' 등의 음식이 나오고 '덜 익었다', '계산서

좀 갖다 달라' 등의 말이 나오므로 '식당'이 적절하다.

**07** 여인이 'It's too rare for me.'라고 했다.

**08** Man이 'Would you like me to bring you another one?'이라고 하자 Woman이 'That's O.K. I need to be going.'이라고 했다.

**09** 'I promise I will be your first customer.'라고 했다.

**10** 불만족을 말하고 있으므로 '안 좋은 점'이 나와야 한다.

**11** 'be not satisfied with'는 '~에 만족하지 못하다'라는 의미로 불만족을 나타내는 표현이다.

**12** ② try+to부정사: ~하려고 노력하다, try+동명사: 시험 삼아 ~해 보다 ③ stop+to부정사: ~하기 위해 멈추다, stop+동명사: ~하기를 멈추다 ④ regret+to부정사: ~하게 되어 유감이다, regret+동명사: ~한 것을 후회하다 ⑤ remember+to부정사: ~할 것을 기억하다, remember+동명사: ~했던 것을 기억하다

**13** nevertheless는 '그럼에도 불구하고'라는 의미이므로 'Thus(따라서, 그러므로)' 정도로 바꾸는 것이 적절하다.

**14** ① the way와 how를 함께 쓸 수 없다. ② in → on ④ when → where ⑤ where I lived in → which I lived in 또는 where I lived

**15** (A) 주어가 I이므로 myself (B) I've에 연결되어 완료형을 만드는 had (C) '사람들이 이걸 사길 원할 거라고 생각해?'에 대한 대답이므로 customer가 적절하다.

**16** 뒤에서 다빈치가 요리사로 일했다는 내용이 나오며 마지막 부분에서 'Da Vinci believed that people would soon appreciate his creative cooking.'이라고 했으므로 'creative cook'이 적절하다.

**17** ⓐ painter → painters ⓑ in → of ⓒ even decorated → were even decorated ⓔ when → where

**18** ㉠ 앞에서 '손님들이 불만족스러워했다'라고 했으므로 결과를 나타내는 'As a result' ㉡ 뒤에서 '그런 일은 절대로 일어나지 않았다'라고 했으므로 'Unfortunately'가 적절하다.

**19** 주어진 문장의 'For example'로 (D)의 앞 문장에 대한 예를 들고 있으므로 (D)가 적절하다.

**20** 앞에서 'da Vinci never became a successful cook'이라고 했으므로 ⓓ는 'creative' 정도로 고치는 것이 적절하다.

**21** 영작하면 'He spent a lot of time cooking all kinds of food.'이므로 7번째 들어갈 단어는 cooking이다.

**22** 다빈치에게 주어진 여러 가지 일 중에서 요리를 향한 그의 열정을 설명하면서 창의적인 요리를 만들고 주방에서 사용할 새로운 기계들을 발명하였다는 내용의 글이므로 ②번이 적절하다.

**23** 사람들이 다빈치의 요리를 좋아했는지는 알 수 없다.

**24** 'He was given a chance to pursue his passion for cooking.'이라고 했고 'He created machines that could crush vegetables and pull spaghetti. He even made a device that could scare frogs away from the water tank.'라고 했다.

**25** ① pursue ② destroyed ③ device ④ engineer ⑤ passion 이 들어간다.

**26** 주어진 문장의 'As a result'로 (E) 앞의 내용에 대한 결과가 나오므로 (E)가 적절하다.

**27** 'be used to+(동)명사'는 '~에 익숙하다'라는 의미이다. 주어가 복수이고 시제가 과거이므로 'were used to'가 적절하다.

## Lesson 6 (기말)

```
01 ①  02 ⑤  03 ①  04 ④  05 ④  06 ⑤  07 ①  08 ①
09 ⑤  10 ⑤  11 ②
12 (D) This is the house where ghosts live.
13 ④  14 ⑤  15 ①  16 ②  17 now[Now] that
18 That's the reason why he hasn't finished the painting,
19 ③  20 ⑤  21 ②  22 ⑤  23 ②  24 ③  25 ④  26 ③
27 ⑤  28 ⑤  29 ⑤
```

**01** 모두 접두사 un-을 붙여 반의어를 만들 수 있지만, convenient는 in-을 붙여 inconvenient로 반의어를 만든다.

**02** ⑤번에는 'reasons'를 'kinds'로 고쳐 '한꺼번에 다섯 가지 종류의 음식을 요리하는 것은 어렵다'라는 의미로 쓰는 것이 적절하다. all at once: 갑자기, 한꺼번에

**03** 뒷부분에서 'It's too rare for me.'라고 했으므로 'I'm not satisfied with the steak.' 정도로 고치는 것이 적절하다.

**04** 'I thought you were interested in science.'라는 말에 'I was but not anymore.'라고 했다.

**05** 맛있다며 어디서 샀는지 묻자 (D) 직접 만든 거라고 답하고 (A) 정말이냐며 팔아도 되겠다고 하자 (C) 사람들이 이걸 사길 원할 거라고 생각하는지 묻고 (B) 물론이라고 답하는 순서가 적절하다.

**06** by itself: 저절로, 스스로

**07** 여자가 휴대전화를 왜 샀는지는 알 수 없다.

**08** 주어진 문장의 'It'이 (A) 앞의 'the steak'를 가리키므로 (A)가 적절하다.

**09** '빵, 샐러드, 스테이크' 등의 음식이 나오고 '덜 익었어요', '계산서 좀 갖다 주세요' 등의 말이 나오므로 '식당'이 적절하다.

**10** 배우가 되고 싶다는 말에 (d) 놀라며 과학에 관심이 있다고 생각했다고 하자 (a) 그랬었는데 더는 아니라며 영화 배우가 되고 싶다고 하고 (b) 배우가 되고 싶은 게 확실한지 묻자 (c) 그렇다며 최선을 다하겠다고 약속하는 순서가 적절하다.

**11** 여성은 'It's too rare for me.'라고 했다.

**12** 관계대명사 that은 전치사 다음에 쓰지 못하므로 관계대명사를 쓰려면 in which가 되어야 한다. <조건>에서 반드시 관계부사를 사용하여 고치라고 하였으므로 in which 대신에 where를 써서 고친다.

**13** ① at the place 삭제 ② tomorrow 삭제 ③ are people → people are ⑤ the way와 how는 함께 쓰지 않고 둘 중의 하나만 쓴다.

**14** (A) 앞의 내용에 대한 '결과'가 이어지므로 thus (B) 앞의 내용과 상반되게 역접으로 이어지므로 however가 적절하다.

**15** • The house가 선행사이므로 where • the day가 선행사이므로 when이 적절하다.

**16** 앞에서 'He spent a lot of time cooking all kinds of food'라고 했으므로 ⓑ는 'wasted' 정도로 바꾸는 것이 적절하다.

**17** now that: ~이기 때문에, ~이므로

**18** 배열하여 영작하면 'That's the reason why he hasn't finished the painting.'이다.

**19** 'be used to+(동)명사'는 '~에 익숙하다'라는 의미이다.

**20** (A) as (B) of (C) like (D) with가 들어간다.

**21** '최후의 만찬'에서 어떤 종류의 음식을 찾을 수 있는지는 알 수 없다.

**22** creative: 창의적인, 창조적인 innovative: 획기적인

**23** 주어진 문장의 'also'로 보아 (B) 앞에서 나온 역할에 이어지는 것이 자연스러우므로 (B)가 적절하다.

**24** 주어진 문장과 ⓒ: 형용사적 용법 ⓐ, ⓓ: 명사적 용법 ⓑ, ⓔ: 부사적 용법

**25** 고등학교를 졸업하고 대학에 가므로 ⓓ는 After로 바꿔야 한다.

**26** (A) 음식에 흥미를 가졌기(interested) 때문에 최후의 만찬을 바탕으로 한 그림을 맡았다고 하는 것이 적절하다. (B) 그림 속 식탁 위에 어떤 음식을 올릴지 결정하기 위해 모든 종류의 음식을 요리하느라(cooking) 많은 시간을 썼다고 하는 것이 적절하다. (C) 다빈치가 요리하느라 많은 시간을 썼다고 불평(complained)했다고 하는 것이 적절하다.

**27** 'He was not only a great painter but also a creative cook.'이라고 했다.

**28** ⓐ years → year
ⓑ artistically → artistic
ⓒ used to → were used to
ⓓ painting → painted

**29** (A) 앞의 내용과 상반되므로 however (B) 결과가 이어지므로 Therefore (C) 뒤에서 '그런 일은 절대로 일어나지 않았다'라고 했으므로 'Unfortunately'가 적절하다.

## Lesson 7 (기말)

> **01** ⑤ **02** ③ **03** ① **04** ② **05** (1) 선물 (2) 현재 **06** ③
> **07** ③ **08** ④ **09** The early bird catches the worm. **10** ⑤
> **11** ④ **12** ④ **13** ④ **14** ⑤
> **15** It would be great if there were men as wise as Birbal.
> **16** ② **17** ⑤ **18** ③ **19** ② **20** ④ **21** ③ **22** ③ **23** ③
> **24** ④ **25** ① **26** ③ **27** ②
> **28** (A) precious (B) speechless **29** ①

**01** 접미사 '-less'는 '~이 없는'이라는 뜻이다. speechless: 말을 못하는, (충격 따위로) 말이 안 나오는

**02** 그대로 해석하면 '초조할 때 불안해 보이기는 어렵다.'라는 뜻으로 어색하다. unnatural을 natural로 고쳐야 한다.

**03** (B) 한국 노래 부르기 대회에서 노래를 해야 한다는 말에 (D) 행운을 빈다고 하자 (A) 다리 한 쪽을 부러뜨려야 한다는 말인지 묻자 (C) 잘 하길 빈다는 뜻의 표현이라고 알려주는 순서가 적절하다.

**04** 'Yesterday is history, tomorrow is a mystery, and today is a gift.'라고 했으므로 ②번이 적절하다.

**05** 'present'는 '선물'이라는 뜻과 '현재'라는 뜻이 있다.

**06** 학교의 영어 팝송 부르기 대회에서 노래를 해야 한다는 상대방에게 '행운'을 빈다는 말이 적절하다.

**07** 앞에서 'Well, you should always live for today.'라고 했으므로 'past'를 'present'로 바꾸는 것이 적절하다.

**08** 'Well, you should always live for today.'라고 했다.

**09** The early bird catches the worm.: 일찍 일어나는 새가 벌레를 잡는다. → 부지런해야 성공한다.

**10** 'Everyone in my family is good at dancing.'이라고 했으므로 'dance'가 적절하다.

**11** (C) 학교의 영어 팝송 부르기 대회에서 노래를 해야 한다는 말에 (A) 행운을 빈다고 하고 (B) 다리 한 쪽을 부러뜨려야 한다는 말인지 묻자 (D) 잘하기를 빈다는 뜻의 표현이라고 설명해 주는 순서가 적절하다.

**12** 뒤에 명사(design)가 이어지며 완전한 절이 나오므로 소유격 관계대명사 whose가 적절하다.

**13** 가정법 과거는 'If+주어+동사의 과거형(be동사는 were) ~, 주어+조동사의 과거형(would, could, might 등)+동사원형 …'의 형태로 쓴다.

**14** certainly: 확실히, 꼭, 반드시

**15** 가정법 과거는 'If+주어+동사의 과거형(be동사는 were) ~, 주어+조동사의 과거형(would, could, might 등)+동사원형 …'의 형태이다. as wise as ~: ~처럼 현명한

**16** '말이 안 된다'는 주어진 문장 다음에 '어떻게 지혜를 항아리에 넣

을 수 있는지' 묻는 말이 나오는 것이 자연스러우므로 (B)가 적절하다.

**17** 뒤에서 '깨지 않도록 조심해 주십시오.'라고 한 것으로 보아 ⓔ는 'precious' 정도로 바꾸는 것이 적절하다.

**18** 뒤에 명사 necks가 나오므로 소유격 관계대명사 whose가 이끄는 절이 선행사 two pots를 수식하도록 하는 것이 적절하다.

**19** ⓑ는 Raja Birbal을 가리키지만 나머지는 모두 Akbar를 가리킨다.

**20** 각각 (A) were → was (B) who → whose (C) interested → interesting이 되어야 한다.

**21** 'On the day of his burial, he escaped through the tunnel and hid in his house.'라고 했다.

**22** ⓒ는 과거시제로 쓰여야 하므로 hide의 과거형인 hid가 되어야 한다.

**23** a number of = many

**24** 문장의 주어는 a man이므로 was가 적절하다. 부사구 'Among them'이 문두로 나가서 '동사+주어'로 도치된 문장이다.

**25** 'Akbar looked inside the other pot and found a pumpkin just as big as the pot.'라고 했다.

**26** 'You can see for yourself.'라고 했다.

**27** to부정사의 부정은 'not+to동사원형'의 형태이다.

**28** (A) 가치 있고 중요하며 낭비되거나 부주의하게 사용되어서는 안되는 것. (B) 보통 충격을 받아서 일시적으로 말을 할 수 없는.

**29** (A) at은 비교적 좁은 장소 앞에 쓰이고 in은 넓은 장소 앞에 쓰인다. (B) famous for: ~로 유명한 (C) with: ~을 가지고

# Lesson 7 (기말)   2회

| | | | | | | |
|---|---|---|---|---|---|---|
| **01** ③ | **02** ① | **03** ⑤ | **04** present | **05** ④ | **06** ① | **07** ② |
| **08** ⑤ | **09** ① | **10** I wish I could dance like you. | | | | **11** ② |
| **12** ① | **13** to have Birbal near | | | **14** ② | **15** ⑤ | **16** ① |
| **17** ③ | **18** ④ | **19** ③ | **20** ③ | **21** ⑤ | **22** ① | **23** ③ | **24** ② |
| **25** ② | **26** ① | | | | | |

**01** • find out: 알아내다, 풀다, 발견하다
  • unusual: 흔치 않은, 드문

**02** 각각 (A) up (B) out (C) on (D) of가 들어간다.

**03** Anna가 좋은 표현들을 많이 아는 이유에 대한 언급은 없다.

**04** 'gift'가 '선물'이라는 뜻이므로 같은 '선물'이라는 뜻을 가지면서 '현재'라는 뜻도 있는 'present'가 적절하다.

**05** 기타를 잘 친다는 말에 이어 (B) 고맙다며 언니에게 배웠다고 하자 (D) 정말이냐며 언니도 기타를 치는지 묻고 (C) 학교 밴드에 있다고 답하자 (A) 굉장한 가족이라며 자기도 기타를 칠 수 있다면 좋

**06** 사람들이 '어제는 역사, 내일은 미스터리, 그리고 오늘은 선물'이라고 말한다.

**07** 자신이 소망하는 것을 'I wish I could+동사원형' 형태로 말하는 것이 적절하다.

**08** 뒤에서 'Do you mean it's better to hand it in even though it's late?'라고 반문하고 있으므로 ⑤번이 적절하다.

**09** 시험 공부 하려고 아주 일찍 일어났다는 말에 ⓒ 잘했다며 일찍 일어나는 새가 먹이를 잡는 법이라고 하자 ⓐ 아니라며 일찍 일어나는 새가 빨리 지친다고 하자 ⓓ 일찍 일어나는 게 싫다는 말인지 묻고 ⓑ 정확히 그런 뜻이라는 순서이다.

**10** 'I wish I could+동사원형 ~' 형태로 자신이 소망하는 것을 쓸 수 있다.

**11** 'Every dog has its day.'는 직역하면 '모든 개는 자기의 날을 갖는다.'라는 뜻으로 우리말의 '쥐구멍에도 볕들 날 있다.'에 해당한다. ① 오늘은 이만 끝냅시다. ③ 잠 잘 시간이다. ④ 열심히 공부할 시간이다. ⑤ 천 마디 말보다 한 번 보는 게 더 낫다.

**12** 모두 소유격 관계대명사가 들어가야 하지만 ①번에는 주격 관계대명사가 들어가야 한다.

**13** liked의 목적어로 to부정사를 쓰고 him이 전치사 near의 목적어가 되도록 한다.

**14** ⓐ What → Whatever ⓓ which → where ⓕ which → that

**15** 가정법 과거는 'If+주어+동사의 과거형(be동사는 were) ~, 주어+조동사의 과거형(would, could, might 등)+동사원형 …'의 형태로 쓴다.

**16** 'I've been asked by my king to bring him a potful of wisdom.'라고 했으므로 ①번이 적절하다.

**17** ask의 목적격보어로 to부정사가 적절하다.

**18** 주어진 단어를 모두 한 번씩 사용하여 알맞게 배열하면 'can't be taken out without breaking the pot'이 된다. 그러므로 ④번 breaking이 정답이다.

**19** ① 형용사구 → 부사구 ② 가정법 문장이 아님. ④ 복수 명사의 소유격으로 officials'가 적절함. ⑤ 조동사 뒤에는 항상 동사 원형이 와야 함.

**20** ⓐ give sweets him → give him sweets 또는 give sweets to him ⓑ to say → say ⓓ having → to have ⓔ wisely → wise

**21** 뒤에서 'live these years over again'이라고 했으므로 ⑤번이 적절하다.

**22** 'I can't believe it's time to say goodbye.', 'I hope I can see you again.'에서 ①번이 적절함을 알 수 있다.

**23** '어떻게 했는지' 묻는 <보기> 문장은 (C) 다음에서 답하고 있으

므로 (C)가 적절하다.

**24** (가) 가정법이므로 were (구어체에서는 was도 가능함.) (나) 무엇이 있는지 묻는 것이므로 의문대명사 what (다) without의 목적어로 동명사가 적절하다.

**25** 'It would be great if there were a wise man like Birbal in our country.'라고 했으므로 없다는 것을 알 수 있다.

**26** 'I still remember the time when we went camping together.'라고 했다.